# AFFRONT TO MERITOCRACY

# AFFRONT TO MERITOCRACY

## STORIES OF OVERLOOKED TALENTS, IGNORED ABILITIES, AND HIDDEN TRUTHS

**MARK JONES LORENZO**

SE BOOKS
Philadelphia | Pittsburgh

Ψ
SE BOOKS
5307 West Tyson Street
Philadelphia, Pennsylvania 19107
www.sebooks.com



Published in full-throated defiance of Yog's Law—thus this book's publication might be termed an affront to meritocracy.

Cover design and art, as well as all illustrations in the text, by Mark Jones Lorenzo.

Manufactured in the United States of America.

10 9 8 7 6 5 4 3 2 1

Library cataloging information is as follows:

Lorenzo, Mark Jones
Affront to meritocracy : stories of overlooked talents, ignored abilities, and hidden truths / Mark Jones Lorenzo.
p. ; cm.
Includes bibliographical references.
I. Title
1. Education—Mathematics. 2. The Teacher's Role—Narratives and Theory. 3. Hitchcock, Alfred, 1899—Criticism and Interpretation. 4. Film Studies—General. 4. Anthropology—Cultural Studies. 5. Computer Science—Algorithms.
PN1998.3.H58 F53 2014
814.5401'53097—dc22
20134426568

ISBN: 978-1-492-31615-2

*For my Mother and Father,*

*And in memory of my Grandfather*

# ACKNOWLEDGMENTS

The great twentieth-century physicist Richard Feynman once said, "I'm smart enough to know how dumb I am." Humility is the antidote to hubris. Writing a book is self-imposed and mostly isolating work, so I am grateful to those who encouraged me through this grueling labor of love while always keeping me humble. To my teachers,[*] students,[†] friends,[‡] and, especially, parents: thank you for piercing my mind's echo chamber to help make this manuscript a reality. I am, as always, in your debt. Any mistakes present in the text are solely my own.

[*] Louis, Ned, Shekhar, Jonathan, Bella, Joie, Susan, David, Fred, John, and, especially, Tom and Lisa: there wouldn't be a book at all without you.

[†] Ali, Nicole, Zoe, Abigail, and, particularly, Madi: without all of you, the book wouldn't be nearly as good.

[‡] Yan, Bob, Rich, Joe, Gavin, Mike, Bridget, Craig, Anthious, Jenna, and, of course, Carolyn: my thinking evolved greatly by bouncing ideas off of you all.

# CONTENTS



## PART I: POPULAR ESSAYS



## PART II: ACADEMIC ESSAYS

## PART III: EXPLICATIONS



## PART IV: REVIEWS OF BOOKS AND ARTICLES

## PART V: REVIEWS OF FILMS



## PART VI: RUMINATIONS

## PART VII: SHORT STORIES



## APPENDIX

# AN AFFRONT TO MERITOCRACY:

## When talent or ability is disregarded.

# A Note on the Text

In his essay collection *Farther Away*, novelist Jonathan Franzen notes that the author with the most influence over his writing is, well, himself. He has a point and, to that end, the pieces in this collection build off of one another and are reprinted in substantially the same form as they originally appeared elsewhere (although some of the writings are new for this collection or have not appeared publicly before). Small errors have been corrected, the writing has been freshened, and asides and footnotes have been added or better fleshed-out.

Rather than organize by subject matter—by, say, math, education, film, and so on—AFFRONT TO MERITOCRACY is written discursively and arranged organically by the style or type of writing. The first section, "Popular Essays," contains long-form essays with a bent toward entertaining the layperson. In the second section, "Academic Essays," different kinds of academic styles of writing pervade. "Explications," the next section, contains pieces that are narrow in scope but overflowing with detail, whatever the subject matter may be. The following two sections, "Reviews of Books and Articles" and "Reviews of Films," are self-explanatory, though reflections on books and films are not restricted to these two sections. In the penultimate section, "Ruminations," short-form writings on a hodge-podge of topics are presented. Finally, the "Short Stories" section contributes several works of fiction, and a multi-part Appendix rounds things out.

Affronts to meritocracy, among other kinds of affronts, run as overarching themes throughout the text. Oftentimes, however, pieces contradict one another; this is due less to some sort of cognitive dissonance on my part but rather more because of an evolution in or reevaluation of my thinking.

The year that each piece in the book was originally penned is noted parenthetically at the end of its respective chapter. Feel free to read the works in any order—but I hope you run into a few pieces that interest you.

# PART I

# POPULAR ESSAYS

# 1.

## MATHEMATICAL CERTAINTY AND THE PROSECUTOR'S FALLACY

The Sixth Amendment to the U.S. Constitution guarantees that the individual accused "shall enjoy the right to a speedy and public trial, by an impartial jury[*] of the State…." But can any trial truly be a fair one for the accused if members of the jury aren't mathematically literate?

Math seems to be one of the most challenging subjects in large part because an intuitive sense of number isn't necessarily familiar vocabulary to most people. In his influential text *Innumeracy: Mathematical Illiteracy and Its Consequences* (1988), John Allen Paulos[†] laments this "inability to deal comfortably with the fundamental notions of number and chance," using the term "innumeracy" as a catchall descriptor of this "plague" (as he terms it). Paulos, though, describes this widespread phenomenon as afflicting "otherwise knowledgeable citizens"—i.e., adults in our society, those same adults who sit on juries.

It's this lack of familiarity with notions of chance that could adversely impact the search for justice in a courtroom. In the chapter "Probability and Coincidence" in *Innumeracy*, Paulos presents the case of *People v. Collins* (1968), in which an interracial couple (a rarity in 1968) was charged with robbery. According to the California Supreme Court,

> On June 18, 1964, about 11:30 a.m. Mrs. Juanita Brooks, who had been shopping, was walking home along an alley in the San Pedro area of the City of Los Angeles. She was

---

[*] Contrary to common belief, nowhere in the Constitution is the accused afforded the right to a jury of his or her peers. Rather, the "jury of one's peers" line originated in the Magna Carta.

[†] Paulos is a long-time mathematics professor at Temple University who has published quite a few math books for the layperson, of which *Innumeracy* is probably the best known.

> pulling behind her a wicker basket carryall containing groceries and had her purse on top of the packages. She was using a cane. As she stooped down to pick up an empty carton, she was suddenly pushed to the ground by a person whom she neither saw nor heard approach. She was stunned by the fall and felt some pain. She managed to look up and saw a young woman running from the scene. According to Mrs. Brooks the latter appeared to weigh about 145 pounds, was wearing "something dark," and had hair "between a dark blond and a light blond," but lighter than the color of defendant Janet Collins' hair as it appeared at trial. Immediately after the incident, Mrs. Brooks discovered that her purse, containing between $35 and $40 was missing. About the same time as the robbery, John Bass, who lived on the street at the end of the alley, was in front of his house watering his lawn. His attention was attracted by "a lot of crying and screaming" coming from the alley. As he looked in that direction, he saw a woman run out of the alley and enter a yellow automobile parked across the street from him. He was unable to give the make of the car.... The latter then saw that it was being driven by a [black male], wearing a mustache and beard. At the trial Bass identified defendant as the driver of the yellow automobile....*

Before continuing, we need to define the probabilistic ideas of *independence* and *dependence*. Two events are considered *independent* if the occurrence of one event has absolutely no impact on the occurrence of the other. Likewise, two events are classified as *dependent* if the occurrence of one event does have an impact on the other.†

If it is the case that two events are independent events, to find the probability of both events occurring we simply multiply the probability of the first event occurring by the probability of the second event occurring. For example, to find the probability of flipping successive heads using a single fair coin, simply multiply one-half—the probability of obtaining a single head—by one-half.

---

* *People v. Collins*, 68 Cal.2d 319, 66 Cal. Rptr. 497, 438 P.2d 33 (1968).

† A good example of the distinction between independent and dependent events can be found in statistician Nate Silver's interesting text *The Signal and the Noise*: he describes faulty bets in the real estate market which (likely) led to severe financial crisis.

Thus, the probability of obtaining two heads in a row with a fair coin is one-fourth, or a 25 percent chance. Critical to observe here is that if the two coin flips were not independent of each other, we could not simply multiple the probabilities together to get the probabilities of the successive events; rather, we would have to rely on calculating the values using what are termed *conditional probabilities.*[*]

Suppose we could accurately assign probabilities to real-life events,[†] such as the probability of a man having a mustache, a woman having a ponytail, or an interracial couple in a car. In fact, this is exactly what the prosecutor proceeds to do in the court case. Here are the characteristic probabilities the prosecutor came up with:

- Yellow automobile: 1 in 10
- Black man with a beard: 1 in 10
- Man with a mustache: 1 in 4
- White woman with a ponytail: 1 in 10
- White woman with blond hair: 1 in 3
- Interracial couple in an automobile: 1 in 1,000

The prosecutor argued that these characteristics were all independent of each other—e.g., whether or not a woman has blond hair has no effect on whether or not a black man has a beard. Therefore, with the assumption of independence made, it is a simple matter of multiplying all of the characteristic probabilities together to get the probability of observing a yellow car, a man with a mustache, a woman with a ponytail, a woman with blond hair, a black man with a beard, and an interracial couple in a car: 1 in 12 million.[‡]

---

[*] For a more complete discussion on independence versus dependence in probability calculations, pick up and read through any introductory statistics textbook. *Elementary Statistics* (11th ed.) by statistician Mario Triola is an especially good choice, with probability theory presented in a cogent manner.

[†] Sometimes this is subjectively done—there is a branch of probability loosely called "subjective probability"—but it would be more beneficial to gather data from observation or experimentation first if possible.

[‡] Note that all of the characteristics separated by commas in the sentence have implied *ands* between them—we wish to find the probability not of any one of these events, but of *all* of them taken together.

One in 12 million! Incredibly unlikely—and the jury interpreted this probability to mean the following: the odds that the couple on trial—who fit all of the characteristics enumerated above—were *not* the culprits was 11,999,999 to 1. Surely seems like beyond a reasonable doubt. With that kind of ostensible mathematical certainty, the jury convicted the couple of the crime.

Except that the assumption of independence doesn't hold in this case,* so the probabilities cannot simply be multiplied together. The case ended up being appealed to the California Supreme Court, which overturned the verdict. Here's why: even supposing that independence *did* hold in this case, and that the chances of finding a couple with all of the aforementioned characteristics was 1 in 12 million, we can't restrict our attention to *all* couples in the Los Angeles area, of which there would be several million couples, when considering the probabilities; instead, we need to examine just those couples in the Los Angeles area which have the *enumerated characteristics*. Of that subset of all couples (ones which would be interracial, with the white woman having a ponytail, the black man having a mustache, and so forth), of which there are around thirteen, the convicted couple is just one: thus, a one-in-thirteen chance, must greater than reasonable doubt.

Another way to look at this argument is like this: the 1 in 12,000,000 figure represents the chance that all of those events could have occurred together *if in fact the couple was innocent*. But since there certainly existed more than one couple with all of those characteristics—a dozen more, perhaps—then the probability that the couple on trial is in fact the guilty couple drops to the point where they are no longer guilty beyond a reasonable doubt.

The prosecutor's error has a name: the *prosecutor's fallacy*. And *People v. Collins* is not the only example. Mark Buchanan, in an article for *The New York Times*,† expounds on how juries can jump unwittingly to unfounded mathematical conclusions, even when being presented with presumably ironclad DNA evidence:

> [S]uppose that police pick up a suspect and match his or her DNA to evidence collected at a crime scene. Suppose that the likelihood of a match, purely by chance, is only 1

* Beards and mustaches aren't independent, among other characteristics.

† "The Prosecutor's Fallacy," from May 16, 2007.

> in 10,000. Is this also the chance that they are innocent? It's easy to make this leap, but you shouldn't. Here's why. Suppose the city in which the person lives has 500,000 adult inhabitants. Given the 1 in 10,000 likelihood of a random DNA match, you'd expect that about 50 people in the city would have DNA that also matches the sample. So the suspect is only 1 of 50 people who could have been at the crime scene. Based on the DNA evidence only, the person is almost certainly innocent, not certainly guilty.

Now we're back to the subtle notion of conditional probability, which was mentioned earlier. Conditional probability "restricts" the sample—it narrows the potential people who could be considered a part of the sample by attaching a limiting condition. In Buchanan's example above, the potential pool of people is narrowed considerably by the restriction that only those who match the DNA profile be considered a part of the probability calculation.*

In fact, statistician Mario Triola defines the prosecutor's fallacy this way: "[It] is a misunderstanding or confusion of two different conditional probabilities: (1) the probability that a defendant is innocent, given that the forensic evidence shows a match; (2) the probability that forensics shows a match, given that a person is innocent."†

Prosecutors are not the only profession guilty of mishandling conditional probability (and mathematics in general). Doctors frequently make the same sorts of mistakes with conditional probability, especially when discussing results of tests for diseases. For instance, consider diabetes. The American Diabetes Association says that about 5.9 percent of Americans have the disease. Now, suppose a new test to detect diabetes is developed that is 98 percent accurate for people who have the disease, but only 95 percent accurate for those who don't. Suppose you obtain a positive result on the test—how worried should you be?

---

* But it is convenient in Buchanan's example that the likelihood of a random DNA match isn't that low. Compare this 1 in 10,000 chance to, for instance, the Robert Chae murder trial, in which the chances of a DNA match were 1 in one septillion (which is ten to the twenty-fourth power). Since there are only around seven billion people on the earth today, chances are effectively zero that the DNA matched anyone other than one of the culprits.

† *Elementary Statistics* (11th ed.), p. 174.

When being presented with a positive result for diabetes, most people would assume that there is very little chance that they didn't have the disease; after all, the test is "98 percent accurate for people who have the disease." From that statement alone, it would seem that there's only a 1 in 50 shot that if the test comes back positive it's in error.

But this superficial reasoning misses an important point. First, assume independence holds with this diabetes test—i.e., assume that the physical act of taking the diabetes test has no impact on whether the person being tested has the disease or not (this is a safe assumption). Next, consider that there are two ways in which a positive test for diabetes could arise here: (1) If the person being tested actually does have the disease, and the test is correct, or (2) If the person being tested does not actually have the disease, and the test is incorrect.* In order to determine the probability that if you obtained a positive result you in fact have the disease, we have to divide the probability of case (1) by the sum of the probabilities of cases (1) and (2).

The probability of case (1)—If the person being tested actually does have the disease, and the test is correct—is the probability of a randomly selected individual having diabetes (0.059) multiplied by the probability of the test being accurate for those who have the disease (0.98), which turns out to be 0.057, or 5.7 percent. The probability of case (2)—If the person being tested does not actually have the disease, and the test is incorrect—is the probability of a randomly selected individual *not* having diabetes (0.941) multiplied by the probability of the test being *inaccurate* for those who don't have the disease (in other words, showing a positive result that's, in actuality, false; this probability is 0.05), which turns out to be 0.047, or 4.7 percent.

To obtain the final answer—the probability of actually having diabetes given a positive result—take 0.057 and divide it by the sum of 0.057 and 0.047. The quotient is 0.55, or 55 percent—basically a coin flip, which is a startlingly counterintuitive result.

Understanding why the answer to the diabetes question isn't 98 percent and also how to obtain the correct result of 55 percent using the mathematical ideas of independence and conditional probability are far from trivial, best-left-for-the-genius-mathematicians

* This latter case is termed a "false positive."

tasks that have no bearing at all in real life.[*] As we have already seen, a firm grasp of these kinds of probabilistic ideas can spell the difference between near-certain conviction due to "mathematical certainty" and ultimate acquittal due to reasonable doubt.[†]

What's more is that the prosecutor's fallacy is not the only named species of innumeracy in the courtroom. There's also the defendant's fallacy, the interrogator's fallacy, and the jury observation fallacy, among others.[‡] All are the result of failures of mathematical and probabilistic reasoning, and all have the real-world consequence of injustice due to faulty mathematical logic. In fact, could we go so far as to say that innumerate juries are *ipso facto* not impartial? If not quite a violation of the Sixth Amendment might there be an Equal Protection Clause issue here?

Putting this aside, how do we correct the problem? Short of jury education classes—which, even if they did exist, would likely focus on the processes of the law rather than the subtle ideas of probability theory—presenting the content in high school mathematics classes (and perhaps even a brief mention in a social studies class or two) seems like the best bet, and therein lies an important nexus of civics and mathematics education—and perhaps a cure for a persistent innumerate affront to a judicial-system meritocracy.

(2011)

---

[*] There are even subtler ideas that cause perplexity with conditional probability. One of them is called the "confusion of the inverse," which means that the "given" statement is erroneously reversed. So, in the diabetes problem above, instead of calculating the probability that you have diabetes given that you obtained a positive result, you mistakenly find the probability that you've obtained a positive result given that you have diabetes.

[†] The Buchanan *NYT* article also details the infamous Sally Clark and Lucia de Berk convictions.

[‡] For complete explanations of these types of fallacies and more detailed forays into conditional probability, along with a primer on Bayesian inference, read through "The 'Jury Observation Fallacy' and the Use of Bayesian Networks to Present Probabilistic Legal Arguments," by Norman Fenton and Martin Neil.

2.

# Signing and Speaking in the Space-Time Continuum

"Albert Einstein's Theory of Relativity says that time is relative to the inertial frame in which it is measured, not that it is subjective.... But one aspect of Einstein's theory does have a counterpart to the psychology of time, at least as it is expressed in language: the deep equivalence of time with space."

So begins Steven Pinker's section about constructions of temporal language in his amazing book *The Stuff of Thought: Language as a Window into Human Nature* (2007). Pinker, a professor of psychology at Harvard and a noted linguist, seeks to make transparent—by decoding the use of tenses, prepositions, nouns, and verbs in spoken language—that which is usually opaque: the ways in which the human mind goes about constructing mental models of time, space, and relationships. His focus, though, is not on sign language; in fact, sign language of any sort merits only a single mention in his 499-page tome, in a chapter on deconstructing curses ("There has even been a report of a deaf sufferer of Tourette's," Pinker relays, "who produced 'fuck' and 'shit' in American Sign Language [ASL]").

My contention, however, is that sign language deserves pride of place in the chapter entitled "Cleaving the Air," in which Pinker presents a comprehensive systematic study of time-and-space metaphors, tenses, and aspect. (Unless otherwise stated in this essay, take the term "sign language" to mean a manually coded English system.) In deconstructing everyday spoken language, Pinker unwittingly describes as metaphor some of the forms that signers express explicitly—by, quite literally, "cleaving" the air with their hands. The most obvious of these forms is tense, so it is there that we shall begin.

"We...see that the meaning of tense (location in time) is like the meaning of spatial terms.... [Thus] [t]he best way to understand the language of time is to depict it, naturally, in space. Consider a line that runs from the past through the present moment to the future. Situations (that is, events or states) can be represented as segments along the line," he writes. Pinker proceeds to draw a line in the text illustrating that very idea: the past to the left (behind) the present moment, the future to the right (in front of) the present moment. The farther to the left of the present, the farther traveled into the past, and vice versa.

A very similar time diagram visually explicating tense appears in the appendix to *The Joy of Signing* (1987) by Lottie Riekehof. "A sign does not change to show tense as is the case in the English language where words frequently show tense by a change in spelling.... It should be remembered that there is a visual time line that the signer should keep in mind. The future is before you and the past is behind you.... The larger, more slowly, more to the back the sign for 'past' is made, the greater the distance in the past is meant." The physically exaggerated "push to the past" motion behind the signer relays that the action or event has already transpired; likewise with the forward movement signifying the future.

A more nuanced version of the diagram appearing in Riekehof's text, but this time with an ASL bent, appears in the online article "A Survey of ASL Tenses" by Karen Alkoby.[*] After elucidating the two types of time signs in ASL—the Lexical Tense Markers and the Time Adverbials—a drawing with a human figure at the center, surrounded by perpendicular axes of "Height" and "Location," is explained: "The time signs have a relative location on the timeline, which agrees with their meaning. In addition to the timeline, the height defines the coordinate system of the sign location.... The timeline is indicated on the illustration... as starting from Far past, Past, Near past, Present, Near future, and Far future respectively with the vertical lines from left to right."

But the past, present, and future tenses simply cannot account for all constructions of the English language. As Pinker explains in *The Stuff of Thought*, "We need to introduce a third moment in time: not just the event you are talking about, and the moment at which you are speaking (that is, the present moment), but also a *reference time*: an event that has been identified in the conversation and that is serving as the 'now' for the actors in the narrative." So, according

[*] The article, accessed June 22, 2010, can be found online at http://facweb.cti.depaul.edu/research/techreports/TR00-002.pdf

to Pinker, if, say, I am describing to a friend what my teacher taught in class last Wednesday, then last Wednesday is the "now" for my teacher—i.e., the reference time—despite the fact that it's not the "now" for me.

Pinker's point is that spoken language struggles to get across these complicated ideas, since, to account for reference time, in addition to the past, present and future tenses, two more are needed: the pluperfect (for example, *She had climbed the tree*; here, the reference event is located before the present moment of speaking) and the future perfect (*She will have climbed the tree*; here, the reference event is located in the future, after the present moment of speaking). Needless to say, these tenses with reference events often introduce awkward constructions into spoken language.

Two lines of inquiry should be immediately apparent: (1) Does sign language have a reference event "placeholder" to allow for the pluperfect and future perfect? and (2) Might all five tenses be more naturally expressed kinesthetically by signers than orally by English speakers?

Let's tackle the first question first. According to Donovan Grose, "[In ASL], the Perfect Tenses, indicating an event occurring before a reference time, are marked by a single downward movement of the head, glossed here HN."* Grose continues:

> Previous analyses claimed that this same nonmanual [i.e., head and body movements, facial expressions, or the like] was an optional marker of conditionals (Liddell 1986), and a marker of closed events (Nowell 1988). The current study accounts for the function of the HN as a Perfect Tense marker.... This approach argues that all finite clauses encode for three temporal points. These temporal points are: the time of utterance (S), understood as either Speech or Sign time, the reference time (R), and the event time (E). These three points generate two relationships, one between S and R time (S/R) and another between R and E time (R/E). These points may be simultaneous, as S and R are in the Present Tense, or they may be ordered sequentially. In the Perfect Tenses, E occurs before R (E_R), re-

---

* From the essay "A Nonmanual Marking the Perfect Tenses in ASL," available online at www.ub.edu/ling/tislr8/Grose.doc (accessed June 22, 2010).

> gardless of the relationship (S/R). This allows for Perfect Tenses in the Past, Present and Future.

Thus, events needing a reference event to be located properly in temporal space can be distinguished from the "time of utterance" (in other words, the present moment) through the use of the HN (head nod), a nonmanual behavior (part of the language not communicated using the hands). So, then, everything Pinker detailed about the pluperfect and future perfect is accounted for (in ASL, at least).

As for the second question posed—if the expression of tenses can be more naturally expressed by signing than speaking—let's go back to *The Joy of Signing* text. Telling stories involves characters, whether these characters have acted upon their worlds in the past or will do so in the future. The act of signing models these prospective "realities" of story through the use of pointing at actual objects or into space to represent other objects (not present in the signing space), spatial relationships, and events. As Riekehof explains, "Signs are placed in specific locations if a story is to be told effectively. Example: A tree is placed on your right. A child walks toward the tree coming from the left, then climbs the tree.... It is important to remember where you have put the tree or you might have the child climbing a tree on the left that you have originally placed on the right. *Keep the visual image alive in your mind* [emphasis added]." Furthermore, as Riekehof tells us, the signer herself could "become" the characters present in the story being told. Through these signing techniques, one-to-one correspondences between the physical space immediately around the signer and perhaps even the body of the signer herself are established with events and reference events in a story or anecdote, quite apart from the "present moment." Whether such "painting a picture in the air" of a story or anecdote is a more natural way to communicate is open to debate, but one thing seems certain: using the spoken word to convey mental perceptions of time and space loses something in the translation that signing—signs can trace out time and space in, well, time and space—does not.

There is another, more subtle language construct related to tense that Pinker discusses: aspect. It's best to let him explain:

> Time is encoded in grammar in two ways. The familiar one is tense, which can be thought of as the "location" of an event or state in time, as in the difference between *She loves you*, *She loved you*, and *She will love you*. The other timekeeper is called aspect…; it can be thought of as the *shape* of an event in time. Aspect pertains to the difference between *swat a fly*, which is conceptualized as instantaneous…; *run around*, which is open-ended; and *draw a circle*, which culminates in an event that marks the act's completion. [his italics]

Let's summarize, then. The "shape" of an event in time is its aspect, and aspect can be an instantaneous event; an event that has no fixed beginning or fixed ending; or an event that either has a fixed beginning and no fixed ending, or the reverse (such as *drawing a circle*, which has an endpoint).

Aspect is naturally conveyed by signers simply by signing the verbs—the question of whether the temporal endpoints are fixed or not is largely "built in" to the signs themselves. Take the sign for "Hit, Impact, Strike": As Riekehof describes it, "Strike the left index finger (which is pointed upward) with the right 'S' (palm-side left)." Contrast that with the sign for "Climb": "Place the curved 'V' hands before you, facing each other; move them upward alternately in stages. (To climb a rope form 'S' positions, hand over hand, as in actual climbing)." A hit, impact, or strike is a "momentaneous" (Pinker's word) event, an event that lasts but a mere instant in time—as the mutual sign for these three words conveys. Climbing, though, is open-ended, and the sign for the verb climb permits the signer flexibility in communicating this aspect. There are countless other examples of verbs in sign language that reveal their aspect by very the hand and arm movements needed to construct their signs. The temporal aspect of ASL is exhaustively analyzed in *American Sign Language: A Teacher's Resource Text on Grammar and Culture* (1980) by Baker-Shenk and Cokley. The text breaks down temporal aspect into four inflections—over time, regularly, long time, and over and over again—which make manifest the duration or frequency of the action being examined.

We have, of course, only scratched the surface of tense and aspect in sign language. Beyond unpacking these linguistic components of signing, a good grasp of parts of speech is paramount to properly understanding signers—especially in ASL, where so much communication is implied (and thus left "unsaid") and signs are continually evolving and being consolidated. As Alkoby explains,

> As a native signer of American Sign Language (ASL), I find that I must often verify the tense of sentences with a sign language interpreter because improper use of the ASL tense can lead to a severe miscommunication. For example, in [the paper] *Legal Ramification of an Incorrect Analysis of Tense in ASL*, a deaf plaintiff misunderstood when he was asked "Did you understand when you were signing the paper at [Company A] that you were borrowing money and agreeing to pay it back?" The plaintiff responded, "Yes" because he thought the question asked if he understood at the time when he was signing the paper.

Miscommunications aside, as long as proper care is taken, the notion of a space-time continuum functions as more than just a metaphor for sign language—it is the *sine qua non* of signing itself.

(2010)

# 3.

## Website Filters, Social Networking, and Constitutional Rights

In the Supreme Court case *U.S. v. American Liberty Association* (2003), the then-newly passed Children's Internet Protection Act (CIPA), a congressional bill introduced by Arizona Senator John McCain, was upheld. CIPA was written to limit access to pornographic and objectionable Internet materials at public libraries (and schools) by requiring filters at these locations—lest their federal funding ceases. As the majority opinion of the Supreme Court case succinctly declared, "Because public libraries' use of Internet filtering software does not violate their patrons' First Amendment rights, CIPA does not induce libraries to violate the Constitution, and is a valid exercise of Congress' spending power."*

But the question of what exactly the software installed on these public computers should filter, and what should be left unfiltered for public consumption, is ill-defined. (The acid test for obscene material was famously earlier but unhelpfully explained by Justice Potter Stewart: "I know it when I see it.") As then-Chief Justice Rehnquist explains, "By connecting to the Internet, public libraries provide patrons with a vast amount of valuable information." However, he continues,

> there is also an enormous amount of pornography on the Internet, much of which is easily obtained.... The accessibility of this material has created a serious problem for libraries, which have found that patrons of all ages, including minors, regularly search online for pornography.... A library can set [blocking or filtering software] to block categories of materials, such as "Pornography" or "Violence".... When a patron tries to view a site that falls within such a category, a screen appears indicating that the site

---

* *U.S. v. American Liberty Association* (2003), page 2. The full text of *U.S. v. American Liberty Association* is available online at www.supremecourt.gov.

> is blocked.... But a filter set to block pornography may sometimes block other sites that present neither obscene nor pornographic material, but that nevertheless triggers the filter.[*]

Anastasia Goodstein, in her book *Totally Wired: What Teens and Tweens are Really Doing Online* (2007), adds to Rehnquist's criticism of Internet filters by referencing a report from the Brennan Center for Justice at the New York University School of Law. ""They [the filters] continue to deprive their users of many thousands of valuable webpages, on subjects ranging from war and genocide to safer sex and public health.""[†]

And therein lies the problem. Democracies must always juggle the protection of a citizen's individual rights with the protection of society's rights at large, and often those protections are at cross-purposes. The First Amendment frames this tension as one of not *forcing* freedom of speech, but rather of not *abridging* it—a non-interference clause (what government should not do), rather than a guarantee to intervene (what government should do).

It's a fool's errand to argue that U.S. citizens have some sort of First Amendment right to consume Internet pornography at public libraries—notwithstanding the infamous legal battles of *Hustler* publisher Larry Flynt—especially considering the online accessibility of pornography to not only adults but to minors as well. Public libraries, and certainly schools, should never function as a pornography distribution venue.

But the more interesting and less clear-cut questions center on whether these filters should block social-networking sites such as Facebook; because the first popular online social-networking site, called Friendster, arose only shortly after the Supreme Court ruled CIPA constitutional, it was not mentioned in the Court's discussion of website filtering. Unlike pornography, social-networking sites are not in and of themselves lacking in educational or social value; rather, these sites' societal benefit (or harm) results directly from their use (or misuse).

One of these important uses is what Anastasia Goodstein describes as "trying on different identities" and, like many of these

---

[*] Ibid, pages 7-8.

[†] *Totally Wired* (2007), page 137.

new technologies arising from the creation of the Internet, is a double-edged sword. "Social-networking sites…give teenagers a virtual stage on which to try out different aspects of their identities as well as to perform and show off for their peers."[*] Adults may recoil in horror at the prospect of teenagers experimenting in a public space with their identities, but, as Goodstein explains, "Trying on different identities is also simply a part of growing up," and certainly was a feature of pre-Internet teens' lives.[†] After all, as Shakespeare famously wrote in *As You Like It*, "All the world's a stage, / And all the men and women merely players."

Yet this online "stage," as it were, can be used for nefarious ends, both by other teens and by predators. Consider a new twist on an old childhood theme: bullying. Instead of the big kids shaking down the diminutive ones for their lunch money, young people are increasingly going online to taunt, harass, and torture their prey—and it's not necessarily the big kids who are doing the bullying. "Unlike offline bullying, anyone can cyberbully….It's virtual, and therefore it has a disembodied, anonymous nature so teens can't fully see or experience the reaction of the person they are bullying."[‡] And social-networking sites offer would-be bullies a perfect forum—replete with space for public postings on users' virtual walls—to perform their harassment.

As bad as this so-called peer-to-peer "flaming" is, though, the more publicized danger of social-networking sites is that of the predator angle: that sexual predators may be perusing social media pages, "shopping" for teenage prey, as one might peruse pages in a store catalog. In 2007, for example, a teen was lured online by a sexual offender via a MySpace account. As the local *Bradenton Herald* explains it, "The Florida incident comes just a day after a new state law took effect making sex offenders register their handles for [w]eb sites such as MySpace.com."[§]

However, "[t]he fear and the attention being given to this issue are way out of proportion with the extremely low number of abductions or sexual assaults being reported in which MySpace has

---

[*] Ibid, page 63.

[†] Ibid, page 66.

[‡] *Totally Wired* (2007), page 82.

[§] http://www.bradenton.com/local/story/161853.html, accessed November 13, 2007.

been said to play a role."[*] Yes, adults are posing as teens on these social-networking sites, and yes, there's been a small minority of teens who have been lured into communicating and meeting with sexual deviants, but, as Anastasia Goodstein puts it, "[A]s soon as they figure [out that the person they are writing to isn't who he says he is], they're over it. They will block him or not write back. They're not as scared as adults are for them...."[†]

Maybe not, but to assume that the overwhelming majority of teens will both act responsibly on social-networking sites and also block any unwanted advances from predators seems a bit naïve. Teenagers, and especially the youngest among them, are only beginning to learn about the ways of the world, and, as neophytes, dangers lurk around every corner—especially in a de-facto take-all-comers virtual space like Facebook.

Ironically, while teens can display their "polished identities" (a term coined by the youth-culture researcher Andrea Graham) online—and be who they want to be—predators can create their own online avatars to be who *they* want to be, so teens must be vigilant and know both what to look for and what to avoid. Ignorance isn't bliss in this case—no teen should be allowed to post a profile on a social-networking site without at least having been exposed to some sort of educational primer on the pitfalls and perils of social-networking space. One such primer can be found on the website wiredsafety.org, the self-proclaimed "world's largest Internet safety and help group." A section of the site is devoted to discussing social-networking sites like Facebook. Warning individuals not to post pertinent personal information online, wiredsafety.org goes on to encourage parents to speak to their children about using such sites responsibly. Wiredsafety.org also brings up a rather interesting unintended perversion of these social-networking sites: "If you find that your child has a profile on the [w]eb site, you should review it. It's amazing how much you can learn about your child by reading their profiles."[‡]

Since teens' profiles are, in many cases, available for public consumption, what teens wish to hide from their parents—and per-

---

[*] *Totally Wired* (2007), page 72.

[†] Ibid, page 73.

[‡] http://www.wiredsafety.org/internet101/blogs.html, accessed November 13, 2007.

haps would have, had they been born a decade earlier—suddenly is available to be viewed and analyzed by mom and dad. These kids' ostensibly private lives are no longer opaque—they are transparent to their parents, teachers, and guidance counselors alike, and this is on balance a good thing. A youth threatening on his Facebook page to bomb his school, murder his ex-girlfriend, or buy and sell illegal drugs can be exposed with relative ease; likewise, a teen contemplating suicide who posts online her ruminations on the meaningless of life and the beauty of death can be sought out and offered help. The text and graphics these youth author on these pages online eliminates debate—there is no ambiguity in a message such as "I'm going to shoot all my enemies in the school tomorrow." The content posted on these webpages are virtual smoking guns.

Let's return to our original point of contention: Should these social-networking sites, like online pornography, be blocked by libraries and schools? Well, it's already happening in some schools. Because "[t]he media has been saturated with coverage of MySpace, [m]any more schools have blocked access to the site and expelled or suspended students who have posted inappropriate content."[*] And a new companion law to CIPA, called the Deleting Online Predators Act (DOPA), proposed in 2006 by Pennsylvania Representative Michael Fitzpatrick, would prohibit access to a "commercial social networking website or chat room through which minors may easily access or be presented with obscene or indecent material [and] may easily be subject to unlawful sexual advances, unlawful requests for sexual favors, or repeated offensive comments of a sexual nature from adults."[†] In the congressional record, Fitzpatrick himself explained the relevance of his bill: "The Department of Justice recognizes child pornography as a precursor for pedophiles and is often linked to online predators. According to Attorney General Gonzales, one in five children has been approached sexually on the Internet."[‡]

---

[*] *Totally Wired* (2007), page 74.

[†] http://thomas.loc.gov/cgi-bin/query/z?c109:H.R.5319, accessed November 13, 2007.

[‡] http://www.govtrack.us/congress/record.xpd?id=109-h20060726-41, accessed November 13, 2007.

The provisions of the law, though well intended, are a bit draconian. Whereas CIPA was clearly designed to stem the tide of pornography and extremely gruesome images, DOPA seems at first glance geared more toward protecting teens from themselves—which might come dangerously close to violating the free speech clause of the First Amendment since the young (and old alike) who can't afford the technologies that permit this new form of virtual socialization and public address would not be allowed to access them at public libraries or schools. As California Representative Diane Watson explained, "The bill would curb Internet usage as a means to protect children, a counterproductive method to achieving such an important goal. Rather than restricting Internet usage, parents, teachers and librarians need to teach children how to use our ever changing technology."[*]

Furthermore, teachers who create blogs for discussion of texts, Wikis, or even educationally-related Facebook or the now-mostly-defunct MySpace pages—educators who are what Anastasia Goodstein calls the "trailblazers," those utilizing the most up-to-date technologies to enhance their pedagogy—would be dramatically affected by the passage of a law restricting or cutting off the very lifeblood of their classroom innovation.[†]

There are problematic aspects with the bill's wording, too. For example, consider DOPA's definition of social-networking sites: "[a site that] allows users to create web pages or profiles that provide information about themselves and are available to other users."[‡] Except this broad and loose description covers more than just social media such as Facebook; sites such as *Yahoo!*, in which users can provide information about themselves on their own personal profile pages, fall under this definition as well.

Finally, the technologies available online are transforming faster than bills like DOPA or CIPA can keep up with. There always seems to be a new danger that each bill misses, a new kind of online medium that people find ways of using creatively—or de-

---

[*] Ibid.

[†] In terms of using MySpace in an educational manner, even libraries quickly got on board; take a look at http://www.myspace.com/pawtucketlibrary to see what I mean (well, take a look if the website's still there!).

[‡] http://thomas.loc.gov/cgi-bin/query/z?c109:H.R.5319, accessed November 13, 2007.

structively. This is the battle that the well intentioned must fight: the struggle to be relevant.

And that, unfortunately, is the salient point. Good intentions aside, these kinds of laws have the effect of keeping the Internet out of the hands of the right people while still permitting the wrong sorts of people—i.e., those with a prurient interest in shopping for young prey—unfettered access and uninterrupted service. Those who want to lure children will hardly skip a beat just because Facebook is blocked at their local library. They'll surf online with their cell phones; they'll find another venue or circumvent whatever laws are on the books.

Educating minors of online dangers is a much better way to combat the problem. It's simply far more effective to have a society of technologically savvy and knowledgeable young people than a society of young people who have been perpetually prevented access to the Internet for their own "protection." After all, the Internet, like a gun, is simply a tool that can be used by individuals for good or for ill; in fact, Internet regulatory proposals and gun control laws resemble each other. As the brilliant text *Freakonomics* (2003) frames it, gun control laws like the Brady Act lack teeth and are "feeble" largely because they don't prevent those who shouldn't be anywhere near a gun from having one and instead impede access to firearms of those who actually follow the rules. Until Internet-safety laws correct their own version of this fallacy, they will be an impediment to well-meaning individuals and an affront to society at large.

(2007)

# 4.

## Mediation and Conflict Resolution in High School

Conflict, as noted in the essay "Mediation in the Schools" by David Trevaskis, is not necessarily synonymous with violence, despite the connotations the word frequently conjures up in people's minds. "However, unresolved and lingering conflict frequently leads to violence, interfering with productivity and the quality of life in schools and the community." Addressing a conflict through a mediation process wraps a messy, real-life event around an intellectual framework that *ipso facto* presupposes that the situation can be mediated or, at the very least, has the possibility of a mediated solution. That mediation, or some type of conflict resolution, can apply to a variety of conflict-type situations a high school teacher might encounter is far from clear. In addition, it also presupposes that someone—either involved in the dispute or outside of it—intervenes with some sort of mediation in a timely way; it is far from a given that people, even teachers, have such foresight and can interject themselves accordingly.

In order to grapple with the benefits and potential downsides of mediation, and thus form a cogent position on such kinds of school conflict resolution, it is necessary for me to describe a major, multi-student conflict I encountered in my own high school classroom in my second year as a teacher* which culminated in vicious name-calling and threats directed towards fellow students. Because I have retained most documents extant about this conflict, I can rely on primary-source material in presenting vignettes.

The conflict had its roots in my fourth period classroom—a class of twenty-three twelfth graders nervously itching to wrap up the school year. With only about twenty class days left before finals,

---

* I had a bit of a sophomore slump.

Y.,[*] an Asian-American female, K., an African-American female, and J., a white female, were at the center of the conflict; A., a white female, and M. and C., also white females, were secondary parties. Y. and J. were friends, as were A. and C.; K.'s prior relationship to the individuals listed in more complicated and is not necessary to relate in order to understand the conflict, except to note that she, J. and Y. rarely if ever interacted in my class.

As Y. explained it in a "Classroom Grievance"[†] paper she later delivered to me,

> On April 30, K. walked into Mr. Lorenzo's 4th period class and asked for a college recommendation. Mr. Lorenzo remarked that it was quite late in the school year. I said, "Tomorrow is May 1, when we all decide where to go to college," K. turned around to me and told me I was smart mouthed. "You always have something smart to say to me, why don't you stop being such a b----." Mr. Lorenzo asked K. to leave but she refused, saying that I instigated her and that I'm always "smart mouthed." In the course of this school year I have not held any conversation with K.... I was very upset with her comments....

That night, I received an e-mail from J., who was very concerned about what had transpired in class. J. wrote that she just

> wanted to express my feelings about class today. I think what happened was terrible and obnoxious and truthfully I feel that there is very bad tension in our class. I don't know why there is tension between people in our class and how to stop it, or if it can even go away, but I feel that you could have done something more as a teacher. I know you can't stop people from arguing or disliking each other, but you can punish people or kick them out of class when they are verbally assaulting someone else in the room. I'm not just saying this because Y. is my friend.... It's really not fair for some students to feel unsafe in school in terms of being picked on. Classrooms have to be safe spaces where

---

[*] Each student's name here has been replaced with a pseudonym consisting of only her first name's first letter.

[†] I present a stylized version of the conflict in a poem called "This Play's a Wreck" later in this book.

> teachers won't allow that kind of thing. I don't even feel comfortable speaking up in class because even on [this past] Friday when I tried to speak I was called a nerd and told to shut up. I just can't stand that this stuff goes on in high school and I wish that you could do something to prevent it from continuing. This kind of stuff happens in so many of my classes, not just this one. But this whole situation is distracting me from learning.

Needless to say, things didn't get much better over the next couple of days. Realizing that I had to stop the proverbial bleeding immediately, I devised a set of classroom rules—rules that were obvious, and rules that had been enumerated to my pupils previously though never quite in writing this way, but explicit rules nonetheless. I wrote up my list of directives on a single page and made a copy for each member of the class. Here is some of the document:

> There are less than 20 class days left for seniors. On May 30, seniors who do not meet the criteria for exemption will take a senior final examination. The days prior to the senior final will be devoted to reviewing material covered during this semester. But before that time, the following common-sense rules and dictates must be followed:
>
> - Students in this class will not talk ill or disrespect their peers.
>     - Penalty for non-compliance: A warning, followed by a detention. For each successive violation in a single class period, either an In-School Suspension or immediate removal from the class, or both—dependent on the circumstances and the teacher's discretion.
> - Students in this class will not publicly humiliate other students, either within the room or without.
>     - Penalty for non-compliance: A warning, followed by a detention. For each successive violation in a single class period, either an In-School Suspension or immediate removal from the

> class, or both—dependent on the circumstances and the teacher's discretion.
>
> - Students in this class WILL treat others with respect.
> - Students in this class WILL continue to learn new material, up until the very last senior day, with no more than minimal resistance.
>
> No one in this classroom is beyond reproach. Each one of us must do his or her part to create a safe, productive environment conducive to learning and tolerance and to improve our current circumstances. With your help, I look forward to completing this school year in a positive, hopeful manner.

Picking up with Y.'s description of the events, she wrote that

> On Wednesday, May 2, Mr. Lorenzo handed out a list of classroom rules. He gave the class approximately seven minutes to read over the rules and sign the bottom portion acknowledging that we understood and would follow the rules. He had a section for comments, but he made it very clear any comments should be written and not verbalized. C. repeated several times that she wished to talk to Mr. Lorenzo about the new rules, and that they were "ridiculous." Mr. Lorenzo repeated several times that he would talk to her after class, but she would not let up, so he took her outside and talked to her. He then continued with the day's lesson. The rest of the class progress [sic] normally.

But, alas, this détente wouldn't last long. By the next day, the undercurrent of tension was forcefully made manifest by some frustrated students. Y. explains:

> On Thursday, May 3, several students acted out. Mr. Lorenzo began the class by continuing the quiz review from the previous day. He stopped his lesson when M. cursed. He asked her to stop. He then asked her to leave the classroom and go to the [nearby administrator's] office. He outlined his rules sheet handed out [the previous day noting] that anyone removed from class would go to [the depart-

> ment head] in the office. M. refused. She told Mr. Lorenzo to write her up if he so chose, but she would not go to the office. She walked out of the classroom. Mr. Lorenzo procured a write-up sheet and filled it out, he then continued to go over the review packet, he instructed the class to complete a section of activities. K. asked to go to the bathroom, and Mr. Lorenzo let her. The rest of the class proceeded to do the assigned activities.... C. then proceeded to curse so loudly so that Mr. Lorenzo could hear. Upon hearing the cursing, Mr. Lorenzo asked C. to leave. She said "I don't fu----- care. I'm sitting here doing my work, that tattletale little b---- is sitting there doing nothing, and you're doing to kick me out." She then left the classroom. C. sat behind me, so I could not directly see who she looked and or directed her comment towards, but I believe it was towards me.
>
> Mr. Lorenzo procured another write-up sheet and filled it out. K. returned from the bathroom and gathered her belongings, while yelling "if anyone here has anything to say they should fu----- say it to my face. Every time I leave the classroom someone has something to say, one, two, and three, f--- you," and she left. The one, two and three, was in my opinion directed towards J., F. [another student friendly with J. and Y., but not a factor in this conflict], and myself. I do not know what instigated this comment from K.... A. then said "she'll beat you're a----." A. then asked to go to the bathroom, and Mr. Lorenzo let her go. She returned about ten minutes later cursing and Mr. Lorenzo was forced to write her up also.

That night, I received a second e-mail from J. not only recapitulating the details of the day, but also describing her feelings, hopes, and fears.

> Although 4th period is still a little bit rocky right now, I feel like it is changing for the better. Today, everything really came to a head and I admit I was made very uncomfortable by comments made by three of the girls that were written up today but, I feel that it is worth it if everyone else in the class can benefit in the long run. I don't really care that some people are angry with me or if they don't like me because of my standing up to them. The reason I

> wanted to write this e-mail is simply to have documentation of the threats made in class today. I wanted to bring them to your attention, not to be addressed or anything, but only as a warning in case something happens to myself or any of my other classmates that were threatened. Today A. said she would, "beat their a----" referring to myself and Y. She said she would do this at the end of the year because she won't get in trouble. While Mr. Lorenzo was talking with Y. outside for a minute, A. also got angry at something F. said and said, "I'll punch you in the f----- face." When K. came into the room after being sent out at the beginning of the period, she also threatened that she would physically harm F., Y., and myself.
>
> Many other vicious things were said but aside from that, these are the only things that concern me. They probably are false threats but I wanted to make you both aware of them in case something does happen to myself, Y., or F. I would not want anyone to get hurt and then have no way to prove what happened. Again, I don't need you to do anything about these threats and they are probably just nonsense (like all of my friends keep assuring me) but I need you to know that they were made. Although I am feeling that today's events were pretty crazy and immature now, at the time I did feel threatened and I am still not sure whether to believe if something bad will happen to myself or my fellow classmates or not.

Let me end the suspense: the threats made were never delivered upon. The remaining class days were relatively uneventful, but the incidents attracted the attention of a member of the school's parent-teacher organization—which just happened to be, unfortunately for me, J.'s father. In e-mails addressed not to me but to my department head through these trying days, he juggled both roles: that of a parent concerned for his daughter's safety, and of a community leader, interested in the general welfare of the students at the school. So that another perspective is represented here, let's take a look at some of what he wrote immediately after the escalation of the in-class rhetoric.

> There is a serious problem in Mr. Lorenzo's fourth period class. A few students are so discourteous and disrespectful

> to their fellow students and to Mr. Lorenzo that my wife, my daughter J., and I have concluded that the remaining students are being robbed of the education that they expected to gain when they scheduled the class. J. and her classmates have a right to learn, but that right has been violated. However, due to intimidation by the rude and disruptive students, J. and her classmates feel helpless to change the situation without help from your Department. Please let me know what steps you plan to take to convert the deteriorating situation in fourth period to an exemplary learning experience for the final month of this school year. The majority of the students certainly deserve it.

Although he was unquestionably right to add his voice to the chorus of individuals frustrated about the situation, and I appreciated his perspective on things, I wish that his letter had been addressed directly to me rather than to my department head.

Could mediation have worked here? In order to address this, we need to unpack the question. First of all, what do we mean by "worked"? What would we be hoping to accomplish via mediation, or some conflict resolution process? Next, we need to determine the timing for such a mediation process—i.e., by the time the situation became chaotic, was it too late for repair? In other words, if such mediation or conflict resolution (or conflict "management") might have staved off conflict, how, exactly, do I know *when* to intervene, and could there be some sort of training process so that I and other teachers could learn to timely recognize the symptoms and signs of an inevitable coming-to-blows of the pupils in my classroom? And, finally, am I really the best person to orchestrate the mediation, or could another adult—or even student—run it? Let us focus and expand on each of these questions in turn.

If a conflict mediation process has "worked," what does this imply? Perhaps the best way to answer this question is to look at a mediation that didn't work. In 1986, President Ronald Reagan met with General Secretary Gorbachev in Reykjavik, Iceland, to negotiate arms controls between the two superpowers. As described in *Dutch: A Memoir of Ronald Reagan* (1999) by Edmund Morris, the summit took place over the course of several days, and the negotiations kept getting tripped up over details such as the United States' right to build a missile defense shield and the abolishing of different types of nuclear weapons. "'I've said again and again the SDI [missile defense shield] wasn't a bargaining chip,' Reagan said, annoyed by the smile. 'If you are willing to abolish nuclear weapons, why are you so anxious to get rid of a defense against nuclear weapons?'" Annoyed, Gorbachev demanded that everything else was off the table unless Reagan agreed to end SDI. Morris describes what happened next:

> There was a long silence. Reagan slid a note over to Shultz [the Secretary of State]: *Am I wrong?* The secretary whispered, "No, you're right."
> "The meeting is over," Reagan said. He stood up. "Let's go, George [Shultz], we're leaving."
> . . .
> They strode out into a wet glare of television lights. Reagan headed straight for his car.
> "Mr. President," Gorbachev said, no longer smiling, "you have missed the unique chance of going down in history as a great president who paved the way for nuclear disarmament."
> "That applies to both of us."
> "I don't know what else I could have done."
> "You could have said yes," Reagan said.

These negotiations on a world stage failed, ultimately, because neither party was willing to budge from entrenched positions on the subject. While mediations and negotiations that might transpire in a school will never have such far-reaching consequences, Reagan and Gorbachev's failure to come to some sort of agreement helpfully illustrates for us how mediation and conflict resolution should not be conducted. Success cannot be achieved if parties to the mediation view it strictly as a zero-sum game.

"The Story of Little Red Riding Hood and the Wolf, Retold Through Negotiation" (by Crawford and Bodine, 1996) demonstrates, through a narrative familiar to most, why simply getting two disputants to sit down together, à la Reagan and Gorbachev, isn't enough to ensure success. By the time the Wolf and Red Riding Hood get to the fifth step of the negotiation—evaluate options—they have already put themselves in each other's shoes, so to speak, so that the agreements that are codified during the final step of the process are not only possible but have *organically* arisen from the dialogue. This is the only way a "success" can be achieved: when the parties to the dispute simultaneously arrive at a mutual, non-imposed solution.

This, of course, then begs the question: how would "success" have been defined if some kind of mediation or negotiation were to have taken place between the agitated and frustrated members of my tumultuous classroom? Following the "Little Red Riding Hood and the Wolf" negotiation story, we can imagine that there would be quite a few different arguments heard in step 2—points of view. One of the common threads running through the primary documents detailing my class's conflict is the presence of some slight or perceived insult that Y. directed towards K.; this appears to have been a trigger mechanism, but, because the scope of the insults and threats so quickly expanded well beyond these two individuals, there certainly was latent hostility in the class—and this hostility may not have germinated in my class but simply found full expression there. Much of what causes conflict in schools, after all, has as its root events that have transpired outside of the classroom.

We certainly couldn't expect, after a negotiation between Y., K., J., A., and C., for everyone to exit the meeting as best friends. We could expect, and might define success, as (1) allowing all individuals to have an opportunity to listen to their respective grievances and their perceptions of one another without an audience (their non-involved classroom peers), which such a mediation should perforce permit, (2) agreements to not threaten, intimidate, or mock each other, and (3) an explicit avenue whereby future issues between disputants could be readily and quickly addressed prior to further escalation (such as with private meetings with the teacher). Any chance of success, of course, would have rested on those involved agreeing to not only participate in the mediation but also to abide by the resultant agreements. After the incidents in my classroom occurred, I didn't get together with the disputants but rather simply unilaterally disseminated a list of rules for students to follow—or else.

When those rules were handed out, I distinctly remember thinking that it was simply too late to explore any other way of dealing with the problem other than transforming my classroom into a gulag—anything less would be simply rearranging deck chairs on the *Titanic*. But ruling with an iron fist is inimical to my nature; "procuring" (as Y. put it) write-up sheet after write-up sheet to deal with disruptions was, as the vignettes illustrated above, merely a stopgap solution to a larger, systemic problem. Instead of addressing the causes of conflict, I was only reacting to the effects—which is unsurprising, since "[s]chools have attempted to manage interpersonal conflicts among students, teachers, and administrators by various models of discipline, such as referrals to the principal's office, detention, suspension, and expulsion," as Trevaskis writes. Would mediation have worked, or was it already too late? Were things already beyond hope when the rules were distributed, or did it only become a truly "non-negotiable" situation immediately following the recitation of the riot act—that next day, when the true insults went flying?

All of these questions center on timeliness—namely, whether and when it might be too late for mediation or conflict resolution to be viable, whether it's a voluntary process or not. Mediation presupposes that one who has the power, authority, or knowledge to conduct mediation is also cognizant of the proper time to engage in mediation; timing is everything, and a mediator intervening at the most opportune time is paramount to the success of the process.

In order to impart the skill of intervening at the correct time—early enough before chaos erupts, but late enough that the actors in the conflict can be identified—it seems that the mediator-in-training should be exposed to a wide variety of hypothetical conflicts. (This assumes, of course, that the mediation is involuntary; if it were voluntary, the mediator would not need to concern him- or herself with any sort of judgment about when to step in. Because I have structured my thinking about conflict resolution around a seminal event much earlier in my teaching career, we'll consider involuntary mediation in this brief discussion of timeliness.) In the training manual *The Conflict Manager Program: Peer Mediation for High Schools*, much space and print is devoted to hypothetical situations. Many of these training exercises largely focus on how to manage the disputants during the mediation process, but others work around the edges, exposing trainees to the roots of the conflict prior to hashing through any sort of conflict mediation session. In addition, the activities in the text called "Constructing I-Messages" and "Culture and Conflict Discussion" also move towards viewing conflict outside of a small room with two actors and onto a larger canvas of misunderstandings, misinterpretations, and miscommunications among people. Perhaps there should be more activities in this vein; also, anyone training to be a conflict mediator in schools might find it useful to spend time observing places in the school in which students are closest to being "themselves," such as in the lunchroom or the courtyard. Ultimately, though, the skill to know when to intervene before a blowup occurs will develop with experience.

Back to my fourth period class: If I were a trained conflict mediator, and my students in that class simply *knew* that, they might have approached me to deal with the situation privately. Walking around with the label "mediator" may have precipitated that which (I know now in retrospect) I sought: a preemptive solution to a nasty eruption. Furthermore, if our school had—and had publicized—a team of adult conflict resolution managers, some of the students in my fourth period class might have sought their help in dealing with the conflict. And, extending these ideas even more, suppose that most classrooms, including mine, had students who had been trained as mediators, and their peers knew it; this may have fostered a completely different, constructive reaction among the students—both those trained as mediators and those who simply knew of peer mediation—in my classroom. The conflict resolution skills that those mediator students learned wouldn't only be valuable in a high school setting, but in their later adult lives as well.

What I am describing, however clumsily, is the development of a different kind of culture in my school and others like it, a culture of listening, understanding, non-violence, interconnectedness and community. This is a culture in which the onus of timely intervention wouldn't be placed squarely on the teacher. According to Trevaskis, "[T]he job of educators today is to teach our children how to handle all of the conflicts that arise in creative and constructive ways. Too many forces in our culture reinforce the opposite message, that conflict is somehow bad and something that we must avoid."

Project PEACE is a program designed to reduce violence and conflict in Pennsylvania's schools by "teaching students how to discuss and mediate disagreements peacefully. It empowers children, who are still in their formative years, with the important life-skills that promote constructive communication, problem-solving, critical-thinking and self-esteem. *Children become active participants in governing behavior in their classrooms by taking on the role of mediator and using the mediation process* [emphasis added]," Trevaskis says. Perhaps that's part of what went wrong in my fourth period class: students didn't taken ownership over the classroom environment and, instead, left that all to me. Although I was the authority figure in the room, their perception of that figure—as one who simply metes out punishment, delivers praise, and "controls" the kids—may be (or should be) anachronistic in today's school milieu.

And there is at least some research to back up the effectiveness of peer mediation. Consider the article "Conflict Resolution Education: The Field, the Findings, and the Future" by Tricia Jones: "The research on peer mediation, especially at elementary levels, confirms that mediators gain social and emotional competency from this experience and that schools can gain from improved classroom and school climate. Those impacts are much less evident with peer mediation in middle and high schools," Jones writes. Possibly by the time students make it to high school, their preconceptions and assumptions about their peers and environment are too set for any kind peer mediation, seen by them for the first time, to have much of an impact. But as the article goes on to note, longitudinal analyses of conflict resolution education would be especially helpful to confirm this. As Marian Vollmer explains in her essay entitled "Partnering Character Education and Conflict Resolution,"

> Essential to the mediation process is the creation of foundation abilities for conflict resolution. Grounding conflict-resolution strategies in teaching ethical behaviors through commonly accepted character attributes successfully facilitates this process. Emphasis has been placed on teaching the basics of conflict resolution as early in a child's life as possible, such as during the elementary grades….

Therefore, to effectively create a culture of peaceful mediation of conflict in high schools, that kind of culture perhaps must be advanced when children are very young, well before their preconceived notions of the world have become static and non-malleable.

Short of going back in time to reform students' elementary school lives, this culture of non-violence can be fostered in high schools in part by putting in place anti-bullying programs. Recall J.'s statement about "safe spaces" in her first e-mail to me: "It's really not fair for some students to feel unsafe in school in terms of being picked on. Classrooms have to be safe spaces where teachers won't allow that kind of thing. I don't even feel comfortable speaking up in class because even on Friday when I tried to speak I was called a nerd and told to shut up." Instead of examining the unfortunate events of my fourth period as an example of a failure to mediate a conflict, perhaps it should be considered through the lens of a failure (on my part) to prevent bullying.

A more intrepid teacher would have proactively followed the "Individual Interventions" section of the "Bullying Program Elements," also by David Trevaskis:

- Intervening on the spot when bullying occurs;
- Holding follow-up discussions with children who are bullied;
- Having follow-up discussions with children who bully;
- Sharing information with staff;
- Involving parents of children who are involved.

Ironically, I ultimately did, to one degree or another, address most of these bullet points but merely as a reaction to events rather than in a proactive, proscribed manner; for instance, the parent of a child was involved—but only because he had e-mailed my department head, not because I informed him of the rapidly deteriorating situation and his daughter's unwitting involvement in it.

Nevertheless, preventing bullying, like promoting a culture of non-violence and conflict resolution, requires more than just a timely intervention in a single bullying event while ignoring the causes and the environment around the bully and the bullied.* In his first e-mail, J.'s father correctly noted that he and his wife, as well as "every responsible parent justly expect [this high school] to be an excellent learning environment, just as it was when we both graduated from [it nearly thirty years ago]." But then he went on to claim the following: "Nothing has occurred during the past twenty-

---

* Bullying can be considered an affront to meritocracy, especially in a school, since bullied students do not permit themselves to flourish creatively, socially, or academically since so much time, energy, and resources are spent worrying about and overcoming—or failing to overcome—the bullies. The bullied reside in a playground of lost potential, complete with swords of Damocles hanging above their heads.

five years that can excuse such an unacceptable situation." His dogmatism blithely ignores the facts on the ground, the ever-shifting realities of high school education in America. Much needs to be done to improve not only my high school but also others across the country. Simple platitudes will not do; leaving it all in the hands of the teachers will not do; putting the onus of responsibility on the students to "just stop it and behave" will not do. It will take a concerted effort and commitment among all stakeholders—teachers, students, and parents alike—to create a classroom, school, and community that's positive, welcoming, and tolerant, a truly "safe space" that J. longed for but never quite experienced.

(2008)

# 5.

## Juvenile Justice, Animal Abuse, and Animals-as-Therapy

In *True Notebooks* (2003), writer Mark Salzman's meditation on teaching experiences in Central Juvenile Hall in East Los Angeles, one of his students in creative writing, an adjudicated juvenile named Kevin Jackson, reads aloud to his small class a piece he wrote about a dog he knew years before. "Around when I was nine or ten me and my friend Arthur had a puppy named Sparkie. Well," he continues,

> really Sparkie wasn't our dog, he belonged to someone who lived up the street from me. When they would go to work me and my friend would climb the fence and steal their dog for a few hours to play with him and then we would return him before the owners knew he was even gone. But one day when I went over there to get him he wasn't there.... Even now I still wonder what happened to the dog. I wonder if Sparkie and I were to cross paths again, would he remember who I am?

The irony of the story seems lost on everyone. Here is this future juvenile offender stealing a dog—not to abuse it, but to enjoy its company. It's a bizarre tale, made all the more bizarre by a Juvenile Justice Bulletin, published around the same time Kevin wrote about Sparkie, summarizing studies which document the links between animal abuse and youth violence—studies which show, in fact, how improbable Kevin Jackson's story really is.

In "Animal Abuse and Youth Violence",* author Frank Ascione explains the purpose of his Bulletin: "The past two decades have witnessed a resurgence of interest in the relation between cruelty to animals...among youthful offenders.... This Bulletin reports on the

---

* http://www.ncjrs.gov/html/ojjdp/jjbul2001_9_2/contents.html, accessed on August 22, 2007.

psychiatric, psychological, and criminological research linking animal abuse to juvenile- and adult-perpetrated violence." The studies he cites and the statistics he reports are eye-opening. Consider: after defining the notion of "cruelty to animals," Achenbach et al. used what's called an "Achenbach-Conners-Quay Behavior Checklist" to collect reports of "problem behaviors" among 2,600 boys and girls aged 4 to 6 who had been referred to mental health clinics; a control group of non-referred children constituted a representative sample of comparison based residence, socioeconomic status, and ethnicity. The results? "In their statistical analysis of individual ACQ items, Achenbach and colleagues noted that cruelty to animals was significantly ($p < 0.01$) higher for referred youth, boys, and younger children."

So Achenbach demonstrated a statistically significant* linkage between cruelty to animals and mental-health referrals. But what about violence? Mistreatment of animals at a young age is suspected to play a role in later violent behavior. Ascione frames the potential connection this way:

> Animal abuse and interpersonal violence toward humans share common characteristics: both types of victims are living creatures, have a capacity for experiencing pain and distress, can display physical signs of their pain and distress (with which humans could empathize), and may die as a result of inflicted injuries. Given these commonalities, it is not surprising that early research in this area, much of it using retrospective assessment, examined the relation between childhood histories of animal abuse and later violent offending.

Although the notion of "retrospective assessment" is questionable—without conducting longitudinal studies in which we follow those who have and who have not committed animal abuse and

---

* Generally, a $p$-value lower than 0.05 indicates that a researcher's claim has been demonstrated—i.e., that there is statistical significance; the Achenbach study reported a $p$-value of less than 0.01. Note that even a $p$-value of effectively zero does nothing to establish causation—only a well-controlled and properly designed experiment can demonstrate a cause-and-effect relationship (in most cases; exceptions include Jerome Cornfield's retrospective analysis of smoking and lung cancer and other kinds of epidemiological studies).

document, through the years of following the participants, their instances of violent behaviors, we really can't confidently correlate animal abuse and later violence—the point is clear: an individual's inability to engender empathy perhaps prevents him from treating living creatures as more than just objects, things to be damaged or destroyed at a moment's notice. The theory essentially goes: If you hurt animals, then why wouldn't you hurt people, too?

But Michael Schader doesn't seem to agree. In "Risk Factors for Delinquency: An Overview"* Schader correctly observes that "[r]esearchers have concluded that there is no single path to delinquency [among juveniles] and note that the presence of several risk factors often increase a youth's chance of offending." Although vaguely mentioning "physical violence," animal abuse is not cited in Schader's piece as a potential risk factor.

Of course, the very act of abusing animals can land juveniles in trouble with the law. Websites such as *pet-abuse.com*† have detailed juveniles' legal run-ins due to the abuse of animals. In Lawrence, Massachusetts, for instance, teens were arrested for participating in dogfighting training in 2006; and, also in 2006, the distressing story of a 14-year-old boy who killed his parrot with a firecracker is documented. The article "America's Abuse Problem"‡ by Cindy Adams relays a rather gruesome story of a 10-year-old boy's abuse of his eight-week-old puppy. Needless to say, the abuser landed himself a conviction in juvenile court.

The Cindy Adams article also points to a disturbing new nexus leading to violent behavior in children: "For many years, a classic triad of enuresis (bedwetting), pyromania (fire setting) and animal abuse was cited as symptomatic of troubled children and adolescents. This seems to be giving way to a new classic, however: the triptych of child abuse, childhood animal abuse and later deviant behavior against humans."§

---

* A U.S. Department of Justice document.

† Accessed on August 22, 2007.

‡ Presented on the ASPCA website: http://www.aspca.org/site/PageServer?pagename=edu_resources_america, accessed August 22, 2007.

§ In fact, there even seems to be a nexus between pyromania and childhood animal abuse! In the Journal of the American Academy of Child & Adolescent Psychiatry, a short article entitled "A Study of Firesetting and Animal Cruelty in Children: Family Influences and Adolescent Outcomes" (July 2004) found

Cindy Adams then goes on to detail a famous study by Alan Felthous and Steven Kellert (1985) which observed and studied 152 men (with 102 of them serving time in federal jails). The researchers concluded that "[c]ruelty to animals during childhood occurred much more often among the aggressive criminals than among the non-aggressive criminals or non-criminals." In other words, the researchers observed a difference of *degree* in terms of aggression between those who had performed abuse on animals and those who hadn't. Realize, however, that this study apparently also relied on the data-gathering process of so-called retrospective assessment, which calls into question the results; after all, can we really trust the animal-abuse claims of these ignoble miscreants?

However, in a publication several years later called "Childhood Cruelty to Animals and Later Aggression Against People: a Review" (1987), Alan Felthous and Steven Kellert further their arguments of the abuse-violence link. "Studies using direct interviews to examine subjects with multiple acts of violence point to an association between a pattern of childhood animal cruelty and later serious, recurrent aggression against people," they claim. Unfortunately, the problem of "direct interviews" again casts doubt on their conclusions since the memories of these convicts may not be entirely trustworthy.

Has the legislative branch of our government caught up with and assimilated the mountains of research studies, anecdotes, and policy proposals that those documenting this sad confluence of animal mistreatment and youth violence have promulgated? In a word, yes. Take the Missouri House of Representatives, for example. In House Bill 1279*—Animal Abuse by Children—the court is required to "order counseling or behavior-specific psychological treatment for a child adjudicated for engaging in behavior…pertaining to animal abuse." The bill pays respect to the research on animal abuse and juvenile violence by stating that "the link between cruelty to animals and other forms of violent behavior has been well documented. This activity is often a stepping stone to acts of violence upon people. These children need psychological

---

that "family variables increase the likelihood of childhood firesetting and animal cruelty and…these behaviors are related to adolescent delinquency."

* The full text of the bill, accessed August 22, 2007, can be found at http://www.house.mo.gov/bills02/bilsum02/commit02/sHB1279C.htm

help immediately, rather than waiting for the problem to escalate." Other state legislatures are looking into adopting similar proposals.

If it is agreed that juveniles—and, by extension, adults—who abuse animals lack the ability to empathize, as noted by several studies above, perhaps a controlled exposure of animals to those juveniles who are already locked up might help them develop these skills which they so sorely lack. Indeed, this philosophy of animals-as-cognitive-therapy has been put into practice in at least one state—New Mexico—in at least one juvenile detention center—the Youth Diagnostic and Development Center. Tamara H. Ward, Community and Social Service Specialist of the Development Center, describes the experience of using dogs to "facilitate change in juvenile delinquents" in a program called Project Second Chance.* Recognizing the link between the "red flag" of animal abuse and later violent behavior, Project Second Chance was designed to expose delinquents to shelter dogs with the express purpose of furthering empathy development among these juveniles. The juveniles write journals and are interviewed by the staff over a period of six months to a year. The juveniles in the program are also given animal-themed scenarios to discuss, such as this one:

> A very little baby bird was in her nest waiting for her mother and father to return with food. She was eager to see them so she wiggled to the edge of the nest. But she made a mistake, went too far, and fell out of the nest. She landed on the ground below the tree, all alone. She didn't know how to get back on her nest because she was too young to fly. If you were the baby bird, how would you feel? Would you feel alone? Frightened? Sad? What other feelings would you have?

The adjudicated juveniles discuss with staff members the so-called "dimensions of empathy," such as emotion and compassion, and even assume the role of a dog, "answering as the dog would, expressing feelings as the dog would," although the document doesn't make clear exactly what this process entails. Although no data are readily available on the efficacy of Project Second Chance, it does

---

* Tamara's full observations and discussion of the program is available at www2.vet.upenn.edu/research/centers/cias/powerpoint/Ward.ppt, which was accessed on August 22, 2007.

seem that this seemingly silly notion of juveniles-as-animals might engender empathetic behavior and lead to some sort of rehabilitation among the detainees if executed correctly.

Which takes us right back to Kevin Jackson in Mark Salzman's *True Notebooks.* Recall that the juvenile delinquent had written a story about Sparkie, a dog he "stole" from a neighbor day after day not to harm but simply to be around and play with. Author Salzman is advised and guided in Central Juvenile Hall by the omnipresent Sister Janet Harris, an elderly woman with the energy and time to devote to helping juveniles in the lock-up facility. Early in the book, when Salzman asks Sister Janet to inform him of who'll be attending his start-up creative writing class, the Sister describes Kevin Jackson this way: "Kevin Jackson is shy, it takes a while to get to know him, but he's one of the nicest boys you'll ever meet. You'll like him right away." As the text goes on to show, Sister Janet's assessment proved correct. Could Kevin Jackson's docility, his politeness, his lack of aggression, be a result of those afternoons he spent getting to know Sparkie years ago? Of course, we can't be sure. But based on the research and testimonies suggesting the connection between animal abuse and youth violence, and the corollary—that exposure to animals might lessen the potential for juveniles to engage in injurious behavior whilst increasing their empathetic responses—we certainly can't rule it out, either.

(2007)

# 6.

## Perpetuating Genius and Stupidity: The Persistence of the Myth of Galois

Shakespeare, had he lived about two centuries later, would have certainly reveled in scripting the details of such a story. A young mathematical prodigy, living in heady and tumultuous times, consistently rejected at every turn—by his teachers, other mathematicians, and society at large—turns to revolutionary practices and politics, in a rebellious fit of rage. After threatening the life of the king in the restored Bourbon dynasty in post-1789, post-Napoleon France, he is jailed for an extended period of time and yet manages to fall in love—with a prostitute, no less. After an attempt on his life is averted, and after eluding spies and royalist agents in search of him because of his radical republican stances, he faces a contemporary in a duel—and is left to die alone in a field. The night before he dies, however, he transcribes, for the first time, the sum-total of his theories of mathematics, including Group Theory; his corpus—which has breakthroughs as revolutionary as his politics—the world of math has not seen the likes of since the singular Euclid assembled his *Elements*.

Although Shakespeare never got the chance to write this mythological narrative of Evariste Galois—the nascent mathematician and French radical the story speaks of—in novel-size, at least two authors did: Leopold Infeld, in 1948, and Tom Petsinis, in 2000. Infeld's book, *Whom the Gods Love: The Story of Evariste Galois*, concentrates on the machinations of the politics of betrayal—the text frames Galois as a young man caught in a deathtrap of lust and conspiracy. With police spies after him near the end of his life, Galois, considered one of the most dangerous and explosive persons of the rebellious republicans, succumbs to the antagonistic forces seeking to destroy him.

In *The French Mathematician*, by Petsinis, the story is much the same: a promising mathematician torn from the sciences finds refuge in radicalism—after his father is framed by local town folk and commits suicide. Interestingly, the text is in first person from the point of view of Galois; his supposed-emotional reactions to life events both major and minor are detailed fully.

Neither novel purports to be an accurate rendition of the minute-by-minute details in the life of Galois, but each has underpinnings in fact. Thus, events that comprise the great mythology of Galois—such as his furious night-before-the-duel spent scribbling down his proofs; his almost-clockwork-like attempts at breaking into the cloistered mathematical society of the day, along with the repeated rebuffs; and the network of mysterious royalist agents continuously keeping track of his whereabouts—are assumed sacrosanct. And yet the fictions that these two authors believe they are writing are more pervasive than they claim.

Between the times that these two novels were published, an article appeared in the periodical *Mathematical Monthly* debunking much of the myth of Galois' life and times in which the novels were based. Entitled "Genius and Biographers: The Fictionalization of Evariste Galois," by Tony Rothman (1982), the article is not so much revolutionary as it is cynical; it reads almost as snark,* and yet is ingenious in its approach and synthesis of the disparate pieces of the mathematical puzzle of Galois.

Rothman spends much space discussing whom he considers the original mythmaker: Eric Temple Bell. In 1937 Bell, a former mathematics professor and one-time president of the esteemed Mathematical Association of America, wrote a seminal work in math history entitled *Men of Mathematics*. The book is a collected biography; each chapter contains a biographical portrait of a famous mathematician, with a little bit of mathematics thrown in for good measure. The text is lucid and fluid—Bell brings his considerable descriptive talents to the fore to capture personalities. More than halfway through the text, the chapter "Genius and Stupidity" appears. Galois is the subject, and, by bringing a greater sense of urgency to some of the young mathematical prodigy's series of unfortunate

---

* For more on snark—including the history and culture of the term (it was coined by Lewis Carroll, a mathematician posing as a writer)—read *New Yorker* editor David Denby's entertaining slim volume *Snark*.

events, Bell, the flamboyant storyteller, manages to lose much of the truth in fanciful prose and—worse yet—hagiography.

The truth—or at least a smattering of the documents and personal writings of Galois—was fully available to Bell. As Rothman explains,

> The primary source of information, containing eyewitness accounts and many relevant documents, is the original study of Paul Dupuy, which appeared in 1896. Dupuy was a historian and the Surveillant General of the Ecole Normale.... [T]hose who use Dupuy as their sole source of information must make mistakes. Nevertheless, this original biography is much more complete and accurate than subsequent dilutions and contains more information than a reading of Bell... would even suggest.

Bell, of course, made liberal use of Dupuy's work—yet, as Rothman says, he did not even once quote from it. Instead, he culled bits selectively, at one point even egregiously altering the timeline of events in Galois' life to better fit the narrative thrust of his chapter. (I am referring to Bell's description of Galois' political activities. Rothman says, "[C]hronology is rearranged, events are omitted and others invented in increasing quantity, until the end of his account is *largely fantasy*" [my italics].) Much of the article catalogs Bell's offenses against the facts that he was nonetheless privy to about Galois' life.

Despite—or because of—the sacrifice of detail to paint the more intriguing portrait, the chapter, and the book, made a mark. Although it is difficult to establish exactly how influential any book was or is, Rothman notes that mathematician-physicist Freeman Dyson's imagination was sparked by the mythically tragic story of Galois, a story of unlimited potential and of fate and circumstance interfering. He goes on to quote from Dyson's book *Disturbing the Universe*: "[M]y head was full of the romantic prose of E. T. Bell's *Men of Mathematics*.... The most memorable chapter is called 'Genius and Stupidity' and describes the life and death of the French mathematician Galois, who was killed in a duel at the age of twenty." Rothman also credits Bell's Galois chapter for creating and propagating the legend and the myth of Galois, which—as I will demonstrate below—holds sway in some popular mathematical literature to today. And, to paraphrase Rothman, the fact that the same errors of history will fire the imagination of future generations of mathematical students will, unfortunately, not be in doubt.

In 1993, after seven long years of toiling away in his attic in almost absolute secrecy, Andrew Wiles believed that he had finally proved one of the most notorious and elusive riddles in all of mathematics: Fermat's Last Theorem. Scribbled in the margin of a copy of the Diophantus' *Arithmetica* by Pierre de Fermat, a jurist and part-time avid mathematician in seventeenth-century France, it read (using modern parlance): with $x$, $y$, and $z$ as integers, there are no solutions of $x$ to the power $n$ plus $y$ to the power $n$ equals $z$ to the power $n$ where $n$ is greater than two. A short time after Wiles formally presented his proof of Fermat to the mathematical community, errors in his logic were found. Eventually, though, Wiles, a professor at Princeton University, corrected them (almost entirely by himself), and Fermat's Last Theorem was indeed unequivocally shown to be a theorem.

But, as Wiles has said, the proof could have only been completed in the twentieth century. The rapid development of layer upon layer of abstract mathematics, such as topology, graph theory, game theory, and scores of others—and even forays into the logic and ontology of mathematics itself, meta-mathematics, with such revolutionaries as Kurt Gödel and Paul Cohen—characterized many of last century's advances in the field.* Like Newton before him, and perhaps even more so, Andrew Wiles stood on the shoulders of giants to accomplish the heretofore impossible.

One of those giants was Evariste Galois. Galois, some 150 years before Wiles' proof of Fermat's Last Theorem, arrived at Galois theory, a mathematical method used in part to transfer sets of infinite collections to finite ones. After spending much time juggling the complexities of elliptic curves and modular forms to arrive at a proof of Fermat, Andrew Wiles decided to try something different, detailed in Amir D. Aczel's best-selling book, *Fermat's Last Theorem: Unlocking the Secret of an Ancient Mathematical Problem.*

---

* For the best historical treatment of the trends of mathematical thought over the twentieth century, see *Mathematics: The Loss of Certainty* (1982) by Morris Kline. Math simply isn't as black and white as you might initially suppose.

> After two years of getting nowhere, Wiles tried a new approach. He thought he might *transform* the elliptic curves into Galois representations, and then count these Galois representations against the modular forms.... This translation of a problem constitutes an immense step forward, since a finite set of elements is so much easier to handle than an infinite set. [original italics present]

The profundity of the move was not lost of Wiles, who had been straining for years to work his way out of complication after complication.

Aczel's book has many other examples of clear, metaphorical, and commonsensical explanations of mathematics utilized to solve Fermat littered throughout. There are also scattered biographies of many mathematicians whose results or help contributed to the final proof, such as Nick Katz, a contemporary of Wiles' and the only person whom he chose to tell about his proof-in-progress, in addition to Pythagoras, the ancient Greek mathematician.

There is also a rather lengthy biography of Galois. Although Aczel's explanations of mathematics seem relatively sound—albeit very simplified—his description of Galois' short life contains many of the same errors as Bell's chapter on Galois. Before enumerating these errors, it is necessary to note that Aczel's text was published some fourteen years *after* Rothman's article on the fictionalization of Galois went to print.

Only two paragraphs of Aczel's section on the young mathematician go by before the first questionable statement arises. "Unfortunately," he says, "[Galois] was not to enjoy any recognition in his tragically short life." If recognition is taken to mean that the general public knew about his prowess in mathematics, then this statement is correct. However, the sentence before speaks of the young Galois' mastery of current mathematics and development of cutting-edge math of the day—certainly topics that the layperson would not be accustomed to assimilating or understanding or, perhaps, even being aware of. Thus, the statement is probably implying professional recognition, which Galois did indeed receive. Rothman's article says that Augustin-Louis Cauchy, a French mathematician who unsuccessfully attempted to prove Fermat's Last Theorem, gave praise of Galois' solution for the Grand Prize in mathematics and even personally encouraged him in his mathematical pursuits. And Auguste Chevalier, another noted mathematician, was Galois' best friend and ultimate securer of the young prodigy's place in the annals of mathematical legend—it was he whom Galois sent his mathematical papers to before he was killed in a duel.

Aczel then proceeds to completely disregard primary source material and stick to the script of Bell's "Genius and Stupidity." When describing Galois' ill-fated attempts at passing his entrance exam into the Ecole Polytechnique, he recalls one of the popular myths. "When he realized he was going to fail the second and last permissible attempt … Galois threw the blackboard eraser in the face of his examiner," Aczel writes. It shows Galois as quite the rebel—except for the fact that it never happened. Rothman explains:

> Legend has it that Galois, who worked almost entirely in his head and was poor at presenting his ideas verbally, became so enraged at the stupidity of his examiner that he hurled an eraser at him. Bell records this as a fact but according to the little-known study of Joseph Bertrand the tradition is false…. [I]n response to [the examiner's] questions, [Galois] replied merely that the answer was completely obvious.

Needless to say, Galois' reaction to the failure was hardly that of physical assault.

It is directly implied in *Fermat's Last Theorem* that, as legend has it, Cauchy lost Galois' submission to him of some of his breakthrough mathematics. However, once again, the historically erudite Rothman trumps Aczel. "…Rene Taton," Rothman tells us, "has discovered a letter of Cauchy in the Academy archives that conclusively proves that he did not lose Galois' memoirs but had planned to present them to the Academy in January 1830."

Continuing, there is yet another legend transcribed as fact by Aczel. Consider the following passage:

> Out of school, Galois started offering private lessons in mathematics. He wanted to teach his own mathematical theories, outside of the French schools, when he was all of nineteen years old. But Galois could not find students to

> teach—his theories were too advanced; he was far ahead of his time.

Although he was certainly far ahead of his time, he did find students to teach—almost forty of them, according to Rothman. However, as Rothman also points out, the teaching activities did not last for long because of Galois' radical politics.

Although we have covered barely three pages of Aczel's biographical section on Galois, there are more factual errors to be found. "While on parole," he writes, "Galois met a young woman and fell in love. Some believe he was set up by his royalist enemies who wanted to put an end to his revolutionary activities. . . ." Only someone with a less-than-complete record of primary documents believes that Galois was set up in any way. Recall that the two novels about Galois mentioned at the beginning of this essay, *Whom the Gods Love* and *The French Mathematician*, used conspiracy theories as a basis for much of the intrigue in the fabricated plots of Galois' life. Yet there was never any conspiracy; Rothman, examining primary documents (such as extant letters to and from Galois), demonstrates this.

Another famous legend propagated by Bell of the final days of Galois centers on the young woman he fell in love with. Aczel writes, "[T]he woman whom he got involved was of questionable virtue [i.e., a prostitute]." In one of the most startling sentences of Rothman's article, the prostitute theory is disregarded: "Any presumption that she was a prostitute must at this point be disregarded as a complete figment of Bell's imagination."

Finally, in the most famous and most incorrect legend of them all, Galois is said to have written the entire body of mathematical theories he ever produced in a single night, the night before his fatal duel; Aczel presents this as fact. According to Bell's description, Galois spent that entire night writing his "scientific last will and testament." Bell continues: "Time after time he broke off to scribble in the margin 'I have not time; I have not time,' and passed on to the next frantically scrawled outline. What he wrote in those desperate last hours before the dawn will keep generations of mathematicians busy for hundreds of years."

And again, Rothman debunks. In another of his direct and unambiguous sentences, he sets the record straight. "Galois had indeed helped to create a field which would keep mathematicians busy for hundreds of years but not 'in those last desperate hours before the dawn.'" Check off another affront to the historical record.

The sheer number of Aczel's identical errors with Bell is astounding; in a matter of six pages, we have discovered at least six inconsistencies with primary source material. The critical reader automatically should call the credibility of the entire text, from a historical perspective, into question. If so much was so wrong with the story of Galois, how can we completely trust other sections and other biographies in *Fermat's Last Theorem*?

Putting that text aside, we next turn to another bestseller, *Fermat's Enigma: The Epic Quest to Solve the World's Greatest Mathematical Problem*, by Simon Singh, a physicist. This book is much more detailed than Aczel's, walking through much of the math instead of just cursorily mentioning the results as Aczel does.

But some of the errors first made by Bell reappear, despite the overwhelming evidence to disregard them. "Sensing that he was about to be failed for a second time … Galois lost his temper and threw a blackboard eraser at Dinet, scoring a direct hit," and "The night before the duel Galois attempted to write down all his mathematical ideas" are two of the most obvious culprits. He also claims that "Historians have argued about whether the duel was the result of a tragic love affair or politically motivated…" which seems a bit too inconclusive of a statement, considering the synthesis of relevant documents that Rothman presents in his article. Although the myths contained in Singh's work about Galois are certainly not as egregious as those in Aczel's, one is still discouraged by their presence.

Last century, there were at least two specific times that the works of Galois reached a popular, non-mathematical audience in an accessible format: with the publication of the widely-read *Men of Mathematics*, and when Fermat's Last Theorem was proven (in fact, Andrew Wiles' proof made national headlines, including a feature story on the front page of the *New York Times*). Bell's book arrived before Rothman's seminal article, and the two Fermat books discussed here, after. And yet, at least some myths of Galois remained in tact, perpetuated to more and more potentially unsuspecting people.

Even in two recently published *dictionaries* of mathematics for a general audience, the mythos of the ill-fated genius is promulgated. In *The Harper Collins Dictionary of Mathematics*, falsities of Galois' life are unabashedly proclaimed. The dictionary states that published papers were intentionally lost by Cauchy—recall that was shown by Rothman to be a myth—and that "Galois was killed in a duel, probably provoked by royalist or police agents…" notwithstanding the evidence to the contrary. And in *The Biographical Dictionary of Scientists: Mathematicians*, despite being much more careful with facts than *The Harper Collins* dictionary, errors are made surrounding the circumstances of the duel that cost Galois his life.

Although we could continue searching out texts and plucking out errors, let us instead address the central question arising from both Rothman's article and this essay: Why do these historical myths continue into contemporary times, fighting as they do against the letters and documents and accounts that debunk them?

Lord Alfred Balfour famously observed that history doesn't repeat itself so much as historians repeat each other. So, perhaps the myths recur as a result of lazy scholarship; or they endure to stimulate interest in a popularly perceived "dry" and difficult subject; or the myths continue because of simple ignorance. Or maybe the almost supra-natural story of Galois, the genius' genius, needs some context in our cosmology—maybe a call to popularly known archetypes—to be both believable and understandable to a wide audience (after all, how many of us can personally relate to such genius?). In part, this is what Rothman believes. Here is what he says of Bell's overall account of Galois:

> It is a myth devoid of such complications as a protagonist who is faulted as well as gifted. It is a myth based on the stereotype of the misunderstood genius whom the conservative hierarchy is out to conquer. As if the befuddled hierarchy is generally organized well enough for persecution. It is a myth based on a misunderstanding of the method by which a scientist works: as if a great theory could be written down coherently in a single night.

Bell, then, "saw his opportunity to create a legend"—and did—in Rothman's final analysis.

The persistence of the myths after Rothman's article, though, seems to speak to a deep-rooted lack of confidence on the part of mathematicians and others popularizing the discipline to a mass audience. Although the texts discussed in this essay are not enough to qualify such a proposition as axiomatic, it appears that the need to manipulate facts to create the "misunderstood genius" narrative with Galois is indicative of two fears running in parallel: (1) That a non-mathematical audience won't be able to relate to or appreciate the extraordinary genius of Galois unless he falls into readily recognizable "genius" biographical categories (in other words, popular archetypes),* and (2) That a non-mathematical audience will find the materials boring unless there's something spectacular and enticing to tell.

Mathematics is not perceived as an art, with masterpieces, but as a cloistered science, inaccessible to the mainstream. As author-mathematician William Dunham rightly states in *Journey Through Genius*, mathematicians throughout the ages "did not feel compelled to justify their work with utilitarian purposes any more than Shakespeare had to apologize for writing love sonnets instead of cookbooks or Van Gogh had to apologize for painting canvases instead of billboards." Imagine if the mathematicians had apologized—we would all be much poorer today. So, instead of mathematics writers offering figurative apologia to non-mathematical readers by myth-making and sensationalizing, perhaps math—and specifically, the story of Evariste Galois—should be presented just as it is, banality and all.

(2002)

---

* Taking some of these archetypes of great mathematicians to task is David Foster Wallace: in his history of infinity *Everything and More*, Wallace notes, with respect to mental illness, "The cases of great mathematicians with mental illness have enormous resonance for modern pop writers and filmmakers. This has to do mostly with the writers'/directors' own prejudices and receptivities, which in turn are functions of what you would call our era's particular archetypal template."

7.

# The Alchemist

## In Search of John Tukey, the Man Who Transformed Statistics into Science

I initially encountered John Tukey while preparing to teach my first college statistics class. Well, *encountered* probably isn't quite the right word here; Tukey had been dead at that point for ten years, technically not quite making it out of the twentieth century, and I didn't encounter *him*, I encountered words written *by* him. But they were sage words, words which expressed exactly what I wanted to express to my class, certainly better than I ever could.

And I should be even more specific: by "encountered" I mean through Google. I suppose it's a pity that that's how we stumble upon words now, as ethereal letters glowing on electronic screens rather than typeset and plastered on the printed page. And yet there's something decidedly old-fashioned about searching through text online, scrolling up and down rapidly to separate the chaff from the wheat: somehow we have more in common now with the ancients who unraveled scrolling parchment or papyrus, or even a nineteen-seventies microfiche operator who dizzyingly scanned hundreds of pages of newspaper print by masterfully spinning knobs like a topflight deejay might spin old vinyls. No sense in sounding like a Luddite, though. Let me share John Tukey's words:

> Statistics is a science in my opinion, and is no more a branch of mathematics than are physics, chemistry and economics; for if its methods fail the test of experience—not the test of logic—they are discarded.

It's only later I realized whom this luminary was, and how important he was to the science of statistics.

Notice the key word: *science.* How, exactly, could statistics be a science? Wasn't it a math? Well—yes and no. Tukey's quote lays bare the empirical nature of the discipline of statistics: unlike in, say, geometry class, where the logic of the results is paramount—it's where most students first see proofs, after all—in statistics we see if the mathematical models fit the data well (at least that's what Tukey's saying we should do), rather than treating the real world as an inconvenient distraction to be swatted away in a heady pursuit of abstract mathematical modeling.

On June 16, 1915, in New Bedford, Massachusetts, John Wilder Tukey* was born. He was the only child of two highly literate teachers, Adah M. Tukey (née Tasker) and Ralph H. Tukey. Adah and Ralph met in high school; their classmates had voted them most likely to give birth to a genius.

Ralph Tukey always had a deep sense of humor and a wonderful way with language. He earned a doctorate from Yale in Latin. Ralph's first teaching job was at William Jewell College (established in 1849 by members of the Missouri Baptist Convention), which then had an exclusively male student body. When World War I broke out, Ralph Tukey—along with most of the younger faculty—resigned to permit the established faculty to keep their jobs. Later, he taught at and eventually became principal of New Bedford High School.

Tukey was homeschooled by his parents, and he did not begin any sort of formal education until he was admitted to Brown University. His mother Adah did most of the homeschooling since—although her qualifications were second to none—married women were prohibited by law from working as teachers in Massachusetts.

* Pronounced "Tuke-ee"; at Princeton graduate school, his nickname was "The Tuke."

Adah adopted a Socratic teaching style with the young Tukey, rather than a more straightforward and conventional "drill-and-kill" approach. She asked questions as answers to his questions, developing in him an intellectual curiosity that would last a lifetime. And, to further Tukey's blossoming education, New Bedford (luckily) had one of the most comprehensive libraries around—it even stocked research journals, and Tukey wasted little time in poring through them.

Tukey's academic background was in chemistry—he earned both undergrad and grad degrees in the subject from Brown—so I suppose it's no surprise he brought a more empirical, inductive, perhaps even utilitarian mindset to bear on statistics. Make no mistake, though: Tukey was no slouch when it came to mathematical proof or mathematics in general. He was so good at abstraction as a college student that his friend Richard Feynman (later to go on to be one of the most famous physicists of the last century and a world-class polymath in his own right) poked fun at Tukey's (and mathematicians') love of logically proving "trivialities."

Feynman was not afraid to rib Tukey. In his autobiographical *"Surely You're Joking, Mr. Feynman!": Adventures of a Curious Character* (1985), Feynman describes an interaction that he, Tukey, and several other mathematicians had one afternoon in a lounge in Princeton.

> [I] ... overheard some mathematicians talking about the series for *e* to the *x* power... [which is] very simple [to calculate]. I mumbled something about how it was easy to calculate *e* to any power using that series (you just substitute the power for *x*).
>
> "Oh yeah?" they said. "Well, then what's *e* to the 3.3?" said some joker—I think it was Tukey.
>
> I say, "That's easy. It's 27.11."
>
> Tukey knows it isn't so easy to compute all that in your head. "Hey! How'd you do that?"

> Another guy says, "You know Feynman, he's just faking it. It's not really right."

But Feynman wasn't faking it—he had a trick, involving two parts memorization, two parts approximation, and one part pure blind luck. (His method bears some resemblance to his more famous safe-cracking exploits at Los Alamos during the Manhattan Project.) Later, as their friendship developed, Tukey and Feynman, through informal experimentation, came to realize that different people do not keep time in their heads in quite the same way.

But more serious, and productive, were Feynman, Tukey, and Bryant Tuckerman in forming the Princeton Hexaflexagon Committee devoted to the topological study of hexaflexagons, a subset of flexagons, papers models that can be folded ad infinitum revealing new and repeating faces with each iteration. Of course, somewhat ironically, hexaflexagons, and the mathematical study of them, are brutally abstract—and at least somewhat antithetical to the later interests of both Feynman and Tukey. Tukey ended up writing his doctorate in topology. By the start of the World War II, though, Tukey had left behind the pure deductive abstractions of topology (his 1939 doctoral dissertation was titled "Denumerability in Topology") in favor of bombs and bullets.

With little interest in statistics before the war, Tukey did an about-face when he joined the Fire Control Research Office (FCRO) shortly before the Japanese bombing of Pearl Harbor. The FCRO was focused on calculating the trajectories of artillery, ballistics, and the like. According to David Brillinger, Tukey's greatest biographer,*

> While working at FCRO, Tukey had many meals and interactions with Charlie Winsor. These proved a major inspiring influence on Tukey's ensuing career interest in data analysis. Winsor was a Harvard engineer, but because of his Ph.D. in physiology he was known as an "engineer-turned-physiologist-turned-statistician." To quote Tukey: "It was

* Read Brillinger's *The Annals of Statistics* lengthy article "John W. Tukey: His Life and Professional Contributions" (2002) for a one-stop shop for all things Tukey. It's the closest the deserving Tukey has come yet to getting a biographical-book treatment of his life.

> Charlie and the experience of working on the analysis of real data, that converted me to statistics."

In addition to his real-data approach to statistics, perhaps simply seeing Winsor have his hand in so many disciplines inspired Tukey to later avoid the common trap of the academic: specialization.

Though the Second World War came to a close, Tukey didn't stop engaging in real-world national-defense projects; in addition to code-breaking (which he did during the war as well), Tukey helped get the Nike, a surface-to-air missile, off the ground. Brillinger again: "It required a systems solution to which Tukey was so profoundly suited: the integration of ground-based tracking radar, computers, and communications with an airborne missile."

As the Cold War heated up in the middle of the twentieth century, nuclear weapons testing proliferated, their use against civilian populations appearing increasingly likely. To help staunch that eventuality, nuclear test ban treaties were negotiated. In order to determine compliance, though, scientists had to have some way of differentiating between seismic events caused by earthquakes and those precipitated by atomic blasts (underground or not)—and Tukey was instrumental in devising methods for fruitfully examining the time-series data of seismograms.

Tukey was also well suited to studying the intersection of health and the environment; for instance, he led a committee to investigate the effects of fluorocarbons in the ozone layer. And Tukey brought statistics to bear in civic projects on the U.S. decennial census and election forecasting (especially in the 1960 Kennedy-Nixon race, a nail-biter of an election), helping to improve estimates and fill in gaps in incomplete data sets.

But why did Tukey consider statistics a science, rather than a math? In probably his most famous article, "The Future of Data Analysis" (1962) in *The Annals of Mathematical Statistics*, Tukey notes that "[t]here are diverse views as to what makes a science," but he nonetheless enumerates three criteria: (1) "Intellectual content"; (2) "Organization in understandable form"; and (3) "Reliance upon the test of experience as the ultimate standard of validity." "By these tests," Tukey claims, "mathematics is not a science since its ultimate standard of validity is an agreed-upon sort of logical consistency and provability."*

Unlike mathematics, data analysis is a science since it "passes all three tests," the upshot being that "[d]ata analysis must use mathematical argument and mathematical results as bases for judgment rather than as bases for proof or stamps of validity." In other words, let the data do the talking—don't fit the data to the mathematical models.

Tukey also pointedly addresses how statistics—and, more specifically, data analysis—should be taught: move away from rigidity and *cookbookery*,† and admit that "it [data analysis] uses judgment." Through observation—examining the data at hand, replete with all its real-world variability—and experimentation—seeing which mathematical models fit the data, a process akin to falsification rather than logical proof—Tukey had squarely set the paradigm as *science*, rather than math, for data analysis and statistics at large—though the abstract mathematical models of statistics, and their underpinnings, still relied on classical proof for justification; the approach to problems, though, had shifted. It was an affront to the mathematical establishment.

By the early 1960s, Tukey had been at Princeton for more than twenty years, and a full professor of mathematics more than ten. He was teaching a wide variety of classes—some at the elementary level, such as exploratory data analysis, and others on more advanced research topics.

His teaching style was unique, "strikingly original in presentation and content," according to J. A. Hartigan, one of his former students at the time. Hartigan tells of the many new words used during lectures, words like *orstat* for order statistic and *hinge* for median. Nevertheless, "more than the new words, there were new, different ways of thinking about the subject matter. He always aimed to shake you out of old ways of thinking." Also, Tukey always wel-

---

* Although, foundationally, mathematics as both a consistent and provable discipline has always been on shaky ground. Read the book *Mathematics: The Loss of Certainty* (1980) by Morris Klein for the salient details.

† The pejorative of statistics as merely a "cookbook discipline" is the bane of statisticians everywhere.

comed questions during class, and would often prompt his students to ask them. In fact, his questioning style may have come about because he was homeschooled in a way that encouraged the young Tukey to ask many questions so as to learn the content on his own.

Tukey would warn those he taught of the *over-utopian* nature of textbook problems and how a random sample of values oftentimes isn't *utopian*. In other words, idealized, non-real-world, pre-constructed data isn't realistic data.

Perhaps the best description of what sitting in one of Tukey's classes was like comes from Peter McCullagh, who was a graduate student at Imperial College in London when Tukey was invited to give a seminar there. After being introduced, "Tukey ambled to the podium, a great bear of a man dressed in baggy pants and a black knitted shirt.... An array of coloured pens bulged from his shirt pocket," which were necessary for his one-of-a-kind style of data analysis.

> Carefully and deliberately, a list of headings was chalked on the blackboard. The words came too, not many, like over-weight parcels, delivered at a slow unfaltering pace. For the most part, the words were familiar individually, but as phrases they seemed strangely obscure.... When [the list on the board] was complete, Tukey turned to face the audience and the podium, a long desk of the type used for demonstrating chemistry or physics experiments. "Comments, queries, suggestions?" he asked the audience, each word seeming to take a full minute to deliver. As he waited for a response, he clambered onto the podium and manoeuvred until he was sitting cross-legged facing the audience. This activity must have taken a full minute, but there was still no response.*

As the silence prevailed, Tukey reached into his pocket to grab a bag of dried prunes and proceeded to eat them, slowly, one at a time. Finally, after a while of this, a man in the front row finally punctuated the silence, and the considerable tension which had developed in the seminar room, to ask Tukey a question. To many in the lecture room that day, the number-of-prunes-till-a-question had

---

* From "A Memory of John Tukey as Teacher" (2003) by J. A. Haitian in *Statistical Science*.

seemed a test of the audience's intelligence: the more prunes eaten, the lesser the average smarts in the room. "My impression is that [Tukey] liked to play games his way to get people to figure out for themselves the things that he already knew.... Whatever the explanation, he was much more successful with individual students than in seminars or formal lectures." But the record says otherwise. Taking a closer look at one of those lectures* will help us take the measure of the man.

It is November of 1964. Tukey is invited to give a talk at the 125th Anniversary Meeting of the American Statistical Association (ASA), held in Boston. Many mathematicians and statisticians are present at the banquet. Tukey sits at the head table and consumes his by-now customary portion of skim milk.

After the dinner, Tukey rises to the podium and speaks. His talk, later titled "The Technical Tools of Statistics" when reprinted in the *American Statistician*, was customary for its prescience, sprinklings of pithy aphorisms, and use of neologisms (he loved coining terms). Rather than focusing on the design of methods to collect data, Tukey turned his attention strictly to the analysis of data.

Tukey began his speech by asking three questions of his audience: "What have our technical tools been? What are they today? What can we see of what they are to become?" He continued: "The assessment of the future is always chancy. Who knows this better than a statistician? Yet experience has taught us that it is usually well to extrapolate so long as we go only a modest distance and do what we can to ensure adequate caution.... Accordingly, I shall focus on the future, saying little about the past, and less about the present."

He noted that statisticians have often had to possess a "split personality," since, although they work daily within a sandbox of mathematical numbers and symbols—"probably the most secure things in human life"—they also have to openly exercise caution at the interpretation and promulgation of their results, which stem from the uncertainties and variability inherent in real-world data.

* Most of the source material for the following two sections of this chapter comes from the "Memories of John W. Tukey" webpage at Bell Labs, accessed on January 20, 2013, and found online at cm.bell-labs.com/stat/tukey

"[T]he tools of the statistician have been sharpened on the grindstone of algebra and hammered out on the anvil of mathematical models," he said.

Tukey then introduced the idea of marking time by eighths of a century (25 years) for the purposes of the lecture. For instance, the ASA, at the time of his speech, was ten-eighths old (125 years old). Why count this way? "Since we still learn to count on our fingers, by tens...." This brings to mind another of Tukey's rather esoteric methods of counting. He disliked using traditional tally marks since he believed that a mistake with tabulating could easily be made. So, instead, he promoted the dots-in-a-box method that, coincidentally, was also a means of counting by tens. First, draw four dots as the vertices of a square (four dots represent four tallies); next, draw the four sides of the square, connecting the vertices (four lines represent four more tallies); finally, insert the two diagonals of the square (two more lines represent the final two tallies).*

Thoughts of new ways to dissect data should lead naturally to machines—specifically, to then still-new electronic computers. "By two-eighths ago one could see the shadow of the programmable calculator on the outside of the window," and, then, "[t]here was a war, and a [John] von Neumann; it took only half an eighth to bring the program-self-modifying calculator to reality...." And this was followed by the idea of *software* (a term that Tukey may have coined, but not during this lecture)—the notion that a piece of hardware need not be tethered to only one algorithm for life. Statisticians must leverage the capabilities of the computer, and do so quickly—lest the young will have scant interest in the field.

Tukey also put pride of place in the connection between hardware and *brainware*, the latter term meaning "the minds of those who know what is wanted," when examining data. And he excited his crowd by speaking of the potential of computer graphics to analyze data sets, noting that computers will become indispensable to

---

* More about this and other Tukeyisms can be found in "The Picasso of Statistics" chapter in David Salsburg's book *The Lady Tasting Tea: How Statistics Revolutionized Science in the Twentieth Century* (2001). As Salsburg points out, "Nothing had been too mundane for Tukey to attack with original insight, and nothing is too sacrosanct for him to question.... Like Picasso going from cubism, to classicalism, to ceramics, to fabrics, John Tukey marched across the statistical landscape of the second half of the twentieth century," leaving little unchanged in his wake.

the statistician because of their speed and ease of data visualization. He admonished his audience, though, by noting that he knew of no one using the visual-display capabilities of computers well, and by predicting that in the next eighth of a century statistics is going to depend heavily upon the capabilities of the computer because a computer could "fit the apparent desires of the data," rather than the other way around—a key theme of Tukey's still-developing model of exploratory data analysis (EDA). (About five years earlier Tukey had said, "We need not sit loosely in the saddle of data," perhaps his "first utterance on data analysis," according to then-graduate student Arnold Goodman.)

And to those who would warn of the pitfalls of computing, namely with respect to a lack of clarity, Tukey issued a warning: "The tool that is so dull that you cannot cut yourself on it is not likely to be sharp enough to be either useful or helpful." In other words, Tukey wanted statisticians to dive headlong into computers so they would have the opportunity to fully take advantage of their benefits, despite the risks. He even suggested the creation of a computer language for data analysis, going so far as to say that he'd create it himself if no one else did. (Of course today there are numerous computer languages with the requisite statistical bent, such as SAS or SPSS or S, which Tukey later influenced the development of, or S's popular descendent R.)

Michael Tarter, who saw Tukey's speech, said tellingly, "The banquet was part of the first meeting I attended after receiving my Ph.D. degree. As is no doubt common, buyer's remorse was beginning to set in. In an after-dinner speech [Tukey] predicted much of what has since then actually happened to our field and this was enough to dispel any doubts on my part concerning career choice." The lecture was a success.

Ironically, though Tukey was one of the biggest proponents of computer use at the time, he didn't utilize computers very much for his work—and when he did, the results weren't necessarily useful. For instance, graduate student Alan Gross recalls the code of a FORTRAN computer program Tukey handed him, probably for an IBM 7090, which was nearly unintelligible. "FORTRAN ignores arguments that aren't used, so he made each subroutine's argument list into a sentence with commas between the words. Typical John!"

Unfortunately, Tukey's unique personal style was not fully appreciated by everyone he met.*

"People are different," Tukey was fond of saying. Yet even with his legendary New Englander ethos, and his homespun, folksy and spare manner, Tukey could occasionally be passive-aggressive and almost abrasive when it came to getting his points across. Kaye Basford, a former colleague of Tukey's in the late 1980s, warmly relays a story about him that nonetheless has a bit of an edge: "[Tukey] didn't make you feel inadequate when you couldn't keep up with his line of reasoning. He would just give you three of four of his papers to read and then expect you to understand his viewpoint and discuss the pertinent issues the next morning."

Tukey had a years'-long clash with sex researcher Alfred Kinsey; Tukey objected to Kinsey's sampling methods, which hardly met the standards of random sampling, the ideal method of data collection. Both Kinsey and Kinsey's wife Clara found the statistician very disagreeable, Clara going so far as to say that she would have liked to have "poisoned" Tukey. Although Kaye Basford puts a positive spin on Tukey's seemingly lack of tact by saying, "What a way to get the best out of people by having them strive to live up to those expectations!" his smothering force of argumentation seeps through.

Bea Chambers, who worked with Tukey at Bell Labs in the math research department—Bell Labs being one of, effectively, two full-time jobs Tukey held down, the other being Princeton professor—tells of her first meeting with Tukey. After programming a computer to produce some numbers for analysis, Chambers showed them to Tukey. He took a quick glance at the printouts and said, "This won't do. There cannot be any negative numbers in the results." But for Chambers, a newly minted research mathematician, Tukey's reputation didn't precede him (yet). She continues:

> Did I know Tukey was a genius? Of course not. So, I countered with, "Why not?" Tukey said, "SIT!," so… I sat. Then, Tukey explained what the problem was all about, what he was expecting to find, and he explained all this in

---

* And, with that, we (slightly) ease out of hagiography.

> a simple and straightforward way. OK, so I agreed the numbers could not be negative.... [She explained to Tukey how she approached the problem.] Tukey pursed his lips for a few seconds, then, he looked at what I had done, told me what was wrong, told me how to correct it, gave me a little smile, and left.

If not quite condescending, Tukey was quite sure of himself with Basford and Chambers, both women. Alan Gross, a graduate advisee of Tukey's in the 1960s, describes a scene of embarrassment (on Gross's part). "Finally, John never wasted a minute of time. There were several occasions when he had to drive somewhere and would invite me along to discuss whatever it was that we had to discuss," Gross said. "I remember one time when he said he had to go to his home to get something for his wife [Elizabeth, whom he met while teaching a folk dancing class] who was spending the day at an auction. (I'm embarrassed now to say that) I responded in mock horror, 'What. You let her go to an auction alone?' His quiet, terse response [was], 'She's selling.' Little did I know then that Elizabeth was an antique dealer and professional appraiser, and John was a feminist, too."

Tukey, who lived through women's rapidly expanding workforce roles during World War II, the ages of *The Feminine Mystique* and women's liberation movements and the Equal Rights Amendment, acquitted himself quite well on women's rights, though he wasn't marching on the picket lines; if not quite a feminist, Tukey worked at a time when many of his male cohort refused to help or even deal with their fellow women professionals.

Another of Tukey's female students, Karen Kafadar, remembers a gruff but enthusiastic, collaborative and intellectually generous man during their first meeting at Princeton. After the chairman of the mathematics department at that time (the early 1970s), Geoff Watson, told Kafadar that Tukey had something for her to work on, she "timidly approached Dr. Tukey following a 411 class (the famous 'undergraduate' course attended to by even full professors), introduced myself, and reported Watson's directive. He broke into a big grin and said, 'Wait here.'" Shortly thereafter, he returned, sporting his "trademark black T-shirt whose pocket held the usual Bic 4-color pens," and told Kafadar, "Read this and then I think you'll see that we have a lot of computing to do." In her recollection, Kafadar pays special attention to the word "we" in Tukey's statement—which he pointedly used instead of "I"—noting that "John Tukey chose his words very carefully." Ultimately Kafadar and Tukey had a fruitful mathematical relationship: he became her doctoral dissertation advisor, making her one of his "children," as Tukey often referred to his thesis advisees. (And Kafadar had six "children" of her own, giving Tukey, her academic father, even more "grandchildren." Tukey never had any biological children.)

His intellectually generosity sometimes knew no bounds. Full of ideas, Tukey simply "threw them out, and let others work on them," Kafadar remembers.

> Many of them have taken people 20 or 30 years to work out why they perform so well. Consistent with that characteristic, he never used his own name for his ideas, procedures, or methods. They were always the "Duckworth test", or the "Bruceton test", or "Winsorization", or "decigalt" ("for Francis Galton,* who started so many

---

* Sir Frances Galton (1822-1911) was one of the most creative and controversial figures in mathematics. He came up with the statistical ideas of correlation and regression to the mean. (He also arrived at the notion of eugenics—thus, Hitler was one of his greatest admirers.) When visiting a livestock fair for fun in the early 1900s, Galton witnessed a bizarre game hundreds of people were playing: they would each guess the weight of a slaughtered ox. Galton was surprised to find that, though no single person guessed the correct weight exactly, the averages of their guesses (specifically, the median; the mean ended up being even closer to the truth), was very close to the mark: "the middlemost estimate expresses the *vox populi* [the voice of the people], every other estimate being condemned as too low or too high by a majority of the voters." This idea of using aggregate responses from people, contemporarily called the "wisdom of crowds," or crowdsourcing, has been found to be at least as good as responses originating from any individual in the group. In 2009, British magician Derren Brown famously predicted the "Midweek Lotto Numbers" live on Channel 4 television in England. The odds of guessing the numbers correctly were around 14 million to one. He said he used the wisdom of the crowd approach: "I gathered a panel of 24 people who wrote down their predictions after studying the last year's worth of numbers. Then they added up all the guesses for each ball and divided it by 24 to get the average guess."

Crowdsourcing has also found application in more serious endeavors, such as diagnosing illness. As the *Time Magazine* article "Web MDs: Social Media are Changing How We Diagnose Disease" explains, social media sites like Facebook are being used to capture a wide variety of hypotheses from people

> things")…. The other characteristic of his personality that always impressed me was his constant encouragement to his students…. He always knew just the right thing to say to make his students feel better.

More than simply not taking credit for his own ideas by refraining from affixing them eponymous labels, Tukey would often do the mental heavy lifting, behind the scenes, for projects that needed desperately to get done. In the 1960s, there was a call to compile a statistical citation index, a first-of-its-kind massive undertaking. Tukey headed a team of eminent minds, but "did a lion's share of the grunt work," said then-student Alan Gross. "Everywhere he went in those days, he had 10 or 15 side-inches of journals under his arm. He would attend seminars, and spend the whole time copying references out of said journals onto data entry sheets." Gross's description of *side-inches*, by the way, pays homage to another of Tukey's neologisms: the *side-foot*, which measures a stack of printed computer output—"When I said we should be using computers by the foot, I did not mean by the running foot of output paper. I meant, rather, by the 12 inches of thickness of stacks of printout" that statisticians are calling the *side-foot*, Tukey said—but which was, by and large, a term never widely used.

Even if the heavy lifting of a project wasn't exclusively of the mental variety, the relentless Tukey would often intercede to finish the task. In the late 1970s he was called to action by a citizens' group near Princeton. The group was up in arms about how traffic patterns would be affected by a proposed development. Research, in the form of traffic counts, were required. Phyllis Marchand, a member of the group who later went on to become a successful mayor of Princeton Township, remembers:

> Imagine my surprise when Professor John Tukey, the Donner Professor of Science at Princeton University, and one of the most influential statisticians came over and offered to do the job. A man who could command hundreds of dollars an hour for statistical consulting and analysis had agreed to sit in a lawn chair and count cars as they passed by. John Tukey, with all his fame, volunteered his exper-

---

about illnesses to surprising effect. And all because on a lark one hundred years ago Frances Galton visited a livestock fair.

> tise, and without calculators, computers or any fancy technology, sat on a chair at the designated spot on Route 206 and with a pad of paper and a pencil counted the cars and trucks as they traveled past. I smile as I think of that image.

Marchand also fondly recalls how active both Tukey and Elizabeth were in donating their time and energy into "raising money and raising consciousness about environmental sensitivity, quality of life, and historic preservation" at Princeton.

The end, when it came, found Tukey's mental powers as strong as ever. Tukey had lost his wife, Elizabeth, several years before; at her eulogy, he sadly said, "One is so much less than two."

At eighty-five years of age, Tukey was still very much involved in the academic community, "was able to work with statisticians in the Princeton area as well as correspond with other statisticians all around the world, and he also continued some of his consulting work," as Luisa Fernholz—a fellow statistician who got to know Tukey well in the last half-decade of his life—writes, despite Tukey having suffered from a stroke. She continues: "It seemed as if this could have gone on indefinitely, but it did not happen that way. It all stopped in the first hour of July 26, 2000."* The polymath was no more.

To be completely honest, my first encounter with Tukey—or at least with his work—much predates the start of teaching my first college class. It goes back to middle school, with the introduction, in a math class, of box-and-whisker plots (boxplots) and stem-and-leaf plots (stemplots), the old graphical standbys for quick-and-dirty displays of small data sets. Boxplots quickly became so popular that Texas Instruments, for their newly minted TI-80s graphing calculator series, permitted users the option of displaying them.

Tukey arrived at boxplots, stemplots, and other clever graphs in his groundbreaking book *Exploratory Data Analysis* (1976). Tukey thought of exploratory data analysis as "detective work": "[Tukey]

---

* From "Remembering John W. Tukey" (2003), in *Statistical Science*.

believed the exploration of data is best carried out the way a detective searches for evidence when investigating a crime. Our goal is only to collect and present evidence. Drawing conclusions (or inference) is like the deliberations of the jury."* The scientist-as-detective, the mathematician-as-scientist. Tukey's wide range of interests, as well as his sheer genius, allowed him to see one process as another, to connect seemingly disparate disciplines, to make mathematical metaphor. Tukey, whose academic background was in chemistry, engaged in a bit of alchemy when he transformed his next love—mathematical statistics—into a science.

"Exploratory data analysis can never be the whole story, but nothing else can serve as the foundation stone—as the first step," he wrote. My first step in teaching my college statistics class was to establish an intellectual framework—and Tukey's science approach, discovered through a chance encounter online, would end up serving me, and my students, quite well.

So thank you, John Tukey.

(2014)

* Found in *Statistics: Informed Decisions Using Data, 4th ed.* (2013), by Michael Sullivan, III.

# PART II

# ACADEMIC ESSAYS

# 8.

## A Clash of Complements: Comparing Mathematics Curricula

The pendulum swings back and forth, barely missing its target's skin, yet inching closer and closer in frightening periodic fashion. Before long, critters eat away at the ropes restraining the object of the pendulum's wrath, and successful escape is made—with no cuts or bruises to boot.

This narrative—based on Edgar Allen Poe's short story "The Pit and the Pendulum"—roots a first-year unit of the Interactive Mathematics Program (IMP), a reformed math curriculum designed to replace traditional mathematics curricula in high school. But it also, in a way, serves as a metaphor for the sometimes-violent pendulum-like shifts in mathematics educational paradigms through the past half-century that led to IMP's creation.

IMP was, in part, designed as a reaction to the Back-to-Basics movement that dominated the milieu of mathematics pedagogy in the United States. In brief, after the launch of the space satellite *Sputnik* by the Soviet Union in the late 1950s, rigorous curricula were implemented emphasizing mathematics and science in American schools; and with the impetus of civil rights movements in the late 1960s and early 1970s, the focus shifted to the needs of the individual student, and more constructivist-type pedagogies—such as New Math, with its set theory, relations, and abstract structures—were brought to the fore (Huetinek and Munshin, 2000).

New Math garnered much criticism from both within and without the educational community. "Many elementary teachers," Huetinek and Munshin (2000) explain, "already insecure in their own mathematical knowledge, failed to fully understand or appreciate the mathematical implications of the structural approach [of New Math].... Exacerbating their lack of content knowledge was the fact that insufficient professional development was provided to support the change" (p. 5). In other words, New Math broke down because overwhelming numbers of teachers failed to appreciate the epistemological differences of the new curricula.

As a result of the maelstrom, the pendulum swung back towards a return to more "traditional" math education approaches—but not before radical pedagogic methods were tried, such as Open Classrooms, Alternative Schools, and the like. As Ryan and Cooper (2000) explain in their history of education text *Those Who Can Teach*, achievement tests and SAT test scores dropped significantly throughout the 1970s, and "many parents, politicians, and educators argued that the schools had tried to accomplish too much and had lost sight of their basic purposes. A return to the basics seemed to be the cry of the late 1970s and the early 1980s" (p. 369).

It was in this tumultuous and reactionary environment that IMP took shape. In 1989, with a grant from the California Postsecondary Education Commission, the Interactive Mathematics Program was born. Rather than functioning as a dissent to the Back-to-Basics envelopment, the grant was bestowed to restructure and recalibrate the existing three-year core math curriculum in California. By 1992, after successful field-testing in several California schools, the National Science Foundation conferred a multimillion-dollar grant for IMP; NSF Award Number 9255262 called on IMP's project coordinators and developers to expand and implement their NCTM *Standards*-based reform program far and wide. And, to avoid breakdown à la New Math, much of the grant money was designated to go towards teacher training and professional development. The rest of the money, according to the grant abstract, was earmarked for meta-studies of IMP's efficacy, the composition of auxiliary materials for the program, and rewrites and revisions of the curriculum. NSF funding, more than anything else, prevented IMP from turning into a math-reform-program du jour and allowed it to flourish and quickly gain mainstream traction.

IMP, after several permutations, eventually came to be considered a reaction to the traditional curriculum of mathematics (for some evidence of this, although the site's not easily accessible anymore, one need look no further than the website *mathematicallycorrect.com*, which contains a corpus of polemic on the ostensibly nefarious effects that IMP has had on unsuspecting pupils). In order to better conceptualize what IMP was reacting against, it is necessary to review, albeit briefly, the history of the traditional curriculum.

A history of the traditional mathematics curriculum is much harder to come by than a history of IMP, since the notion of a "traditional curriculum" is amorphous and difficult to define. Although there is no obvious way to gauge dominant paradigms in mathematics—it is easier to realize effects in their wake—the traditional curriculum, through the last couple of decades, usually can be pegged to be the majority's approach to teaching math. For instance, a "traditional curriculum" immediately post-*Sputnik* might be considered to be New Math, despite the many radical elements of the New Math approach (at least as compared to today's conventional wisdom). And, by the late 1980s, curricula and basal textbooks spawning from the ideas and ideals of the dominant Back-to-Basics movement can be accurately labeled "traditional" for the time.

Huetinck and Munshin (2000) define the current "traditional approach" using two criteria: teaching by telling, and assigning pupils to groups (p. 4). Note that instead of defining the traditional curriculum by enumerating taught topics, the authors bring it into relief by mentioning types of pedagogy. Other authors, such as Mackey (2002) and Datta (1996), have conceptualized the traditional curriculum as antithetical to reform curricula such as IMP—thus, they tell what it is by telling what it isn't. In the context of this essay, however, the traditional math curriculum will be considered that which contains contemporarily canonical subjects presented in year-long, non-integrated courses—e.g., algebra class, geometry class, precalculus class, among others—and, in general, is characteristically mile-wide, inch-deep (in other words, little depth to lots of mathematics taught). The math covered in traditional curriculum classes includes such topics as factoring and two-column geometry proofs, all conveyed to students in a more or less abstract fashion via teaching by telling. In addition, the traditional curriculum will be endowed with further detail by references to The Third International Mathematics and Science Study's (TIMSS's) video of the American classroom, widely considered to be representative of traditional approaches: an article in the education periodical *Phi Kappa Deltan* by TIMSS researchers Stigler and Hiebert (1997), for instance, mention that the study was constructed in large part to observe paradigmatic American teaching.

◆ ◆ ◆

Latent and manifest differences between the contemporary traditional curriculum and IMP abound: there are contrasts in philosophical approach, construction of curriculum, the role of problem solving, interaction with other subject areas, use of mathematical manipulatives, degree of emphasis on rote, graphing calculators and computer use, homework, assessment, standardized-test scores, and even political connotation. Let's examine each of these in turn, beginning with the philosophical differences.

"In essence," explains Freitag (2002), "the role of the teacher [in IMP changes] from a giver of information [as in a traditional classroom] to a facilitator, and well-developed IMP activities should be used since they promote learning through discovery and experimentation" (p. 1). A "giver of information," the *modus operandi* of today's purist traditional-curriculum instructor, is akin to a behaviorism philosophy of teaching. "Behaviorists consider a young child's mind to be a blank slate," or, as John Locke—who originated the notion—describes it in Latin, *tabula rasa* (Huetinck and Munshin, 2000, p. 46). The traditional teacher who underpins his practice on *tabula rasa* considers himself the know-all authority in the classroom, with an obligation to "fill up" his students' empty heads with facts until their young minds are bursting at the seams. Although this sounds a bit extreme, a segment of the TIMSS video illustrates: the American teacher was a sage on the stage, supplying all the information without fail—even preemptively providing a formula ideal for pupils' self-discovery in a later class—and students were not allowed to be active interlocutors, only passive receptacles. Perhaps the most succinct explanation for the practice of the traditional curriculum teacher lies in an article by Schifter (1996): The traditional approach assumes that "people acquire concepts by receiving information from other people who know more; that, if students listen to what their teachers say, they will learn what their teachers know; and that the presence of other students is *incidental* to learning" [emphasis added] (p. 494).

The IMP instructor, however, believes that the presence of other students is more than just critical to the learning of new concepts: it is the *sine qua non*. As a facilitator, the IMP instructor does not base his practice on *tabula rasa* but rather on a humanistic, constructivist methodology: humanistic, because he considers the differences of individuals in the classroom, and constructivist, since he recognizes that different students often learn commensurate knowledge in incommensurate ways.

"The constructivist approach to teaching requires establishing a community of mathematics learners" (Huetinck and Munshin, 2000, p. 50). Although there is some debate about what constructivist teaching actually means—as Huetinck and Munshin (2000) note, it has come to be a virtual panacea for those defending reformist teaching—I will stay in line with the stance taken by the NCTM *Standards*, which can be adequately summed up by Schifter (1996):

> [Constructivism] is a perspective that informs the principles guiding the current movement for mathematics education reform: that individuals necessarily approach novel situations by interpreting them in the light of their own established structures of understanding; that the construction of new concepts is provoked when those settled understandings do not satisfactorily accommodate a novel circumstance; and that this constructive activity is not simply an individual achievement but embedded in and enabled by contexts of social interaction. (p. 494)

Constructivism, then, can be said to underpin the philosophy of teaching in IMP classrooms. To more clearly see constructivism in action, it is necessary to reference a videotaped math classroom—but, this time, not one from the TIMSS study.

In the Public Broadcasting Station (PBS) series *Life by the Numbers* (1998), class periods from *The Pit and the Pendulum* IMP unit in Philadelphia's Central High School were shown in edited segments. Actor Danny Glover, the host of the multi-part series, intoned that while watching the IMP class, it is not immediately clear whether it is an English, physics, or arts-and-crafts course. Throughout the unit, students, both in groups and individually, were required to literally construct their own pendulums (analogous to the one described in Poe's short story), collect data on their pendulums' periodicity, and, by the conclusion of the unit, enact the climatic portion of "The Pit and the Pendulum" for a captive audience of ninth graders. The unit is shown to at once involve the community of mathematics learners and yet also capture the interest of the individual pupils; the unit, then, can be considered an apotheosis of constructivism, fulfilling the criteria for the constructivist classroom—and, as such, being anathema to *tabula rasa* and the traditional teaching-by-telling approach of mathematics instruction.

*Life by the Numbers* demonstrated some of what *The IMPlementation Center* (the official website of the Interactive Mathematics Program) explains are qualities that separate the IMP curriculum from the traditional curriculum—or, for that matter, from other math-reform curricula. "The IMP curriculum is problem centered," their website says, "[and] [u]nits of the IMP curriculum generally begin with a central problem or theme. Students explore and solve that problem over the course of the unit.... Solving a particular unit problem often requires concepts from several branches of mathematics." Recalling *The Pit and the Pendulum* unit—which is centered around a single problem, that of "whether the prisoner in Edgar Allen Poe's classic story would have enough time to escape the blade on a 30-foot pendulum that will reach him in only 12 more swings," as described in *The IMPlementation Center*—students are required to import data-collection skills into their math classrooms.

Other units in the IMP curriculum besides *The Pit and the Pendulum* also betray that same constructivist *raison d'être*, and are indeed rooted in the same principles. The units that constitute the IMP curriculum, as a whole, contrast sharply with that of the traditional curriculum. "The critical difference," according to Schoen (1993), "between the IMP curriculum and conventional multiyear mathematics curricula lies in the fact that IMP materials are problem based, rather than topic based" (p. 2). Look through traditional texts in algebra, geometry, or precalculus, and this topic-based construction is immediately apparent. Although we will examine a lesson in a traditional textbook later on, it is important to note that, in general, traditional texts—and, by extension, traditional curricula on which they are based—attempt to cram in as many topics as possible, lest something potentially critical be left out. However, the topics tend to be disjoint from unit to unit and chapter to chapter, and, quite frequently, topics are not integrated and merely left hanging after they are discussed—despite the fact that the NCTM *Standards* suggest that topics should logically interconnect.

The NCTM *Standards* also state that probability theory should be given just as much emphasis as algebra, but often probability units are tacked on to the end of traditional texts, and not all traditional instructors teach it. IMP, however, incorporates probability, algebra, and geometry, among others, into just the first year of the curriculum. As Schoen (1993) details it,

> The first year of the [IMP] curriculum incorporates five units—*Patterns in Mathematics, The Overland Trail, The Game of Pig, The Pit and the Pendulum,* and *Shadows*—each of which takes five or six weeks of class time. In the course of these units, students develop and work through important mathematical concepts and skills, by using concrete planning problems from the settlement of the American West, games of chance, literary and empirical models of periodic motion, and estimates of the relative length of shadows. The units include work on problem-solving strategies, geometric and number patterns, the use of variables to express generalizations, graphing, algebraic expressions, systems of equations, probability, quadratic equations, curve fitting, normal distributions and standard deviations, and trigonometric functions. (p. 2)

In other words, by the time these ninth grade IMP students complete their first year, they will have had exposure to a majority of the skills and concepts *listed for the eleventh grade* in the NCTM *Standards.*

By the end of the second year of the curriculum—after completing such flowery-named units as *Do Bees Build It Best?* and *All About Alice*—students will have worked on problems that "involve the comparison of populations, the areas of polygons and the volumes of regular prisms, relationships between doubles and halves in passages from Lewis Carrol's *Alice in Wonderland*, and the maximization of profits from a simple cookie store" (Schoen, 1993, p. 2).

The last two years of the curriculum, which continue to be structured around integrated yet disconnected units, further extend and refine the mélange of skills and concepts pupils have already been exposed to in IMP during the ninth and tenth grades. An especially noteworthy real-world unit during the third year is called *Pennant Fever*, which asks students to calculate the probabilities of wins and losses of baseball teams; recall that probabilistic concepts were first introduced in the first year of the curriculum.

The flip side of the self-contained units in IMP, however, is best described by Freitag (2002): "Students are not asked to learn a skill if it is not needed for the unit problem, and practice exercises for skills are scarce. In fact, the IMP curriculum has almost no skill or manipulation problems or exercises" (p. 1). Freitag (2002) elucidates a key difference between IMP and the traditional curriculum, that of the role of problem solving. Somewhat dogmatically, IMP has few skills' practice exercises, instead preferring to stick to the script of its problem-centered units. Although each unit begins with a central question and culminates in a climatic demonstration of the answer, skills—as an end in and of themselves—are not emphasized.

Flipping through the archetypical traditional mathematics textbook, the emphasis on skills drills is evident: at the end of each section (and sections are small and discrete and tightly focused), there are many, many problems recapitulating the skills taught in the section in multiple ways, with IMP-like application problems relegated to the very end of the homework lists. Problem solving per se is not given top priority; rather, mastery of mathematics skills (such as factoring and expanding equations, among others)—and not necessarily concepts—is primacy in the traditional curriculum.

Problem solving in IMP, however, is almost to the exclusion of all else. There are Problems of the Week (POWs),* open-ended problems, long-term problems, story-oriented homework problems, overarching unit problems, group-application problems, spiraling-content problems, logic problems, history problems. And, whereas traditional problems emphasize answering questions by using a specific mathematical algorithm or method, nearly all IMP problems do not place restrictions on the student to utilize any particular mathematics to solve them. In the "Concepts and Skills for the IMP Curriculum" section of *The IMPlementation Center* website, the mathematical content covered in each of the years is detailed. Each year has at least a modicum of algebra, geometry, trigonometry, probability, statistics, and logic covered, and several of the years have extra mathematical topics.

IMP problems not only require that pupils to integrate their math knowledge—i.e., mathematics that was discussed in other units could come into play to help solve problems in later units, a characteristic of IMP's spiraling curriculum, in which "fundamental ideas are developed and redeveloped in [a] spiral fashion, becoming deeper and wider" (Tanner and Tanner, 1975, p. 429)—but they

* For a detailed look at two POWs, see the Appendix.

also sometimes call upon subject areas other than math to solve them. Data collection, analogous to the kind normally found in science classes such as physics, is necessary for predicting and systematizing the periodic motion in *The Pit and the Pendulum*, and de facto history lessons are served up with creative assignments such as "Sublette's Cutoff" and "Getting the Gold."

As we've already seen, entire units, such as *The Pit and the Pendulum* and *All About Alice*, are interdisciplinary, since they are structured around narratives otherwise thought to be confined to English classes. And in *The Pollster's Dilemma*, a fourth-year IMP unit, notions from political science are explored in enough detail that pupils should be able to explain statistical concepts of polling to unsuspecting voters.

Throughout the four-year IMP curriculum, lots and lots of writing is required: homework, POWs, group work, and other assignments entail written explanations and reflections from pupils. In the POW write-ups, for instance, students must answer the following questions: Did you enjoy working on the problem?, Was the problem too hard or too easy?, What grade would you assign yourself for your work?, and Why do you think you deserve that grade? Oral presentations are also sometimes engendered by problems, with each and every student required to make at least one oral presentation each year. With IMP, then, writing and presenting are no longer confined to English and public-speaking classes.

In terms of integrations with other subject areas, the traditional curriculum falls short compared to IMP. Although occasional problems in traditional texts tie into a historical or real-world context, they are usually reserved for end-of-section explorations—and many teachers may not cover or assign them. In-class activities and lectures also rarely focus on interdisciplinary ideas—think of the math-skills-only style of the American teacher in the TIMSS video—and there is not typically any writing or oral presentations in traditional classrooms.

The same can be said for the use of mathematical manipulatives. This is not to say that there are absolutely no manipulatives utilized in the traditional classroom besides chalk, the blackboard, and the overhead, but the majority of skills and concepts are reviewed that way. Recall, once again, the sage-on-the-stage routine of the American instructor in the TIMSS study: there was no exploration of concepts by students—which is something ripe for mathematical manipulatives—so manipulatives were rendered unnecessary.

"IMP does not rely on the traditional instructional strategies that emphasize group lectures and discussions and individual, paper-and-pencil seat work. Instead, IMP relies on group problem solving… [and] manipulative materials, which reveal the physical reality that underlies many abstract concepts" (Schoen, 1993, p. 4). Since the majority of IMP problems are applied and real-world, manipulatives are *sine qua non* and wholly appropriate; they further the conceptions of solving problems in the ways that mathematician George Polya described in his seminal work, *How to Solve It* (Huetinek and Munshin, 2000). It should be noted, however, that the large degree of abstractness of traditional mathematics classes makes it potentially more challenging for effective manipulatives to be constructed.

A mathematical manipulative that the traditional classroom does make use of is the graphing calculator. But there are frequently explicitly designed problems that call upon pupils to use the calculator, which renders the calculator a specialized tool to be utilized only in certain situations. Ditto for the computer, a device rarely spotted into math classes.

Students make use of the calculator quite frequently in IMP as well, but are rarely expressly told to do so (after learning the rudimentary calculator skills). For instance, consider an IMP assignment culled almost at random: "The Locker Problem." It is a problem of recursion, and, although it asks what happens when large numbers of lockers are open—and an answer could perhaps be found quicker on a calculator—the assignment does not explicitly command students to solve the problem using their calculators; instead, as *The IMPlementation Center* website explains, "calculators are always available to students, and the students decide when to use them. They come to regard the calculator as simply another tool to use, like paper and pencil, in working on problems." Computers are used as well, as Schoen (1993) describes, in various ways.

When students do IMP homework, they often don't have access to computers or even graphing calculators—but the homework can usually be completed without this technology. Yet Mackey (2002), in her overview of IMP years one and two, classifies the homework as a weakness of IMP. In the teacher's manuals, she points out, homework answers are not present; in addition, homework is usually long and detailed, thus making it difficult to grade in bulk. Also, she says, the homework does not always reflect what was covered in the lesson or in the class, leading to some disconnect. Finally, Mackey (2002) notes that there is too little practice for students to really be competent at important mathematics skills—but "I am not an advocate of 40 problems a night of 'drill and kill'" (p. 14).

The "drill and kill" approach is often the method of choice for traditional instructors, though. In most traditional texts, there is a preponderance of drill problems, while there are very few application problems; that ratio is inverted in IMP's curriculum.

Since there is a ready-made surplus of drill problems at the end of textbook sections, assessments are typically easier for teachers to construct in traditional classrooms; but traditional instructors' assessments vary tremendously—some have lots of drill problems, whereas others have more applied queries. IMP assessments, on the other hand, are notoriously difficult to create, since questions on the tests must accurately reflect what's been taught and assigned for homework in class to be fair (and in IMP, most problems are applied and have multiple steps). But these are ephemeral concerns, since the IMP texts help teachers construct their assessments. The assessments customarily have two parts: an in-class section and a take-home section. A teacher's assessment description for year two reads like this:

> Tell students that today they will get two tests—one that they will finish in class and one that they can start in class and will be able to finish at home. The take-home part should be handed in tomorrow. Tell students that they are allowed to use graphing calculators, notes from previous work, and so forth, when they do the assessments. (They will have to do without graphing calculators when they complete the take-home portion at home unless they have their own.) (Fendel, Resek, Alper, and Fraser, 1998, p. 229)

The end-of-unit assessment description above applies to the *Solve It!* unit. The in-class assessment for *Solve It!* has few problems, and the take-home assessment has a single, multi-step query. Other units have similar assessments.

Do the assessments—and, for that matter, the entire IMP curriculum—adequately prepare students for standardized tests? According to Huetinck and Munshin (2000), they do: "In general, evaluations show comparable or better results on standardized, norm-referenced tests by students in these programs compared to students at the same level in traditional programs" (p. 143). Examining the results of several studies will help flesh-out the authors' statement.

In "Comparison of IMP Students with Students Enrolled in Traditional Courses on Probability, Statistics, Problem Solving, and Reasoning," Webb and Dowling (1997) assessed pupils using multiple-choice and free-response questions culled from the Second International Mathematics Study (SIMS). The researchers performed three comparative studies with several grade levels of students; in all of the studies, IMP students outperformed traditional-curriculum students by large margins, although the researchers concede that the total number of pupils assessed in the studies was relatively small.

Staples (2001) narrowed the focus to just two classrooms—one traditional and one IMP—in "Characterizing Differences Between Two Mathematics Classrooms Using 'Reform' and 'Traditional' Curricula." A traditional algebra class was compared with a second-year IMP classroom in the study. And, although Staples (2001) does not provide any quantitative evidence of this, she comments that "[b]oth courses were taught by well respected, experienced teachers at the same school who had established productive learning environments in their classes and positive rapport with their students" (p. 1). In fact, most of the research is anecdotal, and it is based almost entirely on classroom observations and student interviews. However, Staples (2001) does observe some general trends in the philosophies of the classrooms, despite making no manifest judgment on their efficacy. In the traditional class, Staples (2001) claims, students do not perceive themselves as sources of mathematical knowledge, but in the IMP classroom, "students saw themselves as 'knowers' of mathematics" (p. 3).

Boaler (2002) also investigated the differences between IMP and the traditional curriculum in a narrow scope—the research was conducted at a single school. The study, "Stanford University Mathematics Teaching and Learning Study: Initial Report—A Comparison of IMP 1 and Algebra 1 at Greendale School," found no significant differences in test scores between IMP and traditional pupils. Nevertheless, Boaler (2002) discovered differences in students' attitudes towards the two types of curricula:

> In our questionnaires we included a number of items that probes students' motivation, looking specifically for an intrinsic interest in mathematics. The results indicated that the students taught in different ways are developing different motivations. For instance, the responses of the Algebra 1 students indicate a stronger orientation towards grades, while the IMP students display higher levels of intrinsic interest. (p. 6)

Boaler (2002) delights in sprinkling the rest of the study with pupils' quotes emphasizing these stark affective contrasts.

Even noted mathematics professor E. F. Wolff (1997)* joins the chorus with his article "Summary of a Matched-Sample Study Comparing IMP and Traditionally-Taught Students on the Stanford Achievement Test—9th Edition at Central High School, Philadelphia, PA." Wolff (1997) found statistically significant differences in students' performance on the SAT-9s favoring IMP students (the SAT-9s have mathematics, science, and reading content on them), with the caveat that "[d]ifferences in student performance after 4 years of IMP [the study only assessed students after two and a half years] should be investigated," with more research to better confirm the claims (p. 4).

Of course, not all studies are in agreement that IMP classrooms produce better standardized test-takers than traditional classrooms. Bishop (1997), in "California 1992 and 1996 SAT Scores for IMP Schools," reported on the declines of average SAT scores in schools running the IMP curriculum. Although I do not wish to marginalize dissenting voices on the efficacy of IMP—and there certainly are some (once again, the *mathematicallycorrect.com* website, despite many ad hominem arguments, contains some noteworthy dissents centering on the notion that any criticism of IMP is reflexively judged to be politically incorrect)—the Bishop (1997) piece was one of only a few that is not obviously pure polemic.

---

* He is one of the featured mathematics educators of the *Life by the Numbers* episode mentioned earlier.

Polemicists often grab results from one study or another and run with it merely to stir controversy, which brings to the surface yet another point of contention between IMP and the traditional curriculum, namely, that of political connotation. IMP and other like-minded reform programs are poised to change the established strictures of math education, and, rather unsurprisingly, with potential change comes resistance.

In an article entitled "Updates on Math in Escondido" (2002), IMP is unfavorably discussed. "[T]he math [in IMP] seems almost secondary," with "social engineering content" emphasized instead of mathematics (p. 2). The piece dismisses the IMP curriculum as radical iconography in lockstep with leftist concerns: "Looking through the pages you find problems based on radical environmentalism, HIV/AIDS instruction, child abuse... 'finding the perfect group,' and many others. Much of the material is highly questionable.... This is very stupid stuff" (p. 2). In other words, the article pulls a bait-and-switch: it shifts the debate about the effectiveness of IMP—i.e., Is there learning of mathematics going on?—to an ideological realm, placing the entire IMP curriculum on the extreme left of the political spectrum, thus debasing the curriculum wholesale because of its supposed-political sympathies.

Some other articles criticizing IMP—such as Datta's (1996) and Mackey's (2002), both mentioned above—also present the reform program as necessitating a lurch to the left; but this sort of explicit debate of the political merits seems relatively confined to the traditionalists opposed to IMP who seem to believe that they are bravest of souls, holding back the barbarians at the gates of august pedagogic tradition. Perhaps the criticism evinced by the self-aggrandizing traditionalists of IMP is best captured by Pogrow (1996) in his introductory paragraph on education reformers. "Those responsible for this avalanche of reforms have taken the perspective that there are problems with the education establishment, problems with society, problems with the political structure, problems with current practice—in short, problems with everything except reformers and their proposed reforms" (Pogrow, 1996, p. 657).

When defenders of IMP talk of the traditionalists, they frequently present them as staid, dogmatic and rigid, but do not necessarily label them as rightwing or reactionary; support for this can be found in, among other places, "The Need for Change" section of *The IMPlementation Center.*

Finally, note that in this charged environment, there doesn't seem to be many agnostics: the traditional-versus-IMP debate polarizes people. These pedagogical issues—which, as they get closer to being resolved, may dictate the flow and direction of mathematics education—do not necessitate a middle ground.

The many differences between IMP and the traditional curriculum can be better brought into relief by constricting our focus and examining, in detail, two commensurate lessons from IMP and the traditional approach. The IMP lesson will be culled from a year-two text, and a first-year algebra book will supply the traditional lesson.

The student text for the first unit of the second year of IMP is very thin—it's only about one hundred pages in length, and it covers about a month's worth of class periods. The *Solve It!* unit reintroduces students—after a long summer break—to the rigors of high school mathematics. Review assignments dictate the classroom's topics for the first couple days of the school year. The *Solve It!* student text alternates between classwork, homework, and other assignments; other than an appendix, there is no reference, explanatory or other extraneous material—the student manual follows the flow and contains problems relating to the content of the classroom topics discussed daily (the student text demarcates "sections" with day numbers. For example, the first portion of the book has assignments and homework for days one through five).

The *Solve It!* student manual is also illustrated prodigiously. The visual design of the assignments is ostensibly to make them more enticing to students, although they frequently do not serve any utilitarian purpose relating to the assignments (as, say, diagrams describing the dimensions of a structure in a geometry word problem might). Significantly, though, the illustrations and pictures are quite often of women and minorities engaged in mathematics. The ubiquity of women and minorities in the pictures indeed hints at the political connotations assigned to IMP by the traditionalists.

The algebra text also has illustrations, but they are sparse and banal by comparison and usually serve a problem-based or utilitarian function. *Elementary Algebra: Structure and Use* is a textbook suited to students with little formal background in algebra. Nearly five hundred pages in length, the book will be with pupils the entire school year.

*Elementary Algebra* is structured, for lack of a better term, traditionally. Instead being split up according to class periods, as the IMP student handbook is, the traditional text is divided and subdivided by topics and subtopics. The first chapter details natural numbers, with separate sections for equalities and inequalities, properties of addition and multiplication, combining like terms, and algebraic expressions. Other chapters systematize the mathematics of integers, quadratic equations, polynomials, factoring, rational numbers, algebraic fractions, exponents, and radicals. Sections begin by formally and abstractly defining the topics or terms required for the problems presented, and continue by giving examples of their use in the math milieu. *Elementary Algebra*'s sections conclude with scores of practice problems, with the more challenging problems, such as applications, at the end of the lists of problems. The section formats do not vary throughout the book.

The distributive law is the central topic of Section 1-5, entitled "Distributive Properties." With somewhat turgid prose, the seven-page section begins: "We now introduce another important property of the natural numbers, a property that involves both multiplication and addition, called the distributive property" (Barnett and Kearns, 1990, p. 32). The words "distributive property," and many others throughout the book, are in bold, propagating the notion of a definitional—as opposed to an applied—organization of math. Since this is their first exposure to an algebra textbook, students' conceptions of algebra, and of high school mathematics, will be formed and influenced by this formalistic approach.

In the IMP student handbook, on the other hand, there are only a few bolded terms. The style of the lessons is largely conversational, with stories and situations setting up the classwork and homework problems. In the Days 13-21 section, there is a classwork and homework exercise that has students discovering the distributive property geometrically instead of by the traditional algebra-only approach. "A Lot of Changing Sides," and its corresponding homework, "Why Are They Equivalent?" and "One Each Way," contains a couple of multi-step applied problems and several traditional-style drill problems. The geometric and algebraic concepts in the problems are anticipated in the introduction to the section, which nicely presages algebraic geometry: "In mathematical work, you often need to be able to switch smoothly from one algebraic expression to an equivalent one.... You may be surprised to see that you can often use geometry to find equivalent algebraic expressions" (Fendel, Resek, Alper, and Fraser, 2000, p. 36). Addressing students personably—"You may be surprised," instead of intoning "We now introduce," as the traditional textbook does—establishes a non-threatening comfort zone around the potentially intimidating mathematics.

In the *Solve It! Teacher's Guide*, very specific lesson plans—one for each day of class—are given to the instructor. An Outline of the Day in each of the lessons specifies the activities for the day; in general, homework assigned the previous class is discussed, new material is revealed (either by the teacher or, more commonly, by students working alone or in groups), and homework for the next class is distributed.

In the lesson for Days 13 and 14, the classwork and homework is on the distributive property. The lesson is described in conversational form. For instance, under the subheading "Why are they equivalent?" teachers are told to "[p]oint out to students that they can't possibly check all possible values for $x$ to confirm that $2(x+1)$ and $2x+2$ always give the same result. Inform them that in their homework tonight, they will be looking at and evaluating three proposed explanations of why these expressions are equivalent" (Fendel, Resek, Alper, and Fraser, 1998, p. 98). And in "Introducing the activity," instructors are supposed to "[h]ave students read the introduction and Question 1 of the activity, or perhaps have a volunteer read this material aloud to the class. Then ask students to explain what exactly they are being told to do. Be sure that they identify the two steps of drawing a sketch [for the distributive property link] and finding an expression for the near area" (Fendel, Resek, Alper, and Fraser, 1998, p. 98).

Dialogue to espouse, questions to ask, student reading to be assigned, discussion topics to bring forth, talking points to speak, diagrams to draw, and connections to mention are described in incredible detail—the teacher is told precisely what to ask, say, and do in the *Teacher's Guide* throughout the lessons. Perhaps the lessons are a little too scripted. And yet answers to classwork and homework problems are not supplied to the instructor. Although there isn't total rigidity (teachers are occasionally *suggested* to do or say certain things), sticking to the fully-realized lesson-plan script seems primacy in IMP.

Lesson plans are not laid out in the *Elementary Algebra* text; rather, teachers are free to use whatever examples, definitions, and other problems they see fit in class—and they are also free to assign whatever homework problems they wish, whether they be of a drill type or of an applied kind. (They can even borrow IMP problems!) But with this freedom of instructor expression comes a tendency and propensity to structure classes around dictation, replete with example after example to show pupils on the board or the overhead. (It's how most instructors learned the math when *they* were in grade school, after all.) The instructor's text for *Elementary Algebra,* in which teachers are supplied the answers to almost every problem, encourages this sort of sage-on-the-stage behavior. Whereas the *Solve It! Teacher's Guide*—although largely telling teachers what to do and when to do it—supplies instructors with a plethora of structured activities for both individual students and groups, the *Elementary Algebra* teacher's text merely supplies teachers with a pool of drill problems for discrete topics (e.g., factoring, the quadratic equation, etc.).

In the "Distributive Properties" section in the traditional text, the teacher assumes a "fallback" position of sage on the stage. A Trends in International Mathematics and Science (TIMSS) study video illustrates this archetypal American instructor: although he was not teaching the distributive property, he dictated drill example after drill example to his students. He predicated his classroom not on students' constructivist self-discovery of mathematics, but on covering as many examples of the different abstract properties as possible—bringing the notion of mile-wide, inch-deep teaching to life—with an emphasis on terms and definitions, and none on application or multi-step word problems. One can imagine that same TIMSS instructor teaching Section 1-5 in *Elementary Algebra*: most questions posed to his class would be drill and definitional (for example, What is the numerical coefficient? What are like terms? What's the rule for combining like terms?). In addition, he would assign many of the endless supplies of problems at his disposal for homework, but the problems would likely be uniformly single-step mechanical ones.

The IMP lesson on the distributive property, however, would be more akin in structure and tone to the TIMSS video's Japanese math teacher's classroom. The teacher's class was constructivist, posing a single, multi-step problem for students to solve that implicitly taught them some of the abstract rules of triangles. Likewise, the IMP lesson for Days 13 and 14 do the same: the activity "A Lot of Changing Sides" is introduced, and students in groups play with the notions of the distributive law indirectly—the property "isn't formally stated until students have dealt with the ideas for several days" (Fendel, Resek, Alper, Fraser, 1998, p. 97). The homework for Day 13, which brings together the ideas of the distributive property, is called "Why Are They Equivalent?" There are only four questions, and all require students to write explanations.

By the time Day 14 rolls around, the homework is discussed and elaborated. Students are polled to check for agreement in answers. The distributive property is more formally introduced, although geometry is the means and the method: the areas of squares are shown to be equivalent (and the homework assigned in the previous class dealt with this geometric exploration in its applied problems). The class is split into groups for presenting answers to the entire class of the geometric applications of the distributive law, and, finally, homework systematizing the algebra of the distributive property is assigned, due the next class.

Days 13 and 14 have an arc of development in which students, in a social dynamic, are exposed to problem situations in which the abstract laws of the distributive property reveal themselves to be *implicit* in solutions. The traditional lesson of the distributive property, though, turns this presentation on its head: instead of allowing pupils to inductively discover the rules of math buried in the problems, the traditional instructor deductively teaches the rules at the start, and then has the students apply those rules to solving problems. Math, instead of a process of discovery and exploration and—indeed—play, literally becomes one of dependence; without having the rules and definitions and algorithms for specific types of problems at the ready, the traditionally-taught student rightly wonders, how can the problems be solved?

Indeed, the most glaring difference between the IMP and the traditional curriculum distributive property lesson, and IMP and traditional curricula overall, is in the levels of dependence students have on their instructors for learning the mathematics (in fact, in this respect, IMP might even be considered an antecedent to the modern "flipped" classroom, in that the onus to learn lies squarely on the students' shoulders). In traditional lessons, students, in full *tabula rasa* mode, are entirely reliant on their instructor to dictate the rules and terms of the math at all times. Students are left to merely passively soak up the mathematics and spit it back out in assessments.*

IMP's pupils discover math more or less on their own terms. They have at least a modicum of independence of mathematical discovery. This is not to say that all students in traditional curricula are abject failures at truly understanding math, and all pupils in IMP are resounding successes. Some students are successful under the tutelage of the traditional curriculum; others are not. But IMP's most glaring characteristic, for better or worse, is that it confirms to students what they suspect anyway: that their math teachers are not indefatigable be-all, end-all purveyors of math knowledge, but are continually open to the process of mathematical discovery as well.

(2002)

---

* And, in terms of high-stakes testing (such as to determine Adequate Yearly Progress), traditional, non-IMP classrooms which teach "to the test" hurt the validity of these tests: this is termed Campbell's Law—"The more any quantitative social indicator is used for social decision-making, the more subject it will be to corruption pressures and the more apt it will be to distort and corrupt the social processes it is intended to monitor," as social psychologist Donald Campbell explained his eponymous law—and its profound consequences in education are presented with aplomb by Diane Ravitch in her book *The Death and Life of the Great American School System*.

The problem is less that using quantitative tools to drive decisions is not well-intentioned (although, remember: the road to hell is paved with good intentions)—after all, a way to combat nepotism and thus to further meritocracy in not only education but in all fields is through removing as much evaluative subjectivity and guesswork as possible—but more that what and how we measure, compounded with confounding difficulties such as Campbell's Law and the like, make the resultant measurement data more shrouded in mystery than we initially suppose. The solution is *not* to simply stop using quantitative tools because they're imperfect: this is a case of letting the perfect be the enemy of the good. Rather, when drawing inferences, consider not only how the data were collected but what data were collected—do they present a complete picture? For instance, suppose you need to have cardiac surgery and have a choice of two nearby surgeons: Surgeon A and Surgeon B. Furthermore, suppose 87 percent of Surgeon A's patients survive while only 61 percent of Surgeon B's do. Which surgeon would you choose for your operation? The question is not rhetorical since the summary percentages do not give a full picture of the data: perhaps Surgeon A only agrees to operate on the easiest cases.

# References


Barnett, R. A., & Kearns, T. J. (1990). Elementary algebra: Structure and use, fifth edition. New York: McGraw-Hill.

Bishop, W. (1997). California 1992 and 1996 SAT scores for IMP schools. Mathematically Correct.
Retrieved November 12, 2002, from the Internet:
http://mathematicallycorrect.com/impsat.htm

Boaler, J. (2002). Stanford University mathematics teaching and learning study: Initial report—A comparison of IMP 1 and algebra 1 at Greendale school. Philly Mathematics.
Retrieved November 11, 2002, from the Internet:
http://www.gphillymath.org/StudentAchievement/Reports/Initial_report_Greendale.pdf

Datta, S. (1996). A nation afraid of mathematics: The San Francisco example. Mathematically Correct.
Retrieved November 12, 2002, from the Internet:
http://mathematicallycorrect.com/impsf.htm

Fendel, D., Resek, D., Apler, L., & Fraser, S. (1998). Interactive Mathematics Program: Solve it! Teacher's guide. Berkeley: Key Curriculum Press.

Fendel, D., Resek, D., Apler, L., & Fraser, S. (2000). Interactive Mathematics Program: Solve it! Berkeley: Key Curriculum Press.

Freitag, M. (2002). The Interactive Mathematics Program: A report.
Retrieved November 11, 2002, from the Internet:
http://jwilson.coe.uga.edu/emt669/Student.Folders/Frietag.Mark/Homepage/Welcome/IMPreport.html

Huetinck, L., & Munshin, S. N. (2000). Teaching mathematics for the 21st century: Methods and activities for grades 6-12. Columbus: Merrill.

The IMPlementation Center. (2002). The IMPlementation Center.
Retrieved November 19, 2002, from the Internet:
http://www.mathimp.org/

Mackey, K. (2002). An overview of IMP Years 1 and 2. Mathematically Correct. Retrieved November 12, 2002, from the Internet: http://www.mathematicallycorrect.com/imp.htm

"Making a Difference." Life by the Numbers. PBS. WHYY, Philadelphia. April 1, 1998. Pogrow, S. (1996). Reforming the wannabe reformers: Why education reforms almost always end up making things worse. Phi Delta Kappan, 77(10), 656-663.

Ryan, K., & Cooper, J. (2000). What is the history of American education? In K. Ryan and J. Cooper (Eds.), Those who can teach (9th ed.) (pp. 355-393). Boston: Houghton Mifflin.

Schifter, D. (1996). A constructivist perspective: On teaching and learning mathematics. Phi Delta Kappan, 77(7), 492-499.

Schoen, H. L. (1993). Report to the National Science Foundation on the impact of the Interactive Mathematics Project (IMP). Retrieved November 11, 2002, from the Internet: http://facstaff.wcer.wisc.edu/normw/NSF%20IMP%2093%20Scan.pdf

Staples, M. E. (2001). Characterizing differences between two mathematics classrooms using "reform" and "traditional" curricula. Retrieved November 11, 2002, from the Internet: http://tigersystem.net/aera2002/viewproposaltext.asp?propID=6519

Stigler, J. W., & Hiebert, J. (1997). Understanding and improving mathematics instruction. Phi Delta Kappan, 79(1), 14-21.

Tanner, D., & Tanner, L. (1975). Curriculum development: Theory into practice. New York: Macmillan Publishing.

Webb, N., & Dowling, M. (1997). Comparison of IMP students with students enrolled in traditional courses on probability, statistics, problem solving, and reasoning. Wisconsin Center for Education Research, School of Education, University of Wisconsin-Madison. Retrieved November 12, 2002, from the Internet: http://facstaff.wcer.wisc.edu/normw/comparison_of_imp_students_with_.htm

Updates on math in Escondido. (2002). Mathematically Correct. Retrieved November 12, 2002, from the Internet: http://mathematicallycorrect.com/twocity.htm

Wolff, E. F. (1997). Summary of a sample-matched study comparing IMP and traditionally-taught students on the Stanford Achievement Test—9th Edition at Central High School, Philadelphia, PA. Philly Mathematics. Retrieved November 11, 2002, from the Internet: http://www.gphillymath.org/StudentAchievement/Reports/SupportData/CentandGirlsSAT9.pdf

# 9.

## The Curious Case of Causation: Confusing Correlation and Cause and Effect

In order for high school statistics students to appreciate the importance of experimental design, *Principles and Standards for School Mathematics* (2000) expects them to "understand the differences among various kinds of studies and which types of inferences can legitimately be drawn from each" (p. 401). More generally, if students are to draw proper conclusions about the relationships between variables, they must have a good handle on the distinction between correlation and causation.

Teaching this distinction presents a dilemma for the high school statistics instructor. Whereas in all previous secondary mathematics classes leading to statistics (or Advanced Placement Statistics) students have been inculcated in the closed-system nature of math—even if real-world problems are presented to students, they are still likely part and parcel of an axiomatic approach to the discipline—in statistics, the collection and analysis of data applies mathematical tools to a "messy" reality and imposes a need to acknowledge and conform to the rigors of science.

As Carl Gauss famously observed, mathematics is the handmaiden of science; John Tukey, the groundbreaking twentieth century statistician who revolutionized exploratory data analysis, might have argued that science is the handmaiden of statistics. "John Tukey taught that Statistics is more a science than it is a branch of Mathematics.... Statistics is held to the additional standard imposed by science. A model for data, no matter how elegant or correctly derived, must be discarded or revised if it doesn't fit the data or when new or better data are found and it fails to fit them" (Velleman, 2008). Statistics is often called the science of data, after all.

Even though numerous methods of descriptive statistics are presented to students in pre-statistics math courses, such as boxplots, dotplots, histograms, outlier tests, and the like, and forays into the display and analysis of bivariate data consume time in algebra classes (with the creation of scatterplots, the calculation of correlation coefficients, and the construction of least-squares regression lines), the "burden" of science is not often discussed—and ideas of causation versus correlation are at best merely glossed over, rarely given anything more than cursory treatment—leaving statistics teachers to contend ultimately with palpable confusion in their classrooms about this wrinkle once any sort of inferential statistics is broached in the curriculum.

Velleman (2008) implores statistics teachers to nip this problem in the bud immediately: "We should teach students to resist jumping to conclusions, extrapolating, and proposing explanations for associations that assume causation." So, statistics students must become adept at suggesting realistic lurking variables. There might not be a formulaic or algorithmic way to conjure up a third or lurking variable explaining an apparent relationship in a bivariate data set, as there is a step-by-step process to obtaining the correlation coefficient of two variables, but students understanding the distinction between causation and mere correlation is not only critical, it is of a piece with statistics as a science and not just a math. As Paulos (1992) states, "[T]oo often people become mesmerized by the technical details of correlation coefficients, regression lines, and curves of best fit and neglect to step back and think about the logic of the situation" (p. 57).

I became aware of these statistical-thinking curricular deficiencies in "pre-statistics" courses only when I taught statistics classes of my own. Pleased that students were already comfortable with the correlation coefficient—save for a *z*-scores' derivation of the calculation of *r*—I was surprised by their bewilderment at the caution not to confuse association with causation, at having to propose logical lurking variables, and at having to think in such a non-quantitative way in a math class.

Beginning with the most obvious sets of variables that were correlated but not causal did little to help students identify faulty cause-and-effect in later, less obvious bivariate data sets. Specifically, during class discussion, my students had trouble identifying what causal relationships implied, proposing alternative explanations for these relationships, and understanding why values of the correlation coefficient can't measure the likelihood of causality.

For instance, early on in class discussion, a television and life expectancy activity from Rossman, Chance and von Oehsen (2002) was presented. The in-class activity has students calculate the correlation coefficient of the number of people per television set by country and the life expectancy of these countries. After discovering the value of *r* to be close to negative one, the authors ask: "Since the association is so strongly negative, one might conclude that simply sending television sets to the countries with lower life expectancies would cause their inhabitants to live longer. Comment on this argument" (p. 194). The following responses would be typical:

> "Of course one doesn't cause the other. It's just because the countries with more TVs have more money."
>
> "No! If that were true, then instead of food drops on poorer countries we should do 'TV drops' on poorer countries."

These responses indicate that not only did students realize that there was no cause-and-effect relationship, but they also understood the bizarre consequences of assuming the relationship actually was causal.

But later, slightly less obvious problem situations confounded my students during class discussion. In an activity entitled "Evaluation of Course Effectiveness," Rossman, Chance and von Oehsen (2002) describe a college professor's systematic study of the efficacy of his freshman learning-skills course. The professor examines two variables in his study: students' grades in his course, and their final college GPAs. Because *r* is found to be close to one, the professor "concludes that his course must have had a positive effect on students' learning skills, for those who did well in his course proceeded to do well in college," and vice versa (p. 202). Whereas my students readily pointed out the faulty logic in the televisions-versus-life-expectancy activity, they had trouble (1) recognizing his conclusion was fallacious at all, (2) discounting the high *r* value as evidence of causality, and (3) arriving at plausible alternative explanations for the strong association.

After the lessons were wrapped up, I formally assessed my students. The six-question quiz I disseminated on the correlation coefficient contained two questions dealing solely with association versus causation. These two questions, both adapted from Brase and Brase (2003), were stated as follows:

1. Suppose it is discovered that there is a high positive correlation in the United States between teachers' salaries and annual consumption of liquor.
    a. Explain what a cause-and-effect relationship here would imply. Then explain why a cause-and-effect association between these two variables is unlikely.
    b. Can you think of an alternative explanation for the strong association? Write a few sentences addressing this.

2. Is it possible to use the chirping of a cricket to predict the outdoor temperature during the summer? The correlation coefficient between chirping frequency (number of cricket chirps per second) and outdoor temperature (in Fahrenheit) of a random sample of crickets was calculated to be 0.732. Based on the value of *r*, would you conclude that there is a cause-and-effect relationship between these two variables? Justify your answer.

Student responses elicited by these questions ranged from the convoluted and the confused to the ridiculous and the (unwittingly) silly. It is instructive for us to examine these responses, for they betray a number of errors of statistical thinking.

For example, students seemed to be puzzled by the direction of cause to effect. Here is a representative response to the chirping cricket question: "No, you can't. No one can ever prove temperature actually causes crickets to chirp." Although right to dismiss the cause-and-effect relationship between the two variables, the student misread the implied (but faulty) causal chain: chirps-cause-temperature. This kind of response wasn't confined to the cricket question: although less obvious, teachers' salaries are supposed to predict annual consumption of alcohol, not the other way around. Nevertheless, here are some mistaken answers students gave to part (a) of the liquor question.

> "A cause-effect relationship would mean that the more annual consumption of liquor in the U.S., the higher the salaries teachers will get."
>
> "The more a teacher drinks the more they [sic] get paid. A teacher who drinks would not be effective."
>
> "This would imply that the higher the teacher's salary, the more that teacher drinks. This is very illogical because drinking high amounts of liquor would not constitute a pay increase."

Another student figuratively threw up his hands when he wrote, "If a teacher had a high salary, then he would drink a lot or if a teacher drinks a lot, then he has a high salary." Since all of these pupils seemed to have had trouble differentiating between the predictor (explanatory) variable and the predicted (response) variable, they confused the direction of cause to effect. There is certainly some merit in recognizing that it is often unclear which of two variables might be the cause and which might be the effect. Huff (1954) terms this a *post hoc*[*] fallacy: "In some of these instances cause and effect may change places from time to time or indeed both may be cause and effect at the same time. A correlation between income and ownership of stocks might be of that kind," since the more income earned, the more stocks purchased, and the more stocks purchased, the more income obtained (p. 89). Disentangling the effect and the cause with stocks and income is effectively impossible.[†]

Several of the quiz answers above are notable for another reason besides their misstatement of the direction of cause-to-effect. Their responses are largely "restricted" in scope; instead of interpreting the "annual consumption of liquor" to mean annual consumption among *the entire population of the United States*, these students took it

---

[*] Referring to *post hoc ergo propter hoc*, meaning after this, therefore because of this. Just because A occurs and then B occurs doesn't mean A *caused* B.

[†] One is reminded here of Kurt Vonnegut's *Timequake*, where the great novelist plays with cause and effect by having his characters relive a portion of their lives.

to only apply to teachers. Many other pupils' responses to part (a) of the liquor question betrayed that same narrow focus, such as

> "A cause-and-effect relationship here would imply that due to teachers making more money, they will consume more liquor. This is unlikely because it does not make sense that would be the case."

> "It would imply the more teachers are paid, the more they drink. This is unlikely because it's untrue, teachers don't drink more when they're paid better."

> "A cause-and-effect relationship would imply that teachers consume more liquor because they make more money. This is unlikely, because liquor consumption has nothing to do with how much money one makes—poor people drink too."

No student here claimed that there actually was a *causal* relationship between alcohol consumption and teacher salaries; contrariwise, no student claimed the variables were unrelated. In part (b) of the liquor questions, students were asked to conjure up a third variable that might explain the relationship between the other two. Frequently, pupils strained to explain the relationship, making causal leaps into the wild blue yonder.* For instance, consider these fallacious, convoluted "explanations":

> "This could be due to teachers usually being stressed or depressed so they desire more alcohol. And they also have summers off to drink. So they're laying them back when it's hot."

> "An alternate explanation is that older teachers are more likely to drink more."

> "Public school teachers have higher salaries than private school teachers and since public school teachers usually have worse students they may drink more."

---

* Behavioral economists Daniel Kahneman and Amos Tversky have researched faulty causation inference and attribution, among many other topics; see *Thinking, Fast and Slow* for more.

> "The longer teachers work, the more they get paid. So as they get older, their salaries get higher, as well as possible liquor consumption. Either that or the longer teachers work, the higher chance they have of getting a class that will drive them crazy and cause them to drink more liquor."

During a class discussion of the relationship between foreign language study and SAT score in high school, students easily pointed out a lurking variable: intelligence. An analogous understanding of the idea of a lurking variable, a third variable in the "background" which explains the connection between the other two, is shown in the following response to the liquor question: "Teachers with higher salaries tend to have higher positions, thus they have more responsibility and stress. People with more stress tend to drink more." Despite the narrow focus, the notion of "stress" as an explanation of the relationship between the variables seems at least somewhat plausible. Other pupils, though, got hung up on esoteric economic concerns when fingering potential third variables.

> "There may have been a tax decrease on liquor that year which prompted an increase in consumption that ironically [?] fits with teachers' salaries."

> "With more people buying liquor, the country makes more $ [money] off taxes, and teachers are paid from taxes."

> "Jobs are making it through depression so the teachers drink more. So recession would be a confounding variable."

> "When teachers get higher salaries, the economy is probably doing well so more people buy liquor."

These responses strain mightily to make connections between seemingly unrelated phenomena. Only the last response above approaches the most likely truth: that as teachers' salaries are rising, everyone's purchasing power is probably increasing, leading to more discretionary spending on liquor (among other items).

Not every pupil answered both parts of the liquor question incorrectly. For instance, here is one student's answer to both parts:

> "It would imply that teachers drink more due to the fact that they have more money. They are probably unrelated variables: there is likely a confounding or lurking variable explaining the relationship."
>
> "Perhaps the standard of living goes up, so everyone has more money to spend on everything, including liquor. If teachers' salaries go up, it's likely that other salaries go up, too."

Although this last student answered both parts of the question correctly, take note of a subtle problem (apparent in several other responses as well): the conflation of "lurking" variables and "confounding" variables, despite their ostensible differences. This is a persistent error of language in both classroom discussions of causation, experimental design, studies' analysis, and the like, and on written evaluations.

The quiz revealed another persistent error in pupils' thinking. Take a look at these three responses to the cricket question:

> "No, not cause/effect, because it has only a moderate relationship and to prove cause-and-effect you need [an *r* value] above 0.8 or below –0.8."
>
> "I would say this is not a pure cause-and-effect relationship, because the correlation is not very close to 1, and you wouldn't say one is directly associated with it—but it certainly is an indicator."
>
> "It doesn't necessarily cause it but the scatterplot would show a strong association anyway, so maybe it does."

Despite repeated injunctions during class time to disregard the value of *r* when jumping to conclusions about cause and effect—and, by extension, to ignore any linear patterns shown on a scatterplot as indicators of causality—these responses all rely on *r* as evidence either for or against causation. It appears that some pupils intuit that the closer the absolute value of *r* is to one, the higher the probability there is of a cause-and-effect relationship between the variables, until—presto!—causation is proven with $|r|$ equal to one. Perhaps the notion of numbers-as-measurement is too ingrained, too strong, too intuitive for students to cast off easily.

On the other end of the spectrum, several students either refused to even entertain the possibility of cause-and-effect—under *any* circumstances—or implied that the two weren't dissimilar enough to merit comment. These types of answers to the cricket question bordered on the existential. Paulos (1992) states that, when considering association and causation, "…the philosopher David Hume maintained that in principle there is no difference between the two" (p. 56). Hume might have been proud of this student's response: "No, the association just implies causation. Assume that they are the same thing, since no one can ever prove temperature actually causes crickets to chirp anyway." Or this one: "No, you are never able to conclude a cause-and-effect relationship because it cannot be fully proven that one causes the other."

But at least these students were thinking critically! Some chose to repeat, as answers to all of the questions, "Association never implies causation, association never implies causation"—as if it were an incantation to be delivered upon the faintest whiff of the words "cause and effect."[*] Unfortunately this kind of response, although technically correct, is rote and not thought through. Students must be open to the possibility that cause-and-effect may be proven, not be reflexively against the prospect; otherwise, the vagaries of experimental design, without allowing for causation-as-explanation, will be foreign to them.[†]

For students to properly draw inferences from data they must, in part, appreciate the distinction between causation and correlation. Since understanding these distinctions is a *sine qua non* of statistical

---

[*] But it's *not* an incantation, thus this last part of the sentence has an "if it were…" subjunctive case rather than an "if it was…" indicative case grammatical construction.

[†] Students might also want to consult the marginally famous *xkcd* comic how a student was broken of attributing causality to anything at all because of his time as an Advanced Placement Statistics student—even to the point of wondering if the statistics class actually broke him of the habit or if that was merely correlation as well.

thinking,[*] pupils should be exposed to these ideas early on, in the academic years prior to taking a statistics class. Perhaps my students' errors cataloged above would have been lessened or eliminated by treatment of inferential ideas in prior math classes.

Surely anytime a correlation coefficient is discussed or calculated in a pre-statistics course, such as in Algebra 2, the notion of association versus causation—and a clear warning not to confuse the two—should be made: Just because identifying the differences between correlation and causation imposes the burden of science[†] in math class isn't an excuse to simply ignore these differences. Thinking critically about data should not be the exclusive province of statistics students.

(2009)

[*] Data drives decisions: misidentifying mere correlation as causation results in false conclusions about data, which may in turn lead to misinformed decision-making—and whole hosts of affronts to individuals or groups.

[†] For more about science itself, read the brilliant book *Superstition: Belief in the Age of Science* (2008). Author Robert L. Park traces the beginnings of the scientific method to a solar eclipse over the ancient Greek city of Miletus in 585 BCE. "What distinguished the eclipse…from every previous eclipse of the Sun by the Moon was that it had been predicted [by Thales of Miletus].… Thales understood what had happened and made use of the event to state the law of cause and effect, perhaps the most brilliant insight of all time.…" Superstition was superseded by a scientific causation.

# References

Brase, Charles H., and Corrinne P. Brase. *Understandable Statistics: Concepts and Methods* (7th ed.). Boston: Houghton Mifflin, 2003.

Huff, Darrell. *How to Lie with Statistics*. New York: W.W. Norton, 1954.

National Council of Teachers of Mathematics (NCTM). *Principles and Standards for School Mathematics*. Reston, VA: NCTM, 2000.

Paulos, John A. *Beyond Numeracy*. New York: Vintage, 1992.

Rossman, Allan J., Beth L. Chance, and J. Barr von Oehsen. *Workshop Statistics: Discovery with Data and the Graphing Calculator* (2nd ed.). New York: Key College, 2002.

Velleman, Paul F. "Truth, Damn Truth, and Statistics." *Journal of Statistics Education*, Volume 16, Number 2 (2008).
Retrieved November 11, 2009, from the Internet:
www.amstat.org/publications/jse/v16n2/velleman.html.

# 10.

## Fitting into Kaplan's Suit: An Algorithmic Transcription of Hitchcock

If it is agreed that Hitchcock* seeks the inherent simplification of "life" into definable, discreet units—a magnification and projection of empirical, overarching cosmological truths underpinning a contextualized reality—then mathematics, and specifically the algorithmic method, may be utilized logically as an explorative apparatus. However, it is not necessarily the case that the films *seek* this notion. Therefore, before constructing machinery that realizes such algorithmic underpinnings and churnings—if there are, indeed, such root structures—it is obligatory to defend, with reasonable credibility, the veracity of inherent segments of constructed-ness, or structure, of Hitchcock, and the limitations of such a realization henceforth.

At the most basic, rudimentary level, breaking films apart into constitute discrete units for examination, which is necessary for an algorithmic process, betrays the sense of wholeness and unity that the sum of those parts—or more than the sum of the parts—propagates: in essence, the parts in separation disqualify the whole as a complete, functional, fully-realized "organism." For instance, examining the complementarity of Judy and Madeline or Judy and Midge as separate from their contexts, from their wholeness, necessitates the deconstruction† of the essence, or at least *an* essence, of *Vertigo* (1958); furthermore, since "essence" is inherently not definable in the sense of elements of construction, its loss cannot be accounted for by more discrete examination.

---

* Here, and throughout the rest of this essay, we refer not specifically to director Alfred Hitchcock himself, but rather to the Hitchcock oeuvre and its inherent associated attributes, traits, correspondences and relations.

† Deconstruction here is not meant quite as Derrida originally presented it—his writings which are the genesis of the notion of deconstruction form a rich discourse (in the sense of Foucault) that might be a bit ill-fitting here—but more along the loosely general lines of "breakdown."

Indeed, arguably, there are two parts of Hitchcock: the parts and the whole. Quantification of the whole is impossible since by definition any examination or investigation relies on a part, or parts, extracted from the whole. Thus, a cyclical paradox, à la the hermeneutic circle, presents itself: inspection of the parts of the film shrouds the wholeness, and, contrapositively, a viewing of the whole merges or dismantles or shadows the parts. Both the parts and the whole cannot be examined simultaneously, and it is impossible to grasp the sense of the whole using algorithmic/deconstructionist methods. This is somewhat unlike phenomenological perception, which has more dynamic focus but surprisingly similar methodological drawbacks as our parts/whole complex. As the Done Ihde, when detailing the "programmatic and general features of phenomenological inquiry," concedes,

> I have employed typical philosophers' devices. I have analyzed a totality into components and introduced a simplification. The simplification was a visual model of what is global and complex. I am quite aware that gains in clarity may be offset in richness. What is pushed to the background or, worst, forgotten, may complicate the investigation in the future. In spite of that, I shall take a take yet another step towards simplification....*

Despite us also seemingly being between the Scylla of simplification and the Charybdis of heuristic impregnability, the discrete parts of Hitchcock are available for inspection based on a definitional calculus. This is the essential axiomatic approach that precedes the use of algorithms: accept as true a precise-as-can-be statement—e.g., distinct parts of Hitchcock can be considered for examination—and derive consequences.

Considering the parts of the films, a new, multi-structured query arises: What is a "part," and is there an indivisibility to those parts—a kind of "lowest common denominator"—defining a part? Mapping mathematical algorithms onto film posits an important consideration: the potentialities for one-to-one correspondences between the worlds of algorithm and film. Certainly there is some-

---

* Done Ihde, *Experimental Phenomenology: An Introduction* (New York: State University of New York Press, 1986), p. 67.

thing lost in the translation, akin to the transposition of tableaux to printed, ostensibly descriptive word; yet the breaking-down of Hitchcock into algorithmic form yields aggregate benefits of insight and increased ease of description, first and foremost of dynamic/static systems' interplays and relations in temporal space.

It should be noted, though, that a translation is at best a sketch or afterimage of the original's intentions—think Plato's Allegory of the Cave—and, likewise, the algorithmic methodology applied to Hitchcock is at best a translation of distinct parts. Thus, the algorithms, which are facsimiles, can only be assumed to have correlative properties to the originals. In other words, correlations can be firmly established using algorithms—i.e., this could mean this, that could mean that—but undeniable links between constituent parts of Hitchcock using algorithmic methods cannot be demonstrated for three reasons: parts either exist by themselves or do not exist at all (they are fused together and do not exist as distinct, manipulative entities from the whole); the translation from Hitchcock into algorithm can never be in perfect synchronicity; and parts are concretized or become defined presumably by the algorithms themselves.

Returning to the nature of a discrete part, we shall consider a part after it has been translated into algorithm, since any attempt to discuss a part of a film requires translation into a language of some sort, which an algorithm is: indeed, the discussion of the transcription of Hitchcock into algorithm is a translation, a facsimile, of the algorithmic translation itself. At the risk of introducing a circular definition, an algorithmic part is such a part of Hitchcock that is capable of being translated into algorithmic form.* More specifically, then, the problem of what is suitable for translation into algorithm emerges. An algorithm is a series of linear steps leading to a resultant of some sort, whether that resultant be actual output or simply the progression of the steps themselves (we will stay away from more complicated computer science distinctions, such as whether our algorithms can be run with a Universal Turing Machine); this implies causality, which is the major motivator of the algorithm. Algorithms do not necessarily have to be confined to

* This is an inclusion/exclusion relation—implied here is that there are parts not capable of being systematized into algorithm. We consider the whole a contained "part" which, as mentioned, cannot be made into algorithm.

narrative issues, but narratives are the obvious direct expression of causal structures in film. Hence algorithms, because of their linearity, can be considered de facto narratives.

An example will suffice to demonstrate the utilitarian nature of the algorithm in Hitchcock. Recall the multiple identity transformations of Roger O. Thornhill, the protagonist of *North by Northwest* (1959): an ostensibly innocent man pursued by those who do not believe he is who he says he is, Thornhill adopts his doppelganger's *raison d'être* so to speak, and allows himself to be transformed—and transforms—into the cipher of George Kaplan, the secret agent for whom he is mistaken. And whereas before his mistaken identity Thornhill lived unwittingly a life of quiet desperation (as Henry David Thoreau might have said), afterwards, although he continues to push the rock uphill for time immemorial like Sisyphus, he is happy (as Albert Camus might have said).

Hitchcock scholar Robin Wood, in his analysis of *North by Northwest*,* segments the film into three ephemeral movements (or parts) built on the "main stages in the evolution of the hero's attitude"; and, in a commensurate way, the following algorithm, based on basic narrative/character instances from *North by Northwest*, also splits the Thornhill developments of identity into several discrete steps (or parts):

(1) Thornhill = Culturally-Constructed Identity
(2) Thornhill = Kaplan
(3) Kaplan = Thornhill
(4) Kaplan = Dead
(5) Thornhill = New Identity

This mélange of algorithmic theory and narrative/character description is clearly too liberal and amorphous in its construction; in terms of understanding, little is gained with the translation of the thread of Thornhill's identity through the diagesis since the narrative context is not explicitly defined in the algorithm. Despite the numbers present before each line denoting the causality axiomatically implicit in the narrative, the algorithm is too loose: it is unclear what "=" denotes, what "New Identity" refers to, or how the flow

---

* Robin Wood, *Hitchcock's Films Revisited* (New York: Columbia University Press, 1989), pp. 131-141.

of time—the element that permits causality—is accounted for, with the exception of the monikers of enumeration. It is also ontologically untenable and sociologically cringe-worthy to affix labels like "Culturally-Constructed Identity" onto individuals, even fictive ones, without recourse to elaborate ancillary suppositions about notions of culture.*

Since we have used—and will continue to use—"Culturally-Constructed Identity" as a descriptor of Thornhill at the commencement of the narrative, a definition must be in order. Robin Wood supplies it: in his chapter on *North by Northwest*, he declaims Thornhill's reliance on the fast-paced New York cultural milieu for purpose. Roger Thornhill is a person who

> lives purely on the surface, refusing all commitment or responsibility (appropriately, he is in advertising), immature for all his cocksureness, his life all the more a chaos for the fact that he doesn't recognize it as such; a man who relies above all on the exterior trappings of modern civilization—business offices, cocktail bars, machines—for protection, who substitutes bustle and speed for a sense of direction or purpose....†

Despite Wood's description of Thornhill's total buy-in of the cultural trappings, the notion of a "Culturally-Constructed Identity" is a terribly imprecise descriptor.

So, in sum, the root problem with the algorithm is that its conventions have not been explicitly and satisfactorily defined; further along in this essay, such conventions will be elaborated, and more specific and detailed algorithms will be synthesized with the same raw material, but for the purposes of our present argument, let us continue to refer to what we shall henceforth call the "Thornhill Algorithm." First of all, note that the algorithm reads left to right,

---

* For more on this, pick up at random nearly any anthropology or sociology paper written during the last fifty years.

† This passage is found in Robin Wood, *Hitchcock's Films Revisited* (New York: Columbia University Press, 1989), p. 134. Note that a constant theme in Wood's writings is the questioning—and often debasement—of implicit cultural artifacts and assumptions; his recurring references of F. R. Leavis' critiques and challenges toward established staid strictures in academe are part and parcel of this propensity.

then top to bottom—this is not a trivial observation, since attempts to read the above algorithm in contrary ways lead to fallacies and mutations of intended meaning. As it reads now, it is both a step-by-step description of the transformation of Thornhill and "instructions"—on a meta-level—for that change. The output is a New Thornhill, but, more than that, it is the inputs, or the agents of change in the narrative—Kaplan, Death, and so forth—that the output is of causal consequence.

Second, the equals-sign convention ("=")—the assignment of the properties of one "object" to another; in this case, the objects are both characters and types of identities—functions as a panacea of sorts, at once simplifying and complicating the translations of the algorithm. To conceptualize the notion of the equals sign in force, examine lines two and three of the "Thornhill Algorithm": to the left of the equals sign is an object (character) that assumes the properties of the object (identity) to the right: in this loosely defined algorithm (the algorithm is, recall, loosely constructed to allow for an easier dissemination of the notion of the "parts" of Hitchcock, and the potentialities for an algorithmic translation of those parts), assignments of identity are capable of being made to characters. This is a recurring trait of the algorithm.

Third, noting that objects to the left of the equals sign are not static but dynamic and variable by definition—because various properties are conscripted to the left-of-the-equals-sign objects throughout the causal structure, they are receptors of change—we can denote these objects as *variables*. Thornhill and Kaplan both appear to the left of the equals sign; both objects are variables requiring and necessitating assignment or assignments transmitted from the object to the right of the equals sign.

And, finally, objects to the right of the equals sign have properties—static properties—that will be assigned instantaneously to the variables to the left of the sign; despite their static quality, they are effectors of change to the objects to the left of the equals sign simply by virtue of their fixed properties (fixed, that is, at the time of transmission). Thus, "Dead" is a static conception assigned to Kaplan, and "Culturally-Constructed Identity" is a set of traits set forth for Thornhill. (Importantly, the order of the assignments is critical.) The significance lies in the assignment and/or mapping of characters to characters: in the case of Thornhill to Kaplan or Kaplan to Thornhill, one character (object) is the variable, or the receiver, in the algorithmic equation, and the other is the transmitter object—and the transmitter, during the "sending process," is static and unchanging. Recall our earlier nature-of-a-part inquiry: the part, we now see, is the static transmitter: at this instant in the narrative or diagesis, the transmitter object cannot be reduced further, lest the "message" is distorted, the properties it transmits not fully elaborated; despite the seemingly-open definition of "New Identity" or even "Dead"—two transmitter objects in the "Thornhill Algorithm"—the reduction of the assignment objects is not possible otherwise assignments do not occur and narrative logic ceases. Extending this, it is apparent that even "Thornhill" and "Kaplan," when to the right of the equals sign, function solely as transmitters that alter the characteristics of the variables. Thus the conventions of object transmitters allow for the empirical revelation of irreducible parts in Hitchcock, namely, the distinct parts.

Nevertheless, as already noted, there exists a kind of amorphous quality to the constructs: "New Identity" and "Culturally-Constructed Identity" are open-ended and vague, despite their being irreducible by definition. We are able to increase specificity about these terms—and other terms that follow from them—only so far as written communication allows; there will always be an ambiguity, a sense that a part has not been wholly defined or grasped at in enough detail. But it is unnecessary to fully enumerate the makeup of the parts or the variables to work with them; this is akin to the fields of mathematics and computer science, where, as long as a level of detail is accepted as adequate beforehand—essentially, a line in the sand is drawn—the results of infinitely small or inherently non-definable building blocks are, *ipso facto*, manipulated without harm or error. (Think of the "black box" in science or engineering—we do not need to be able to describe the box's innards to make use of its functionality.) However, since we, as we shall observe, are not totally clear on that essential "something" that is in the irreducible makeup of a part of Hitchcock (a transmitter object, recall, is laden with irreducibility), to ease the sense of the "something" potentially missing, an undefined constant will be supplemented in the following algorithmic example to each object where deemed appropriate. The "something" is akin to a placeholder or a marker for the unknowable. It is also somewhat analogous to physicist Albert Einstein's utilization of a "cosmological constant" to account for the then-unknown expansion of the universe in his

Special Theory of Relativity.* When the "something" is seen in action in the algorithm below, its functionality will be more readily obvious.

Assimilating the traits and conventions we have observed in the "Thornhill Algorithm," a more complicated version of the algorithm, with more universally applicable and better-defined conventions, will now be introduced. The semantics and notation of the following "Thornhill Algorithm" are not entirely arbitrary, but rather follow a latent logic rooted in conventions of computer science coding. The algorithm is composed of *pseudocode*,† an import from computer science denoting code that cannot be run by a computer, but can be read and assimilated readily and easily by humans (although "real" computer code, such as C++—euphemistically referred to as "object-oriented code"‡—or Visual Basic code, can also be read by humans, it tends to not be as clear as well-written pseudocode. Also, the pseudocode writer can play hard and fast with the conventions so long as the code is rigorously logical and consistent).

The following algorithm essentially captures the same notions of *North by Northwest* detailed in the previous algorithm. The level of detail is higher, however, and elements not present before surface with this example:

(1) Define Type: Something = {Something as Something}
(2) Define Type: True_and_False = {False, True, Unknown}
(3) Define Type: Identity = {Culturally_Constructed as True_and_False, Part_of_Living_Person as True_and_False, Something as Something}

---

* The cosmological constant was Einstein's attempt to compensate for what his equations were telling him was true: that the universe was not static but expanding. When observations later confirmed this truth, Einstein exclaimed that the cosmological constant was the biggest blunder of his career. Modern research, though, has shown there might be a place for the constant after all.

† For an introduction to computer programming, see the Appendix. It might also be beneficial to read the chapter "A Mathematical Approach to Alfred Hitchcock," presented later in the book.

‡ For more about the natures of object-oriented programming and design, and algorithms in general, refer to the following text: Daniel Appleman, *How Computer Programming Works* (Emeryville, California: Ziff-Davis Press, 1994), pp. 105-143.

(4) Define Type: Character = {Living as True_and_False, Guilt as True_and_False, Identity_of_Character as Identity, Something as Something}
(5) Thornhill as Character
(6) Kaplan as Character
(7) Begin:
(8) Thornhill = {Living = True, Guilt = False, (Culturally_Constructed = True, Part_of_Living_Person = False, Something = Something), Something = Something}
(9) Kaplan = {Living = Unknown, Guilt = Unknown, (Culturally_Constructed = False, Part_of_Living_Person = False, Something = Something), Something = Something}
(10) Thornhill = Kaplan
(11) Thornhill.Living = True
(12) Thornhill.Identity_of_Character.Part_of_Living_Person = True
(13) Kaplan = Thornhill
(14) Kaplan.Living = False
(15) Thornhill.Identity_of_Character.Part_of_Living_Person = True
(16) End.

Hierarchy is the key concept that structures the conventions of this pseudocode. By hierarchy, we refer to the top-down approach of computer programming: like a nesting doll, in which larger, identical dolls literally grasp and contain others, there is an interdependence—and yet still clear differences between the assorted objects—of the code. (For the sake of completeness, note that the pseudocode bears strong resemblance to C++, a contemporarily pervasive computer language. C++'s antecedent, called C, was formed exclusively by Dennis Ritchie in 1972. In computer language terms, C++ and the pseudocode are deemed "structured code.") Also, elements present in the film—Kaplan, Thornhill, and more—are enumerated specific attributes in the hierarchical composition. Because of the complexity of the algorithm, each line will be examined in detail.

(1) A "type" is defined. This first "type" of variable, or kind of variable (denoting the attributes that this variable contains), is the analogue to Einstein's cosmological constant mentioned earlier: a "something" that cannot be demarcated but nevertheless ex-

ists; it is a commodity that is beyond definition in a structuralist approach to film, since it cannot be related to structure(s) of any sort. It is also the clearest expression of a correlational "margin of error" in the pseudocode approach: if the "something" could be measured in magnitude, its complement would correspond to the degree of accuracy that this methodology contains. More specifically, if the magnitude of "something" was *x* percent, then its complement, one hundred percent subtracted by *x* percent, would total the percentage of accuracy that this "something" possesses. Also observe the recursive and reflexive (in the sense of reference to the self) nature of this line: the "something" is of type "something," thereby eluding the quandary of a specific quantity of "something."*

(2) "True_and_False," a type of variable, is defined. For the sake of maintaining a patent link to the standards and strictures of the computer science milieu—and also for clarity's sake—all of the variables' names are continuous; in other words, they have no spaces separating alphanumeric characters (instead of calling this variable type "True and False," the underscore character is used to link together the words: "True_and_False." This is simply a naming convention in modern programming languages and has no impact on the conceptions conveyed by the algorithm). The "True_and_False" variable type, which other variables, such as the Kaplan and Thornhill variables, will make use of later in the algorithm, has a trinary structure since there are three possible values it can assume: true, false, or unknown. The definitional utility is clear: in cases where either another character or the spectator—in other permutations of such algorithms—is unsure of the guilt of another character or of themselves, the "unknown" moniker can be assigned. Essentially, the trinary structure is a double-binary composition: known or unknown guilt, and, if guilt is known, then guilty or not guilty (true or false). This structure of assigning guilt is not unprece-

---

* Perhaps the idea of this "margin of error" is best laid bare by what Einstein said about mathematics: "As far as the laws of mathematics refer to reality, they are not certain, and as far as they are certain, they do not refer to reality." We cannot use models, mathematical or algorithmic or otherwise, to perfectly model the world; in *Critique of Pure Reason*, Immanuel Kant similarly maps the limits of human knowledge of *noumena* as filtered through our senses.

dented in Hitchcock analysis. Peter Wollen demonstrated the belief of guilt from several vantage points of characters, and the dynamic nature of known/unknown guilt between characters, utilizing notational, algorithmic-like methods.[*] Indeed, some of this essay is inspired by his semiotic examination strategies; his "Wrong Man Story" and "Mole Story" can be converted to algorithmic form with rapidity using the conventions of algorithmic pseudocode presented here. Of course, the true/false/unknown options work with more than just guilt; in this algorithm for instance, "True_and_False" is utilized with life and death in the "Living" variable on other lines of the algorithm.

(3) A third type of variable is defined—the variable of identity—and it is given attributes' characteristics of the notion of identity (but, as already discussed, the reader will probably not find its definition adequately comprehensive or meaningful here). "Culturally_Constructed" is an attribute of identity—and it is a "True_and_False" variable type; so "Culturally_Constructed" may take one of three forms: true, false, or unknown, as dictated by the "True_and_False" variable type mentioned previously. Next, "Part_of_Living_Person" is defined, also as a "True_and_False" variable type. This attribute will be used for the Kaplan/Thornhill character, but it could also, perhaps, be adjusted for other films in the Hitchcock oeuvre. Recall *Vertigo*: Judy assumes the identity of Madeline, a dialectically deceased and fictive character, for Scottie. (Extending this, imagine an algorithm amalgamating the livingness of non-identity Judy with the fully-realized-yet-dead Madeline, or one accounting for the continuing impact on characters that murdered Marion has in *Psycho* [1960]: the algorithms could allow for mapping the dynamism in non-corporeal personages—in other words, there would be literal influence from the grave systematized.) Finally, the "Something" attribute is denoted as part of the variable of identity as a fail-safe mechanism to account for everything—it represents that which is unknowable about the essence of identity (unknowable psychologically, anthropologically, sociologically, etc.) but nevertheless exists; refer to the explanative de-

---

[*] Peter Wollen, *Readings and Writings: Semiotic Counter-Strategies* (London: Verso, 1982), pp. 40-48.

scription of line (1) for more information. Summarizing, line (3) of the algorithm demonstrates notions of hierarchy: "Identity" has attributes associated with it ("Culturally_Constructed," "Part_of_Living_Person," and "Something"), and those attributes are associated with more specific attributes (true, false, unknown, and "something").

(4) Another variable type (to be also used later in the algorithm) is defined: "Character," which is composed of attributes analogous to the "Identity" variable. "Character" is incommensurate with "Identity," however; "Identity" is a subset axiomatically posited in the pseudocode of the more expansive "Character," which takes into account the activity of the character from which the identity is underpinned. "Living" and "Guilt," two "True_and_False" variable types, are present in the "Character" definition. "Living" is determined by mortality: simply, is the character that the variable is associated with living or deceased? The "Guilt" of the character that the variable is linked to is the marker for his/her guilt (despite that guilt can change throughout the course of the narrative, the algorithm is only in a definitional stage; the narrative, or "flow of time," that the variables and parts will pass through in the algorithm has not yet commenced. This will begin on line [7] and extend to line [16]). "Identity_of_Character," the third attribute of "Character," is classified by "Identity." The "Identity_of_Character" is of type "Identity" (recall line [3], where the description of the "Identity" variable type is presented). And the fourth attribute of "Character" is "Something," the essential unknown ingredient that emerges with our discrete-form examination of Hitchcock.

(5) "Thornhill," a name for a variable, is denoted as a type of "Character," labeled in line (4). "Thornhill," unlike "Identity" or "Character," is not a new type of variable, but a variable associated with a defined type: "Character," in this case. Therefore, "Thornhill" has all of the attributes of an "Identity" variable, but there is no "Thornhill" *type* of variable, only the "Thornhill" variable. This is significant for the generality and transportability of the algorithmic conventions to other situations; if the algorithm were too specific—and a "Thornhill" type of variable is much too specific—then the pseudocode's terms and notation becomes terribly situation-specific and less useful and transportable.

(6) Another "Character" variable is named: "Kaplan." "Kaplan" has the same attribute potentialities as "Thornhill," since they are both "Character" variable types; in other words, both "Thornhill" and "Kaplan" contain the variable properties of "Living," "Guilt," "Identity_of_Character," and "Something," although they will not have the same initial values (true, false, etc.); the algorithm will define the values of their characteristics differently.

(7) The algorithmic "flow of time" commences with "Begin." Now, variables and types that were defined before this line—in lines (1), (2), (3), (4), (5), and (6)—become dynamic and can interact with each other on an algorithmic "playing field." The interaction halts on line (16) with "End."

(8) The "Thornhill" characteristics, at the initiation of the narrative of *North by Northwest*, are classified. The true and false monikers follow an order dictated by the type of variable "Thornhill" is (a "Character" variable). The line is self-explanatory in its variable assignments.

(9) "Kaplan," as "he" is known at the commencement of the narrative of *North by Northwest*, is characterized. This algorithmic line statement, like in line (8), is self-explanatory.

(10) The defined characteristics of "Kaplan" at the beginning of the algorithm—his guilt, mortality, and so forth—are assigned to "Thornhill." Earlier in this essay, the conception of a "part" was discussed, and a part in Hitchcock was shown to roughly match the objects to the right of the equals sign. In the case of this line, then, the part is "Kaplan," because his attributes' characters are static: they are assigned directly to "Thornhill." "Thornhill" now has the equivalent characteristics of Kaplan originally defined on line (9); the "Thornhill" attributes classified on line (8) no longer hold true: "Thornhill" has been altered by "Kaplan."

(11) This line of the algorithm alters a characteristic of "Thornhill" to account for the fact that he is indeed alive. His "Living" status has been altered from unknown (Kaplan's status also, and "Thornhill" acquired it in line [10]) to true. It takes two: Thornhill acquires a life force only with the input of Kaplan.

(12) Another characteristic of "Thornhill" is changed to take into account that his identity is "part of a living person," as the

variable reads. This is in direct contrast to the attribute awarded to "Thornhill" by the "Kaplan" assignment of line (10).

(13) At this point in the algorithm, "Thornhill" becomes the "transmitter" object because it is to the right of the equals sign (as elaborated upon earlier) and thus is the "part" in the pseudocode statement. "Kaplan" is now the variable and is dynamic, acquiring the attributes of "Thornhill"—in essence, this line of the algorithm accounts for Roger Thornhill literally embodying George Kaplan, fitting into his suit at the abandoned hotel room, voluntarily capturing his transient "life force" with Kaplan serving as the personality and Thornhill as the body and voice—and the formerly fictive Kaplan thus achieving the status of a living, breathing, fleshed-out flesh-and-blood person.

(14) In the restaurant near Mount Rushmore in South Dakota, Roger Thornhill, who for all intents and purposes is George Kaplan, is shot—and killed. The attribute of "Living" is switched from true to false to account for this development.

(15) This line directly corresponds with the somewhat ambiguous line (5) of the first conception of the Thornhill Algorithm: "Thornhill = New Identity." This is a conception of the new identity Roger Thornhill has mustered from his brushes with death and his fish-out-of-water scenarios: he has retained most of Kaplan's bravery and debonair, and embodied it into a mortal individual not "culturally constructed" (Kaplan is not culturally constructed, according to the criteria enumerated previously. Rather, Kaplan is mostly simultaneously constructed with and by Thornhill in a kind of dialectical process of giving and taking attributes from each other—which is reflected in the reciprocity of the algorithm's equivalence statements). Rather than the status quo ante, there's a new equilibrium in Thornhill's life.

(16) "End" concludes the dynamic section of the algorithm that initiated with "Begin," and also wraps up the entire algorithm.

The pseudocode algorithm at first blush perhaps seems needlessly complex, but its complexity (and consistency) allows it to have a high degree of precision. In addition, it demonstrates *and* reflects much of the dynamism of the Kaplan and Thornhill characters in the narrative flow of *North by Northwest*. The discrete units, or parts, appear in the algorithm, and their usefulness in understanding the ever-changing characters through the narrative temporal flow is apparent. In addition, the structure of the algorithm is close in terms of conventions to the computer language C++, so the logic of the code, perhaps even more deep-rooted than examined here, envelops Hitchcock in a latent layer of logic.

Furthermore, the building blocks of the pseudocode put forth are capable of handling an effectively infinite number of Hitchcockian constructions: this is true because of the universal conventions demonstrated. For example, "Identity" might be defined in a substantially different way—with different attributes and different notions of what "true" and "false" constitute—whilst being loosely constrained in the logic of fundamental narrative definitions of identity. Venture into a realm of too much axiomatic arbitrarity, though, and the code loses meaning and analysis power despite its consistency.

Other objects besides characters could be presented and defined in the algorithms, such as notions of love and even romance (by creation and classification of appropriate attributes), depending on the requirements of the specific film or films the algorithms represent.

Also, the algorithms do not have to be limited to narrative explorations of character, but can be extended to, for instance, the dynamic nature of space, sound/silence, randomness, tableaux and emotion through a temporal flow. Although the most efficient algorithms at this point seem to be those rooted in and dependent on narrative contexts—and therefore time—other types of effective pseudocode may be possible and even desirable for study in certain circumstances in the Hitchcock corpus.

A criticism of these algorithmic methods might be that they are merely metaphors that "degrade" or "distort" the truth of Hitchcock; taken even further, it might be argued that an algorithmic approach gives us merely a description, rather than an explanation, of these film worlds.* But reading Hitchcock's corpus as an algorithmic document is simply akin to other types of readings: consider reading *North by Northwest* as a moral fable. Has anyone seriously taken as a point of departure on writing about Roger Thomhill—

* I.e., the descriptive-versus-predictive argument. Expanding the algorithmic methods of translation to include conditional structures—dynamically testing the truth or falsity of states of variables—would bring more predictive power.

and, by extension, Mr. Kaplan—that his development through the narrative neatly corresponds to Kierkegaard's Stages on Life's Way?

Hardly a close reading of *North by Northwest* is necessary to nod one's head in agreement at the obvious parallels: Does Thornhill at the beginning of the film live purely on the surface (i.e., the Aesthetic Stage)? Check. Does he, though a series of unfortunate events (a great alternative title for *North by Northwest* which has, of course, already been lifted for the popular set of children's stories) come to appreciate the reciprocal nature of care (i.e. the Ethical Stage)? Check. And does Thornhill ultimately take a leap of faith by coupling with a mate he truly cares for, by posing as Kaplan for her safety—to overcome the hopelessness and despair that sets in upon realizing the futility of ethical behavior (i.e., the Religious Stage)? Indeed. These questions are annoyingly rhetorical.

A fictional character like Thornhill seems tailor-made—like one of Kaplan's ubiquitous suits—for a Kierkegaard treatise, considering the philosopher's propensity to construct an underlying theoretical basis by utilizing archetypes. Plus, Kierkegaard spoke of crop rotation, and Thornhill is chased by a crop-dusting plane. Certainly not a coincidence![*]

In short, reading a Hitchcock film as a moral fable strikes one as just as valid as reading it as an algorithmic one. And the possibilities for algorithmic exploration of Hitchcock are (literally) limitless, since the algorithms themselves are suited to many permutations of attributes, characters and objects. The inherent complexities of the semantics of the algorithms might reward with filmic insights perhaps previously unrealized or unexplored.

(2003)

---

[*] Perhaps Thornhill suffers from existential angst early in the picture because of the multifarious life choices he faces—in terms of his practice of serial monogamy especially. Too many choices lead to anxiety and dread. As Kierkegaard wrote, "When I behold my possibilities, I experience that dread which is the dizziness of freedom, and my choice is made in fear and trembling." Thornhill "eliminates the choice," so to speak, and thus quells his anxiety, by settling down (finally) with a *sole* mate, Eve.

# 11.

## An Examination of the Non-algebraic Properties of Mathematical Knots

### 1. INTRODUCTION

This essay will summarize a topological branch of mathematics called knot theory. It is intended as an introduction for readers who have baseline knowledge of mathematical proof, and who are also relatively familiar with another branch of mathematics called graph theory—thus, the reader is expected to have a working knowledge of problem solving techniques of graph theory. In addition, the essay will serve as a summary of important past results in knot theory and its current applications to the field of biological research.

Although knot theory utilizes explicitly algebraic results (replete with difficult notation), most algebraic symbols have been neglected in favor of more visual and intuitive demonstrations. In addition, because some knot theory proofs are directly reliant on more complex concepts such as groups, fields, point sets, etc., they are not included here.

This essay refers to terms associated with knot theory by their most common definitions; for example, although several sources have been examined in the preparation of this work, the most common names associated with operations or results are used.

### 2. THE CONCEPT OF A MATHEMATICAL KNOT

What is a mathematical knot? In order to fully understand what the question is asking, let us explore the notion of a knot in terms of what the reader will already be familiar with: everyday real-life knots, such as knots in shoelaces. Assume that a shoelace-like knot takes the following form:

*figure 2-1.*

(Note that the dashes on either ends of the knot in *figure 2-1* signify that we are only looking at a localized section of the "string.") This projection of the "shoelace" above is not a *mathematical* knot since only knots in closed form are considered; in other words, the knot must be a closed-form loop connected "piece of string."

Notice that if the string is not connected, any knot can be deformed, or manipulated, into any other knot-like representation. Thus no matter how complex the knot structure is, if the "knot" is not in a closed form, the knot is equivalent topologically to any other non-closed "knot."* Here is a simple visual demonstration to demonstrate that any two open-form knot structures are topologically the same:

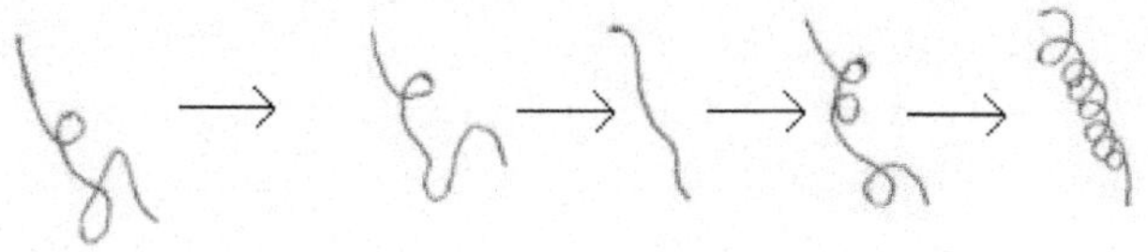

*figure 2-2.*

* Equivalent in terms of shape. Topology deals with objects being "topologically equivalent," which means that the objects can be transformed continuously into each other with points on both objects or surfaces having a one-to-one correspondence. For instance, because a baseball and a cube have no "holes" in them (termed "genus zero"), they can be, using topological rules, transformed into one another. A coffee cup and a donut (or torus) are also considered topologically the "same" object because they can be transformed into one another (the coffee cup and the donut are denoted as "genus one" because they have one "hole" each in them). We can generalize this to claim that any object with genus zero requires one "cut" to separate it; any object with genus one requires two "cuts" to separate it; any object with genus $n$ requires $n+1$ "cuts" to separate it. Thus, the study of topological equivalence, on a fundamental level, relies on an object's "holes" and "cuts" as starting points to create taxonomies. For more on topology and a host of other math topics, read David Bergamini's *Mathematics* (1967), a delightful for-the-layperson treatment of the discipline.

It is important to notice how the open-form loop can always be transformed into the single, non-looped or "knotted," string.

We will only, from this point onward, consider closed-form looped knots. Knots are real objects; they exist in three dimensions. Therefore, we must find a way to represent "crossings," or overlaps of the string, in two-dimensional space. If no regard is made to overtop or underneath crossings, this is the form a two-dimensional knot projection takes:

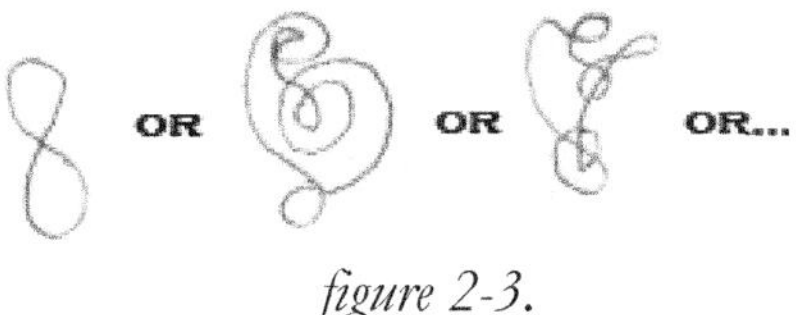


*figure 2-3.*

Because the knot projections in *figure 2-3* do not denote type of crossings (overlaps of the string), the knot representations in two dimensions here could be represented by many different permutations in three dimensions; for example, in the left-most knot diagram in *figure 2-3*, there is the single crossing that could be shown, in three dimensions, to have two possible forms:

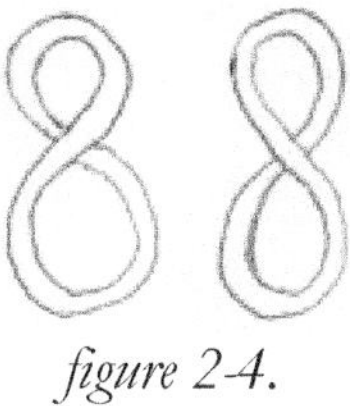

*figure 2-4.*

We see that the knot classification is dependent on the crossings (overlaps); therefore, let us formalize a method of drawing knots in two-dimensions based on knot projections while taking into account crossings (overlaps). Below are the same two mathematical knots in *figure 2-4* drawn with crossing type shown:

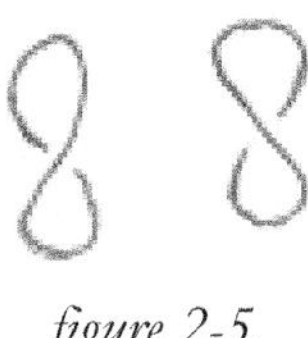

*figure 2-5.*

We have now represented the two-dimensional projection of the knots in *figure 2-4* with crossings (overlaps); we have represented a knot on the plane, or in $\mathbf{R}^2$. Please note also that the "strings" we have been referring to are one-dimensional and have zero thickness; the knots are not dependent on the thickness of the string, only the way the string is arranged.*

## 3. INTRODUCTION TO THE UNKNOT

We will now examine the unknot, also termed the trivial knot. Just like the open-form knots in *figure 2-2* can always be transformed into each other, any representation of the unknot can be transformed into any other representation of the unknot—i.e., all unknots can be made into a closed-form loop. The knots in *figure 2-5* can be transformed into such a loop, as shown here:

*figure 3-1.*

We now know enough about the unknot to show which knots are topologically equivalent to the unknot.

THEOREM 1. *Any knot with 0, 1, or 2 crossings is the unknot.*
PROOF: We shall examine the cases individually to discover that this statement holds. For zero crossings, demonstration is trivial: zero crossings is represented by *figure 3-1*, the unknot. For one crossing, there are two possible representations, as shown in *figure 2-5*; both can trivially be transformed into the unknot. For two crossings, we must consider the four possible cases:†

---

* Questions to the curious reader: What is the genus of *any* knot? Do *all* knots have the same genus? Hint: Think about how many "cuts" it requires to separate a knot—is a knot analogous to a torus (the donut), requiring two cuts, or does a knot only require one cut?

† There are four cases because at each crossing there are two possible projections, so since there are two crossing places with two projections each, 2x2 = 4.

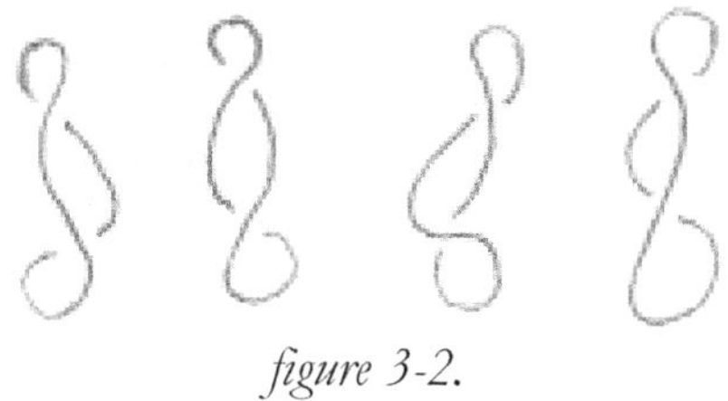

*figure 3-2.*

*Figure 3-2* displays the cases of two crossings, which can all trivially be "twisted" at the ends to make the single-loop unknot shown in *figure 3-1*. Therefore, any knot with zero, one, or two crossings is the unknot. ▌

THEOREM 2. *Any knot $k$ with $n$ crossings can be made to have $n+m$ crossings, which can always be deformed into the original knot $k$ with $n$ crossings.*

PROOF: Take any knot $k$. Pick a local segment of $k$ that has no crossings. Make $m$ trivial crossings on that segment—trivial because they do not influence the minimum crossing number of $k$, or the fewest number of crossings a knot can contain while still being that representation of the knot (for the trivial knot, the minimum crossing number is zero).

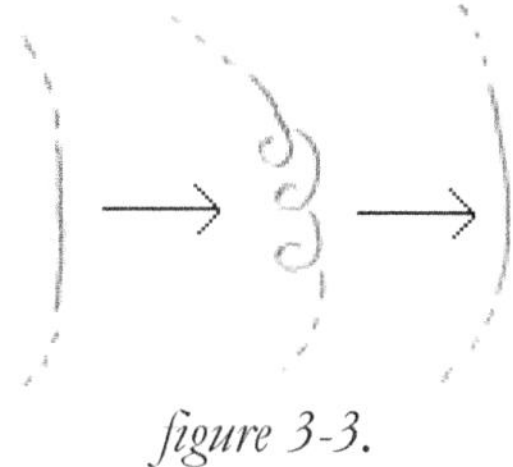

*figure 3-3.*

Since the $m$ crossings on the local segment of knot $k$ are trivial, we can simply "untwist" them to back to what we had before the addition of crossings, and thus we have the knot $k$ with $n+m-m = n$ crossings. ▌

## 4. THE REIDEMEISTER MOVES

Note that, from the proof of Theorem 2, there are certain "moves" we can execute on the knot which do not influence the minimum crossing number of the knot; in other words, manipulating the knot in specific ways does not change the original representation of the knot before it was manipulated despite the possible addition or subtraction of crossings.

Kurt Reidemeister, in 1927, proved that any of the five knot "moves" do not influence the crossing number of the knot.[*] In fact, all arrangements of a knot $k$ are built from these five moves, as detailed in [2]:

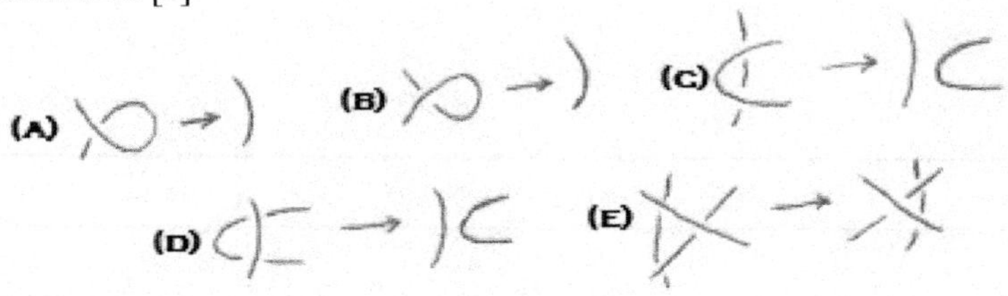

(A) (B) (C) (D) (E)

*figure 4-1.*

*Figure 4-1* displays the Reidemeister moves, as they are commonly called. All moves are performed on localized sections of the knot. Part (a) and part (b) demonstrate that crossings in an overlap form can be "untwisted" to a single strand (locally); these first two moves were used to prove Theorem 2. Parts (b) and (c) show strands "separated" from each other (locally). Part (e) demonstrates the ability to, under that specific permutation, "slide" a strand past several crossings (once again locally).

Although the standard proof that only these five moves are sufficient to transform one knot into another (and the corollary, that two equivalent knots are equivalent because they were transformed using Reidemeister moves) is beyond the scope of this essay, it is important to notice the elegance of the moves; there exists order in chaos in a way, because even though there are an infinite variety of topologically equivalent knots to one specific knot, all equivalent knots can be constructed with a discrete number of moves. A simple proof that the five Reidemeister moves are all that is necessary to construct equivalent knots is left as an exercise to the reader.[†]

---

[*] These are called topological invariants, or properties that do not affect the topological structure of the object.

[†] The reader may wish to read through *Knots: Mathematics with a Twist* by Alexei Sossinsky for a simple but thorough primer on knot theory.

## 5. RELATIONSHIP WITH GRAPH THEORY

Knot theory has several key similarities with graph theory. For example, an important concept in graph theory is isomorphism, which reveals that two graphs are the same graph; we have already encountered knot theory's own isomorphism: demonstrating that two knots are really the same knot.

Let's show that these two knots are equivalent:

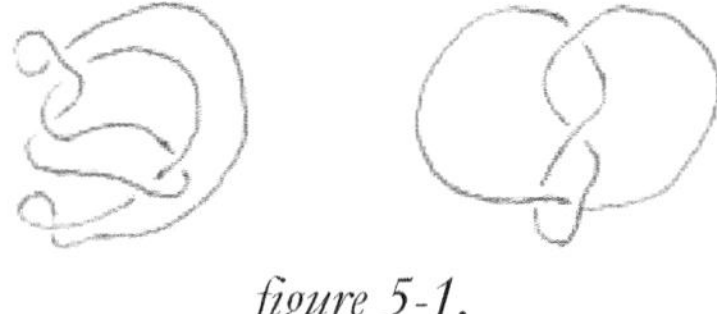

*figure 5-1.*

We will use Reidemeister moves to transform the first knot in *figure 5-1* to the second, proving that they are really the same knot (note that these knots are redrawn and altered a bit from [1]):

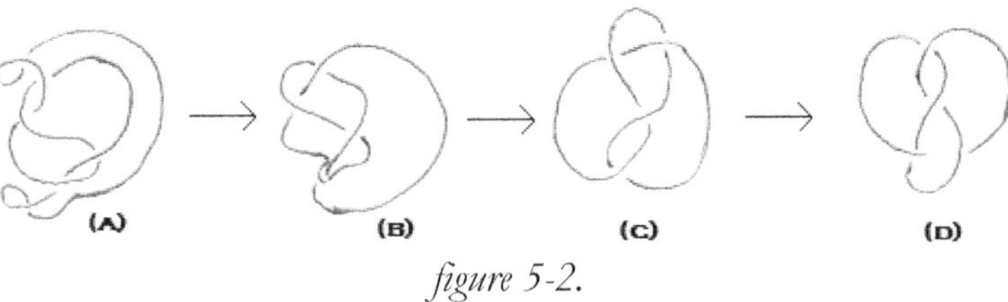


*figure 5-2.*

For *figure 5-2* parts (a) to (b), we eliminated the "twists" in the knot by using Reidemeister moves (a) and (b). For *figure 5-2* parts (b) to (c), we used Reidemeister moves (c) and (d), and then used Reidemeister move (e) to reshape the knot. For *figure 5-2* parts (c) to (d), we simply flipped the knot over. We are now left with topologically equivalent knots.

Can we use Reidemeister moves to show that these two knots below (called the left and right trefoil knots) are the same?

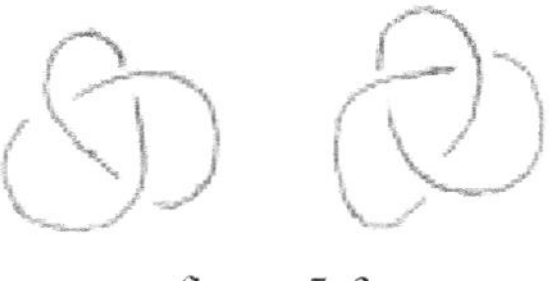

*figure 5-3.*

Although initially it appears counter-intuitive, the left and right trefoil knots are not the same knot; they cannot be deformed into each other using the five moves.*

Similar to the idea of "directed graphs" in graph theory, knot theory also has knots with direction orientations. Pick a point on the knot and decide on a direction. Orientation of a knot follows from this. Here is a diagram of an orientated knot, redrawn and altered from what is shown in [1]:

*figure 5-4.*

Of course, this orientated knot is also the unknot (simply use moves [a] and [b] to deform).

Planar graphs (graphs that are in the plane) and knot theory are also related. We can create knots from planar graphs, and also planar graphs from knots. We can turn a knot projection into a planar graph by shading the knot projections (not including the infinite region) in a "checkerboard" manner, as detailed in [1].

Next, inside the shaded checkerboard regions, we insert a vertex of the graph, and between regions, connect the vertices with edges, which gives us our planar graph—planar because the knot projection in on a plane ($\mathbf{R}^2$), and the graph construction is also planar.

Plus signs populate each edge of the planar graph; this is because we must know, if we are to transfer the graph back into the knot, if a knot crossing associated with that edge is "over" or "under." The planar graph with positive signs (or negative signs to denote "over" or "under") is called a signed planar graph, because of the crossing connotations. (It is apparent that the knot-to-planar-graph construction resembles the "duel graph" construction in graph theory.) Having the power to transfer knots to graphs is extremely important; the link between the two seemingly disparate mathematical

---

* As an exercise, attempt to transform the right trefoil into the left trefoil (or the reverse)—notice that there is not a one-to-one correspondence of the "string strands" between the two knots.

topics allows us to transfer different types of problems from one discipline to another (and therefore we have extra tools to help us solve problems in graph theory and knot theory).*

Analogous to planar graphs, the Hamiltonian circuits of graph theory can also be transferred to knot projections; essentially, we must determine if the Hamiltonian circuit is unknotted or knotted in the graph. The graph is "embedded," or the edges are made to pass under or over other edges in the graph, as if the edges were the strings that constitute knots (in other words, the edges have crossings; the crossings are over or under other edges in the graph). A possible algorithm for creating a knotted Hamiltonian circuit might look like this:

(1) Begin the circuit at a vertex;
(2) Choose the first edge of the circuit;
(3) Choose the second edge of the circuit, which is adjacent to the first edge;
(4) Check to see if the second edge intersects the first edge on the plane (this particular graph representation on the plane, not just the "planar" representation of the graph [if there indeed is a planar representation]);
    a. If the two edges intersect, treat the edges like the "strands" of the knots, and decide (arbitrarily) which "strand" (or edge) will be "under" and which will be "over" the other; go to step (5);
    b. If the two edges do not intersect, go on to step (5);
(5) Choose the third edge of the circuit, which is adjacent to the second edge;
    a. If the third edge intersects with any other edges, create an "over" and "under" portion of the edges, analogous to (4a); go to step (6);

* Question to the reader: Can *any* knots be constructed from non-planar graphs? Attempt creating knots from the *k5* and *k3,3* graphs; showing, perhaps using Reidemeister moves, that no knots can be constructed from these two non-planar graphs is equivalent to showing that all non-planar graphs can never have any knots associated with them (since all non-planar graphs are not planar because of the existence of a *k3,3* or a *k5* [or both] in the graph).

b. If the third edge does not intersect with any other edges, go to (6);

(6) Continue the process of adding adjacent edges and checking if the edge intersects with any other Hamiltonian circuit edges previously constructed;

(7) Return to the original vertex in (1) with adjacent edges to create the entire knotted (or trivially knotted) Hamiltonian circuit.

Gordon and Conway proved in 1983 that the embedded *k7* graph (a complete graph with seven vertices), no matter how the embedding of edges in the graph is created, always contains a Hamiltonian circuit that is knotted (in other words, cannot be made trivial; but this is not the case for the *k5*, since there are certain knotting-permutations that make a Hamiltonian circuit in the *k5* trivial; see [1] for more details).

## 6. COLORABILITY

We will now introduce the concept of knot colorability, which differs significantly from graph theory's definition of the same. A strand of a knot is a segment of a knot between two crossings that does not have any crossings in-between. *Figure 2-5*, the two one-crossing unknots, show examples of strands: each picture of the unknot is composed of two strands. The trefoil knot (*figure 5-3*) has three strands.

If a knot is colorable, we must be able to color all the knots strands (choosing between three colors for each strand) such that at any knot crossing either all three colors are used or only one color is used at all strands intersecting the knot crossing. Here is an example of a properly tri-colored trefoil knot (with different numbers indicating different colors for the strands):

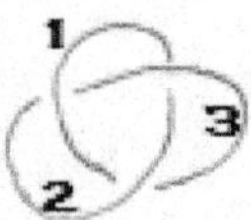


*figure 6-1.*

At each crossing, we have three strand-intersecting colors: 1, 2, and 3. In addition, each strand is, of course, colored uniformly (one color to a strand).

Using colorability, we can prove that the tri-colorable trefoil knot is distinct from the unknot—i.e, that they cannot be transformed into each other and thus are different knots.

THEOREM 3. *The trefoil knot is not the unknot.*
PROOF: The trefoil knot is tri-colorable, as shown in *figure 6-1*. The unknot is not tri-colorable in any projected permutation (the reader can see this by examining this essay's third section's diagrams of unknots and attempting to tri-color the trivial knots; all attempts are futile). Thus, we have shown that because the trefoil is only tri-colorable and the unknot is not tri-colorable, they are distinct knots and cannot be transformed into each other. ▮

A key theorem of knot theory builds off of Theorem 3: If a knot is colorable, then all diagrams of that knot are also colorable. See [2] and [4] for more details on the theorem and on colorability in general.

## 7. UNKNOTTINGS AND CROSSING NUMBERS

We will now look at unknotting numbers and crossing numbers using the trefoil knots.

DEFINITION: Unknotting number, or *u(k)*, is the quantity representing the fewest number of crossings that need to be changed (or removed) on a knot *k* to deform the knot into the unknot.

THEOREM 4. *The u(k)=1, or the unknotting number is one, of the trefoil knot.*
PROOF: Let us examine both cases of the trefoil knot (there are two trefoil knots: the left and right trefoils). *Figure 5-3* shows both left and right trefoils. Looking at the left trefoil, we see that we only need to remove one crossing to make the trefoil the unknot. Why? Because we proved earlier using colorability that the trefoil knot and the unknot are distinct knots (Theorem 3). Thus, the *u(left trefoil)*≠0. We also earlier proved that any knot with two or fewer

crossings is the unknot (Theorem 1). Therefore, we must remove one crossing to obtain the unknot, so *u(k)*=1 for the left trefoil. For the other trefoil knot (the right trefoil, also displayed in *figure 5-3*), the crossings are reversed, but the same properties of the left trefoil apply, so *u(k)*=1 for the right trefoil, and *u(k)*=1 for the trefoil in general. ▮

DEFINITION: Crossing number, or *c(k)*, is the fewest number of crossings a knot can have and still be that particular representation of the knot (we have informally mentioned crossing number already).

THEOREM 5. *The c(k)=3, or the crossing number is three, for the trefoil knot.*
PROOF: We know from Theorem 4 that the *u(trefoil)*=1, so it follows that the number of crossings must be equal to or greater than three (because the unknot has a maximum of two crossings, and the trefoil's unknotting number is one, so 2+1 = 3 or more; we will answer the "3 or more" part with the application of crossing number to the trefoil in this theorem). Furthermore, if we begin with the standard representations of the trefoil knot (examine *figure 5-3*) and use the results of Theorem 2, then it is clear that either:

(1) A trefoil knot with greater than or equal to three crossings has "trivial" crossings which, using a series of Reidemeister moves, can be eliminated, leaving us with three crossings, for *c(trefoil)*=3;

(2) Or a trefoil has greater than three crossings, which cannot be made trivial, therefore the knot is not a trefoil knot anyway.

So, a trefoil knot has *c(trefoil)*=3, or a crossing number equal to three. ▮

THEOREM 6. *u(k)≥c(k)-2 if and only if c(k)≥3 relates the crossing number to the unknotting number.*
PROOF: We know that if *c(k)*≤2 then *u(k)*=0. Also we know that if *c(k)*=3, then *u(k)*=1 (i.e., the trefoil knot, the only possible knot to fulfill this requirement). Thus, we see that *u(k)* ≥*c(k)*-2 if and only if c(k)≥3. ▮

## 8. ADDING AND ALTERNATING

There are several disparate topics in knot theory that require discussion for completeness; these topics will be discussed very briefly but in enough detail for the reader to be exposed to their fundamental ideas.

We begin with a question: If a knot *k1* with *c(k)*=4 is composited, or "added," to a knot *k2* with *c(k)*=3, will *k3* (added knots are called "factor" knots) have a *c(k)*=7? Answer: It depends. Let us look at two knots where this relationship would hold:

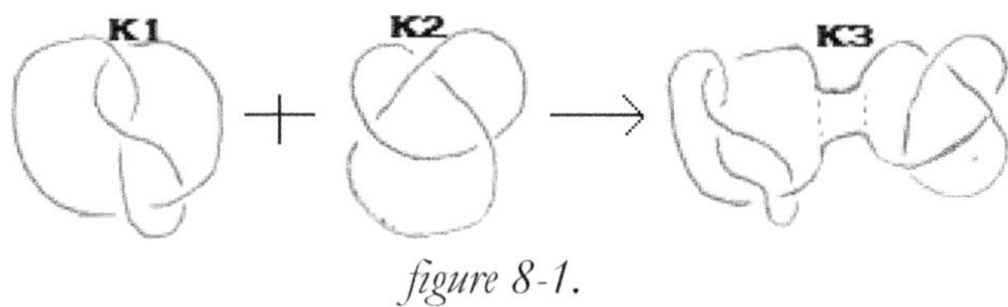


*figure 8-1.*

As *figure 8-1* shows, adding the two knots gives us *c(k3)=c(k1)+c(k2)*. However, *c(k1)+c(k2)=c(k3)* only when we join the knots at single strands of *k1* and *k2*, not at other crossings. Also, even if we do add at single strands of the knots and stay away from the crossings, we cannot always be sure that the equality will hold. Please note that "adding" a trivial knot to any knot will retain the original knot's crossing number.*

Next, we discuss "alternating knots." In an alternating knot, at each crossing a strand alternates its position—either on the top of or on the bottom of another strand—all the way through the knot (of course, to see any alternation, we must orientate the knot). Starting at any crossing and following through the entire knot, note how each crossing alternates in the knot diagram, redrawn and modified from [1]:

---

* Question to the reader: What is incorrect about this argument to show that *c(k1)+c(k2)* does not always equal *c(k3)* (in other words, why is this proof trivial)? The equality will not always hold; let us examine an example. Adding a knot with two crossings (a trivial knot) to the trefoil will not make the crossing number of the composite knot 2+3 = 5; rather, since the two-crossing knot can be deformed into a knot with zero crossings, the crossing number of the new composite knot will simply be two, because "adding" a trivial knot to any non-trivial knot will retain the original knot's crossing number. Hint: Examine the crossing numbers of the aforementioned knots.

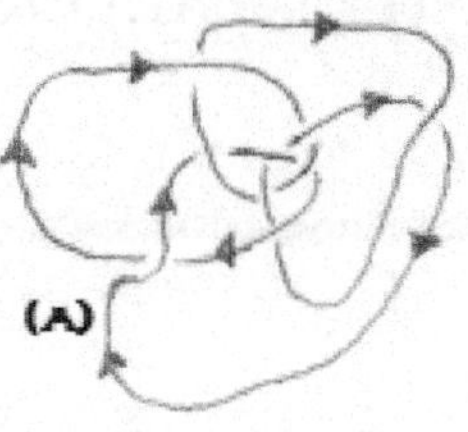


*figure 8-2.*

If we start at the labeled crossing (a) an label it with a "1," and go on to the next crossing and label it "2," and continue this labeling, all around the knot, each crossing will have two labels. Since we began the labeling at "1" and each crossing has two labels, we have 1+(2*k*-1), an even number, as the last crossing number. Note that there will be an equal number of odd and even labels in the knot diagram. Of course, we can form a whole series of relationships around the evenness-oddness of crossings (analogous to graph theory: the Euler cycle is an excellent example). This type of labeling is called Dowker notation.

If a signed planar graph has the same sign associated with each edge (either all positive or all negative), then the corresponding knot projection is always alternating.

## 9. MODERN RESEARCH AND OTHER KNOT FORMS

Only a handful of years old, research into a branch of knot theory called "Virtual knot theory" (discovered by Kauffman) takes a simple knot crossing concept and generalizes results about it. A "virtual crossing" is defined by [3] to be a crossing that is "not really there" in the diagram (thus the moniker "virtual"), and it is represented by a "4-valent vertex" with a denoting circle:

*figure 9-1.*

As shown in *figure 9-1*, by not drawing the strands in a way to determine if they are "under" or "over" each other, the orientations of the crossings (either "under" or "over") become unimportant here.

Interestingly enough, if a non-planar graph is made into a knot projection using the methods described in section 5 of this essay, the knot automatically contains virtual crossings (we cannot tell the orientation of some of the crossings; recall that planar graphs lent themselves to constructing knots with "classical," or standard, orientation).

We can also generalize the Reidemeister moves with the addition of virtual crossings. For a complete description of the generalized moves and other results of Virtual knot theory, consult [3].

Can knots be studied in higher dimensions? If a knot is made in four dimensions, with a two-dimensional projection signifying a fourth dimension by using colors, projections of knots might be trivial: we can simply "pass" the colors of the strands through each other and end up with the trivial knot each time. Other approaches need to be considered.

Instead of using the one-dimensional "strings" to construct the knots, we might use spheres made from smooth manifolds ("smooth" manifolds denoting that the manifolds, or a set's collection of objects, are differentiable); see [1]. We can generalize even more (going into five-space, where 3-spheres can be manipulated); thus, the study of knot forms in higher dimensions is not trivial if we increase the dimensions of the "strings" from which the knots are originally made.

## 10. REAL-WORLD APPLICATIONS

Is knot theory just an abstract form of mathematics, replete with useless puzzles and rules, or can it be applied to empirical reality? Over the past century, knot theory has been found to be surprisingly usefulness in biology.

There are applications of knot theory to Deoxyribonucleic Acid (DNA) analysis. DNA is, of course, in the shape of a double helix and is constructed of rungs of molecules bonded together (its structure is given full description in [1]). But DNA is not ladder-like but tangled. The molecular strands are made up of sugars and phosphates; each sugar is bonded to one of four bases: Adenine,

Thyamine, Cytosine, and Guanine. A always bonds to T; C always bonds to G.

For the DNA to copy, the tangled—and "knotted"—molecules must be read and understood correctly. Topoisomerases are enzymes that manipulate DNA topologically. The topoisomerases have their own Reidemeister moves, so to speak, that like knot theory's Reidemeister moves do not topologically alter the arrangements of the molecules.

Although equating topoisomerases' function to Reidemeister moves is ultimately a superficial comparison, it is not entirely incorrect and effectively demonstrates the surprising connection between knot theory and biology.*

Knot theory also has applications in protein analysis, mechanics, and quantum physics.

## 11. SOME OPEN PROBLEMS

Just like in every other field of mathematics, knot theory has a rich tapestry of open problems. Since the field is relatively young (compared to graph theory, for example), it is surprising that many of these open problems, which at first glance appear to be very simple to understand, have not already been solved; however, perhaps because of the especially visual nature of knot theory, the problems are unusually difficult. For example, there is no "simple" algorithm to determine if any knot $k$ is the unknot,† let alone *any* algorithm to tell if two knots are topologically equivalent. Here are several more open problems, taken directly from [1], which can be understood by the reader:

(1) Can we find a way to generalize the notion of colorability in order to show that the unknot is not simply a composition of two non-trivial knots?

---

* For the curious reader, episode three of the PBS documentary series *Life By the Numbers* (the episode is titled "Patterns of Nature") presents, in a brief segment, knot theory's applications to biology in terms of analyzing certain deadly viruses and their structures.

† There is, though, a circuitous 130-page algorithm thanks to Wolfgang Haken (of Haken and Appel fame, the mathematicians who in 1976 put an end to the four-color problem in graph theory with a brute-force computer proof).

(2) If *k* is a knot with an unknotting number of 1, is there always a crossing in any minimal-crossing projection that we can change to make *k* the unknot?*

## 12. CONCLUSION

Knot theory, when first arrived at well over a hundred years ago, was not intended to be used in any real-life applications. Without any such "useful" applications, knot theory has deep and often beautiful results. Distinguishing knots, coloring knots, and analyzing knots all follow from some general rules about knot invariants. No clear applications outside the abstract field were intended.

However, as is frequently the case with mathematics,† some startling connections were discovered between knot theory and chemistry, biology, and physics only in the last quarter-century. Knot theory is used currently in the effort to slow virus replication and might perhaps help us better understand our universe.

(1999)

* Recall that removing any of the three crossings from a trefoil transform it into the unknot.

† I.e., the discovery of math tools (in an abstract form) preceding their usage in other fields (in a more applied form); consider Riemann geometry and Einstein's application of the non-Euclidean form of geometry fifty years later in his theory of relativity. Paul Dirac once said that to preview the physics of the future, one only need to look at the mathematics of today.

## REFERENCES


[1] C. C. Adams, *The Knot Book*, W. H. Freeman, New York, 1994.

[2] D. W. Farmer and T. B. Stanford, *Knots and Surfaces*, American Mathematical Society, 1991.

[3] L. H. Kauffman, "Virtual Knot Theory," Europ. J. Combinatorics, 20 (1999), 663-691.

[4] C. Livingston, *Knot Theory*, Mathematical Association of America, 1993.

[5] "Mouse's Knot Theory Homepage," no longer extant on the Internet.

# 12.

## Ghosts in the Darkness: A Look at Dark Matter

If one asks what the universe made of, despite centuries of pioneering scientific progress, only an incomplete answer can be given. Everything visible in the universe—stars, planets, nebulae, quasars, pulsars, galaxies, and star clusters—constitutes less than ten percent of the cosmos. So what is the rest of the universe made of? Dark matter, a non-luminous matrix, is theorized to compose the remaining ninety percent. Astronomers and cosmologists realize that accurate predictions of planetary, galactic, and celestial motions cannot be made without properly recognizing and categorizing the looming presence of dark matter.

Vera Rubin and her associates at the Carnegie Institute of Washington were among the first to notice paradoxical events in the cosmos caused by dark matter. Stars in outer orbits of galaxies, they discovered, were rotating around their galactic centers nearly as fast as stars closer to the nucleus of the galaxy, a violation of Kepler's law. The law states that bodies nearer to the core of an object will rotate around that object faster than bodies farther away from the core. If dark matter did not exist, stars in the outer orbits would be pulled from their periodic paths and launched into space. Dark matter forms a protective "shield" around the galaxies, keeping the masses from breaking apart (Bartusiak, 1996).

But what is this invisible, elusive substance made of? By conducting a review of research over the past decade and a half, this essay will explore the theories and experiments of cosmologists, physicists, and astronomers examining dark matter. At present, there are two major hypotheses that have arisen to explain the structure of the non-luminous substance. The first theory states that the invisible mass is composed of matter containing protons, electrons, and neutrons. MACHO, which stands for Massive Compact Halo Objects, is the collective term used to label this "baryonic" explanation. Baryonic matter is any real or observable substance in the universe, such as white dwarfs, brown dwarfs, planets, or asteroids. Therefore, anything cataloged as existing matter is considered a baryonic substance (Bartusiak, 1996).

WIMP, or Weakly Interacting Massive Particles, is the acronym for the second theory, which claims that dark matter is made of non-baryonic theoretical particles. The theoretical particles seem to exist only in mathematical formulas (with few exceptions). The examples in the picture below illustrate the differences between the baryonic MACHO matter and the WIMP non-baryonic matter. WIMPs are represented by theoretical particles (on the right), and MACHOs are displayed as three potential forms (on the left; recall that baryonic matter can exist as any real, quantifiable matter): Saturn, an atom, and even a Volkswagen.

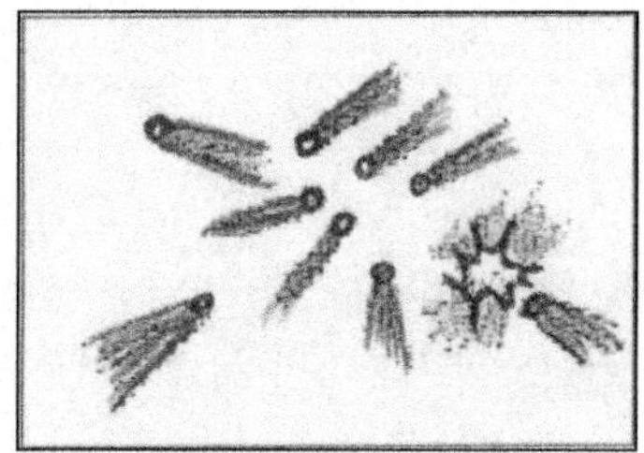

Astronomers support a MACHO baryonic composition, perhaps because they wish to be able to observe and quantify objects that are visible, analogous to stars and asteroids. Cosmologists and physicists, being in more mathematical fields of research, believe in a theoretical-based particle universe (Bartusiak, 1996).

In 1986, the first MACHO experiments were conducted. A Princeton Astronomer named Bohdan Paczynski proposed a method to detect the presence of dark matter. Called "microlensing," it relied on massive amounts of observation into the visible portions of the universe from earth-based telescopes. If the dark matter were composed of MACHOs, then the gravity from the non-luminous objects contained in dark matter would, as Croswell notes, "magnify or 'microlens' the star's light, bending what would otherwise be diverging light rays" (p.42). Therefore, any star with dark matter passing in front of it, relative to our observation point (the earth), would brighten beyond its normal magnitude for a designated time period. The microlens effect is illustrated in the following diagram.

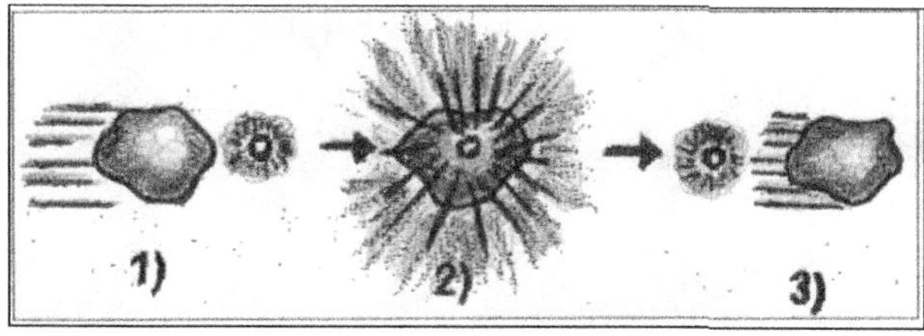


At 1), dark matter (represented by the "blob") is moving to the right, and is about to pass over the star. In 2), the dark matter has covered the star, and the brightness of the star has increased dramatically. At 3), the "blob" of dark matter has passed over the star, and the star has returned to its normal magnitude. The duration from normal to bright to normal again can take anywhere from fractions of a second to hundreds of years. The intervals of magnitude changes in stars can be used to determine the specific composition of dark matter. The longer the time frame, the denser the composition of dark matter. For example, if the star observed remained bright for three months, the mass of dark matter would be approximately 1.4 solar masses.[*] Therefore, since the MACHO theory indicates that dark matter is composed of real and detectable matter, dark matter with a solar mass of 1.4 is made of neutron stars (Croswell, 1996). Microlensing, if detected in any stars, could be used as a powerful tool to demonstrate dark matter is composed of MACHOs. But for the method to work properly, thousands of stars have to be continuously observed for long periods of time in order to detect any changes in their magnitudes.

Microlensing search-runs were begun in the early 1990s. Several groups of scientists attempted to prove microlensing could detect the presence of MACHO matter. OGLE (Optical Gravitational Lensing Experiment) and DUO (Disk Unseen Objects) were the two major groups dedicated to proving the existence of baryonic matter with lens experiments (Glanz, 1996). Success was announced in 1996. At least fifty percent of the universe was said to be made of MACHOs, claimed the astronomers at a press conference in San Antonio. But, as Glanz points out, some members of the MACHO teams declared that the data gathered were "too sketchy to really settle the dark matter issue" (p. 595). Are their results accurate or faulty? Is microlensing really a viable method to

[*] One solar mass is equal to the mass of our sun.

detect MACHOs? Only a handful of microlensing events were detected by the groups. Is this enough to prove the existence of baryonic matter in the non-luminous matrix?

More recently, the label of dark matter as non-luminous has fallen under question. A very faint luminous halo was discovered near the spiral galaxy NGC5907. Sackett notices it had the "same spatial distribution expected for the galaxy's dark matter" (p. 124). Did the faint light reveal dark matter—or simply more stars? The results from the NGC5907 discovery support one of the many types of MACHO baryonic matter dark matter might be composed of—namely, faint stars. Richard J. Rudy et al. reports on their discoveries, claiming that the halo is "a collection of stars with near-solar abundances of heavy elements, along with many low-mass stars" (p.159). Many conclusions about the nature of the halo have been considered, and promptly ruled out. The faint light could not be from an ordinary stellar halo, since the wavelengths are not typical for that halo. In addition, the infrared colors suggest a star distribution that is not typical (Sackett, 1997). If the halo is composed of faint visible stars, a form of baryonic matter, then a MACHO theory might be more tenable.

Instead of looking for faint stars or other types of visible MACHOs, Ikebe et al. decided to find invisible proof of the MACHOs. X-ray experiments were conducted, attempting to establish the dark matter arrangements by looking for areas of higher density. Ikebe et al. mapped the Fornax cluster's dark matter using the x-ray method (West, 1996). "They have shown quite convincingly that dark matter distribution in Fornax is a mixture of two distinct components on different scales, one associated with the cluster as a whole and the other, smaller one belonging to the giant galaxy," according to West (p. 401). Therefore, dark matter has a similar arrangement that defines luminous matter.

While x-ray and other MACHO experiments were conducted at various laboratories around the earth, another entirely different theory was simultaneously developed. What if the dark matter were composed of particles that have mostly not been detected? According to cosmologists and physicists, WIMPs, the elementary theoretical particles, make up dark matter. Although the WIMPs are mathematical models and not truly detectable objects, their presence would explain a great many cosmological events of the past. For instance, the Big Bang theory, which posits that the universe was formed from a single particle that exploded and expanded, works better with a WIMP process than a MACHO one, simply because the Big Bang was a very smooth event, and baryonic matter could not form galaxies with uniform initialization (Naeye, 1996). To visualize the Big Bang, imagine blowing air into a deflated balloon. In this example, the air represents the WIMP particles. If the air is blown at a continuous rate, the balloon can be expanded to maximum size efficiently. Now imagine inflating a limp balloon with marbles. The marbles represent MACHOs. Can the balloon now be *smoothly* expanded to a large magnitude? Probably not. But the Big Bang, according to cosmologists, was a smooth occurrence. Therefore, it appears more likely, according to the WIMP hypothesis, that non-baryonic particles make up the entire universe since they were present from the very first cosmological event, the Big Bang. The theory is logical, but nearly all of the elementary WIMP particles have not yet been discovered.

The only elementary particle as of this writing that has been detected is the neutrino. For every proton in the universe, there are approximately one billion neutrinos. Staggering numbers of the particles pass through the Earth at any given second. If neutrinos have any mass at all, their sheer numbers might account for all of the dark matter. Oscillation, a process by which neutrinos change into other types of neutrinos, can occur only if the tiny particles have mass (Mukerjee, 1994). Experimenting for oscillations in neutrinos can reveal if the neutrinos have mass.

Baha A. Balantekin and other scientists at the Los Alamos National Laboratory used a particle detector to catch these oscillations of neutrinos. The experiment was called the "Liquid Scintillator Neutrino Detector." Billions of neutrinos were shot into a particle accelerator. If neutrinos can change type, they would transform into one of three forms: the muon, tau, or electron neutrino. But the particle detector is only thirty meters long, so the particles must change their association within the thirty meters, or mass will not be detected (Murkerjee, 1994).

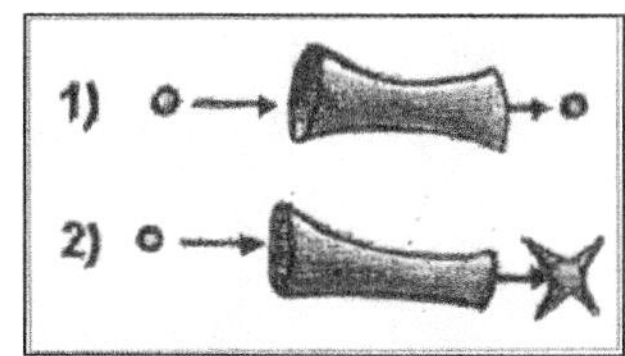

The simple diagram above illustrates two possible results of the Los Alamos Oscillation experiment. The circles represent neutrinos, in their original states. The star represents a neutrino that has changed form. The two tubes symbolize the thirty-meter particle accelerator. At 1), a neutrino is injected into the tube and emerges at the right of the structure as its original form, a neutrino. Therefore, the experimental result at 1) indicates that neutrinos have no mass, because the neutrino did not change its association. But at 2), the neutrino enters the particle accelerator and exits as a new particle. The second experiment's result points to neutrinos having mass—since the neutrino changed during the journey of thirty meters inside the particle accelerator. In addition, 2) reveals that dark matter is composed of neutrinos, since the near-infinite number of neutrinos with any detected mass at all can account for all of the dark matter in the universe. But the experiment raises a serious problem: If a small distance limitation of only thirty meters is imposed on catching the WIMP elementary neutrinos' shifts, can oscillations really be examined?

Cosmologists have begun a search for another WIMP elementary particle, the axion (named after a detergent), at the Lawrence Livermore National Laboratory in California. Axions are very light particles, with less mass than neutrinos (if, indeed, neutrinos have any mass at all). A powerful magnet installed inside a cavity at the laboratory attempts to detect the axions. The cavity is very cold, registering at hardly 1.5 degrees Celsius above absolute zero. The temperature must be extremely cold in order to find the axions (Naeye, 1996). The success of the experiment has been limited and more study is required.

Other WIMPs being considered besides neutrinos and axions are Zinos, Winos, Photinos, and supersymetric particles. These are all exotic theoretical dark matter particles, and none of the Winos, Zinos, or other particles has been detected by conventional means (Bartusiak, 1996).

But sometimes convention doesn't stop experimentation. A physicist at the University of California in Berkeley, named Daniel Snowden-Ifft, began looking for dark matter WIMPs in an ancient mineral called mica. Like footprints, trails of elementary particles would be left in the sentiments. But a print would be visible only if the elementary particle collided with the atomic nucleus of another atom (Travis, "On the track….", 1994). The impacts are similar to the results a miniature bullet would incur if it tore through the mica eons ago. A "pit" is an ancient footprint of an elementary particle that collided with an atomic nucleus. Since the mica is over a billion years old, there should be many such collisions, according to the theory.

But, at best, searching for collisions in mica can only eliminate possible theoretical particles (and still leave others as potential suspects comprising dark matter). The scientists at Berkeley have examined many pieces of mica and have had only limited success (Travis, "On the track....", 1994). However, this is a low-cost approach to detecting WIMPs. In addition, the mica method is visible proof of the actions of exotic particles, instead of mathematically "perfect" WIMP theories explaining the composition of dark matter.

Instead of using rocks to support a WIMP theory, scientist Francesco Paresce and his colleagues at the European Space Agency commissioned the Hubble Space Telescope to detect the presence of elementary particles. The telescope was pointed to a specific cluster of stars called NGC6397. Paresce expected to see many stars in the images. Pictures were taken of the cluster, but many stars were absent from the projected amounts. Red dwarfs, which were expected in moderate quantities, were also mostly absent from the photographs (Travis, "Massive problem of....", 1994). Both predictions were incorrect, but what would this prove about dark matter?

The absence of red dwarfs indicates low mass stars cannot constitute a major part of the dark matter in the universe, which effectively refutes a portion of the MACHO theory. Therefore, astronomers have one fewer baryonic matter component to claim as proof for a MACHO universe. In addition, as Travis observes, "[D]ata from a dense cluster reveal that the number of such stars [red dwarfs] drops off precipitously when they get small and faint, making them an unlikely dark matter source" ("Massive problem of....", 1994, p.1319). Once again, if red dwarfs are not a dark matter component, then another possible form of baryonic matter is eliminated.

Some scientists are arguing against both the MACHO and the WIMP theories, and have instead attempted to solve the problem of the composition of dark matter by looking into the past. Dark matter may not even exist at all, and the odd movements of some celestial bodies that seem to be best explained by the non-luminous matter can be accounted for by other means. The cosmological constant, first proposed by Albert Einstein in the early twentieth century, claims that the universe increases its energy content by simply existing through time—and the "dark matter" is only the added energy (Naeye, 1996). Therefore, dark matter is composed of neither WIMPs nor MACHOs, but is simply additional energy influencing the motions of celestial bodies.

But Einstein himself later discounted the cosmological constant (he called it the biggest blunder of his career, though modern research has shown the constant might have a place in cosmology after all), so application of the anti-MACHO/WIMP theory seems unlikely. Because the many experiments into the composition of dark matter have revealed either direct or indirect evidence of MACHOs and WIMPs, it seems probable that ninety percent of the universe is made of a substance called dark matter.

Dark matter might also be potentially composed of *both* MACHOs and WIMPs. Baryonic matter and non-baryonic matter have been detected in the matrix, so why not? Although it appears possible that dark matter could be made exclusively of either MACHOs or WIMPs, why would there be overwhelming evidence to support both microlensing experiments and the pits found in mica, for example?

The Big Bang needed non-baryonic matter to generate galaxies smoothly. Yet x-ray methods have detected different levels of organization of dark matter, similar to visible structures. Red dwarfs have been eliminated as baryonic matter, but the luminous halo indicates the presence of faint stars. Once again, it appears both theories have merit.

Whatever the conclusion turns out to be, the search itself is extremely important. Since the dawn of astronomy as a science, luminous glowing objects have been cataloged, and the overwhelmingly large dark portion of the universe has been ignored. For the first time, that remaining ninety percent of the cosmos is being examined—so possibly, one day, we can figure out what the universe is made of.

(1998)

# References

Bartusiak, M. (1996, October). The new dark age of astronomy. Astronomy pp. 36-39.

Croswell, K. (1996, October). The dark side of the galaxy. Astronomy pp. 40-45.

Glanz, J. (1996). Is the dark matter mystery solved? Science. 271 (5249), 595-596.

Hewett, P., and Warren, S. (1997). Microlensing sheds light on dark matter. Science. 275 (5300), 626-627.

Kanipe, J. (1996, October). Dark matter and the fate of the universe. Astronomy p. 35.

Mukerjee, M. (1994, August). Missing matter found? Scientific American p. 22.

Naeye, R. (1996, October). Ghosts in the cosmic machine. Astronomy pp. 49-53.

Rudy, R.J., Woodward, C.E., Hodge, T., Fairfield, S.W., and Harker, D.E. (1997). The peculiar colours of the halo light in the edge-on spiral galaxy NGC5907. Nature. 387 (6629), 159-161.

Sackett, P. (1997). Strange colours peek from a dark halo. Nature. 387 (6629), 124-125.

Travis, J. (1994). Massive problem of missing dwarfs. Science. 266 (5189), 1319-1320.

Travis, J. (1994). On the track of dark matter in mica. Science. 265 (5172), 607.

West, M. (1996). X-rays reveal heart of darkness. Nature. 379 (6564),401-402.

# 13.

## Lend Me Your Hands: A Look at Palmistry

The efficacy of palmistry is a question of at most limited anthropological interest. The relationship between the palmist and the subject is, however, worth investigation; the dynamics explicitly bear a striking resemblance between two other notable "interpreter-subject" associations, that of the psychiatrist-client and the shaman-patient. In this essay I will show, using four transcribed case studies, that the palmist-subject interaction is akin to the medicine man's or the psychiatrist's interplay with his clients. In addition, I will demonstrate that although some of the interests of the subjects are predictable, others are personal and hence unpredictable (or, in anthropologist Edmund Leech's terms, "personal symbols").

There are four case studies. For the first two, a palm reading methodology consistent with the text *How to Read Palms and Fingerprints* was implemented. For the other two, nearly all of the "axioms" of palmistry (at least according to the book) were reversed or changed; for instance, where the "inward life line" would denote a "greatest happiness on familiar grounds" tendency, a corollary reading is a "greatest happiness away from grounds you are familiar with." The inward life line reading, though, is dichotomous: either there is happiness on familiar grounds or there is not.*

Non-dichotomous readings are rules that are not easily reversed—the different types of fingerprints are an example. Having long nails, meaning the individual has an "artistic approach, but is

---

* The realization that there could be more than one opposed reading was a consideration. For example, the opposite of the inward life line reading could also have been "you shall find your least happiness on familiar grounds." However, adopting a strictly negative reversal methodology to each of the dichotomous-type reading rules could have rendered the process discouraging to the subjects during the last two interviews, and in turn potentially damaged the relationship being formed between the palmist and "client."

overly sensitive," is not readily reversible. Thus, the nail axioms (and other rules analogous to it, like skin texture, for instance) were simply switched with other "nail definitions." The reversed and refigured palmistry was used consistently with the final two subjects.

With several of the subjects, I took line-by-line notes; although writing notes during a conversation impacts on the flow and perhaps content of the dialogue, I tried to minimize these effects by writing as quickly and discreetly as possible.

*She is a nineteen-year-old college student with an interest in theater and English. I have personally known her for almost two years; in addition, I am close with the subject.*[*] *She has never had a palm reading before. I was permitted to take almost line-by-line notes; what follows are selected excerpts from the extended conversation.*

AUTHOR: Before we start, I want to ask you your feelings on this whole thing; by that I mean, What do you think of palm reading?

SUBJECT: I've never really thought that much about it, but I really don't buy the whole thing, because it seems really unrealistic.

AUTHOR: Unrealistic?

SUBJECT: Yeah, unrealistic, because, I don't know.... I really don't think that your palm can tell what happens to you in the future. Come on.

AUTHOR: I want to tell you first that I've never done this before, but I've studied a book on the subject and I think I know it pretty well.... I mean, I've tried it on myself and it seems to be pretty accurate.

SUBJECT: Okay, we'll see. I don't know; go ahead.

AUTHOR: ...[Reading palm] It seems like, in the past, you've had some personality changes.

SUBJECT: Yeah, that's true. Last spring, I was like a stronger, different version of myself here today. I never thought that about this before.... I mean, it seems really odd. But that's true—I did have some personality changes, especially since last spring.

AUTHOR: I think that because your life line is straight, sort of, you need, well.... It's saying to me that you need more warmth in your personality, and....

SUBJECT: Okay, I see what you're saying.

---

[*] She would later become my fiancé but—for reasons that I obviously could not read on her palms—not my wife.

AUTHOR: ...and you are relatively self-centered and selfish.
SUBJECT: Maybe, I don't know. I've been trying to do away with that lately.
AUTHOR: Yeah.... Let's talk about how long you'll live.
SUBJECT: I'll probably die when I'm thirty, right?
AUTHOR: It appears that you will live until you are about 65.... I've also noticed that according to your thin life line, you will be prone to serious illness at around that age.
SUBJECT: Oh, great. I mean, I guess I see it though. That's about how old my uncle and aunt lived.
AUTHOR: Also, what is really interesting is....
SUBJECT: Like when I was in the hospital last spring because of [an illness].... Yeah, that prone to serious illness [thing] is believable.
AUTHOR: Interesting. So you find what I'm saying to be accurate?
SUBJECT: I guess, so far, yes, it is.
AUTHOR: ...let's get on to some more stuff about your future love life.
SUBJECT: Maybe some good news?
AUTHOR: You will have a few delightful romances; you can expect at least one really serious relationship in your life.
SUBJECT: I hope so. I haven't really had much success yet, as you know. I'm ready for the right person right now, whenever he comes along....

Before proceeding to the next subject, there are several comments to be made about subject one's conversation. First, before the palm reading begins, the subject is clearly skeptical about the palm reading; notice how she almost sarcastically states, "Okay, we'll see [if it works]." She is clearly unimpressed by the notion of a palm read. However, by the final part of the transcript (on romance), she has forgotten, or at least temporally suspended, her disbelief. Although as a palmist my performance was (hopefully) far from perfunctory, certainly it was not extraordinarily effective. What caused the subject to betray her initial notions of palmistry?

One line in particular characterizes her proclivity and desire to believe. After asking her if she found the reading generally true, she responded with, "I guess, so far, yes, it is." It is skepticism's "last stand"—and the beginnings of the Forer effect and confirmation bias, cognitive errors that will recur with other test subjects. Because a great number of the comments the palmist stated appear valid, the subject responds with greater enthusiasm and willingness to "mold" the remaining elements of the conversation into her own applied truths. For example, consider the final comments on romance. How palmistry's interpretation of her future love life is truthful to her is unclear; the subject admits she has been unable to "find the right person"; yet, although the palm reading seemingly is an insipid, inaccurate interpretation, the subject diverts from the reading into talking about her views, her feelings, her beliefs.

Former magician-turned-skeptic James Randi, in the documentary *Fooling People*, explains her bias best: "The person *wants* the palm reader to succeed." Perhaps the need for reading success results in a transformation of memories and assumed personality traits into a "molded fit" for the read. If this is an accurate analysis, then as the palmist (attempting to look for feedback from the subject), am I "fooling" the subject into believing that I (or the text) am accurate, or, more interestingly, is the subject unconsciously fooling me to assume a falsely composed personality and historical profile simply to maintain harmony and avoid conversational discord?

*He is a twenty-year-old communications major. Like the first subject, he has never had a palm reading before. Because I was not granted permission, I did not take notes during the conversation.*

There were several noteworthy items to emerge from the conversation with this subject. He appeared somewhat convinced, especially midway through the conversation, that I was accurate in my predictions. The interplay ran very much like a question and answer forum; for example, he asked the question, "How long will I live?" and I, using the exact words of the text, responded. Therefore, the conversation was somewhat "cold"; I did elicit an "autobiography" of the subject, in a sense, throughout the palm reading (as with subject one, when there was a clear tendency towards constructing an autobiography to fall in line with my predictions). Yet his openness about his life and personality was disparate and inconsistent. Sometimes wildly inconsistent, in fact:

AUTHOR: Your palm tells me that you will not be very wealthy.

SUBJECT: I think I see what you are saying. I've had some money before, but not a lot.... Money has not been easy to come by at all. I guess it won't be in the future either!

AUTHOR: ...You will tend to move around a lot to many different places as you get older.
SUBJECT: Should be no problem.

His responses are banal and terse. Should we, as anthropologists examining the conversation, be concerned with the content or the actual delivery of the lines? If we follow anthropologist Bronislaw Malinowski's example with analyzing myths, the manner of recitation is crucial—not only the subject's speaking methods, but also the palmist's. The subject constructs an identity with the manner of his responses; subject two's quip about money is more mocking than serious. As a psychoanalyst I could claim, using the manner of his responses toward money, that he treats the concepts of wealth with insolence, or possibly money is an irrelevant factor in his life.

Subject two has fashioned an identity for himself with two contradictory lines about the same basic notion (wealth). Subject one was also concerned with money, albeit on a less significant scale. The same reading was "correctly" (according to the palmistry text's rules) elicited by the palmist to her: "Money will not be easy to come by." She responded with apparently little interest—but she did respond. However, subject two was clearly more motivated by the concepts of riches. The merging of the private symbol and the public symbol into the personal symbol takes full effect in this case (anthropologist Gananath Obeyesekere's idea). Money is a public symbol; it marks social status. With subject two, though, we see the emergence of a personal symbol, too.

As an analogue between the commonality of the private and public symbols, consider the separation between the sacred and the profane. Although they are seemingly discrete (though complementary) categories, neither can exist without the other; rituals that permit category jumps are bridges between the separations. Without venturing into the validity of Obeyesekere's argument of the personal symbol or Leech's thesis about the separation and constituents of private and public symbols, we can say with some assurance that private and public symbols, like the sacred and profane, cannot exist without one another. In addition, there must be a way to bridge the gap between them (again, with things such as rituals).

Money is at least a somewhat important factor in most people's lives because it is a symbol of status. Yet money represents more with subject two than just status—money has personal significance.

(Also, subject two does not explicitly claim that wealth is of personal interest; it could be deduced later from the tone and dialogue of the conversation.) The private symbol* of money was brought forth publicly by the reading, albeit implicitly. The bridge between the private and public symbols constructed by the palmist has been effected; money is a personal symbol for subject two, then, because it marks group status and other isolated notions.

Before moving on to subject three, let us now make a comparison between the sacred and profane, the private and public symbols, and the palmist and the subject. All three are dichotomous and require a bridge to venture between them. The sacred and profane need the ritual; the public and private need the personal symbol (or at least the personal symbol that is derived from them); and the palmist and the subject need the elicited constructions of identity from the subject and the textual authority of the palmist, in addition to the subject's willingness to believe in the predictions and the palmist's ability to appear accurate and authentic. As Leech states, emotion is produced from the ritual; it also appears that emotion is produced from the palm reading. Therefore, the systematic construction of the identity of the subject by the subject and the palmist derives emotion. Let us explore this concept further with subject three.

*He is a twenty-five-year-old actuary from the Ukraine. Four years ago, he immigrated to the United States. He is a rigorously logical thinker, and tends to treat anything in the realm of the supernatural as irrelevant; if there is success in predictions, he says, it is because of chance. The axioms of palmistry have been reversed and otherwise modified for him (without his knowledge). I took nearly line-by-line notes. What follows are selected excerpts.*

AUTHOR: As you know, I will be attempting to read your palm. From it, I think I can tell you things about yourself, your future, your history.

SUBJECT: I am familiar with it. Go ahead.

AUTHOR: Turn over your palm first; I want to see your skin structure. See, it's rough.

SUBJECT: What does that mean?

AUTHOR: Well, you see how it's a bit rough here? It means you have a vivid mind and a good intuition.

---

* Here meaning a repressed concept located in the unconsciousness.

SUBJECT: What else?
AUTHOR: You also have good taste in things.
SUBJECT: I don't know if I have good taste, but that's interesting about the intuition part. That's true, because I wouldn't.... Yes, I can think of many examples of my so-called good intuition.
AUTHOR: Give me some.
SUBJECT: I can remember how, just last week, Christy said I should... solve the problem of calculating reserves, and I immediately thought of John's solution from a year ago.... I was quite pleased that I was right.

The palmistry predictions appear to evoke an emotional response from the subject, namely, pride. Is the subject expressing a "conceited nature" (an autobiographical element) by the confirmation of his "keen intuition?" Perhaps. His response, then, is affective* despite his inherent logical nature. The emotion is the bridge between the palmist and subject; his prideful commentary creates the link between the two people. (I can see if I am correctly analyzing him, and in response he can give me a kind of moral support or feedback to continue the session.) It is akin to the psychiatrist-patient survey.

Another significant element to notice is his memory construction. Observe the connection he creates between an assignment from "just last week" to a solution from a year ago. The narration is in terms of two distinct time periods, yet both connect the concept heuristically. In remembering, the subject selectively associates elements of his immediate and long-term past to create a version of the past, but certainly not a disinterested version. Perhaps the emotion of pride triggered the past's constructions; if this is correct, then we can make the connection that Berg, who states that emotion produces the ritualizing, is valid. Can both Leech's ritual-creates-emotion and Berg's emotion-creates-ritual notions be analytically accurate here? The binary relationship between emotion and ritual (like that of culture and man) is inexorably tied. One needs the other to exist (analogous to private and public symbols and the palmist and the subject, as discussed earlier). Without the affective, there is little point to the event—in other words, as Malinowski argues with respect to myth, there is little point to living

* By affective, I am referring to "affective states," a concept in psychology.

and engaging in activities without the emotional elements attached. Therefore, we can safely claim that a synthesizing of the subject's identity comes in part from his emotional response toward the readings.

Of course, with subject three, the palmistry system was reversed and otherwise altered. Did it make a difference at all in the palmist's believability? Assuming that the secret of the alteration was not betrayed by my tone or speech, there is no recognizable difference between the subjects due to the change of the text's rules. Subject three sought, like the other individuals, to respond favorably toward the palmist's readings; he justified the (false) readings by memory constructions that are true to him and conform and reinforce the matrix of the palmist's predictions.

The palmistry text is deliberately vague. Obviously, a great many characterizations can apply to a great number of people. Is it because of the vagueness of the "axioms" themselves that the altered rules (which are also applicable to a great many people) appear to have equal efficacy? Although the rules' designated vagueness is purposefully designed to fit a broad spectrum of subjects, the subjects' willingness and desire to see the palmist's success is culpable for the "false" predictions ringing "true." Rather unsurprisingly, subject four had similar results to the "false" propositions.

*The final subject is a fourteen-year-old coworker. I have known him for a year. He is interested in a wide variety of subjects, and he told me he was quite open to the possibility of palm reading telling some truth about his life. Because of the location, I was unable to take immediate notes.*

Even though his life line was thin (which, again, according to the palmistry text denotes a predisposition to health problems—like Theodore Roosevelt, whose life line, unlike his girth, was famously thin), I reversed the prediction and told him that he will "be very healthy until much later in life, with the proper exercise and regular visits to the doctor." The subject proceeded to tell me about his frequent visits to the dentist and doctor this year, and his mild health problems. But instead of contradicting the analysis, here is what he said: "I can see how I wouldn't have any health problems for a long time. I just need to make sure I don't go too far off track like I did this year." I also told him he is strong-willed and independent, even though that contradicts the text's interpretations. He readily agreed and told me a story about his trip to summer camp two years ago confirming the statement. It does not seem that subject four had any suspicions that my palmistry statements were not in line with the text's. He, like subject three, responded favorably to "false" (i.e., inconsistent with the text) statements about his future, past, and personality; we could argue that similar to subject two, a personal symbol emerged here ("personal" because he demonstrated the concept had a personal locus): health. Recall the subject's grouping of his health concerns: "I just need to make sure I don't go too far off track like I did this year." He synthesizes his memories into a "bundled" relationship based on commonality; it is the palm reading that is the catalyst for the bundling.

Would the same personal symbols have emerged if the first two subjects were palm read with the reversed system, and the last two subjects with the original system? Clearly, this cannot be tested, so a hypothetical answer is all that is possible: Perhaps, assuming that the similar topics were discussed, like health, riches, having an independent nature, and the like. The mentioning of content that has personal significance to subjects cues them into giving exposition on these personal symbols. Regardless of the specifics of the palmistry statements, the homeostatic relationships will tend to keep their form.

As author Susan Baur explains, "[Because the past molds the present], identities [keep] running true to form.... [A]ll recollections, not just earliest memories, are flexible constructions, and... individuals feel a strong but unconsciousness need to modify them in order to justify their present attitudes...." Have we seen these constructs—these homeostatics—in each of the four subjects here? With subject one, romance was an important factor. After the palmist informs her that she "will have a few delightful romances," the subject constructs a version of her past (no successful romantic relationships) and couples it with a possible future ("I'm ready for the right person right now"). Note the pessimism of her response despite the positive nature of the palmist's prediction. The past molds the present, regardless of the content of the palmist's speech. In fact, we could, without difficulty, imagine subject one's statement with a complementary palmistry (i.e., the reversed method). Assume that the reading was, "You will not have much luck in the romance department." Her current response, "I haven't really had much success yet, as you know," is equally valid. Her romantic identity, regardless of the prediction, will remain relatively consistent.

A construction of biography and identity is created, of course, with the palmist and subject's conversation. Let us compare the palmist's methods with the shaman's. The subject in both cases must have at least a modicum of belief in the process. This is not to say, for instance, that the palm reading must be an effective exploration into the subject's psyche or past; it simply means that the subject must (at least slightly) buy in to the palmist's ability to read palms. Anthropologist Levi-Strauss denotes a parallel notion in shamanism: the patient must have a strong belief in the shaman's ability to heal.* Also, he explains, the shaman is required to at least give the appearance of belief in his own techniques. If the palmist overtly doubts his methodology (in full view of the subject), certainly the subject will take heed and follow suit; the palmistry session will consequently be fruitless.

But the palmist is unwilling to go as far as the shaman to demonstrate effectiveness. For example, consider the famous shaman Quesalid; his physical props to "suck the disease or illness" out of the patient are well documented. In the healing sessions, the shaman is a completely dominant figure. He dictates the flow, content, and structure of the conversation, the healing techniques, the *performance*. The shaman gives the patient a vocabulary to understand illness; he literally "puts words" into his patient's mouths.

The palmist does not resort to measures as extreme; he will probably not use props or devices to portray explicitly the effectiveness of the reading as the shaman does. In addition, although the palmist does indeed put words into his subject's mouths, the subjects are allowed input and are also permitted to direct the flow of the readings. (The palmist ultimately, though, directs the dialogue.) In this respect, the palmistry sessions more closely resemble psychiatric ones.

---

* Perhaps, because of the placebo effect (and simply waiting out illness), the shaman actually does appear to heal the patient. And, if a shaman of today would sneak in some of the West's advanced medical techniques during a healing, the patient might be impressed enough to truly believe in the supernatural powers of the shaman. Shades of Arthur C. Clarke here: "Any sufficiently advanced technology is indistinguishable from magic."

Also, the shamanistic healing process requires not only the shaman but also a group supporting the patient (as Levi-Strauss details). The palmist does not require the imprimatur a group setting might convey, but instead leans on one-on-one interactions—akin to psychiatry.

The psychiatrist also tends to listen to his patients more than he speaks to them. With palmistry, the subject and palmist both listen and converse. Unlike the psychiatrist, the palmist allows the subjects to draw their own conclusions from the palmistry (the system in psychiatry is reversed; the psychiatrist listens to the subject and then gives a "reading"; the palmist, though, gives a reading and then stands back as the subject subconsciously molds the reading to fit his personality or history).

There is interplay* between the palmist and subject; reexamine the four subjects' dialogue with the palmist (me). Although mostly the palmist directed the conversations, the subjects had an active part in the dialogue. The palmist must work off of the subjects' statements.

Also, as the conversation progresses, the subjects are more willing to agree with the palmist—and consequently modify their memories or expressed feelings about themselves—because they have an investment in the conversation, coupled with a desire not to interrupt the urgency of dialogue between themselves and the palmist. The subjects construct a neo-biography in real time that not only conforms to the subjects' already past notions about themselves but also conforms to the content of the conversations.

Nevertheless, there were certain content areas of memory and identity with which subjects were especially concerned. As discussed above, one of the subjects was interested in romance; another, interested in money; yet another, in problem-solving independence; and another, in health. Romantic possibilities, riches, and health are certainly rich areas of cultural interest.

However, the degree of emphasis on those specific areas with the respective subjects (as discussed earlier in the subject analyses) function as personal symbols as well because they have more than a superficial impact on the subjects' lives. The cultural assumptions

* Which might be compared to a tennis match; the palmist always "serves," though.

about riches, for instance, has with subject two become more than just a status symbol, but a symbol of personal significance.

The outlier in the palmistry experiment is subject three. Because he is from another country, and has only lived in the United States for several years, can we really include him in the analysis of personal/public symbols? A desire to be an independent thinker is a hallmark of our culture. However, how can we assume that he is not simply reciting Ukrainian tropes about independent thinking, whether he realizes it or not? Because he gives a specific meaningful example: independent thinking is relevant to his personality, and he interprets the palm read to reaffirm his perceived abilities in the area.

The personal symbols of the subjects might be best described using anthropologist Victor Turner's conception of Ndembu symbolism: "[Symbols] elicit emotion and express and mobilize desire.... [A] single symbol represents both the obligatory and the desirable" (from the book *Ritual and Belief*).

The personal symbol of subject two both "elicits emotion" and "mobilizes desire"—he has contempt toward riches (emotion attached), and money is also an "obligatory" symbol (perceived in terms of the entire cultural system). Health and romantic issues prevalent in two other subjects also almost precisely fit Turner's definitions (romance elicits emotion, and is obligatory, or expected, in society; the notion of health produces emotion [in subject four], and is also obligatory and desirable).

Although four case studies is a small sample size, it is nevertheless enough to demonstrate the emergence of symbols and concepts of identity of personal relevance (removed from notions of a more cultural interest), the interaction and linguistic interplay between palmist and subject, the subjects' insertion of affective interest, and the "bridge" subjects and the palmist construct.

The motivation behind the subjects' fascination with predictions and personal construction of identities, though, is a more difficult question—why are people attracted to palm readers at all? Perhaps there is an innate or subconscious archetype that explains their interest. If so, then learning of our past and present, and confirming our own suspicions about who we are and who we will become, is a built-in mechanism of *Homo sapiens*.

(2000)

# 14.

## Religion Is Utilitarian: A Look at *In Sorcery's Shadow*

Religion is certainly utilitarian.* If nothing else, religion serves as a *limiter* of culture, which engenders tension—since culture, by definition, is a force of expansion: culture moves one's concerns from kin and tribe to the mass of humanity; but, analogous to an axiomatic mathematical system, religion—in both its creed and the actual manifest practice of it—sets up a woven cultural system of rules and practices for its members. Religion dialectically "constricts" culture, but what, precisely, is religion? Let's look to anthropology for answers. Religion, as anthropologist Clifford Geertz states, quite literally defines reality for believers. Geertz creates a bipartite "division of labor" of the functional relationship of religion to culture. Religion creates models "for" reality—in other words, a "for" model resembles an architectural blueprint *for* reality (and for building reality). Religion also creates "of" reality—ways of understanding and conceptualizing reality. Thus, religion, according to Geertz, is something by which we *understand* the world and something by which we *build* the world. (He also argues that although models for reality exist independently of man, models of reality are almost uniquely characteristic of man.)

*In Sorcery's Shadow: A Memoir of Apprenticeship Among the Songhay of Niger* by Paul Stoller presents several important questions to the reader that can perhaps be analyzed with Geertz's "for" and "of" framework. The first of these questions—How far can we go in the quest to understand other peoples?—is deceptively complex.

Interpersonal relations, conceptions of morality, and the like, are defined, albeit latently, by a religious system present. Therefore, a direct answer to Stoller's query is: as far as possible to fully under-

---

* As in "pragmatic"—*not* in the sense of J. Bentham and J. S. Mill's philosophical idea of utilitarianism, of furthering the greatest good for the greatest number of people.

stand the religious system (and, thereby, understand the reality) of the culture. Since the religious system defines the people, and is shaped by the people, fully comprehending the religious system of the culture *should* lend itself to understanding.

Let us briefly turn to E. E. Evans-Pritchard's article "Men Bewitch Others When They Hate Them." Effectively, Evans-Pritchard argues that the notion of witchcraft in society is a "valuable corrective to uncharitable impulses." Evans-Pritchard believes that the system of witchcraft is a social corrective with a double function: fear others' retribution (keeps individuals in line morally) and fear accusations of witchcraft (keeps individuals on a "non-polluted" path). But Evans-Pritchard's description of the functions of witchcraft—which resemble Geertz's of and for models—are theoretical and created, clearly, from a distance and "other" perspective (in other words, he does not believe in the witchcraft he is examining). Therefore, has Evans-Pritchard gone *far enough* to understand the structural-functional relationship of witchcraft in Azande society? His methodology, although not fully detailed in the article, is quite similar to Stoller's initial conceptions of how to engage in fieldwork. But, as Stoller quickly discovers, informants lie to their anthropologist observers because they (at least the people of Songhay) proudly wear a "So what's the difference?" attitude.

Could Evans-Pritchard's data and fieldwork in Azandeland be a model for a specific type of reality that the Azande *wish* the anthropologist to perceive? Said differently, could it all just be a show? "One kills something thin in appearance only to discover that on the inside it is flat," Stoller points out. Therefore, it seems unlikely that Evans-Pritchard's non-immersion in Azande life is sufficient for him to understand the Azande—understand both their models "of" and "for" reality.

A full immersion in the culture for the observer is impossible (take a look at the very beginning of Stoller's text, with the short parable about the log). But certainly, at least, models of a "for" reality should be fully understood by the anthropologist. There must be at least a description of the profane and the sacred in the society, and pollution concepts (as described by the anthropologist Mary Douglas) must be understood, or at least detailed. Perhaps after fully absorbing the cultural functions of a society, social and psychological functions will be recognized, as Geertz describes.

Has Stoller gone *too far* in his quest to understand the Songhay? No—at least, probably not. The model "for" reality—"rooted [of]… no less distinctive 'mental' dispositions"—is mastered by Stoller. His involuntary chanting after an "attack" leaves him partially paralyzed, and his confrontation of Dunguri shows an understanding of an aspect of the model "for" reality (certainly more difficult to grasp for an anthropologist than the model "of" reality, since the model "for" model is rooted in mental dispositions). Stoller has transcended Evans-Pritchard's understanding of Azande society because he has *experienced* a mental motivation without axiomatizing it—as Evans-Pritchard surely would have done.

It is ethical for ethnographers to become apprentice sorcerers in their attempt to learn about sorcery? Examine Bronislaw Malinowski's new conception of the myth to find an answer. In "The Role of Myth in Life," Malinowski correctly assesses the problematic nature of exclusively examining a myth's narrative without looking at the way the text is recited. "The limitation to the study of myth to the mere examination of texts has been fatal to a proper understanding of its nature [because] studied alive, myth… is not symbolic, but a direct expression of its subject matter." In other words, in order to fully grasp the significance of myths, which have as much meaning in recitation as in the content of the texts themselves, the ethnographer must *hear* the stories.

Analogously, it is necessary for the anthropologist studying sorcery to actually hear, see, and partake in the practices. Can the anthropologist simply study texts on sorcery and create an accurate conception of the religion? Hardly; consider the passage in *In Sorcery's Shadow* in which the Sohanci says, "Bam bam bam, bum, bum, bum," to designate a "warning to those who have betrayed a man." We, as readers, do not understand or *feel* the inflections of the words, or witness the context of their impact (and thus mere texts without performance don't allow for the experiential presentation of rituals, myths, or the religion itself); although religion is utilitarian, it certainly is not the intellectual pursuit of its members that texts and content without performance displays. As Malinowski observes, an intellectual, logical definition of myth, and religion, "would create an imaginary, non-existent class of narrative, the etiological myth, corresponding to a non-existent desire to explain, leading to a futile existence as an 'intellectual effort.'" However, it is *ethical* for the ethnographer to go to any length—e.g., become the sorcerer—to understand sorcery? Geertz's conceptions of religion, and how an anthropologist should understand religion, perhaps give a clear answer to the question (although the answer is implicit): yes, since the quest is to fully comprehend the cultural system and understand the religious phenomena as well as possible (and understand the two models of religion). Only when the anthropologist *becomes* the sorcerer can he begin to fully realize the mental dispositions of the sorcerer and thus understand deep-seated notions about the cultural functions of sorcery.*

And what of the motivations as ethnographers—are they seekers of knowledge, or self-actualization, or power? Perhaps the motivations of ethnographers are just another step up from the telling of myths. As Levi-Strauss describes in "The Structural Study of Myth," myths are a part of human speech. Myths can be classified into "bundles of relations," he says, that, taken as a whole, create new meaning (analogous to language, where phonemes are simply indeterminate sounds that are "bundled" together to create meaning). Myths, in this framework, are a higher-level language. Is the ethnographer, by studying a culture, constructing "bundles of relations" of cultural viewpoints and dispositions that he is creating or engaging in a new level of knowledge or, indeed, language? Conceptualizing a model "of" and a model "for" reality (like Stoller valiantly attempted to) exposes the ethnographer to a comparison of culture—whether it be a dichotomous comparison or not—that a person living in a single culture is not privy to.

Ethnography is more than just a quest for knowledge, or power, or self-actualization; rather, the motivation for ethnographers may be a need, or desire, to engage in a bit of a "forced" comparison of the ethnographers' cultures—and a comparison of the two models of reality—to see a "higher" cultural function. For instance, consider: Where does Stoller belong on the cultural spectrum after he has lived half of his adult life in another culture besides the one he grew up in? His conceptions of cultural functions are, like the hearing and telling of myths, a new "bundled" language of the meaning "of" and "for" reality, both mentally and physically.

(2000)

* But "becoming" isn't always feasible. Consider the hijras: Serena Nanda, author of the ethnography *Neither Man nor Woman: The Hijras of India*, believes that the hijras, who emasculate themselves, are an alternative gender.

# 15.

## Dead Before Death: A Glimpse at the Near-Death Experience

The concept of the near-death experience, or NDE, is now a bit of a hackneyed cliché. Consider the fairytale-like nature of the event: A person, incapacitated and unconscious, travels "outside of his body" to view himself (in a third-person perspective). He ascends into a "heaven" of unbearably bright atmosphere and large, exaggerated shapes (such as a cylinder, tunnel, or a halo). Next, he encounters a "being" who invariably asks a question about his earthly life. After he is instructed to return to earth because it is "not his time yet," he recovers from the trauma or illness and seeks knowledge and understanding of the experience for the rest of his life. And another question invariably rises: Why? (It is a multi-layered query, of course; "Why" not only applies to the "post-mortem" experience of the absorption of knowledge but also of the motivation behind the entire experience.) If we assume the stance of functionality (i.e., that these types of "events" have a specific subconscious purpose), which admittedly might be false, then the NDE must be some type of physiologically reactionary mechanism. Of course, this does not explain the NDE's structural makeup or consistency among different groups of individuals.

In addition, notice how easily the NDE lends itself to narrative description; it resembles a character-centric novel or film.* Also notice that the NDE cannot be witnessed or visualized by anyone

---

* A character begins the causal chain with one set of assumptions about the nature of his life, and, through a series of impactful personal events, reforms and changes his conceptions. There are many examples in modern fiction of this kind of story: *A Separate Piece* and *Pale Horse, Pale Rider* lend themselves appropriately (and, interestingly enough, *Pale Horse, Pale Rider* has an NDE-style event near the end of the novel after Miranda catches the flu). Most big Hollywood films have this character-centric structure; consider everything from *Citizen Kane* to *Jackie Brown* to *Beavis and Butt-Head Do America* (which, coincidently, also has protracted NDE sequence).

*except* the person actually having the experience (thus, it is not testable under standard laboratory conditions; a scientist could not purposely induce a near-death state in an individual, by invoking a trauma, to obtain an NDE description).*

But the NDE does not externally resemble the standard subconscious imagery we all experience: the dream. The essential difference is the cause-effect logic; dreams have little causality from one "segment" or "section" to another; in other words, there is little reasoning behind the visualizations' connections (but, obviously, as a psychoanalyst would state, there is an abundance of explanation for the types and locations of the events and objects in dreams). But the NDE, as described above, carries a clear "plot line" through the imagery, and everything in the NDE builds toward a clear "ending."

Another main difference between the NDE and the dream is the recollection process. Usually, dreams fade quickly from memory or are not recalled at all. The NDE fades from memory more analogous to a real, lived experience. For instance, a major event in a person's life, like a wedding, will be remembered appropriately: as something experienced during waking life. Likewise, the details of the NDE are recalled as if they were traumatic events that occurred in a conscious state. Distinguishing dreams from NDEs, neurologist Oliver Sacks notes that the NDE is in fact physiologically a close cousin of the *hallucination*, rather than the dream.

> Both OBEs [out-of-body experiences] and NDEs, which occur in waking but often profoundly altered states of consciousness, cause hallucinations so vivid and compelling that those who experience them may deny the term hallucination, and insist on their reality….
>
> But the fundamental reason that hallucinations—whatever their cause or modality—seem so real is that they deploy

---

* Although the NDE is, itself, falsifiable. Because postmortems often have out-of-body experiences (OBEs), several U.S. hospitals have placed an ever-changing sign of text, hidden on the ceiling in a hard-to-reach spot, which a floating postmortem might see. So far, no one who has reported an NDE at these hospitals has also reported seeing the letters on the sign at the time of the experience.

> the very same systems in the brain that actual perceptions do.

This essay will be divided into two parts. The first part will discuss the motivations of the NDE and will place the experience in a conceptual framework with which to analyze it efficiently. The second part will describe the reform processes of postmortems (which, as we will see, bear some resemblance to the health food movement). My analysis will not be Freudian (Freud assumed that the "dream work" was a conscious retelling of the dream in narrative, according to the anthropologist Jonathan Church), although it is obvious that some facets of the NDE lend themselves to sexual idioms (going through a tunnel, as "Enders" often do, can be compared to a womb, as Obeyesekere so eloquently describes in his 1981 text *Medusa's Hair*).

Two individuals will be denoted as archetypal and their experiences will be examined, with names and identifying details removed; their NDEs are of a piece with the vast majority of accounts, one way or another. Also, both of their experiences capture the most common elements present in the postmortem lifestyle. It is not my intention to bombard the reader with endless examples of case accounts, as could easily be done, but rather to focus on common empirical components of the NDE and post-NDE and use them as a springboard to relating the NDEs with ideas and concepts of anthropological and psychological theorists. (We will at least begin to discover why the proverbial NDE apples don't fall too far from the theoretical trees.) Both NDE postmortems we shall examine are American, so when I refer to "society" or "culture" I am broadly talking about American society. Although many people from other societies have indeed had similar experiences, we cannot so easily justify this essay's analysis of those subjects' NDEs without more elaborate suppositions.

The Internet as a tool to help identify the experiences will be used, since the first archetypal subject, Leanne, and many other people like her, have utilized the Internet to seek acceptance and share in the commonality of their experiences (this reinforces the "validity" of their NDEs and functions as the "group acceptance" required for healing from the event).

◆ ◆ ◆

Pseudonymous Leanne did not undergo a traumatic event—the usual catalyst for NDEs. Rather, her NDE was induced by a hypnotic experience. Although not a typical trigger for an NDE, Leanne's experience nevertheless illustrates many of the characteristics of the typical NDE. She posted her experience online. Parts of it will appear here with some identifying details removed.

> I saw the exterior of the hospital where I was born in 1946. It was snowing. I saw the admittance area next. Then, from above, I saw a baby with dark blue eyes lying on a cold, hard, black and white tile floor. I was lying on a delivery room table that stood on a black and white tile floor.
>
> I was viewing myself from above and experienced no feelings except to observe that the baby was moving its eyes back and forth with curiosity. I had stopped breathing directly after birth and went back into my body as Sister Lisa (delivery nurse) picked me up and cradled me to her breast. I felt very content and safe.

Leanne goes on to describe how she was brought to her mother's recovery bed by Sister Lisa. Her father, though, was not there—although she sensed her grandmother's presence. "My mother did not want me, though; she wanted my father." She continues:

> This first intense feeling resulted in my decision to return Home…again. I began moving backward and was surrounded by a cylinder of swirling white-gray fog. A doctor leaned over and looked into the cylinder at me. I continued to [go] back into the cylinder and saw a bright blue sky at the other end.
>
> A dolphin, whom I instantly recognized as my guardian angel, was leaping over a puffy white cloud. I told him that I was not going to stay down there, that I was coming Home.

The dolphin/angel attempts to convince Leanne of her need to "go back" to an earthly domain. After Leanne balks, God Himself, bearded and dressed in a white robe, appears and telepathically instructs her to return "Home." She reluctantly agrees, vowing to "learn her lesson so well" that she'll never have to return to "this world."

After emerging from the cylinder of white-gray fog, Sister Lisa embraces Leanne. Here's how Leanne later makes sense of her journey:

> It's impossible to explain the feeling of overwhelming love and acceptance that I felt, but others who have experienced an NDE have no need for an explanation—understanding shines in their eyes. I felt as if "Home" best captures what I went through. I can only compare it to what has been described to me as the "alpha state" in meditation.

Many personal and private symbols emerge in her account. Sister Lisa is clearly a private symbol; there is little, if any, publicly communicative value in her presence. But what of the dolphin (the "guardian angel")? Is there any overt meaning? The dolphin is an abstraction, and also probably a private symbol, originating psychogenetically. There is one obvious public symbol, however: "Then a white bearded figure [God] in a white robe appeared in the distance...." How does the subject know it is God (in the Judeo-Christian sense)? Like the monk who shaves his head because of a repetition of rules instructing him to do so, Leanne assumes a publicly shared meaning and creates a common image of the figure. There is little or no personal motivation in the appearance of the apparition.

Her characterization of Home, however, is a personal symbol. Home has a very intrinsic meaning for the subject. Therefore, Home assumes the status of a personal symbol because it has both publicly communicative value and personal significance. And, even more important, the ease at which public, private, and personal symbols emerge from the NDE account is startling. That the NDE explicitly taps into the reservoirs of the individual's conceptions of symbolism cannot be mere coincidence.

The appearance of family members has parallels with Karen McCarthy Brown's descriptions of Vodou spirits and Obeyesekere's analyses of Buddhist/Hindu cultural constructions. As the text *Medusa's Hair* describes, family members often play the role of emissary to the gods. In Leanne's NDE account, the subject's mother acts out an important role, although not quite that of spokesperson, as is the case with Buddhist/Hindu family members. Nevertheless, the mere presence of family members gives, like in the Obeyesekere text, justification and believability to the entire experience, at least to the postmortem.

The NDE is also an expression of personal identity very much like the Hindu/Buddhist possession states. Leanne, in this example, is seeking to properly define her place in society.* There is a kind of revitalization of the common mythological constructions of the West. (Angels, heaven, God, and saints come to mind as some typical mythological constructions.) Because she lives in a highly demythologized society—which gives little credence to myth models or myths themselves—perhaps the subject required a reaffirmation of "illogical" mythological concepts in a very "logical" way.

In essence, the only way a person as highly secularized and demythologized as an American could more readily accept mythological abstractions is with her senses: sight, sound, smell, proprioception, etc. These senses lend empirical validity to the improbable; in the case of the NDE, the expression "I have to see it to believe it" best characterizes the necessity of the visualizations to be as immediate, as *real*, as possible.

This leads directly to the next question: Is the NDE a "modern myth"? Surely myths, in a conventional sense (by "conventional," I am referring to the myth forms in "primitive" societies. For example, the retelling of the Oedipus myths) are not going to be accepted readily by a society as cynical or as unbelieving as our informational/technological contemporary society. The once sacred myths of the Judeo-Christian Bible have, in our current societal state, become profane and ubiquitous, and they are rarely treated as historical accounts rather than parables—even if one regularly attends an organized place of worship. Simply put, many people have a very hard time believing something that is not readily observable or testable or falsifiable.

---

* By this I mean the American culture is so loosely defined that the only real label we can give it is shallow at best: the pursuit of happiness and/or the acquisition of material wealth and success. In addition, small group structure, which plays such a pivotal role in smaller societies, such as foraging societies, in almost nonexistent in the U.S.; alienation among people, not group solidarity, is more common. It is especially because of the neolocal residence patterns of families, which are primarily due to economic motivations.

Thus, assuming that we, as humans, need myths in order to resolve contradiction and create understanding of the world around us, we have fed our new empirical cravings by creating the mythological constructs in an "observable" world, namely, the NDE. Although this is perhaps a radical proposition, it nevertheless aids in explaining the genesis of the experience. And, as we will discover later, individuals who have encountered the light are more willing to accept the metaphysical.

Samuel, let's call him, is a history professor who ruptured his appendix while with a class in England. After several days in the hospital, he finally decided to, as it were, give up and accept death. Upon losing consciousness, he had an OBE.

The following are selected excerpts from a tape-recorded interview Samuel had in front of a university in the San Francisco area describing the NDE (which was posted online).

> [After leaving my body], I [floated] down corridors and saw other doctors frantically running somewhere, I don't know where, and I also saw people waiting in the waiting rooms, which I passed overhead as well.
>
> I began to hear whispers and voices, distorted, behind me and in all directions. I was really scared.... I didn't know what was going on.... But suddenly, a white angel, who I believe was perhaps the Virgin Mary, came and rescued me.

The Virgin Mary takes Samuel in hand (or in something), and they pass through a long, dark tunnel. Upon emerging, there are "many bright floating lights flickering at high speeds, all orbiting a very large bright light" that he is "sure" is Jesus, and overwhelming happiness falls over Samuel.

Samuel's NDE compares favorably with Leanne's. The tunnel, the light, the feelings of pleasantness—all of these characteristics are shared in both accounts. Although some of the constructions of angels are profusely different (e.g., Samuel certainly does not claim to have seen a dolphin), the presence of a corporeal being to escort the "dead" person to the supreme single power (the god) occurs in both accounts. Also, the floating and observation of self is common. In fact, looking through many descriptions of NDEs, we find that although the circumstances surrounding the experiences are often dissimilar, the elements described in them are frequently the same.

We can use anthropologist Rodney Needam's conception of the recurrent appearance of witch characteristics as a starting point for explaining the NDE commonality. "[T]he image of the witch," he says, "is autonomous and can be conceived as an archetype of the unconscious imagination." Furthermore, the "notion of a psychic constant [sic] in the form of an autonomous image to which the human mind is naturally predisposed" is the most effective way to explain the witch's recurring features.

Transplanting Needam's conceptual framework to the NDE appears valid. Applying it, the human mind is "naturally predisposed" to observing lighted images and god-like apparitions, coupled with the odd archetype for observing one's own image from the outside.* Although it is perhaps an avoidance of presenting a testable solution to the witch quandary, Needam explains the synthesis of images using ambiguous medical terms: "A conceivable process is that these contrasted cerebral functions combine in an imaginative tropism, a synthetic response to natural foci of attraction among phenomena, whether social or physical, and that the product is the archetype." Applying this unwieldy explanation teaches us nothing about the motivation behind an individual's NDE. Nor does it give us a solution for the distinct lack of variability among NDE descriptions, except to say that the brain is chemically and organically predisposed to create "synthetic" images corresponding to the causal chain of events of the NDE—which is a less narrative-like and more physiological (or neurological) explanation (unless we commit to argument that the brain neurologically has a penchant for narrative structure, which might have a basis in fact).

---

* Why are most accounts of NDEs relatively recent? Because cardiopulmonary resuscitation was developed the middle of last century and, before that, revival after cardiac arrest was extremely rare. NDE-like experiences can also be produced by epileptic seizures. Famously, Fyodor Dostoevsky said that during at least one of his frequent seizures he "touched God."

Therefore, while not totally agreeing with Needam, we can, at least loosely, use his notion of the archetype to explain the prevalence of common images and events in the experience. Let us define the NDE as follows: It is a reactionary archetype designed to *create meaning* and *resolve contradiction* about a process that still largely eludes modern definitions of understanding: death. And, once again, the NDE functions as a type of myth—as something designed to insert meaning where no obvious meaning exists. The brain is a three-pound processor designed largely to analyze patterns and resolve meaning—even if those resolutions take the form of mythical confabulations.

Note that Samuel, like Leanne, assigns symbolism to objects he cannot quite understand. For instance, consider the Christian religious characters that appear in his experience. Samuel admits at the beginning of the interview that before the NDE, he was very secular. During a time of crisis, his subconscious mind recalled images and figures that are essential to assigning meaning to the process of death (at least "essential" in the Judeo-Christian religious sense). Hence, this is why the NDE is a reactionary or reflexive mechanism—it "regresses" the individual to mythological constructs he has long since discarded as irrelevant in our secular, modern world.

Extending this argument further, we note that both subjects have religious-orientated experiences, despite their secularization in our demythologized society. Could the neo-religious symbolism displayed in their NDEs be a revitalization ritualistic process? Certainly, the NDEs are renewals of previous values from generations' prior (as a revitalization ritual implies). But they also take on a distinctly altered personal form; religious liturgy is not as important to postmortem subjects, it appears, as are holistic religious or spiritual feelings. Thus, in the transition from the past to the present, since the institutional context of the mythological forms of conventional religious values (the Judeo-Christian creed) were altered, the expressed form by individuals, through the NDE experience, was also altered.

In addition, just as the belief system of the postmortem changes (we will discuss shortly the new sets of values postmortems tend to adopt), it might be argued that the expression of religious symbolism during the actual NDE is a direct reflection of the institutional state of religion in the society of the individual. In essence, the NDE is an outlet for acceptable religious narration in our secularized society. (So, religion is usually associated with death and times of crisis; the NDE is both a crisis and a death experience, and, therefore, religious symbolism is associated with it.)

In Samuel's account, we see the almost fervent speak about a common Christian religious figure. His near-default association of *light = Jesus* is proof of his personal need to, in a time of crisis (and lack of understanding) recall, and revitalize, the institutionally blanketed religious doctrines.* Of course, the same comparison can be made with Leanne, who discovers similar "standard" religious figures. Common Christian characters are used to explain the unknowable.

We see a similar feature with Kalu Kumara, the Black Prince. As Obeyesekere describes, when the female future ascetics begin to have erotic dreams with another male individual (are the dreams perhaps a sexual cry for help? Obeyesekere never says), it is reflexively attributed to invasion by the Black Prince. A ubiquitous mythological figure is used to diagnose a common ailment.

Much ink has also been spilled in texts such as *Life After Life* and *At the Hour of Death* to diagnose the entire NDE religiously in terms of the Bible, as a shaman using mythological texts might "diagnose" a patient. For example, after quoting several well-chosen Bible passages, Raymond Moody, the person most responsible for the popular conceptions of the NDE as we know it today, declares, "Notice that in both of these passages there is the strong suggestion that a resurrection of the physical body will occur...." The context of his statement is unimportant; what is essential to observe is his use of Christian religion to analyze and explain. Where contradiction or exception occurs, as is the case with NDEs, there is a return to mythological propositions to fill in the gaps, despite (or in spite of) our living in a demythologized society.

We will now return to Lenanne; what follows is the account of her spiritual and emotional awakening after the NDE. Notice her new, pronounced outlook on her life.

---

* It is also a kind of subjectification, using cultural constructs to obtain new personal meaning. However, the cultural constructs used are not as readily accepted in our mainstream society as, for instance, gods are in Buddhist/Hindu society.

> As for how the experience has changed my life, initially, it saved my life because I was approaching [a] spiritual death.... I would also like to say that my experience has resulted in my becoming a doctor or a teacher, but I immediately became obsessed with spiritual/psychological astrology. Since most readings are done for free, I've no dreams of wealth and fame. I also practice the craft with a great sense of responsibility, and I stress that we make our own choices and create our own destiny. I suppose that astrology is my way of being a spiritual teacher....

What has most obviously changed in Leanne is not her behavior, but her awareness of a viable alternative to her behavior, in the sense of spirituality; she recognizes that a secularized mechanism with which to understand the world is not her only option. She must reconcile her post-"death" feelings with those acceptable or understood (at least somewhat) in society. In other words, engaging in what Obeyesekere calls "fantasy" to reconcile the personal experience is futile: "Through fantasy the patient attempts to bring about a resolution of his psychic conflict as well as an inner integration of personality. But this must fail, since inner integration, to be successful, must be matched with an outer integration with society." Leanne must not create private, socially uncommunicative symbols to deal with the aftermath of her NDE, but must instead use objectification (a public expression of emotion) to permit reconciliation and synthesis.

There is also creativity in her expression. Although her post-NDE feelings of "love" and "pleasantness" tend to direct an interest in many spiritual activities, the characteristics of her spiritual awakening are creatively chosen by Leanne—and the characteristics she chooses are her externalized emotional responses to the experience.

Her creativity has an analogue with the concept of sexuality in Hindu mythology; renouncing sexuality in Hindu culture gives rise to "powers" in other forms. Renouncing a wholly secular lifestyle for Leanne after the NDE gives rise to her new "powers" of spirituality.

"I am not religious in the traditional sense, however, my spirituality continues to grow and transform," she notes. Therefore, although her NDE was a bare-bones interpretation of Biblical mythological figures (like saints and God), interestingly enough, although she accepts the spiritual values, she rejects the standard Judeo-Christian religious ones. The revitalization of religion by the NDE, if there is indeed such a revitalization, is not religion-specific, it seems. The NDE brings about in the individual a religious awakening not really specifically or conventionally religious.

Analogous to the heath food movement, where there is an almost binary division between the manna and the taboo, the postmortem gains an understanding of the spiritually "good" and spiritually "bad," which are treated as Manichaean. "I accept all religions if practiced with love," Leanne claims. A cosmology of the postmortem experience can start to be built by this statement. "Love," as ill-defined as it seems to be by her account, is a major motivator behind the placement of items in the "good" or "bad" spiritual categories.

Death itself, although in the health food cosmology would be considered taboo, appears surprisingly enough in the "good" category of the postmortem's creed. The subject tends not to have a fearful or apprehensive attitude toward the process but instead considers it a necessary completion of a cycle. Leanne reflects this attitude with her talk of "destiny" and "karma."

But there are many similarities with the health food cosmology that surface. "Working against the body and nature," "dependence through mass production [of values]," and "fragmented/artificial/cold" are all oppositions, just like in the health food movement.

The cosmology of the post-NDE gives people a way to think about their world, as the myth models of secularized religion (by this I mean the skeletal religious symbolism known to, if not practiced by, secular individuals) give people a way to process the actual near-death experience. To create the cosmology, then, elements of Judeo-Christian mythology are utilized, applied, and then somewhat discarded in favor of a revised methodology, namely, the bipartite categorizations of "good" and "bad."

Commonly, there is a separation between the profane and the sacred in our culture ("sacred" meaning overtly religious, mythological, or supernatural phenomenon). Certainly one of the most important functions of the post-NDE cosmology is the integration of the profane and the sacred; in fact, "profane and sacred synthesis" can be considered in the "good" category of the cosmology. Like with syncretic religion Vodou practitioners, the profane and sacred elements become hard to distinguish in the postmortem's lifestyle. Leanne recognizes the inherent contradictions of astrology and rationalism, but she also explains her forced acceptance of both roles and the positives that have emerged from their union.

Samuel's system of belief after his experience is similar to Leanne's. Notice his focus on knowledge in the aftermath of the NDE in the following excerpt, taken from the latter part of his talk at the university near San Francisco.

> After my near death experience, I sought out knowledge of every kind. Knowledge was the key thing up there. If you come into my house, you'll see stacks and stacks of books on almost every subject—I have tried to be as diverse as possible. I've realized that the gaining of knowledge is the most important thing, more important than money, or even life on this Earth....

In Samuel's postmortem cosmology, knowledge is the essential ingredient. Like Leanne's "love," Samuel's "knowledge" becomes a motivator for change. The Hindu ascetics also have motivations for change—they wish to cease having sexual intercourse with their husbands.* Likewise, Samuel's need for knowledge becomes a manifestation of his desire to deal with the experience and its implications; in other words, his requirement to reorient himself to his common cultural surroundings—he cannot simply go back to his pre-NDE understanding the world, because the experience was both traumatic and enlightening for him—assumes the form of a symbol: in this case, knowledge (and, in the case of Leanne, love/spirituality).

Samuel even claims to have "stacks and stacks of books on almost every subject" contained in his home. Is he, by assuming the cosmology of "knowledge acquisition," merely displacing the trauma of his near death experience? Perhaps, but this seems to be too pat of an explanation. More likely, Samuel truly believes that

---

* Although this is a generalization of their reasoning, it seems largely plausible and might certainly be a valid catalyst for asceticism.

knowledge acquisition is "manna".[*] Leanne also sought knowledge in the form of spirituality. Although Leanne's and Samuel's cosmologies appear to diverge (one with spirituality and the other with knowledge), they both nevertheless have similar beliefs in the "good" and "bad" categorizations mentioned earlier. Knowledge is most certainly placed in the category of the spiritually "good."

Shamans give their patients a vocabulary with which to think about themselves and their illnesses. Obeyesekere correctly states that the analyst must successfully integrate the patient on three fronts: society, culture, and personality. The NDE "victim" frequently does not have the benefit of integration on two of the three fronts: society and culture. Therefore, how can there be a reconciliation of personality without support from the other two elements in the triptych? Before Raymond Moody's *Life After Life* was published in 1975, there was only rudimentary general societal knowledge of the NDE or its aftereffects. The text, despite its ultimate analytical simplicity about its subject matter, still managed to open up a cultural dialogue. NDEs became relatively acceptable to discuss, albeit not completely.[†]

Since *Life After Life*, there has been an explosion of materials about the near-death experience. Books such as *Embraced By the Light*, by Morse, and *At the Hour of Death*, by Osis and Haraldsson,[‡]

---

[*] Though we have labeled Samuel's experience as archetypal in many ways to the general NDE population, we cannot ignore his profession—that of a professor. As such, certainly he had some interest in knowledge for knowledge's sake prior to his NDE.

[†] Although Moody's book was not the first research done on the subject (a Swiss Alpine climber, after a trauma on the slopes, wrote his account of an NDE in the late 1800s), it was among the first popularly acknowledged studies and led to a ballooning of publicly documented accounts.

[‡] And, more recently, *Proof of Heaven*, by neurosurgeon Eben Alexander, which is perhaps the most unconvincing of the lot. Alexander leans on his professional expertise to explain away any natural reason for his NDE; his lack of measured brain activity while in a comatose state is his "proof" of heaven. But as Oliver Sacks explains in a sharp critique of the book in *The Atlantic*, "The one most plausible hypothesis in Dr. Alexander's case, then, is that his NDE occurred not during his coma, but as he was surfacing from the coma and his cortex was returning to full function. It is curious that he does

discuss the impacts and implications of the NDE. But most texts on the subject have a common fatal flaw: they begin by assuming that the NDE is a real journey, not a psychologically symbolic one, and proceed to show, rather defensively, why the NDE must be a true afterlife experience rather than some sort of dream or hallucination. These books, then, are counterproductive to understanding the NDE.

Instead, we look to the Internet. Although group meetings to talk about near-death accounts are quite rare—Samuel's conference notwithstanding—and people will frequently not talk publicly about NDEs if they have had one, since openly discussing death is still mostly taboo, the Internet has opened up an anonymous forum for the dissemination of descriptions of near-death experiences. So with the advent of online access to discuss such experiences, people who have had NDEs tend to post their stories on the Internet. People can claim they have seen the afterlife without fear of retribution or opprobrium from coworkers or acquaintances; in addition, the commonality of accounts posted on the web encourages the experiencer—through a sort of neo-group acceptance—to share and relate.

The factor of group acceptance of NDEs on the Internet is in its own way a question of efficacy. It is not appropriate to claim that "real" group discussions (that is, group discussions with actual people present) are more effective than Internet postings and message boards. However, it is correct to state that Internet dialogue is better suited to this kind of trauma, which requires anonymity (once again, few who have had NDEs wish to be publicly outed leading to, perhaps, humiliation, despite the limited cultural acceptance of NDEs).

But what becomes of people who have lived out the rest of their lives with the knowledge of the existence of an "afterlife" of sorts, because they have viewed it firsthand? According to most accounts, they develop a new cosmology for understanding and navigating the world. Regardless of the reason why the cerebrum actuates these archetypal visions during traumatic stress, the result of them is clear: the individual who has visited the Great Beyond is given a modern myth model.

---

not allow this obvious and natural explanation, but instead insists on a supernatural one."

In our demythologized society, comprehending and analyzing a very complex, very unknowable world is terribly desirable—even if the tools used to understand the world are affronts to the scientific method. Alourdes leans on her myth models and mythological gods to make sense of her environment. In *Medusa's Hair*, Obeyesekere's subjects use their Buddhist/Hindu traditions (and the personal application of the traditions) to understand their world. The text *In Sorcery's Shadow* describes a Nigerian society completely dependent on myth models to grasp the reasoning behind events both large and small. *Ritual and Belief* examines a multitude of societies (everything from modern applications of witchcraft to the witchcraft in Salem) and, implicitly, myth models are "running the show." If our society has myth models, they are surely not in the conventional sense and are ambiguous and ill defined.* But after an NDE, the postmortem has been unwittingly supplied a ready-made myth model with which to understand the world—which is certainly an enviable trait in any secularized society.

(2000)

* It seems that mega-popular films such as *Star Wars* have given the West many of its myth models, despite our knowing that these stories are fictions.

# 16.

## Developmental Differences in the Classroom

For an instructor to view his or her students as homogenous is not only counterproductive but also an affront to individuality. Nevertheless, although all children and adolescents are different, they certainly have many similarities, especially within a specific culture. Therefore, an appropriate balance must be reached between treating students as a homogeneous and a heterogeneous group. The theories of developmental differences can assist instructors in realizing their own proper equilibrium.

Consider the initial attempts to view child development in a theoretical framework. The child, according to John Locke, is a *tabula rasa* (blank slate), totally shaped by his or her experiences in life (Berk, 2000, p. 12). If a teacher adopts this kind of perspective, then an unrealistic notion arises: if all children in a class can be made to have the same experiences, they likely will view the subject matter in an analogous way.

American psychologist John B. Watson (and B. F. Skinner) founded the school of behaviorism. Behaviorism derives in part from Locke's conception of teacher control: the "environment is the supreme force in child development. Adults [can] mold children's behavior in any way they [wish]" (Berk, 2000, p. 20). Like the idea of *tabula rasa*, behaviorism is a rather extreme analysis of the level of control the environment has over the individual. Nevertheless, many instructors, interested in issues of regulation and subordination in the classroom, adopt philosophies of the behaviorist stance; the pragmatic value is minimal, since the notion of the homogeneous classroom that can be controlled by the teacher is mostly unrealistic.

At the other end of the spectrum of individualistic determination versus external loci of control is the cognitive-developmental theory of Piaget. The sensorimotor, preoperational, concrete operational, and formal operational stages characterize the theory; in essence,

Piaget makes the case that the four stages are "inevitable"* in the development of the individual, assuming that the developing person has experiences in which they "actively manipulate and explore their world" (Berk, 2000, p. 21). The work of Russian psychologist Alexander Luria demonstrates, albeit not entirely, the veracity of Piaget's framework. Luria (1976) conducted a plethora of experiments with people in a technologically "unadvanced" society in Asia at different stages of schooling. In the abstraction and generalization tests, individuals with no schooling (and thus no real exposure to the school-type techniques of generalization and abstraction), no matter their age, scored poorly, and those with more schooling, no matter their age, scored progressively better. To make a generalization, it almost appears as if schooling furthers the development of individuals on a Piagetian scale; in other words, school is the place to facilitate the active manipulation and exploration of a child's world, thus leading to greater levels of cognitive development (in the Piagetian framework). Luria (1976), though, does almost nothing to prove that the four stages of Piaget are dependent on the age of the cognitively developing individual.

However, Luria (1976) tempers the work of the behaviorists and Piaget (the all-environment versus all-individual cognitive indicators) by somewhat supporting the Vygotskian sociocultural approach: that social interaction in a culture is a necessary ingredient in development (Berk, 2000, p. 26). It is only when the more "primitive" people are exposed to the culture implicit in school—that of the importance of operations, generalizations, formulas, and ideation—that they are capable of demonstrating skills in those content areas. In essence, both the environmental influences of behaviorism/Locke and the individual discovery method of Piaget interact in the Vygotskian method.

If teachers adopt the Vygotskian approach of the importance of social interaction in a culture, then group activities in class are appropriate because they further cultural-social interaction and thus cognitive developmental skills. But not all group activities are appropriate; as Berk (2000) observes, research has discovered that only cooperative learning, or explicitly working toward a common goal in a peer group, is effective in abetting development (p. 265).

---

* Although how inevitable seems open to debate, considering Piaget arrived at these ideas after closely observing his own children.

Extending the Vygotskian approach, culture, according to Goode (2000), fashions thought processes; the researcher compares European Americans to East Asians in several situations. Notably, the two groups viewed identical images of fish but in entirely different (and probably) culturally defined ways. Goode (2000) lends credence to Vygotsky by demonstrating a cultural correlation and latent cultural developmental construction in ways of thinking. Instructors appreciating differences in culture can possibly better understand motivation of cognitive description in students originating from different countries or varied cultures.

Social representation develops and is developed by language, according to Vygotsky (Berk, 2000, p. 260). Language facilitates cognitive development, and cognitive development facilitates language as well. Teachers must be aware of the importance of emphasizing language development in their early-grade classrooms.

However, not all agree that an instructor has more than a modicum of control in constructing a complex palette of language for students to assimilate. Pinker (1994) discusses a child's instinct for language development, given a social milieu. Pinker (1994) wrestles with the question of complex language as innate, because the ubiquitous nature of complex language lends itself to such a notion. "[C]omplex language is universal," he states, "because *children actually reinvent it* [his italics], generation after generation—not because they are taught, not because they are generally smart, not because it is useful to them, but because they just can't help it" (Pinker, 1994, p. 32). The Pinker (1994) analysis suggests two important points: that children in a social environment will construct forms of complex language because of utility, and that adults who compose languages in pidgin cannot envelop the pidgin with the complexity young people can (in the form of creole). This suggests a kind of "zone of proximal development" (a Vygotskian notion) with complex language. Pinker (1994) notes this: the "successful language acquisition [of an individual] must take place during a critical window of opportunity in childhood" (p. 38). In this way, all of a teacher's young children in class are a group with homogeneous language needs: they must be socially exposed to each other (whether in the form of cooperative groups or other activities) in order to ensure an acceptable development of language—and not just with pragmatics, the social component of language, but with the other components of complex language as well, including phonology, semantics, and grammar. The Pinker (1994) perspective of language (which derives from a Vygotskian-like view) is a compromise position between the behaviorist perspective, which states that language is acquired through conditioning, and the nativistic perspective, which claims that language is biologically based (Berk, 2000, p. 359).

Although the door closes after a certain point in a child's life in terms of the ability to easily grasp complex language development,* it is unclear whether this also occurs with a host of other physiological elements. For example, Nelson (1999) notes that in terms of brain development, unless there are extreme instances of chronic deprivation, a child is able to develop normally under most sets of circumstances. Berk (2000) lists a large number of factors that could affect physical growth—heredity, nutrition, malnutrition, obesity, and diseases, among others—yet she freely admits that adolescents' "poor diets do not have serious consequences if they are merely a temporary response to peer influences and a busy schedule," i.e., the adolescents would develop normally physically one way or the other despite diet (p. 194). This relative invariant of physical development implies that teachers do not have to worry about their students' physical development (within reason). Knowing overall that boys grow at a slower rate than girls in their early teens, for instance, could squelch a teacher's classroom fears about a short male and a tall female (Berk, 2000, p. 178).

Intelligence, however, is an issue that teachers must take note of constantly in the classroom, since there are many available theories to conceptualize it. Spearman's theory of general intelligence and specific intelligences (*g* and *s*) is especially effective because of its definitional simplicity yet pervasive application (Berk, 2000, p. 317). Thurstone also conceptualized a descriptive view of intelligence; his contains seven primary mental abilities: spatial visualization, word fluency, rote memory, number, reasoning, perceptual speed, and verbal meaning (Berk, 2000, p. 317). There are more contemporary theories as well mentioned in Berk (2000): consider as examples Cattell's theory of crystallized intelligence (p. 318), Carroll's three-

---

* The "Matthew effect"—where the rich get richer and the poor get poorer, only here in terms of vocabulary and reading skills rather than money—may have something to do with this.

stratum theory of intelligence (p. 319), and Sternberg's triarchic theory of intelligence (p. 321).

Although an individual's intelligence does not necessarily correlate with his or her group's intelligence, instructors must be aware of group differences, not to stereotype or explain away, but to note potential strengths and weaknesses synonymous with groups. Neisser et al. (1996) makes the case that group differences can make a difference. For instance, with gender, Neisser et al. (1996) states, "While some tasks show no sex differences, there are others where small differences appear and a few where they are large and consistent" (p. 91). There are apparent differences in ethnic groups' measured intelligence as well, although Neisser et al. (1996) notes that these differences cannot necessarily be attributed to actual lesser intelligences among ethnic groups.

In order to better understand motivation and behavior, an instructor must also be cognizant of the emotional and social development of groups of people, like teenagers, who they may have as students. As Sapolsky (1997) points out, teenagers, much like primates,* feel a need to fit in to a social group of their peers. In another article, Erikson (1968) speaks of the adolescent's identity crisis. And in a third piece of research, Hine (1999) describes the contradictions present in Western society about the role of the teenager. All of the articles demonstrate that instructors' view of teenagers in their classrooms must be carefully considered in order not to hinder their students' emotional and social development as they slowly become adults.

The list of developmental elements that a teacher must be aware of in a school classroom goes on. The connection between gender and morals, for example, is unclear. In a piece by Wark and Krebs (1996), Carol Gilligan's conception of justice-versus-care-based moral judgments is examined as it correlates to gender. They find that it is not necessarily the case that females make more care-orientated judgments, and males make more justice-orientated judgments. A teacher, however, should use the results of the Wark and Krebs (1996) article with discretion, since Gilligan's ideas are still very much in vogue.

With respect to culture, parenting styles can be very different and can dramatically shape the type of child teachers eventually teach.

---

* No equivalence implied.

The text by Small (1998) demonstrates the parenting cultural disparity. In Japan, most mothers agree on a set of parenting rules (consider the so-called tiger mother, although this is largely a Chinese construct); in America, parents constantly refine or alter rules, and even children of the same household are not necessarily raised the same way. Teachers who consciously recognize that individuals may be different *because* of these kinds of cultural assumptions are in a good position to be effective with a wide variety of students.

(2001)

# References

Berk, L. E. (2000). Child development (4th ed.). Boston: Allyn and Bacon.

Erikson, E. H. (1968). Identity: Youth and crisis. New York City, NY: W. W. Norton & Co.

Goode, E. (2000, August 8). How Culture Molds Habits of Thought. *The New York Times.*

Hine, T. (1999). The rise and fall of the American teenager. New York, NY: Avon Books, Inc.

Luria, A. R. (1976). Cognitive Development: Its cultural and social foundations (Lopez-Morillas, Martin & Solotaroff, Lynn, Trans.). Cambridge, MA: Harvard University Press.

Neisser, U., Boodoo, G., Bouchard, T. J., Jr., Boykin, A. W., Brody, N., Ceci, S. J., Halpern, D. F., Loehlin, J. C., Perloff, R., Sternberg, R. J., & Urbina, S. (1996). Intelligence: Knowns and unknowns. American Psychologist, 51(2), 77-101.

Nelson, C. A. (1999). How important are the first 3 years of life? Applied Developmental Science, 3(4), 235-238.

Pinker, S. (1994). The language instinct: How the mind creates language. New York: Harper Collins. Chapters 2 & 9.

Sapolsky, R. M. (1997). The young and the restless, The trouble with testosterone, (pp. 75-90). New York: Scribner.

Small, M. F. (1998). Our babies, ourselves: How biology and culture shape the way we parent. New York: Anchor Books. Chapters 3 & 7.

Wark, G. R., & Krebs, D. L. (1996). Gender and dilemma differences in real-life moral judgment. Developmental Psychology, 32(2), 220-230.

# 17.

## High School Gender Differences in Mathematics Ability

There is a significant variance in the proposed explanations of the gender-related discrepancies in test scores of high school mathematics students. Nevertheless, there is general agreement, at least among the research literature examined here, that gender is indeed a strongly correlated variable in the differences observed in mathematics scores among male and female students.

For example, Stumpf and Stanley (1996) claim that over time, the gender differences in not only math but in other subjects measured by standardized tests (e.g., Advanced Placement tests) have decreased. In the mathematical sciences, male students have higher scores overall; in the humanities, such as language and English literature, female students scored higher. Although the gap has shrunk over the past ten years, part of the convergence in scores on the examinations can be attributed to higher participation rates. More males signed up for humanities-orientated tests, and more females signed up for mathematical-scientific exams over the observed time frame in the study. The more gender-balanced participation was found by Stumpf and Stanley (1996) to account for some, but not all, of the achievement variance.

Hedges and Nowell (1995) also examine gender differences in a variety of school subjects among older teenagers. But they are more specific than Stumpf and Stanley (1996) in that they disaggregate by school subject area. For instance, data in Hedges and Nowell (1995) demonstrate a female bias in reading comprehension, vocabulary, perceptual speed, and associative memory tests; in mathematics, science, social studies, spatial ability, mechanical reasoning, electronics information, and auto and shop information exams, males did better than females. Hedges and Nowell (1995) also note that the male scores had more variability than the female scores. In other words, females, in their test scores in all subject areas, tended to cluster around a more narrow range of results than males.

In an article by Gallagher et al. (2000), several studies are mentioned that investigate the large male variance and different gender ability levels further, specifically with respect to mathematics. Two standardized examinations, the SAT-M (the mathematics section of the Scholastic Assessment Test) and the GRE-Q (the quantitative section of the Graduate Record Examination), are examined. Also, students were demarcated into two samples: high ability and average ability individuals. Gallagher et al. (2000) continues the deductive trend of the articles presented in this literature review: in a Piagetian-like approach, the problems of the SAT-M and GRE-Q are broken down into two kinds: concrete and abstract. The more concrete problems are shown to favor females, and the more abstract queries are shown to generally favor males.

The studies in Gallagher et al. (2000) also differentiated problem-solving strategy use by gender. "Specifically, female students were more likely than male students to correctly solve conventional problems using algorithmic [step-by-step] strategies; male students were more likely than female students to correctly solve unconventional problems using logical estimation or insight" (Gallagher et al., 2000, p. 167). Marked gender divisions were also discovered in types of problem presentation; males generally were stronger in multiple-choice questions, and females tended to do better than males in the free response format. The implication that strategy use may be directly related to gender in mathematical ability is explored further by Gallagher and De Lisi (1994). Only high ability students are examined. In addition, the SAT-M is the exclusive math examination employed in this study. Instead of classifying solution strategies into the dichotomous concrete and abstract categories as Gallagher et al. (2000) does, Gallagher and De Lisi (1994) enumerate a comprehensive list of strategy types including, but not limited to, algorithmic; insight with an algorithm; logic, estimation, or insight; plug in options; and guessing. Males excelled at unconventional problems, because they utilized more appropriate flexible problem-solving strategies (such as logic, estimation, or insight), and females generally did better at the more conventional problems using algorithmic methods.

The study by Gallagher and De Lisi (1994) also examined, broadly, affective qualities in gender differences in mathematics. The use of conventional strategies in solving problems was correlated negatively with positive feelings about the subject. Since females tended to employ more conventional strategies while solving problems from the SAT-M, females' attitudes toward mathematics were generally more negative than males' attitudes.

Honing in even more specifically on the reasons why males tend to excel on certain parts of the SAT-M, Casey, Nuttall, Pezaris, and Benbow (1995) examined spatial ability by gender and its influence on test scores; three-dimensional mental rotation was the skill investigated. With females, mental rotation ability was strongly correlated with mathematical aptitude. But with males, the variance of spatial ability as a predictor variable in math aptitude was much larger, leading to less significant results. Recall that both Hedges and Nowell (1995) and Gallagher et al. (2000) observed larger variances in male achievement in the school subjects tested. Interestingly, gender differences in the SAT-M were eliminated when the mental rotation ability variable was statistically adjusted. Casey et al. (1995) suggest that mental rotation ability may be the key "underlying mechanism for the pattern of relationships and gender differences" in the SAT-M (p. 704).

Finally, taking both spatial skills and affect a step further, Casey, Nuttall, and Pezaris (1997) attempted to find the most fundamental properties of the gender discrepancies in the SAT-M. Casey et al. (1997) note that self-confidence (but not math anxiety) and spatial ability contribute most or all of the male advantage in the SAT-M. Although self-confidence is a strong contributor to the advantage, mental rotation was found to be twice as influential of a variable. Synthesizing some other results, Casey et al. (1997) makes the case that a greater aptitude in spatial ability allows more unorthodox and non-algorithmic strategies to be utilized by students. This, in turn, leads to more problem-solving flexibility, more self-confidence, and better results. Thus, since males appear to have the advantage in spatial ability, they ultimately have the advantage in SAT-M problem solving.

Despite the publication dates, the articles selected follow a very clear deductive (general to more specific) line of reasoning. Moreover, the studies, taken as a whole, suggest two interrelated ideas: fundamental gender differences in mathematical ability exist, yet the differences can be narrowed to several key elements. Casey et al. (1997) even claims that the differences in spatial ability could be eliminated through interventions at a young age (more emphasis with females playing with blocks, etc.). Therefore, unsurprisingly, none of the studies reviewed directly answer the question, Are there differences in mathematical ability caused exclusively by gender? Yet, the articles all discriminate various degrees of gender variations in mathematical ability. In doing so, some of them at once support and contradict each other.

As an example, consider Stumpf and Stanley (1996), Gallagher and De Lisi (1994), and Casey et al. (1997). Stumpf and Stanley (1996) make the case that participation of males in tests stereotyped as female-orientated and participation of females in tests more commonly stereotyped as male-orientated has resulted in more appropriate samples to measure gender differences in standardized examinations.* (Recall that the Stumpf and Stanley [1996] study focused on high school tests analogous to the Advanced Placement exams.) Stumpf and Stanley (1996) also claim that, examining the trends of all the tests scores over a decade, gender differences have narrowed significantly. Social and environmental factors are suggested to be causes of the convergence. As more females filtered into the mathematics Advanced Placement preparatory classes for instance, they amassed more self-confidence and more social acceptance. The Vygotskian approach of environment is evident here.

In Gallagher and De Lisi (1994), participation is noted but not treated as a causal factor. Instead, conventional and unconventional strategies, and their effects on the efficacy on problem solving and attitude, are examined. Gender (unwittingly) dictates the type of problem-solving strategy to be used. There is literally no individual control over the problem-solving strategies. In essence, according to Gallagher and De Lisi (1994), the strategies employed, and thus aptitude in mathematics, cannot be altered by environmental effects (environmental effects influence aptitude in Stumpf and Stanley [1996]) or individual will. Instead, strategy use, and by inference mathematical achievement, is static.

Casey et al. (1997) assumes a different, third argument, about the malleability of mathematical aptitude. Acknowledging the impact of the environment and spatial ability, the dynamic nature of both is demonstrated by Casey et al. (1997). Therefore, according to this

* Could so-called stereotype threat, arrived at by Claude Steele, where females are primed ahead of the test with negative characteristics of their gender's ability vis-à-vis mathematics (wittingly or not), be a contributing factor to the discrepancies in math scores? It is certainly something worth considering.

model, the individual male or female has at least a modicum of control (or agency) over his or her aptitude in mathematics. Although the extrinsic-versus-none-versus-intrinsic control of mathematical aptitude is not a perfect fit in describing the top-down theoretical frameworks of all the articles examined in this literature review, it nevertheless serves as a fair description.

The female-concrete and male-abstract tendencies discovered in several of the articles are also notable, because they point to a (perhaps) fundamental difference in mathematical reasoning due to gender. However, the methods to ascertain the strategies used by students are very problematic. In the Gallagher et al. (2000) study, male and female individuals were asked, while solving problems, to "think aloud" (p. 168); the students were audio taped during the "think aloud" problem-solving sessions. Later, after transcribing the audiotapes and considering their contents, the researchers placed the individuals' types of problem-solving strategies into different groups. The construction of the taxonomy, and the assignment of the male and female students into those groups, seems somewhat arbitrary.

For example, an "algorithm strategy" is defined as the following: "Solutions that consist primarily of computational strategies generally taught in school" (Gallagher et al., 2000, p. 170). First of all, how can Gallagher et al. (2000) be entirely sure that all or even some of the algorithms placed into this category are appropriate? In addition, not all computational strategies taught in school are necessarily entirely computational; some strategies may involve some insight (and the very fact that a student chooses to use one algorithm over another displays insight). A mélange of algorithmic strategies may have been used by the student, and perhaps the strategies may have been combined in creative and outstanding ways (perhaps even some of the students had synesthesia, confounding the study's results); yet, because of the definitions in the study of the types of strategies, this creativity will be overlooked.

Also, I call into question the recitation of the problem-solving methods by the students. Surely the students do not have the same depth or experience in metacognitive demarcation as Gallagher et al. (2000) or other researchers have. Therefore, the students may falsely interpret solution strategies, thereby rendering data invalid or questionable. Even the exclusive use of high ability students (as in the first part of the research) does not rule this out as a concern.

The tests of spatial ability (mental rotation ability) in Casey et al. (1995, 1997) also are highly questionable. Because both articles' premises—that spatial ability is significantly different by gender (and is a direct cause of gender differences in scores on the SAT-M)—are dependent on demonstrating true gender spatial ability differences, I find it disturbing that the actual empirical testing and grading for the skill is so briefly examined. With the exception of a single example of what questions on the spatial examination look like (in Casey et al. [1995, 1997]), no further detail is provided. Without appropriate documentation, it is difficult for a reader to have any more than the most general idea of what the researchers are describing as "spatial ability."

Several articles also measure affective and attitudinal attributes in mathematics among male and female students. In Gallagher and De Lisi (1994), affective variables are not used in constructing the thesis of the female-concrete-versus-male-abstract dichotomy of problem solving. They are merely framed at the end of the argument to suggest possible causes for the use of conventional schemata, and, conversely, to suggest that poor attitudes toward math are caused by the use of conventional strategies.

But in Casey et al. (1997), measured affective traits are designed to support the thesis that both mental rotational abilities and self-confidence are comprehensive predictors of mathematical aptitude. The "math self-confidence" variable is treated like any other empirically measured variable in the article, despite the fact that the tools and methodology used to gather affective responses are not present. Affect is not described as simply an artifact of test results in Casey et al. (1997), nor is it pulled from another source. Therefore, since the conclusions from the article rely so heavily on a connection between affect and mental rotation ability, and it is not clear how the affective or attitudinal was differentiated, the results suggesting the gender differences must be questioned.

A latent paradigm is kept alive in all of the articles, namely, that there are gender differences in mathematical ability. Although the articles do not entirely agree on what exactly those differences are, and if they are indeed caused by qualities specific to gender and not environmental treatment of gender or self-perception related to gender (or stereotype threat), they all conclude that there is a significant correlation between gender and mathematical ability. Because several studies discussed here connect possible environmental-gender correlates, these correlates should be mentioned briefly.

Gallagher and De Lisi (1994) state, "[F]emale students are more likely than male students to use solution strategies provided by the teacher and, as a result, are less likely to do well on novel problems for which they have not learned a specific solution strategy" (p. 210). Note that this directly relates back to the Gallagher et al. (2000) definition of the algorithmic strategy: a problem-solving method which is taught in class. It also relates to the Stumpf and Stanley (1996) discussion of more females entering science/mathematics classes in the sense that the more algorithmic strategies can be assimilated by females (because as more females enter these Advanced Placement classes, they become more common and more comfortable in the classes), the better (to a point) females do in the examinations. This was offered by Stumpf and Stanley (1996) as a possible explanation for why females' scores significantly improved in the mathematical sciences during the time period measured in their study.

Gallagher et al. (2000) mentions the possibility that the gender-skewed results may be flexible with proper strategy training. If problem solving—and a demonstration of the differences between abstract and concrete problem solving—was a more stressed element of mathematics curricula, Gallagher et al. (2000) argues, then perhaps females would equal or even surpass males in most kinds of math problems on standardized tests like the SAT-M.

An application, then, for professionals in the field of teaching mathematics to high school students would be to demonstrate a plethora of mathematical problem-solving strategies. Perhaps if all students had more exposure to different kinds of strategies, they would make appropriate use of them; also, students require a "playground" of sorts in the classroom with math. They should not be afraid to utilize the concrete (or conventional) algorithms or the abstract (or unconventional) strategies to solve a problem. A student's access to experimentation, and a mathematics teacher's role as a facilitator, not a sage on the stage, should better propagate the playground with which to try out various methods on different problems. According to Gallagher and De Lisi (1994) and Casey et al. (1997), higher levels of confidence and persistence were associated with the employment of more divergent, abstract problem solving. If this type of problem solving is promoted properly in the classroom, then students should experience an increase in confidence and positive feelings toward the subject. Also, if spatial ability (mental rotation ability) is consistently demonstrated to be a strong cause of the gender variance in SAT-M scores, then activities that strengthen spatial ability should be promoted, starting even in elementary school. Females' success at standardized tests (such as the SAT-M) must be promoted in classes because of the future consequences of the test scores, such as college admissions and job opportunities.

For now, though, further research must be performed to determine the nature of the gender differences in more detail. As repeatedly mentioned, the importance of spatial ability must be confirmed to a stronger degree. Also, affective concerns must be measured and studied. How strong of a factor is attitude? Can attitude truly be improved by having students use abstract problem-solving methods (this was only inferred in several articles)? Students participating in a study that asks them to talk about their solution strategies should be made aware of the metacognitive analyzing methods used by the researchers. Perhaps the students could better refine their own dialogue detailing solution methods.

Other studies need to examine more causes behind the types of strategies used. Also, do parents play a role in strategy use? do teachers? do other students? Finally, a fundamental question must be answered: Are there inherent physiological/neurological differences between males and females that, acting in concert, can be said to cause these mathematical differences in the first place?* If the mathematical discrepancy is rooted in genetics (or epigenetics), then the process of improving mathematical scores may need to be approached from an entirely different perspective.

(2001)

---

* Of course, this is the intractable nature versus nurture argument, originated by Sir Francis Galton. As described in the amazing book *The Lady Tasting Tea* (2001), Galton was fascinated with heredity and inheritance. One of the many data sets he studied was that of the heights of children of really short couples and of really tall couples. Galton noticed that these heights tended to what he called "regress" toward the mean height of the entire population (otherwise we'd have only really tall and really short people in the population).

## REFERENCES


Casey, M. B., Nuttall, R., & Pezaris, E. (1997). Mediators of gender differences in mathematics college entrance test scores: A comparison of spatial skills with internalized beliefs and anxieties. Developmental Psychology, 33(4), 669-680.

Casey, M. B., Nuttall, R., Pezaris, E., & Benbow, C. P. (1995). The influence of spatial ability on gender differences in mathematics college entrance test scores across diverse samples. Developmental Psychology, 31(4), 697-705.

Gallagher, A. M., & De Lisi, R. (1994). Gender differences in scholastic aptitude test – Mathematics problem solving among high-ability students. Journal of Educational Psychology, 86(2), 204-211.

Gallagher, A. M., De Lisi, R., Holst, P. C., McGillicuddy-De Lisi, A. V., Morely, M., & Cahalan, C. (2000). Gender differences in advanced mathematical problem solving. Journal of Experimental Child Psychology, 75. 165-190.

Hedges, L. V., & Nowell, A. (1995). Sex differences in mental test scores, variability, and numbers of high-scoring individuals. Science, 269. 41-45.

Stumpf, H., & Stanley, J. C. (1996). Gender-related differences on the College Board's Advanced Placement and achievement tests, 1982-1992. Journal of Educational Psychology, 88(2), 353-364.

# 18.

## Three Theories of Education in the Mathematics Classroom

The three major theoretical positions of education—psychoanalytic, behavioral, and humanistic—each, albeit with widely different approaches, conceptualizes a system or model based on "axioms" (or rules) to explain human behavior. Two of them, the humanistic and behavioral approaches, are nearly opposites. The behaviorist approach is predicated on apparent causes to predict responses irrespective of the individual, while the humanist approach searches for meaning and motivation based on individuality. Examining only hypothetical situations, the efficacy of the humanistic view seems strong; however, empirically, the behaviorist view, although perhaps dependent on too many generalities about the homogeneity of behavioral responses, might be the most effective methodology to adapt in the classroom.

Humanistic theory is grounded in a set of positive ideas and ideals. Developed as a reaction to the other two existing popular positions, its overriding impetus is in the recognition of the personal, the individual, and the ability to chose. Essentially, "[humanistic theory] stresses not so much people's biological drives as their goals; not so much their past experiences as their current circumstances; and not so much environmental forces as perceptions of those forces" (from the book *Psychology in Teaching, Learning and Growth, 5th ed.,* by Hamachek, p. 26). There is the inherent assumption of faith in the individual in this theory—a person can intrinsically determine his own "self" and the consciousness that follows without extrinsic environmental stimulants dictating "correct" perceptions. In other words, the freedom to interpret, integrate, differentiate, and dissect external experience is permitted for each individual.

There are five basic assumptions of humanistic theory. The assumptions are not dogmatic rules, but rather general guiding ideas mostly resembling a sort of catalog of philosophical thought: Humans are sentient creatures; they have the freedom of choice; they have interpersonal relations that define them; they are more than just mere biomechanical units; and they have purposeful intent. In addition, and somewhat paradoxically, implicit is that humans cannot be specifically described by any strict rules at all: the definitions have a purposeful inclusiveness (meaning the assumptions do not discriminate or divide people into various groups) and generality. But they offer no clear methods to dissect human behavior. The ambiguity of the definitions is so great that each person subscribing to the five principles will likely have a different view of what they mean, compounding the ambiguity of the definitions even more. Continuing this line of reasoning, some of the criticisms associated with humanistic theory are apparent: a free-for-all results when "implementing" the postulates outside of the theoretical framework in which they are based, resulting in little empirical value.

For instance, consider a high school classroom. Since the self (the self-concept) is the root of the theory, it becomes the teacher's prerogative to understand each student's perceptions of himself and environment in order to be effective *for that particular student.* Certainly the motivations behind the humanistic theory are well intentioned; for the teacher to have knowledge about what works best with each of his pupils is a great asset. But the goal is especially unrealistic because of the time and energy demands exerted upon the teacher. Since the student-to-teacher ratios in typical public high schools are around thirty-to-one, the teacher is simply outnumbered—he cannot teach the lesson and explore each person's intrinsic interpretations of sentience, interpersonal qualities, and relationships with the school environment, especially in a single class period or block. In addition, many students do not wish to be exposed to a "psyche dissection," further complicating the teacher's efforts to understand the individual.

Another issue with the implementation of the theory in schools arises: the students' ability to be conscious of and engaged in a diversity of possibilities. "[T]hrough their [the students'] capacity to make choices they will develop the sense of self necessary..." (Hamachek, p. 31). The unmentioned element of experience plays a key role in determining the ever-changing perceptions of all people, including students. Therefore, to state arbitrarily that students can determine the best methods of learning for them (intrinsically, within the self) seems misguided. Indeed, students will develop self-concepts in part because of their choices over time.

But to claim that students even know that choices in certain situations exist and that they can benefit from them to create a sense of self (and assist the humanistic-orientated teacher in teaching them) assigns too much responsibility to the students—and the pressure of responsibility to learn one's self might *itself* be detrimental to establishing the sense of identity in the students. In a geometry class, for example, to probe students about how they best understand proofs—visual or written—before they even learn proofs is self-defeating to both the student and the teacher. (The teacher will present the proofs incorrectly to some students, and the students will unnecessarily have extra struggles understanding the material.) Although the humanistic theory initially seems like a commonsense approach to conceptualizing human behavior, the flaws and fallacies of the approach probably outweigh any pragmatic value.

Unlike humanistic theory, behavioristic theory emphasizes pragmatism. Behavioristic theory is based on empiricism—how people react to environmental stimuli, not how they feel about those stimuli, is the core issue. The theory, formed largely by John B. Watson, describes environmental impacts on human behavior. "[T]he proper starting point for understanding people is through the study of *behavior*—what they do, not what they think or feel" (Hamachek, p. 17). Predicting effect based on cause is at the root of the theory; intrinsic motivations behind actions take a back seat.

Conditioning takes the behavioristic theory off of the pages of texts and into observable reality—something that, as mentioned earlier, the humanistic approach cannot do effectively. Behavior that is positive or "has a satisfying effect" (as Hamachek puts it) will be learned by the individual; behavior that has consequences or negative effects is less likely to be learned.

Classical conditioning is really a type of training. For example, a psychologist might "train" an individual to fear speaking if that person were given electric shocks every time he vocalizes anything (an extreme example, obviously).* Immediate results in a laboratory

---

* Maybe not. Recall Stanley Milgram's psychology experiments on obedience, or Walter Mischel's marshmallow experiments. Psychologists love coming up with perverse experimental conditions; this was well satirized in the films *The Five-Year Engagement* and *Ghostbusters* (speaking of marshmallows…). In

probably would be observed—the person under observation simply would not speak. But when the behavior (in this case, silence) is not reinforced (when the person who reinforces the behavior is no longer present), "extinction"—the technical term—of the behavior may eventually result. In this example, when the person finishes the test and is free of the electric shocks "programming" him, he will most likely begin speaking again. Pavlov's dogs would be proud (well, only if they had been conditioned to be proud).

The other type of conditioning in behavioristic psychology is termed operant conditioning. Operant conditioning "involves a selection, from many responses, of the one that habitually will be given in a stimulus situation" (Hamachek, p. 20). The conditioning is dependent on appropriate behaviors within the environmental context to achieve rewards or punishments. Back to the classroom: if a teacher rewards students with praise whenever they operate correctly in a learning environment (e.g., answer a problem correctly, behave appropriately and consistently, or maintain regular attendance), they will be likely to engage in the behavior again. The result of the reinforcement is observable and not ambiguous; the students are conditioned to responses that net them reward.

There are two kinds of reinforcements: positive and negative. Positive reinforcement is geared toward gaining something positive from a behavior, while negative reinforcement is predicated upon avoidance of negative consequences. Put simply, positive reinforcement has a net gain for the individual while negative reinforcement has a net loss for the individual.*

---

addition, psychologists enjoy naming rather obvious biases. A random example: the "availability heuristic." There should be a named bias for their propensity to slap a name on every perceived bias.

* Studying the effects of positive and negative reinforcements is not so simple due to a tricky statistical concept called "regression toward the mean," probably first noticed by Francis Galton while investigating heredity. The behavioral economists Amos Tversky and Daniel Kahneman also studied regression toward the mean, finding it among cadet pilots in the air force. Frequently, after a good landing, a cadet is praised—and his next landing isn't as good. And after a bad landing, a cadet is reamed out—and his next landing is better. Although these results, taken together, would seem to suggest that positive reinforcement isn't effective while negative reinforcement is, rather, these results illustrate regression toward the mean: a natural tendency to "go backward," or regress, to the mean value of the population.

Of course, in behavioristic theory the idea of personal freedom, so stressed in humanistic psychology, is a non-factor. Free will does not exist in behaviorism; every person's behavior is merely a product of a variety of responses dependent on environmental conditions. The theory dehumanizes people. Individuals are treated as homogeneous computers to be fed a program; input the data, describe the variables, and a predictable output follows. (This recalls the determinism of Laplace's demon.) The results of using the behavioristic approach, while sometimes quite effective, raise ethical concerns. Does authority reside with one person or a group of people to deliberately control the environment to invoke responses? How can a behavior be intrinsically motivated once the "experiment" is complete? Can human behavior be so simplified and predicted that the actual responses we are seeing from stimuli are definitively caused *by* those stimuli? Does behavioristic psychology revoke a person's freedom, or does the individual have a choice whether or not to respond to the environmental controls?* In what learning situations is it appropriate for a stimulus-response system to be used?

Operant conditioning is, on a very general level, behavioral conditioning. Electric shocks or other negative stimuli afflicted on a student if he fails to answer a problem correctly are obviously not possible nor desirable in a high school classroom; this would probably lead to negative reinforcement, or the avoidance of the pain—i.e., not coming to class at all. Restricting our attention to just the mathematics classroom in high school, should the student "operate" correctly in the mathematical world presented, he would receive positive reinforcements.

An argument against the approach is that it fails to instill intrinsically a desire to learn mathematics beyond the external motivators of carrots and sticks. However, it seems that a technical subject such as mathematics is tough to present in a way that both motivates the mass of students on an intrinsic level and teaches them appropriate procedures on an extrinsic one. At the risk of entering into a debate about the nature of teaching math, I will say that a behavioristic approach of stimulus-response is the best a teacher

---

* And if the person does have such a choice to be conditioned, to be programmed, then doesn't that render behaviorist conditioning no more than a parlor game?

could hope to achieve with nearly all of his students on a secondary mathematics level.

Let me illustrate my point with another example from a geometry class. Assume proofs have been presented for the first time and that the high school students are just starting to get accustomed to their rigid logic and syntax. It is early January, midterms will be given in two weeks, and the curriculum states that students must be proof-ready before the midterm. Suppose there are thirty students per class. Taking all these real-world conditions into account, a behavioristic approach might be the most effective. There is nary enough time to gauge the intrinsic understanding and motivations of all or even some of the students.

Math has little "gray area"; the subject, at least on the level of high school geometry, is such that statements can (almost) always be shown to be either true or false (there is little debating in high school mathematics as there would be in, say, social studies). (It is somewhat ironic that the high school subject most removed from the real world is probably best taught using the most empirical, real-world system.) Even without the added time constraints mentioned in the above example, a certain amount of mathematics must be covered before the end of the school year—that's simply the reality of teaching. The pragmatic value of the behavioristic theory is that the approaches of conditioning and stimulus-response likely work on greater numbers of people faster than the ambiguous and ambitious postulates of humanistic theory: The two theories are a clash between optimism and realism. The humanistic approach is a cluster of sentimental elements without a structured, rigorous methodology grounded in science or the scientific method. The behavioristic theory describes tools that work (to a certain degree) to allow for students' progress, even if those students tend to find the subject perfunctory. Perhaps as a teacher subscribed to a more humanistic viewpoint, I could get a minority of my students over time to intrinsically develop good mathematical skills, with a large portion of my time devoted to a small number of students' feelings toward learning. But as a behavioristic teacher, a majority of my students could achieve at least some competence in mathematics, depressingly the most realistic objective possible.

(2000)

# 19.

## Synthesizing a Model of Pedagogy

Humans might be thought of as *infinite* creatures. Their synthesis of the biological and mechanical is beyond mere complexity; their nervous systems interact on a level simultaneously discrete and continuous with the rest of the body. Intelligence is result of these interactions: it is an ill-defined concept that gives impetus for sentient functionality. Several theorists have proposed models for conceptualizing human intelligence. Spearman, in 1927, famously suggested that intelligence is based on general and specific factors; intelligence is the resultant of two variables' interactions, according to Guilford (1967); and in 1985, Sternberg proposed the most contemporary model: the three major components of intelligence. But these panoply of theories are not mutually exclusive; taken together, they offer a comprehensive and panoramic description of intelligence.

Beginning with Spearman's conceptualization, we immediately note the superficial simplicity of his argument. The theorist claims that intelligence is a hierarchy of factors: one general (*g*) factor and multiple specific (*s*) factors. The *g* factor functions as a reserve base of intellectual power for the variety of mental tasks an individual must perform. Since it is not a specialized intelligence element, the general factor is used to perceive high-level associations and connections. To accomplish a multiplicity of tasks, *s* factors are utilized; they are factors especially engendered to handle specialization. Some people may have high *s* factors in mental arithmetic, for instance, while others could be quite skilled in reading or mentally "hearing" music on paper.

Two significant assumptions about human intelligence are advocated in the Spearman model. First, the theory suggests that every individual has a finite amount of intelligence. In other words, humans are limited intellectually. It is interesting to note how much this assumption resembles modern computing theory. All computers have a finite (countable, not infinite) quantity of memory. The memory can store discrete bits of information in varying proportions. For example, two different computers starting with the same amount of free memory might be used in different respects: one computer could contain a mass of image files and the other might have a virtual storehouse of audio files.

Spearman's theory does not imply that all people begin with the same quantity of "memory" (intelligence) with which to divide up into varying *s* factors. Nevertheless, he does claim that two individuals with an equal amount of the general factor can have varying proportions of *s* factors (with the "sum" of the two individuals' specific factors equivalent in value). The theory lends credence to a commonsense notion many people have about intelligence: that people immensely talented in different areas (Einstein in theoretical physics and Chopin in piano composition, for instance) might be equally intelligent, albeit in different disciplines.

Second, the model is built on a framework of simple hierarchy. As the 1995 Hamachi text *Psychology in Teaching, Learning and Growth, 5th ed.*, explains, "Usually…the more *g* factor a person has, the more *s* factors are at his or her command" (p. 138). To illustrate the concept, let us create two hypothetical frameworks: assume that Person X is of average intelligence and Person Y is on a genius level. Person X has a smaller *g* factor than Person Y. Person X has fewer *s* factors than Person Y does as well; an intellectual hierarchy removed from the individuals themselves is present. At the lower, average level, Person X's *g* factor (which contains the specific factors "branching" off from it. The general factor supplies the *s* factors with intelligence from a reserve storehouse of intellectual power) has less "mass" and thus less dependents can be formed from it. Person Y has a more massive general factor than Person X, so he has more room for the dependent "branches" of the *s* factors. Effectively, if a person's general factor has a large mass, then there are a great number of *s* factors.

This model is adept at conceptualizing overarching notions about intelligence. It is simple, yet it allows for great latitude and complexity in application; nearly everyone's skills can be justified with Spearman's system. Also, it attempts to submit reasoning for why some people have different distributions of intellect, yet appear equally smart: because of different specific factors. The theory does not pigeonhole intellectual ability, either. Unlike Thurstone's system for instance, which enumerates seven rigid categories for intelligence (which Thurstone assumes are mutually exclusive but in reality overlap and are not exhaustive by any means), Spearman's model takes into account a literally infinite number of intelligences in an infinite number of combinations. The Spearman system is not necessarily useful in testing or measuring intelligence because it allows for a huge amount of diversity. However, it is effective in resolving general patterns of intellectual ability because of its latitude in defining different kinds of intelligence.

Guilford's model complements Spearman's in the sense that elements of intelligence progress from general to specific. However, unlike the Spearman's theory, the Guilford conception treats intelligence as a series of ever-changing causes and effects. The "structure-of-intellect" model is complex only because of the magnitude of combinations of interactions of intelligence. The model is best described in visual form, as shown in *Psychology in Teaching, Learning and Growth* (figure 5.1, p. 141). Two variables are inputted in the model: what we think about and how we think about it. The interaction of the two variables produces a result. There are five operations (the way we think) and four contents (how we think). The results of each of the twenty possible variable interactions (five multiplied by four) are restricted to six different products, making the total number of cognitive abilities equal to 120 (twenty multiplied by six). Although many of the labels for the three dimensions of possibilities are ambiguous ("systems," "cognition," and "units" are good examples of this), the system as a whole has merit—it suggests that there are quantifiable processes inherent in thought.

Especially significant are the convergent-divergent properties of the mental-operations variable. Convergent thinking "focuses on one answer or solution," while divergent thinking "explores new possibilities" (Hamachek, p. 140). Although the difference between convergent and divergent thinking is not quite akin to the difference between non-creative and creative abilities (and does not imply that a person with little divergent thinking will not be creative), solutions to problems will likely be more conservative using convergent thought.

This model is especially effective because it describes the minute-to-minute, second-to-second cognitive processes of the mind. Instead of talking about overall types of intelligence, as Spearman's theory does, the Guildford model paints a picture of intellectual operations. It attempts to describe a cognitive "motor"—fuel enters in (the operations and contents), and out comes the energy to drive the mind (the products). The three dimensions are dependent on an implied fourth—time—with which to allow the processing of the information into products. Of course this is a realistic conception, since all thought requires time.

Synthesizing Guilford's and Spearman's theories, we discover that the three-dimensional structure-of-intellect model details the processes and mechanisms of the *s* factors of intelligence. An analogy to explain the meaning of this linkage of models is necessary: consider the Spearman theory to be a "low-magnification" image of intelligence, and the Guilford model to be a "higher magnification" display of intelligence. More detail is apparent in the Guildford conceptualization, but the overall picture of intelligence is not as clear (as it is in Spearman's system) because the "magnification" of our "object," intelligence, has increased. Think of the structure-of-intellect model like imaginary gears and pulleys that propel the *s* factors in Spearman's model.

Accepting this synthesis as reasonable, to make our composite intelligence model truly functional a third theory must be added. Specific factors derive from general factors, and the Guilford model motivates specific factors. The *s* factors, however, have no structure or classifications; they simply randomly "dangle" from the *g* factor. Grouping the *s* factors by type into a series of classes is accomplished with the Sternberg theory.

Sternberg's model is the most contemporary of the three, originating in 1985. It also is the closest to empiricism in the sense that it recognizes that not everyone intelligent has a rapid mind; the argument states, "[b]righter people tend to be more reflective in their efforts to understand the terms and parameters of problems," which can take a great deal of time (Hamachek, p. 144).

Intelligence is a triad of components for Sternberg. The first type is componential intelligence (analytic intelligence): the aptitude people exhibit in taking tests (e.g., Graduate Record Exam, Scholastic Aptitude Test, Medical Boards, etc.) connects with this area. This is the "uncreative" intelligence; it is the application of deductive or inductive reasoning with existing facts and information to process the data to form somewhat standard and predictable general or specific results. Students with high grade point averages in school tend to have a high degree of this analytic intelligence.

The second kind of intelligence is given the moniker of experiential, meaning a creative form of intellect. This is also based on the use of inductive and deductive reasoning but in a much more creative fashion. Individuals with experiential intelligence tend to be the artists and artisans, physicists and mathematicians (not actuaries or accountants, though; those professions require a much more componential form of reasoning), writers and musicians, teachers and professors. The classification of experiential intelligence is divided into three parts. Selective encoding, or the ability to pick out and concentrate on critical information; selective combination, or the combining of disparate pieces of information together to inductively construct larger relationships; and selective comparison, or the ability to reexamine and reinterpret something's functionality compose the triad of experiential intelligence. Each part of experiential intelligence has different means to achieve the same end of creativity.

Contextual intelligence is the third type of intelligence in Sternberg's model. It is the practical, commonsense, real-world kind of intelligence. Essentially, these are street smarts. People good with interpersonal relationships and negotiation skills have a high level of contextual ability. Politicians tend to have extremely high levels of this intelligence, but then so might con artists or businesspeople. Of the three categories of intelligence in this model, this one is the most difficult to quantify since it is the least academic in nature.

Although the model does pigeonhole types of intelligence, it is encompassing enough and exhaustive enough to account for almost everyone. (Although it admittedly is much more specific in defining aspects of intelligence than the Spearman model by not enumerating all academic qualities, as Thurstone's model does, the theory correctly accounts for more than just book smarts.) Also, the model is very effective in casting a template for the design of a fair and encompassing intelligence test. While a Thurstone or even a Gardner methodology would design questions testing each person's aptitude in seven basic subject areas (numerical ability, musical intelligence, etc.), a Sternberg-based examination, which would not be subject-specific, could test how an individual synthesizes and deduces from information presented.

Reexamining our composite model of pedagogy, the Sternberg system gives general classification to the multitude of *s* factors. For example, if a person has most *s* factors in musical ability, we could argue (although perhaps I am stretching the limits of the models in combining them this way) that all of that individual's music *s* factors are grouped in experiential intelligence. If another person was, say, an extremely popular and likeable person in whatever environment he was in (but was not particularly academically talented), we could claim that most of his *s* factors were located in the contextual intelligence group. And if a third person was a medical doctor, he perhaps had a strong concentration of *s* factors in the componential area. Furthermore, the competence of the persons just described (the musician, the likable individual, and the doctor) could be the direct result of the mass or size of their general factors (recall that the more massive the general factor, the more *s* factors are possible, according to Spearman). The minute-to-minute functions of the different *s* factors of these individuals in their Sternberg model categories of ability are well described by Guilford.

Although I have only examined these three theoretical viewpoints of intelligence on a limited scale, the ease at which they mold themselves together and complement each other is astonishing; intelligence viewed as a combination of these three models describes an inherently dependent and complex and infinite "universe" *within* each individual. (After all, as physicist Michio Kaku and others have detailed, the human brain is the most complex object in the universe.) In addition, all of these "universes" are dissimilar, despite the fact that they rely on the same components. The notions of intelligence are so difficult to measure that a true test to quantify people's intellectual skills, whatever they may be (or however they are defined), will likely never come to pass.

(2000)

# 20.

## The New World and Education: A Historical Perspective

The notions of "government" and "influence" are both structured in dynamism; essentially, what is considered to be influential—in a positive, negative, or neutral sense—is constantly being reinterpreted and redefined through a temporal lens, and the historical foundations of government also are continuously reanalyzed in an analogous sense. The difficulty, in the analysis of history, is in the negotiation of an effective balance between a formulation of history with underpinnings in the past and in the present, according to Edward Carr in his classic text *What is History?* Nevertheless, the conceptions and interplay of government and influence, though always in a process of revision, can be contemplated in a discourse about American education—as long as we are cognizant of the historical basis for the arguments.

For example, consider the influence of government during the pre-Revolutionary era as discussed by Ellwood Cubberley in *Public Education in the United States*: The colonies were divided into a triad based on two essential features, space (land distribution) and immigrants' origin, and the governments—of the Massachusetts/Puritan area (New England), the middle colonies (such as Pennsylvania), and the southern colonies (for example, Virginia)—operated in virtual independence of each other; their perpetuation is explained by the author as mostly rooted in the import of Old World ideas from the immigrants who settled in the particular locales.

Cubberley presents the past as a series of finite-length conflicts between opposing ideas or forces, one of which more closely correlates with both a chronological impression of "progress" and a present-day paradigm—and that particular idea or force unambiguously "wins" the historical conflict and is allowed to perpetuate. The Christians' ideas physically and metaphysically conquered the Romans' and the Greeks' methodologies; the Protestants forced the Catholics into capitulation in the long run in terms of an educational structure, since "[u]nder the new theory of individual responsibility promulgated by the Protestants the education of all became a vital necessity," as Cubberley explains; and the system of education propagated by the Puritans and the New England colonies directly resulted in the public school pedagogy currently present—because in some overarching ways, such as the mandatory placement of schools in communities with certain numbers of people (by judicature, with The Old Deluder Satan Act), the dissemination of standard texts to students (such as the *New England Primer*), and other broad features Cubberley enumerates, the Puritan's society of learning is vaguely reminiscent of education in contemporary times.

Contrary to Cubberley, Joel Spring, in *The American School, 1642-1996*, promulgates a discourse of near-malignant deliberateness to the government's influence over public schools, and of the formation of public schools in general; whereas the former views government (and society) in the past as having a penchant for rooting out "inappropriate" ideas and ideals—inappropriate to the sense of "progress," or inconsistent with the current state of educational and societal affairs (since the current times, in Cubberley's linear analysis, are at an apogee or are an apotheosis of progress)—the latter recognizes the "attempt to ensure the domination of a Protestant Anglo-American culture in the United States," as Spring says. The fear of domination by others outside of the Anglican-Protestant culture led to a series of cultural-homogenization government initiatives in some of the colonies (for instance, the banning of German language documents in Pennsylvania) and a drive to formally recognize the primacy of the English language in the disparate schooling systems by such notable individuals as Benjamin Franklin. "Let the first Class learn the *English* Grammar Rules, and at the same time let particular Care be taken to improve them in *Orthography*," Franklin wrote, in his influential treatise on the proposed curriculum of the English School.

Overlap these two constructions of the influence of government in the American educational milieu—Spring's demonstration of a myopic class ensuring its own perpetuation as the primary reason for much of the methods and structure of the contemporary public school system, and Cubberley's progress-determinism theory—with the more subtle, dialectical approach presented by Kaestle. (Note that even the title of Kaestle's piece, "Between the Scylla of Brutal Ignorance and the Charybdis of a Literary Education," explicitly frames a dialectical context metaphorically with a mythical play between opposites.) Kaestle defines government as a passive "arbitrator" between opposition groups, such as conservatives and liberals (however they happen to be designated through time and space), ready to adopt the emerging consensus positions, or dominant positions, as universal schooling became the norm. Examining Kaestle's explanation of the mass schooling debate reveals this back-and-forth struggle between groups: "The vigor of this conservative position [no mass schooling] put advocates of mass schooling on the defensive in the early nineteenth century." Then, he continues, "[b]y 1825 the opponents of mass schooling, not the advocates, were on the defensive." This shift was not caused by government initiatives, or laws, or exploratory programs, but by vigorous non-government collectivist debate and deliberation. Therefore, government, according to Kaestle, did not have a direct influence in the direction of education, but was only responsive to dominating arguments or trends (and the shifting trends may or may not be classified as "progressive" per se—as long as we think of the word progressive in the modern sense, not as in the "Progressive Movement"*).

The historian Gerald Gutek organizes his *An Historical Introduction to American Education* around individuals, some of whom resided in government, who were powerful influences in the direction of American education. He posits that if government did mold the educational system in any way, especially in America's early years (prior to the onset of universal education), it was because of the ingenuity of a select few forward-thinking individuals in the U.S. government. The biographical sections on Mann, Jefferson, Harris (the archetypal superintendent), and others demonstrate this propensity of Gutek's—the author frames his historical theses around individuals and their respective contributions to the educational milieu of America.

So, in summary, the portraits constructed by the historians of government's influence in American education leave much ambiguity: Is the government (and education) driven by an almost deterministic progress, as Cubberly suggests? Or is it what Spring claims:

---

* Take a look at Jonah Goldberg's *Liberal Fascism* for a thorough explication of how the term "progressive" has nefarious connotations throughout American history.

a powerful force dedicated to the homogenization of the young in a Protestant ethic via the public schools? Perhaps it is a passive machine, ready to eventually adopt and implement collectivist notions, as Kaestle explains? Or is Gutek—who frames discussions of history around the influence of progressive individuals, some situated in government—correct? By the mid-twentieth century, the influence and power of the American government over the general course of education is relatively unambiguous: Consider the desegregation of the schools, the curriculum changes as a result of the Soviet's overt scientific progress, and the implementation of landmark laws for the education of children with disabilities (such as Public Law 94-142) as examples. Also, the influx of social experts, the initiating of meritocracy, and the economic-market dictums related to educational activity were all sanctioned and promoted by the government. Although government did have some quantifiable influence recently, it is ultimately unclear how much of an effect it had on education during the United States' "formative" years (i.e., at least prior to the Civil War); consequently, because of the ambiguity, government did not have the biggest overall influence on education.

In contemplating something that could claim the moniker of "the biggest overall influence on education," it is imperative to consider a single circumstance that spawned many changes or had a significant enough impact in the past that the manifestation is strongly correlated with the present makeup of American education. As Bernard Bailyn, in *Education in the Forming of Society: Needs and Opportunities for Study*, notes, the past doesn't necessarily "blend" into the present but is in large part not reconcilable with the present; in other words, the contemporary categorizations or distinctions, as Cubberley envisages them for instance, may be largely invalid since history does not necessarily proceed in a linear, clear line of progression (therefore, notions of determinism or progress are implicitly repudiated by Bailyn because he postulates that history may take many "twists and turns").

Directly criticizing the likes of Cubberley, Bailyn states, "The modern conception of the public education, the very idea of a clean line of separation between 'private' and 'public,' was unknown before the end of the eighteenth century." Thus, the transformation from a largely private to a largely public educational paradigm in America cannot be considered the "most significant event" in the sense searched for, since the private/public distinction was later categorized with the benefit of a retrospect *derived* from the present: "[That] the past could be differentiated from the present mainly by its primitivism, the rudimentary character of the institutions and ideas whose ultimate development," as Bailyn says, were already known, is an erroneous methodology of some historians. Edward Carr also notes a similar pattern of reductivism among certain historians in *What is History?*

However, Bailyn does conceive of a single event that relatively unambiguously shaped the future of education: the adaptation to a new land, since utilitarian purpose was assigned to the pedagogical institution. Because of the move to the New World, according to Bailyn, there was a "rapid breakdown of traditional European society...." This breakdown forced the supplementation of religion, family values, etc., into a new setting: the school. The breakdown was evinced by the laws passed requiring children's obedience to their parents; the loss of prestige due to the menial labor forced on elders; and the new edicts requiring parents to educate their children or face penalties. As Bailyn and others (e.g., Joel Spring) explain, the fear of an anarchy of the young, the loss of values of religious and moral descent, and other unforeseen effects from the transplantation of Old World society to the New World prompted an overriding impetus for stringent levels of control over persons—and that control ultimately became a major basis for the educational system of the United States. And, even more important, the schools—in the difficult, harsh living conditions of the colonies, in which the pragmatic was assigned increasing emphasis—became of a practical use: the transcription and propagation of an indigenous culture. "[E]ducation not only reflects and adjusts to society; once formed, it turns back upon it and acts upon it," Bailyn writes. As the imported Old World educational system adjusted to the new sense of space that the colonists obtained from their transportation to the New World, and also modified itself to accept and indoctrinate other identities or cultures into an homogeneous template, American education—a dynamic entity—gradually shaped and transformed the landscape; through the eventual universality of education, it became a dominating force of influence in our society.

(2001)

# 21.

# Affront to Meritocracy

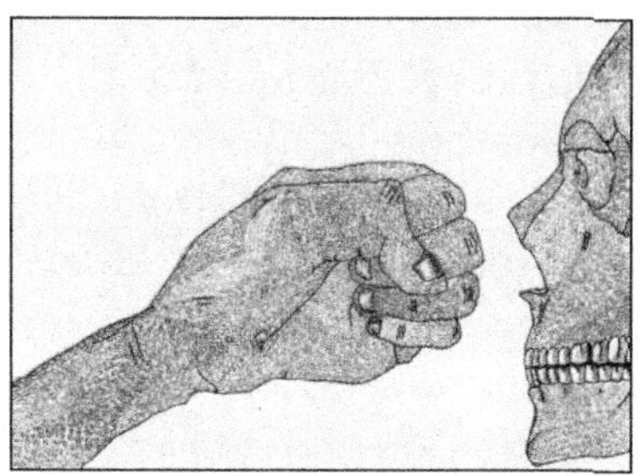

## Grade Inflation in the Early Aughts

"The historian is necessarily selective," according to Edward Carr (1919) in his classic text, *What is History?*, since "a hard core of historical facts existing objectively and independently of the interpretation of the historian is a preposterous fallacy…." In other words, not only overt historical analysis is considered interpretive—a mere arrangement of facts, however seemingly self-evident to the historical context they may be, also betrays a sense of *selection*. Also, causality in a historically engendering format necessitates *construction*—either from the historian, the context, the body politic of the notions, or other latent and manifest factors. Thus, from this enumeration of methodology, two layers of historical propagation emerge: the capturing of "relevant" facts and the contextual linking, associating, and explaining of those facts. It is with tracing some of this interpretive anchor—and the tones and types of rhetoric through a mostly contemporary chronology, since the language in the articles may betray at least an ancillary dynamic epistemology from which some of the implicit reasoning or causality emerges—in the so-called modern conservative media's discourse of grade inflation that I am most concerned.

The media, utilized in this essay, are largely Internet-based. The hegemony of dialect and idea that the Internet contains is astounding and seemingly contradictory to the supposed-penchant the medium has for egalitarian-individualized expression. This hegemony, which therefore perpetuates a mostly homogeneous milieu—by dominance and repeat of facts—works more or less as an initial filter of facts that Carr (1919) discusses: that which is selected, in part because of a tendency to invigorate the reader and maintain interest, achieves primacy over less "stimulating" facts. To label this a "survival of the fittest facts" (in other words, those facts which contain the most interest are the most read and thus gain ascendance over the demonstration of an idea—somewhat through the ubiquity caused by incessant promulgation) is perhaps too simple, clichéd (does everything in life have to be at least metaphorically Darwinian?) and incomplete a comparison. Instead, the process is more analogous to Carr's narrative about the text *Stresemanns Vermächtnis*: the histories and facts present eventually gain dominance because of the unavailability, loss, or undocumented texts of other viewpoints and other facts. That which is extant speaks for the generations.*

Causality functions in an analogous sense. When a historical explanation becomes entrenched in the cosmology of a culture, and present influences thus dictate a sense of the past, conceptions of the past may be transformed—since the past is largely driven and understood by memory.† If the causality of any history, or connections between any set of facts, is ubiquitous in an environment, the burden of proof is on the dissenting historical author to reshape or reinterpret memory and the past from a differing perspective. Since certain ideas (or facts) can be broadcast with both incredible frequency and bulk resulting in other ideas (or facts) to recede into the background or assume an ancillary role, the Internet does not permit the sort of idealistic equal-time discourse that it purports to accommodate.

---

* For a more nefarious view of how historical discourse is made, consider what Edward Said wrote in the *Nation* article "The Public Role of Writers and Intellectuals": "[T]here is a social and intellectual equivalence between [the] mass of overbearing collective interests and the discourse used to justify, disguise or mystify its workings while at the same time preventing objections or challenges to it....They are staples of the dominant discourse, designed to create consent and tacit approval." Said probably goes too far here—serendipity seems just as likely a motivator as backroom conspiracy.

† The Paul Klee painting *Angelus Novus* is a famous visual expression of memory in historical construction; the angel in the artwork perceives and understands the present with the aid of a past that he is literally facing.

Given these suppositions to the exploration and examination of Internet media, *grade inflation* will now be examined. Essentially, grade inflation is a phenomenon that distorts or removes any differentiation between "good" students and "exceptional" students (Mansfield, 2001). Grade inflation is based on norm-referenced grading; in other words, instead of primarily fixed standards (also called criterion-referenced grading), grade inflation operates with a floating standard, or with no obvious standards at all (Jesness, 1999). The phenomenon occurs mostly at educational institutions of higher learning, and specifically, at Ivy League universities such as Harvard (Oppenheim, 2001).

The modern conservative* media's documentation of grade inflation almost invariably presents an antagonistic image of the manifestation. For example, Feulner (2001), writing for the conservative *townhall.com*, states that grade inflation removes accountability from higher institutions, "[a]nd our colleges [thus lose] touch with reality" (p. 1). Beaver (2000) notes a lowering of academic standards supposedly symptomatic with the influx of grade inflation. And Radosh (2000) compares Harvard University to a summer camp: an environment for the instruction of mere socialization skills. The lack of variety in the tone of the media is not to be ignored, since it reconciles with the grounds of homogeneity of rhetoric mentioned earlier—however, it should be noted, the articles and histories obtained are most certainly not comprehensive; a selection of articles (and facts in those articles) was required for this essay.† (Furthermore, the scope of this essay, or the blanket of historical facts that it covers, most certainly does not fully reconcile with the scope of the conservative pieces gathered; there is overlap, but the scope is not inclusive of all factual content of the articles.)

Understanding the ways in which the conservative articles are framed assists in comprehending their assumptions about the natures of grade inflation. The texts read consistently like reactionary pieces, constantly fighting and struggling to emerge from the

---

* Although a trenchant criticism of the essay you're now reading might be that it paints the "conservative movement" with a too large a brush, note that when it comes to the issue of grade inflation there has been surprising widespread and long-standing agreement amongst its diverse factions. A seminal conservative text illustrating this—from a not-quite conservative author—is *The Closing of the American Mind* (1987) by Allan Bloom.

† Shades of Carr's trap that always awaits the would-be historian.

"hole" they find themselves in. In other words, the confluence of material in the conservative texts—overall—assumes a conscription of skepticism on the part of the potential audience/readership engendered by the topics. This quality to the texts underpins the arguments presented: possibly analogous to the responsibilities of a dissenting historical author promulgating conflicting notions (in other words, different from the paradigms), the rhetoric relies on a pragmatic ideology, anathema to wantonness, to shape a holistically logical-sounding plea. But there is also a sense of "struggle," and thus affect, present in much of the discourse—a struggle between a morality fostered in a rose-colored conception of a "moral" past and a less-moral, invariably more liberal* present. (The struggle suffusing the conservative pieces extends to railing against the so-called liberal media itself—as if the fourth estate were a fifth column.)

To make the struggle less abstract, a "hero figure" with maverick qualities is discussed: Harvey Mansfield. Professor Mansfield of Harvard University has been "ticking off liberal colleagues for years," Feulner (2001) explains (p. 1). The professor is described by Oppenheim (2001) in the following light: "[He's] a renowned scholar of political philosophy who has a certain knack for finding trouble" (p. 1). Another article mentions "his [Mansfield's] years of courage in the face of moral intimidation may finally be drawing real blood from his countless foes" (p. 1). This dichotomous individual-versus-unappreciative/ignorant-outsiders philosophy has at least a modicum of precedent with certain histories.

For instance, almost analogous to Gutek (1991), who places a primacy on historically "influential" individuals and their paradigmatic struggles against the rising tide of the status quo, many of the grade inflation articles frame a hero—Harvey Mansfield—against an academic world of ever-more liberal conventions (once again, see Feulner, 2001; Oppenheim, 2001; or Kurtz, 2001, among others). In this way, a narrative is propagated that shapes the present and perhaps the future: by placing Mansfield's actions in an idealistic context, the milieu he traverses is at worst corrupt and at best inept or incompetent. The story element in the construction of this issue is an especially appealing read, since most of us are frequently

* "Liberal" in today's sense of the term (i.e., "progressive" or left-leaning)—not "liberal" in the Burkean sense.

exposed, and thus already acclimated, to the narrative forms of the moral hero/loner against the world; consider the narrative paradigm of the Western film as an example. Utilized in the context of grade inflation, where a good-against-evil diagesis can be temptingly and simplistically drawn, a discussion of grade inflation is distorted and undergoes selection commensurate with the necessary features to compose the archetypal narrative (for a more complete elaboration on these narrative paradigms and their derivations, see Giannetti, 1999).

Even more interesting is the dual nature of this particular character construction: There is Professor Mansfield the character, detailed in many of the conservative pieces, who is single-mindedly consumed with reforming a morally decaying institution (and slaughtering sacred cows), and Professor Mansfield the author of several articles, who opines autobiographically. As an analogue to this, consider the discourse on Benjamin Franklin and Thomas Jefferson in Gutek (1991). Both individuals are presented as reformers in a resistant culture of educational mediocrity (see the chapter "Education During a Revolutionary Era," in Gutek, 1991). Then, Franklin's and Jefferson's *own words* are reprinted, and there is certainly not an obvious cognizance of their own importance or ultimate "influence" running through the texts. Mansfield,[*] as opposed to Franklin and Jefferson, is being cited as "influential" contemporaneously while authoring his own pieces about that which he is famous and controversial for—leading to some fascinating presentation that can be roughly described by what Carr (1962) has explained as a "continuous process between the historian and his facts" (p. 35).[†]

The Mansfield "controversy" the conservative texts speak of is rooted in two features. First, the Harvard professor, because of his disaffection with the grade distributions at the university—nearly half of the undergraduate students receive an A or an A- grade,

---

[*] In terms of the conventions of this essay, Mansfield the character will not have a date of publication after his name, but Mansfield the author will, immediately following his name, have a date moniker customarily used for citing author's texts.

[†] See Mansfield (2001) for his patterns of reaction and historical synthesis: ideas framed with such statements as "I certainly got attention," "I was pleased," and "I should be asking" display both the professor's awareness of scrutiny and innate pleasure he takes at being in the grade inflation debate.

with most of the other half of the student body achieving Bs or Cs—instituted a policy of two grades for his classes: one "transcript" grade (the inflated grade), and one "real" grade. The "transcript" grade is public knowledge, conferred to vocations and institutions that review the student's achievements. The "real" grade is an indicator derived by a set of fixed standards Mansfield deems appropriate; students, when obtaining their "real" grades, gain a cognizance of their own true achievement, according to Mansfield (Oppenheim, 2001). The "real" grades, then, are more closely correlated with teacher-perceived student achievement than the "transcript" grades.

Second, Mansfield, to justify his two-grade methodology, issued a series of statements about the causes underpinning grade inflation. He cites the university's establishment of affirmative action as a major motivator: "When affirmative action opened Harvard's doors to a large number of minorities in the early 1970s, white professors were unwilling to give black students Cs to avoid giving them a rough welcome. At the same time they didn't give Cs to white students to be fair" (Oppenheim, 2001, p. 2). Here's the upshot: aside from the fact that there is no statistical proof of this,* and also that the perceived "grade inflation" may actually be a natural outgrowth of a variety of benign statistical effects such as increasing aptitude (à la the Flynn Effect), age, gender-distribution differences, and implementation of course withdrawals policy (see the research article by McSpirit & Jones, 1999), Mansfield's (2001) argument is based solely on his personal *memory* of history.

Memory allows the benefit of retrospect but also the disadvantage of removal from events. To see the distorting effects of memory on history, we need to look no further than Cubberley's (1919) text: he presents the educational history of America as part and parcel of its own transformation. In other words, the shaping of American education—that of schools "gradually…transformed from instruments of religion into instruments of the state," as Spring (1997) explains the historian's thesis (p. 8)—occurs organically and intrinsically, proportional to a sense of progress that Cubberley (1919) has envisaged. But since "we can view the past, and achieve our understanding of the past, only through the present"

* Mansfield (2001) notes that Harvard will not allow archived student transcripts to be viewed or disseminated.

(Carr, 1962, p. 28), an assumption not considered by Cubberley (1919), he views contemporary institutions as naturally springing forth from a linear conception of the past, as if a personified past were almost *aware* of its ultimate place in the present. The retrospect quality of memory, in this way, forces Cubberley (1919) to a unilateral, myopic view of a past anxiously awaiting its convergence with a more positive, sophisticated, "destined" present.*

Bailyn (1960) explains that Cubberley's (1919) clear lines of progression between the past and the present are faulty, specifically with the Puritan precursor theory (Cubberley [1919] posits that the Puritan's educational system was a direct-line ancestor to the public school). Sectarian religion became of great importance because of the new difficulties adjusting to the sense of space the colonists obtained in the New World (Bailyn, 1960). And yet, "Cubberley…told a dramatic story, of how the delicate seeds of the idea and institutions of 'public' education had lived precariously amid religious and other old-fashioned forms of education until nineteenth-century reformers, fighting bigotry and ignorance, cleared the way for their full flowering" (Bailyn, 1960, p. 10). It is apparent that Cubberley, according to Bailyn (1960), utilizes two of the attributes conservative texts also assume: the construction of a narrative of hero-reformers and the qualities of memory to form an edited, combined, and compressed image of the past.

In the past—specifically, the 1950s—*Plessy v. Ferguson*, the separate-but-equal facilities edict, was ruled unconstitutional by the Supreme Court in *Brown v. Board of Education of Topeka*, leading to the desegregation of public schools (Ryan & Cooper, 2000). That these events occurred is beyond dispute, of course. Nevertheless, just as Cubberley (1919) takes an event, like the Law of 1647, and—noting its requirements of schools in areas with certain numbers of people—declares that the enactment of the law is an event that "represent[s] the very foundation stones of which our American public school systems have been based" (p. 18), Professor Mansfield generalizes a present effect based upon past events.

---

* Sounds a bit Hegelian, doesn't it? Carrying things closer to our time, it reminds one of Fukuyama's *The End of History and the Last Man* (1992): forgive my simplification of this sort-of conservative author's famous book, but history didn't exactly end with the wrap up of the Cold War.

The desegregation of the schools did cause an influx of African American students into higher education (detailed in the chapter, "Education and Integration," in Gutek, 1991), as the professor suggests. This is his key event, in the same sense as one of Cubberley's (1919) key events in his historical thesis was the Law of 1647. Then, however, Mansfield's (2001) memory constructs the rest: "Because I have no access to the figures, I have to rely on what I saw and heard at the time. Although it is not so now, it was then utterly commonplace for white professors to overgrade [sic] black students.... From that, I inferred a motive for overgrading [sic] white students, too" (p. 4). Regardless of whether or not Mansfield (2001) is "correct" about such resultant effects of affirmative action, Mansfield is a maverick figure in the dynamic conservative narrative since he is changing the structure of what can be said—by changing commonly accepted conceptions of the past. As Popkewitz (1987) states, "Our questions about the present require that we recognize that the present is not just our immediate experiences and practices. Part of our historical consciousness is to recognize that the past is part of our everyday discourse, structuring what can be said..." (p. 1). (Popkewitz [1987] then attempts in his piece to somewhat counteract the effects of memory by constructing a history based on many events and few causes.) The Internet medium, by producing works that support and supplement the Mansfield (2001) claims with great frequency, both initializes and propagates the selection-of-ascendant-facts process.

Mansfield (2001) and others mention different explanations for grade inflation besides the influx of students after the implementation of affirmative action. Sympathy between professors and protesting students during the Vietnam War is posited as the point of emergence of grade inflation by some conservative articles (e.g., Bauer, 1997). However, conservatives may have a vested interest in this argument beyond grade inflation; as Spring (1997) notes, Richard Nixon was elected president of the United States at a time when there was "conservative reaction to student demonstrations and the demands of the civil rights movement" (p. 388). Is this argument of the causality of grade inflation simply a post-Vietnam War justification of the "righteousness" and the "morality" of those who supported the war (possibly an offspring of the "Silent Majority")? Nixon (1990) himself has historically framed the student protesters in a negative light: "The incident [his meeting with students protesting] was typical of the emotions tearing the country apart during the Vietnam War. It was worse among those who had avoided or evaded the draft, because deep down they had a guilt complex" (p. 250).*

The Vietnam War and Affirmative Action arguments can be denoted on the "right" in a contemporary political spectrum; they are both conservative arguments coinciding closely with modern conservative stands (some current conservative thought is discussed in Spring, 1997). Although the next major argument presented can also be considered on the right side of the political spectrum, it is more "left" than the previous two—i.e., more "liberal" of a supposition. Surprisingly, perhaps because grade inflation is such a new issue, or possibly because the issue is currently framed too contentiously, there is no leftist response from the "traditional sources" that I could gather (by traditional sources, I mean publications that customarily disseminate American leftist thought. Some examples are *The Nation*, *The Progressive*, and others). Therefore, the following argument for grade-inflation causality functions as a more "liberal" response.

The third argument is the positing of an economic-historical causality. Portraying colleges as a business in a market composed of a single commodity—students—Beaver (2000) claims, "The major change incurred by the decision to recruit more students from a declining population was the lowering of standards.... To reach recruitment goals, colleges began accepting less-qualified students" (p. 1). And to retain those less qualified, universities resorted to grade inflation, so attrition rates did not skyrocket (Beaver, 2000). However, an irony is present: conservatives, who have historically supported the marketplace and *laissez-faire* economic practices (see Spring, 1997), must then object to the consumerism which causes colleges to compete for more students and the lowering standards to attract them (according to an *Economist* article titled "All Shall have Prizes"). Most of the conservative discourse thus far has not recognized this significant contradiction. Nevertheless, the rhetoric denotes the notion's place on the political spectrum: It is the contradictory nature of the argument that has led me to place this

* Richard Nixon loved to play armchair psychologist when ascribing motivations to people's actions. Listen to some of his hundreds and hundreds of hours of White House tapes to see (well, hear) what I mean.

grade inflation causal explanation to the left on the political spectrum of the Vietnam War and the Affirmative Action arguments, since it is not entirely consistent with conservative ideological suppositions.

Wilson (1999) delves into more detail about the consumerism of college, in a proposal somewhat reminiscent of the "Cardinal Principles of Secondary Education" report (present in Gutek, 1991). He first summarizes a 1998 article by a Professor Perrin of Dartmouth, which discusses the university's quandary: "[When] Dartmouth noticed that its students weren't doing as well in the competition for graduate-school admissions as they deserved to," professors began to raise student's scores—simply because students went there (Wilson, 1999, p. 2). Wilson (1999) also suggests another factor causing grade inflation. There was a "triumph of the consumer's perspective in the institutional culture of the academy, replacing the authority of professional judgment, much weakened by the '60's rebellion, with the authority of student wants" (Wilson, 1999, p. 3). In other words colleges, based on Wilson's (1999) theories, are almost cosmopolitan stores, betraying their idealistic flavor for an "entertainment" value engendered by a want of students' business on the one hand, and a sense of institutional guilt on the other (i.e., guilt for not giving their students high-enough grades, simply because they attend top-tier colleges). This is in contrast to the 1970s ideals of education, that "instruction based on student interest is contrary to the idea" of proper education (Spring, 1997, p. 394).

In his chapter entitled "Meritocracy: The Experts Take Charge," Spring (1997) details the emerging class of experts, at the end of the nineteenth century, that attempted to remove the variability in institutions such as schools so that the creation of human capital could be scientific and orderly. But grade inflation represents or reflects a shift in the importance of these experts in the academy—who then dealt on a macro level with scientifically constructed "strata of people" as mere cogs in the mechanisms of society. There are several sources to support this change. Gutek (1991) describes the discourses about the nature of high schools following the upheavals of the revolutions in the 1960s: "Was it [the schools] to be an institution whose primary purpose was academic preparation for college bound youth [i.e., the experts' management of human capital]? Or, was it to be a multi-purpose institution that sought to meet the social, psychological, emotional, and economic needs of American adolescents?" (p. 114). Dealing with such issues as student affect and psychological needs represented a move towards more individualized instruction in schools. Ryan & Cooper (2000) mention diversity and other issues that forced a more individualized—and much more variable—approach to schooling following the 1960s; the experts, who customarily dealt with demarcated "orderly" groups in the past, had to be redefined to deal with the randomness and chaos of the individual.

However, comparing the state of contemporary universities to the past—at the time of the influx of the experts—is a complicated proposition. In one sense, as Spring (1997) describes, the meritocracy of the experts was rooted in more pragmatic than humanistic disciplines (the Morrill Act of 1862 is cited as evidence); and this follows today's shift to broaden collegiate appeal to a more practical curricula (e.g., influenced by the business world) (Beaver, 2000). But in another sense, the university of today is a clear affront to the meritocracy of the past: in a corporate-dominated environment, the ivory tower finds itself not at the helm of an American society coordinated by experts as it once was, but in a more dubious position: as a servant of market forces.

The anachronistic notions of meritocracy, then, are distinct from the *modern* conceptions of meritocracy, which are largely restricted to an academic milieu: "Meritocracy" is entrenched with new connotations.* Grade inflation—either the "true" or vestigial presence of it—isolates the academy further from the rest of society, because it calls its accountability into question (Feulner, 2001), an accountability that "attempted [during the 1970s] to restore power to the professional educator," *not* to the "traditional" experts (Spring, 1997, p. 389).

Kaestle (1976) discusses the dynamism in modern conservative political ideology characterized by the adoption of anachronistic/status-quo notions applied to new, ever-shifting realities. Unsurprisingly, the current discourse on grade inflation reveals similar, contemporary patterns. Conservatives adapted to the contemporary educational-multicultural hegemony, and the loss of the Protestant domination in classrooms (discussed in Spring, 1997), by embracing

* As a related concept, note how Hamilton (1989) traces several words and their usage through a historical chronology and discovers a dynamism in classroom construction, based upon the changes of the meaning of words.

a sectarian, isolated approach—akin to what Bailyn (1960) describes that happened in pre-Revolutionary America—to education. Their traditional values, and moral education, long the dominant paradigm in American education, found a new home in the mandates of multiculturalism: One culture, according to cultural relativism, is morally equivalent to any other, and thus can be disseminated in isolation as long as other cultures are respected. Spring (1997) discusses this adaptation more thoroughly (also see Kaestle [1976] for examples of how those on the left and the right can support the same issue for totally different reasons).* Perhaps an influx of outside experts and neo-scientific management, roughly analogous to the late nineteenth-century's trend, will be a reactionary mechanism appearing in future conservative discourse to counteract grade inflation and restore the original epistemology of the meritocracy as the society of America with a locus in the university.†

(2001)

---

* Taking the Kaestle (1976) explanation of left-right common support but generalizing it to a more removed, tertiary level, if the market-forces explanation truly finds a place in modern liberal canon, we can envisage a scenario in which liberals and conservatives not only support the elimination of grade inflation—the same issue—but support it based on the same *background causality*: however, they support *that* causality for different reasons.

† What is an undergraduate degree worth if grade inflation is rampant? The question is not meant to be rhetorical. It seems that the university perpetuates itself in two ways—through obtaining funds (whether from the great mass of students, or the savings incurred through the use of graduate students, or the donations of alumni) and "creating" acolytes who more or less never leave academia—the undergrad degree is not so much about the individuals per se but really about feeding the monster. I don't mean to attach a negative connotation to this idea; rather, it seems to me that the university has every right, along with the corporation, to both survive and thrive any which way it can. We have all permitted this to happen, as individuals and as a collective: it goes back to the notion of the universal culpability of humankind, a favorite theme of Alfred Hitchcock. Maybe the university and the corporation really aren't antithetical at all and it might even be considered ironic that the corporate donations and the corporate structure of large academic institutions go to funding anti-corporate research that in turn perpetuates the "system" (the "system" is tough to unpack) and, in fact, grade inflation debates are merely a chimera of which *credential* inflation—a notion that applies to academe's employees—is a case in point of a larger problem which, alas, is well beyond the scope of this chapter.

# References

Bailyn, B. (1960). Education in the forming of society: Needs and opportunities for study. New York: Vintage Books.

Bauer, H. H. (1997). The new generations: Students who don't study. LSU.edu website.
Retrieved September 20, 2001, from the Internet:
http://www.bus.lsu.edu/accounting/faculty/lcrumbley/study.htm

Beaver, W. R. (2000). Cheapening college: Sending more high school graduates to college will improve neither their prospects nor the economy. The Hudson Institute.
Retrieved September 20, 2001, from the Internet:
http://www.hudson.org/American_Outlook/articles_sm00/beaver.htm

Carr, E. (1919). What is history? The George Macaulay Trevelyan lectures delivered in the University of Cambridge, January-March 1961 (pp. 3-35). New York: Alfred A. Knopf.

Cubberley, E. (1919). Public education in the United States: A study and interpretation of American educational history. Cambridge: Houghton Mifflin.

Feulner, E. J. (2001). As simple as abc. Townhall.com.
Retrieved September 20, 2001, from the Internet:
http://www.townhall.com/columnists/edwinfeulner/printef20010711.shtml

Giannetti, L. (1999). Understanding movies (8th ed.). New Jersey: Prentice Hall.

Gutek, G. L. (1991). An historical introduction to American education (2nd ed.). Illinois: Waveland Press.

Hamilton, D. (1989). Towards a theory of schooling. London: Falmer Press.

Jesness, J. (1999). Why Johnny can't fail: How the "floating standard" has destroyed public education. Reason Online.
Retrieved September 20, 2001, from the Internet:
http://www.reason.com/9907/fe.jj.why.html

Kaestle, C. (1976). Between the scylla of brutal ignorance and the charybdis of a literary education: Elite attitudes toward mass schooling in early industrial England and America. In L. Stone (Ed.), Schooling and society: Studies in the history of education (pp. 177-191). Baltimore: Johns Hopkins Press.

Kurtz, S. (2001). Crimson truths: Reality has a hearing at Harvard. National Review Online.
Retrieved September 20, 2001 from the Internet:
http://www.nationalreview.com/comment/comment-kurtzprint030201.html

Mansfield, H. C. (2001). Grade inflation: It's time to face the facts. The chronicle of higher education.
Retrieved September 20, 2001, from the Internet:
http://chronicle.com/free/v47/i30/30b02401.htm

McSpirit, S. & Jones, K. E. (1999). Grade inflation among different ability students, controlling for other factors. Education Policy Analysis, 7(30).
Retrieved September 20, 2001, from the Internet:
http://www.epaa.asu.edu/epaa/v7n30.html

Nixon, R. (1990). In the arena: A memoir of victory, defeat and renewal. New York: Simon and Schuster.

Oppenheim, N. D. (2001). Grading on the Harvard curve: Harvey Mansfield's irony goes unappreciated. The Weekly Standard, 6(3).
Retrieved September 20, 2001, from the Internet:
http://www.weeklystandard.com/magazine/mag_6_24_01/oppenheim_art_6_24_01.asp

Popkewitz, T. (1987). The formation of school subjects and the political context of schooling. In T. Popkewitz (Ed.), The formation of school subjects: The struggle for creating an American institution (pp. ix-x, 1-24). New York: Falmer Press.

Radosh, R. (2000). Liberal intellectuals and affirmative action. Front page magazine.
Retrieved November 6, 2001, from the Internet:
http://www.frontpagemag.com/archives/radosh/2000/rr12-18-00p.htm

Ryan, K., & Cooper, J. (2000). What is the history of American education? In K. Ryan & J. Cooper (Eds.), Those who can, teach (9th ed.) (pp. 355-393). Boston: Houghton Mifflin.

Spring, J. (1997). The American school, 1642-1996 (4th ed.). New York: McGraw-Hill.

Wilson, B. P. (1999). The phenomenon of grade inflation in higher education: Meeting of the governor's blue ribbon commission on higher education, Longwood College. Front page magazine.
Retrieved November 6, 2001, from the Internet:
http://www.frontpagemag.com/archives/academia/wilson04-13-99.htm

# PART III

# EXPLICATIONS

# 22.

## Subtleties Abound: A Closer Look at *Punch-Drunk Love*

In his *New Republic* essay "After Disenchantment," art critic Jed Perl serves up a critique of art in a postmodern, disenchanted world ruptured by the ravages of seen-it-all, done-it-all. A disconnectedness, he claims, pervades the milieu—and an "entire aesthetic" is based on people's inability to "weave things together." Where form once followed function, now there is neither form nor function, but merely a distinctness of events, notions, motifs. "The magic has not gone out of art, but there is little sense of how magical acts can add up to a magical atmosphere, and how that atmosphere can become a part of ordinary life."

Film, which Alfred Hitchcock recognized as a sort of panacea of art—which has multiple and disjoint mediums acting in concert—sometimes allows for the seemingly disconnected to connect, without force or deliberateness. *Punch-Drunk Love* certainly has a bit of what Perl called "the magical acts which can add up to a magical atmosphere" in an almost anachronistic, Romantic-era sense.

The tone of *Love* has an undercurrent of brash optimism, à la Romantic period works. The destructive is always countered with the constructive: consider the Jeep flip juxtaposed immediately by the dumping of the harmonium onto the street—Barry Egan (played by Adam Sandler, in his best performance to date) has no control over the destruction of the Jeep, but eventually repairs the harmonium.

Or consider Egan's destructive behavior. Although it causes many complications for the protagonist, eventually it comes to serve him constructively: he protects "his girl" from the band of blonde brothers.

The splitting-apart, combining-together motif permeates so much of *Love*. When Lena (Emily Watson) takes off for Hawaii—thus destructing their uneasy makeshift union—Barry follows her and re-constructs their romance via a heart that literally cradles the interior of the silhouette of the couple's embrace.*

Continuing, we note that the very act of destructing for constructive purposes also rules the day. Barry's obsessive and yet fruitful quest to obtain a million frequent-flier miles is effected by culling and cutting UPCs from pudding. We note that Lena's broken—i.e., destructed—car is the impetus for the construction of a relationship she so (self-destructively?) desperately wishes; she, at the start of the film, hands him the key to her car—and her heart—for him to start.

The influx of a myriad of color—red, blue, cyan, violet, magenta, in a patterned-swirl—that breaks up the movie (destructs it) at several points connect and form developmental logics around Barry's destructive behavior: when the first transition occurs five minutes into the film, the screen merely shows colors besieged by randomness and stars stuck pointlessly on the screen. No reason, no explanation; things are just there, seemingly disconnected. But with time comes purpose. Near the end of the film, when Barry finally has focused his destructive rage constructively to protect his love, and the same swirls of colorful randomness appear, titles denoting his precise destination (Utah) pop up. Order from chaos, constructive motion from uncontrolled destructive pointlessness. Suffice it to say, it is a kind of multi-textured character development.

More instances abound of destruction reforming and reconfiguring into construction: the rage Barry has at his seven sisters, expressed beforehand as violence upon objects, transforms into oral diatribes and invective that aggressively and pointedly fight against sibling abuse; the near-violence that quells with a simple "that's that" from the sex-phone-line ringleader; the oddly-charming and frighteningly violent pre-lovemaking-ode Barry and Lena impart each other.

And yet the magic of these events, themes, motifs and constructions does indeed add up to a magical atmosphere, akin to the Romantic conceptions of unabashed style that Perl discusses in his piece.

The magic can be felt in Jon Brion's lush score (Brion's offbeat music for the brilliant *Eternal Sunshine of the Spotless Mind* [2004] and

---

* The official movie poster frames the shot of this scene in an ironically purposeful, almost winking-like manner.

*I ♥ Huckabees* [2004] are equally impressive); in the cinematography—especially in Hawaii, which Barry amusingly notes to Lena, "Looks just like Hawaii"—which progressively saturates the screen with more and more contrast as the build up to the shouting-match climax nears; in the multiple layers of themes and meanings—hardly touched upon here; and in the flawless acting of the cast, which I would be remiss to not mention.

*Love* is organic in a way, developing in unexpected and original ways, flirting with chaos at times and yet bounded by the conventions of less atypical films. As Jed Perl says of the artist Braque, "In Braque's writings the mysteries of art turn out to be organic processes—processes of growth and transformation." The line between *Punch-Drunk Love* and many other movies in the genre of romantic comedy* follows from this: where other films may have characters and elements undergoing growth, *Love* has an interlocking of growth and transformation, forming the magical atmosphere of Barry Egan's life that is at once surreal and yet, somehow, familiar and ordinary.

(2002)

* An uneasy fit for this nuanced, tough-to-categorize film.

# 23.

## *American Beauty*: In Defense of the Status Quo

Lester Burnham (Kevin Spacey) is what many of us fear we will become: a middle-aged, disgusted, dissatisfied loser given precious little respect and appreciation but also lacking the impetus to do anything about it. From nearly the first shot of *American Beauty* (1999), we are led into what Lester terms his "pathetic little life." After his daily "high point" in the shower, Lester heads off to work in a Mercedes driven by his domineering wife Carolyn (Annette Bening). While with Carolyn, he regresses to infantile, child-like behavior—for instance, in the automobile, Lester assumes the rear seat and quickly falls asleep as a newborn might while Lester's daughter rides shotgun.

As *American Beauty* wears on, Lester encounters a beautiful, albeit seemingly shallow, high school teen girl Angela who is best friends with his daughter. Angela is (perhaps) the eponymous Beauty of the title. Also, Lester meets his new next-door neighbor Ricky at a social engagement with his wife; drug-dealing Ricky quickly becomes something of a role model to the disaffected protagonist. After a series of adventures, Lester is a changed man. Because throughout the narrative Lester manages to transform into an adult—and ultimately appreciate his family and make peace with his place in life—with the assistance of the teen beauty and the young drug-dealing neighbor, Lester is, in effect, the filmmakers' mouthpiece for a paradoxically full-throated defense of the suburban institution of marriage.

If the numerous roses throughout are meant to represent beauty in the form-content relationship of the film (as the title *American Beauty* suggests), then we can associate most appearances of American beauty roses with "beauty" in Lester's life at those moments in the movie. Look no further than the angelic fantasy sequence in Lester's bedroom for an example. Lester, framed in the mid-shot (breaking the rule of thirds), is transfixed at the ceiling, with rose pedals slowly trickling from above the camera into the frame.* In the following shot, we assume Lester's viewpoint to observe teenage Angela, also in the center of the shot, affixed onto the ceiling surrounded by rose pedals.

Contrast Lester's erotic "rose" representation of Angela with his perception of Carolyn, his wife. When we first see his spouse, she is picking and cutting roses in an outdoor garden. While scenes with Angela are oftentimes overflowing with American beauty roses, this first scene with Carolyn contains only a single, dull-colored cut rose. The wilted, severed rose is analogous to the severed hopes and dreams of our hero's life; he *once* saw beauty in Carolyn (thus, the explanation of the presence of the rose at all) but the beauty has withered into total impotence in the face of her power—perhaps the visual metaphor of her cutting the rose represents her castrating Lester, making Lester the wilted rose in this scenario.

The appearance of the rose with Carolyn, though, prefigures a major narrative development of her husband. The shots framing the wilted rose juxtaposed with Carolyn not only might represent a kind of history of their relationship, but a harbinger of a "rosy" future. Cutting to near the end of the film, right before Lester is shot, he tenderly takes in a picture of his wife and child in the company of a bouquet of American beauty roses—he has found his beauty. Thus, Lester has come full circle; superficially at least, he has realized that despite his family's, and especially Carolyn's, flaws, there is nothing ultimately more fulfilling than the standard suburban family unit. More deeply, though, Lester, by attempting a radical change of lifestyle but failing to find a better way to live, has conformed to a set of cultural expectations of American life—namely, the structured married lifestyle, replete with a literal white-picket fence.

Carolyn has also, by the end of the film, arrived at a similar place. Despite her liaison with the King (played pricelessly by Peter Gallagher of later *The O.C.* fame), Carolyn decides that what she has with Lester was more important—indeed, better—than her exciting

---

* It's likely the roses aren't even there but, rather, are computer-generated. Why shoot anything for real anymore when a team of cubicle geeks can digitally render worlds of the imagination and thereby circumvent the laws of nature? Pretty soon, we'll have a new Marilyn Monroe movie—completely visually indistinguishable from, let's say, the incredible *The Seven Year Itch*. Or maybe a new James Bond movie starring Sean Connery, circa 1964? Or maybe you'd prefer Roger Moore? or Timothy Dalton? Coming right up!

but ultimately unfulfilling tryst with the King. Her near-mental collapse after Lester's discovery of her affair suggests this (although I suppose we could argue that she was simply upset that she was caught, but her behavior toward the end of the film likely refutes such an analysis). After Carolyn discovers Lester's corpse, she has her most emotionally revealing moment: she falls on her husband's clothes in the closet; notice the strong form-content relationship here—Carolyn gathers up what she has "lost." Carolyn, like Lester, has come full circle and has discovered that the institution of marriage was/is the strongest and most fulfilling bond in her adult life. Therefore, she also conforms to a suburban set of expectations about structured married life as surely as her husband does.

Even Carolyn's next-door neighbor, the Colonel, is forced to conform to the expectations of marriage, at least in public. Despite his repeated beatings of his son and, we assume, his wife, the Colonel displays an outwardly strong loyalty to the cultural expectations of the institution of marriage and of sitting for the "standard" family meals. His slight deviation from these expectations—his kiss of Lester—forces the Colonel to protect his rapidly crumbling cultural edifices in the only way he knows how: by destroying the object of his deviation.

Likewise, Lester and Carolyn eliminate the objects of their deviation from the cultural norms of marriage. Carolyn decides (after she is caught with the King) to "cool things off for a while" with her not-so-discreet lover. Lester, after realizing that his character change has occurred despite (or in spite of) not having sex with Angela, consciously decides to discharge his fatherly duties—by becoming a surrogate father to Angela, a role requiring a maturity he doesn't seem to have until those closing moments of *American Beauty*. By Lester assuming a parental role, he is (again) furthering the defense of the cultural institution of marriage: the father must be a father figure, and, for this to occur, he must behave like an adult. Lester acquires this newfound maturity right before he dies. Thus we have another reason why the protagonist lovingly embraces the picture of his family: he has learned to not only be a "proper" husband but a "proper" father as well.

Let us once again focus on Lester's character development. Because our "hero" (if you can call him that) begins the film with one idea about his life—that his marriage is terrible, but without a clue what to do about it—and concludes the film with another—that his marriage, despite its ups and downs, is a wonderful and multifarious adventure—we can say Lester has traveled on a cyclical journey of sorts; in other words, he used to believe that life could not be worse but eventually believes that life couldn't be better.

In the classic *The Wizard of Oz*, Dorothy experiences a similar reaffirmation of the beauty of what she has—she finds there's no place like home. In the year of the film's release, 1939, *Oz* was designed to comfort the fears of the citizens of a country facing another World War, the tail end of Depression, and other potential calamities off in the horizon.

Our crises now include a war on marriage. Ever-increasing divorce rates bring this reality home to American families. "There's no place like home" translates, in *American Beauty*, to "There's nothing like suburban marriage." We are being urged to calm down, take stock, and recognize the beauty inherent in traditional marriage, despite its many deep-seated flaws.

Is *American Beauty*, which presents us with two middle-aged main characters who come to appreciate marriage, a "socially serious" genre film, or is it standard-fare entertainment? According to Peter Lehman and William Luhr in *Thinking About Movies* (1999), "Socially serious dramas usually supply a liberal critique that implies an unquestioned commitment to the value of our most basic cultural institutions.... [thus], there is...nothing fundamentally wrong with the family if we come to our senses and change our ways." This perceptive statement not only supports the idea that *American Beauty* is "socially serious" cinema, but it also nicely encapsulates the theme of the movie: there is nothing wrong with the family that cannot be fixed by a little dose of humility and maturity among the family members themselves.

(1999)

# 24.

## THE ROOTS OF A POLITICAL APATHY DURING ELECTION SEASON

A fervent adherence to conspiracies is usually not the province of a healthy mind. The unhinged might believe that the U.S. government on a remote soundstage, for example, faked the moon landings to gain sort of moral advantage during the Cold War.[*] Besides flimsy or isolated pockets of evidence to support conspiracies, let alone holes in logic usually big enough to fly spaceships through, beliefs like "the government faked the moon landings" should always give the skeptic considerable pause because of the surely herculean difficulty inherent in obtaining the continuing silence of everyone involved. Forget that "the American flag's waving" or that "there's no crater at the landing site" ideas were debunked scientifically years ago—how likely is it that those twelve men[†] who set foot on the surface of the moon—let alone all of the NASA scientists, engineers, and workers—would not have already cracked and let the world in on the secret conspiracy?[‡] More troublesome than the silly conspiracies themselves are the large swaths of people who continue to either be unwilling or unable to exercise skeptical, rational, independent thought.[§] Oftentimes, those same people claim two contradictory things: that the government is on the one hand crafty and clever enough to plan

---

[*] See the slightly ridiculous movie *Capricorn One* for a two-hour thought experiment of how faking a trip to Mars might come about.

[†] To find out what befell the astronauts post-landing, read *Moon Dust: In Search of the Men Who Fell to Earth* by Andrew Smith.

[‡] For an interesting discussion of conspiracies and the tenets of skepticism, consult Guy P. Harrison's *50 Popular Beliefs That People Think are True.*

[§] Not just in the so-called modern world. Some conspiracies are much older than the moon landings' hoax. Consider one of the oldest and most fruitful conspiracies: that of Jews controlling the world. Such Jew-baiting goes back centuries; new life was breathed into the idea by the Tsars in the early twentieth century, sandwiched between the Dreyfus affair and the rise of Hitler, in the form of the mass produced screed *The Protocols of the Elders of Zion.*

and execute such mass conspiracies, but on the other hand too dumb and mismanaged to do anything right. Cognitive dissonance indeed.

The pleasure of the conspiracy theory is in the power of explanation: the world and (at least some) events in it suddenly and seemingly make sense, logic and Occam's razor be damned. The conspiracy theorist also has cover for failure—if others are secretly in control of his fate, he cannot be blamed for his mistakes. The appeal of conspiracy theories is not lost on me. When I was in eighth grade, I distinctly recall my industrial arts teacher declaring recycling a "myth" because he had once surreptitiously tailed a garbage truck around his block, only to find the sanitation workers change the sign on the side of the vehicle to read "Recycling Truck" before they swung around the block again to collect the recyclables. The myth is that recycling is always environmentally friendly,* rather than that recycling doesn't exist.

I truly *wish* I could believe that this country was controlled by a bunch of wizened white-haired, balding, elderly men in smoke-filled boardrooms barking orders to their frazzled twenty-something blonde female secretaries. I wish that I could pin the blame for this vice or that failure of mine on Person/Group *X*—oh, how easy it would be to simply affix responsibility to others! How simple it would be to claim that if not for that monster of a leader—who obviously spends his vacation time consorting with his nefarious cohorts (who currently reside somewhere between the sixth and seventh of Dante's circles of Hell)—I and my poor, weak, infirm, feeble friends would rise, like light-creamed milk to the top of a cup of coffee, to the peak of free-market heights; there would be no zenith we couldn't reach.

Except that the world just doesn't seem to work that way. Ineptitude, semi-competence, and mismanagement contribute more significantly to the world's ills than all the backroom, boardroom corporate plotting put together ever has. And, notwithstanding the

---

* For example, more carbon dioxide may be produced from driving trash to the nearest recycling plant and processing it than by simply burning the trash without any transport. See *Confessions of an Eco-Sinner* by Fred Pearce for a fascinating exploration of this and other ecological ideas. (Here's another idea from the book: did you know that bananas are an endangered fruit and might die out completely if we're not careful?)

Peter Principle, the reason is simple: Americans may be fond of conspiracies, but they are also smart enough not to be led lemmings-like to the edge of a cliff by those individuals who are so obviously and explicitly neo-fascists or nitwits. To wit: After Barry Goldwater gave his infamous "Extremism in the defense of liberty is no vice" speech, people handed JFK's former vice president a landslide of Democratic proportions. (The Daisy television commercial helped a bit, too.) And when Walter Mondale admitted, in the 1984 convention, that he would raise taxes on the American people, people overwhelmingly stuck with the Gipper. (Honesty isn't always the best policy.) One a Neo-fascist, the other a nitwit—and both duly denied a shot at leading the free world.

But the question arises: Doesn't George W. Bush, to put it mildly, snugly fit into one of those two above-mentioned categories? And, if he does, then why was he permitted to take the reins of leadership? First, in 2000, Mr. Gore easily surpassed Mr. Bush in the popular vote—as Mr. Gore has publicly reminded us innumerable times.[*] Second, as the Democrats are fond of pointing out to us information-overwhelmed denizens, We the People have a chance of correcting America's historical trajectory by ejecting W. (or Dubya) out of his command-and-control seat this 2004 presidential election season.

To replace W. with a self-aggrandizing Washington bureaucrat (read: John F. Kerry) isn't necessarily the correct course of action, though. Howard Dean has done much for the Bush campaign during his campaign for the nomination: recall all of Dean's criticisms of Mr. Kerry during the primaries about the Massachusetts senator's acceptance of special interest funds and his cronyism akin, at least in part, to the Devil Who Wears Prada (read: George W. Bush).[†] Bush probably doesn't wear Prada, but it's nevertheless a great and topical moniker, I think.

"The Real Deal" is commensurate, and has always been this election season, with Mr. Dean. How pathetic of the Democratic Party

---

[*] Imagine if Gore had been elected: Republicans would have been the party in opposition to war post-9/11, with the Dems all-guns-blazing. History turns on a coin flip.

[†] Mr. Bush later explained all of his actions as president in his self-aggrandizing memoir *Decision Points*. It's become like a broken record to say, but: the only presidential memoir worth reading is U. S. Grant's.

that they prematurely ejected the former Vermont governor before his time; how awful that the Party sold out on nonsensical notions like "electability." That's pure bunk because electability is super tough to predict. Turns out hypocrisy find just as comfortable a home in the Democratic Party as in the Republican establishment.* And for that, the Dems simply don't deserve my vote.

I also tired of being reminded, during the Democratic Convention,† of the great social programs that rank-and-file Democrats spearheaded through the years. Although the country is greatly in their debt for some of them—but not all; recall that it was a Republican, President Dwight D. Eisenhower, who appointed Supreme Court Justice Earl Warren, one of the most so-called liberal activist judges of all time,‡ although Ike later regretted the choice—we could as easily recall the great accomplishments of Republican eras past, such as the abolition of slavery and Reconstruction. Is there a time limit for such brazen (albeit occasionally legitimate, on both sides) bragging? If it's saleable, perhaps there isn't.

Howard Dean, à la Hillary Clinton in 1992, had it right in his campaign: the next great social experiment for America, one, if successfully executed and *smartly* publicized, might seal the Democratic Party's victories in the next six presidential elections, should be and must be universal healthcare (single-payer is the *sine qua non*). Kerry has said little about this most important of issues, afraid as he is of scaring away those independent voters who hear government sponsored healthcare and reflexively think of the supposed health care rationing in the social democracies of Europe.§ If Kerry does dis-

---

* But as Jonah Goldberg has sagely pointed out in at least one of his many *National Review Online* articles, just because someone is a hypocrite doesn't necessarily mean that what he is saying or preaching is incorrect.

† The only noteworthy event of this year's convention was the keynote address given by rising young political star Barack Obama. Kerry handpicked him, skipping over more traditional choices, to deliver the speech.

‡ Although we could make a case, as has been done in books like *The Living Constitution* (by David A. Strauss), that the Warren Court's rulings on issues like desegregation were simply a natural evolution of the legal precedent and common law (originally a British notion) of the mid-1950s, rather than some sort of activist agenda.

§ Health care rationing occurs in the U.S. all the time (and has throughout the twentieth century as well)—it's just not called "rationing." For instance, there's rationing by income, medical history, gender, and occupation, and

cuss healthcare, I, and the rest of America, will be listening intently—simply because health care in this greatest of lands should be a right, not a privilege, and if our tax cuts are going to be rescinded, shouldn't they be spent for our most pressing societal need?

There's a deeper problem with Kerry. It's pretty much impossible for any politician, throughout his or her career, to be consistent about the issues. For example, when George W. Bush ran for congress in the late 1970s, he ran as a pro-choice candidate. Politicians modify or contradict their stances based on prevailing political winds, or due to deep contemplation, or perhaps because of familial tragedy—needless to say, when whole swaths of ideologues flip ideologies as a result of political expediency or unforeseen events, it's tough to assign the burden of dissent to a single political soul.

None other than Ronald Reagan was hypocritical in this regard; his famous pronouncement that the Democratic Party left him and not the other way around hardly takes into account the Byzantine twists and turns of the two (now) major parties' core issues and constituencies. Who could have predicted that African Americans would ultimately turn out in droves in support of the Democrats—the party, in name if not in spirit, in opposition to Lincoln's quasi-Abolitionist Republican Party of 1860?

So Senator Kerry cannot be faulted, *ipso facto*, for his ever-shifting positions on some issues—and any disinterested observer would surely agree that he has repeatedly changed his positions throughout this campaign. All politicians must be chameleons: during primary season, they must appeal to their base, only to turn "moderate" come election time (but a leopard never changes his spots: all those in the know know how their candidate *really* feels about the issues). But Kerry *can* be faulted for claiming otherwise, just as the president can be fairly criticized for his unacknowledged flip-flops (despite their often extenuating circumstances).

In a *New York Times Magazine* profile of the senator, Kerry rather unbelievably claims that his "prescience" about the shadowy world of terrorist groups facilitated his calm composure post-9/11—"September the eleventh did not change me," he said. Kerry did indeed pen a book in 1997 called *The New War* about non-state ac-

---

rationing by race used to be legal as well. Consult *Health Care for Some* by Beatrix Hoffman for more information.

tors who violently disrupt societies. But his book was about the drug trade, not terrorism.

I suppose I want to hear that he changed. I want to hear that he views the world differently, or that he views his obligations as a legislator differently, or even that he views his duties as a citizen differently. I want to hear that he's a human being like the rest of us. Bush flip-flopped on nation-building: in the second debate against Al Gore during the 2000 campaign, Bush expressly warned of the dangers of nation-building and the hubris that such a foreign policy would imply. He wanted a "more humble foreign policy." But John Maynard Keynes once said, "When the facts change, I change my mind. What do you do, sir?"—and on the eleventh of September, the facts definitely changed. We are now engaged in the most complicated and expensive nation-building exercise since our post-WWII reconstruction of Europe and Japan. Bush changed: he more resembles the candidate he ran against last election than his status quo ante-self. Bush changed: whether you believe he's a puppet of plutocrats or a Churchillian figure, his administration's actions speak to that change, as does the near-total lack of dissent in the GOP.

Some have said that Kerry's home state of Massachusetts is a liability, a kind of liberal albatross that the opposition can hang on the senator. The last time the Democrats nominated a politician from Massachusetts for president, he came off as a technocrat, fairly or not. Michael Dukakis had built a lot of momentum going into the 1988 presidential debates.* When answering a tactless question posed by moderator Bernard Shaw about what he might do if his wife Kitty were brutally raped and murdered, it's generally accepted as conventional wisdom† that Dukakis's nonplussed reaction be-

* Well, sort of: he looked overmatched when filmed riding a tank some weeks earlier. George W. Bush looked vaguely ridiculous with his "Mission Accomplished" flight suit on in 2003. These kinds of military-themed staged political photo-ops never quite come off well, do they?

† The great economist John Kenneth Galbraith coined the phrase "conventional wisdom," meaning it to refer to that which is "simple, convenient, comfort-

spoke of his inability to appear human. Rail against that hypothetical rapist, Mr. Dukakis! Similarly, rail against the terrorists, Mr. Kerry! They aren't hypothetical! Certainly don't tell me that your core wasn't altered in the slightest by these attacks on our soil. Our retaliations for them these last three years don't mitigate the impact they've had on our national psyche, our national soul.

Michael Douglas's character Andrew Shepard, in the chronically underrated film *The American President* (1996), said the presidency is all about character. I would modify that to read the *perception* of character. And my perception of Mr. Kerry's character is one of, frankly, indecisiveness; his sclerotic approach in responding to the Swift Boaters is sad. He has only himself to blame if he loses in November.* I mostly agree with the president's oft-repeated proclamation that at least we know where he (Bush) stands, even if we don't agree with him,† but we don't quite know where Kerry stands. Bush has done an excellent job of facilitating and promoting a positive perception of his character, if not his policies, among a plurality of the electorate. Whether the perception lines up with the reality is hard to say.‡ But if the president does win in November,§ it will not be because of his policies—after all, he's been a near-complete failure domestically, in my view—but it will be because he's managed the heretofore impossible: turning this election into a referendum on his opponent's innumerable weaknesses. Call it the power of incumbency, of TR's bully pulpit. Just wake me up when it's over.

(2004)

---

able, and comforting—though not necessarily true," according to Steven Levitt, author of *Freakonomics* (2003).

* Here's a trick if the Democrats wish to snag a presidential victory: secretly sponsor a charismatic conservative or libertarian third-party candidate to the tune of millions—nay, billions—of dollars. That third-partier will safely split the vote of conservatives, leading to an easy Democratic victory. (It's happened before: see Perot, Ross.) Hint: For all you actual conservatives out there, this strategy works the other way around, too.

† And plenty of conservatives don't—he doesn't exactly conform to a Burkean ideal.

‡ But not for Jon Stewart, who has fashioned an entire career out of doing a single thing well: catching hypocrisy among pols.

§ Spoiler alert: Bush won.

# 25.

## Analysis of an Uncast Vote

*Constraints*: We shall only be examining votes in a single state during a presidential election year—the results that lie herein could conceivably be extended to other types of elections—and the candidate, either Republican or Democrat, with the highest number of votes is considered the victor in that individual state's contest. We will exclude third-party candidates because our mathematical model is not only simpler and more cogent with a two-party supposition, it is just as valid—since the political culture in the U.S., at the time of this writing, does not lend itself to viable third-party candidacies in presidential elections.

*Definitions*: Let us first define $r$ as the number of Republican votes and $n$ as the number of total votes ($n$ must be positive); let us also set $d$ to equal the number of Democratic votes or, alternatively, $d = n-r$.

*The Even Total Votes Case*: If the total number of votes cast (not counting my own uncast vote) is even, we shall see that the probability of my single vote altering the election results is negligible—it is $1/(n+1)$, where $n$, recall, is the total votes cast.

Let us consider the case of $n = 2$. When two votes are cast, there are three possibilities of vote totals:

$P_1$ => $r = 0$ and $d = 2$;
$P_2$ => $r = 1$ and $d = 1$;
$P_3$ => $r = 2$ and $d = 0$.

Only with $P_2$ is there any potential impact afforded to a single uncast vote—in this case, a single vote for either the Republican or Democratic candidate will determine the winner of the election in the state. In general, no matter how high $n$ is in any given election, when $n$ is even, there is only one possibility out of $n+1$ possible vote totals of a single uncast vote having an impact. The derivation of this, which may be calculated inductively, is left as an exercise to the reader.

*The Odd Total Votes Case*: If the total number of votes cast, not counting my own, is odd, we shall see that the probability of my single vote altering the election results is also negligible—it is $2/(n+1)$, where $n$, recall, is the total votes cast.

Let us consider the case of $n = 3$. When three votes are cast, there are four possibilities of vote totals:

$P_1 \Rightarrow r=0$ and $d=3$;
$P_2 \Rightarrow r=1$ and $d=2$;
$P_3 \Rightarrow r=2$ and $d=1$;
$P_4 \Rightarrow r=0$ and $d=3$.

If either $P_2$ or $P_3$ occurs then there is a potential impact afforded to a single uncast vote—in this case, a vote for either the Republican or Democratic candidate may tie the contest. In general, no matter how high $n$ is in any given election, when $n$ is odd, there are two possibilities out of $n+1$ possible vote totals of a single uncast vote having an impact in the election. The derivation of this is once again left to the interested reader.

*Margin of Error*: Utilizing our probability definitions above allow us to determine, *post hoc*, the precise potential impact of a single extra vote as long as we know $n$ (observe that we do not need to know $r$ or $d$). However it is unrealistic to assume that we shall know the precise number of votes to be cast prior to an election; thus, we must append to our mathematical model an allowance of a margin of error.

Let us define $M_I$ as the minimum total of a future $n$ value, and $M_f$ as the maximum total of a future $n$ value, where $M_f, M_i \in \mathbb{N}$. So that the following formulas hold, both margin of error values must be set to even numbers (they could just as easily be odd, but minor modifications to the equations below would have to be undertaken). Also, to simplify matters, let us assume that each of the potential *n*'s in the margin of error has an equal probability of matching the "true" final vote total. That is,

Probability of any given *n* in the margin of error is $M = \frac{1}{M_f - (M_i - 1)}$, since there are $M_f - (M_i - 1)$ total terms.

Now, let's define the following variables:

$$u \in \{\mathrm{N} \mid x \text{ is even}\}$$
$$v \in \{\mathrm{N} \mid x \text{ is odd}\}$$

This now leads us to:

$$P = M \cdot \left( \sum_{u=M_i}^{M_f} \frac{1}{u+1} + \sum_{v=(M_i+1)}^{(M_f-1)} \frac{2}{v+1} \right),$$

where $P$ is the probability of a single uncast vote making a difference (we are essentially calculating an expected value given a set of votes over a certain interval).

Since $P$, as $n$ gets large, is small, we can use a relatively simple formula to approximate it for a large $n$. We must first note that there is a 50 percent chance that $n$ will be even, and a 50 percent chance that it will be odd. Therefore, assuming we select an *even*-numbered $n$ somewhere between $M_i$ and $M_f$, we can claim that

$$P \approx Q = \frac{1}{2}\left( \frac{1}{n+1} + \frac{2}{(n+1)+1} \right),$$ where $n$ is sufficiently large.

Finally, we observe the following:

$$\lim_{n \to \infty} P - Q = 0.^{*}$$

(2006)

* An obvious criticism of this essay might be that "if everyone thought this way, no one would vote—rendering the math here meaningless." In philosophy, this would be termed the free rider problem blowing up into a "tragedy of the commons." But people don't usually make decisions based on math. (Plus, this essay is a satire along the lines of *The Journal of Irreproducible Results.*)

# 26.

## All Swans are White: Products of Odd Numbers are Always Odd

Let's first informally see that the product of an odd number* multiplied by an odd number will always turn out odd. Try calculating 7x9, or 3x7, or 15x3—all these products are odd. Of course, if we want to *prove* that any odd number times any odd number is odd we cannot go about testing the products of all of the numbers in the universe, since there are infinitely many; but if we could arrive upon one set of odd numbers that did *not* result in an odd product—in other words, if we encountered a *counterexample*—that *would* be sufficient to prove that the statement "Any odd number multiplied by any odd number results in a odd product" is false. As philosopher David Hume once said, "No amount of observations of white swans can allow the inference that all swans are white, but the observation of a single black swan is sufficient to refute that conclusion."

But there are no black swans here. To see why, we must generalize the product of odd numbers. First consider any odd number as the quantity $2k+1$, where $k$ is any integer.† Now, $2k$ will *always* be an even term of $2k+1$, since 2 multiplied by any integer is even. For example, if $k$ is equal to 3, then $2k = 2x3 = 6$, which is even. Plug in other integers for $k$ if you remain unconvinced.

Since $2k$ is an even term, 1 added to $2k$ will result in an odd sum. Another way to see this is to note that any term multiplied by 2 must be divisible by 2, and all even numbers are divisible by 2, so $2k$ must be even and one more than $2k$ must hence be odd. Thus, $2k+1$ represents a *generalized* odd number.

Now let's multiply a generalized odd number by another generalized odd number. If the product we obtain is also odd then we

---

* Note that by using the term "number" here and throughout this short essay we always mean integer.

† Any positive or negative whole number.

have demonstrated that any odd number times any odd number always results in an odd product, which is what we claimed initially.

Since $2k+1$ is a binomial expression (i.e., two unlike terms), when multiplying two binomials together we will use the "FOIL" method from middle school (first, outer, inner, last):

$$(2k+1)(2k+1) = 4k^2+2k+2k+1 = 4k^2+4k+1$$

The result can be factored slightly, as shown below.

$$4k^2+4k+1 = 2(2k^2+2k)+1$$

Since there is a 2 multiplying the quantity in parentheses in the first term of the factored product, we can say that $2(2k^2+2k)$ is divisible by 2—and is therefore even. If $2(2k^2+2k)$ is even (which it is), then 1 added to that quantity must result in an odd sum. So we have demonstrated that any two odd numbers multiplied together always results in an odd product.

What about multiplying more than two odd numbers together—how about three, four, five, or more? Let's call the "or more" $n$. Essentially, we have to multiply $(2k+1)$ by itself $n$ times and examine the product.

We can utilize the binomial theorem, which allows us to quickly see that:

$$(2k+1)^n = (2k)^n+n(2k)^{n-1}(1)^1 +[n(n-1)/2]\,(2k)^{n-2}(1)^2+\ldots+(1)^n$$

Since a 2 can be factored out of every term except for the last term—which is just 1, because $(1)^n = 1$—all terms except for the last are divisible by 2 and hence even, with the last term making the product of $(2k+1)^n$ odd. Therefore we have shown that the product of any number of odd numbers will always result in an odd number. Q.E.D.

(2000)

# 27.

## Too Clever by Half: Charting the Course of *The O.C.*'s Decline

Remember Act Three, Scene Four of *Hamlet*? You know, where Hamlet stabs the eavesdropping Polonius—"A bloody deed! almost as bad, good mother, / As kill a king and marry with his brother"—and the play's falling action begins? Things are never the same for our tensed-up characters, since their lives unravel and complications ensue. Polonius's death precipitates the decline.

We can sort of contrast this writer-intentioned descent with the much-popularized and parodied television show trait of jumping the shark* which is, of course, anything but writer-intentioned. Somewhere in the muddled area demarcating these two notions lies the edifice of Marissa and Ryan's mid-first season *The O.C.* relationship, perhaps the dumbest pairing of sensual-tension-laced leads since—well, since ever.

And it's a shame, since the show had such early potential. But that which is great often unwittingly sows the seeds of its own demise. Frankly, watching septuagenarians consummate their relationship in a nursing home with hospice awaiting eagerly to barge in† might be more interesting than witnessing Marissa and Ryan, since their first Ferris wheel kiss, dodge increasingly pointless bullets threatening their separation. Even an "exciting new loner" named Oliver—who might as well have been called, to be less subtle and more clever, Artifice—was introduced for one purpose: to create tension in a relationship which disingenuously screams of destiny.

On-screen consummated "destiny relationships" generally haven't had a good history. Remember *Moonlighting*? Or how about *Dawson's Creek*? Recall the near-implosion of *Creek* after Dawson

---

* That things-are-never-going-to-be-the-same moment, originally referring to The Fonz (Henry Winkler) jumping over a shark on the sitcom *Happy Days*.

† For what this might look like, imagine *The Notebook* with no flashbacks.

and Joey kiss at the end of the first season: their meant-to-be relationship lasted all of three episodes till the show's writers wisely distanced the two. Or, better yet, think back to the near-awful abbreviated third season of the up-to-then stellar *Felicity*, when viewers were forced to watch the machinations of Felicity and Ben's avoidance of communication; that's what marked the creative decline of the show, not Ms. Russell bobbing her hair.*

Look, there's simply no way to spin this: The falling action, à la *Hamlet*, has already begun on at least one *O.C.* plotline. It may and probably will ultimately suffocate the show, which has more often than not promulgated original and unpredictable situations, if it's allowed to perpetuate. Consider Summer's awfully unlikely fixation with Seth or Seth's banter with Anna: these are relationships with vitality and no hint of a shark fin. Banality is never a threat when Anna and Seth play with Captain Oats (disclaimer for the uninitiated: Captain Oats isn't a metaphor for some new bizarre, unsanctioned teenage pleasure, but simply a doll). And, after all, Seth and Summer, a *prima facie* relationship of destiny, at least in Seth's mind, did not hook up (yet); instead, Anna and Seth did, leaving the audience to wonder rather than experience—which was, *ipso facto*, the right course of action. No need to stultify us with unfulfilled expectations.

Therefore, writers of *The O.C.*: please allow the falling action to quickly run its course, and let Marissa and Ryan pine away for each other without ever again being together, otherwise there'll be more than just a vengeful Prince of Denmark to deal with in the mix.

(2004)

---

* The creative decline of *Felicity* did not coincide with the ratings decline. Ratings slid at the start of the second season, ostensibly due to the character Felicity's curly chopped top, but there's a confounding variable: the show moved that season to the different and less viewer-friendly timeslot of Sunday night.

# 28.

## A Thinly Veiled Western: *In the Heat of the Night* as Ethnography and Metaphor

All of the elements are there: the reluctant hero; the transient nature of the protagonist; the lawless, out-of-the-way town; the showdowns; the preponderance of guns; and the like. The Western narrative paradigmatic structure does not detract from *In the Heat of the Night* in any case, but it does—in a formulaic way—surrender some tension and render large portions of the diagesis passé.

For instance, consider the first third of the film, in which Virgil Tibbs, ever the loner, arrives by train. He encounters resistance on all fronts: he's arrested, then shunned and ignored. It is the spouse of the murdered Mr. Colbert who demands that Tibbs be kept on the case and not permitted to leave—à la the damsel in distress that, in the archetypal Western, clings to a perceived savior.

As an African American in a de facto segregated area, Tibbs can be a participant observer efficaciously (and hence an effective detective), both above the fray and yet inexorably linked to the fates of some denizens. He is unlikely to confuse the forest for the trees. Anthropologically, he might be the best fictional ethnographer of a post-antebellum, post-Reconstruction, pre-Civil-Rights-legislation* Deep South because of his positional points of interest and disinterest to the mores and culture; I wouldn't be surprised if half a dozen film doctoral dissertations over the years were built on that very notion.

Interestingly, Philadelphia is presented implicitly as a bastion of racial tolerance, togetherness and placidity in the movie, which in retrospect seems far from the case. Contrast the implicit Philadel-

---

* The film is set right around the time that Martin Luther King, Jr. penned his famous "Letter From Birmingham Jail," probably the most effective persuasive essay of all time.

phia with the explicit Mississippi: likewise by exposition, *ipso facto*, we are led to believe that—with the obvious exception of the opening murder—the town is an exemplar of placidity and pastoral serenity,* albeit segregated nefariously.

For the middle third of the film, when Tibbs is instructed dialectically to both leave and stay as the town grapples with the ugliness of its ossified social structure by confrontations with the commanding presence of the police detective, we could make all sorts of antiquarian connections—consider the parables in the Old Testament; Oedipus, who, analogous to the townsfolk, cannot see the obvious truths; and Freud, in which Tibbs can play the part of the Deep South's superego, lots of people can play the id, and Chief Gillespie can be the ego to sort it all out—but this seems to be both ancillary and besides the point, and also gives *In the Heat of the Night*, a relatively straightforward Western, a bit too much credit.

Note that it is with the arrival of Tibbs that the town reverts to a classically Western one; everyone, from the Sparta Chief of Police to the Mayor, falls in line with the tired archetypes. That's what saves *In the Heat of the Night* from being a complete retread of a Western,† since it is only with the impetus of the protagonist's arrival that the characteristics which define the Western paradigm are allowed to defile Virgil Tibbs and consequently wake us from our complacency, if only in a rather blasé way.

(2002)

* For proof of this, consider the empty jail cells in the police station. Either crime is a rarity, or "justice" is delivered swiftly.

† For a much sharper, more observant (though satiric) look at a similar milieu, watch the classic Mel Brooks comedy *Blazing Saddles* (1974).

# 29.

## Title Cards Tell the Story: Cut to *2001: A Space Odyssey*

Few films have received the critical adulation of *2001: A Space Odyssey* (1968)—it has the (deserved) gloss of perfection. Between the innumerable books, articles, and Internet discussions, there's a copious corpus out there.* Rather than sift through all this content, which is a Sisyphean task, let's focus on a small, almost throwaway yet important aspect of *2001*: its title cards.

Why do three title cards (ignoring the opening and closing credits sequences which are punctuated sublimely by Richard Strauss's Also Sprach Zarathustra)† appear at almost incongruous plot locations? The first, which describes the ascent of man, opens a sequence of primitive, *Homo erectus* man-apes foraging for food and struggling to survive. Until the imposing monolith appears, the man-apes are indistinguishable, in terms of behavior, from the other animals surrounding them—which, as a point of comparison, are shown naturally interacting with the man-apes in the barren habitat. The "ascent" of man, according to the filmmakers,‡ is the acquisition of both patterned and organized behavior; either the appearance of the monolith, suggesting to the man-apes that the environment can be consciously altered, or an actual "power" that the monolith instigates over the man-apes facilitates the behavioral change. Ultimately, though, the direct cause is beside the point, but

---

* One of the best: a book published on the year of HAL's "birth" called *HAL's Legacy: 2001's Computer as Dream and Reality* documents the progress made so far—in terms of sight, hearing, intelligence, etc.—in realizing the multifarious aspects of A.I.

† This Strauss piece's second-most-famous use? As the entrance music for legendary professional wrestler Ric Flair, used because it "projected the exact image I wanted—classical, yet futuristic" (from his autobiography *To Be the Man*).

‡ The construction of the narrative of *2001* was very much a collaboration between Stanley Kubrick and Arthur C. Clarke.

the result of the monolith's appearance is not: the man-apes have shed their ape-qualities and become men, gaining the ability of mental displacement and conscious intent. After the much praised (and much imitated and mocked)[*] tossed bone jump cut, the audience is transported perhaps a million years into the future. Yet there is no title card. The absence of a title card here suggests that while technological advancement has accelerated greatly, mental *capacity* for advancement (not the notion of technological "progress," which has increased linearly) has remained static.[†]

Following the surprisingly insipid performances of individuals whom the audience initially presupposes are lead characters,[‡] a second title card appears: "The Jupiter Mission." On the spacecraft headed towards the biggest planet to investigate a radio transmission from an unearthed monolith,[§] we observe the first signs of a higher intelligence—but, ironically (I guess), it is not a human one. Computer HAL's development into a purposefully malevolent machine presages humanity's final leap to a transcendent state of being at the film's end. And since "his" transformation occurs at the midpoint of *2001*, the "Jupiter Mission" also functions as a structural and thematic center.

Astronaut Dave Bowman's "Beyond Infinity" journey in the final third of the film, denoted by yet another title card, transitions *2001* to the contemplative. The first two parts of this *2001* triptych have functioned as almost "commonplace" filmmaking, at least as compared to the final sequence. Although the visuals in the first part of *2001* are unique, the documentary-like feel and the terse acting styles give audience members a common point of reference with other contemporaneous movies. The second segment of *2001* also is not entirely original either, because despite HAL's characterization, viewers have indeed been introduced to evil machines in

---

[*] E.g., *History of the World, Part 1*, among other films.

[†] Perhaps a *Star Trek* quote is in order. After Kirk dines Khan in probably the best-ever *TOS* episode "Space Seed," Khan—who has been in cryogenic freeze for hundreds of years—notes, when giving the captain his take on the future, "Oh, there has been technical advancement, but how little man *himself* has changed."

[‡] A false assumption. The film does not have readily identifiable main characters besides perhaps the computer HAL, despite what the silly sequel *2010* would have you think.

[§] Well, more precisely, an un-*mooned* one.

films before 1968. In addition, the almost comedic "unplugging" of HAL is well played but is not wholly original.

But with the final third of *2001*, audiences have no point of reference, little to compare. Dave Bowman is reborn into another not only mentally superior but mentally *different* form (much like the man-apes' evolutionary snap to humanness). The pastiche of lights, colors, and sounds projected on-screen[*] mark humanity's shedding of limits and an optimistic rebirth in the form of the Star Child, perhaps Kubrick's prefiguring of an imminent Singularity.[†]

(2000)

[*] The entire "journey" sequence of geometrical patterns and flashing colors may be a nod to the hallucinations caused by the then popular LSD, a hallucinogenic substance, since *2001* was released in the drug's heyday—the experience of the "journey" is psychedelic. See Oliver Sacks' *Hallucinations* for more.

[†] Rumors of the Singularity being "near" are greatly exaggerated (notwithstanding cochlear implants and the like), with apologies to both Twain and Kurzweil. For a concise essay exposing the cracks in Kurzweil's thinking, check out "The Closing of the Scientific Mind" by David Gelernter in *Commentary*.

# 30.

## *CITIZEN KANE*: THATCHER OVERSHADOWED

Young Charles Foster Kane, after removal from his household, is dominated by Thatcher, his guardian. However, without ever having any explicit exposition in the plot, the association shifts through time—Kane becomes the dominant individual. In particular, one scene at the beginning of the classic film *Citizen Kane* (1941), through a direct form-content relationship, effective lighting, and the usage of depth of field, encapsulates this changed interaction.

As a Christmas present, Thatcher gives a new sled to young Charles. Of course, Charles is not impressed by the gift, but he nonetheless sarcastically chimes in, "Merry Christmas…"—there is a cut—"…and a Happy New Year." A temporal ellipsis of nearly twenty years passes from the beginning of the sentence to its end. The audience's new image of Kane's guardian is of a very aged man with white hair—which nicely blends in with the snow falling outside the window beside him.

The time jump is motivated by audio; despite the synchronous audio between the two time frames, there is a dramatic contrast of some visual elements, but a unity of others. The unity is, of course, the presence of Thatcher; the contrast is Thatcher's presentation: he is shown as a looming, dominant figure before the ellipsis: notice his extreme low-angle framing as he hands Charles the sled. Proxemics also plays a role to further Thatcher's dominance. Although Kane and Thatcher are perhaps no more than a meter apart, the distance between them is greatly heightened by director Orson Welles' use of space—the audience cannot discern exactly how far apart the two figures are because of the lack of spatial orientation in the scene caused by the immediate low angle (of Thatcher) to high angle (of Kane) jump. (Also note that the cut from Thatcher to Kane and then back again to Thatcher twenty years hence is a shot-reverse-shot type of composition.)

Lighting contrast is minimal between Thatcher and the background (overall, both the inside background and Thatcher are lit darkly; also, Thatcher's hair color matches the immediate background color). The frame is tightly divided into two parts: Thatcher on the left side and a background plane on the right. The shot of Thatcher is also a bit canted over, or rotated, to one side. In addition, the background plane is somewhat important to the scene; in it, on the right side of Thatcher, we can see a Christmas tree. The audience realizes that Kane has received a gift (of a sled) from Thatcher because it is the holiday season.

After the temporal jump, Thatcher and the snow background outside the window are lit brightly, and once again there is little contrast between the wealthy guardian and the background (but the lack of contrast is with bright areas, not dark ones; also, Thatcher's hair color has now changed to white, matching the bright background). A direct form-to-content relationship is in evidence here; the form is a visual image of Thatcher's white hair, and the content is the temporal difference between the shots—the form is directly related to and readily assists the audience's understanding of the content of the sequence.

The juxtaposition between the two time periods is heightened by the reverse lighting in the space (by reverse, I am referring to the change in lighting between the inside of the house that Thatcher was shot in low angle at, and then the immediate switch to a relatively brightly lit [at least near the window which Thatcher is standing next to] office building) and the several common bright elements (viz., the snow and brightness outside the window reminds the viewer of the Kane's household shown only several seconds before [several seconds in screen time, of course]).

The audience sees Thatcher, now an aged man, dictating a letter to Kane about his holdings. Although Kane is not in the room, it is apparent in the mise-en-scene that there has been, in the twenty years since we last saw Charles, a shift in dominance between the guardian and the guarded. After the temporal ellipsis, Thatcher is no longer shot from a low angle; he is framed only from eye-level or high angle shots in the sequence (this, of course, emphasizes the change; although Welles does not necessarily imply throughout the film that any person shot from a high angle is automatically a dominant figure, the contrast between the low angle shot of Thatcher and the high angles twenty years later strongly suggests that there was indeed a change in dominance).

When the audience first observes the white-haired Thatcher, the frame is divided into two elements: Thatcher and a window; both elements seek to orientate the viewer to the sudden shift in time. And both elements recall the reverse shot: the low angle shot of Thatcher twenty years before placed the guardian on the left side of the frame; now, he is on the right side. This juxtaposition of elements cues the viewer to appreciate the temporal difference.

Outside the window, which has an effectively infinite depth of field, we observe snow and buildings (we realize quickly that we are no longer in a rural area; we also understand that the season has not changed—it is still winter, so the statement "and a Happy New Year" sounds completely appropriate). The depth of field is mostly consistent between the two time periods, although twenty years later we have a slightly larger depth of field simply because we can see out the window.

On the other side of the frame, in the foreground plane of action, there is a medium close up of Thatcher, but not a visual match of the Thatcher that took Charles away from his home—this Thatcher has white hair. Thus, within a couple of seconds of screen time, the audience realizes that a good chunk of story time has elapsed. Thatcher's next statement, about Charles's twenty-fifth birthday, focuses our perception of exactly how many years have passed.

Therefore, it is the *audio*, not the visuals, which cue us precisely to the difference in diagesis time. The editing between the two shots is critical—it matches up the first part of Thatcher's sentence twenty years before with the final part of his sentence twenty years later. The two shots placed side-by-side have created a new meaning for the audience. In these two shots, at least, Eisenstein's famous A+B = C equation applies.

The lighting in Thatcher's dictation scene appears realistic but is somewhat stylized. As the guardian walks from one part of the room to the other (whilst speaking), he falls in and out of shadows of light. He face momentarily appears and disappears because of the lighting contrast between him and the space. The form-content relationship is apparent here; because we realize that Thatcher is not talking directly to Kane, but rather dictating a letter to him, the lighting implies that Thatcher, in the decades that have passed, has remained "in and out" of touch (and control) with Charles.

Also notice Thatcher's proxemics in the space as he walks around the room. He always maintains a fixed distance from the man he is dictating to (who is always darkly lit and whose face the audience never sees—which cues us to largely ignore the character). Essentially, the frame is divided between the two men; they never share the same portion (or side) of the frame.

Despite Thatcher's changing lighting as he strolls around the room, he is almost always brighter than the man he is dictating to, further reinforcing Thatcher's importance and the other man's lack of importance in the space. (In fact, the mise-en-scene cues us to associate the man with Thompson; we also never see Thompson's face in the frame throughout the film.)

Thatcher's new, impotent relationship with Kane is dramatized by Thatcher's visual expressions: they range from disgust to anger through the sequence. For instance, after another temporal ellipsis motivated by audio (which carries Charles's response to Thatcher's letter about his monetary holdings), Thatcher realizes that Kane only wishes to run a newspaper. Notice the continuity of action between the Thatcher's letter and Charles's response. We remain within the same space, but once again, like the previous ellipsis, the time frame changes, although it is not more than a week later in story time.

In addition we realize that once again the content of the audio, not the visual presentation of the office space, initiates the temporal jump. The audio is not consistent between the two sequences, however. Thatcher is the main speaker before the temporal ellipsis, and after the jump in time, the "unknown man," whom we have never heard before, is now speaking, although he is still not shown (there is a new character present in the space next to Thatcher but he is not lit brightly so, though intrigued, we largely ignore his presence).

Comparing the two temporal jumps in the scene thus far, we realize that they are both motivated nearly entirely by audio; however, while the first temporal jump is consistent with the content of the sentence spoken, the second is not. If not for the audio discontinuity, then, the time difference would be difficult to discern despite the slight change in camera position (to an eye-level shot of Thatcher) and the new character standing next to Thatcher. Even the proxemics are the same between the time jumps. Thatcher, prior to the jumps, sits down in his chair. After the jumps, Thatcher and the man whom Thatcher is dictating to are in the exact same space.

Instead of giving the audience a specific time ellipsis value, analogous to the first jump, Welles apparently believes that the more important information to gather between the two time frames is not the time jump duration itself (which, again, is probably a week), but rather Kane's response to the letter. Therefore, the director is implying that during the first ellipsis, the audience should be concerned about the difference in time, and, in the second, we should pay attention to the content of Kane's response.

After reading Kane's statement, Thatcher repeats the final sentence in disbelief: "I think it would be fun to run a newspaper." He looks directly at the camera, and delivers a direct address: this creates a visual impact that does not necessarily cause us to sympathize with the guardian but certainly allows us to take notice of his feelings about Charles's actions.

The visual and temporal rhythms of the scene are very fast-paced. Although every cut signifies a change in time (which is an editing stylistic feature and will be continued into the next sequence: the newspaper montage), the camera moves back and forth continuously to follow Thatcher's movements; the scene has a kind of "rhythmic heartbeat" because Thatcher, even while sitting, is still moving in his chair.

A montage sequence* follows Thatcher's glance at the audience. But the montage, analogous to the temporal ellipsis, is motivated by audio: several notes of the soundtrack begin playing to assist our change in perception (and cue us to respond to an abstracted version of reality in the form of a montage sequence). The screen dissolves to a camera dolly pullback of approximately a dozen people, all dressed in black, reading Kane's newspaper. Because it is a dolly shot, and the camera is moving, an arc of expectation builds: what

---

* Although the montage sequence that dissolves into the screen is not technically part of the scene, it is an integral part of this mise-en-scene analysis because it neatly parallels, visually elaborates on, and completes the arc of development of the dominance-impotence relationship established between Kane and Thatcher. Thus, because of its importance to the mise-en-scene, a brief analysis of the newspaper montage sequence follows in the main text.

will be at the end of the shot? Will there be the payoff? Although we are in a stylized, music-filled montage sequence, there is indeed a payoff to the shot. The audience sees, at the back of everyone in the space, Thatcher, quite angry with the publisher of the newspaper, read the headline and dispose of the paper. Thatcher stands out visually for several reasons. He is the only person in the space speaking; he is the only person in the space moving; he contrasts with the lighting of the space; he is dressed differently than the homogeneously blackly dressed individuals in front of him; and we observe more of his facial features that any other person in the frame. Therefore, though Thatcher is not facing the camera, he is the central focus of the shot, the one we pay attention to most.

Like the temporal ellipsis, which allowed us to quickly orient to the time frame partly due to Thatcher's repeated appearances, the montage sequence does not disorientate us also because of the presence of Thatcher. In each quick cut of the montage, Thatcher is there; in addition, his actions and verbal tone are similar. In each segment of the montage, Thatcher throws down the *Inquirer* after reading the headline (which he never approves of).

The montage sequence, a series of ideas irrespective of time or space, accelerates us through the story. It functions as a type of idea-orientated temporal ellipsis; in other words, both time passes during the montage and also an idea dependent on time is presented. The sequence obliquely describes the *Inquirer*'s development into a perceptive, hard-hitting newspaper that ultimately is very popular with the public and a force to be reckoned with in the city. Also, Thatcher does not approve of the politics of the paper; this is explicitly conveyed by his actions in each segment of the sequence.

Finally, after the montage concludes and the music stops playing, we have a transition back to "reality," or normal time: the audience is behind Thatcher, in a somewhat similar shot to the montage sequence's visuals, with Thatcher holding another one of Kane's newspapers, reading the headline. It is because of the visual and audio commonality that we can accept the transition back to a standard temporal space. Instead of throwing the newspaper, Thatcher slowly moves it off the frame revealing Kane framed with a high shot (he is in the middle of the frame).

The framing of Charles from a high angle recalls his similar framing as a boy in the company of Thatcher (immediately preceding the temporal ellipsis): from a high angle. In that prior scene,

Thatcher's dominance over the boy is shown. But now, with the twenty-year jump (and Thatcher's loss of control over the "wild" Kane), the framing serves as an ironic commentary on the new dominance-impotence relationship between the two men. The shot, then, simultaneously reminds us of the prior relationship and orientates us to the new one. It is Kane who is the center of attention now; he is lit brightly and in contrast with the background (and in focus).

Although the dominance-impotence relationship between Kane and Thatcher is neither explicitly mentioned nor developed again through the remainder of the movie, the mise-en-scene in the newspaper montage sequence and Thatcher's office sequence set a tone for the rest of the film. What Kane, and the audience, eventually realize is that the only person the newspaper baron was able to establish dominance over was his former guardian. Kane is presented as a dominant figure only ironically—because of his utter lack of control over the chaotic world he alone unwittingly creates for himself.

(1999)

# 31.

## Mirror, Mirror: A Look at Jane Smiley's *The Age of Grief*

A mirror is a very revealing thing. Worlds which may not have been visible at first glance appear with the aid of a reflection. In Jane Smiley's novella *The Age of Grief* (1987), a metaphysical world is presented with extensive mirror imagery. Smiley creates a family, the Hursts, full of a rich history and terrifying inner demons. To the uninformed observer, the Hursts' lives appear stable. But the mirror imagery Smiley utilizes alerts the reader to growing problems. The *ironic middle* (a term used by the main character), or comfort zone, is degrading within the family. And the mirror, by presenting an abstract realm to that main character, furthers the problems in the Hurst household.

The reader meets Dave, the protagonist, who is a professionally successful middle-aged man with a wife, named Dana, and three children. He and Dana are both dentists, and they have a private practice in a small town. Because of a substantial accumulated wealth, the Hursts are able to afford a summer home. But as successful as Dave is, he cannot operate without a tool to assist his dentistry: the mirror. Dave, as a dentist, relies on reflections to keep his job, since in order to scan a mouth for problems he must interpret the images of teeth by using a tool that is essentially a mirror on a stick (it's called a mouth mirror). He probes mouths with the device during long workdays; therefore, he takes reflections for granted—he realizes that the mouth mirror allows him to view hard-to-reach or difficult-to-see places, allowing him to practice his craft. As he cleverly points out to the reader, if he is an artist, his greatest work is never seen (sans mirror).

Dana also makes use of a mirror. In addition to being a dentist, she is also a respectable singer, having performed in the opera *Nabucco*. Dave is convinced she has fallen in love with a member of the production, though he has little evidence. While driving Dana home after her last performance in the opera, she says, "I'll never be happy again." Why will she be unhappy? Because she cannot be close to her potential new love interest or because her moment of operatic glory is over? The answer is unclear, so Dave glances up at her through the rearview mirror of his car for hints.

Apparently, he sees another side of Dana only revealed by the mirror—a Dana in love with another man. The mirror, in Dave's eyes, supports his conclusion that she "fell in love with one of her fellow singers, or maybe it was the musical director." But can his analysis be substantiated? Dave's use of the mirror is questionable. The mirror reverses her image, so, therefore, her physical features are backwards. In addition, the mirror distorts her face slightly. The distortion is more prominent than the mouth mirror Dave uses in his dentist's office every day, because of the larger distance between the object being viewed (here, his wife), and the mirror.

Thus, Dave, taking the mirror's image for granted, thinks he has witnessed an entirely new side to his wife—a side so deeply in love with another man that she can "never be happy again." But is the mirror displaying his wife's guilt of infidelity or simply revealing a sorrowful facet of Dana (as the car's warning describes, "objects in mirror are closer than they appear"; could Dana be close enough to the rearview mirror in order to avoid appearing distorted to Dave?)? Of course, just as Dave uses a mirror to probe people's mouths, he uses the rearview mirror to figuratively probe Dana; he never directly asks her, "Do you have a love interest?" but instead examines her with a device he believes will reveal the "cavity" in their relationship.

Does he see the truth in the car's rearview mirror, or is his truth simply a reversed distortion? Although he is a very proficient dentist, quite good at using reflections to analyze and correct problems with teeth, Dave's view of the images in a mirror outside of the dentist's chair is potentially inaccurate. In order to establish a case for his inaccuracy, we must examine Dave's spouse in more detail.

Dana, an opposite of Dave in nearly every respect (she is more of the "fatherly" figure, with Dave the sensitive, more maternal parent in the relationship; their names even mirror each other) might be properly thought of as his living reflection. Dana, like a mirror, reveals Dave's characteristics. However, Dave does not correctly predict what his reflection, Dana, thinks of his own personality. While visiting their summer retreat, Dave's spouse voices an odd remark. "'You know,' she said, 'you scare me a little. You always have." Dave fails to see the attribute; in fact, the narration alerts the reader that in fact *Dana scares Dave*. Thus he has perceived himself incorrectly in the "living mirror" (that being Dana); his initial analysis was reversed and distorted. If his use of reflections is faulty outside of the dentist's office, his belief about Dana's infidelity is possibly wrong as well.

Dana is not the only person in the family who benefits from being looked at as a mirror. As author Marian Nelson points out, the couple's references to their children "suggest that the children are mirror images of their parents." Lizzie, the oldest, is an abstract reflection of Dave's pent-up emotions. She repeatedly feels ill during automobile journeys. Dave always stops the car and pulls over to the shoulder of the road. He helps Lizzie out of the vehicle, in anticipation of her vomiting. But she never does; her continual near-climax of full-blown sickness reflects Dave's near-confessions of his fears to his wife. Just as Lizzie is never quite visibly sick (and probably will later develop emetophobia), Dave is never quite openly truthful about his belief of his wife's infidelity.

Lizzie's pseudo-sickness allows Dave to have another chance at examining his wife through the mirror, in an attempt to support his conclusion of infidelity. While driving back to the city with his children in tow and Dana riding in another vehicle behind him, Dave once again glances in his rearview mirror.

> At stoplights, my glances in the rearview mirror gave me a view of her unyielding head. At one point, when I looked at her too long and missed the turning of the light, she beeped her horn.

Dave looks at his wife and sees aggression; he is clearly afraid of her. For Dave, each viewing of his wife's reflection is a virgin one; the mirror gives him an opportunity to probe into the emotions of his wife, which are normally in a hard-to-reach location, like a cavity lodged in the underside of a tooth. He can carefully look at the woman he married with the protection a barrier (they are both not in the same automobile) to prevent her from telling him the inevitable, or so he thinks: that she has a romantic infatuation with another man. But note the distance between the mirror and Dana; as the story progresses, and Dave consistently uses the mirror, it appears that the further away an object is from the mirror, the more distorted the object appears.

Before Dave really has a chance to examine Dana through the mirror though, Lizzie puts a stop to his probing. "Lizzie said that her stomach hurt." His oldest child's sickness is a mirror image of Dave, bringing back to the fore his emotions about Dana's potential lover. His fears and difficulty with his marriage will continue; the trip to their summer home did nothing to alleviate the pressure in the relationship. Dave's response to Lizzie's stomach pain furthers this analysis: "I said, 'You can stand it until we get home.'" Dave has every intention of continuing the obsession, right back to the doorstep of his city home.

During yet another "revealing" automobile journey, Dave peers in his rearview mirror—and this time examines his children with the probe:

> I couldn't resist looking at Lizzie and Stephanie again and again in the rearview mirror. They were astonishingly graceful and attractive, the way they leaned toward each other and away, the way their heads bent down and then popped up, the way their gazes caught, the way they ignored each other completely and stared out the windows.

Dave uses the mirror to distance himself from his own family, just as when he viewed his wife in the mirror to see her face for the "first time." It is like he is peering into a dollhouse world, like he is looking at his own family from the outside. Dave believes in the power of the mirror to present him details not readily apparent. "I felt as if I had never seen them before" is his response to the revealing reflection. "Seeing" the children is important to Dave because they represent a kind of permanent bond between husband and wife. In addition, as Nelson notes, the offspring can be thought of as representing mirror images of family members. Therefore, Dave, possibly in an attempt to understand Dana, looks at the children as a "part" of Dana. But any emotions or feelings his wife contains have been filtered and degraded through a system: Dana, to the children, to the mirror, and finally to Dave's eyes. The mirror has distorted an already distorted image. Furthermore, the distance factor (the length between the object being observed through the mirror and the mirror itself, as repeatedly mentioned) continues to play a key role in the amount of distortion.

Dave utilizes the mirror in two ways: to inspect hard-to-see places (the backs of teeth, the features of his children) and to create a protective barrier between himself and the object he wishes to observe (Dana, the children, Dana through the children). But, just as Dave does in the dentist's office, he uses the mirror to examine the problems and features that are difficult to spot, not to distance himself from the reflections in the mirror. Rather, he creates a barrier between the objects in the mirror and himself simply to effectively analyze the images. But in creating the barrier, he increases the distance between the object being viewed and the mirror, thus decreasing the efficacy of the mirror. Therefore, the mouth mirror Dave employs during dentistry barely distorts the images of posterior segments of teeth, since the distance between the objects being viewed and the mirror is small. Conversely, Dave's probe of Dana between vehicles is fairly ineffective because of the distance between his wife and the rearview mirror.

Dave is the principal player; he simply needs a weapon, the mirror, to help him handle his problems. Analogous to a sword or an old-fashioned pistol, the weapon is effective at close range only. Dave, lacking skills of vocal articulation, requires another means to understand a person besides speaking. The mirror gives him a gateway to explore a person's feelings (a hard-to-reach place, like the back of a tooth). The mirror "balances" his lack of speaking skills. If there is a problem with a person, he wishes to understand it—but he will not vocalize his inquiry. Dave wields the mirror weapon to probe and dissect Dana, his children, and other people's mouths.

But are Dave's observations accurate, or only backwards interpretations of reality? Jane Smiley wisely chooses not to reveal the nature of the mirror's truthfulness. Dave has essentially lived by the mirror; his job relies on the device for every examination; and its penetrating abilities paradoxically further the decay in his personal life while they help halt decay in teeth in his professional life. But the mirror also shows him another side to his children, images that are beautiful and graceful. Is a new perspective opened up to Dave with the mirror? Is the mirror an asset to Dave, even with the problem of the distance factor, or does it arrest him emotionally? Does the mirror create the fantasy of infidelity, or merely confirm it?

Does the mirror perpetuate Dave's paranoia? In fact, does Dave's use of the mirror *cause* the cavity in his relationship in the first place? Like a visit to the dentist, the answers to these questions may be both helpful and terrifying.*

(1998)

* Some answers do come in the very odd movie *The Secret Lives of Dentists* (2002), based on the novella. Comedian Denis Leary plays Dave's inner voice.

# 32.

## A Proof in the Inner City

Even from about three blocks away, the tall, angular, and dark planes forming the contours of the exterior of the school were clearly visible. The houses and buildings and eyesores surrounding the school were at most half its height—Baud High School (a pseudonym; all proper names in this essay are pseudonyms) dominated the skyline and blocked direct sunlight from my view. Only through the small and perfectly square windows at the highest floors were shimmers and projections of bright yellow light from the sun allowed to reach me. Several smokestacks on the roof, releasing dark billows that contrasted with the blue-gray sky of the early morning, added even more altitude to Baud High School's six stories. The school's stature appeared imposing in the surrounding chaotic urban landscape of inner city Philadelphia.

I parked my car in the rear lot. Entry to the school at the early hours is easier from there, Assistant Principal Thomas Baker had told me. Walking the path from my car to the rear entrance, I accidentally stepped onto a small pile of junk food wrappers soaked in some rainwater from the downpour the night before.

My first impressions of the school were crystallizing before I had any human contact. I immediately thought that the school was typical for the city, for the environment. I also thought of the "savage inequalities" of Jonathan Kozol. "We're definitely not like other schools in the city—there's something special and different about our school and our students," the assistant principal explained to me over the phone several days before my visit. "You'll see, and I'm sure you'll notice the differences."

But there was a dissonance between his briefing and what I saw before me; nothing positive he had said was registering in my mind as I opened the rear double-doors. Besides the influences of the media—who construct mostly negative, war-zone-like images of America's inner city schools—the lucid Mike Rose book, *Lives on the Boundary*, which unflatteringly describes several urban schools (an example is the Maravilla district where he has some of his formative pedagogic experiences), certainly had an influence on my expectations.

The context of the community also figured into my first impressions. The socioeconomic level of the area, judging from a brief visual survey, was not particularly high. Weathered brick row homes and alleys surrounded the perimeter of Baud High. Early-model automobiles lined the potholed, narrow streets. The school's webpage, which has only one isolated shot of the exterior of Baud High, does not discuss the economic situation of the neighborhood—but that situation was clearly in disrepute, at least compared with many suburban areas.

There was a dramatic visual contrast when I stepped inside the school, though. The lobby, lined with clear glass cases of models of bridges, robots, and various kinds of vehicles, was bright and airy. Baud High values technology—this was immediately apparent.

The school is vocational, and students must pass an exam to gain entry. The paper-and-pencil test, according to the school's website, is designed to differentiate students based on "real-world skills and applications in technology and the industrial arts." To be admitted into Baud High School, prospective students must excel in a "testing meritocracy" designed to include or exclude them into the school's community. The school is not a take-all-comers institution, like many others in the inner city (à la magnet schools).

I went to the elevator and pressed the "3" button—the math department was located on the third floor. Exiting the elevator and glancing around the long and narrow corridors, the lack of posters or flyers on the walls was striking: the dull beige walls were bare. The rows and rows of identical lockers that lined the walls were the most interesting visual stimuli. The chaotic landscape outside of the school—the potholed streets, the makeshift houses, the billows of smoke—contrasted with the order and the structure inside of the school—like the models displayed in the lobby and the rows and rows of lockers in the halls.

The math department, located in a single, expansive room, had two new Apple computers resting on the center of a long table. The impression of a technological community was furthered by the presence of these contemporary machines. I met the math department head, Dr. Bradley, and the other teachers. Before my first observation (scheduled for the first period of the day), I listened to the early morning chatter in the math department. The teachers joked incessantly with each other; their energy level was quite high, and smiles were everywhere. Did they actually *enjoy* working here? I wondered. I had assumed, because of descriptions in the Mike Rose text mentioned earlier—and also the subversive book by Paulo Freire, *Teachers as Cultural Workers*, which presents teaching as a perpetual struggle—that inner city teachers used all of their energy to handle the various pressures of the school, but certainly not to joke around. After all, more than half of the school year had elapsed, and these teachers must certainly have been tired from their daily trials and tribulations.

The light mood in the math office did not extend into the classroom, however. I was assigned to follow Mrs. Barnes into her eleventh-grade geometry class. We walked there together, and she told me what to expect: "These kids are just *not* where they should be. I'm not far enough into [the year's curriculum].... We need to move faster, and they need to understand a lot more than they do now."

Taking a seat at the back of the room, I was able to see the layout of the classroom clearly. A computer resided at one end of the class (next to Mrs. Barnes' desk), and a microwave was on a table at the other end. The presence of these electronics added to my impression of Baud High as a technology center. The desks in her classroom were arranged orderly in five rows and five columns and were evenly spaced apart. Students, as they entered the room, took packages of food in a crate next to the door and lined up at the microwave to heat them up. During this time, the students were quietly talking, asking each other questions (inaudibly from my location), and Mrs. Barnes was preparing the lesson. She wrote a proof on the whiteboard—which asked students to confirm if a certain triangle was isosceles—while students clustered together and ate their food.

Ten minutes into the class, most of the thirty students had arrived but had still not settled down. Mrs. Barnes, in a loud tone, policed the students to their seats. "Get to your desks and quiet down!" "Miss, I need a pencil," a student said. "That's Miss *Barnes*. Here's a pencil—but give it back to me at the end of the period."*

* I wonder if she would have corrected the student if an adult observer (i.e., me) hadn't been in the room—after all, it was midway through the school year; shouldn't the students have known by now *not* to call her just "Miss"?

Nearly the entire class' population was composed of minorities. This was my expectation, since the demographics of the area suggest a largely minority population. The school's website also described the student body as mostly minority.

About fifteen minutes (!) into the class period, after the students were calmed and seated, Mrs. Barnes began the lesson with a brief review of the definition and properties of isosceles triangles. There were no real world examples talked about, and there were no visual demonstrations. She walked around the front of the room and, in a loud voice, posed questions for students to answer. "What's special about the isosceles triangle compared with other triangles?" "If two of three of their sides are the same length, what does that imply about their angles?" Students signaled that they had an answer by raising their hands. Two or three students called out answers, but were quickly reprimanded by Mrs. Barnes.

When she was finished with the oral-questioning session—I suppose that she was satisfied that the basics of the triangle's properties had been addressed—students' attention was directed to the proof on the board. geometry is a unique subject in the mathematics high school curriculum because of proofs. Algebra, precalculus, and statistics are usually not examined on an advanced enough level in standard high school curricula to permit extensive excursions into the world of proof. But to prove theorems in geometry requires comparatively little mathematical knowledge on the topic, and nearly all geometry classes have some treatment of the notion of proof by the middle of the academic year—which, again, was when this observation took place.

Let me be frank: my expectations were low. Although some students, who participated during the oral-questioning session, enumerated the properties of the isosceles triangle, proof was an entirely different story, an entirely different way of thinking. Especially high school proof, which not only requires an excellent grasp of deductive, logical, and algorithmic thinking, but also necessitates a knowledge of conventions: the "givens," the "statements," and the "conclusions." Whereas in more advanced mathematics proofs are surprisingly informal and loose—as long as the mathematical statements logically and correctly reconcile—proofs in high school geometry are rigid and allow little creativity; the rules and the rules of the rules, so to speak, are strictly defined and must be mastered by pupils.

I did not suspect that anyone could completely prove the statement on the board. It was not especially easy, since several intuitive leaps were required to solve it. The transitive property—if A equals B and B equals C, then A equals C—was the linchpin of the proof. An awareness of complementary and supplementary angles was implicitly needed in at least one statement. And a complete understanding of isosceles triangles was essential otherwise the proof would be effectively meaningless: without explicitly noting that the statements in the proof demonstrated all of the properties of the isosceles triangle, the proof would be unfinished.

"So who wants to prove that this triangle is isosceles, based on what we have here?" A single volunteer raised her hand. Mrs. Barnes called her up to the whiteboard. To my amazement, one minute and five lines later, the student correctly proved the theorem.

The event must be put into perspective, however. Since I did not observe the class period prior, I cannot be entirely sure that Mrs. Barnes didn't go over the same proof in the previous class—and the student simply repeated what she had already seen. After all, this could be part of Mrs. Barnes' theory of practice: show students difficult procedures with examples, ask them to repeat the answers to those same examples, and hope that the students truly understood what they were doing. She might believe that knowledge is learned that way. But there was no mention from anyone that the proof was covered earlier.

And the next example Mrs. Barnes used in class makes this scenario of "repeated proof" unlikely. Mrs. Barnes opened up her geometry text for the first time during the period and culled a proof from the chapter to write on the board. "Here's something you haven't seen yet: I need someone to solve this proof about vertical angles and the isosceles triangle," she told the class loudly.

A different student volunteered, and he also quickly solved the proof on the whiteboard. Mrs. Barnes did not criticize the solution, but she did not congratulate the student for the correct proof, either. She merely said, "Correct, take your seat, and now let's take a look at what homework you all had to do for today."

The last five minutes of class were spent discussing homework due for the next class period. Although she only assigned five problems, one of the students in class complained. "I protest," he said.

A quick retort followed: "You can protest all you want, but you're still getting it to do for tonight!"

Although Mrs. Barnes' class had a high level of student involvement with mathematical knowledge, the class had a low level of teacher-student interactivity. She definitely did not have a buddy-buddy-type rapport with her students. She was the clear sole authority in the room, and there was little that would alter her plans for the class session. She also solely controlled the flow of knowledge in the room and the way that the knowledge was presented to her students, whether it was by showing examples of problems, questioning them on mathematical properties (like of an isosceles triangle), or other means. The students' relationship with the text passed through her—for instance, she told her pupils specifically which homework problems to tackle. And her word was final: she assigned a specific number of homework problems, and a student's protest could not convince her otherwise. To Mrs. Barnes, the classroom was not a democracy, but an autocracy, with her solely in charge of all its attributes.

Following the class, Mrs. Barnes spoke to me about her authority. "My first-period class is always well-behaved and listens to me; that is my best class." No mention at all of the proofs, of the students' progress at understanding the mathematics, of the amazing performances of several of the students—only a statement about issues of control.

Although "control" is an objective of all teachers for obvious reasons (without control over a class, teachers cannot teach), Mrs. Barnes' theory of practice appeared to be built primarily on the notion of control. Control over the direction and *specific* math problems shown to the class, and control over the students' behaviors. For instance, preempting the students from eating their own food in class—by supplying them with food—is a method of control. Giving them food to eat, in case they didn't have any breakfast in the morning, also is a means of control, of ensuring that they have enough energy to be awake and aware for the entire class period. Complaints of "I'm hungry" were not heard, since food was readily available. Mrs. Barnes eliminated the problem of hunger for her early morning first-period class by providing the cure—food.*

---

* Whether or not she *bought* the food, rather than merely supplied it, I never found out.

The explicit routines that Mrs. Barnes had in her class—the food distribution and the oral-questioning session are examples of this—helped her gain and maintain control over the class. In each class, Mrs. Barnes told me, students could expect the food, and they could expect the questioning session. The routines helped Mrs. Barnes set classroom expectations: the routines were not a surprise to her pupils, because the routines were stable and consistent. Notions of control and routine are thus closely related.

The classroom routines may have also been beneficial to the inner city students. After class, Mrs. Barnes explained to me that the most stable influence many of these teenagers have in their lives is the classroom. School, because of the routine itself, is a refuge for kids, a counterbalance to the chaos of the outside world. Mrs. Barnes conceives of herself as a guardian *in loco parentis* of this stability role of the school; she wishes to ensure that the routines, at least in her classroom, remain consistent and stable so that the school is truly anathema to the chaotic environment her students may encounter when they leave. Students should be able to count on her to be there and to be ready. The role of Mrs. Barnes-as-guardian in the school also impacts the community outside of the classroom, since she defined the school as a refuge for teens subsisting in the outside world. (And, as a related point, the idea of an orderly "technology center"—which Baud High strives to be—sharply contrasts with the chaotic environment outside of the school; it places the school into relief vis-à-vis the rest of the community.) This type of guardianship is also counterpoint to educational theorist Paulo Freire's conception of teachers "mothering" students, which is an exclusively classroom function with negative, passive connotations. The teacher-as-guardian role has active, positive connotations because of its community benefit, and it is an important feature of Mrs. Barnes' theory of practice since it describes her role as a teacher.

Nevertheless, the quest for teacher control over a class—even if it comes as the result of routines—cannot be the overriding or driving factor of a lesson, of the presentation of knowledge. Mrs. Barnes' control of her students was impressive but was perhaps at the expense of teaching mathematics.

Her strict routines for class control impacted the methodology of her presentation of knowledge. Mrs. Barnes had very specific math objectives for the period: Introduce (or reintroduce) the properties of an isosceles triangle; demonstrate several proofs to the class members; discuss the homework from the night before; and assign new homework. Although a teacher must always have objectives in a lesson plan for each class period, it is not effective to treat the lesson plan as sacrosanct. Presenting mathematics cannot be just another "routine," commensurate with distributing food. Plans are made to be broken—or at least modified. Mrs. Barnes' pedagogic methods may have appeared to have effective results—the dramatic ways that the students solved the proofs gave me that impression—but I was left unsure of how many students really understood what was going on.

To get her pupils to complete work, Mrs. Barnes threatened her students with sanctions. For instance, after examples culled from the previous night's homework were placed on the whiteboard, Mrs. Barnes told her students, "When you take the PSSAs [Pennsylvania's set of standardized exams], you'd better know how to do these problems, and do them fast or you'll be in deep trouble!" For the remainder of the class period, Mrs. Barnes continued to associate mathematical knowledge with the handling of more advanced mathematical queries. Mrs. Barnes' ability to explicitly tell students about the bigger picture, about the purpose behind the lessons—that they are preparation for upcoming standardized exams—is a feature of her theory of practice, since she's orienting the students to the placement of mathematical knowledge in the "real-world" (i.e., the world outside of the confines of this specific classroom). Knowledge counts—insofar as without having the knowledge, a student is unable to handle the more advanced ideas (required for assessments). Extending this notion further, we can claim that Mrs. Barnes believes that knowledge builds on itself, in a linear fashion, like stepping stones: without knowledge "A," there can be no knowledge "B"; without knowledge "B," there can be no knowledge "C"; and so forth. For example, an understanding of arithmetic is needed before comprehension of algebra is possible, and a comprehension of algebra is required before precalculus can be tackled. According to Mrs. Barnes, this scaffolding approach is how knowledge is obtained by her pupils.

But the actual teaching strategy that Mrs. Barnes utilized to help students learn the content seemed inappropriate for the topic of proofs. Given the setup of the room that day (i.e., the facing-forward seating arrangement), and the proof she placed on the board at the beginning of class, I expected a lecture session on some proof fundamentals (which in itself is not the most appropriate setup because proofs, I believe, must be taught and learned in a self-discovery method. An example of a teachable self-discovery method for proofs is the Interactive Mathematics Program at Central High School* and some other high schools around the country). Instead, several students participated in what was largely an exclusionary session for rest of the class; by "exclusionary" I mean that most students were excluded from any type of mathematical self-discovery. But the excluded students also were not the empty vessels urgently waiting to be filled by the teacher (the *tabula rasa* of philosopher John Locke's conception), since Mrs. Barnes did not lecture her students on mathematics.

Instead, Mrs. Barnes dictated the terms of instruction—her knowledge, and her presentation of that knowledge, is what counted in the classroom. She placed specific problems on the board, in an order of her choosing, for volunteers to complete. Students who participated and volunteered on a regular basis probably did well in her class (I am making this judgment based on the performances of the students who did volunteer), while the excluded majority, who were the silent students, probably did not do especially well. (This "excluded majority" perhaps accounts for the dissonance between what she said to me on the elevator before the class—that the kids are not where she wants them to be—and the performances on the white board I saw that were breathtaking. That "excluded majority" is the mass of students she was referring to.)

An "excluded majority" of students in her class may have formed simply because of ineffective formative assessment—Mrs. Barnes didn't appear to have an efficient way to formatively assess her students. Formative assessment is a teacher's informal observations and snap-second judgments of students occurring during instruction but prior to formal assessment. When her students volunteered to solve proofs, Mrs. Barnes was only able to assess the student volunteers' abilities. During the question-and-answer session she was able to get some sense of her around thirty students' aptitude in the mathematics, but most students did not participate. Also, she didn't collect the homework, or even check to make sure

---

* See the chapter on the Interactive Mathematics Program for more information.

that her students completed it. Formative assessment is critical in the classroom because a teacher must know if her pupils understand the material during instruction so that adjustments can be made.

Another important element of her theory of practice, then, was time: completing specific objectives according to a defined timetable ensured that the material was adequately covered. Mrs. Barnes was very aware of the element of time—her comments in the elevator to me before class about "being behind" are evidence of this theory of practice. The oral-questioning session was the closest to any sort of unplanned teacher-student interaction that I observed during the class that could have altered her timetable for the class period. Although other teachers could have an oral-questioning session and—because of the responses of the students—change the lesson or the emphases of the class period, Mrs. Barnes did not seem to have any intention of modifying her schedule. The proof that she wrote on the whiteboard before the questioning session began is the same proof that she asked the class to solve after the questioning session ended.

Some students were able to keep up with Mrs. Barnes' timetable. The students who completed the proofs clearly understood what they were doing. That was one of the greatest strengths of her theory of practice—the handful of students that participated and kept up with Mrs. Barnes' teaching obtained a comprehension of proofs. But as Paulo Freire, in *Teachers as Cultural Workers*, explains, teaching is a dialectic of thesis, antithesis, and synthesis between all students and their teachers. In other words, teachers and students must learn from each other if there is to be real and democratic learning. It was this type of learning experience—one that takes into account each student's unique learning needs for the open-ended mathematical material of proof—that was most sorely lacking in Mrs. Barnes' class, and was so sorely needed.

(2002)

# 33.

## The Doctor's Calling: A Look at Technology in the Mathematics Classroom

Walking closer and closer to a sensor attached to the overhead projector, James, a student in Mr. Ringol's* class, watched as a distance-versus-time graph relative to the sensor popped up inside a calculator window that was electronically fed through the projector. Although James didn't quite match the original graph that Sherri, another student in the class, had made, he came quite close and seemed pleased with his attempt.

Using electronic sensors called Calculator-Based Rangers, or CBRs, students in real-time can produce graphs of equations—such as distance-versus-time or acceleration-versus-time—by moving away from or closer to the relative placement of the sensor. The students can attempt matching each other's movements, as James tried to do with Sherri's, or can compete against the computer by trying to match a randomly drawn graph. Either way, the CBR is on the cutting-edge of mathematical pedagogy because it explicitly allows students to control the mathematics presented—and learn about what they're presenting by controlling it. The CBR is the ultimate in interactive algebra demonstrations, getting the students intimately involved with the concepts. But what sort of class would support its use? What kind of school culture would have CBRs and promote such intense student involvement?

Driving up the seemingly endless hilly road in dense, thick fog, Lower Providence High School was not yet visible—it was shrouded in a white mist along with everything else around it on this cold March morning. As my car began leveling out near the top of the hill, pieces of the school began popping out from the fog surrounding them. First, a wall; next, what appeared to be the top corner of a building; then, a whole red brick side.

---

* A pseudonym; all proper names in this essay are pseudonyms.

Lower Providence High is located in a small suburban neighborhood in Southwestern Pennsylvania. The school's website describes the 18,000-member community as "relatively affluent, mostly professional people." The mist surrounding me largely prevented an inspection of the exterior of the school.

The path to the entrance—one of six, I later counted—was a spotless narrow concrete walkway surrounded by symmetrically landscaped bushes that placed the path into relief. The rich, formal arrangement of textures making up the outside of the building—the brick, the stucco, the shingle—presented themselves to me as if shouting, "This is a serious house of learning!"

The seriousness, present in spades on the outside, extended itself and permeated throughout every room, corridor, and hallway I saw in the interior as well. The lobby wall displayed rows of plaques of "Hall of Fame" awards—for individuals who "made a difference in the betterment of the community through knowledge and deeds." There were sports trophies too, but the plaques were placed in a prominent position, most likely to be the first things seen upon entering the school.

The math department was a sanctuary of seriousness. I was introduced to the department head, Mr. Walls, and other teachers as they arrived. Tons and tons of books and workbooks lined the shelves, which seemed to extend infinitely high.

I was introduced to Mr. Ringol, otherwise known as "The Doctor" (I didn't quite understand the explanation given to me of why he goes by this nickname[*]). My first class of the day's observation was to be with him, so we talked about what he had planned for his ninth-grade algebra class that I was going to observe.

"We're covering slope and applications with slope," he told me. He said that he places a primacy on student involvement and on learning concepts. "It's not as important that my kids come out of the class knowing how to calculate the slopes of lines for the rest of their lives as it is important that they *get* the concept of slope," he said, slowing down and stressing the word "get." "It's important

---

[*] Maybe his first name is Doctor, like the most disreputable American surgeon of all time, Dr. Doctor Bliss: the man, perhaps more than anybody else, responsible for the death of President James Garfield. Read the wonderful *The Destiny of the Republic: A Tale of Madness, Medicine and the Murder of a President* for more.

that they understand what a slope is, and how graphs can show *movement* and *reality*."

The Doctor's theory of practice—according to his conception of it—revolved around concepts more than skills. Although he needed students to master enough skills to handle in-class examinations, standardized tests, and future mathematics classes, he wanted his students to understand the underpinnings of the skills. Sounds simple, but it is of course notoriously difficult: it is common for people who have had algebra classes to forget their contents quickly, since they're unlikely to need algebra later on in their post-school lives.

When the bell rang, the students filtered into The Doctor's room like moths to a flame. The walls of his classroom were filled with posters and signs about math, and, specifically, about the TI-83/84. (The TI-83/84, made by Texas Instruments, is currently the most popular calculator in public school mathematics classes.) There was a single computer in the corner, next to the teacher's desk. The students' desks were arranged in a semicircle, and there were about twenty desks. Blackboards dominated two of the walls, and an overhead projector was in front of one of them.

The students were very, very noisy, talking to each other, texting on cell phones, talking to themselves—although they sat down in their seats quickly, they didn't settle down quickly. The Doctor, meanwhile, set up the materials he was going to use for the period: the overhead, the calculator, the CBR, the textbook, etc.

"Okay, okay, okay—settle down. Time for me to check your homework; get it out," he said. Within a minute, the loud talk became a steady whisper, and homework was on everyone's desk. Mr. Ringol spent about fifteen seconds at each student's desk, examining the homework, pointing out certain parts of the students' notebook pages, and marking up his own notebook (he denoted whether or not students had completed their homework). Why use so much time at the beginning of the period? "This is usually the only chance I get to interact with each and every student during a class period," Ringol told me.

The students' quick silence when the homework was checked underscored the school's emphasis on academics. These pupils are continuously academically pressured—the school's culture places the onus on the students to academically achieve. The mechanism that caused students' silence, then, was not so much Mr. Ringol's innate prowess at controlling teenagers, but rather cultural and extrinsic factors—namely, pupils' fear of school-wide academic retributions.

After finishing, Mr. Ringol stood up in front of the classroom and asked for a volunteer. "You know my rule: I promise that I won't make you do anything that makes you look stupid or silly—or smart." The class laughed, and two people raised their hands. Mr. Ringol's joke underscores his awareness of some latent assumptions of teenagers. A hesitancy to volunteer could be caused by shyness or a fear of embarrassment—which is why he said that he wouldn't make anyone appear to be "stupid" or "silly." But students may also fear looking *intelligent* in front of their classmates, which Mr. Ringol noted in his comment. The rankings and orderings that occur in schools, discussed in detail in the "Sorting" chapter of the Sizer and Sizer book *The Students are Watching*, is a pressure students must bear, especially in this school which emphases academics so strongly. For the most part students do not want to call attention to themselves in maters related to academics—either positive or negative.

The use of humor to convey that truth is also a control mechanism in a way: The truth revealed in the comment shows the students that the teacher understands their predicament (with volunteering in this case, but it could be used in other ways, as Mr. Ringol did later in the class), sympathizes with their positions, and is reasonable enough to construct a classroom activity that takes into account basic student perspectives. To force a student to actually do something embarrassing in front of his or her classmates would be ill advised, since it might cause the student to be ostracized by peers and lead to the student resenting the teacher. In addition, from a pedagogical point of view, it would be counterproductive: it seems unlikely that any student could learn material by being embarrassed.

The humor also relaxes the students, making the class less intimidating; thus the students have less resistance to learning. Of course, a classroom that is too relaxed may not be motivated enough to work; Mr. Ringol's call for volunteers—which puts students on-edge—coupled with his humor—which relaxes the students somewhat—creates a classroom equilibrium: Not too much, not too little—a Goldilocks approach. The humor, then—a mechanism for relaxation and control—is also a part of Mr. Ringol's theory of practice. He did not explicitly mention this tactic to me in our conversation before the class period; therefore, it probably spontaneously occurred during instruction for him. If the class isn't quite in equilibrium, Mr. Ringol will use some standard teacher-speak—like "settle down," which he said when he wanted to check homework—or will utilize humor to shift the classroom into equilibrium again.

Formative assessment, the dynamic assessment that occurs during instruction, also helps to maintain equilibrium in the classroom. The minute-to-minute needs of students in the classroom cannot entirely be predicted. This is why lessons cannot be "prepackaged" uniformly for every classroom—a point that theorist Paulo Freire, in *Teachers as Cultural Workers*, makes. If a teacher uses standardized or prepackaged lessons, they must not be implemented myopically (i.e., without taking into account the specific needs of the classroom's pupils). Although the CBR activity is prepackaged (by Texas Instruments, as an option to their instructor-TI-83/84s), Mr. Ringol asked for volunteers, and, as discussed, asked in a way conducive to maintaining equilibrium in his classroom.*

"Sherri, come up here and walk back and forth in front of this [the CBR sensor]." As Sherri walked, the sensor plotted points on the distance-versus-time graph based on her distance from the CBR. Mr. Ringol asked for another volunteer—James came up—and he was asked to match Sherri's graph with the same distance-versus-time walk.

Mr. Ringol turned the CBR off and sat down on one of the unoccupied students' desks. (Although he was a fairly young teacher, he was tall and imposing and, I assume, somewhat physically intimidating to his students. Sitting in a student's seat may have, like the humor, made the class less intimidated of him.) A discussion ensued about what it all meant. "James, why didn't your graph match Sherri's?" "Because I didn't walk exactly like her, my distance was different, I mean." Mr. Ringol pointed out different sections of the

---

* Just because the latest pedagogical technological fads are installed in classrooms or handed to teachers hardly guarantees that the effectiveness of instruction will improve. This just doesn't mean CBRs—interactive whiteboards especially come to mind as well. Mr. Ringol was adept with the CBR, but, even if he didn't have access to the technology, I suspect his students would have still learned the concepts. Good teaching always transcends technology.

graphs on the overhead—parts that represented varying slopes, which implied changes in speed and thus acceleration or deceleration—and brought these notions into the discussion. He suggested them tacitly, and coupled them with other questions. "Why is this section of the graph going up faster than this section? What were they doing differently? Anyone?"

Class participation in the discussion session was high. Students did not have to raise their hands to participate—they could simply call out, as long as they didn't interrupt other speakers. The removal of the hand-raising convention sped up the discussion; more individuals could participate, and students' response times were quickened since they didn't have to wait to be called on. Although this rule was not explicitly stated, it was clearly known by the students this far into the year (more than halfway through). A weakness of this organizational strategy is that it presupposes that all students perform better and are apt to participate more in an "open forum," which is not necessarily the case: some students may actually prefer the formality of the hand raising and feel less pressured this way, feel less anxiety to compete for attention.

After the discussion winded down (it was about ten minutes long), Mr. Ringol organized the class into groups of three—by who sat next to each other—and handed out a worksheet and a CBR to each group. He explained the group activity, which was essentially an intuitive, calculator/CBR-based activity to discover more about the nature of slope and functions, and the class split up by group and went to different locations in the classroom. For the rest of the period, which ended thirty minutes later with the sound of the bell, the groups worked on the activity. The noise level in the class rose dramatically; it was not always clear if the students were talking about work or merely talking.

If they were just "merely talking," then a significant problem of his group-selection method was exposed: creating groups based on who sits next to whom is faulty since friends are likely to sit next to each other in a class, and friends have a tendency to socialize (since they are used to socializing outside of the class—that's why they're friends in the first place). Group selection by random methods might have been more effective; plus, people who aren't used to talking together would be forced to, strengthening the cohesiveness of the class.

There was very little lecture in the class period that I observed. Mr. Ringol expected his students to figure out many of the new concepts—but not the new skills. The little lecture there was, interspersed between the discussion session and the group activity, elaborated on skills, not concepts; the concepts were impressed upon the students in the informal discussion and the group activity.

Mr. Ringol's theory of practice shifted the "burden of knowledge" to the students by placing them in groups and by demanding a high level of student participation. The students' knowledge counted, but the teacher defined the students' relationship vis-à-vis the text and the mathematical material, since he structured activities around his interpretations of what was important to learn and what was not as important. Mr. Ringol was a sieve through which pupils received knowledge; he was a facilitator through which mathematics was transmitted. The text was utilized solely, it seemed, as a reinforcement of knowledge learned from the sieve rather than as something to defer to, as something sacrosanct.

Because of the dynamic relationship with mathematics he constructed for his students; because of his willingness to engage pupils in self-discovery activities (as he did with the CBRs); and because of his maintenance of the classroom equilibrium, I consider the pedagogic methods in his class (that I observed) to be an overall success. But not everything was perfect, as I have mentioned.

His use of technology in the classroom was very effective. Not only did he choose the "token participants" to demonstrate the CBR's functions, but he gave *each group* a CBR with which to experiment. All students, then, could have some hands-on experience with the technology, yet not be forced to perform in front of other classmates, as Sherri and James were. (Of course, if a school does not have access to or money to purchase such technology, then all of this explication is one big moot point.)

The discussion session was also especially effective because of the seating arrangement. Recall that Mr. Ringol sat facing the semicircle-desk organization of his pupils. He could clearly see all his students; each student was "in the front row," so to speak.*

---

* Educational theorist Lisa Hennon has documented the historical "convergence of discursive elements" in the designs of classrooms and schools. For example, as Dr. Hennon writes, "According to architectural and educational studies of school buildings and design, a 'flexible learning environment' is

I also learned, however, that the construction of groups must be more carefully considered. His cursory groupings probably were not the most effective possible from a pedagogical standpoint, since friends were likely to be seated next to each other—and they ended up organically grouped together. The high level of socialization suggested to me that random groupings, or ability-level groupings, would have made learning more of the focus of the CBR activity.

In addition, his low emphasis on traditional lecture methods may not have been beneficent to every student. Although the variety of mediums he used to demonstrate the mathematics was noteworthy, not all of his students may have been comfortable with the heavy emphasis he placed on non-traditional instructional methods. After all, future math classes these students have in high school—they were only in ninth grade—will not necessarily be commensurate with the sometimes-esoteric approaches Mr. Ringol adopted. Then again, they may be: the school is an academic bastion, judging from the school's value-systems I observed in the lobby, among staff interactions, on the website, and in other places. Mr. Ringol may be comparatively conservative in his instructional approaches in the school. Either way, the interest the students displayed in the technological and interactive presentations of mathematics in The Doctor's unique classroom will not be something soon forgotten.*

(2002)

---

'interactive' and promotes 'active' learning through a sense of 'community....' The overall aim is to promote active participation and learning by providing the physical conditions that foster in students and staff a sense of having a personal stake in the school" (from the article "School Architecture, Curriculum, and Pedagogy: Shifts in the Discursive Space of the 'School' as Forms of Governmentality" [1999]). Mr. Ringol's classroom certainly fostered that sense of ownership and active participation through his use of space.

* I later asked Mr. Ringol if he had any teaching advice for me. Here's (in part) what he said: "I suppose that this job is absolutely impossible, like a marriage is, or raising children is, or I suppose writing a novel is, or like a lot of other things that get 'done' somehow despite their nutty complexity and unimaginable difficulties. I don't want to scare you but of course this job is scary and requires a certain disposition that may not be a completely learned behavior. But I press on."

# 34.

## A Taste of Discovery Learning

A cognitive transition occurs in tenth grade mathematics. Up until then, math builds linearly, school year after school year, gaining complexity but not truly leaping into another plane of thought. But tenth grade brings, for many students, geometry. And interwoven in the study and understanding of geometry are proofs, the building blocks of higher mathematics. It is the first time students are required to think deeply about *why* mathematics actually works logically, instead of blindly following rules that may seem rather disjoint.

A class period or series of class periods that introduces the concept must be appropriate and effective. Anecdotally, adults frequently mention proofs as a turning point in their feelings about math (from mostly indifferent to negative) or as a reaffirmation of their belief of the "utter uselessness" of mathematics.

No teacher of mathematics or mathematician would argue that proofs are an easy concept to grasp for the uninitiated. However, since the topic is a catalyst for bad feelings, perhaps its instruction should be refined.

Mathematics and the real world outside of the classroom rarely collide overtly, especially for young people. With proofs, the little link that can be found with math and the outside world evaporates, since proofs are the building blocks of higher abstractions. At the level of high school geometry, proofs largely exist for both their own sake and the sake of building bridges into ever-greater complexities in the subject.

Using psychologist Jerome Bruner's "Discovery Learning," a method of constructivist inquiry-based instruction, with an introductory class period or series of class periods in proofs for students seems to be a wise choice: students, with some instructor prodding, could realize the altered thinking necessary to not only grasp proofs but inherit some level of mastery in them as well. The ability to handle the material would presumably displace much or all of the common negative student reactions.

The tact of guided discovery is pragmatic. A pure Discovery Learning approach would largely be misplaced here, since students would quickly become frustrated with the reasoning behind the proofs and the assumptions underlying them. Guided Discovery allows the students to reach for a lifeboat if they need it, and they likely *will* need it.

The following is a lesson plan for an introduction to proofs built around the six-step framework of Bruner's Discovery Learning method.

*Step 1: Expose students to warm-up exercises.* I would begin the class by asking the question: "Can anyone think of a math problem that they couldn't solve?" This might get several reluctant responses, especially if I directly call on people to answer. Next, I would pose this question for discussion with an immediate neighbor (in other words, people sitting next to each other in the class would have to form a consensus about the answer): "Can anyone think of math problems that have not be solved, by anyone? In other words, are there any problems out there that even the smartest people are unable to solve?" I would suspect that no group in the class would answer in the affirmative; nearly all students believe (at this point in their academic careers) that math is the ultimate example of a static, complete subject—if they have even thought about the ontological foundations of math at all. They likely believe there is no fluidity or dynamism in the discipline, since all it seems to consist of is textbooks with letters and numbers in them (and math instructors who have all answers to the problems posed in the texts).

Before having students engage in any thinking outside of their comfort zone, it is imperative to dispel their most commonly held assumptions about math as a static subject. Admittedly, this is a tall order, but the essence of proofs is not necessarily in obtaining an end result, but a possible means to an end, since the end may not exist at all in higher mathematics.

I would briefly discuss the case of Andrew Wiles. Wiles is the Princeton University mathematician who took eight years of his life to solve a 300-year-old problem (he solved it not hundreds of years ago, but as recently as 1994). While discussing this with my students (and asking them specific questions about their thoughts as I describe the story of Professor Wiles' solution), I will stress that the problem looked relatively easy. It is called Fermat's Last Theorem, and it states that the following equation cannot be solved (where *n* is an integer):

$$x^n + y^n = z^n \text{ where } n > 2.$$

Wiles proved that this statement could not be solved for any integer greater than two. But he didn't attack the problem with large calculators or computers or extraneous equipment. He solved the problem using a pencil, paper, and his mind. And he took 150 pages of math statements to do it.

An important idea for students to realize is that a math problem that is small doesn't necessarily take a short length of time to solve. Conversely, a problem that is lengthy and complex doesn't necessarily require a large amount of time to contemplate. For instance, a problem with many variables and numbers such as,

$$5x^2 + 78x^2 + 3x^2 + x^2 + 56x^2 + x^2 = 0$$

has an extremely easy and quickly found repeated-root solution (without any calculation) of $x = 0$. The more macro-level question of how a mathematician can realize when a problem is going to be simple to solve—or not so simple—must be introduced in the next step of this Discovery process.

*Step 2: Emphasize contrasting features.* What makes proofs different from the mathematics that the students have been accustomed to up until this point in their academic careers is the thinking process involved. "Are there any rules in everyday life that are unbreakable and out of human control?" I would ask them. "Gravity" might eventually emerge. I'd quickly obtain a classroom consensus that gravity is a rule that we must respect and abide by.

"But how, then, do planes, birds, and helicopters fly and 'defy' the rule of gravity?" Assuming no one can explain why, I will talk to my students about air pressure, and ask them to remember what it feels like to place their hands outside of a car window while the car is in forward motion. If your hand is slightly tilted at an angle away from the direction of the motion, I'll explain, air pressure will build up on the palm, causing your hand to lift. Although the rule of gravity is not ignored, it is temporarily overcome in favor of a stronger force.

In the same light, the world of mathematics has rules, or axioms, that cannot be broken. But, by working with those rules in an analogous way as a plane or a bird works with gravity and air resistance, a problem can be solved. Although the metaphor is a bit crude and isn't exactly a thorough descriptor of proofs or the proof process, all students are familiar enough with gravity and flying machines and animals to obtain the basic idea.

In addition, students must realize that proofs are different from other types of problems they have been exposed to. Discussing puzzle pieces as yet another metaphor for regular math problems and proofs (to emphasize the contrasting features between the two different kinds of mathematics) is appropriate. As an example of a non-proof mathematics problem, consider adding two numbers together. Illustrating this using puzzle pieces, we first must understand that an individual puzzle piece cannot be broken down into more than piece; it is indivisible. In addition, a puzzle piece adjoins to another only in pre-determined locations. These rules of puzzle building cannot be changed. Accepting these axioms, adding two numbers together is analogous to snapping two puzzle pieces together.

A proof, however, is much more complex. Since a proof requires a direction and an assimilation of varied rules in mathematics, an analogous puzzle pieces' metaphor would probably be closer to a more complex construction—e.g., an automobile or a house. Now, with these assemblages, the constructor must not only take into account the intricacies of puzzle pieces' rules (the sides where they snap together, the sizes of the pieces, and so forth) but must also consider the overall picture of the object being constructed. Two modes of thought must occur for successful completion: a micro-mode, which considers the step-by-step procedures, and a macro-mode, which handles the overall direction of the building process.

The difficulty levels involved in simply snapping two pieces together to create a bigger piece and fashioning a house or an automobile are obvious; because of the multiple thinking skills required, the house or automobile is much more complicated, and so too are proofs as compared to other math problems. The differences between proofs and non-proof problems will be introduced in later steps of the Discovery process.

*Step 3: Encourage students to make intuitive guesses using information they already know.* By this step in the process, it is imperative to avoid describing the abstractions of the proof and actually begin to demonstrate one. Since this is geometry class and not a more advanced topology or analysis class, a visual geometry proof is suitable.

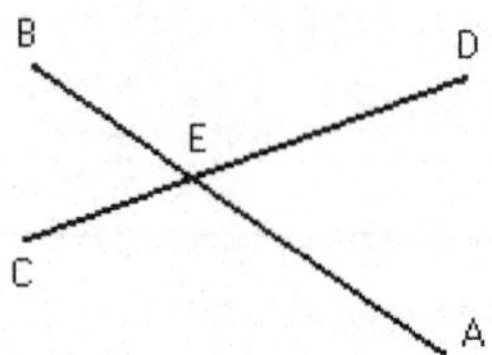


By this point in the geometry year, the students should have seen many diagrams like the one above. They should know the most basic facts about how to read the diagram. (Realizing that AB is a line segment and CD is also a line segment and that AB and CD intersect at point E must be immediate observations by the time proofs are first presented.) Students also must have been exposed to the following rules of Euclidian geometry:

1. Angles can be added together and subtracted from each other, just like other quantities.
2. Quantities equal to the same or equal quantities are always equal to each other (and interchangeable).
3. Two straight lines can intersect at only one point, if they do intersect; if two straight lines do not ever intersect, then they are parallel lines.
4. The sum of the angles on a straight line is equal to 180 degrees.
5. If two lines intersect, the vertical angles formed are equal.

One of the rules above was derived from the other rules; the other four rules must be accepted as true because they are analogous to the indivisible puzzle pieces described in the previous Discovery Learning step. After presenting the diagram and the five rules to my students, we will discuss them as a class. I will make it clear that one of the rules can be broken down into a series of steps using the other four rules (but the other four rules cannot be broken down any further).

*Step 4: Ask questions and let students try to find the answers.* Specifically looking at the diagram and the rules associated with it, I would pose them queries that would lead them to discover which of the five rules requires proof (i.e., which one is built from the other four rules). "Do you believe that you could ever describe a way to show for sure that two lines intersect at only one point? How could we do that?" Other questions might include the following: "How many degrees is a circle? If we cut the number of degrees on a circle in half with a line, does that show that angles on a line are 180 degrees? Can we break that down any further? Quantities that are equal are interchangeable—but why? Does it have to do with the definition of the equals sign? How do we really know that if two lines intersect, the vertical angles formed from the lines are equal?"

Asking students what the obvious rules are as compared to the not-so-obvious axioms is a key element to discovering the identity of the rule that requires proof. With another group exercise designed to pick out the least obvious rule of the five, one rule should presumably emerge as disjoint from the other rules: If two lines intersect, the vertical angles formed are equal. This statement is not self-evident. If the students are unable to reach that conclusion, then a discussion will ensue in the classroom. It will be initiated with more questions from me. "Why is this rule [of the vertical angles] the least obvious conceptually of the bunch? Why does this rule not visually follow from the diagram?" are some potential contextual questions.

*Step 5: Stimulate awareness by encouraging students to consider consequences.* Since students have seen diagrams similar to the one presented above for most of the school year in geometry, considering the consequences of the removal of each rule separately is a jumping off point for arriving at the logic necessary to show that the fifth rule requires proof. For example, the deletion of the rule "if two straight lines intersect, then they intersect at only one point" would wreck havoc with the essence of a line. If two lines intersected at more than one point, the lines could not possibly be what we know to be lines in Euclidian geometry.* The lines, if they intersected at more than one point, could not be straight—changing the definition of the lines themselves. Since the consequences of removing the rule adversely affect the entire logic of geometry, the rule is a vital building block of the discipline. Similar causal features can be found with the other rules.

But it is with the fifth rule (if two lines intersect, the vertical angles formed are equal) that if untrue wreaks the most havoc. Since the fifth rule requires proof (a series of step-by-step instructions built from at least some of the other rules), claiming that the fifth rule is false is comparable to claiming that the forces of air pressure could never overcome the forces of gravity (recall we discussed air pressure exceeding the forces of gravity in an earlier Discovery step). If that were so, then not only could planes, helicopters, and birds not be able to fly, but air pressure itself, in a variety of manifestations, would not act the same way: balloons would not be able to be blown up with air, for instance. In other words, an entire structure would immediately collapse like a house of cards. Realizing the effects that the nullification of the vertical angle rule would have on geometry sets students up to examine the step-by-step process used to build the rule.

*Step 6: Encourage learning through doing and actual involvement.* Before beginning the procedures necessary for the completion of this step in the learning process, please notice how little math has been done up to this point. Although a relative mastery of some types of geometry proofs will indeed require practice eventually, it is most important that students realize that with proofs they are not dealing with an immense number of calculations but with ideas and logic. Ultimately, the more that this is stressed, the better.

The involvement step in Bruner's process is the point at which we move into some abstraction. This is unavoidable; proofs are by their very nature abstract. Admittedly, because of the intense abstractions, it is at this stage that students are most likely to ask, "What good is this in the real world, anyway?"

---

* In other words, geometry on a two-dimensional surface, such as a tabletop or a piece of paper. Not surprisingly, in higher mathematics, geometry can exist in an infinite number of dimensions. But that will not be considered here since the topic is typically beyond the scope of a high school geometry class.

We must prove that the two opposite angles in the diagram are equal to show that the fifth rule is true. (Please refer back to the diagram.) We know that lines AB and CD intersect at point E. This is apparent on the diagram (and based on another rule). Because angles on a straight line add up to 180 degrees (a rule states this), the angles AED and DEB equal 180 degrees. This also means, using the second rule, that angle AED equals 180 degrees subtracted by angle DEB (because AED + DEB = 180 degrees, and, subtracting DEB from both sides, AED = 180 – DEB. This is simple algebra that students should have picked up in algebra class from a previous term). Now, because angles on a straight line add up to 180 degrees (same rule used before) angles BEC and DEB added together give 180 degrees. Manipulating that equation, we find that angle BEC equals 180 subtracted from angle DEB (because BEC + DEB = 180 degrees, and subtracting DEB from both sides yields BEC = 180 – DEB). By definition, since angle AED = 180 – DEB and angle BEC = 180 – DEB, angles AED and BEC equal each other (since we can replace equal quantities with each other; if two quantities have equal contents, then they are equal themselves).* We have proven that the two angles are equal, and, consequently, proven that if two lines intersect, the vertical angles formed are equal.

Students may inquire, "But how do we know it always works? Haven't we just shown it *only* for those two angles, but not necessarily *any* two?" Since all diagrams and angles that have this form could be "plugged" into this proof, we have shown it for all possibilities, I will explain.

The proof might be difficult for a student exposed to this type of logical structure for the first time. It is important for students to observe that all of the proof's steps made use of the other four rules and nothing else; there are no sudden leaps present, only a coupling of axioms in a deliberate order. This step in the Discovery process should be relegated to at least one forty-five minute class period, maybe even two, depending on the progress of the class in understanding the inherent assumptions behind the proof.

Since this step requires student involvement, other similar proofs that follow the basic structure of this one (and make use of no new axioms) could be presented to individual students or groups of stu-

---

* Recall that this is Euclid's first common notion: "Things which equal the same thing also equal one another."

dents. Using this proof as a template for a barrage of in-class and take-home proofs to solve will help students grasp the underlying logic. With enough examples, students can move on to more complicated proofs and differently structured ones, but not with rapidity.

It is interesting to note that Japanese educational instruction of mathematics bears similarities to the Discovery Learning approach. In her article "Japanese Education," author Merry White describes a Japanese school's introduction of cubing numbers to fifth grade students. The students are required, in groups, to prove how and why cubing a number works. During the process, the Japanese children learn about cubing's relation to volume, measurement, and other real-world quantities, thus permitting them an understanding not only of the mechanical process of cubing, but the reasoning behind the concept as well.

Assuming that American students could concentrate for "more than eight minutes" (as Neil Postman asserts in his piece "Order in the Classroom") on discovering the origins of mathematical concepts such as proofs, pupils have an excellent chance of understanding proofs' relation to exceedingly complicated math notions. Therefore, this Discovery Learning approach to proofs for American public schools must be considered, simply because of its efficiency as a tool for students to acquire that often-elusive big picture.

Proofs are not word problems, but logic problems, replete with their own specialized methods of attack. The deductive approach to problems (going from general to specific) is required; in essence, students use general rules to find specific properties. The detailed deductive critical thinking process that these kinds of proofs necessitate is a trait that will be useful for students in all academics, even if a geometry class is their last formal exposure to proofs.

(2000)

# 35.

## ORDER AND DISORDER IN *THE WRONG MAN*

At the start of Alfred Hitchcock's *The Wrong Man* (1956), Manny's (Henry Fonda) life is shown to be mathematically ordered; he even mentions to Rose (his wife, played by Vera Miles, who would later costar in *Psycho* [1960]) the connection between his musical mind and mathematics. Manny never arrives home late without calling ahead; he never drinks, smokes, or participates in disorderly conduct of any sort.*

Let us consider the acts of the movie as mapped onto a classical narrative paradigm. The first stage of the *evil in a good world* narrative paradigm—i.e., the threat to an ordered world/transgression or contract with evil—begins when Manny arrives at the local bank and is mistakenly fingered as the hold-up man. This first stage of the paradigm comes to fruition as Manny arrives home: now, through the forces of the law, he is explicitly aware of the threat to his ordered world (and he also, in a sense, comes into contact with evil: the evil of the ignorant law). The descent to hell/emergence of evil into a good world occurs during the "stripping phase"—Manny is striped of his already flimsy identity; he descends into the hell of an ordered world he can no longer participate in (or play in—he is a musician who plays the bass). By the time Manny reappears in an ordered world (in *his* ordered world), there is a complementary banishment of Rose to the depressed underworld; it is almost as if *she* is now being punished for Manny's foolish belief: that one can obtain any more than a modicum of control over one's life. In addition, the actual hold-up man is punished.

---

* The notion of disorderly conduct takes on a new connotation when we consider Manny's persecution and prosecution: the legal system ultimately accuses Manny of behaving in a disorderly fashion with respect to the rule of law. Hitchcock's personal paranoia of the police and the law probably stems from a childhood experience: to teach him a lesson, his father arranged for young Hitch to be temporarily locked in jail.

This same narrative paradigm can also be applied to *Vertigo* (1958), albeit more clumsily. For instance, there are several key part of *Vertigo* that can be classified as the threat to an ordered world: Scottie's (James Stewart) discovery of his own physiological vertigo during the opening chase; Scottie's meeting Lester (Tom Helmore); Scottie's encountering of Madeline (Kim Novak); or Scottie's breakdown. But perhaps the best fit of the paradigm is with Scottie's mental disorder after he witnesses Madeline's death: there is both a transgression or contact with evil (evil in the expression of Madeline) and a threat to the ordered world (although Scottie's world is hardly ordered: by his own admission, he is a wanderer). The decent into hell/emergence of evil into a good world occurs during the dream sequence: Scottie subconsciously realizes, as the manifest artificiality of the images in the dream sequence demonstrate, that he has been duped: evil has come into his good (?) world. He subsequently descends into a personal hell that neither Mozart nor Midge (Barbara Bel Geddes) is capable of retrieving him from. Finally, the discovery of Judy-as-Madeline resumes a semblance of order/control in Scottie's life—he has solved the mystery* of Gavin's wife's "supernatural possession," successfully completing his detective work—but Judy, for her transgressions, is banished to the underworld, and so is Scottie: he must live (or die?) with the fact that through his actions (or inactions) he has killed three people by movie's end.

A more complicated but revealing narrative paradigm to map onto *The Wrong Man* is the first of two paradigmatic feminist narratives. The initial stage, woman-discovers-self trapped in gender roles defined by patriarchy/woman-as-guilty, is evident in Rose, albeit subtly. The image of Rose on her bed, submissive to Manny and his idea of the proper and "efficient" familial structures (he posits: the family will manage; the kids will do this and that; etc.), crystalizes a visual metaphor of this narrative paradigm. Also, woman-as-guilty overtly presents retroactively when Rose begins her breakdown, blaming herself for Manny's arrest. The second part of such a feminist narrative structure—woman struggles against gender stereotypes and oppression/violence—occurs during the search phase in *The Wrong Man*: Rose (and Manny) attempts to recapture the pseudo-order that

---

* Or is it a puzzle? Author Malcolm Gladwell, in *What the Dog Saw: And Other Adventures*, explains the distinction: a *mystery* is present when we have too much information, a *puzzle* when we don't have enough.

once existed in her life; however, she quickly gives up and begins a new route toward a "recovery" (this sense of recovery associates with what Hitchcock scholar Robin Wood refers to as the therapeutic theme in Hitchcock)—a refusal to be an ordered servant of patriarchy. Finally, the woman finds liberation in bisexual nature/punishment paradigm is best encompassed by Rose: she rebels against the double bind she finds herself in: she cannot accept Manny's pseudo-sense of an ordered marital life as non-fictitious, nor can she relate to the law (feminist scholar Tania Modleski's so-called female double-bind); she must escape both through madness.

The feminist approach can also be molded to conform to *Vertigo*'s narrative. Unlike *The Wrong Man*, there are two main female characters it applies to: Madeline and Judy, but both not completely. Women-discovers-self trapped in gender roles defined by patriarchy: Madeline is trapped by the spirit of Carlotta, who was driven away by exclusion in a patriarchal world. Judy is also trapped by a gender role, that of an "easy" woman, who will do most anything for love and money. The second feature of such a narrative paradigm—woman struggles against gender stereotypes and oppression/violence—is empirically demonstrated with Madeline's indecision and struggle to climb the bell tower: she must decide if her love for Scottie overwhelms her desire to die. Interestingly, this is also a point in the plot where Judy encounters the second stage of the paradigm. She must struggle against her oppression (in the form of Elster) and determine if she loves Scottie enough to cease the Madeline role, or at least reveal it to him. Finally, Judy finds expression/liberation (for a time) in a bisexual nature—with Madeline (and, conversely, Madeline finds liberation in a bisexual* nature through Judy; after all, it is only through Judy that Madeline exists). Both are punished with death for their transgressions. (2001)

---

* A useful way to examine how views of sex and gender are constructed is to look at a deviant (i.e., different from "norm") group: transsexuals. In our Judeo-Christian society, like Noah's Ark, everything comes in twos—including sex and gender. Our society is strictly dichotomous, binary: there is the sacred and there is the profane, and they should not be mixed. There is certainly no "middle" gender, and anything other than male or female is considered strange and rejected. According to ethnographer Serena Nanda, "Transsexualism has been defined in such a way as to reinforce our cultural constructions of both sex and gender as invariably dichotomous." Transexualism is considered a transitional state en route to full maleness or femaleness.

# 36.

## *Vertigo* and the Feminists

"Hitchcock manages frequently to dramatize an identification with his female characters," Alfred Hitchcock scholar Robin Wood writes in his *Hitchcock's Films Revisited* (1989), "that must deny all but the most singlemindedly [sic] sadistic male viewer any simple pleasure in the violences to which they are subjected." In other words, Wood stresses that the viewer, whatever the gender, in much of Hitchcock is forced to identify in some parts of the films, at least, with the female. This is apparent in *Vertigo* (1958). Although the female(s) here is guilty as well, the identification is ultimately more ambiguous, more in the realm of the kind of feminine spectator vantage point that Wood partially argues for later in his text utilizing *Vertigo*: "… Hitchcock continues to shoot the film essentially from Scottie's [James Stewart] viewpoint, even though he is fully aware that our emotional identification must now be with Judy [Kim Novak]." Tania Modleski, in her book *The Women Who Knew Too Much* (1988), submits a much more persuasive thesis of the female perspective (especially in her chapter on *Blackmail* [1929]): that of clear ambiguity. She posits that Hitchcock is ambiguous toward the female, and thus the camera is sympathetic yet almost takes personified pleasure, in a sense, when the female is punished; this is the essence of an "uncertain" subjective feminine viewpoint present not only in *Vertigo*, but in most of mature Hitchcock. Not quite a purely "male gaze."

In *Vertigo* the viewer is seemingly made to identity with a male perspective throughout the first half of the film. However, before entering into any discussions of ideological or narrative issues, it is important to reiterate comments from Wood and especially Modleski that somewhat debunk the myth of the explicitly "pure" male persona embodying the first seventy-or-so minutes of *Vertigo* because it weighs in so heavily with the issues of spectator identification. Wood says, "The shot [of the posy floating on water in front of Madeline] can also be taken as an imaginative-subjective shot from Scottie's viewpoint.... [Thus] the shot links the two consciousnesses, and we are made to feel that the image has much the same significance for both." Wood concedes, then, that the viewer can be coerced into understanding the perspective of Madeline, even at this early stage of the film (she has not yet uttered any dialogue). This is an especially crucial concession: in effect,* the audience is able to discern at least a modicum of Madeline's point-of-view (whether Madeline is "real" per se is irrelevant to this line of reasoning) without a line of dialogue from her—and Hitchcock (or the screenwriters/interventionists, depending on your theoretical framework) establish her with others' (mostly males') exposition. This male buildup of the image of Woman and of the notion of her submission figure heavily into Scottie becoming fully cognizant of his ultimate fantasy, that of shaping (and exploiting) his own version of Woman (with some help from Gavin and Pop Leibl) in Madeline Number Two.

All of the subjective identification that is evoked within the audience is made fully possible and credible by outsiders' (males') construction of character. Like Wood, Modleski also notes the Madeline subjective shot of the posy, but assigns more credence to it; she notes the identification that Madeline induces: "she becomes the very figure of identification, which here is realized in its most extreme and threatening form in the idea of possession."

Modleski continues to even deeper realms, analyzing the essence of Madeline's creation: "[despite his attempts to gain control over her] Scottie will find himself repeatedly thrown back into an identification, a mirroring relationship with her and her desires [death, for instance]." This is the narrative subtext of *Vertigo* that shines a great deal of light on the ideological issue of women's place in society: men create/construct the image of women, who, as Modleski frequently notes, are outside of the so-called patriarchal society; then men seek identification with their own creation; finally, not finding that identification, women are left without acceptance in the patriarchal world, men are left with an emptiness of character (characteristic of Roger O. Thornhill [Cary Grant] in *North by Northwest* [1959]), and the process restarts.

---

* Notwithstanding that this section of Wood's book was composed prior to the author's feminist awakening (though Modleski still has many disagreements with him).

The narrative forces the spectator to identify with the female in three main characters. The aforementioned Madeline-identification is present; *Vertigo* conjures up identification with Judy and her predicaments in the final part of the film as well. The narrative orderly lays out her problematic bind and her weakness of character. Judy, as the quintessential modern female in *Vertigo* (ignoring Midge [Barbara Bel Geddes], who projects too much of an overtly motherly quality to fall into the same category as Judy, Robin Wood notes this: Madeline and Midge are never on screen at the same time because of the incompatibility of the worlds in which they live), is presented as capable of being endlessly manipulated by men. Scottie also assumes a female role (very much like L. B. Jefferies [James Stewart] in *Rear Window* [1954]) in several ways. Modleski points out one of these feminine traits: "Scottie's faulty vision provides additional proof that he now occupies a feminine position, in that Hitchcock frequently impairs the vision of his female protagonists in one way or another."* The detective has been forced into a double bind, in a way, in patriarchal society; like Rose's rebellion against the patriarchal world in *The Wrong Man* (1956), Scottie too descends into madness to escape.

*Vertigo* also presents something more latent and indeed perverse about the female in our culture (or at least the contemporary culture of the film): there are two basic types of females needed by men: the motherly and the fantasy (using psychoanalytic theory these two types are roughly correlated with the superego and the id in men, respectively). Judy and Midge are motherly; Madeline is fantasy. (And, interestingly, both Judy and Midge *wish* to be the fantasy.) The plot of *Vertigo* hinges on a mother's love and the fantasy's ability to pull a man outside of his reality (of the reality of mother). This bipolarity underscores the essential female double bind: the notion of Woman is in and of itself a dialectical manifestation simultaneously in and out of a patriarchal system, on the one hand rejected and on the other hand desired by the men who "paint their portraits."

(2001)

---

* *Notorious* (1946) also overflows with examples of this.

# 37.

## The Dark Nothingness in Hitchcock

There is a dark nothingness lurking deep within the characters of Alfred Hitchcock's films. The most direct metaphorical expression of this hollow, dark nothingness is the middle initial of "O" in Roger O. Thornhill (Cary Grant) of *North by Northwest* (1959); the "O," as Thornhill annoyingly explains to his captors, stands for nothing;[*] and the letter O is a hollow letter, visually; it looks very similar to the number zero. Thornhill is defined not by himself but by his setting, at least at the start of the narrative; the complex network of social, business, and family (specifically his mother) associates reflect him back to himself—thus establishing what the manifestation of Thornhill is in his reality. Much of the Hitchcock corpus posits that it is only in the literal or figurative death of a person that he or she truly becomes an individual, a being, a presence—someone who can be understood as disjoint and ontologically distinct from the societal mirrors that continually reflect his or her images.

*Psycho* (1960) is built largely around this premise. Marion (Janet Leigh) is simply an image in an endless hall of reflective cultural mirrors (much like the double mirrors that scare her sister Lila [Vera Miles] in Norman's room). Marion's life, as defined in the first forty minutes of the film, has become a futile exercise, a fool's errand. She has stolen money; she has, for all intents and purposes, a dead-end job and occupation; she is relying on the slim hope that Sam (John Gavin) will marry her; and she seems desolate and alone, with no use for friends. Her literal death makes her important, noticed, and in the mainstream of patriarchal society (her entrance into patriarchal society occurs since her motivations and personality underpinnings are taken seriously by a web of people, including Arbogast, Sam, and her boss). The irony is that her death gives her

[*] Kind of like Harry S. Truman—the "S" stands for S.

the significance that she longed for in life.* Marion is no longer constructed by the reflections around her; the postmortem Marion is the center of attention. Furthermore, it is not until her death that her peers and we know her; this is a remarkably important concept in Hitchcock. One thinks immediately of *The Trouble with Harry* (1955) as a poignant expression of this: Harry was an insignificant, unimportant, and irrelevant human being lodged at the fringes of society. The gap (the figurative one by his absence and the literal one by the holes in the ground made for his repeatedly dug graves) created by his death reverberates in the lives of both the people who knew him alive and people who did not. The death creates an imbalance in the social network that sends shock waves to large numbers of individuals. His identity in life was precarious at best (this much we know about him, based on his wife's comments). But in death, he "experiences" many sensations: he is admired (Sam draws him); he is touched (by everyone—they throw him in and out of a grave, repeatedly); he is cared for (many graves are dug for him. Also, he is bathed and dressed); and he is talked about by everyone in the town. Marion is, in death, also bathed, cared for (she is wrapped by Norman [Anthony Perkins]), carefully buried, and talked about. Suddenly, the nothingness of these individuals' identities in life becomes something more than nothingness in death. Perhaps because no longer functioning as societal mirrors (since

---

* Hitchcock scholar Thomas Hemmeter explains Marion's need for attention thusly: "Both [Marion and Norman] respond to their social condition by retreating into fantasies which offer illusory transformations of their lives.... Seen one way, Marion's theft makes no social sense: she who wants broader community acceptance in a respectable marriage to Sam directly violates community values with her theft and runs away.... Seen in another way, however, her desperate act does make sense: as a culturally grounded fantasy, ... [which] leads her into a world of violence," culled from the article "Horror Beyond the Cinema: Cultural Sources of Violence in Hitchcock's Mid-century America" (2003).

In that same article, Dr. Hemmeter argues the merits of the late-century Gus Van Sant *Psycho* remake. The remake, he says, "returns us to the earlier world of Hitchcock's *Psycho*, not to attempt an emotional or aesthetic reprise of the original but to present a contemplative reflection on the cultural realities stimulating both films." Point taken. Nevertheless, Van Sant's film, unlike the original, commits a cardinal sin: it's boring. Give me *Psycho II* (1983) any day—Anthony Perkins is always entertaining.

they are dead), everyone is forced to take heed and notice them: they no longer reflect back.

Scottie (James Stewart) loses Madeline/Judy (Kim Novak) at the end of *Vertigo* (1958). She (or they) can no longer reflect back Scottie to himself. His identity, consonant nominally with the living presence of Judy/Madeline, disappears into mostly nothingness without her.

A character does not have to die a literal death; he or she may die a figurative one to become an individual. Thornhill and Manny (from *The Wrong Man* [1956]), by becoming aware of the mirrors engendering blatantly false constructions of character, recognize the precarious nature of their identities, and learn to counteract the mirrors' effects, at least somewhat (although a full counteraction cannot occur, it seems, unless the character is literally dead).

The question arises, though: If all characters in Hitchcock (and by extension, all of us) are defined by the self-reflexivity of others' interpretations and reflections of us, then *who are we*? Can we exist, then, alone, without others? Norman proves that identity cannot be stabilized by isolation; Thornhill proves identity cannot be kept in balance by constant (superficial) social contact. However, as *Psycho* and *The Trouble with Harry* demonstrate, holes form in a social network with the literal death of a character. Therefore, each person can be metaphorically associated with a link on a chain that if broken off forces a new chain to be formed to compensate (Sam marries Harry's ex-wife; the killer is caught in *Psycho*, which would not have happened if not for Marion's death and the subsequent investigation of her death). I am reminded of the rudiments of mathematical chaos theory: though this metaphor has been beaten to death through overuse, it is said that a single butterfly flapping its wings somewhere in Asia can create enough of an atmospheric disturbance to ultimately cause a hurricane to form in the Gulf of Mexico.* Hitchcock characters' deaths, figurative and to a much more significant extent literal, engender those same sorts of disturbances in the social atmosphere that they, however tenuously, belong.

(2001)

* We owe the butterfly effect metaphor to mathematician Edward Lorenz.

# 38.

## Marital Relationships: The Search for a Normative Impulse in Alfred Hitchcock

In the contemporaneous timeframe of *North by Northwest*'s and *The Wrong Man*'s releases (the mid-1950s), marital proclivities dictated and defined a great majority of the familial structures in this country, significantly more than at present. At least in part, the ultimate and eventual drive toward the seemingly normal impulses of the heterosexual marital union that Roger Thornhill (the protagonist of *North by Northwest*, played by Cary Grant) and Manny (the lead of *The Wrong Man*, played by Henry Fonda) experience derives from latent cultural assumptions inherent in both of their characters. However, it is not so simple as to state that they blatantly accept the cultural constructions without question, without resistance, and with resignation, by the end of the two films; both Manny and Thornhill undergo cathartic events in their narrative lives; for both, an understanding and appreciation of the potentialities, paradoxes, and quandaries of matrimony—an institution defined so overwhelmingly by outside forces of society invading one's inner character—transpire only after their own redefinition by similar external, societal forces. It is only through their "creation" as individuals in the narrative that Thornhill and Manny assume more than a modicum of control over their marriages/marital relationships and are capable of actively striving, by mostly internal loci of control and not by cultural determination, toward a real normative impulse (and not an overtly culturally defined one): the heterosexual marriage.

Before examining several individual segments of *The Wrong Man* and *North by Northwest*, it is necessary to define the notion of a "normative impulse." Marxist scholar of Alfred Hitchcock Robin Wood, in *Hitchcock's Films Revisited* (1989), states, "[G]reat art strives—however implicitly—toward the realization of norms" in a society, in a culture. "It is a matter of the nature of creative impulse, which, to flourish, must be rooted in at least a potential normality to be striven for, values by which to live." Wood argues with vigor that a sense of true alternative normative values beyond the psychotic or the "underworld," so to speak, are not present in Hitchcock's art; instead, in the oeuvre, perhaps because of the commercial nature of the films, or possibly because the matter wasn't explored with seriousness, the striving for norms symptomatic in the characters are mindlessly aligned with typical bourgeois lifestyles. Wood later claims that even *Family Plot* (1976), one of the most overtly "positive" films in the Hitchcock cannon, does not offer substantial normative alternatives. This certainly seems true on the surface: although there is a new sense of respect for each other inherent in Blanche (Barbara Harris) and her lover at the end of the film (after capturing the thieves and recovering the diamonds), the impetus behind it is a fabrication and an act. However, Wood fails to note that for the first time in the narrative the relationship is not forced but consciously chosen by both characters. This new dynamic of a "chosen relationship" (and not a forced one), that of Blanche's mate becoming another of her believing "clients," and Blanche assuming the role of a psychic actress, is a consequence, but not the motivation behind, the stasis of the coupling. Although new "breakthrough" norms that Wood would prefer observing are indeed not overtly present, the sense of a sort of "relationship resignation" that existed throughout the picture has mostly dissipated.

Another relevant example occurs in *Rear Window* (1954): Jeff (James Stewart) and Lisa's (Grace Kelly) balance, or steady-state, present in the final shot, certainly did not exist in most of the earlier scenes. Although the film demonstrates feminist Tania Modleski's notion of the ever-present double bind of the female (through Lisa's forced performance of the antithesis of her true likeness for Jeff; recall that she reads a book on the Himalayas until he falls asleep, and then she switches to a much more characteristic favorite read, *Harper's Bazaar*), the propensity of the redefined (at least compared to earlier in the movie) successful heterosexual relationship cannot be overlooked. If Hitchcock (or, as Wood would put it, the "interventionists," sidestepping the notion of an auteur) could not find anything more creative than the eventual heterosexual coupling of his central characters in his films (the bourgeois norms), then why do his characters always establish such a sentient, active balance in their relationships? To be more specific: Why does Lisa even bother to act for her partner, and Jeff bother to care about her? Why does Blanche in *Family Plot* plan elaborate ruses to arouse male impulses of "struggle to keep one's mate happy"? Why doesn't Hitchcock simply place his central characters at the end of films in resignation of their relationships, rather than having them ultimately actively and consciously choose to be in them? Because the normative impulses that the individuals in many of the pictures strive for are these redefined, *redeemed* relationships, which are not quite "normal" in a sense, but rather self-aware; they certainly bear little resemblance to their earlier counterparts: relationships driven by a sense of passive resignation to the implicit and explicit demands of society. In both *Rear Window* and *Family Plot*, these normative impulses are fulfilled in large part by the female, by choice, trapping herself in a double bind: neither female in the two films can truly be "herself" with her partner. The entrapment of the female is necessary for the active balance. *North by Northwest* and *The Wrong Man* are strikingly dissimilar to the two aforementioned pictures in the achievement of the same ends of normative impulses. Both utilize a narrative process I will refer to as the *creation of the male individual* to achieve the ends of a balanced, active, chosen (and not resigned to) relationship with their mates.*

The *creation of the male individual* is best defined as a psychoanalytic paradigm narrative structure with three overarching pieces: First, a main male character and another unseen character (defined by other people only) are disjoint; next, the male protagonist "catches up with" and "fuses" with the embodiment/outside definition of the other, unseen character: for all intents and purposes, he *becomes* the other individual; finally, the main character sheds the other culturally defined person but is irrevocably changed in the process. It is only through this change of character, this near-creation of individuality, that the male's marital relationships become active and balanced. Both Thornhill and Manny are shells of people at the beginning of their respective narratives; it is not until being told they are someone else, someone they never knew, and are then "forced" to embody that other person, that they are able to see and understand

---

* I assign a specific moniker to the process only because both films overtly have it in common. Therefore, the procedure cannot be considered an anomalous one-off, something unique to a single film.

the sense of a steady-state necessary in their relationships. This, of course, is much different than the female characters' alterations in *Family Plot* and *Rear Window*: in those films, the females choose to alter themselves and be placed in the double bind. The males in these films experience culturally-defined rebirths, in a way, out of their control; but after shedding their skins, they understand how to avoid resignation to the culturally defined heterosexual relationship and redefine it to their liking: they appreciate the power of cultural norms, and seek to take an active role in their own lives outside of others' definitions. The sense of recognition that a marital relationship requires active control and balance, and not passive acceptance, is the alternative normative impulse that Wood nonetheless claims is not present in the Hitchcock corpus.

In order to demonstrate this, let us first establish that both Manny and Thornhill conform to the *creation of the male individual* psychoanalytic paradigm narrative structure defined above. Then, by comparing several scenes from each of the two films, the new sense of active control and direction must be shown in their relationships. And, finally, it is necessary to observe that the new relationship control is correlated with their newly created characterizations.

Roger O. Thornhill, at the start of *North by Northwest*, is an empty shell—he exists merely as a cog in a wheel of an ever-churning capitalistic market-exchange machine. He has been married twice, but both marriages ended, we assume, because of his lack of character and lack of a character. The path of least resistance, then, at least with relationships with potentialities for marriage, is one of no control for him; his identity, or lack thereof, extends into passivity in relationships: to further this notion, consider the domination his mother exerts over him. After being mistaken for George Kaplan, someone who doesn't exist, and through the course of the story by becoming the essence (and defining the essence) of Kaplan, Thornhill becomes sentient, almost self-aware of the constructions of his own life: he witnesses firsthand the power of societal definition: everyone tells him he is Kaplan, and he begins to "fit into Kaplan's suit," so to speak, and become the espionage agent. Kaplan supplies the personality, Thornhill supplies the body and voice; they are two parts of the same whole. (We could extend these metaphors even further, but this is unnecessary; the general idea is clear.) Thornhill subsequently sheds the Kaplan identity (Kaplan is killed) and acquires a new, self-aware one; a semblance of balance is restored in his life, and he is overtly more conscious/dynamic/sentient in his personality and decision-making.

Manny, at the beginning of *The Wrong Man*, has similar characteristics to Thornhill's initial onscreen conception: he is hardly defined as an individual, only as set of mathematical regularities. Manny believes he can control his life by fulfilling a carefully calibrated set of routines every day. But one evening while returning home from work he arrested for a crime he did not commit. Like Thornhill, he is an innocent man wrongly accused—this, a recurring theme in Hitchcock, is the most basic structural commonality between the two films. Because he is a shell of a man, the new "criminal Manny" is relatively easily externally constructed: everyone tells him he is the thief that committed the burglaries; when tested by the police, he even exhibits the same handwriting and commits the same written blunder (*draw* for *drawer*). Manny's ordered life is decomposed, released into chaos, and redefined in an orderly way by the law enforcement complex. He embodies the robber, a man he has never met, for most of *The Wrong Man*. After the eventual shedding of the thief through prayer (the robber "dies" in him, as Kaplan dies in Thornhill), the picture culminates with Manny's new understanding and awareness of the suppressions inherent in his stay-at-home wife, and the fragility of her world; for Manny, the ordeal is over—he has lost the identity of a criminal. But, as his wife Rose (Vera Miles) points out, "That's fine for [him]." Manny is one step away (but clearly headed toward) from the same sort of sentient control over culturally constructed phenomenon that Thornhill obtains at the conclusion of *North by Northwest*; he begins to realize that the rules and regularity imposed by the marital institution were unbearable for all involved in the partnership. For the first time in the marriage, Manny considers the implications of the regular, axiomatic approach he has to marital relations (and his life as a whole), and the necessary methodology that must be adopted to restore balance. And he consciously chooses to regain the balance—he realizes that he cannot continue to live day in, day out, the way he has before—and, as the end titles reveal, the couple "recovers."

Thus, both main protagonists conform to the narrative paradigm of *creation of the male individual*. Several scenes in the two films demonstrate, through contrast, the new implicit control Manny and Thornhill have over their marital relationships.

In *The Wrong Man*, consider the scene at the start of the film: after Manny makes some faux bets on the horses, he returns home to his wife. When he enters her room (the film space is established with effective shorthand: the rooms are noticeably cramped and small), she is lying on their bed. The room is sparse, and the lighting creates black and white contrasts in every shot. The sparseness of the room could be taken to denote her mental state: she doesn't have all her marbles. More appropriately, the room's lack of décor symbolizes the emptiness of Manny's character and the falseness/precariousness of the stability of his marital union. The overhead shots and odd-angle shots of the couple during their dialogue emphasize their lack of control over a chaotic world. Compare this scene to a later, complementary one, when Rose is still awake and Manny arrives home: "I know what we are going to do," she says. "We'll lock all the windows and the doors and keep them out." In order to retain some semblance of control, she effectively locks herself in the house; in order to give herself the impression of control over their nine-year marriage, she has done just that: locked herself in the house. Manny does not realize this dynamic has been disturbed; when, at the beginning of the movie in their bedroom he confidently claims that "everything's going to be okay," he is blissfully unaware of the lack of control both of them have in their lives and in the instability of their marital union: Rose cannot "lock" everyone out in order to maintain stability. Both Rose and Manny presumptuously believe that the external, culturally constructed world is tamable—Manny through his ordered lifestyle of routines and musical/mathematical sense (he even explicitly mentions his math proclivities to Rose), and Rose through her retreat.

Manny's implicit behavior—that his marriage is simply another equation, another orderly aspect of his life—is rendered meaningless by his descent into dystopia. By being thought of by everyone else as someone whom he isn't, Manny realizes that the order in his life, even his identity itself, is extraordinarily precarious. In order to retain some of that order, he prays*—a seemingly illogical and anti-

---

* Perhaps the reason why the presence of religion/confession in this film seems so much more like a banal expression of belief rather than actual belief itself (as Robin Wood pointedly observes about both *I Confess* [1953] and *The Wrong Man*) is its perfunctory narrative use. Although I usually do not feel as if I should pose counterfactual "What if?"s, it strikes me as relevant to do so

scientific action, yet a crucial one: Manny sheds his alter-ego and obtains an individuality; he, in essence, is no longer just a microcosm of the outside world (by this, I mean his structured/ordered lifestyle at the beginning of *The Wrong Man* reflected the institutions he existed in).

He also realizes that, just like prayer (an un-mathematical, irrational act) ordered the chaos his life had become, new, conscious actions must be taken to order the chaos of the dialectic (the Hegelian notion of the existence of the play of opposites) of his marriage to Rose. In the final scene of the movie, marital balance is not restored. However, Manny begins to gnaw away at discovering how best to restore the lost equilibrium. The intense contrasts present in the sparse room of their home have given way to more muted distinctions between white and black in the mental hospital space: the strict, regimented, culturally defined order of their marriage was disturbed, and the realities of it—that there must be some sort of significant adjustments to their relationship—are displayed by the bleeding of white and black colors: chaos and order must coexist in order for a dialectical world, a dialectical marriage (the presence of two opposites: the male and the female), to truly function.

*The Wrong Man*'s tone is decidedly serious and solemn; contrast this with *North by Northwest*'s tone, which is comical and urgent. Consider the scene in the police station: a drunk Roger Thornhill is hesitantly permitted to call his mother. As Robin Wood notes, "At the police station, he tells his mother on the phone, very emphatically, 'This is your son, Roger Thornhill'—as if he had been brought to the point of doubting it." Wood says that Thornhill's identity is precariously defined at best. Like Manny, Thornhill is a microcosm of the world he exists in—the urgent formal/ordered machinations of capitalistic society; and, like the society itself, he is an empty shell, devoid of purpose, of masculinity (a generous de-

---

here, largely because of the religious "loophole" of salvation in the final cut. What if Manny had not prayed for a miracle—would evil still have been brought from the shadows into the light? What if Manny had been better established as a man of faith? What if the narrative had fashioned a more appropriate context and setting for the transcription of faith, namely that of the potentialities of the supernatural (in other words, the logic of faith as a healing system is suitable only if such underpinnings are present in the filmic structure)? If these issues had been addressed, the leap of faith required to accept the faith-based solution to Manny's predicament would ring less hollow.

scription of Thornhill: he is a boy in a man's body, dominated by maternal forces). The emptiness and sparseness of the police station (the colors are muted; the walls are bare) serve as underpinnings for the advertising man's identity; he hardly exists at all apart from the settings defining him. He is a construction in a constructed world. Although the plot does not display his propensity for destroying marital relationships, the narrative and exposition make it clear: he is too boring, too formal, too external to handle the internal dynamics of a marital relationship in anything more than a passing, passive sense—hence his multiple divorces.

Thornhill's embodiment of Kaplan changes that, however; his unwitting (and eventually by conscious selection) spy identity, analogous to Manny, enables the advertising man to perceive society from the outside in. Left to his own devices in the cornfield, for example, his perspective shifts to something beyond money and other superficialities that he seemingly never brought into question before: his own survival.

When Thornhill decides to continue playing the Kaplan role for Eve's sake, the mise-en-scene changes, quickly, from dark to light. After Thornhill agrees to the professor's request to resume being Kaplan, the screen lights up—it denotes that he has "seen the light," and realized that the important things in life are not necessarily money or success, but human relationships and love.

The progress of Thornhill's at conducting his relationship—from that of an immature externally defined boy-man, to a mature, responsible, and sentient being—is visually confirmed in two related scenes. After sneaking onto a train and encountering Eve (Eva Marie Saint), he is stashed him away inside the foldout bed; but she does not join him there. At the end of the picture, after becoming "Mrs. Thornhill," Eve and Thornhill consummate their new marriage together on the foldout bed, "For old time's sake," as he says. He is now mature enough to be an equal participant in his third marriage; one supposes that his other two wives dominated him, like his mother does. With Eve, there is a true partnership, and a true understanding of what the term "partnership" entails, that Thornhill did not possess with wives one and two: he cannot be a formal capitalistic machine, devoted simply to financial success, to consummate a successful marriage, but rather he must be a selfless individual dedicated to the partnership that a marital union requires. Only through the falling away of that capitalistic identity through the assumption of the Kaplan identity, and the subsequent participant-observer status to "normal" society that the essence of Kaplan demands, could Thornhill realize the rules in a milieu outside of his financially-driven environment. Kaplan allowed Thornhill to view "himself," in a way: he formerly was akin to the mindless people who laugh at him in the elevator—unaware of external forces outside the money market.

Both Thornhill and Manny lose their innocence about the sense of (dis)order in the world and in relationships. But from that loss, they inadvertently gain a *creation of the male individual*: they embody a new identity and self-awareness. And by obtaining the knowledge of precariousness, they gain the power of choice. Thornhill certainly does not have to get married again, but he *chooses* to; he chooses to strive toward the bourgeoisie normative ideal of marriage but with his (and Eve's) rules, not the rules of the externalities (there seems to be a fairly clear notion presented in *North by Northwest* that Thornhill and Eve will have a more successful marriage than Thornhill's prior two). Eve and Thornhill have both recognized that, in a sense, the rules of society have let them down and left them unfulfilled. Eve wishes to "fight for her country," but her dedication seems half-hearted, continuing only because nothing better has come along. Thornhill's life is also a parable of the unfulfilled; he has made money, but much of it goes to alimony. By the conclusion of the picture, Thornhill and Eve realize that marital relationships are chaos—yet both want to be together anyway.

Likewise, Manny in *The Wrong Man* recognizes that, through obtaining the identity of an externally constructed person, "orderly" life and "orderly" marriage is ripe with chaos and randomness. And, with this knowledge, he makes a choice: to continue his marriage, seek a new balance, and find a new way to control the chaos, if indeed it can be controlled. This is the subtle normative impulse, a higher ideal, values by which to live, that Wood searches for in Hitchcock's art (at least with respect to the films mentioned): characters are fully aware of the (mostly) untamable chaos of heterosexual marriage, yet desire it anyway.

(2001)

# 39.

## Man-as-Woman: The Strange Case of *Rear Window*'s L. B. Jefferies

*Rear Window*'s (1954) L. B. Jefferies (James Stewart) is certainly not an archetypal male protagonist of 1950s cinema. Looking at the gender-cultural assumptions of the time reflected through the spectrum of several popular movies, the dichotomous divisions of strong-male and gentle-female are quite overt on the screen; relegating a John Wayne-type principal character as the apotheosis of the ideal of maleness of this time period, James Stewart's character is neatly complementary. He is a sort of ironic commentary on men, a "projector" of the potential fallibility of male rationality, a character the audience comes to know way too intimately. More significantly, and perhaps controversially, exhibiting these traits ultimately allows Jefferies to transform into a surrogate *female* in the picture.

When the audience first sees Jefferies, his leg is in a cast; he has symbolically been rendered impotent. Without the functioning phallus, then, he loses a sense of his masculinity (although this by no means renders him a "female"; we cannot assume such a symmetry. Rather, he is defined immediately as *less* of a male). He is also relatively immobile, which forces passivity. A passive nature is more commonly associated with the feminine.* The film has estab-

---

* As support for this, consider the repressive family structure of this relative time frame that Robin Wood discusses in several parts of his masterwork *Hitchcock's Films Revisited* (1989); he mentions, among other points, the American family and its "repressions and sublimations" that occur due to forced ideologies that obscure concepts of underlying truth about women, sexual pathologies, and a host of other latent issues. Also consider his sardonic comment about female status around the late 1940s: "The Second World War saw the release of women from the home and the subsequent efforts to force them back into it."

lished, by visual means, that the character of James Stewart is extraordinarily (for a man) trapped in a repressed situation.

Adjusting to his temporary wheelchair lifestyle, he fixes his gaze across the courtyard to pique his interest. For example, he watches a woman who exercises, drinks, and has gentlemen callers every evening like clockwork. Jefferies names her Miss Torso, and, in doing so, intuits a personality type onto her. (Despite seeing her daily, the audience assumes he has never met her; therefore, by definition, attaching a signifier to a purely visual representation requires a sense of intuition.)

Eventually, Jefferies intuits a murder—not by rational means, but by feelings, by senses, by emotion. He has little empirical basis to deduce that Lars Thorwald (Raymond Burr) has committed any crime: Jefferies does not witness a crime directly, nor does he come into contact with artifacts of a murder. He cannot test his theory of the disappearance of Mrs. Thorwald by active means. Rather, he ultimately must rely on several women around him to assume the non-passive role. Note Robin Wood's statement in *Hitchcock's Films Revisited* about gender methods for solving problems: "[M]en are rational while women are emotional/intuitive" is a gender division in our culture. Jefferies ignores male rationality (because he is rendered passive by the injury and thus cannot test hypotheses about his "dollhouse world," as feminist author Tania Modleski puts it) in favor of female intuition/emotional projection. Whether or not this normally "feminine approach" is a resultant or artifact of forced passivity or is in fact a conscious choice on Jeff's part is unclear.

Regardless, adopting the female approach results in a sanction reserved for females. Modleski, in her chapter in *The Women Who Knew Too Much* (1988) on Hitchcock's *Blackmail* (1929), notes that the female is frequently silenced. "If castration is…always at stake for the male in classical narrative cinema, then decapitation is at stake for the female." Jefferies has little worry about castration, since he has already been castrated, in a way, before the narrative commences; for Jefferies, with post-castration comes a new worry, the worry of the female: decapitation.

Everyone he comes into contact with, from Stella the nurse to Lisa (Grace Kelly), his girlfriend, quickly regards his suspicion as foolish, ignorant, untrue. In effect, he is decapitated. This leads perhaps to a more interesting question: Is the castration of the female (and of Jefferies) caused, in part, by the utilization of intuited, rather than rational, logic? Furthermore, does the passivity usually forced on the female by a capitalistic-masochist society necessitate the use of intuition in favor of rationality for women, since females are in a forced (by society and culture) state of repression and are unable to easily test theories (as Jefferies is unable to because of his pigeonholed passivity and unwitting silencing)?

Furthermore, Doyle, the police detective "assigned" to the mysterious case of Mrs. Thorwald, treats the accusations of Jefferies with little credulity. Jefferies' status, as an impotent (and thus less-than-male) individual, is outside of the law (as Modleski analogously notes of Alice in *Blackmail*). Doyle treats the ruminations of Jefferies' intuited logic with a harsh skepticism—a man, like Doyle, who prides himself on the empirical, the rational, the testable, has little patience for such "feminine intuition" and emotional ramblings. Certainly if not for the immutable bond that Jefferies and Doyle share from their youth, the murder theories would have been dismissed out of hand. Jefferies, then, like women in general, is outside the law on the one hand, but cannot necessarily relate to the criminal (Lars Thorwald) on the other—although the comparison isn't perfect, a case can be made that Jefferies is trapped in a female-like double-bind between the law and the criminal elements in *Rear Window*. He can directly relate to neither; and both worlds, the law and the criminal, shun him (at least the law does until the end of the film—until Jefferies is validated by the male world of the active and empirical: he has to be pushed out of his apartment, out of his passive/intuited logic, in order for the law to believe him).

Of course, Jefferies' "feminine logic" is ultimately validated; if the cold rationality of Detective Doyle had been immediately accepted by all as irrefutable truth, Lars Thorwald would have gotten away with murder. Hitchcock's critical commentary on the fallibility of a purely rational approach to problem solving is apparent here.

Just as Jefferies is forced into passivity in terms of problem solving, he is forced into passivity romantically; Lisa dominates her partner in the diagesis—she stays when she wishes, leaves when she wishes. She dictates the terms of the engagements and has control over the details of their trysts. To further reverse the archetypal male-female/dominant-passive arrangement, Lisa must convince Jefferies to marry her. According to cultural assumptions, the complementary procedure should probably transpire. Consider the ubiquitous narrative (present in numerous fables, fairytales, and the like): Man falls in love with woman; woman is unconvinced man is "right" for her, but nevertheless does not reject him; man, through active means, demonstrates compatibility; and woman and man become serious romantic partners. For Jeff and Lisa, the opposite occurs: Lisa convinces Jeff, through a series of adventures in which she is the star of his voyeuristic show, that she is not the limited two-dimensional person that he at first thought she was but rather an impassioned and adventurous individual he is romantically compatible with.

To assume that the dynamic of their romantic union is as simple as her becoming an adventurous heroine to attract her mate is to betray the true complexity and depth of the narrative. Several ideas can be augmented and elaborated to better further the relationship-gender-structure definition in *Rear Window*. For instance, we can note the following: Lisa eventually compensates (through the acquisition of the typical male characteristic of "activity," for instance) for the loss of Jeff's phallus; in other words, she transforms into what Jeff has "lost," namely, his masculinity, and since there cannot be (by definition of the heterosexual relationship) two "men" in the union, a gender-compensation impetus drives Jeff to embrace female characteristics. Just like in *Family Plot* (1976), where the two main couples link up to form parts of a whole, the necessitation of Jeff's shift on the spectrum from masculinity to femininity results in a corresponding, compensatory repositioning of Lisa on the gender spectrum—to masculinity—to preserve their relationship's equilibrium, as precarious as it might seem.

Continuing this line of thought, it is also apparent, as demonstrated by the last shot in the film (a medium shot of Lisa switching texts), that the relationship, which works only when there is an "equal amount" of male and female, is dependent on Lisa's gender-switching. We can read her shifting from book to magazine as her switch from a public face (necessary to preserve the balance in the relationship) to a private face, necessary to maintain her own individuality. Essentially, she switches on the gender spectrum from male back to female. However, Lisa has now found the appropriate public face to preserve a steady-state (or balance) in the romantic union with Jeff: she must "become" male to compensate for Jeff's newly-acquired female attributes (or perhaps he always had these characteristics, but the forced passivity and acquired impotence of being laid up caused them to emerge), and must remain feminine in private. Of course, now another female double bind is present (and this double bind is correlated with Lisa): Lisa must change her identity for a man, but to delve into this notion any further is probably too far afield. Nevertheless, what must be noted is that Lisa, in order to progress forward in her relationship (and not preserve the "status quo," as Jefferies wants), must engender her own gender transformation.

More to the point, though, is that although Jefferies does not engage in conscious gender switching as Lisa does, he ultimately accepts his predicament, namely, passivity and impotence. Observing Jefferies' inherent pragmatism and optimism in life (he is a go-getter; he is an opportunist; he is an individual who clearly "grabs life"), and his nature to maximize his abilities in every situation he runs into (jumping into the middle of a racetrack to get a picture, although seemingly stupid, pays off: he solves problems by taking advantage of his inherent abilities in whatever situations he finds himself in), demonstrates the most significant and perverse statement of the film. Analogous to Alice in *Blackmail*, who tries as hard as she can but ultimately fails at being "inside" her society, Jefferies demonstrates the predicament of the female in American society during this time period: no matter one's degree of ability, the stigma attached to the lack of a phallus, the forced passivity, and the utilization of an intuited and largely emotional problem-solving methodology all conspire to exclude the woman from ever becoming an equal member of the culture: this is the affront to meritocracy that Hitchcock slyly comments on by using a male character in the narrative rather than a female one.

(2001)

# 40.

# Life and Death

## In Hitchcock's *Family Plot*

In a spectacular opening shot, two words engraved on a headstone are shown to the audience: "Born" and "Died." The camera slowly pulls back to reveal a young teenager with blonde hair carving birth/death dates into the stone whilst blaring rock music is drowning the life out of every other sound in the vicinity.

The movie is *Family Plot*, Alfred Hitchcock's last film (produced in 1975, released in 1976). The birth/death, thesis/antithesis theme (or dialectic) permeates the entire movie, almost to the degree of sacrificing clarity of plot or story* to create narrative parallels. With mathematical precision, Hitchcock constructs a diegesis in which nearly every film element has a corresponding parallel film element.

For instance, there are two romantic couplings in *Family Plot*: Blanche and George, and Arthur and Fran. Although superficially the two couples appear to be opposites—Hitchcock apparently wants the audience to believe the couples are entirely opposite on the surface; for example, Blanche and George have the same hair

---

* We need to be careful conflating the terms "plot" and "story." Recall what novelist E. M. Forster said: "The king died and then the queen died is a story. The king died, and then the queen died of grief is a plot."

color (dirty blonde), and Arthur and Fran have the same hair color (black); also, one couple has a white car, the other, a black car—they are not. Both couples are on a mission for wealth; both use illegal means to obtain riches. Both couples have a dominant partner and a passive partner; and, finally, both dominant partners use their passive partners for personal gain. The line between opposites is further blurred by Fran's blonde wig; with the wig on, Fran's hair color more closely matches Blanche's or George's hair than Arthur's.

Thus, two couples in the film that appear to be opposites are also, in fact, parallels. But, first of all, what does parallelism mean here? In his text *Understanding Movies* (8th ed., 1998), Louis Giannetti writes, "Parallelism is a common principle of design, implying similarity, unity, and mutual reinforcement." It goes without saying that the two couples in the film in a variety of ways fall under the definition of parallelism.

Also: what is the difference between "opposites" and parallels? Opposite, here meaning "antagonistic," is implied by the couples' actions: they are adversaries. Defining opposites in this way, we may define "parallel" similarly—to imply "corresponding" (which also defines the two couples: we see comparative elements and characteristics between them). The two couples work like positive and negative poles of a magnet; they are analogous to two halves of a whole, in a way needing each other to be complete— whilst simultaneously exhibiting contrasting (antagonistic) features.

But more than just the couples are both parallel and opposite. Consider the "Born" and "Died" words carved in the gravestone. Although birth and death are opposites, they are also parallels: one completes the other; even though they are on opposite sides of polarity, and there is a one-to-one correspondence between them—viz. for death to take place, birth must have occurred. After examining *Family Plot*, it is apparent that although each film element has an opposite (which serves as a parallel as well), each film element *requires* its opposite film element (or parallel) to "exist" in the diegesis. Thus, there is a balance (a nearly one-to-one correspondence; almost every element can be paired off with another) of thesis/antithesis elements (which are also parallels) in the film. We will examine key two scenes that display an excess of these one-to-one correspondences of elements between them. In addition, dynamic/static[*] characters (which are an expression of both the parallel and the opposite) will be discussed.

At exactly 1:00 (one hour) into the 2:01 movie, there is a five-minute scene that has a significant plot impact. In a narrative sense, characters' assumptions about their world are altered. From an editing standpoint, Hitchcock momentarily breaks the 180-degree line and experiments with character motion. And because the scene occurs exactly one hour into the film, the "Kidnapping of Bishop Wood" scene is the structural midpoint of *Family Plot*.[†]

After Blanche learns from Mrs. Rainbird that there might be a person—Bishop Wood—who knows the current location of Edward Shoebridge, Blanche informs George of this during a car ride. The next day, George goes to Bishop Wood's church. Before George can speak with him, the Bishop is kidnapped by Fran and Arthur (in full view of the inhibited churchgoers). Next, we see Arthur and Fran discussing the successful kidnapping in their car. However, their success, they say, was tainted by the appearance of George, who they both believe are after them. Fran suggests that Madame Blanche's psychic powers "led" George to the kidnappers. Arthur agrees with his lover's analysis as the car pulls into their private garage, and the scene concludes.

Let's examine the scene in more detail. It begins as George is shown walking briskly up the stairs; the camera is placed at an extremely high angle. Perhaps this high shot is meant to represent a God-like view of George (this seems especially meaningful given that he is walking into a church). The continuous shot of George ascending the stairs visually parallels a future sequence: George's "hunt" of Mrs. Malloney at the cemetery. Examining the move-

---

[*] "Dynamic" here refers, in general, to characters that are "active" in the scene or the film; in other words, they are participating to the development of the narrative in some way. "Static," then, refers to characters that are literally "passive": they do not contribute to the development of the narrative at that point in the film.

[†] "Structural" simply refers to a duration midpoint; because the scene is exactly in the middle of the movie, it literally divides the film into halves. Is it a narrative division (or midpoint), however? Yes, because some characters' understanding of their "world" changes after the scene: It is a turning point for many of the characters.

ments of George, they appear like snake-like; he "slithers" along, perhaps to "bite" the kidnapping couple (since Fran and Arthur believe he is "after them," George has indeed made his presence at the church known)? The small G in the diagram below stands for George; the long arrow maps his movements up the stairs.

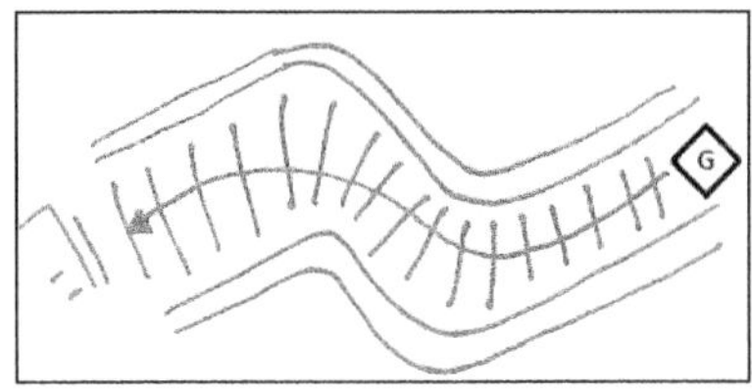


Made manifest by George's snake-like movements, there is a parallel/opposite effect occurring. Examining Genesis from the Bible, we note the evil snake who entices Eve with an apple after God explicitly forbids consumption of food from the garden. Eve (and, by extension, all of humanity) must learn from her mistake of ignoring authority; thus, the snake rebellion of authority is required for "educational purposes." Simultaneously, however, God and the snake represent opposites. George enters the church, a house of God, analogous to the evil snake from Genesis; will he learn a lesson, like Eve did? Yes: after he enters the church, he already has disobeyed authority. With a pipe in his mouth, he blithely asks a church attendant the proper procedure for meeting the Bishop. However, he is clearly forbidden from smoking in the church; thus, he has disobeyed the rules of the religious establishment.

So George has arrived at the church, strictly by coincidence, where Eddie Shoebridge is located; Arthur and Fran, also by coincidence, have stumbled upon George, the "man with the pipe," as Fran calls him.* The two couples (minus Blanche) meeting together is very improbable. But, of course, a different type of logic is at work here: the logic of the narrative has engendered this coincidental meeting.

---

* Sometimes a pipe is just a pipe, but it is interesting that she assigns this moniker to George. The pipe, as previously discussed, is his connection to "rebelling" against God. Remember it is Fran who suggests that Blanche's psychic powers might be legitimate. Psychic powers are an anti-church methodology. Is Fran an "evil" snake? Can we pair up Fran and George (evil snake and Eve) in this way? After all, they are both the "passive" members of the two couples.

One is reminded of *Vertigo* (1958) after Scottie emerges from the hospital: as he strolls along a sidewalk, he "just happens to spot" Judy (Madeline). Hitchcock can almost be seen waving his expressionistic wand—the narrative is like an abstract painting with its own logic, related to but different from reality. (The parallelism is the movie is, of course, similarly expressionistic; in his book, Giannetti states that "Symmetrical parallelism is rarely found in nature: Usually the parallel elements betray a human hand." That human hand is, of course, Mr. Hitchcock's.)

Similarly, George, Fran, and Arthur converging at the same place, at the same time, in a quest for the same person (Bishop Wood), is unlikely (if Family Plot represented the "real" world, which it doesn't, so that act of convergence at common locations is an artifice, and a convenient one). Nevertheless, it is a crucial scene; without it, the narrative for the remainder of *Family Plot* is largely irrelevant (essentially, the movie cannot proceed; it "dead-ends"). By the end of the scene, two characters who were static for the first hour become dynamic: Fran and Arthur. Their assumptions about their world change. In a way, the other main couple, George and Blanche, becomes static. George learns nothing from the kidnapping. Coming into the church, he had a lead as to where Eddie Shoebridge could perhaps be found (given to him by Blanche) but the kidnapping quickly "dead-ends" the pursuit.

George and Blanche have become temporarily static in their quest. But why have Arthur and Fran become dynamic? They realize they are being followed, and, a couple scenes later, they will learn a number of things about their stalking couple by staking out Blache's house at night. After they inject the Bishop and carry him to their automobile, they have an important conversation.

Conversations in cars often equate to character development scenes in Hitchcock's films. Delete the character conversations in cars from *Marnie* (1964), and the film would be terribly jumbled.* In the "mobile" conversations, we learn of Mark Rutland's plan. As

---

* Many would argue it is already jumbled—or at least terrifically artificial. Yet Hitchcock scholar Donald Spoto has almost nothing but praise for the film in his classic book *The Art of Alfred Hitchcock* (1992). Spoto's beautiful prose, though, cannot save the film from an otherwise near-unanimous verdict: it's a dud.

the animal tamer, Mark wishes to trap Marnie in a cage like a wild animal—by blackmailing her into marrying him.

Hitchcock's films after *Marnie*, however, have a dearth of automobile conversations. *Torn Curtain* (1966) has several irrelevant (to the narrative) ones (not, of course, including the bus ride). *Topaz* (1969) and *Frenzy* (1972) do not make especially important use of car conversations, either.

But by his last film, Hitchcock has once again allowed automobile conversations to assume pride of place. Fran and Arthur become dynamic characters in the Bishop Wood scene after their conversation in the automobile because they realize that they are being watched and followed. In fact, there are so many defining "mobile" conversations in the film that we can argue that characters become dynamic while moving and static while still.* Even outside of automobiles, characters in *Family Plot* seem to become dynamic (and realize important information) while mobile. For example, consider George and Blanche's running escape from Malloney: while moving, they realize he wishes to murder them.

"There's no doubt who he's after now," Arthur grudgingly admits to Fran. Then, Fran suggests that Blanche's psychic powers led George to the kidnapping. It is interesting that Arthur even considers the idea, let alone supports Fran's ESP analysis; perhaps he considers the spiritual idea because of his distaste of Bishop Wood and the church as a whole. Psychic powers, though supernatural, are an anti-church methodology. Contrast Arthur to George, who—until the final scene of the film, when his world is shaken†—realizes that Blanche is a fraudulent medium.

The audience, by this point in the film, is perhaps thinking that Blanche's powers did indeed lead George to the kidnapping couple, even though we realize that Mrs. Rainbird suggested the idea. In a way, the audience almost agrees with Fran and Arthur's new belief in psychic powers; perhaps, the audience thinks, Hitchcock has devised the narrative to appear like Blanche's talents as a medium are working in a way unknown even to the medium herself. (Oh, what a tangled web Hitchcock weaves!)

---

* Contrast this with the old saw that car rides/chases stop a movie's plot, rather than further it.

† You might say George appears blanched when Blanche psychically reveals the location of the diamonds to him.

During the rest of the car ride, Fran and Arthur discuss life and death. "He was there, larger than life," Fran says. Arthur answers her with, "Larger than death, you mean." The two statements complement each other; here we have a direct statement of the life/death, thesis/antithesis theme that permeates the movie.

Arthur makes another interesting statement in the automobile. He claims that the Bishop always thought of him as "evil" when he was a child—and he wants the Bishop to "look at me now!" Does this mean that Arthur considers himself super-evil or, contrarily, super-innocent or -successful? His connotation is unclear. But once again we have the life/death parallels and opposites pop up with Arthur's connotation. It could very well be that Arthur considers himself innocent. At the same time, Arthur believes that the Bishop considers him evil. One thinks of the other as evil, and the other thinks of himself as good. Good and evil are, of course, two halves of a whole; they complement each other.

Arthur's conversation with Fran in the vehicle continues to more important matters: While in a dynamic, mobile state (in the moving car), Arthur realizes that in order to be safe Blanche and George must be eliminated. Fran doesn't want to know about his plans, but Arthur expects unity of movement with Fran: "We move as one, nothing held back," he says. "Nothing held back" is in direct contrast to the churchgoers, whom he calls "inhibited." Recall that Fran and Arthur are not inhibited in the church.

Nevertheless, Arthur has captured a distasteful element of his past successfully. Let's look at the movements of characters in the church in a diagram (F stands for Fran; A for Arthur; W for Bishop Wood; and G for George):

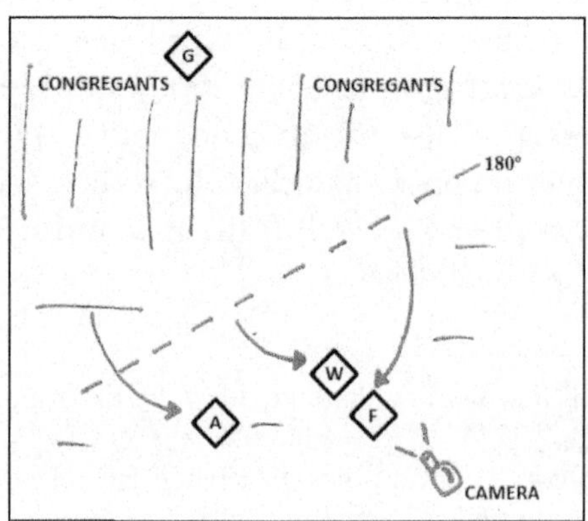

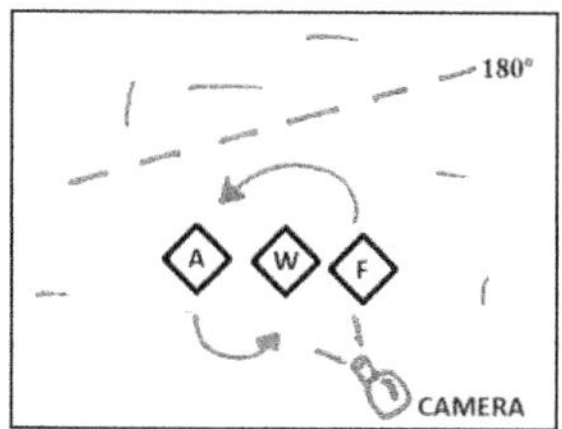


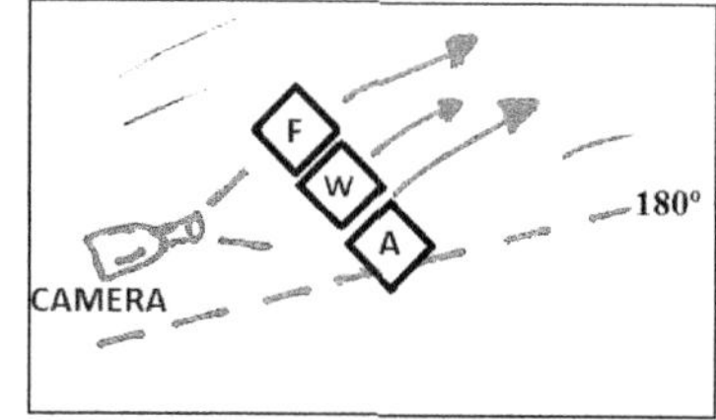


In this sequence of shots, it becomes apparent that by the rightmost diagram above, the camera has (just barely) broken the 180-degree line. Therefore, when Fran and Arthur capture Bishop Wood and remove him from the back door exit, the camera breaks the line.

The 180-degree line separates the dynamic characters from the static characters. The churchgoers, who are static and passive (and are above the line in the first diagram above), literally *cannot* move (or do anything about what they witness); again, to quote Arthur, they are "inhibited." Notice that both Fran and Arthur must cross the 180-degree line to capture the Bishop; while doing so, they go from characters who are as static and as unimportant as the rest of the crowd to dynamic characters who have just engaged in a successful kidnapping.

Thus, the entire church floor is divided into two sections: Dynamic, below the line, and Static, above the line (relative to the overhead mappings, of course). We once again see the contrasting of opposites—between the people above and below the line. George is above the line: he is, therefore, a static character. The George-Blanche couple has been rendered the "impotent" static pair (George doesn't learn anything about Eddie Shoebridge), while Arthur and Fran are the dynamic pair (assumptions about their world change). The Bishop, below the line, can also be labeled as dynamic, because his normal routine of church services is about to change—he'll soon be living in a one-room prison cell.

As Fran and Arthur kidnap the Bishop below the 180-degree line, their movements are extraordinarily deliberate. They trap, using circular movements, the Bishop as if he were an untamed animal. They move with unity, as Arthur expects of Fran. (In fact, their movements are so unified that they seem to resemble the playbook of a football coach: every movement choreographed and executed perfectly.) Their circular movements also can be thought of as a life/death cycle; they have stolen the vitality out of the

Bishop. Perhaps Arthur believes he has captured the "evil" of his childhood.

The scene ends in a parallel, almost reverse movement of George's entrance into the church ("reverse" because George enters the church from the right to the left, and Arthur's car enters the garage from the left to the right): Fran and Arthur's car pulls into their garage, as show in the diagram below.

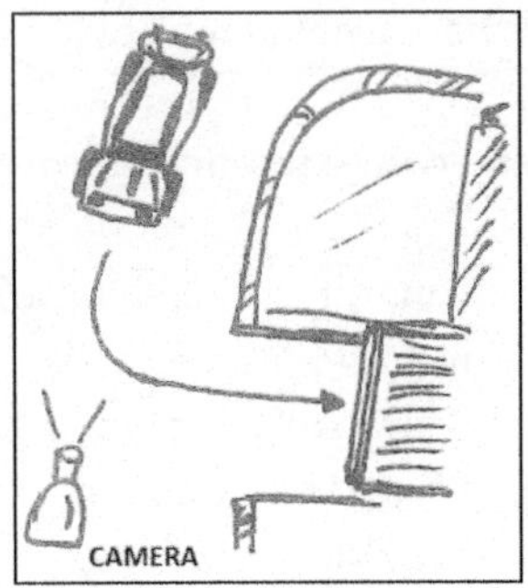


Beginning at the same story location where the first scene concluded (the private garage), the second scene we will examine is 1:40 into the 2:01 movie. Forty minutes of plot have had only one objective: Get Blanche to Arthur Adamson. Once again, analogous to the first scene, the second scene is about five minutes long. Characters' assumptions about their world will once again be upended because of Blanche's discovery of the Bishop and Arthur's discovery of his inheritance (the family plot of *Family Plot*).

Just as Arthur and Fran are about to exit their garage and exchange Bishop Wood for a diamond, they run into Blanche standing outside their garage. Blanche tells Arthur that Mrs. Rainbird "wishes to bestow the Rainbird fortune on him—all the millions and millions of it." The irony is apparent here: Arthur is worth more than the very diamonds he steals.

However, before Blanche can leave, she spots the Bishop, and immediately realizes that Fran and Arthur are the kidnappers. Trapped in the garage, Arthur injects Blanche and incapacitates her. She is taken out of the garage into Arthur's "guest" room.

This scene is what the entire film has been leading up to: the two couples (minus George) meeting to discuss Edward Shoebridge's inheritance. The conversation between Blanche and Arthur is filled with a great many faulty assumptions. Their dialogue does not last for more than a minute. Essentially, the conversation describes the movements of the kidnappings in the two scenes. Arthur forcefully states to the medium that George and Blanche have been "sniffing" and "hunting" them like "wild animals." Of course, it is not George and Blanche but rather Arthur and Fran who hunt like wild animals. Arthur and Fran circled and captured the Bishop in the first scene examined; let's now look their movements in this second scene (B stands for Blanche):

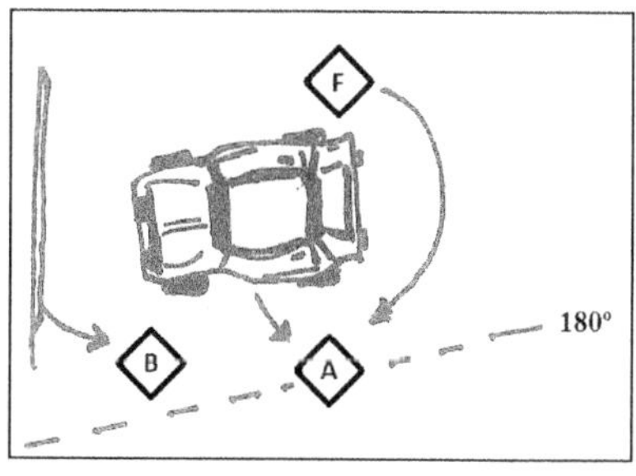


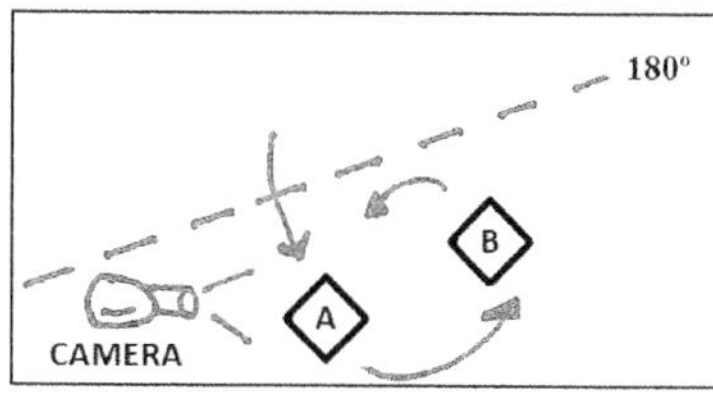


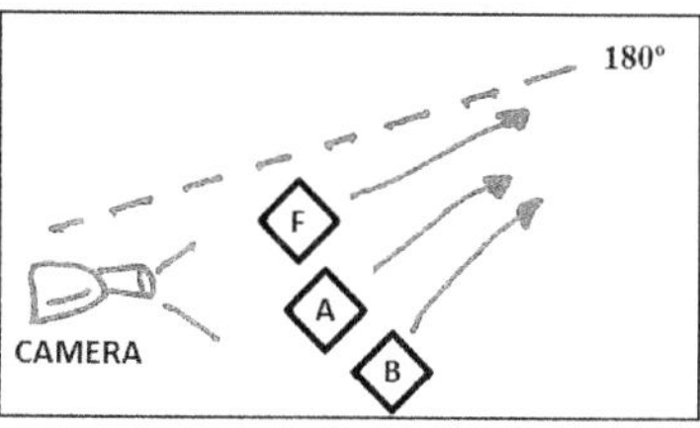


Notice that after Blanche enters the garage, Fran circles around the car, in anticipation of a possible capture. Once again, as they did with Bishop Wood, Arthur injects his victim with a drug, and Arthur and Fran remove Blanche from the garage. Although the camera never quite breaks the 180-degree line, the shots are nearly *identical* to the Bishop Wood capture sequence.

As in that first scene, Arthur expects unity of movement from Fran. There is indeed a similar unity (as shown in the three diagrams above), but Arthur appears more in control. In addition,

Fran's movements seem less deliberate—although they have not planned the capture analogous to the kidnapping of Bishop Wood, Fran appears to resist unity with Arthur. Fran's unity with Arthur does not constitute a reexamination of their identity as a pair, but as frequently occurs in Hitchcock (consider *Strangers on a Train* [1951]) pairs/doubles are displayed throughout the course of the film to be less alike then they first seem. But Fran does not rebel against Arthur, and overall there is still a degree of unity between the couple.

Once again, like in the first scene we examined, the 180-degree line is the dynamic/static physical divider in the scene. Blanche descends to the same position as the Bishop assumed in the first scene.* She is below the 180-degree line, and Arthur, to become a dynamic character like he was in the Bishop Wood scene, goes below the 180-degree line to capture the medium. Everything above the 180-degree line—the car (static, because it doesn't move) and Fran (who essentially refuses to participate in the actual capture)—is as static and as inhibited as the churchgoers from the first scene. Fran, above the line, is physically unable to inject Blanche with the drug; instead, she must pass the needle to Arthur (below the line), who is not "inhibited."

But why does Arthur bother to kidnap Blanche even after she tells him of the fortune he is coming into? It appears to be because she discovers Bishop Wood; however, this is only part of the reason. Blanche has associated Arthur Adamson with Edward Shoebridge. Arthur does not wish to be linked with his troubled past; as far as he is concerned, Eddie Shoebridge was killed with his parents in a fire (hence the fake headstone). Everyone connected to Arthur's past must be punished: The Bishop, by kidnapping for ransom; Joseph Malloney, by death; and Blanche/George, by eventual death. In this scene, Blanche becomes a sort of surrogate Bishop Wood; she is an "evil" connection to Arthur's past.

Then again, there could be an even more extreme reason for the kidnapping. Hitchcock has proven to his audiences that his movies

---

* She *literally* descends. Not only does she fall down, a type of descending, but she also descends into darkness in the prison room. The Bishop, in the first scene, parallels Blanche's movements in the second; he descends as well. Is his kidnapping a direct result of his consideration of Arthur as "evil" a direct punishment from God, thus he symbolically "descends" from his high stature as a Bishop?

have their own logic; this film, in particular, seems to create parallels just for the sake of mathematical precision in the narrative; it is his literal "moving abstract painting" at work. So why did Hitchcock have Arthur kidnap Blanche? Because Arthur was "forced," by Hitchcock's logic devised exclusively for *Family Plot*, to: *Anyone who travels below the 180-degree line in either of the two scenes either is the kidnapped or the kidnapper.* Since Arthur and Fran have already been established as the kidnappers, Blanche assumed a default position of the person being kidnapped. Characters assuming the status of dynamic by traveling below the line in either of the two scenes *creates* a kidnapping. (As an aside, note that Arthur seems to have a fondness for kidnapping characters that start with the letter "B": Bishop and Blanche.)

We know that the two scenes we've examined here are related; most of the elements in the first scene recur in the second. For example, there are common objects present in both scenes: Blanche has her handbag, George has his pipe, and Fran adorns her blonde wig. Also, a variety of shots are similar: for instance, note the close shot of the needle in both scenes.

Yet another common element is the presence of an Einsenstein-type montage in both scenes. As Bishop Wood is being stabbed, the quick cuts (none of which lasts for more than a second) evoke a sense of spatial disorientation for the audience. Similarly, while Blanche struggles in the second scene, the cuts are fast and furious. One is reminded of Eisenstein's *Battleship Potemkin* (1925); the mutiny sequence has a similar montage-style of juxtaposing related images.

Both scenes change the character's assumptions about their worlds. Arthur begins to believe ESP might actually be a viable locator;[*] Blanche learns of a kidnapping her counterpart witnessed; and Arthur learns he is an heir.

---

[*] Maybe he should make use of the former magician and well-known skeptic James Randi to test his theory. Randi has famously put up one million dollars to anyone "who can show, under proper observing conditions, evidence of any paranormal, supernatural, or occult power or event." So far, no takers. Maybe illusionist David Copperfield should give it a try.

Now we must return to the original statement in the introduction: "each film element requires its opposite film element (or parallel) to 'exist' in the diegesis." Is this statement true between the individual elements of the two examined scenes and between the two scenes overall?

Let's see if it holds with respect to individual elements between the two scenes. On a superficial level, Arthur needed "practice" to stab an individual. He received that practice on the Bishop, and later used his learned skills to effectively immobilize Blanche. This is a parallel film element between the scenes.

However, after looking at his movements in the first and second scenes, they appear to be nearly reversed. This is an example of the opposite and the parallel; the individual movements almost form counterclockwise circular paths; yet, between scenes, Arthur changes his orientation from approaching from the left to approaching from the right (relative to the camera position). It is a physical manifestation of the life/death cycle; like two halves of a whole, one element contrasts, yet completes, the other element. Here we have the parallel and the opposite in effect in the scenes. The circular paths are reversed, yet, seen together, they form a complete circle.

After "practicing" carrying the Bishop out of the church, Arthur is now ready to repeat his precise sweeping movement with Blanche—when he removes her from the garage. What he learned from removing the Bishop he uses on Blanche; and, obviously, he knows how to remove Blanche from the garage because of the technique (of removal) he learned from the Bishop.

Also, there are parallels with audience expectation and analysis of Blanche's psychic powers in the two scenes. As discussed before, the chances of George converging at the same place with Arthur and Fran can almost be explained with psychic-locating phenomenon; similarly, Blanche's "discovery" of the kidnapping couple is unlikely (according to "real" world logic, which *Family Plot* does not quite have, as also mentioned before). The audience almost supposes that otherworldly powers led the couples to convergence. But look at how the psychic-assumptions feed off of each other: the audience is conditioned to accept Blanche's meeting of Arthur and Fran in the garage as a realistic and logical plot development because of George's church visit—suspension of disbelief at work!

The two scenes seem to fit like puzzle pieces: every element appears to balance out another one. If we only view one scene in isolation, for example, only George or only Blanche comes into contract with the kidnapping couple; but, examining the two scenes as one whole unit, both George and Blanche have met Arthur and Fran. Isn't it interesting that only one member of the protagonist couple is present in each of the two scenes? The two scenes fit together because they each have a "gap" in them: a missing person (i.e., George or Blanche).

So: the two scenes we have examined in detail "require" each other; since the film eventually leads up to the two couples converging at a common location (at the conclusion of *Family Plot*, both couples converge at Arthur's mansion), the two scenes considered together represent a movement toward the film's resolution.

The two scenes have many balancing parallel features; they also contain opposite elements, like Arthur's capturing movement. In a film like *Family Plot*, where the narrative and structure have been deliberately formed around creating as many parallels (and opposites) as possible, it comes as no surprise that some scenes themselves correspond. With mathematical precision, Hitchcock, for his last film, creates an intricate web of balanced parallel and opposite elements and scenes.

The use of dynamic/static characters is also prevalent. Comparing which characters are dynamic and which are static within the two scenes creates many parallels and opposites. The life/death themes that run through the picture can be called dynamic and static themselves; life, on the surface, is dynamic. Death is static. However, in *Family Plot*, the presence of a character who is dead seems to be more dynamic than one who is alive. After all, it is only after Joseph Malloney is killed (and buried) that George learns anything about the location of Eddie Shoebridge—and the scene gives new meaning to the phrase "Over my dead body!"

Therefore, in a way, the life/death thesis/antithesis themes that for decades had been integral parts of Hitchcock's films finally assume the status of a "main character" in *Family Plot*. The foreground elements in films, which are usually characters, not narrative features (like the parallels/opposites) change in the film. The characters, much like the kidnapped Blanche and Bishop, are rendered as almost impotent cardboard cutouts, which simply serve the purposes of the balancing of parallel/opposite elements. *Topaz* has a similar "character receding" quality to it ("character receding" here means that the characters are shuffled to the background of the film, instead of being lodged firmly in the foreground as the audience's main focus). Thus, the narrative parallels/opposites that are created with mathematical precision have become central, pushing Blanche, Arthur, George, and Fran to ornamental, ancillary elements that serve the purposes of the narrative parallels/opposites, rather than the other way around.*

(1999)

* *Family Plot* clearly isn't the only Hitchcock film with the same tight formalism of main couples. Consider *Rear Window* (1954): it's just as structured, and yet significantly less obvious than it is in Family Plot. As feminist author Tania Modleski notes, "Important parallels are thus set up between Lisa and Thorwald, on the one hand, and Jeff and the wife, on the other." The dominant partner of each relationship, Thorwald and Lisa, respectively, are both also the physically active ones: although it is tempting to group Thorwald and Jeff together (claiming that they are both alter egos; that they are both dissatisfied men in their respective romantic bonds; etc.), and Lisa and Thorwald's wife together (they are both mistreated blonde women; they both have a seeming-propensity to wear the latest fashions; etc.), the more significant, and less superficial, pairing is of the *opposite* sex partners. We observe that Lisa, as an active female, is a criminal element, in a similar vein as Thorwald; and Thorwald is, in many ways, "more of a man" than Jefferies, because Thorwald is ambulatory and has a strong sense of self (by strong sense of self, recall his meeting with Jeff: he is stable and relatively unperturbed by Jefferies' accusations). Thus, negativity is associated with the woman-as-active-person. And negativity is also placed upon male-as-passive-person. Thorwald's wife, despite her death, is a character that other characters feel both sympathy and empathy for. Thus, she has a modicum of power over males and females, in that they seek to discover the cause of her disappearance; however, this control/power is obtained only with her intense suffering/presumed death/death.

# PART IV

# REVIEWS OF BOOKS AND ARTICLES

# 41.

## A Plea for Fixed Standards: A Review of *Jesus Among Other Gods*

In his lively book *Jesus Among Other Gods* (2002), theologian Ravi Zacharias stands athwart the creeping materialism and atheism in the U.S., yelling Stop!

Scientist Richard Dawkins is repeatedly mentioned in the text, along with Jean-Paul Sartre, as rabid proponents of naturalism[*] who, despite their belief in an evolutionary-based morality (indeed, if any at all), fall into a trap of having nothing to compare evil (in the former case) and love (in the latter case) to except their opposites—implying the existence of some sort of supra- or fixed-moral-standards methodology. But where there is thesis, there must be antithesis.[†]

Yet G.K. Chesterton in *Orthodoxy* already best made the point—and Zacharias knows this all too well, since he culls a fantastic passage from that text. In the quoted passage, Chesterton rails against those individuals who precipitate revolution for the mere sake of rebelling, and end up rebelling against nothing at all; Chesterton was mostly addressing the dominant antitheist philosophy of the time propagated by Nietzsche.[‡] Zacharias does a wonderful job recounting the contradictions implicit in the naturalists' take on moral law, and he also nicely summarizes the odd network of rules inherent in Buddhism and Hinduism. But he does not successfully dif-

---

[*] Or the Brights, as mathematician John Allen Paulos terms them in *Irreligion*.

[†] An idea that both Hegel and Marx ran with.

[‡] Let's connect the Catholic theologian Chesterton to the Catholic director Alfred Hitchcock in an effort to understand them both better. As critic Richard Alleva explains in his article "The Catholic Hitchcock: A Director's Sense of Good and Evil" (in *Commonweal*), "The small group of Hitchcock films that do bear witness to a Catholic sensibility (though certainly not to any doctrine) display an almost painful awareness of the Catholic democracy of souls that so engaged G.K. Chesterton, a boyhood favorite of the moviemaker: the certainty that anyone, finally, is capable of anything, any sin, any virtuous act."

ferentiate between a Christian worldview versus any other deistic one as more or less effective of an antidote to naturalism's foibles.[*]

The short story "Those Who Walk Away from Omelas" by Ursula K. Le Guin bears mentioning here. In it, people choose free will[†] over an indefinite, utopian happiness because—besides not countenancing a little boy being locked up perpetually—happiness has no meaning without its opposite, suffering. And *choice* is perhaps a serviceable one-word summary of Zacharias's book.

Zacharias eventually relates suffering and evil as analogous to the suffering of Christ, but he takes Nobel Laureate Elie Wiesel's famous comment about a hanged man wildly out of context—it wasn't supposed to serve as a metaphor for Christ. But Wiesel would clearly agree with Zacharias' criticisms of antinomianism (the notion discussed in relation to the freedom we might have if atheism were proven to be true). Wiesel has famously said elsewhere that "Evil becomes good, inhumanity is interpreted as charity, egoism as compassion," if we all follow adherents of antinomianism—i.e., differentiation and choice are not possible without fixed standards of some kind. But those fixed standards need not necessarily derive from the Torah, Bible, Koran, Bhagavad Gita, the *Star Wars Encyclopedia*,[‡] or whatever, as so-called materialists like Dawkins and

---

[*] Read Joshua Hammer's *Chosen by God* (2000), about the author's brother's single-minded devotion to Torah after a youth spent absorbing Marxist beliefs, to see how living the extremes—in either direction—is a nonstarter toward Truth.

[†] Is there such a thing as free will? Pondering the question is not simply a quaint philosophical exercise. In other words, the answer to such a question may have a truth value—i.e., be answerable. For example, the book *13 Things that Don't Make Sense: The Most Baffling Scientific Mysteries of Our Time* has an interesting chapter devoted to the question of free will. To summarize, fMRIs of investigative subjects' brains have shown evidence of conscious intent to move milliseconds prior to the subjects being aware of conscious intent to move—whence did the decision to move originate? Thus what was once a philosophical problem transitions to becoming a problem of neuroscience. As Ray Kurzweil has noted, philosophy is a kind of "halfway house" for problems that may eventually be subjected to the scientific method.

[‡] The Bible has always seemed to me like *Star Wars*, viz. Episodes 4 and 6: *Return of the Jedi* is simply a structurally cleaner, slicker version of *The New Hope* in the same way as the New Testament is a repackaged, made-for-the-masses version of the raw fire-and-brimstone Old Testament.

another of his fellow "Four Horsemen of New Atheism," Christopher Hitchens, maintain.

I agree with Zacharias (and Chesterton, and Wiesel) that we are not automatons,* programmed by DNA, dependent on determinism, bereft of free agency. There are indeed internal contradictions in naturalism that Zacharias uses successfully against its followers to crack its edifice: but this doesn't necessarily imply, as Zacharias would have it, the veracity of deism, let alone Christianity; even Chesterton, in the beginning of *Orthodoxy*, acknowledges that although Christianity is the best fit for the facts and feelings in life he's encountered, there's still the possibility that another theory or methodology to better explain things remains to be discovered. In this way, Chesterton approaches religion as a best-fit rather than a perfect-fit†—which makes the most sense, since we ourselves are not deities able to accurately measure the truth of absolute claims.

Some mere mortals have tried to measure that truth, however. Recall that philosopher and mathematician Blaise Pascal attempted to construct an airtight argument for belief in God, called Pascal's Wager (or Pascal's Gambit). Pascal argued that one's belief in a deity was a lifetime bet where one had little to lose (what statisticians refer to as the Type I error would be leading a "good" life‡ according to scripture, yet there was no need to) and much to gain—i.e., eternal salvation—while, by not believing, one had much to lose: a miserable afterlife spent in eternal damnation (called the Type II error). Needless to say, there are many holes in Pascal's argument—for instance, would any deity be naïve enough *not* to penalize someone for falsely believing?

---

* Descartes questioned his senses. Although Descartes argued that, from his vantage point, everyone around him could indeed be automata (or zombies), and that the only thing that he knew for sure is that if *he* thinks, he exists—hence, *cogito ergo sum*.

† Even Christian apologist C. S. Lewis observed that Christianity as-is can't possibly be a perfect fit because there are contradictions, such as the following: if we accept that God is omnipotent He cannot be benevolent, since He would not permit His creatures to suffer. Perhaps we can look at religion like Churchill viewed democracy: the worst system, except for all of the others.

‡ Whence does morality emerge? Socrates (or Plato) famously struggled with this question, concluding that the gods aren't necessary to arrive at an independent conception of morality, for there are two possibilities: either the gods decide arbitrarily what is moral (might makes right), or the gods align with what is moral (in which case, definitions of morality are independent of them).

Speaking of mathematics, I am also reminded of the Bishop George Berkeley who in the 1700s famously wrote—when the mathematical concept of the calculus limit was first being fashioned by Newton, Leibniz, and others—that such an amorphous concept of infinitely small "ghosts of departed quantities" surely must be proof of God's existence bearing itself down upon the rational milieu of mathematics—until, within a hundred years or so, the notion of the limit was rigorously mathematically defined without the crutch of apparent God-talk or flowery verbiage.

Why are conditions for life, and intelligent life, just right? Perhaps naturalism or materialism or the anthropic principle is indeed wrong (and are falsifiable, unlike religion), but perhaps also an argument apart from Christianity (or Judaism) will someday arise as a better-fit explanation of the realities of our complex universe.

(2004)

# 42.

## Science or Luck: A Brief Look at Poker Books

It wasn't until I was 25 years old that I played my first hand of poker. But I fancied myself a student of the game for long before then.

Before telling you anything more, let me set the table. By 2003, poker's popularity—especially the Texas hold'em no-limit variety—was through the roof. Conventional wisdom has it that if not for Chris Moneymaker (yes, that's his real name), an accountant and amateur poker player who parlayed an investment of $39 in an online tournament into winning the $2.5 million main event of the World Series of Poker (WSOP), then no-limit hold'em would have never reached the mega-popularity it still enjoys today. Some cold hard facts poke holes in that conventional wisdom, however: if attendance at the WOSP main event is a bellwether of poker's nationwide popularity, then the game enjoyed growing popularity pre-Moneymaker: attendance in the years before Moneymaker's win had been steadily increasing, from below one hundred in the early-eighties Stu Ungar years (Ungar's the only entrant to win the grand prize three times; he was known, at least to a small subset of poker-philes, as the tormented boy genius of poker) to over two hundred by 1992, to more than 500 by the turn of the century. The barrier to entry? Ten thousand big ones, thought to be enough to keep out those who were less than serious about the gambling "sport," back when that kind of money went a lot further than it does now.

In 1998, Edward Norton, Matt Damon and the great John Malkovich starred in a gem of a movie called *Rounders*. The film helped to make two things famous: the WSOP and Johnny Chan. Chan is the Chinese-born wunderkind who cleaned up back-to-back years at the '87 and '88 main events until he was stopped by another up-and-comer, the tempestuous American Phil Hellmuth. *Rounders* glamorized the gambler's lifestyle: Damon's character reveals in a voiceover, at the end of the film, that he's given up everything—girlfriend, law degree, family, respectable lifestyle—to take a shot at the WSOP.*

All fine and good, but does an amateur really have a shot at winning big? Or is it all just luck, shrouded in the illusion of skill? When the WSOPs blew up, in terms of attendance, these past fifteen years or so, so-called professional gamblers (those who earn a living by eking out small margins of victories at countless hands—i.e., the "rounders") were faced with an influx of rank amateurs who in some cases played hold'em more or less randomly, or otherwise approached the deceptively simple game from an online player's perspective, where the careful art of reading tells was a foreign language. So, how did the "professionals" fare at the WSOP? Ever since Moneymaker won—he beat a full-time pro, the sly cigar-chomping Sammy Farha—no main event has been claimed by a professional. So is playing winning poker largely luck, or skill?

Perhaps Mark Twain can help us read the tea leaves. About a century and a half before Moneymaker's win, a famous Twain short story called "Science vs. Luck" grappled with the riddle of luck versus skill. Twain describes a fictional town in Kentucky in which "the law was very strict against what is termed 'games of chance.'" A number of boys had been accused of playing "seven up" (also called "old sledge"), and a lawyer named Jim Sturgis is assigned to their defense. Twain goes on:

> The more he [Sturgis] studied over the matter, and looked into the evidence, the plainer it was that he must lose a case at last—there was no getting around that painful fact. Those boys had certainly been betting money on a game of chance. Even public sympathy was roused in behalf of Sturgis. People said it was a pity to see him mar his successful career with a big prominent case like this, which must go against him.

Sturgis, after several sleepless nights, arrives at a clever defense: perhaps old sledge isn't really a game of chance at all. Perhaps it is a game of *science*. Many witnesses are called to testify to the science-

---

* No-limit hold'em even infiltrated the world of James Bond. In the Daniel Craig debut vehicle *Casino Royale* (2006), Bond forgoes his usual baccarat in favor of hold'em; through fifty years of movies, the famous British superspy has been so modified as to be all but unrecognizable to Ian Fleming's creation.

ness of the game—the basic idea being that the more skill at old sledge a player possesses, the more likely he is to clean up at the table.

But the judge isn't satisfied. "The judge scratched his head over it awhile, and said there was no way of coming to a determination, because just as many men could be brought into court who would testify on one side as could be found to testify on the other." Sturgis, though, has another idea.

> "Impanel a jury of six of each, Luck versus Science. Give them candles and a couple of decks of cards. Send them into the jury-room, and just abide by the result!" There was no disputing the fairness of the proposition. The four deacons and the two dominies were sworn in as the "chance" jurymen, and six inveterate old seven-up professors were chosen to represent the "science" side of the issue. They retired to the jury-room.

The jury members played the game all night. By the next morning, they returned to give their verdict: old sledge was a game not of chance, but of science. "In demonstration whereof it is hereby and herein stated, iterated, reiterated, set forth, and made manifest that, during the entire night, the 'chance' men never won a game or turned a jack, although both feats were common and frequent to the opposition; and furthermore, in support of this our verdict, we call attention to the significant fact that the 'chance' men are all busted, and the 'science' men have got the money."

If only the professionals at the WSOP were so lucky, being busted year in and year out by those who haven't treated hold'em as a science. Except, if author Jim McManus is any indication, these "amateurs" have more than a few tricks up their sleeves. In his brilliant book *Positively Fifth Street*, McManus, like the poet Al Alvarez did years before, writes about the WSOP as well as reporting on the brutal murder of casino magnate Ted Binion. Unlike Alvarez, though, McManus gets in on the action: carefully studying the most famous no-limit primer of them all, *Doyle Brunson's Super System*, as well as T. J. Cloutier's *Championship No-Limit & Pot-Limit Hold'em*, along with practicing by repeatedly playing poker software, McManus enters the main event fray and places an amazing fifth at the final table (in 2000), bested by eventual winner and mathematical polymath Chris "Jesus" Ferguson (he has a Ph.D. in CompSci).

McManus is a case study of using the professionals' own tactics against them: these pros, over the years, were greedy for more than just the chips—they wanted fame, too, and figured one quick way to be known was to spread their gospel as far and as wide as they could by writing books spilling their trade secrets. Not just Cloutier and Brunson. But Hellmuth, Sklansky, Gordon, Hansen, Duke, and Negreanu. And Harrington: the same Dan Harrington who not only won the main event but also later placed fourth and third in fields with thousands of entrants, perhaps the greatest feat in WSOP history (akin to the Bills going to four straight Super Bowls), notwithstanding those with nearly half a dozen bracelets.

Which brings us back to me. I had read through the books, watched countless hours of hands on TV, and even played against my computer (though certainly not to the extent of McManus). I thought I appreciated the subtleties of the game—I figured I understood poker like Clement Greenberg understood Modern art.

But there's a reason Greenberg never took paint to canvas: understanding is not enough. One cannot become an expert simply by studying. Knowing of my love of poker, several teachers I "worked" with (I was a student teacher then) invited me to a game after school one day—not for money, just for bragging rights—at the math department chairman's house. One of the competitors in our game, a math teacher by the name of Gretchen, had poker in her blood: her father had once won a bracelet at a WSOP event.* Another teacher there who knew me well, John, was my mentor.

When my turn came I bluffed with a three-seven unsuited and pushed all my chips in—and was dead to rights, immediately called by both Gretchen and John, who weren't buying it.

There's an old saying in poker: if you can't spot the sucker in the first half-hour at the table, then *you* are the sucker. It didn't take me near that long to realize who the sucker was—I had neither luck nor science on my side. I politely excused myself from the table and drove home. And I never played another hand of poker again.

(2013)

---

* Not the main event—there are many, many satellite events at the tournament each year, not all of them games of hold'em. Win one and you get a bracelet.

# 43.

## Computers Can't Read: A Review of "How We Read"

It is certainly true that the way we read has undergone many transformations. Whether reading on a scrolled parchment, or in a novel, or on the web, we've had to shift our way of thinking depending on what we wish to glean from text. After all, Plato and/or Socrates[*] said that writing and reading aren't even the best way to convey the author's ideas—only the oral tradition can suffice. And with portable reading devices, such as the Kindle and Nook that seem to be all the rage, our way of reading might be more in flux now than in the last one hundred years.

I'm going to put aside for a moment researcher Katherine Hales' notion of machine "reading"[†]—in an article she wrote entitled "How We Read: Close, Hyper, Machine"[‡]—which I strongly object to, and instead mention archival research. Although I am not a researcher, I can imagine the mounds of materials that would need to be parsed through—whether there's Google or some other online search engine or not, the research scholar needs to quickly ascertain what might be relevant to her study and what probably isn't. Because the said scholar doesn't have five lifetimes to do the research, a close reading of all the sources isn't tenable. Point taken.

The point, though, is self-evident, and, as Hayles herself notes, well before the web sprung into being, the research scholar might use the "book wheel, a physical device invented to cope with the information explosion when the number of books increased exponentially with the advent of print." The "scanning" and "skim-

---

[*] Like Jesus, Socrates left behind nothing written—Plato spoke for Socrates through the centuries with the written word. Also like Jesus, Socrates was sentenced to death: by hemlock, though, not by crucifixion.

[†] The quotes I have around the word "reading" aren't there by accident, as we'll soon see.

[‡] Hayles, K. "How We Read: Close, Hyper, Machine." Association of Departments of English Bulletin 150 (2010): 62-79.

ming" of texts on the wheel wasn't close reading, but akin to what Hayles terms *hyper reading*—hundreds of years before the internet.

But surely, though, the physiological process of hyper reading must be unique to the advent of the web! Hayles relays that the "research shows that Web pages are typically read in an 'F' pattern. A person reads the first two or three lines across the page, but as the eye travels down the screen, the scanned length gets smaller...." And hey, if Hayles' article had been written in the 1960s or '70s, I'd bet she would have talked about archivists' eyes' rapid scrolling and scanning—while using a microfiche, the revolutionary way that millions upon millions of pages of text, newspaper or otherwise, were "compressed" for storage. My point? While reading on the microfiche certainly wasn't ever anywhere near as prevalent as reading text online is today, there isn't exactly that much new under the sun. (Although I don't think Ecclesiastes had the microfiche in mind when he penned that line.)

If physiologically we've seen this before, the question then becomes: Is the brain being altered in some way by hyper reading? And, as a follow-up: If the brain is being altered by hyper reading, does that make close reading more difficult to do? From what Hayles reports, it seems like the answer to the first question is yes, and the second question maybe. "[R]ecent studies indicate that hyper reading not only requires different reading strategies than close reading but may also be involved with changes in brain architecture that makes close reading more difficult to achieve," she writes. That sustained concentration is more difficult while hyper reading seems like, well, a no-brainer. The uneven but fascinating book *World Wide Mind* by Michael Chorost discusses, for instance, how repeatedly checking e-mail triggers the same sorts of dopamine-driven pleasure responses in the brain that a slot machine does: the almost random nature of the "wins" (an e-mail you desire) and "losses" (no e-mail, or an e-mail you don't particularly care about) parallels with the game of slots quite neatly. Thus, sustained concentration is dramatically affected. *World Wide Mind* has many other examples like this, of how the nature of Internet has possibly rewired our brains; the hackneyed clichéd "neurons that fire together wire together" is indeed a significant takeaway.

But Hayles doesn't give nearly enough credit to the human brain. It's awfully malleable, as she herself notes: "Supplementing this research [of hyper reading being mentally detrimental] are other studies showing that small habitual actions, repeated over and over, are extraordinarily effective in creating new neural pathways." Hayles goes on to discuss a study in which "volunteers in their fifties and sixties who had never performed Google searches" were asked to repeatedly do so.* Brain scans were performed, showing changes in brain architecture. But, even so, doesn't this cut both ways? Again, the brain is highly adaptable. Practice close reading for a while, free of distractions, the brain will serve its master (or are we subjects of our brains?) well. Want to hyper read? The brain will adapt well to that, too. Hyper reading hardly sounds the death knell of close reading, anymore than close reading spells the end of hyper reading.

This gets us to her next idea: that of students and their seeming disinclination to closely read. Hayles writes that "Bauerlein instances many responses from young people when they encounter difficult print texts to the effect the works are 'boring' or not worth the trouble." Okay, fine. But hasn't this been an age-old problem? English teachers have been trying to get their students to engage with texts well before the internet or text-messaging arrived. Hayles notes this, and also presents a couple of good ideas integrating close and hyper reading along with what was the article's most interesting exploration, that of the "Romeo and Juliet: A Facebook Tragedy" assignment. Vygotsky would have been proud. But, even here, I must criticize: these ideas are a bit disjoint from the rest of her article, which she herself seems to acknowledge by giving them the heading "Synergies between Close, Hyper and Machine Reading," despite there being no other headings or formally identified subdivisions in the article.

Now, onto the part I most strenuously object to: machine "reading."† As Hayles defines it, "Machine 'reading' ranges from algorithms for word frequency counts to more sophisticated programs that find and compare phrases and that are capable of learning." First of all, it's tough to take this seriously when there's a tautology in the sentence: "frequency" and "counts" mean the same thing. Her writing's imprecise here, and despite what we've seen in *The Matrix* and countless other SF films, machine "learning" isn't like

* Where did they find such people? Certainly not online.

† I will continue to put quotes around the word "reading" when it's next to "machine," purely as a form of protest.

human learning—or like any learning, as we conscious entities experience it, at all. Not a good beginning.

And it gets worse: "Given the scope, pervasiveness, and sophistication of contemporary programs used to parse texts, it seems to me quite reasonable to say that machines read.... From my point of view, saying computers cannot read is merely species chauvinism." Species chauvinism? This is absurd. Calling computers "stupid" doesn't smack of cultural absolutism or ethnocentrism—we're talking about electronic idiot savants here! No need to pull out the familiar tropes of cultural relativism when speaking of non-human, non-alive, non-thinking, non-reading (sorry!) machines.

So, where to begin to unpack this abject silliness? Let's start with the notion of "algorithms" as something privileged to computers alone. That's not true: algorithms* are merely recipes, many of them mathematical in nature. For instance, in the book *Mathematics 1001*, there is an interesting discussion of so-called hailstone numbers. Here's what they are: pick an integer. If that integer is odd, triple it and add one. If it's even, half it. Whatever you get from that process, repeat: if the result was odd, triple it and add one, and, if even, half it. Keep doing this until you obtain 1. Here's an example:

> Start with 3. It becomes 3x3+1 = 10. And 10/2 = 5. Then, take 5x3+1 = 16. Then, 16/2 = 8, 8/2 = 4, 4/2 = 2, and 2/1 = 1. The process is complete.

That was an algorithm, and a computer wasn't necessary to put it into action. Of course, mathematicians have written computer programs with the hailstone algorithm, because it just takes too long to test many numbers by hand.†

The only way an algorithm can be written for a computer is if there's a way to quantify items in some sort of a finite-length process: which is why a computer is a "genius" at counting words but not so good at counting the times that the "quest" plot appears in all novels and short stories written during, let's say, the Great Depression: that would require the machine actually comprehending

---

* But for more on algorithms in computer programming, see the Appendix.

† By the way, no mathematician has been able to prove that any integer, no matter how big, will always settle on the number 1, like 3 did in the hailstone example above.

the works themselves.[*] Hayles, later in the article, agrees that computers fall far short of comprehension: "the more the emphasis falls on pattern (as in machine 'reading'), the more likely it is that context must be supplied from outside (by a human interpreter) to connect pattern with meaning...."

So, let me translate: machines can't read. They can quantify letters and words (as long as they were explicitly programmed to), present and analyze patterns (as long as they were programmed to by their far-sighted human interlocutors), but they can't read because they can't comprehend anything. Computers can be used as a tool to aggregate large amounts of data, such as texts, and human beings themselves can have fun themselves decoding the patterns that computers present.[†] After all, the best use of such machine "reading" Hayles can come up with is an analysis of *Time* magazine covers—but, even here, the analysis was done by human beings after the patterns were organized and disaggregated by computer algorithms written by human beings. Computers didn't "read" anything, unless we completely redefine the meaning of the word "read."

And there's the rub. Computers are very limited: they have no problem quantifying things, as long as there are things to quantify. The problem comes with *qualifying*: how absolutely terrible computers are at this! Since close reading is largely about qualifying, rather than quantifying (admittedly, hyper reading might have a quantifying element to it), computers generally can't tell you who killed whom and why in *Romeo and Juliet*, only that the word "Romeo" appears 310 times in the play.

---

[*] Well, maybe not: in 2011, IBM's supercomputer Watson demonstrated a fairly sophisticated "understanding" of text while competing on *Jeopardy!* So sentience may or may not be required for machine "comprehension." Thus, a computer might be able to pass the Turing test despite lacking sentience. See Ray Kurzweil's book *How to Create a Mind* for more information. Also read novelist Richard Powers' 2002 short story entitled "Literary Devices" for an eerie prediction of Watson's methods of language analysis. The short story is a follow-up piece to Powers' masterful novel *Galatea 2.2*.

[†] Remember the late '90's controversy over the *Bible Code* (by Michael Drosnin)? That was machine "reading" at its finest. Patterns in the Old and New Testaments were found statistically, later decoded and interpreted by human beings as predictions. A famous prediction was that the end of the world would come in 2006. Luckily, Armageddon hasn't arrived yet.

Thus, Hayles' article ultimately fails to convince since she misses elucidating that fundamental distinction between quantification and qualification, as well as how her close, hyper, and machine reading categories are affixed to that spectrum. The closer the type of "reading" is to a kind of quantification, the better a computer would perform it (checking to see if Zipf's law holds in a series of texts, for example, or checking a pamphlet's Flesch readability level), and the closer to qualification, the worse. Human beings might not be able to readily scroll through thousands of texts per second, but at least we have a chance of understanding what these texts mean—i.e., we can *read.*

(2011)

# 44.

## Innocence Stolen: A Review of *A Girl's Life Online*

Who is to blame for thirteen-year-old Katie Tarbox's pubescent online infatuation, romantic attachment, and eventual ill-conceived Texas tryst with the much-older-man "Mark"? Is it her mom? her stepfather? the online child predator, "Mark" (his real name is Frank)? Or is it Katie herself? Katie Tarbox, in her cogently written, revealing, and ultimately deeply disconcerting book *A Girl's Life Online* (2001), smartly chooses not to tackle this difficult question directly, but we shall. Let's hear the case against each of these suspects in turn, seeing if we can successfully pin the bulk of the blame on the culprit who callously stole Katie's earliest teen years.

Is her frequently absentee mother to blame for the events that stole away years of Katie's childhood? Perhaps Katie's attachment to and romantic interest in "Mark" was mostly a function of a rebellion against or reaction to her mother. After all, her mom isn't exactly presented in a good light by Katie. After relaying that her mother not only worked full-time, but "really became a workaholic" about the time Katie turned eleven years old, Katie explains that much of her self-worth, and the self-worth of her parents, was a result of how well Katie performed at swim meets. In addition, after the real-life encounter in the Texas hotel room between her daughter and "Mark," her mother isn't especially supportive of Katie; at the swim team meeting convened shortly after the encounter, Katie's mom says, "[It] is Katie's fault and not the fault of the chaperones here." But as the dedication page of the book makes clear, Katie doesn't fault her mother retrospectively for these maternal lapses in judgment. By the end of the text, Katie's mom is shown to be supportive of her daughter (sending her off to a new school for a fresh start, recommending counseling sessions and medication, and the like), but the sense that her mother is a bit self-centered continues to leave a bad taste in the reader's mouth long after finishing *A Girl's Life.*

How about her stepfather, David, who seemed to be much more interested in playing the role of Freud than the role of father? How much blame can be affixed to him? Not much, it seems. It's difficult to assign responsibility to someone Katie never really utilizes as a parental resource. Although he is not her biological father, he was (at least physically) always there for her: taking her to school every morning, taking her to the police, taking her to the FBI for depositions. But David is forced to view Katie through an impenetrable barrier—illustrated, rather ironically, by their car ride to the FBI: "The police car we rode in was equipped with a barrier that turned the backseat into a rolling jail cell.... I, of course, had to be the one who sat back there while David rode in the front." Katie simply never opens up to her stepfather, and his comments and analysis of his stepdaughter's life and situation invariably end up sounding more like he's reading out of a psychology textbook than speaking about someone he's ostensibly a guardian to.

Possibly "Mark," the child predator himself, is the one most to blame. He is certainly the easiest target, and he undoubtedly shoulders quite a bit of the responsibility. In a letter he wrote to Katie prior to his sentencing, he says that "I was the adult, not you. I should have acted like an adult. You were not at fault here." Nevertheless, if he's not a situational child predator but rather a preferential pedophile, there's an argument to be made that in fact his actions were at least partially out of his control. Unfortunately the nature of his illness and his actions were not sufficiently explored in the text, although Katie does make it clear that "Mark" had a pattern of luring young girls—and at least one young boy—for sexual encounters, lending at least some support to the theory that "Mark" may in fact be a preferential pedophile (there is a disturbing extensively legal taxonomy, by the way).

Finally, we have to entertain the idea that Katie herself is most to blame—after all, she was by any measure complicit in the chain of events that led to her meeting her virtual beau in real life. "Alone with him [online] while the world was dark and sleeping, I felt like I was involved in an intimate little conspiracy.... [T]here was also something excitingly illicit in this moment," she claims. And, after her encounter with "Mark," Katie admits, "I had also been part of what happened in Texas. I was a mature person. I was just as responsible for this as he was."

Katie's certainly the person most blamed by others for the encounter. Consider her stepfather's reaction after "Mark" pleads guilty: "'Feeling guilty for screwing up a man's life?'" Or her sister Abby's harsh judgment of Katie: "'I'm really disgusted with you,' she told me, over and over. 'You've ruined our family.'" Even her supposed old friends pin the blame for the incident on Katie: "To them I wasn't the victim of a crime who deserved compassion. I had been stupid, or maybe seductive, and placed myself in danger. I was a bad influence." Can all these people be wrong? Well, in a word, absolutely. Katie was indeed at least somewhat responsible for her actions, but she cannot be faulted for "Mark"'s continued pressuring of Katie to meet with him, and his physically taking advantage of her when they did in fact meet in a Texas hotel room. "The truth of the matter was that I should have known better," she writes, and this may be true—but still, she certainly didn't deserve to lose two years of her young life to a traumatic child predatory experience. Her childhood was unfairly taken from her.

So who is to blame? Who bears the most responsibility for the incident and the fallout from it? There's certainly enough blame to go around. The brilliance of Katie Tarbox's subtle and heartbreaking book lies in her refusal to give pat answers to these sorts of questions and to instead present the realities of a teen's life's struggles and pains and confusion as they really are: complicated, messy, ever-changing, and ultimately unanswerable.

(2007)

# 45.

## A True Horror Story: A Review of *A Child Called "It"*

At the conclusion of *A Child Called "It"* (1995), author Dave Pelzer casually notes that "What you have just read is a story of an ordinary family that was devastated by their hidden secret," ongoing child abuse. But for anyone who's actually read this monumentally disturbing book—the endless passages describing accounts of beatings, torture, and cruel and unusual punishment inflicted upon young David Pelzer by his sadistic and mentally deranged mother while other family members not only stood by but acted as enablers is by turns horrifying and disgusting—his family can be described as anything but "ordinary."

This most *un*ordinary family has, as its head, a mother who, early in her marriage, is a preternaturally creative cook and years later is brutally creative at cooking up new ways to deeply humiliate and hurt her son David. Each chapter highlights a new low for David. From starvation to drowning to burning to suffocation, the incidents read more like fiction conjured up from horror master Stephen King[*] than real life tales.

Here's just one example, culled at random, from the chapter titled "The Fight for Food":

---

[*] Interesting, but unrelated, aside: in his brilliant autobiography, *On Writing* (2000), King relays an anecdote about how he nailed his many publication rejection letters to his bedroom wall: "By the time I was fourteen … the nail in my wall would no longer support the weight of the rejection slips impaled upon it. I replaced the nail with a spike and kept on writing." Rejection is a common theme in publishing nonfiction, too. *The Emperor of Scent* unsparingly details the labyrinthine, Kafkaesque world of blind-peer review; this amazing book centers on the misunderstood contemporary olfactory scientist Luca Turin and his repeatedly futile attempts at budging the scientific conventional wisdom enough to allow for dissemination of his radical theories of smell. Turns out Thomas Kuhn's famous detailing of the scientific paradigm is sometimes tragically apt.

> Without hesitation I opened my mouth, and Mother rammed the cold spoon [filled with ammonia] deep into my throat. Again I told myself this was all too easy, but a moment later I couldn't breath. My throat seized. I stood wobbling in front of Mother, feeling as if my eyes were going to pop out of my skull. I fell on the floor, on my hands and knees. *"Bubble!"* my brain screamed.

Replace the word "Mother" with "Jailer" in the above passage, and you might get a prisoner of war's account of the horrors of captivity. Indeed, there is an ongoing internal dialogue throughout the text whether David's experiences more closely resemble that of a POW's, or a slave's. Consider: "This whole charade of living like a slave had come to an end"; "The section where Mother ordered me to sit was covered with rocks about an inch in diameter. I lost circulation in much of my body, as I sat on my hands in my 'prisoner of war' position." Even Valerie Bivens, the social worker who pens a short chapter at the end of *A Child*, throws her two cents in when she writes, "We see the child's perception as he moves through a horrifying continuum, from an idealistic family life to becoming a 'prisoner of war' in his own home."

But whether David was effectively a POW or a slave is almost beside the point. How could David's father allow Mother to perpetrate such terrors on his own son? Of the many undercurrents running through the story, this one may be the most disturbing. Father is diminished, rendered entirely impotent to stop the abuse. For instance, after telling him than Mother had stabbed him in the gut with a kitchen knife—and yet *still* ordered him to wash the dishes—Father's non-response is breathtaking in its subjugation: "'Well...you ah...you better go back in there and do the dishes.'" David's father, his ostensible protector, cowers in fear at his wife's demented behavior towards his son. Father is worlds away from the mythic Superman-like figure David repeatedly mentally conjures up of him, and Pelzer expertly depicts his dad's fall from grace in *A Child Called "It."*

The book isn't perfect, however. Mother is rendered as too much of a caricature, as an embodiment of pure evil and selfishness, and because of this many unanswered questions about her remain long after the last page is turned. Chief among them is Mother's transition from loving to loathing: one chapter ends with a recounting of the blissful memories of a family vacation to the Russian River, while the next starts with a description of the Russian-like Gulag David finds himself trapped in. There little segue, and almost no explanation, for the motivation behind Mother's turn to evil, short of cursory description such as "About this time, Mom's behavior began to change radically," and a description of the reasoning behind her proto-abusive "mirror treatment" tactic.

This is a minor quibble, however, which doesn't overshadow what is an incredibly powerful and painful portrait of a survivor of a hell like no other—and the very fact that Pelzer managed to bravely document his unique childhood hell is a major step toward keeping it that way.

(2007)

# 46.

## Courtroom Farce: A Review of *Don't Pee on My Leg and Tell Me It's Raining*

In a book replete with anecdotes, policy recommendations, and amusing section headings, Judge Judy Scheindlin (Judge Judy) purports to expose the dark underbelly of our society, stripping away the "veil of secrecy that has protected a social system run by reality-impaired ideologues." But *Don't Pee on My Leg and Tell Me It's Raining* (1996) only occasionally succeeds at fulfilling this lofty goal. Let's restrict our attention to just one chapter of the book to see why Judge Judy's effort is at best a hit-or-miss affair.

The third chapter, entitled "Judicial Diversity Doesn't Mean a Mixed Bag of Nuts," begins promisingly enough. After presenting an anecdote designed to illustrate the "life and death decisions" that judges in family court have to hand down on a daily basis, Judge Judy rails against a perceived lack of judgment she believes is apparent amongst a large contingent of judges, especially in the mid-level appellate courts. "Too often," she claims, "these [judicial] appointments are based not on ability and wisdom, but on political expediency, payback, race, gender and other 'politically correct' criteria. That is absurd."

But the anecdotes that follow her claim of wanton judicial absurdity due to inappropriately appointed members of the bench do next to nothing to support this accusation. In fact, the elements of race, gender and politically correct politics are simply dropped in favor of presenting colorful stories of "juvenile criminals who laugh at the law when higher courts reverse their convictions." If the chapter had simply leveled a charge of illogic on the mid- to higher-level courts' rulings, claiming that their decision-making process had gone awry for some unknown reason, her anecdotal evidence would have fit the bill. She presents the heart-wrenching story of Mr. Knowings to further her case that the appeals court in New York "seems to be in competition with itself to accommodate criminals." But implying that there is some clandestine, shadowy process of selecting justices based on "cultural diversity" is stretching matters a tad too far without presenting some real evidence—which, of course, she doesn't.

Even though the Knowings story (and others like it) is used to dramatic effect, and helps to further her points and flesh out her arguments, the use of anecdotes in place of raw data, as policy and behavior experts would use, casts doubt on her conclusions. She maligns these experts in an earlier chapter, saying that "[p]oliticians, sociologists, psychologists, and social workers have scrambled to find the magic key that will reduce violence in America," implying a distrust of conclusions drawn from a collection and analysis of data; and, in a later chapter, she complains, "[W]e have legions of academics…who will tell you that society and poverty—in short, all of us—are responsible…." Without data, though, how can you support a statement like this: "The intelligent, diligent and caring judges who negotiate the judicial system are also diminished by those who lack qualifications to preside over the lives of people"? Or this: "Some appellate decisions...fail to reflect the reality of our time.... [I]t makes you wonder about the qualifications and fundamental smarts of some of these men and women in black"? Are we to accept the veracity of Judge Judy's appellate-court criticisms on blind faith?

Certainly, though, an appeal to logic and good old-fashioned common sense override the need for data when Judge Judy goes on to say that we need to become more aware of the types of decisions being made and call those judges to account who hand down rulings antithetical to clear-headed thinking. "We might also consider five-year probationary terms for appointed judges, during which the public could watch them, critique them," and let a majority of people decide electorally whether or not judges should retain their seats. Recent history, though, calls into question whether these simple "majorities" of common folk know what's best. Consider the Supreme Court of Earl Warren: the court that struck down segregation in schools, gave citizens accused of crimes certain protections (such as Miranda rights), and laid the groundwork for the civil rights reforms of the 1960s—all decisions which were vastly unpopular with a majority of citizens at the time but which have certainly proven to be just by any measure of human rights and common decency.

It's on the final pages of the chapter, however, that Judge Judy abdicates her repeated calls for individuals to take personal responsibility for their actions. Recall that, only a couple of chapters earlier, Judge Judy vowed to "step down from the bench the first day I have a defendant who comes before me and says: 'I am a leader! I take responsibility for my actions!'" Yet, in two separate instances she recounts with a frighteningly perverse sense of satisfaction, after delivering judgments against two unrelated defendants, she assumes coworkers' names as aliases to avoid these miscreants affixing the blame for their lock-ups on her. Claiming you're someone else—a fellow judge, no less!—strikes one as, well, an attempt to evade personal responsibility for her actions out of a fear of reprisal from criminals. In the latter instance Judge Judy attempts to explain away her behavior by saying that while she has five children and three grandchildren to take care of, Judge Kaplan—whose name she assumes for the benefit of the defendant—is a bachelor who only has "an aged mother who hardly needs him for support." In other words, he's expendable, should the defendant eventually decide to deliver retribution. Judge Judy should be held in contempt for her hypocrisy and blatant disregard of her coworkers.

Obviously, as she notes, "[b]lind justice should not be dumb justice."[*] A regard for logic, a respect for human rights, and a sprinkling of common sense for good measure should all factor in to the hiring of judges and the judicial decision-making process, as the judge rightly claims. "Brain-power and common sense dictate that experience should be the benchmark, not some misguided fairness which may look and sound good, but smells awfully bad...." Based on her patent disregard for data, reliance on anecdotes, myopic belief in the will of the majority, and evasion of personal responsibility when the goings-on in court get rough, with all due respect, judge, you hardly seem to be the one to determine what "smells bad"—in jurisprudential terms, of course.

(2007)

[*] Not quite what the great philosopher John Rawls, with the blindness of his *Original position*, had in mind.

# 47.

## The Money Makers: A Very Short Critique of Milton Friedman

Does a business have *any* social responsibilities? Can an individual in command of a business legitimately spend his stockholders' money to correct the social ills of society? How can a person conclude what the appropriate social responsibilities of business are in the first place? In a famous, insightful, but only partially convincing article titled "The Social Responsibility of Business Is to Increase Its Profits" (*The New York Times Magazine*, September 13, 1970), Nobel winner Milton Friedman fully articulates his anti-socialistic belief of business' only true social responsibility: to make money.

In the article Friedman, a man who would lead a monetarist counterrevolution against Keynesian conventional wisdom,* establishes a set of criteria for determining a businessperson's appropriate position in the workplace as it relates to a phenomenon he calls "social responsibility." People are the only things in the universe that can have responsibilities, he feels. A business "as a whole cannot be said to have responsibilities"—that is personification gone awry. He questions an individual's right to assume the duty of an entire business, since it implies that he alone would control the employee's, the stockholder's, and the customer's money in a fashion not originally intended. Why would the corporate executive be hired in the first place if he were to spend funds for inappropriate (i.e., non-business-related) items? That's just going rogue.

Friedman argues vehemently against any sort of marketplace built on even the faintest whiffs of socialism—Adam Smith's invisible hand, he feels, should rule all. He declares that a business leader who wishes to use money to correct social problems is in fact

* For more on Friedman, Keynes, and the dismal science in general, read the classic *New Ideas from Dead Economists: An Introduction to Modern Economic Thought* by Todd G. Buchholz.

promoting a collectivist doctrine. Government, Friedman argues, already has a system of checks and balances designed to filter money into necessary social causes. Any chief executive acting as a one-man government is "preaching pure and unadulterated socialism." Such an executive is not performing in accordance with the interests of his stockholders or customers.

How can an executive, Friedman asks, possibly know how to use money for social responsibilities? True, the hired individual is probably excellent at managing a company, but what "makes him an expert on inflation," for example? The executive is imposing on the rights of his employees and customers if he initiates a saint-like crusade to fight the world's inequities; he might be nothing more than a demagogue. Friedman concludes that a business executive simply has no authority to spend other people's money for anything other than business objectives, designed to increase profits.

Although Friedman's analysis of the implications of social responsibility is accurate, he fails to distinguish between the viability of hypocritical and honest motives. He states "social responsibility is frequently a cloak for actions that are justified on other grounds rather than a reason for those actions," but fails to explain why social responsibility is wrong in these cases, even though here it might ultimately be designed surreptitiously to raise profits. Friedman asserts that it allows a company to appear more analogous to an individual, rather than a "heartless" capitalistic machine. Yet he still doesn't seem to approve of social responsibility, even in such hypocritical instances, which is an apparent contradiction of his argument. Friedman also fails to mention the increasingly popular idea of viewing corporations as people, with some of the same rights as U.S. citizens under the Fourteenth Amendment. If corporations *are* people, then don't they have social responsibilities too?

Friedman builds a case against honest social responsibility but fails to explain his motives. He specifically mentions government's laggard pace in correcting the social ills of society. Friedman also notes that business is expedient in transporting money to the homeless, for instance. So—what's the problem? He evades by using a philosophical claim: "this argument must be rejected on grounds of principle." Therefore, Friedman implies, a company is not a suitable vehicle with which to perform charity even if it somehow truly has society's best interests at heart.

Friedman proceeds to explain the individual proprietor's situation. He believes it acceptable for the individual to circulate his own money, "but not someone else's." If the chief executive is spending money originally belonging to him, this should not interfere with the business making profits. But Friedman states it does, without offering explanation. It may "impose costs on employees and customers." How so? The individual is using his own leisure time and spending his own money, not his business' money.

Even with the problems in Friedman's article, he does articulate several important points that we would be unwise to overlook. How can an individual, who was hired to deal with the complexities of business, possibly understand the social dilemmas of society? "If they are to be civil servants, then they must be selected through a political process." Friedman is correct. The chief executive, possibly an intellectual out of touch with society's facts on the ground, could not serve effectively as an agent of goodwill. He might simply be too shortsighted to appreciate societal needs—making his engagement in social work an affront to the meritocracy of charitable giving.

In addition, the individual in control of a business might likely not allocate the proper amount to use on social ills. Chief executives are incredibly focused people, naturally geared toward helping their businesses succeed sometimes at the expense of all else (case in point: GE's "Neutron" Jack Welch),* leading to potential conflicts of interest. The homeless person should not have to put his fate in the hands of a businessperson simply because he wields the power of the corporation behind him.

Give the problems of society to the people trained to handle them. The chief executive would have to richly understand the specific needs of a social group before contributing charitably—but by then he would no longer be as ignorant of society and thus might feel uncomfortable being ruthless in the boardroom! Imagine prototypical (?) corporate executive J.R. Ewing (played pricelessly by Larry Hagman), from the classic soap *Dallas*, engaging in philanthropy—sans ulterior motives. The mind boggles at such a notion. Maybe Friedman was on to something after all. (1997)

---

* He might have resented the nickname, but Welch sure earned it: he was merciless—and very effective. If you're interested in such things, you can read through Welch's retrospective justifications in *Jack: Straight from the Gut*.

## 48.

# So Who's Interrupting?

### Issues of Dominance and Control

*You Just Don't Understand* (1990), by acclaimed author Deborah Tannen, delves into the complexity of men's and women's conversations. Tannen is a professional linguist. Therefore, she appears, at first blush, well suited to write about the conversational styles between (and within) the genders.

But why should anyone write such a book in the first place? Tannen's reasons are twofold: First, she wishes to document the differences and distinctions between the two "cultures" of language—men's and women's (essentially, she claims, men and women grow up in different "gender* cultures"). Second, Tannen wants to advise her readers about what might be done to bridge the gap between these male and female conversational cultures.

In her book, Tannen leans heavily on two kinds of "evidence." Personal anecdotes are detailed heavily to clarify or introduce a

* Although I tend to allow "gender" to be synonymous with "sex" in this chapter and elsewhere throughout the book, please realize that I am not unaware of the subtle distinctions between the two terms: "sex" refers solely to biological differences, whereas "gender" is rooted in societal and/or cultural distinctions. Many footnotes notwithstanding, stopping to qualify every instance of the two terms, though, would seriously impede the flow of the writing—as it has done here.

point. In addition, she cites conversational research carried out by herself and others. In the first two chapters, Tannen documents a set of principles and terms that describe the differences between the languages of gender. She claims that there are divergent gender cultural values in style, idiom, motives, and values between men and women. For example, men, according to the author, value independence and status, while women value intimacy and connectedness. Males are adversarial. They wish to be separate, different, and independent, and, at nearly any cost, will compete to obtain the upper hand in a conversation (whether it be with another male or a female).

Conversely, women don't place a primacy on status like men do, instead attempting to form "bonds" with the speaker, whether that be with a man or another woman. Men will tend to play games of "top this"—i.e., men engage in status games with each other: by showing that they suffered through more, are better in some way, or are just generally on a "higher" level than the other person(s) involved in the conversation. Men also will be quick to offer advice, and they will not tolerate individuals accusing them of being incorrect factually.*

Instead of playing status games, women will try to relate to the other speaker. The relating process may include offering similar examples to their conversational partner(s). However, women rarely give advice; instead, they attempt to avoid argument, and usually do not try to take a "one-up" position (i.e., attempt to assume a dominant status). Also, in male-only conversations, there tends to be competitions between men; women may interpret these competitions wrongly, incorrectly assuming that they are perhaps status-orientated endeavors.

In addition, Tannen describes the concept of "differing interpretations" between the genders—she calls this the "metamessage." A metamessage is a subliminal message that travels with its associated verbal message. The manner in which the metamessage is framed by the listener might possibly be a cause of miscommunication; Tannen describes this as a form of "asymmetry," or differing interpretations of communication between the sexes. Essentially, men and women see, hear, and interpret the same things differently.

---

* Tannen describes the much-maligned (mostly) male phenomenon of refusing to ask for directions as a salient example.

In the seventh chapter of *You Just Don't Understand*, titled "Who's Interrupting? Issues of Dominance and Control," Tannen describes issues that crop up when males and females interrupt conversations. She poses a key question: Who interrupts more? According to the author, "the commonly held stereotype [is] that women talk too much and interrupt men." Tannen also claims that any kind of interrupting during conversation can only mean one thing: that the interrupter wishes to dominate the conversation. Tannen has already stated at the beginning of her book that men seek the higher status in conversation; therefore, it should come as no surprise to the attentive reader that men will be shown to interrupt more.

In the section "Do Men Interrupt Women," Tannen explains that much research of conversation interruption simply counts the number of times males and females interrupt conversations. She claims, rightly, that this sort of categorization is too narrow; instead, we must examine the *context* of the conversation interruptions. For instance, is the interruption changing the topic, or is it supporting it? Thus, Tannen wishes to differentiate the interruptions themselves and see if they "violate another speaker's rights" within the context of the conversation. She claims, in the first example she presents in the chapter, that in the male-female conversation, the male did not interrupt the female, because he did not violate her rights. Of course, this example does not support her premise that the male speaker interrupts more.

In fact, in the second example on the same page, the "W," or "Wife," interrupts her husband, and she violates his speaker rights by changing the topic to "salad." This example, of course, again works against her premise of men interrupting more than women, and it also seems contrary to her supposition at the start of the book regarding males' wish to grasp dominance of any conversation (if, in fact, dominance can be construed as interrupting).

The last paragraph of the section further undermines Tannen's "male interrupts more" premise. "It may be," Tannen states, "that one person grew up in a home where conversation was constant.... If two such people live together, it is likely one will overlap" the other. Since she does not specify the "one person" being male or female, it appears that if the female is the "one person" that grew up in the "constant conversation" household, then she will be the interrupter; she will be the violator of her husband's or partner's conversational rights; and she, in turn, will be attempting (one again, according to Tannen's premise) to gain dominance by interrupting. Since gaining dominance is a status device used by males (according to Tannen), a female using it by interrupting cleanly contradicts.

Contrariwise, the next section, called "Interruption Without Overlap," appears to support one of Tannen's premises. She uses research-based material to describe three young children, two females and one male, having a conversation about tongue twisters. After the two females talk about a tongue twister they created, Mark, the young boy, quickly "sets them straight" and lectures the two girls about the "correct" tongue twister: "No. The famous tongue twister is Peterpiperpicked." This example is well chosen to support Tannen's premise of the male offering advice. Mark tells them that they are incorrect, and he also explains to the girls the correct tongue twister that they're trying to emulate. Based on the conversation between these young children, Tannen puts forth another supposition about the art of interrupting: "So it is not the interruption that constitutes dominance but what speakers are trying to do when they talk to each other." However, is a dialogue between three young teenagers really enough to substantiate Tannen's interruption premise for *all* people, regardless of age?

By the third section of her chapter, Tannen begins to trip and fall over her own assertions. In "Overlap Without Interruption," she claims that some people (without distinguishing between male or female) have "high involvement" conversational styles which give "the impression of domination" in a conversation. But how do we know whether an individual's interruption (male or female) is an attempt to gain dominance or simply a projection of a "high involvement" conversation style—and, thus, the ostensible dominance is in reality a form of pseudo-dominance?

There is a noteworthy irony present in the next section, "Successful Cooperative Overlapping." In it, Tannen describes a conversation with her and several of her friends (this is one of the personal anecdotes sprinkled throughout the book which functions as so-called evidence). The irony? The author herself is the interrupter; at nearly every turn she interrupts a male speaker. Thus, Tannen undermines her point with her own involvement—and especially so, given the statement that "[i]t might not be a coincidence that I, the woman, shifted the focus from an abstract, impersonal statement to a personal one" (which is one of the major themes Tannen hammers down throughout: that men often talk in abstract terms while women attempt to relate to the speaker more by becoming extra-personable). For Tannen to act in support of the text's premises during one of her own conversations should not come as a surprise to the reader; instead, the surprise should be that she uses her own conversations to further her (now compromised) theses.

Furthermore, in the next section of the chapter, "Unsuccessful Cooperative Overlapping," it appears that not only the author (a female), but also another male share the same speaking style of taking the abstract and making it more personable during conversation. Consider the statement by Peter, one of the guests in the conversation: "But how did you learn a new sign?" He is engaging in the same kind of Tannen-speak; in other words, he is doing what a woman *should* be doing—making the other male's comments less abstract and more personable by asking a specific question which calls for elaboration. Even Tannen admits to this by saying that "Peter and I use overlap and latching to ask supportive questions." Asking supportive questions is a form of, according to Tannen, relating to the speaker; and relating to the speaker is part of a largely female trait of "connectiveness" described at the beginning of the book; therefore, Peter is acting out the female role despite being male. Peter is thus a glaring counterexample; he is not attempting to gain "one-up" status over the other speakers.

And with her "Cultural Differences" section, Tannen's unwitting self-destruction of her "who's interrupting" premise takes full effect. In perhaps the most laughable sentence of the entire book, the author writes that "nearly everyone agrees that many (obviously not all) Jewish New Yorkers, many New Yorkers who are not Jewish, and many Jews who are not from New York have high-involvement styles...." Of course, claiming that any type of culture (besides the "culture" of gender) has anything at all to do with conversational styles confounds all of Tannen's notions about male and female conversational styles. Since we are all, in a way, from differing cultures, whether they be male, female, Jewish, Christian, Norwegian, or the like, there are simply too many variables to account for to make any kind of generalization about gender language; certain traits that are present with females who are Italian may not be true about females who are Canadian, for instance. Therefore, the book becomes merely a "special case" text for certain individuals, but certainly not for an entire population of Americans, or the population of the world. And that's a danger of leaning so heavily on anecdotal evidence and painting huge swaths of people with an essentialist brush.

However, even more amusing than her stereotyping of Jewish New Yorkers is her statement several pages later. "As a Jewish woman raised in New York who is not only offended but frightened by the negative stereotyping of New Yorkers and women and Jews, I recoil when scholarly research serves to support the stereotyping of a group of speakers." But isn't that exactly what Tannen herself is doing—negatively stereotyping New York Jews in a work that purports to be scholarly? Her point about "recoiling" when "scholarly research serves to support the stereotyping" seems especially humorous—and cognitively dissonant. If we are to take that statement at face value, then we must assume Tannen recoils at reading her own book—since she herself *supports* such stereotyping!

In the sections "Who's Interrupting" and "Uncooperative Overlapping," Tannen goes back to one of her earlier premises: report-talk versus rapport-talk, which she explains as "the characteristic ways that most women use language to create a community and many men use it to manage a contest" (simply an extension of her theme of men's competition and women's need to relate to the speaker). She explains that many men and women feel violated of their speaker rights because of the interruptions. And her arguments hold fairly well throughout the rest of the chapter's sections because she relays seemingly relevant personal anecdotes; for example, she talks about her family experiences between her sisters, father, and mother, and speaks of a fictional (!) story with a heroine named Zoe. Examining her family's experiences and Zoe's conversational endeavors, the author discovers that men tended to treat conversation as a contest, while women viewed it as a chance to learn more about the speakers.

Even though the concluding parts of the chapter are logical enough, mortal damage has been inflicted on the ideas of the chapter—and of the book. The chapter is an anomaly in the text because it brings in cultural issues of conversation, which are not appropriate if the author is to support her start-of-the-book theses. Claiming that culture impacts on conversational style undermines her assertions; a reader can refute every one of her statements about male and female relationships by blaming it on cultural difference or cultural distinction or other confounding variables.

Therefore, more than nearly any other chapter, "Who's Interrupting" is mostly unsuccessful in supporting Tannen's notions of gender-style differences of conversation. If a chapter should be deleted to more strongly support the overall themes of the book, then chapter seven must be removed from the text.

And yet despite the problems with the chapter, *You Just Don't Understand* is admittedly a fun read—though it should not be taken too seriously for several reasons. First of all, it does not have the imprimatur of the scientific or the scholarly; instead, it feels like it was composed on a lark. Examining the lackluster and potentially incorrect documentation at the end of the book shows a less-than-careful attention to academic detail. Although the set of references and notes appears complete, it also appears that the author assumes that most individuals reading the book will not check the notes; consider page 304, note number 116, which says "Mattison, 'Sleeping Giant,' p. 124." How is the reader supposed to locate "Sleeping Giant"? Is it part of a periodical, or is it a novel?

Second, the repeated use of the author's personal anecdotes stains the ideas, because the Tannen is, in many cases, drawing on her own experiences and generalizing them to an entire population of males and females. Is she really the last word on male-female relationships? Just because she is a linguist and has a doctorate does not *ipso facto* make her personal experiences authoritative or representative. Then again, perhaps a segment of the population can indeed relate to her book. After all, it has sold a staggering two million copies to date. What better expression of popular relevance is there?

(1998)

# PART V

# REVIEWS OF FILMS

# 49.

## Where Does Maggie Peyton Place? A Review of *Herbie Fully Loaded*

At least Disney can no longer be accused of filming two-hour commercials for Volkswagen—the '63 Type 1[*] that you see in this film isn't a late-model Bug anymore. But, advertisements aside, how does this contemporary interpretation stack up against its not-so-formidable predecessors? Well, it's not exactly high-concept. Whereas in the original *The Love Bug* (1969) the subtle art of suggestion was deployed to effect convincing anthropomorphism,[†] in *Herbie: Fully Loaded*, we are treated to very explicit cartoon-like demonstrations of Herbie's "intelligent" behavior—Herbie now has eyelids and a very malleable front bumper with which to express his CGI "emotions." These newfound abilities at expression are not used to devastating effect; rather, they belie credibility, distracting us from the story.[‡]

And another thing: Why does Herbie start so many of these movies as a discarded car?[§] In this film, the made-for-television *The Love Bug* (1997), and *Herbie Goes Bananas* (1980), Herbie is rescued from a junkyard. Lindsay Lohan (who plays the main character, Maggie Peyton; her character is a much more of a nod to feminism than Julie Sommars' was in that proto-feminist flick *Herbie Goes to*

---

[*] Until many years after its introduction, Volkswagen didn't formally call the Beetle a "Beetle" or a "Bug"—it was referred to as a Type 1. (The Type 2, by the way, was the formal moniker for the VW Bus.)

[†] Why was it decided to make Herbie a Beetle? Legend has it that when a number of then-contemporary cars were lined up on a lot during casting, people kept reaching over to touch the Beetle—there was an obviously intimate, tactile connection people immediately felt toward the car.

[‡] The rebooted Herbie film is also lacking in American iconography: e.g., whereas the original movie has shots of a twisty ride down Lombard Street, this new movie has…give me a moment….

[§] As film critic Roger Ebert rightly notes, "Why [does] Herbie [end] up in a junkyard, when such a famous car should obviously be in a classic automobile museum in Las Vegas?"

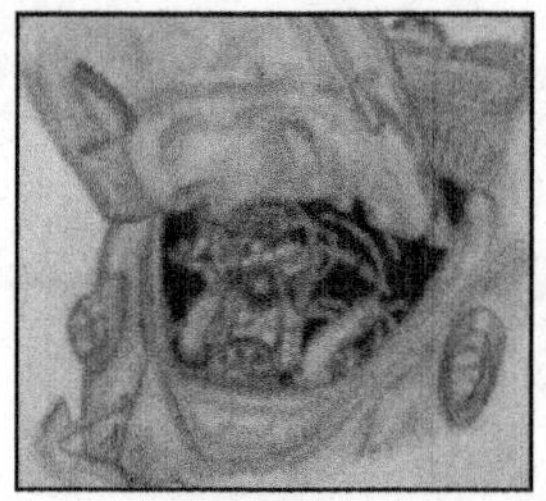

*Monte Carlo* [1977])[*] finds the lovable VW. Even in the original *Love Bug*, Jim Douglas (Dean Jones)[†] purchases Herbie used, not new. Yet I can't imagine any situation that would cause an owner to knowingly divest himself of a living car. What's going on inside that engine of his (Herbie's, of course; see drawing above)? And another thing seems odd to me: where's Mr. Hawk?[‡]

What this movie does do right, at least as compared to its made-for-TV predecessor, is not attempt to give any explanation as to how or why Herbie (and, by extension, the New Beetle he falls for) became sentient. Recall how gracefully the original *Love Bug* treated the matter: In that film Tennessee Steinmetz (Buddy Hackett) imparted a Tao-like wisdom to his "explanation" of the mystery of Herbie, an explanation that amounted to little more than a lament of how machines are getting so complicated that human beings can no longer account for their actions.[§]

Yet the biggest mystery of *Fully Loaded* for me is why the filmmakers chose to focus so heavily on the already overexposed and rather uninteresting milieu of NASCAR. All of the prior Herbie movies effectively rode a fine line between reality and fantasy, but the discord is especially great when Herbie takes to the track against those quasi-racecars—it really strains believability.

---

[*] Especially nice in *Monte Carlo* was Julie Sommars' car: the Lancia called Giselle, a feminine car if there ever was one.

[†] Memorably called "the poor man's Jimmy Stewart if it didn't feel like an insult to Jimmy Stewart, poor men, and whoever a poor man would actually say is his version of Jimmy Stewart" by author Josh Spiegel.

[‡] Alonzo Hawk, played by the late character actor Keenan Wynn, appeared in two Disney vehicles: both *The Absent-Minded Professor* movies and a *Love Bug* film. A single character cross-pollinating two (or more) inter-series films is pretty rare; another example that comes to mind is Ray Nicolette, played by Michael Keaton, who was in *Jackie Brown* and *Out of Sight*—but both of those films' stories were penned by the late novelist Elmore Leonard.

[§] Tennessee also questions his role and place in San Francisco—he's having a spiritual crisis. Previously, the colloquialism-spouting Tennessee had taught English in China, which allows for a few humorous lines in the film. Until Herbie arrives, Tennessee appears restless and languid.

If the filmmakers decide to shake the rust off of Herbie for yet another romp,[*] I would suggest the screenwriters take as their template *The Fast and the Furious* (2001) instead of *Days of Thunder* (1990). A tricked-out Herbie in the world of underground street racing? Now there's a high-concept idea rather than a retread.

If that's not to your liking, how about something more controversial: in the vein of Quentin Tarantino's *Inglourious Basterds*, a counterfactual thriller about Herbie the Love Bug and a band of concentration camp escapees bringing down the man who commissioned (and drew the first sketch of) the People's Car in the first place: Adolph Hitler himself! This sort of movie might be redemptive or therapeutic in a way, since the sordid implications of centering a series of family movies on a machine with a Nazi lineage has never been dealt with head-on.[†] Plus, this new Love Bug movie might be a bit of a psychological thriller, replete with Oedipal undertones: Herbie as Hitler's surrogate son. After all, both proper names start with "H" and have six letters in them each—surely not a coincidence.[‡]

Nonetheless, the juxtaposition of identifiably Jewish people driving Herbie in such a film might be discomfiting; recall comedienne Sarah Silverman's quip that Jewish people driving German cars is "like Take Back the Night," surely the most spot-on analogy since novelist David Foster Wallace said "Calvin Klein ads are to porn movies as jokes are to explaining jokes." So honk twice if you want to see Herbie chase down the Führer.

(2010)

---

[*] And, though a Beetle's average life expectancy isn't particularly good, its maximum lifespan is technically *forever*. But no affront to meritocracy here: all cars have the same maximum lifespan because car parts can be perpetually replaced.

[†] Come to think of it, what a marketing coup Herbie was for Volkswagen: get millions of baby boomers, with no memory of the war, to view the car as cute and cuddly, as an underdog, as—well—quintessentially *American*. After all, Herbie is painted red, white and blue. By *Monte Carlo*, the main villain, who is a fire-breathing, over-the-top German racer, makes fun of the "little American car."

[‡] It is—Buddy Hackett named the car after a skit about a ski instructor.

# 50.

## My Broken Heart: A Review of *Love Actually*

Too much of a good thing isn't always so good. One need look no further than *Love Actually*—tagged as "The Ultimate Romantic Comedy"—to see a fully-realized, non-metaphorical example of this.

This movie's a publicist's fantasy: containing a grab bag of some of the hottest British character actors in cinema today, it's tough to think of a more no-lose proposition. And yet *Love Actually* fails on nearly every level: as a romance, as a comedy, as entertainment for anyone not saddled with the most naïve misconceptions about relationships.

Anytime a film can be compared with the unfortunate *Casino Royale* (1967), there's bound to be trouble; but, regrettably, *Love Actually* and that ill-fated and much-maligned Bond spoof have something major in common: they're both an uneasy mishmash of styles, genres, and well-respected thespians. Consider the cast of *Casino Royale*: Peter Sellers, David Niven, Ursula Andress, et al.—so many stars lending their talents to such creative failure.

In *Love Actually*, it's not that individual scenes with Hugh Grant or Billy Bob Thorton or Emma Thompson are bad per se, it's just that, well, the whole's a far cry from the sum of its parts. There are long stretches punctuated only occasionally by funny moments. But there are so many scenes, with so many leads, that halfway through the film I began to feel a bit like Harry (Alan Rickman), impatiently waiting for Rowan Atkinson to finish those needless flourishes and hand over the boxed-and-wrapped gold necklace. Enough's enough!

The worldview that this movie puts forth is so breathtakingly stupid as to cause audience convulsions: saying "I love you," as the movie critic Chris Orr writes about the film, doesn't automatically mean happily-ever-after begins. You know, if I weren't already a cynic about love,[*] this film would've converted me.

What's more, there's a gratuitous (for me) amount of nudity in *Love Actually*. Ah, but what is love if not, in part, an ode to our nether regions!

Added to farcical notions about love and relationships are farcical notions about plot. Put simply, there are more dangling plot elements when all's said and done than there are ornaments on a Christmas tree (and boy were those trees ubiquitous in this movie!). *Love Actually*'s just too unwieldy for its already-too-long running time.

But as the movie concluded, all was not lost for me, since I learned something important. The next time I see a Nativity scene, I'll know to look for two lobsters.[†]

(2004)

---

[*] Love is like an addiction: the reptilian parts of our brains—i.e., the amygdalae, which process emotions, along with the rest of the limbic system—play tricks on us. So I suppose love's phenomenologically "real," but it's not quite what we think it is. Take a look at the *National Geographic* article from February 2006 titled "True Love" for an artful meditation of our brains' construction of the love emotion. Also consult the chapter "The Hormones of Love" in philosopher Massimo Pigliucci's entertaining "sci-phi" (science-philosophy) book *Answers for Aristotle*. Here's a taste: "...one becomes literally obsessed with the object of his love.... This response, chemically speaking, isn't surprising: dopamine, one of the two chief hormones involved, is the foundation of the so-called reward system of the brain—the very same one that gives us a chemical pat on the back when we do something satisfactory and that also uses the kind of brain receptors that are sensitive to addictive drugs like cocaine. Romantic love literally is an addiction!"

[†] It is impossible for me to view lobsters the same way after reading David Foster Wallace's famous essay *Consider the Lobster*, originally published in *Gourmet*. If you haven't read it, go ahead and read it—now.

# 51.

## Seeing Double Out of One Eye (or: Over-kill): A Review of *Kill Bill*

About twenty minutes into *Kill Bill*, Tarantino's hubristically subtitled "Fourth Film," one-eyed Elle Driver (played by Daryl Hannah) begins whistling a Bernard Herrmann tune from *Twisted Nerve* (1968) as split-screen shots follow her frenetic preparation to murder The Bride (Uma Thurman), who's already in a comatose state after her quite-literal shotgun wedding. The juxtaposition of music and image in the montage is seamless and perfect, and immediately brings to mind Brian De Palma's oeuvre, suffused as so much of it is with analogously visceral tableaux.

And then, unless you've been residing in one of Plato's caves where only vague hints of shadows are visible, a feeling of dread and numbness pervades your entire body as you recall the most damning criticism of *Kill Bill*: endless homages to other films does not necessarily a good film make. From a filmmaker end, it only furthers Mr. Tarantino's already self-aggrandizing disposition; and from an audience end, it creates either/or divisions—either they know what's being referenced, or they don't. And if they, for the most part, don't, does the film work? Does *Kill Bill* work as entertainment, or merely as a ridiculous and bizarre form of postmodern satire?

Unfortunately, despite the lavish praise heaped upon the film, *Kill Bill* is merely ridiculous for the uninitiated. More than perhaps any other widely-distributed film ever released, *Kill Bill* functions solely as a critic charmer, designed expressly to promulgate a sense of wink-wink knowingness among that most pretentious of chattering classes, movie critics. Tarantino, their self-proclaimed savior, has made a piece for them—and, like Paul and the early proponents of Christianity, he expects them to carry his "Thus saith the Lord" far and wide, spreading his infinite movie wisdom to us uneducated unwashed masses.

And I fell for it. I too drank from the cup of knowledge passed around by buying in to the critics' consensus; I too watched gruesome and sadistic violence with a detached and disinterested eye, relishing aesthetic value instead of passing judgment on what is surely uncompromisingly immoral. How can nihilism possibly serve as a proper viewing defense in the face of necrophilia and pedophilia?

It can't and it shouldn't—not even in this post-ironic epoch we're supposedly residing in, not even considering the cartoon-like aspects of the violence (including, appropriately, a segment entirely in anime). I don't care how many esoteric Kung Fu films are paid homage to—there are no excuses for such filth, and holier-than-thou critics ought to know that, let alone Tarantino.

*Jackie Brown* (1997), Tarantino's previous work and his most complete film, was such a beautiful meditation on growing old; it was beautifully written, beautifully acted, and had a mostly-'70's film score to relish. It wasn't a pastiche or imitation of the genre of Blaxploitation, but rather added to its discourse in a mature and thoughtful way.

But, as a few brave detractors have pointed out, *Kill Bill* goes in the other direction. It imitates, lampoons, satirizes its sources. It might be visually stunning, but the movie doesn't respect its progenitors at all. And as sad as *Kill Bill* is, that may be the saddest fact of all.

It finally happened. A high-profile filmmaker has constructed a remake based almost entirely on critical reactions to his initial offering.

In 2003, Tarantino offered up *Kill Bill, Volume 1*, a kinetic romp through an alternate-universe world of betrayal and revenge. Although *Volume 1* was not without its faults (detailed above; there are many), there was at least something to recommend in it: chiefly, its unbridled panache and surprisingly unique visual style.

Yet even critics who approved of the first volume lamented what was surely to come in the second—namely, more of the same hyper, blood-soaked, videogame-like Samurai battles featuring the Bride and those who wronged her. And such a lament certainly didn't seem misplaced at the time; after all, since Tarantino had originally wanted to release *Kill Bill* as one lengthy epic instead of a work sliced into two, wouldn't *Volume 2* just extend the bloodletting another couple of hours?

Tarantino, by the time the first movie was released, had nearly all of the footage he needed for the second volume already in the can—but there was splicing and editing to be done. In interviews through the years, Tarantino has frequently admitted to gauging critical receptions, in detail, to his works; as an example of this, one need look no further than his fascinating discussion of *Jackie Brown* (1997) on the DVD of the same name. In that interview he all but proclaims that pulling the rug out from underneath the critical establishment (and audience) is primacy for him when he exclaims, "Maybe in my next movie I'll blow your mind," even though we probably don't expect him to do so after viewing the somber and sober *Jackie Brown*. He'll demonstrate his genius, he's saying, by showing that, to reverse paraphrase Emerson, inconsistency is the hobgoblin of great minds.

And herein lies the critical fault with *Kill Bill, Volume 2*. As a work that stands on its own, it is plodding, lugubrious, and—although I never thought I'd hear myself say this about a Tarantino film—boring, boring beyond all measure. It is above all, though, a purposeful work of opposition to the first volume—purposeful because its esteemed director seems to have taken the time to read each and every review of his "Fourth Film" and counter each and every expectation the critics had for his next one. In the "Making Of" documentary on the DVD of *Volume 2*, Tarantino even admits as much when he unrepentantly explains that he turned the tables on the audience in this second movie by throwing everyone's expectations for a loop.

Not that there's anything wrong with playing with expectations. A filmmaker worth his name should indeed do that from time to time. After all, Hitchcock secured his place in the pantheon of master filmmakers when he pulled the ultimate trick: killing off his ostensible main character, Marion Crane, only forty minutes into *Psycho*, leaving the audience to scratch their heads in bewilderment. Hitchcock never fooled us quite as much after that.

But one shouldn't make a movie out of dashing expectations, out of, essentially—for all you *Seinfeld* fans out there—"doing the opposite," simply for its own sake. (But is chicken salad on rye untoasted with a side of potato salad really the opposite of tuna on toast?) Tarantino gauged what the opposite of *Volume 1* would be by poring through the reactions to that movie—think of this as the ultimate audience-screening test. And he set out to weave together a movie that's long instead of short; that has an endlessly talky showdown (with Bill) instead of a monstrously action-packed one (with O-Ren); that contains an original score instead of a mishmash of music composed for elsewhere; that has throw-away protracted sequences instead of tight, critical-to-plot scenes; that relies on "suspense" instead of action; that is from the West instead of from the East; and, most of all, that effectively remakes the first volume by allowing the second to narratively stand on its own—which is the ultimate expectation twister, since most of critical press assumed that, despite Tarantino's proclivity of shifting temporal space around in his films, *Volume 2* would wrap up the Bride's revenge saga by her tidily eliminating the remaining three of her former cohorts.

So *Volume 2* is a postmodern, poll-tested work, expertly refined to deliver the blatant opposite of its predecessor. Perhaps it was inevitable that that happened; give a filmmaker a chance at responding to his critics and he's bound to intellectualize the matter. But maybe there's something to be said of creating in a vacuum, of trusting one's instincts instead of listening to a cacophony of voices shouting that they know better.

(2004)

# 52.

## A Cure for the Weary: A Review of *2 Fast 2 Furious*

There's something primal about this movie. Maybe it's because I'm a twenty-something-year-old guy,[*] maybe it's because I'm way too into cars (tricked-out imports, of course). I don't know. What I do know is that *2 Fast 2 Furious* manages to stimulate long-repressed animalistic urges for supreme beauty at the cost of extreme danger, which we're forced to subsume underneath the guise of civilized behavior.[†]

The first, and still best,[‡] *Furious* film did this too. Instead of trying to fashion a movie around the hottest trends of the all-too-short moment, the film created (or at least popularized) the moment.[§] A newspaper article written shortly after *The Fast and the Furious* (2001) made its theatrical release discussed a newly rampant phenomenon of teens, after seeing the film, proceeding to perform donuts en masse in movie theater parking lots.

I suspect that after leaving a screening of the sequel, similar stunts were executed by even the less impulsive among us. And with good reason: *2 Fast* is amazingly visceral, with both car jargon and everyday idiom equally incomprehensible but nevertheless always interesting. Everything in this movie furthers the experience of never-ending acceleration and speed, from engines revving to

---

[*] At the time of originally writing this, anyway. But Father Time hasn't neglected aging me since then.

[†] Freud would have had a field day with this movie.

[‡] By *Tokyo Drift* (2006)—an underrated film in its own right—it seemed that the series was out of gas. But even after an interminable number sequels, the first film, a Rob Cohen picture with limited scope and a hyper-focus on merely street racing—and not exotic locales, crime syndicates, vehicles of all stripes, and the like—still stands tall.

[§] Case in point: MTV at the time proffered an "I'm a Street Racer" episode of their popular *True Life* series.

tachometers flailing to exhaust fumes flaming to Paul Walker[*] never standing still for an instant, à la a video game character from a fighting sim.[†] And it all works—really well.

The editing in the tag-team car race, for instance, is so effective that even though most of the shots are split-second reaction shots of the actors inside their cars we never lose track of the relative placements of the principals. Same for the freeway chases and the night races: the space is established well enough to know where everyone is most of the time. No easy trick, considering all of the scenery rushing by at almost a third the speed of sound.

But maybe all of this is beside the point. Maybe *2 Fast* is a terrible film with blindingly gorgeous eye candy. Maybe I'm incurably sick with lust, like so many other men around my age, for a coffee-can tailpipe, lovely decals, lush spoilers and ground effects, full-bodied fenders, beautifully proportioned rims, 36 by 29 by 36...um, well, better stop there.

Perhaps a cure for this primal sickness could take its cue from *A Clockwork Orange*: force those hooked on street racing to watch import after modified import crashing, all to the tune of Beethoven. Nah, that'll probably be just as fun as *2 Fast*—and, indeed, not a bad idea for the next sequel.

(2003)

---

[*] Unfortunately, the iconic actor would later meet an ironic end when the Porsche he was riding in crashed and exploded, killing him and a friend instantly.

[†] Think of, especially, *Street Fighter 2* by Capcom, the Japanese company whose employees produced the world's best side-scrolling video game strictly in their spare time—namely, *Mega Man 2*. It doesn't take a ludologist to recognize the genius of that sequel.

# 53.

## Frighteningly Conventional: A Review of *A Clockwork Orange*

Although *A Clockwork Orange* is visually slick, and the details presented are at times overwhelming, the narrative/story/plot is surprisingly conventional—we've all seen this kind of stuff before.

"Oh, but the film raises some deep and important issues about our society," you say. Yes, but so does Tuesday night's syndicated repeat of *Star Trek: The Next Generation*,[*] only it doesn't have to show multiple scenes of explicit violence and rape to make its point.

"Oh, but the film is trying to put the audience through what Alex goes through—with all of the nastiness we have to see on the screen—which establishes and furthers the connection we feel with the protagonist, who is at once pure evil and yet sympathetic," you say. Great, but who cares? Just because the great Pauline Kael said that she delights in the "paradoxes" of sympathizing with a murderer-rapist doesn't mean that this is a great film.

"The film accomplishes what it sets out to do, and breaks new ground in the cinema by doing it," you say. I agree that the film accomplishes what it sets out to do—but this doesn't imply that *A Clockwork Orange* is a good film, or that its accomplishments are especially meaningful. I could say that I want to translate the Bible into Esperanto—and I could accomplish that goal—but that doesn't mean that anyone actually cares about an Esperanto Bible besides me, does it?[†] (Actually, the only thing more frightening than watching this overrated movie again would be encountering an Es-

---

[*] Fun *Star Trek* fact: Malcolm McDowell, the scenery-chewing star of *Clockwork*, also later starred as the villain in *ST:Generations* (1994), the first *ST:TNG* movie.

[†] Another fun *Star Trek* fact: *Incubus* (1966), a horror film filmed entirely in Esperanto, starred William Shatner.

peranto Bible. Unfortunately, I'd bet at least one exists somewhere.)

This movie seems more a curiosity now, a historical footnote for those interested in memorizing as much filmic arcana as possible. So here's an answer to a (potential) trivia question, should you encounter it: *Clockwork* was banned from being shown in England for many years after its release because it was Rated X.*

(2002)

* And another fun fact (though not *Star Trek*-related this time): the only Rated X movie to win the Oscar for Best Picture was *Midnight Cowboy*.

# 54.

## Less than Meets the Eye: A Review of *Minority Report*

Eyeballs frame and transfix an awful lot of shots in both *Minority Report* (2002) and *Blade Runner* (1982), two big-budget loose translations of science fiction writer Philip K. Dick's stories. In fact, so do floating billboards, underground scientists and medical operators, photographs, teardrop-shaped passenger automobiles, flying police cars, image-manipulation computers, twentieth-century-style guns, and neo-gothic buildings. Chalk them up to prescient futurists, I suppose.

Then again, come to think of it, the characters and iconography of these two films—separated by a score's worth of years, mind you—bear close resemblance, some of which surely can be accounted for by the similarity between source material, some of which cannot. In both films there's a good cop that appears bad, a reluctant police officer-sans-family as a protagonist, a Bill of Rights-shattering slavery of (for all intents and purposes) humans, a not-so-well-guarded "creator," an obsession with memory and the past, and a preponderance of water and water imagery.

There's also a film noir-like mise-en-scene in both, including, but not limited to, the grainy, almost black-and-white shot compositions; the contrasts and intersections of horizontals and verticals on screen; the billows and streams of bright light forcing their way indoors through windows. Those are features of the genre, though.

So, similarities abound. Are the differences between the films significant? While *Blade Runner* is a sprawling and overly ambitious vision of the near future—recall the flying cars, the transference of much of Earth's population to another planet, and the existence of über-human androids—*Minority Report* is a largely restrained vision: even the holograms don't quite project convincing three-dimensionality.

And, deep into *Minority Report*, when the obviously-CGI spiders are searching through room after room and the viewpoint is omniscient overhead, we see some paradigmatic abodes—and they're not even remotely different from ones today. Also, are we to believe that the only differences in the technological milieu, fifty years hence, are cars with better drag coefficients and the replacement of opaque computers with translucent ones? Even the show *COPS*, with nary a change in the title-credit theme music, is still on-air!

*Minority Report* is optimistic, and almost annoyingly so: whereas *Blade Runner* looks like something out of Dante, *Minority Report*—despite the removal of denizens' civil liberties, despite the underground narcotics dealers, despite the illegal virtual-pleasure-providing shops—is almost perversely positive, like most of the Steven Spielberg oeuvre.* Contrast the narrative arcs of Rick Deck-

---

* There's an old saw about the Stone Age not ending because of lack of stones but because someone thought of a better way. That's what makes predicting the future so hard and these "futuristic" movies ultimately so passé—you never know what unpredictable game-changing event is right around the corner. Consider the story that opens the book *SuperFreakonomics*: since the primary mode of transportation in the late nineteenth century was the horse, urban centers were inundated with mounds and mounds of horseshit. The problem seemed intractable and threatened to eventually overwhelm cities and other population centers. And then *deus ex machina*: a machine called the "horseless carriage" was invented.

A film with a more expansive, fully-realized presentation of the future? *Cloud Atlas* (2012). The first time watching, though, it is challenging to understand, largely because the same actors play many characters. But the conceit of having the actors play multiple roles gets at the heart of what the filmmakers are trying to do: show the progression of different souls through time (homophone alert: note the city of *Seoul* is weaved into different stories through time, too). So, for example, Tom Hanks goes from being an evil doctor with the tagline "the weak are meat, the strong do eat," in the nineteenth century, to a man who rejects Old Georgie's "the weak are meat" worldview and instead helps save humanity in a post-apocalyptic future. And Halle Berry progresses from being completely not in control of her own destiny (she's very briefly a field slave at the start of the film), to the kept woman of an old music composer (not much self-agency), to keen reporter Luisa Rey (who is figuring things out, but still somewhat dependent on others) to Meronym (who helps to save the world). And Hugh Grant, playing against type, simply devolves until he's literally a savage—and nothing more.

And there are so many little clever details throughout, like Tom Hanks playing Cavendish in a within-the-film's-future movie adaptation of Cavendish's nursing home adventures (where he complains about the "ruddy anti-Incarceration Act," like his "real-life" counterpart): especially clever is how Hanks isn't typing his character's adventures using a typewriter, as the over-

ard and John Anderton: one barely breaks even (in Ridley Scott's Director's Cut, at least), and the other metaphorically and almost literally resurrects and reconstructs his family.

Good and evil are improbably delineated in the central characters of *Minority Report*; any and all motives of Anderton inevitably have altruistic ends, even if they don't seem to at first, but those of the elusive villain are always self-serving. In *Blade Runner*, however, conceptions of good and evil are inexorably tied together and can't exist apart (à la Nietzsche); recall Deckard's egocentric and often clandestine motives.

But differences between good and evil are indeed muddled in the utilitarian cogs that turn the wheels of the pre-crime society of *Minority Report*.* There's a pervasive faux profundity, in film actions and words, of the nefarious nature of the pre-cogs' entrapment.

Thus, interesting temporal explorations aside (e.g., the mall chase with the pre-cog), *Minority Report*, unlike *Blade Runner*, is largely irrelevant escapism and an opportunity missed, rather than an effective film-length indictment of the erosion of civil liberties in our culture.

(2002)

---

the-shoulder shots of Cavendish in the year 2012 show him doing, but with an early model Apple laptop, as if future moviemakers (circa 2144) won't quite get the early-twenty-first-century period pieces correct, just like contemporary filmmakers probably don't get, for example, Antebellum South period pieces correct—which is, of course, an ironic commentary on all the scenes in *Cloud Atlas* set in the past. There are layers upon layers here, details upon details, that make the film not only satisfying intellectually (like a puzzle or a clever math problem) but satisfying emotionally, since most (if not all) of the subplots are engaging once you understand what's going on. *Cloud Atlas* is the best film about the future since the spectacular *Children of Men* (2006).

* Ursula Le Guinn, a contemporary of Dick's, explored the consequences of helping the many at the expense of the captive few more effectively in the short story "The Ones Who Walk Away from Omelas."

# 55.

## Wholly Artificial: A Review of *A.I. Artificial Intelligence*

After all of the faith that Steven Spielberg has entrusted in his audiences over the decades—in *Close Encounters*, *Jaws*, and even *Jurassic Park*—you would think that in *A.I.* Spielberg would believe that his audience has at least a modicum of intelligence to assimilate the complex themes of mortality the movie attempts to grapple with.

Unfortunately, he doesn't. Nary a minute of screen time passes before the inevitable dialogic reference to becoming a "real boy," as Pinocchio did. As anyone who's seen the film knows, there are endless *The Adventures of Pinocchio* references. Not only in the dialogue, but also in the thematic structure/content—scenes in the film, like the Flesh Fair, much too closely resemble their fairy-tale counterparts (in this case, the circus in *Pinocchio*).

Referencing *Pinocchio* in futuristic parables is certainly not beyond the pale—and I am not implying that it is, especially considering that I hold *Blade Runner* in high regard—but the sheer volume and frequency of the connections is mind-numbing and displays a total lack of faith in the audience to understand this film's morality play as it unfolds.

There's another rather obvious problem with *A.I.*: the last twenty minutes are terribly misplaced. Although the visuals of a New York in the far future were interesting (but, sadly, rendered obsolete by the destruction of an important landmark several months after this film's theatrical release), the light, happy tone is uncalled for, considering all that came before. In following the story of *Pinocchio* this closely—by assuming that it was this sacrosanct—the forced and awkward conclusion undermines, contradicts, and even competes with the first two hours of the movie.

Chop off the last twenty minutes, and *A.I.* will have a much more consistent tone—albeit with thirty fewer *Pinocchio* references.

(2002)

# 56.

## Disaffecting Banality: A Review of *Requiem for a Dream*

As the once ubiquitous anti-tobacco slogan rants, "Knowledge is contagious." Contemplating this film as a statement of warning against hallucinogens or narcotics would be undermining its integrity and purpose as any sort of work of art—which is the moniker the film so desperately aspires to.

And rightly so. Strip away the power of the images—made possible by a long line of film directors, mind you (e.g., Brian DePalma's split-screens; Paul Thomas Anderson's furious cuts; and, most obviously, the whole of Martin Scorsese's visual inventiveness in *Goodfellas*)*—and what's left is a bit too banal to be construed as anything but a narrative with a strong "moral" center. Like the title itself, pretension and the seemingly-artful rule the day.

That's not to say that *Requiem for a Dream* has nothing to recommend in it. Jennifer Connelly is, as always, almost too absorbed in her role. This is most certainly not a criticism: her balance of the subtleties de rigueur for motion pictures against the dramatics necessitated by the theater would most certainly make Stanislavsky proud.

Ellen Burstyn's Sara is also quite affecting. But her character invariably leaves one with the question, Is loneliness so incredibly dispiriting that malevolent changes are involuntarily effected in response? Yes, I realize that the Promise of the Dream Fulfilled was the catalyst, but the loneliness was surely the underlying motivator of Sara's tailspin.

It is the last twenty minutes that are at once unbearable and yet terribly disingenuous. Forgive me, but when Sara was undergoing the ECT, I couldn't help but recall *One Flew Over the Cuckoo's Nest.* Anyone who's seen that movie knows exactly what I'm speaking of.

---

* Watch *Pulp Fiction* (1994) again to see just how much Tarantino lifted stylistically from Scorsese's masterwork, whether intentionally or not.

Also, *Requiem for a Dream* takes disgusting to new heights with the loss-of-Harry's-arm plot arc. To cringe or not to cringe?—you'll cringe if you can bear witness!

Finally, several shots of Ms. Connelly at the pier overlooking the Atlantic are more-or-less identical—yet are filmed richer and better, with deeper hues and contrasts—to the final shots of *Dark City*, also with Ms. Connelly, filmed some two years earlier. In other words, *Requiem for a Dream* takes some raw material we've seen before and makes it look better—much like the rest of this movie, with its super-stylized and artful don't-do-drugs message, in full-banal surround sound.

(2002)

# 57.

## Heaven Can Wait: A Review of *Star Trek V: The Final Frontier*

Although somewhat unfocused, and certainly much maligned, *Star Trek V* (1989) manages, almost in spite of itself, to be a mostly interesting viewing experience. Many critics have termed the character developments unnecessary; the leads, which even mainstream audiences, by 1989, had become intimately familiar with, are presented in a bit of a different light. Notions in Frost's "Road Not Taken" are discussed latently throughout this film to considerable effect. *Star Trek II* (1982) also gave lip service to the realities of a more "mature" (i.e., old) crew, but certainly with not as much urgency as in this sequel. In a way, we can almost discern the lead actors voicing their personal fears of degradation. *Star Trek V* follows a narrative arc of not only Captain Kirk's maturation (as in the initial sequel), but Bones' and Mr. Spock's as well. The ultimate success of this ageism theme (which will be revisited in *VI*) is all the more impressive considering how it's buried largely underneath superficially perfunctory and disappointing situational comedy which relies much too heavily on disparaging characters.

Film critic Roger Ebert has stated that during the entire running length of the film he only experienced a single moment of "awe" and wonderment: when the Enterprise prepares to enter the "Great Barrier." Although, as he observes, the film takes numerous awkward scenes to build toward that dramatic moment, it is worth noting that the piece-by-piece revelation of Sybok's* mission (of which is noticeably ubiquitous in the *Star Trek* universe; the creator-seeking theme is overused) is well developed and permits the sense of anticipation that is keenly portrayed on-screen. Of course, the

---

* As Trekkers (or Trekkies?—there's still considerable disagreement as to the preferred moniker) know, Sean Connery was heavily pursued to play Spock's brother. As a tongue-in-cheek joke, the Shangri-La planet is named Sha Ka Ree. Get it?

final third of the film is a forced letdown,* because of the unrealistic expectations of the viewer (admittedly made unrealistic by the movie's buildup). *Contact* (1997) has a similar problem at the conclusion of the movie, when Jodie Foster's scientist confronts, literally, her own projected mortality. The devil's in the details.

The film was directed competently, albeit not exceptionally, by William Shatner (not Alan Smithee!). Leonard Nimoy contends in his autobiography *I am Spock* that he respected his colleague's skill at obtaining overtly cinematic-type visuals, emphasizing the opening shots of Sybok as a noteworthy example. Compared to the relatively "flat"-looking images infesting the previous two sequels, *The Final Frontier* is indeed much more visually interesting.

In fact, several shots are so beautiful, such as the aforementioned opening shots of the desolate planet Nimbus III, that they call attention to themselves, which is perhaps distracting in this character-centric picture—though thankfully the footage of the evil "Rock Monster," which can be seen on the extras of the DVD, was edited out of the final cut.

The film's score, by Jerry Goldsmith, enhances the mood; his first score since the original *Star Trek* motion picture, Goldsmith does not work to exaggerate effect or attempt to create emotional dilemmas that are not already suggested by the action on-screen.† *Star Trek V* does, however, use the other four films and two previous television series as support in the creation of conflict—and Kirk's simple questioning of the "Anti-God" (as *A.V. Club*'s Zack Handlen terms him in a wonderful review of the movie) is enough to bring significant contradictions to the fore, à la innumerable episodes of *TOS*. Yet, oddly enough, *The Final Frontier* almost exists disjoint temporally from the other five original-cast films. Therefore, *Star Trek V* can only be truly appreciated by at least moderate fans of the original series—as long as those fans take a deep breath, relax, and aren't too nitpicky when they watch.

(2000)

---

* Except for a single line near the end: "What does God need with a starship?" which surely ranks among the best *Trek* movie quotes of all time.

† A good example of a more recent movie that relies almost entirely on music-synthesizing-emotion is the ill-fated *Mission to Mars* (2000). Needless to say, the "crutch" of music neither assists nor precipitates audience involvement.

# 58.

## All Spaced Out: A Review of *Contact*

Intriguing, creative, but ultimately disappointing best characterizes *Contact*, Robert Zemeckis's 1997 picture. Despite the loving attention to the most minor of details,* the failures rest with logic lapses—and frequently *too much* unnecessary detail.

Classic film theory ("classic" denoting post-D.W. Griffith, post-Eisenstein) states that a shot or scene should conclude when a saturation point is reached. After that threshold is breached, the images become either redundant or tiresome.† *Contact* has numerous shots with this problem. Although meant to evoke contemplative inquiry, frequently they appear to be merely showing off visual effects.‡ *2001* (1968), despite its languid pacing, has meaningful and purposeful sequences that do not become saturated—Kubrick's visuals service a parable, rather than existing for their own sake.

*Contact* also, in its final third, attempts to duplicate *2001*'s sense of wonderment and rebirth, with mostly limited success. Foster's metaphysical visual journey—much like Dave Bowman's trek—is allegorical; like the entire of humanity in *2001*, she must achieve a new level of being (although not truly a new evolutionary status, à la *2001*) by intertwining the spiritual and the scientific. But while the visual metaphors are extremely convincing in *2001* in displaying Bowman's passage through an evolutionary puberty, *Contact*'s seem misplaced and are largely ineffective. The entire final third of the movie suffers as a result.

With its character-centric structure, *Contact* displays some originality but the plot suffers because of its predictability: a woman,

---

* The young Jodie Foster mirror-image shot is especially effective, for instance.

† Thus, *Empire* (1964), Warhol's experiment of an eight-hour single shot overlooking the top of the Empire State building, can be considered quite saturated.

‡ Two examples: the lengthy opening shot and the *Is it real?* journey.

sure of her beliefs, goes through a series of trials and adventures which test her, until she finally realizes her initial focus was too narrow and immature. Through the process, she discovers much about herself. Mythological stories betray the same undercurrent throughout, and many other films have this theme of self-discovery present in their narratives.

Jodie Foster plays a physicist or astronomer of some sort; her stubbornness and narrow-mindedness are acted with aplomb. Foster is as she always is: seamless and believable. Much of the viewer interest in *Contact*'s first half can be attributed to the actor's skill at maintaining a consistently engaging portrayal. In fact, most of the lead performances are especially convincing, although the supporting characters' backgrounds seem at best two-dimensional.

The promise of contact with an extraterrestrial civilization can never match an on-screen, fully-realized vision. In *Close Encounters of the Third Kind* (only the original 1977 version), Steven Spielberg understood the problematic nature of showing the unimaginable and thus wisely permitted the viewer flexibility in conceiving of the unknown. If *Contact* had allowed the same latitude, the movie might be elevated above merely imaginative entertainment.

(2000)

# 59.

## A Diane Lane Triptych

Connie is responsible. That's the take-away from *Unfaithful* (2002), a gut- and heart-wrenching film of the first order. Ostensibly hapless victims of Connie's transgressions are strewn throughout the narrative, with our female protagonist (or is it antagonist?) receiving nary a comeuppance.

Diane Lane's frighteningly affecting performance, though, fights to bring a legitimate dissenting perspective on-screen. Connie and her spouse (played by the irreplaceable Richard Gere) are dialectically trapped in what novelist Jane Smiley termed the "ironic middle." Marriages caught in an ironic middle are not bad per se, but largely lack communicative qualities. In other words, there are truths hidden, things unsaid.

Connie's marriage both latently and manifestly lacks perverse, beyond-the-pale elements—and she has much too much time, as a non-working woman, to consider the fraught potentialities in the deep recesses of her mind; essentially, she is too much an archetype, too typed, to have a wholly distinct personality of her own.

Paul—himself an archetype, of a French lover—supplies Connie with a means and motive to stray. Connie leaves victims in her wake: Paul, her husband, her son, herself. She even repents, in mind and body (recall the scene in which she imagines a different scenario of her and Paul's first meeting). Not to absolve Connie of her culpability or to countenance her actions—and I am not arguing that she had no choice but to cheat, as if some supra-natural force stole her free agency and directed her—but she was weak in mind and forthcoming in body, and her affair quickly became discrete and distinct from the rest of her relationships, as the wonderful *salon.com* review of *Unfaithful* correctly observes. Chalk up Connie's behavior to, on the one hand, her ossified lifestyle catalyzing a defect in the causality department—essentially, she fails to see the consequences of her actions; and, on the other hand, at least a modicum of curiosity and interest spurred by her own—provincial, temporally speaking—ill choices.

*American Beauty* (1999), another contemporary fictive "ethnography" in suburbia, also explored the peaks and valleys—actually, mostly the valleys—of sanctioned and unsanctioned relationships, albeit in a terribly farcical manner. *The Ice Storm* (1997), another mainstay of the genre, had perhaps the opposite problem: it is too ponderous, too preachy. By contrast, *Unfaithful* raises serious questions and courageously supplies some answers in well-acted deeds instead of soapbox speak and holier-than-thou Hollywood morality.

Chalk it up to bad karma: after cheating on her on-screen husband in both *A Walk on the Moon* and *Unfaithful*, Diane Lane receives her comeuppance—she's betrayed by a spouse and a boyfriend in the ponderous *Under the Tuscan Sun*. There's a lesson here, I'm afraid. Frances (played by the ever-more-stunning Ms. Lane), to grow through these painful experiences, must learn to divest herself of emotional expectations from, well, men; after all, in any relationship, there's always one who kisses and one who offers the cheek, and Frances has been kissing one too many cheeks lately.

Indeed, right from the get-go, the whole movie's a veritable didactic presentation of female-world-wary wisdom wrapped in a box and bowtie with all the subtlety of a feminine-hygiene product commercial. *Tuscan Sun* beats us over the head senselessly with themes and metaphors until all the meaning's been rendered moot—and then it pauses for us to contemplate things even further.

For instance, pseudo-profundity abound when Patti, played by Sarah Oh (later to star in *Sideways*, her best movie role), delivers the big Robert Frost-like, Take-the-Road-Not-Taken speech to Frances when she tells her to attend a tour of the Tuscan countryside. Of course, fresh from her spousal breakup and sick of feeling the pangs of discontent, Frances takes things a bit too far and ends up purchasing a three-hundred-year-old villa replete with no running water, deadly insects, steamy toilets, hidden frescos, and collapsing walls. Even a neophyte can recognize the obvious relation between Frances's emotional innards and the house's tenuous structure. "The Fall of the House of Usher" is subtler.

And, in case a lesson or message slips the audience's attention, let's not forget that the wildly annoying character of Katherine—whose only purpose seems to be to spew well-timed aphorisms to our naïve protagonist—is there to remind us. Katherine's supposed to be this all-knowing, independent, liberated woman. If anything, though, she comes off more pathetic than centered; yet Frances appears to look up to her, as if blithely posing in the nude is somehow admirable behavior for a sixty-year-old (or any) woman.

We even have the Montagues and Capulets to deal with! Four hundred years and four thousand poorly executed *Romeo and Juliet* stories later, *Tuscan Sun* generously submits another one to the ledger. When Pawel, attempting to prove his bona fides, tosses the flag which lands squarely on his head during the flag ceremony, I figured that Katherine would pipe up with another well-timed proverb, like, say, Though a tree grow ever so high, the falling leaves return to the ground.

Ever the optimist, I hope that the next time I see an escapist travelogue adapted into movie (expressly to illustrate that home is where the heart is), the first words out of my mouth are not "buyer's remorse." So *caveat emptor.*

It's been a long time—a long time—since I've laughed as hard at a movie line as I laughed at Michael's "clandestine" invitation, post-All-American Beauty contest, to chat with his ostensible girlfriend, Sally (Diane Lane), in *Miss All-American Beauty* (1982): "Meet me in the broom closet at midnight!" Never mind that he screamed it loud enough to be in earshot of contestants at that other beauty—sorry, scholarship—contest, Miss America. And never mind that thirty-seven-year-old Michael shouldn't be allowed within a hundred yards of fifteen-year-old Sally, let alone cramped in a three-by-six broom closet. Wait a minute: I do mind all of those things.

Couldn't a younger actor have been chosen to play Michael? It's irritatingly tough to accept Brian Kerwin's performance as a dopey-in-love, frustrated music teacher when the camera belies his on-screen age.

Even Diane Lane, an actress who rarely phones it in, phoned it in this time. I especially love Sally's bemused reaction when she awakens in a hotel room in New York City: she peers out of the window and literally expresses shock at seeing the skyline—as if, just transported, she didn't realize where she was. This is a career-high level of naïveté![*]

And when she stencils her face blue with eyeliner and beats up the Sally doll (which of course wouldn't be mistaken for her doppelganger; I know it's a TV movie, but couldn't a bit more cash have been budgeted on fashioning an effective likeness? It's supposed to be the protagonist's epiphany and instead it appears as if she's remodeling her '53 Ginny-type), unintentional hilarity ensues. Let's face it: paint the doll's hair flaming red, hand it to Cloris Leachman for thrashing, and a more believable and dramatic performance is rendered!

But, alas, not all performances fall flat. For instance, Sally's father turns in a pretty good imitation of Jimmy Carter in his heyday, and the rather unfortunately named actor David Dukes, who plays über-sleaze Avery McPherson, utters the film's best bit of dialogue: "Sally, you are a queen among queens!" To contemplate further any themes or meta-meanings is to do what biting literary critic Dale Peck has expressly urged his fellow reviewers not to do with bad books: give them an aura of legitimacy. No need for me to be the first to threaten this silly movie with even a thimbleful[†] of legitimacy, so I'll end here.

(2003)

---

[*] Admittedly, this is one of Lane's earliest roles, but still—no excuses!

[†] Using "thimbleful" as an adjective is a characteristic tic of Mick Foley, one of two great writers to emerge from the professional wrestling business (the other being Bret Hart).

# 60.

## Silent War: A Review of *Sound and Fury*

The documentary *Sound and Fury* (2000) drops us in the middle of a long-standing cold war between the hearing and the Deaf worlds, right as a small skirmish heats up into an inter- and intra-familial battle. The daggers-drawn, gut-wrenching debates over cochlear implants exposed on camera are merely red herrings, masking and distracting from the core question: Who wins the future? Since the "future question" can only be thought of—by both the hearing and the Deaf worlds, but especially by the Deaf world, at least as shown in the documentary—as a zero-sum, winner-take-all game, there's little room for compromise.

Pejoratives like "abuse" and "robots" are the salvos in this war: "abuse" by the hearing world to label parents who dare not afford their children with the latest cochlear implants, and "robots" by the Deaf world to imply that any technological sensory-assist amounts to a loss of humanity (and an affront to Deaf culture). Both are obviously extreme, caricatured positions, but the two warring sides are so focused on protecting their turf that they simply cannot hear the only voice of reason in the film: Nita.

Although it's not obvious at first, Nita, through her struggles and her confusion, manages, albeit with mixed results, to formulate with her words, if less successfully with her actions, a compromise path. She straddles a fine line between not angering her husband, upsetting her in-laws, and succumbing to her self-doubts. Nita is the most sympathetic character in a film with very unsympathetic characters, and—with some qualifications I mention below—Nita's words and actions have the most to recommend.

Consider: after visiting an oral-only school, Nita says, "They [the students at the school] don't have any Deaf identity or self-esteem. I want Heather [her daughter] to be part of both worlds: both to speak, and to sign." Nita even seeks out guidance for her own prospective cochlear implant, while simultaneously remaining a stalwart defender of Deaf culture in the face of full-frontal attacks from her sister-in-law. ("So what that I can't hear music?" Nita angrily counters.)

Nita also has to contend with a feisty mother-in-law who no doubt has the best of intentions for Heather. Heather's grandmother is terribly insensitive to Deaf culture; she thinks little of the "emotion of Sign" that her son Peter eloquently elaborates upon, and views growing up deaf as a cruel fate, a Sisyphean torture for a child that should by any and all means be avoided. When speaking to her mother-in-law, Nita acquits herself well, neither coming off as selfish and self-aggrandizing as her husband does nor capitulating to the whims of hearing-world sensibilities. For example, although her husband Peter is rightly afraid that Heather, with an implant, "Won't be part of the Deaf world or the hearing world," he goes too far in suggesting that it's a de facto blessing that his daughter is profoundly deaf, since his implication is that the Deaf world is somehow "better" than the hearing one—the very trait he so despises that is ostensibly present in the hearing community. Nita does not make this mistake and therefore seems, by comparison, refreshingly open-minded about her daughter's future.

Nita is not without fault, however. Her key failure is one of weakness, of casting responsibility around for her decisions. One of the last scenes in the film shows her twisting words while speaking to Heather, making it seem as if she and her daughter had an off-camera adult-to-adult discussion and reached the conclusion that Heather should not have the surgery. Yet it's abject silliness to think that a five-year-old has the wherewithal to consider choices of such import or to make life decisions on the basis of anything much more than a mental coin flip. If she truly wished to have Heather herself evaluate whether to go under the knife, Nita was correct in putting off the cochlear implants till such time as her daughter could make a fully-informed decision. Unfortunately, delay has consequences in the treatment's efficacy, something that Nita doesn't fully grasp like her sister- and mother-in-law do.

Nevertheless, misstep aside, Nita, who is profoundly deaf, is alone in *Sound and Fury* in being able to *listen* to people on both sides of the hearing-Deaf divide. Only though listening to the legitimate grievances of the Deaf community, while also soberly considering the promises held by continuing advancements in technology, will the cold war between the two worlds begin to thaw. (2010)

# 61.

## The Temptations and Shifting Sympathies of *Topaz*

Although generally regarded as a disappointing entry in the Alfred Hitchcock canon, *Topaz* (1969) is, upon closer inspection, a rich viewing experience: a film replete with visual symbols, it has a rigorously constructed plot (with few details wasted), despite no central protagonist or antagonist. The film backdrops the post-Bay of Pigs (*c.* 1962) tensions between Cuba and the United States with a love story in its foreground; but the Cubans and Russians are not necessarily shown to be "evil" Communist dictators, and the Americans are not necessarily shown to be "saintly"; instead, *Topaz* paradoxically distances itself from the politics and policies that the film itself deals with as its main topic.

Images on-screen during the opening of *Topaz* introduce the audience to the catalyst of the adventures. After the blinding white letters of the credits are quickly flashed (with a visual montage of Russian war machines moving swiftly in the background in grainy-looking shots replete with a war-type marching music theme), an ominous message flashes on screen as the camera overlooks a Russian crowd from high above in a long wide-angle shot: "A high Russian official somewhere in the crowd disagrees with the politics of his country." This opening, although not visually similar, nevertheless permits us to recall the first shots of *Psycho* (1960): the camera in *Psycho* effectively "randomly" chooses a building, and a room in that building, to peer voyeuristically into (in *Psycho*, the camera "picks" Marion Crane to observe, but the "subject" for the camera ostensibly could have been anyone present in the skyline shot of Phoenix, Arizona). *Topaz*'s element of randomness is apparent because the dissatisfied Russian official is not specified by the title card; thus, the film could choose any official, analogous to the camera's seemingly random decision to pry into Marion Crane's life in *Psycho*.

*Topaz* begins in Copenhagen. The audience observes a family (husband, wife, and their older daughter) leave a building; a right-to-left overhead tracking shot follows them outside the building and down the sidewalk. We also see an unidentified man watching their movements. Immediately, we are led to suspect that the family is the Russian official's; the family is clearly attempting escape.

The chase sequence between the family and the men pursuing them reverses the cliché: typically, a standard movie chase would be fast, careless, and obvious to spectators on-screen not involved in the pursuit.* Here, however, Hitchcock constructs the sequence of the Russian official's defection to reverse our expectations,† since the defection turns on slow movements and characters' subtle observations of their surroundings rather than fast motion.

The Russian family enters a pottery factory; the Russian agents follow them into the building. A tour is in progress, so both groups follow the tour guide, working hard to blend in. A number of LOR and POV shots occur; first, we see the official's daughter looking off-screen; then, the audience sees a Russian agent with a POV shot (from her point of view), staring directly at the family. Next, there is an LOR shot of the agent, followed by a shot from his point of view; the perspective constantly changes in the space to accommodate several people's points of view. In a way, POV shots become an objective tool of the film; since we see the space from several characters' points of view, the POVs "balance out" in a way, leaving the audience with many different, and often disparate, visual perspectives of the same sequence.

Eye movements become heightened because of the almost casual nature of the scene. Everyone's eyes shift to note his or her locations in the pottery factory (with respect to other characters' places in the tour). Hitchcock capitalizes on the audience's almost hypnotic involvement in the movements of the character's eyes by having

---

* In other words, background individuals in the film are able to clearly see the effects of the chase; consider *The French Connection* (1971) as an example of an out-in-the-open chase (which, of course, disrupts innocent passersby).

† Hitchcock also plays with our expectations of chase scenes in *North by Northwest* (1959). Roger O. Thornhill is almost assassinated in daylight in the middle of a cornfield, instead of at night in a claustrophobic environment (which probably would have been a more typical film sequence). Also, in *Torn Curtain* (1966), there is an entirely silent (except for footsteps) slow-chase sequence, featuring Paul Newman, in a museum.

the Russian official's daughter "accidentally" drop a pottery piece. The sound of the glass breaking, though not loud, jolts the audience and distracts the Russian agents; and the daughter is then able to quickly escape from their clutches.

After American agents retrieve the family, they board a plane and are transported to the United States. The passing of time, and the relocation of the space, is effectively displayed to the audience: The plane in Copenhagen takes off from right-to-left at sunset and, in a juxtaposed shot, lands in Washington in the opposite direction during the daytime. Thus, a temporal ellipsis has effected the relocation of time and space with the two shots.

Boris Kusenov, the Russian defector, is clearly unhappy in America; with overt and exaggerated expressions, he makes his disgust of the country quite obvious not only to the audience but to the other characters in the film. However, as the film progresses, he will give in to the material wealth of the country; seeing his change of character—and the bait of materialistic temptation he can't resist—amplifies the entirely questionable nature of the "missions" and "agendas" of *Topaz*: Why do the characters bother to swear loyalties to nation states when so many of the characters clearly have loyalty only to themselves?*

We are introduced to the ostensible main character of the film, Andre Devereaux, without really seeing or hearing him. Devereaux arrives at a French officials' building in a white car, shown to us with a high-angle overhead shot; as the officials (and the viewers) wait for him to visit their office, the French officials give an exposition of Devereaux's insolence and lack of respect for authority. *Topaz* will repeat this method of introducing important characters dialogically to the audience before those characters actually appear on-screen—in other words, background information of characters, or summaries of characters' importance, is talked about by other individuals on-screen ahead of time; we might deem these "verbally establishing portraits." This technique of introducing main characters is a recurring non-visual motif in *Topaz*.

---

* If we accept the New Wave's auteur theory, then we could claim that some of Hitchcock's main personal statements in the film are the corruption of people by materialism and the insignificance of allegiance to countries. We can extend this to also include loyalty to specific individuals, as will be discussed later on.

The French officials inform Devereaux, a French agent, that the Americans have an important Russian defector. Within the first two lines of Devereaux's response, he stumbles upon what will be the narrative thrust of the film: How did the French government obtain the information of the defection?

Next, there is an interrogation scene of Kusenov by the Americans (Mike, the head U.S. agent, leads the questioning). The queries are fairly standard—and Kusenov displays disgust with everyone—until the question, "Does the word 'Topaz' mean anything to you?" is asked. To signify the change in the tone of the inquiry, a tight shot of Kusenov is shown. He is clearly uncomfortable, not repulsed (as he has been with all of the other queries from the Americans), by the question; the form-content relationship has the style of the Kusenov shot (a high-angle tight close-up) convey the power of the word "Topaz"; Kusenov is rendered impotent by the question, as the high camera angle suggests.

Other camera angles reinforce Kusenov's impotent position. Most of the shots during his interrogation are from table height (all characters in the scene are sitting around a table, except for Mike, the most powerful agent, who is pacing). Nearly all shots of the Americans are from low angles—thus they (the Americans) are made to appear dominant. Since Mike is standing, his low angle shots (from the table height) are the most exaggerated, and therefore he appears to be the most dominant person in the scene. Of course, the form-content relationship emphasizes Mike's controlling position; however, it is not that clear-cut: even though the Americans are shot at low angles, Kusenov has some control over them—after all, he is supplying the answers to their questions.

A call interrupts the interrogation, and Mike is summoned to the telephone. He receives a message from his secretary: Devereaux wishes to have dinner with him. Therefore, in the same scene, we watch all of the (thus far) disjoint movie elements (Devereaux, the Russian official, and the term "Topaz") converge. Mike is puzzled by the invitation, because he had dinner with Devereaux only several nights before, which he explains to one of his colleagues at the inquiry. Analogous to the "establishing portraits" which precede a character's entrance into the film, important and relevant (to the audience's understanding and appreciation of the story) narrative points are introduced beforehand; the film has an exposition-plan-execution form (the exposition, plan, and execution elements in the story or sequence of the film tend to be related by a narrative arc; we will see several examples of this later) to many of the sequences. In this case, the "exposition" is Mike's on-screen explanation that he is bewildered by the dinner invitation because he just recently had dinner with Devereaux. Also, after finishing the telephone conversation with his secretary and returning to Kusenov to continue questioning him, Kusenov floats the name Rico Parra, a high Cuban government official, as a man with information about Russian missile buildups in Cuba; this is yet more exposition for a future narrative scene (and future narrative arc).

The "planning" stage is initiated at dinner with Mike, Devereaux, and Devereaux's wife, Nicole. We find out that Devereaux and Mike "have done things for each other that no other agents in this town would ever do." (Admittedly, that's a very suggestive line!) Devereaux wishes to know more about Kusenov and how the French government got word of his defection. Mike tells him, on the condition of confidentiality—which is obviously an affront to the French government, since Andre is a French agent.

Later, after finding out that Rico Parra has a secretary, named Luis Uribe, who can be bribed (to obtain documents about Cuban missile buildups), Mike intercepts Devereaux in New York. It is in Andre's hotel room in New York that the audience first sees a frequently used visual motif to denote French loyalty: the color yellow.[*] The yellow flowers in the hotel room scream of Devereaux's loyalty to the French, but this loyalty is clearly questionable: Andre promised Mike that he would not speak about their conversation to the French government—and we have a recurrence of the theme of ambiguous allegiance to nation states.

Mike tells Devereaux that he needs him to bribe Uribe to obtain Parra's secret documents because Uribe will not accept money from Americans (since he has no sympathy for Americans). Thus the "planning" stage of this segment of the narrative is almost complete; Devereaux must first see a picture of Uribe, so he knows whom to look for to bribe. The plot becomes too clever by half here, "coincidentally" having Andre's son-in-law's occupation be a

[*] Although this motif was suggested by, for instance, Donald Spoto in the influential text *The Art of Alfred Hitchcock* (1992), it has since become accepted as a part of the "common knowledge" of the film, so I will not cite future references to it.

journalist and sketch artist—why, he even conveniently sketched Uribe when he was as a recent United Nations conference that both Parra and Uribe attended!*

Devereaux seeks a friendly operative, named Dubois, a flower shop owner, to help him bribe Uribe and obtain the documents. Dubois's friendliness to the French agent is emphasized by the color of his clothes: yellow. It must be noted that Roscoe Lee Browne (who plays Dubois) gives by far the most effective performance in the film. While actors Frederick Stafford (Devereaux) and John Forsythe (Mike) often appear as stiff and uninterested spectators to the action—perhaps a consequence of the kind of roles they are playing, that of desensitized secret agents—Browne is active and dynamic throughout his ten minutes on-screen. He steals the show.

Devereaux and Dubois discuss the plan to retrieve Parra's documents in the refrigerator room of the floral shop. Because the audience realizes that Uribe can be bribed, Hitchcock correctly decides that it is unnecessary for the viewers to have to hear the exposition again. But he also realizes that we must see Devereaux giving Dubois the background information about Uribe, otherwise Dubois wouldn't know whom to bribe. So Hitchcock artfully compromises: After Devereaux and Dubois walk into the floral refrigerator (the walls and door are all made of transparent glass), Dubois shuts the door, blocking out the sounds of their voices. The shot is held—it is a silent shot; we can see the two men talking, but cannot hear them—for about a minute, until Dubois and Devereaux emerge from the room.

The shot itself symbolizes something quite subtle. As spectators not caught up in the entanglements of complicated Cold War policies, we have been "shut out" to the world of the spies; the intelligence agents' occupation consists of secret missions; and the closed glass doors function as a metaphor to show that there is indeed spying occurring, but the details of the missions are unclear since we cannot hear them.

Next, the "execution" part of the narrative occurs: Dubois contacts Uribe in an attempt to procure the documents. Devereaux stands across the street from the hotel in Harlem where Uribe and

* But since Hitchcock's films often have an inherent logic somewhat displaced from the notions of reality, perhaps labeling Andre's son-in-law's vocation a too-clever "coincidence" isn't a completely fair criticism.

Parra are staying and watches Dubois' progress. We see a LOR medium close-up of Devereaux watching Dubois; next, we see a telephoto lens long shot of Dubois entering the hotel (which has large glass transparent windows and doors) and calling Uribe. Because a telephoto lens is used, the depth of field is altered and the shot has a kind of voyeuristic quality to it; although we can see Dubois' movements, they are at a distance, and he is framed rather oddly in the long shot (no doubt because of the distortion caused by the telephoto lens).

Uribe comes down to the lobby from the elevator, Dubois propositions him with money, and we do not hear anything; we only see their actions from a distance. Note the parallel structure of this scene and the previous one (with Devereaux and Dubois in the floral refrigerator); in both, we can see action, but we cannot hear it. The audience members watch the expression of an emotion, *temptation*, played out on-screen in one continuous shot (once again, similar to the long take of Devereaux and Dubois talking in the floral refrigerator). Uribe is at first horrified by the offer, but then, after the money is presented, he accepts it.

The visual construction of the scene recalls *Breathless* (1960) by director Jean-Luc Godard. It is well documented that Hitchcock was influenced by the New Wave movement, and even consciously tried to (in the early 1960s, at least) impart a more blatantly "artistic" visual touch on his films while retaining their commercial mainstream Hollywood appeal.* The temptation scene between Dubois and Uribe resembles visually many of the more realistic-looking shots in Goddard's work—because of the telephoto lens filming method, for instance, the space is altered and camera's vibrations and shakes become exaggerated greatly; this makes the scene appear documentary-like.

Also consider a comparison between Hitchcock's directorial style of the mid-1950s and the late-1970s. In *Rear Window* (1954), the director's projection of Jefferies' voyeurism (and by extension the audiences') is visually slick; in other words, even when the shots are from Jefferies' viewpoint through his penetrating camera lens, there is a consistently glossy, controlled, and constructed feel to the images. Yet in *Topaz*'s hotel temptation scene, the visuals resemble

---

* The uneven *Marnie* (1964) is perhaps the most explicit example of Hitchcock's attempt at a commercial and artistic compromise.

newsreel footage; they still, like *Rear Window*, appear constructed, but are less blatantly artificial than in Hitchcock's 1950's thriller. Post-New Wave, the communicative aspects of overt realism influenced films, and Hitchcock was not immune.*

After he gives in to temptation, Uribe and Dubois travel up to Parra's floor to game plan retrieving the vital documents (the telephoto lens long take terminates once we are on Parra's floor). Dubois enters Uribe's hotel room to talk. The shot's composition is unique; instead of a standard eye-level shot-reverse shot, there is a high angle shot of the two men separated by a swinging light bulb that illuminates the room (the shot is reminiscent of *Psycho*, at the moment when Lila horrifyingly discovers Norman's "mother"). Perhaps the light bulb, since it is swinging near and over their heads, signifies their thinking process; after all, they formulate their plans with the light bulb lit directly overhead.

Although we have heard a great deal about Rico Parra in the film thus far, the viewers have not yet seen him—continuing the motif of introducing characters verbally by describing their backgrounds prior to them physically entering the frame. Our first visual introduction to the Cuban official is a memorable one; he brutally removes a person claiming to be his supporter from his hotel room. Uribe and Dubois arrive next at Parra's room, with Dubois claiming that he is a reporter for *Ebony* wishing to take several pictures of Parra. Parra agrees and, while Parra is distracted by the photography, Uribe takes the suitcase with the documents. Dubois and Uribe then escape into Uribe's room without the Cubans (initially) realizing what has happened.

However, the camera stays not with Dubois—who, we assume, is photographing the documents in Uribe's hotel room—but with Parra, who has not yet discovered his missing suitcase. Hitchcock builds suspense while slyly forcing the audience to identify with Parra. Parra sits down at his desk and begins studying some papers; he reaches downward several times (to the location the suitcase was at previously before Uribe swiped it), and we have contradictory

---

* Hitchcock was not the only major commercial director impacted by the movement. Stanley Kubrick, in 1964, framed many shots in the ending sequences of *Dr. Strangeglove or: How I Learned to Stop Worrying and Love the Bomb* with a dark visual undertone using a newsreel-type style.

feelings: we want him to discover the missing suitcase, yet we breathe a sigh of relief when he repeatedly doesn't.*

After Parra discovers the missing suitcase, he proceeds immediately to Uribe's room and discovers Dubois taking pictures of the documents. Dubois jumps out the window; the camera stays in Uribe's room, focused on Uribe: he wears a defeated look on his face. The next shot is a close-up of Parra (looking at Uribe); the audience knows the fate of Uribe.

Outside the hotel room, a more standard chase scene develops (more standard, that is, compared to the movie's opening "chase" sequence) with Dubois on the run from Parra's henchmen. Dubois purposely stumbles over Devereaux, who is still outside of the hotel, and gives him the camera. Parra's main henchman witnesses the exchange (a detail which will expose Devereaux later). Dubois, meanwhile, escapes back to his flower shop unseen, and finishes the project he was working on before Devereaux assigned him the mission of retrieving the documents: a cross with a rest-in-peace sign, all made of flowers. Of course, this is indirectly meant for audience reinforcement that Uribe's implied execution, because of his breach of loyalty to Parra (another instance of questionable loyalty, this time to an individual), did in fact occur.

Devereaux, after seeing the documents (he says that he found them "scary"), decides to go to Cuba to investigate further. He tells his wife, Nicole, of his intentions, and the audience receives yet another character portrait of an as-of-yet unseen person: Juanita, the beautiful widow of a major figure of the Cuban revolution but now, unknown to everyone except a few people, leader of the Cuban underground against Castro and Parra. Nicole suspects that her husband is having an affair with Juanita, and her suspicions are later confirmed.

Devereaux arrives at Juanita's home, and Parra is there (Parra is Juanita's landlord); an uncomfortable discussion occurs, but Parra does not suspect that Devereaux has anything at all to do with the document stealing. Devereaux presents Juanita with a "gift": spy

---

* *Psycho* also has a similar scene. After Norman places Marion's body into her car and rolls the automobile into the motel's adjacent swamp, we *want* the car to sink, even though we have treated Marion as the protagonist throughout the first third of the film (before she dies). Hitchcock confounds audience expectations by leaving us only Norman to sympathize with.

cameras and other equipment. The gift exchange occurs at dinner; the shot is composed with the two characters assuming opposite sides of the frame. Also, the room is backlit (the closed blinds of the room are in the background, and no artificial lights are on in the dining room). In terms of visual tone, the image very much resembles the shot of Carolyn in *American Beauty* (1999) standing alone in an empty, backlit dining room with shades closed after she realizes she is unable to sell a house.

The next morning Juanita and Andre walk outside her house and talk about the resistance; she is wearing yellow, symbolizing her sympathy to the French cause. Next, Juanita meets with a couple labeled simply as the Mendozas, who are operatives for the underground resistance. The spy cameras (used to take pictures of the missiles in Cuba) are hidden in sandwiches in a picnic basket; the Mendozas will have a "picnic" with the "camera sandwiches" near the location of the missiles. Unfortunately for the Mendozas, several birds steal the sandwiches and alert the Cuban guards of the Mendozas' activity (by all of the noise made from the birds taking the food). The Mendozas are captured, but they do manage to deposit the cameras and film in a tube-like fence on the side of the road. In an effective extended take, the Mendozas are arrested by the Cuban soldiers while the equipment is recovered by another member of the resistance.

Somewhat ironically, the film and cameras are hidden again, this time in a chicken (thus, the birds exposed the resistance, and the resistance uses a bird to protect their film and equipment). Later, Juanita and Devereaux eat the same chicken the equipment was hidden in (after the cameras had been removed, of course); this is Hitchcock's morbid humor expressed to the fullest.* The film continues Hitchcock's fascination with birds (in *Psycho*, Norman stuffs

---

* In the *Alfred Hitchcock Presents* episode "Lamb of the Slaughter," directed by Hitchcock, there is a similar ironic use of an animal. After a disgruntled wife (Barbara Bel Geddes, who also co-starred in *Vertigo* and went on to star in *Dallas*, surely the greatest prime-time soap of all time) becomes infuriated with her husband (because he had an affair), she kills him with a frozen leg of a lamb from her freezer. When she hears the police are arriving to investigate, she cooks the leg of lamb, and feeds it to the police; the discussion at the dinner table while the police and his wife consume the well-cooked lamb ironically centers on what type of murder weapon could have been used to kill her husband.

birds; in *Marnie*, Mark has a fascination with birds and other untamed "beasts"; and in *The Birds* [1963], birds attack Bodega Bay).

Devereaux next attends a pro-Castro rally. The style of shooting here clearly echoes Leni Riefenstahl's pro-Hitler propaganda films: Parra is shown from a very low angle when on the speaking platform. Parra's henchman, who witnessed the exchange of the camera film between Andre and Dubois in Harlem, recognizes Devereaux and points him out to Parra. Later that evening, the Cuban official goes to Juanita's house and interrupts their dinner (they are eating the chicken used to hide the camera equipment) to tell Devereaux to leave the country.*

Several planes of action divide up the next shot; Parra arrives at the Mendozas' torture chamber, and they are ready to talk about the resistance (they are nearly dead from the torture). There is a multiple depth of field shot as Parra inches slowly closer to the traitorous couple. An extreme close-up of Parra's ear lets him hear the unfortunate news from the nearly dead Mendozas: Juanita is the leader of the resistance.

The next morning, soldiers and Parra arrive to search Juanita's house for any evidence of a resistance movement. She comes violently out of her bedroom, down the stairs, screaming for Parra to call off the search. As she walks down the stairs, Hitchcock uses a shot reserved almost exclusively for his screen sirens (such as Grace Kelley, Ingrid Bergman, and Tippi Hedren): the forward/backward tracking shot. The camera tracks backward on Juanita as she descends the stairs and alternates to a POV forward tracking shot—the chaotic scene has a dream-like quality.

Juanita has been fingered as the leader of the underground; after she descends the stairs and attempts escape, Rico grabs her arm (the screen simply shows a close-up of his arm, which is held for several seconds for visceral impact). He holds her tightly and faces her; we see a medium shot (waist up) of them both, one on one side of the frame, the other on the opposite side of it. The camera

---

* Consider the following interesting causal chain: Parra exposes Devereaux while he is eating the chicken that was used to hide the equipment to avoid being exposed by soldiers who already exposed other underground rebellion agents because of a couple of untamed birds! The absurdity of the situation reinforces Hitchcock's lack of faith in politics: clearly, in this film, the birds are more in control of the Cold War than the countries are.

begins to slowly rotate around them (a "dance of death") as Parra softly says to her, "You will be tortured, like the Mendozas were. The things that will be done to your body—this body...." Parra slowly pulls out a gun and shoots her in the back to protect her from the torture, out of respect for her; oddly enough, by killing her, he is showing Juanita loyalty, a quality that everyone else in this film lacks at one time or another (Devereaux is not loyal to his wife; Kusenov is not loyal to his countrymen; and Uribe is not loyal to Parra). The next shot is of Parra's gun in his hand, going "limp."*

In one of the greatest single shots of any Hitchcock film, the camera cuts to a directly overhead view of them both as Juanita slumps to the ground; as she slowly drops, her magenta dress expands like a budding flower. This is the sex-death theme expressed brilliantly by Hitchcock: we have witnessed the theme played out many times before, notably in *Vertigo* (1958), *Psycho*, and *Marnie*, but it has perhaps never been as effectively shorthanded—the scene has the paradoxical quality of displaying a sensually beautiful death. The scene also recalls a similarly shot scene in *Vertigo* of Scottie and Judy kissing; in that scene, the camera rotates violently around the couple, making manifest their tumultuous relationship.

Devereaux finds out about Juanita's death before boarding a plane going to the United States; the seats in the plane are all yellow (denoting French sympathy). Devereaux, after arriving in Washington, is commissioned to report back to Paris for a full inquiry examining why he participated in an American mission. The exposition part of the exposition-plan-execution motif occurs again, as Mike informs Andre about the corrupt board of Frenchmen. Mike suggests that Andre meet with Kusenov to hear about the corruption firsthand.

Kusenov has clearly taken the bait of material wealth, as Uribe did earlier in the film. His entire attitude toward American materialism has changed; he even suggests for Devereaux to "listen to his conscience" and stay in America (and not return to face an inquiry). Kusenov explains to Andre that there is a high official French spy ring—called "Topaz"—which is secretly passing off French secrets

* Canadian character actor John Vernon, who plays Parra, doesn't deliver the film's best performance—again, that would be Roscoe Lee Browne—but he is very effective nonetheless. He later went on to star in *Herbie Goes Bananas*, unfortunately for his career.

to the Russians. In yet more exposition for the final third of the film, Andre says that he "must uncover Topaz [before an American delegation arrives in Paris to discuss the Kusenov situation with the French officials] at the risk of my own skin—that's quite a job, my friends."

Andre confronts some of his "friends" at a dinner meeting. Jarre, the man fingered by Kusenov, is carefully watched by Andre. In a series of repeated shots, Andre's head gently peeks around several other people's heads at the dinner table to observe Jarre's reaction to the comments about Topaz. Jarre remains perfectly calm in a series of complementary shots showing the French member of Topaz eating and enjoying his food (in fact, he is the only one in the room with a calm composure, which isolates him; everyone else—who, with just one exception, is not involved in the spy ring—appears flustered by the comments).

Jarre visits Jacques Granville, the head of Topaz (and one of Andre's best friends; he was at the dinner meeting with Devereaux), to discuss options. After Jarre leaves, another person arrives at Granville's house: Devereaux's wife (who sees Jarre leave; this is an important detail, which, like so many other details in the film, will recur for a specific purpose in the narrative). Nicole is Granville's lover, just like Devereaux was Juanita's lover. An interesting "parallel chain" of lovers is created by the narrative: Parra to Juanita to Devereaux to Nicole to Granville, with all adjacent "links" on the chain being lovers; the parallel structure is similar to the love relationships in Hitchcock's chronically underrated *Family Plot* (1976).

Devereaux's son-in-law is assigned by Andre to interview Jarre with the purpose of getting information about Topaz out of him. As his son-in-law walks up the steps to get to Jarre's apartment, the space is established by a quick camera movement: a rotating tracking shot. He sketches and interviews Jarre, but doesn't get very much information. Later, when Andre comes searching for his son-in-law, the space is effectively reestablished by the same shot of the staircase (so the type of shot itself serves as a literal frame of reference).

Devereaux discovers that Jarre was assassinated because he was a risk to reveal information about Topaz. He looks out of Jarre's window to see Jarre dead on top of his car—Jarre was apparently thrown out of his window. The shot visually resembles the first shot of Devereaux, when we see his car through the French official's window.

Because Andre recovered the notebook that his son-in-law used to draw Jarre, Nicole identifies the traitor (she saw him leave Granville's house and immediately made the association; once again, every small detail is presented conveniently to tie narrative loose ends together). She tells Devereaux, albeit reluctantly, of Jarre's connections with Granville.

When the American delegation arrives, Andre informs Mike privately that Granville is the head of Topaz; before the meeting begins with the Americans and the French, Granville is quietly told to leave the meeting. Granville's sense of isolation in the large meeting room is apparent in the form-content relationship of the shots; the camera shows the large space in a wide establishing shot, with everybody in the room appearing small, and there is a slow zoom to a close-up of Granville's face simultaneously as he is told to leave the conference room (the camera pinpoints him, just like the Americans pinpointed the Topaz leader; this is a clear form-content relationship).

Realizing that his career is over, he commits suicide, although his life-ending act is implied, not shown; the camera stays outside his house as he closes the door and fires a shot that is heard, but never seen; in a way, the implication that he is dead is more fully realized and obvious than the implication that Uribe was killed. Nonetheless, notice the parallelism between the presentations of the two off-screen deaths. Also notice that Granville's death takes place behind a closed door (recall Devereaux and Dubois's conversation in the floral refrigerator was another closed-door event). The construction is reversed, though: this time we hear but do not see.

We next see a montage of significant events in the film, coupled with the same marching music from the opening credits, overlaid with a newspaper describing these events in very superficial detail. The newspaper simply declares: "Missile Crisis Averted." A newspaper reader casually tosses the paper down on a nearby park bench and leaves the frame as the film ends (not realizing, as we do—we have been the voyeurs into these characters' lives, after all—the death toll from the "aversion of the missile crisis" or the hardships many people had to go through behind the scenes to "avert the crisis").

In *Topaz*, our sympathies shift frequently for characters; at first, we sympathize with Kusenov, then with the Americans, then with the French, then with Devereaux, then with Parra, then the Cubans, then Juanita, then Jarre, then back again to Devereaux. Therefore, it is difficult to finger a clear-cut protagonist in the film (or a clear-cut antagonist, either). Whom should we root for? The film's lack of a protagonist is odd for Hitchcock; in nearly all of his works, we can easily name a protagonist (*Marnie*: Marnie; *The Birds*: Mitch; *North by Northwest*: Roger; *The Wrong Man* [1956]: Manny). However, just as Hitchcock does not adopt an anti-Communist position in this film—he even frequently presents the Americans as ill-prepared idiots—he does not latch on to a protagonist with which to present the world of the film to the audience (as he does in *Marnie*, for example); instead, he attempts to tackle the Cold War somewhat objectively and without a clear-cut protagonist's eyes for the audience to gaze through. Although this is not his typical style, Hitchcock is ultimately successful in his presentation.

Does *Topaz* deserve its reputation as ineffective, as being some sort of affront to Hitchcock's corpus? Mostly not. However, there are several key problems with the film. Although most of the set pieces taken individually work extraordinarily well (consider the Dubois scene and Juanita's death scene as examples), taken as a whole, the film presents itself as a purposefully made construction, interested in focusing on obscure and unlikely details and blowing them up to link one scene to the next (similarly to the successive coincidences in James Bond films). Devereaux's profession as a sketch artist is a good example of this: having the right sketches of the correct people at the right time seems remotely likely at best and should certainly not determine or largely influence the flow of the plot; in fact, the plot *hinges* on his occupation as an artist to work. *Topaz* is oftentimes less than the sum of its parts.

The film compromises a presentation of reality with a classical Hollywood-type style; some of the scenes look very documentary-like (consider the Dubois-Uribe temptation scene), and the treatment of the material of the Cold War is sometimes believable. However, *Topaz* is also a blatant construction that seems to consciously want to *hide* its constructed form.

The film is also shot inconsistently, as if Hitchcock was attempting every possible camera angle and camera style to show off (although, admittedly, many of his choices are very effective and beautiful; Juanita's death scene is the best example). Some shots are grainy; others are colorful; and still others are high contrast, with many of the shot serving no obvious form-content relationship.

But the film works, and it frequently works very well. It takes a relatively objective stance, and not a popularly biased one, on the Cold War, which is an impressive achievement (considering the year the film was made). Is gives us complicated characters, all with logical and conflicting motivations. It reverses some film clichés, especially with its avoidance of obvious places for action sequences. And the audience does indeed form an emotional attachment, albeit fleetingly, for some of its characters. With its interesting ideas and artful presentation, *Topaz* does not deserve its reputation as inadequate; rather, in hindsight, despite the conclusion of the Cold War, it is a piece of art that has hardly dated at all.

(1999)

# 62.

## *Leaving Las Vegas*: Unfinished Business

Many key elements of *Leaving Las Vegas* seem, superficially, quite cliché: the prostitute with the heart of gold, the alcoholic, and Sin City's presentation itself all, in a lesser film, would be almost unbearably sentimental. However, there are two things in this movie that catapult *Leaving Las Vegas* to the forefront of 1990s' cinema: Elizabeth Shue and Nicholas Cage. Remove the seamless performances of and chemistry between these two leads, and the film itself becomes a cliché.

It is the consistency of performance that enables the two thespians to portray their characters with so much conviction. For instance, this film takes a somewhat different approach than many others to displaying an alcoholism addiction. *LLV* does not require Cage's character Ben to follow a recovery plot-arc through the diagesis: Ben is allowed to drink himself to death. In addition, his lover, Shue's Sera, does not really "learn" anything in the process, and her characterization is not overtly altered. Sera never gives up her life of prostitution, for instance.

The slow-paced nature of the film necessitates (on the part of the audience) a full examination and dissection of the reasoning behind the characters' ultimate attraction to each other. To simply claim that Ben and Sera were both entrapped in a web of loneliness and thus needed one another is not completely accurate, but also not entirely incorrect.

Right from the beginning of *LLV*, we meet up with Ben, an out-of-control alcoholic. The establishing shot of Ben in the supermarket is revolutionary, in a way; instead of establishing the location of the film with a wide-shot pan over a city, for example, the film uses the establishing shot to *establish* its lead's personality. Thus, *LLV* instructs the audience that the importance of the film lies not necessarily with the city itself, but rather with an examination of a character's motivations.

And we immediately notice where his motivations and loyalties lie—with alcohol—in a tracking shot that has an interesting "arc of expectation" which the audience is not prepared for: the camera teases us, for an instant, while Ben is filling up an unseen supermarket cart with bottles of alcohol. When we finally do observe the wagon, the audience immediately notices that Ben is clearly not like (most of) the rest of us: he is only buying alcohol. Is the film being "realistic" by showing a man attaining sustenance solely from alcohol? Not entirely, but the audience is drawn into the unexpected narrative which has its own twisted logic.

In addition, in those first moments of the film, we only hear Ben's whistling; there are no other supermarket sounds discernable in the background. We are being cued into his world. And therein rests the brilliance of the supermarket sequence: not only does it establish Ben's motivation, facilitate the audience's entrance into his reality, and create an arc of expectation, but it does so within a time span of less than thirty seconds.

There is another, similarly character-revealing scene only several minutes later. Once again, analogous to the supermarket, the presentation of the scene is not only effective, but also fresh.

Waiting in line (for the second time) at an airport, Ben is speaking directly into a Dictaphone about his desires and fantasies regarding a flight attendant, who is within earshot. Since she is assisting a patron, and also because Cage is not talking very loudly, she is not tuned into his monologue. However, people behind Ben (and clearly visible in the frame) can easily discern his speech, and all have a look of disgust on their faces. The scene has an odd quality, which many later scenes in *LLV* have—it is simultaneously humorous and revolting.

But the airport scene is also terrifically unique. There is a shot-reverse shot of Ben talking "to" the flight attendant (who cannot hear Ben). While Ben is framed in a medium shot (with others in line visible in the frame), the attendant is framed with a telephoto tight close-up, which has an awkwardly disjointed presentation—the shot suggests, subtly, that Ben's sanity is at question. In the monologue, Ben suggests a sexual fling with the attendant (in relatively graphic detail), and he also talks about pouring bourbon all over her body, perhaps to make the sexual intercourse more enticing for him. Interestingly, in Sera and Ben's failed attempt at intercourse during the final third of the film, Sera pours bourbon over herself to—she hopes—produce the same effect: to make herself sexually desirable to Ben with Ben's choice of analgesic. So while some films have a sex-death theme running throughout them (such as Hitchcock's, De Palma's, or Scorsese's), *LLV* has a more unusual alcohol-sex-death theme.

In most of the outdoor night street shots of Ben in *LLV*, and later of Sera and Ben, the sounds of traffic are not heard. Similar to the original establishing sequence of Ben in the supermarket (where the audience only hears his whistling and no other background din), and also similar to the airport sequence (where we only can hear his monologue into the Dictaphone), the removal of traffic sounds seeks to further envelop the audience into the world of Sera and Ben—and no one else's. Unlike a Hitchcock film, where traffic and street noise are often heard with raised volume (to sound the imposing world closing in), *LLV* silences the outside world (to keep the audience firmly planted in a cocoon).

Within the first ten minutes of the film, the audience has been introduced to one-half of the main characters; after another ten minutes of *LLV*, we are introduced to Sera. She is a prostitute and adopts a different persona for every client, seemingly dependent on what she intuits to be his fantasy affair. Thus, initially, she is not a "real" character to us, but more of a cipher. Even the spelling of her name rings with an aura of superficiality; it suggests an attempt at producing a special or high-class moniker, but ultimately, considering her "multiple personalities" with clients and her employment, is contradictory.

The audience is surely aware that the two characters must meet somehow; the plot must find a way to initiate their (ultimately symbiotic) relationship. Although the choice of Ben randomly almost striking Sera down with his BMW at first appears contrived, it is, under closer examination, entirely appropriate to the logic of the film, if not quite the logic of real life. In a sequence reminiscent of *Taxi Driver* (1976), when Travis, played by Robert De Niro, almost runs over the teen prostitute, played brilliantly by Jodie Foster, he will later become "savior" to, Ben narrowly stops his car in time to avoid running over Sera. On multiple occasions later in the film, Ben constantly refers to Sera as his "angel." Sera's sudden random appearance in front of his automobile indeed supports his angelic feelings toward her—she just, out of nowhere, appeared to Ben though his windshield.

Sera is not an obvious choice for an angelic standard bearer. She is not a savior in the common sense (like antihero Travis in *Taxi Driver*), but instead offers a lonely man unconditional love. A mother also offers unconditional love to her child—and it's not a stretch to claim that he loves Sera more like a mother than a girlfriend.

Ben's ex-wife kicked him out of his house, we learn, and in an interesting and powerful shot, Ben burns his wife's picture (in fact, the shot is so powerful that it is repeated later in the film). Ben also burns most of his belongings. This, of course, symbolizes his break from the past; after he sells his BMW, his past life's destruction is complete, and he can move on—toward his death.

Accepting Sera as a girlfriend or lover is impossible for Ben through most of the film. Ben requires unconditional support, and this explains why Sera acts as more of a motherly figure than a lover or even a friend; Ben needs the company of an accepting person, who will shy away from trying to reform him (and, in fact, she even gives him a liquor bottle as a gift—the "mother" spoils her "child").

*LLV* is not a morality play; it makes few assumptions and contains no obvious judgments about Ben's and Sera's respective problems. This no-moral-judgments stipulation denotes the independence and uniqueness of this film in the '90s: very few other popular films then treated taboo topics such as prostitution and alcoholism with such a detached eye.

The more interesting question is this: Why does Sera wish to be a mother to Ben? Why does she even bother? Although there is no definitive answer given in the film, there are a few possible explanations. Perhaps she needs him to fulfill and boost her ego. After all, his problems are arguably worse than hers, and perhaps Sera needs to see up close a more downtrodden person than she is in order to regain some of her confidence as a human being, and not just as a prostitute. Call this the *schadenfreude* theory; it's not very convincing, however.

Slightly more persuasive: her maternal instincts are piqued because of Yuri's (her pimp) abusive treatment of her. Sera is repulsively submissive to Yuri, and in order to promote her personal need for self-fulfillment in a similar fashion, Sera decides to be a dominant figure over Ben. But this explanation seems a bit farfetched because, although Sera is somewhat dominant over Ben in most scenes—notice how she is always on top in their sexual encounters, for instance—he is hardly dependent or submissive to her; in fact, with respect to her prostitution, he gives her unconditional acceptance.

There is in particular one scene that encapsulates all of the motivations and characterizations of Sera and Ben in the film. In the first third of *LLV*, after Ben has moved in with Sera, we observe her entering the bathroom and not closing the door, whilst simultaneously seeing Ben still lying on the couch. This scene, in many ways, is of a piece with the central thrust of the movie: interpersonal honesty. Ben and Sera can be honest with each other unconditionally. She does not close the bathroom door because she has nothing to hide from him.[*] With any of her other clients, for example, she would never expose or reveal herself in such an honest way. Sera no longer has to build a wall around herself; Ben also, knowing her honest self, does not take advantage of her, furthering Sera's comfort with Ben (a symbiotic relationship of honesty: one's honesty feeds the other's honesty).

In the bathroom, while sitting on the toilet, Sera notes that she is tired of being alone. Once again, as proof of the truthfulness of the statement, notice where Sera says it—in an exposed place. By the final act of the film, after Sera repeats Ben's wife's actions and kicks him out, she realizes, after a series of tragedies, that she is lonely without Ben (she is lonely without someone whom she can be honest with; also, observe that her "confessionals," or honesty monologues, with the psychologist off-screen take place after she has lost Ben for the final time; she still requires the "honesty relationship," but this time it is with a paid professional. Now *she* is the client). After she is raped, beaten, and dispatched from her residence, she wanders the streets of Las Vegas aimlessly. During a montage of lights and glitter in the city, the audience sees an important two-word phrase in bright lights for only a second.

If the bathroom scene encapsulates key characterizations of the film, then the words on the bright Las Vegas sign point to a major theme: "Unfinished Business." Every character in the film, not just Sera and Ben, seems to have unfinished business. Yuri is not yet finished monopolizing Sera's body for financial gain; at Ben's hotel,

---

[*] We see similar bathroom-is-truth shots in the clever *This is 40*, but those are more for comedic effect—toilet humor, if you will.

the checkout attendant is seemingly never finished giving keys and explaining the procedures of the hotel to his patrons; Ben, of course, is perpetually unfinished killing himself; and Sera is unfinished with Ben, the most obvious meaning of the message at that moment in the film.

We can also denote "Unfinished Business" to refer to Ben's unyielding consumption of alcohol and Sera's unceasing prostitution after Ben's death. Despite her "angelic" impression on Ben, he still continues his plan to drink himself to death, and he succeeds; despite her "mother's love" of Ben, Sera continues her practice of the world's oldest profession; thus, we can argue effectively that there is a constancy of character with both Ben and Sera: Ben did not change his plans and Sera did not change hers despite their paths intersecting. Although Ben was only footnote in Sera's life, at least he brought to her, and, equivalently, she brought to him, for a short time, a sense of honesty and happiness—the two qualities most absent from each of their lives.

(1999)

# 63.

## THE FRENCH REVOLUTION: A REVIEW OF *BREATHLESS* AND *JULES AND JIM*

The French New Wave critics and filmmakers such as Godard, Chabrol, Rohmer, Rivette, and Truffaut all wished for audiences to actively appreciate the construction of a film, not only its narrative content. *Breathless* (1959), directed by Godard, radically explores and diametrically opposes "conventional" filmmaking methods (up till that time), especially in its audio-visual style and some parts of its narrative structure. However, it is the later film *Jules and Jim* (1962) by Truffaut that offers the more "reasonable" mainstream-viewer watchable film product, replete with only the subtlest of cues of the radicalism of Godard's work.

*Jules and Jim*, though directly dependent on *Breathless*'s breakthrough mise-en-scene and narrative form, is ultimately a more successful film; while Godard's movie functions more as an experiment (consciously seeking, at every possible opportunity, a chance to break the then-conventional laws of the cinema), Truffaut's is more relaxed, and uses the New Wave films' "awareness" of being a constructed art form to its narrative and entertainment advantage, rather than serving as a liability. Let us first explore *Breathless*'s neo-mise-en-scene and then detail *Jules and Jim*'s greater effectiveness in utilizing these revolutionary techniques.

Instead of opening with an establishing long shot of Paris, *Breathless* begins with a tight close-up of a woman reading a newspaper. Immediately the audience's expectations are disrupted; without establishing the space and location of the movie, the viewer is forced to negotiate a seemingly disrupted flow (even though it is only the beginning of the movie, the viewers come into the film with a set of expectations; in this case, not presenting an establishing shot disrupts the normal flow of expectation and forces the audience to take note of the form and structure of the filmmaking itself, perhaps at the expense of a suspension of disbelief); next, there is a medium shot of a man reading the newspaper. Suddenly, the movie cuts to a medium shot of a woman. Clearly, she is not in the same visual space as the man; she has city traffic behind her. Because we cannot clearly perceive her distance with respect to the man in the previous shot, there is a serious spatial disorientation invoked.

However, how can we assume that there is any type of spatial relationship at all between the man and woman? The issue must be explored in some detail, because it is at the root of New Wave assumptions about the audience.

First, let's agree that the juxtaposition of the two shots (the man and the woman) leads the viewer to link the two individuals in some way, since human beings are natural pattern-seekers, actively looking for function and relationships from form.

Second, Godard does not break the axis of action; if the man and woman were not in the same space, and the filmmaker wished to cue the audience about the spatial discontinuity between them, he would perhaps break the 180-degree line. The line is not broken, though, in these two opening shots, and we therefore assume that there is a spatial relationship between the two characters; thus, Godard, by using a Classical Hollywood Narrative rule that subconsciously forms viewers' expectations about movie space (even if the viewers cannot explicitly define the rule), has "bridged" the audience to understanding this altered form of moviemaking. Godard realizes that he cannot create a film *completely* independent from classical narrative and mise-en-scene techniques; he uses *old* methods to help us deal with the *new* inherent expectations, thereby giving us a frame of reference (the standard techniques) we can utilize to understand this new film form. Within the first few seconds of *Breathless*, the viewer understands Godard's game plan—he will introduce new mise-en-scene, but generally base it on older mise-en-scene techniques with which the audience is familiar.

Several scenes later, after we learn that the man in those opening shots is named Michel and the woman is named Patricia, another new mise-en-scene style is introduced. In a low-angle tracking shot, the camera follows the two characters down a crowded French city street. An absence of sound (with the exception of the characters' conversation and Patricia's "New York City Herald" shouts) accompanies the scene (perhaps to emphasize that we are in Michel and Patricia's world; *Leaving Las Vegas* [1995], for instance, also cuts the background din on most scenes to explicitly portray Ben and Sera's life with no outside interruptions).

The long take of Patricia and Michel has an almost mathematical-like parallelism to it; the camera tracks forward with a medium long-shot of the couple walking away from the camera and their backs facing it; after a lengthy conversation, they turn around and walk toward the camera (the camera reverses and tracks backward) and, eventually, Patricia and Michel are in medium shot range, facing the camera. Godard has cued the audience to expect long, dialogue-laced shots with lots of camera movement and little action; these shots will, with some frequency, reappear in *Breathless*.

Of course, making the scene one long take instead of numerous short shots pieced together adds to the realism of the environment; a stage-play-like feel is given to the proceedings. In this instance, because *Breathless* takes a more "gritty" approach to filming the two characters' conversation (analogous to a documentary), the shot is more reminiscent of, let's say, the Michael Moore "documentary" (and the scare quotes around the word are blisteringly appropriate) *Roger and Me* (1989) or the silly Al Pacino vehicle *Looking for Richard* (1996) or the absolutely amazingly edited and shot Orson Welles project *F for Fake* (1973) than of a strictly fictional narrative.

Godard employs other documentary-style shots in the film. For example, Michel's journey though the bank makes use of a handheld camera tracking shot. The lighting in the film also appears unplanned or lacking in artifice, and therefore akin to a documentary. The audience is cued to believe in the reality of characters' situations because of the realistic "feel" of the aesthetics.

Yet Godard does not entirely conform to a documentary style approach. The frequency of jump cuts implies discontinuous action and unrealistic events; in "real life," there are no jump cuts, and, as we would expect, documentaries by and large do not have a large number of them.

Godard's jump cuts are different from standard-fare jump cuts for a single significant reason: Although there are asynchronous visuals, there is synchronous audio. An excellent example is found in the couple's car trips. In a canted close-up of Patricia in Michel's automobile, there are several jump cuts (which have relatively different visual images [of the background behind Patricia, which changes to signify time has passed] but have synchronous dialogue between the two characters; in other words, the conversation is not disjoint just because the visuals are disjoint). The jump cuts serve to accelerate the narrative along without leaving the audience members confused (Godard does not break the Classical cinematic conventions here with character thought processes). Near the beginning of the film, the director presents Michel's ambitions in one scene composed of several shots. Michel, wearing his gangster-like hat and apparel, stares at a movie poster of Humphrey Bogart, also dressed as a gangster; taking in Bogart's expression and mannerism, Michel subtly cants his face to better imitate the American star. Of course, the audience assumes that Michel believes he is a gangster in the model of the unrealistic gangster film world; also, we assume, at least initially, that he is a shallow presence, as two-dimensional as the poster of Bogart himself. Similar "character defining shots" have appeared in movies before *Breathless* (*Citizen Kane* [1941] is a good example); the technique is not new, and certainly not original; Godard adds nothing to it.

Godard structures the film (as stated before) analogous to a cinematic experiment; in other words, many features of the film exist for their own sake, not necessarily to further the audience's enjoyment or understanding of the film. In a "scene" that stretches on for almost an hour, Godard, essentially in real time, uses the camera to explore Patricia and Michel's ever-changing relationship. Although it is perhaps misplaced to criticize this segment of the film since it does indeed further the character development, the ends simply do not justify the means. Godard appears to use this "realistic" real-time demonstration of the characters in Michel's apartment to display his newfound New Wave narrative techniques. However, what the audience is left with is a mostly boring, excessive dialogue fest that relegates potentially significant character lines to a monotonous level. It's worse than watching a single shot of a stage play. Godard sacrifices entertainment value to show off with a real-time stylistic narrative device.

And it is because of Godard's occasional lapses of directorial judgment, in particular his need to insert unique mise-en-scene techniques ostensibly just for their own sake, that elevates *Jules and Jim*, Truffaut's complementary work, to a superior level; Truffaut does not use the New Wave's new techniques simply to demonstrate that he can, as Godard frequently does; instead, the director employs the methods at targeted points to further a form-content relationship, embellish the audience's understanding of the characters, or add to the aesthetic pleasure of watching the film (yes, we could argue that Godard's insertion of mise-en-scene and narrative techniques add to the "aesthetic pleasure" of watching the film, but most mainstream movie audiences probably would not appreciate the experimental-like quality of the techniques).

*Breathless* is the training ground for *Jules and Jim.* Only several minutes into Truffaut's movie, the viewer notices that, visually, it is more cohesive and smooth than Godard's work (if the audience is explicitly comparing the two films, as I am here). Instead of giving us a potentially confusing situation (as *Breathless* does to begin the film), Truffaut ensures our understanding of the two title characters by presenting us with a montage sequence coupled with narrative exposition of Jules and Jim's friendship.

Is Truffaut assuming the audience is ignorant, unlike Godard, who assumes the audience will make the causal connections between Patricia and Michel as the film progresses? Probably not, because the exposition has the fascinating quality of relaying to the viewer seemingly significant facts about Jules and Jim, yet simultaneously telling us nothing of importance. It is not imperative, as the viewer later discovers, to know the history of their friendship; instead, it is important to understand their character motivations, which the narrative exposition does not explain or discuss. Truffaut has, in a way, tricked the audience; unlike Godard, who attempts to disorientate and orientate the viewer at the same time in the opening shots (to show that, for the rest of the film, the viewer must pay attention to the *form* of the movie), Truffaut is subtle with his intentions. Instead of visually altering our expectations (with us realizing it, as Godard does), he narratively alters our expectations (subtly, likely without us realizing it). He has carefully given us a new set of expectations about the narrative without forcing us to openly pay attention to these new expectations.

He also creatively plays with Jules' and Jim's love motivations early in the film, once again though the use of (this time directly meaningful) exposition. Unlike Godard, who uses a relatively standard technique of displaying a character's thoughts and desires (the poster of gangster Bogart, for instance), Truffaut employs the jump cut visual style. Through the use of narration and asynchronous visual space and synchronous audio (the narrator's voice), the camera quickly shows multiple angles of a beautiful head of a statue that both Jules and Jim fall in love with. The narrator says, "Jules and Jim are gripped by the same face on the statue. They will pursue such a face...." Seconds later, in nearly the same sequence of shots used on the statue, the camera finds Catherine, a woman bearing a significant resemblance to the statue; there is a form-content relationship utilized with the jump cuts. The audience is first conditioned by Truffaut to understand the jump cuts to signify a beautiful object, like the statue; next, the director capitalizes on his audience "training" by paralleling the shot sequence with Catherine's first on-screen images. The form-content relationship holds, and we instantly understand, without even the need for seeds of narration, that Jules and Jim are taken by this beautiful woman.

Later, after Jules and Jim establish a friendship with Catherine, they decide, spontaneously, to race her across the bridge. (This famous scene, among several others in the film, is brilliantly parodied in the Sixpence None the Richer black and white music video of their hit song "Kiss Me.") Of course, there is an obvious form-content relationship here. Catherine's side-view close-up on-screen as she is running signifies her fleeting nature and desire to run away from all relationships and commitments; her premature start of the race denotes her willingness to do anything to win; and her victory (despite her cheating start) indicates her need for attention. Although not entirely unconventional, the race scene lets us understand (somewhat ironically) Catherine more wholly than the other two main characters in the film. Many of her subsequent actions though the narrative come as no surprise to the audience after this deliberate form-content scene.

In Godard's film, sequences of action appear to occur spontaneously without a firm logic behind them. In Truffaut's, though, there seemingly exists a contradiction: spontaneous, random events occur with a clear logical foundation. Consider Catherine's jump into the water. Completely random (the audience should not be able to predict such an action), it is entirely justifiable; because Catherine has lost the attention of Jules and Jim for an instant, she captures it back by "spontaneously" making herself wet. Because of the race scene that preceded this one, the audience accepts her behavior; there is order in her seemingly chaotic actions.

The Great War suddenly grasps Jules and Jim away from Catherine for several years. Because of the historical context of the film, the random nature of that draft is logical as well. Notice that Jules must fight for the German army and Jim for the French; also observe that after the war, the two remain friends. Without getting into a debate about the political feelings of Truffaut, we can make a generalization that in this film, at least, characters' friendships are more important than allegiances to nation states (similarly, consider Hitchcock's *Topaz* [1969]).

After the war, Jim decides to visit Jules in Germany; Catherine waits for Jim at the German train station. Throughout the movie, we revisit the train station, usually with an overhead shot. The repeated use of the shot allows the viewer to quickly reorient spatially. Thus, the overhead shot functions not only as an establishing shot, but also, because it is repeated with some frequency, as a spatial marker for the audience.

When Jim finally arrives at Jules' cottage, they embrace. Truffaut freezes the frame of Jim and Jules' embrace for a split-second. Superficially, the freeze-frame ensures that the viewer will fully appreciate the moment of the reunion; however, the freeze-frame here is used to show that something is not quite right in their relationship anymore. The war has changed both of them; the frozen image is a link between the relationship that once was and the new hardships that they must endure forthwith.

Jim enters the house with Catherine and Jules. With the use of a single sound, Truffaut portrays the tension inherent in the scene. Jules, Catherine, and Jim are all in the living room of the cottage, and Jules swings back and forth on his rocking chair. There is no dialogue for at least a minute. All the audience hears is the rhythmic noise of the squeaky chair, over and over again. Jules, Jim, and Catherine struggle to find words to say to each other while the rocking chair does all of the talking. (This scene will recur several more times in the film.)

Everyone has changed—or have they? Both Jim and Jules are still infatuated with Catherine, even though Jules is (currently) married to her. Catherine, although appearing mature (and not engaging in overtly frivolous activities, such as jumping into lakes) also has not changed her attention-seeking motivations. The ominous narration tells us that "Jim felt something was wrong with Jules's family, but he avoided talking about it." The peaceful countryside setting serves as an effective counterpoint to the tensions between the characters; Jules and Jim both desire Catherine, whereas Catherine merely desires the feeling of being wanted.

Many months pass, and Jim decides (after liaisons with Catherine) to move into Jules' house with her. The ominous narration continues: "Life was a vacation for everyone. But happiness was wearing off." In a remarkable shot, the audience observes what the narrator speaks of. We see a medium-long shot of Jim, apparently bored and unhappy, and in the background, hear two people laughing. The camera dollies upward, stops at the second floor window of the cottage, and focuses on Catherine seducing Jules, and then dollies back downward to Jim.

The film has evolved into a protracted essay on the love triangle between the three main characters. *Jules and Jim* is relatively relaxed in its presentation of three people that apparently have nothing else to do but spend entire days peacefully pining after each other.

Jim, though, must return to France to tell Gilberte, his former love interest, that he is going to marry Catherine. In an interesting shot designed purely for comic effect, the "Train Whistle Girl" (seen once very early in the film) meets up with Jim at a restaurant and delivers to him a monologue at a rapid pace. She is blocked from the audience's view several times by other people who wish to speak to Jim (and Jim, when these other individuals come and talk to him, totally ignores the girl). The comedy is in the form-content relationship; the visuals reinforce her insignificance and utter repulsiveness to Jim; she is masked from us because she is literally too repugnant a sight to behold. (The scene also recalls the physical comedy of placement present in the *Lumière Shorts*.)*

After more exchanges between loves, Catherine craves the attention of Jim once again. In a shot vaguely reminiscent of Hitchcock's *Family Plot* (1976), the viewer observes a high angle long shot of Catherine in her car weaving around trees in circles, while Jim watches through his apartment window. The form-content relationship is strong here as well; her motions symbolize her cyclical swapping of Jules and Jim. She travels far but gets nowhere fast.

Next, in a bizarre scene, Jim confronts Catherine about their failed marriage (and her failed pregnancy). "You tried to change me," he says. "I will marry Gilberte." Obviously, Catherine wants both Jules and Jim at her continuous disposal. "What about me!" she shouts. Then, Catherine pulls out a gun and Jim struggles to gain possession of it. The camera moves into a tight shot of their hands, desperately clawing at the metallic weapon. In order to un-

---

* Speaking of the Lumière brothers, legend has it that when audiences first saw *L'Arrivée d'un train en gare de La Ciotat* (1896), mass panic erupted: people just weren't ready for the illusion of motion pictures.

derstand the motivation for this shot, we must recall the New Wave movement's foundations.

Although the New Wave did make a break with conventional cinema in the late 1950s, New Wave directors did consider several directors in the American studio system auteurs, or authors of films. These auteurs were thought to put their own personal stamp on a film independent of the time period or studio system they worked for. Thus, because there were several admired directors engaged in the Classical Hollywood Style, some New Wave directors consciously borrowed from them.

Truffaut, in the pistol scene with Jim and Catherine, has clearly borrowed from Hitchcock's and Billy Wilder's shooting techniques (both men were considered auteurs). A similar weapon-struggling scene occurs in Hitchcock's *Dial M for Murder* (1953) and Wilder's *Double Indemnity* (1944). Truffaut also had a deep admiration for Hitchcock—after all, he wrote the authoritative book *Hitchcock*, based on his many hours of one-on-one interviews with the Master.

Catherine, throughout the movie, is rarely shown in close-up; perhaps this is to keep her beauty and motivations more of a mystery to us (and implicitly show us that she is a mystery to Jules and Jim as well). But in that last shot of Catherine driving her car into the water (with Jim in it), she is shown in close-up. Perhaps because she has finally acquired her target (Jim) and found her purpose (eliminating Jim, the one man who has finally decided he's had enough of her), she is no longer mysterious to us; the close-up exposes her. In the beginning of the film, Catherine jumps into the lake to gain Jim and Jules's attention; by the end of the film, things have degraded for her to the point where she has to kill Jim by driving into a lake to get his attention—talk about diminishing returns! Catherine's attention-seeking actions symmetrically bookend *Jules and Jim*.

In an ending that perhaps cheats audience expectations, Jim and Catherine are rapidly burned and put into a mausoleum. Finally, the free spirit Catherine, in the form of ashes, is trapped and contained in an urn; ironically, it is Jules, the man with apparently the least amount of control over the woman, who puts her into the vault. The narrator sarcastically states, "She wanted her ashes set free in the wind, but that was not allowed." Perhaps the narration plays more poetically in French.

Both *Jules and Jim* and *Breathless* are breakthrough films; this is not in dispute. However, *Jules and Jim* succeeds by using a liberal dosage of New Wave mise-en-scene methods coupled with an entertaining narrative. *Breathless* only truly functions as an examination of the possibilities of New Wave cinema and the audience's reaction to the new techniques. Both films prove that audiences have the capability of not only completing Eisenstein's famous filmic equation, A+B = C, but of understanding even more sophisticated cinema.

(1999)

## 64.

# Fifty Years

## Of James Bond Films

Former British naval intelligence officer Ian Fleming penned his first James Bond novel, *Casino Royale*, in 1952. Fleming wrote a number of novels and short stories about the secret agent, eventually capturing the attention of President John F. Kennedy—who listed *From Russia, With Love* as one of his ten favorite books. With that big-name endorsement came a surge in popularity. Putting James Bond on the silver screen was the next logical step.

So, in 1961, Fleming sold the film rights to Bond to producer Harry Saltzman, who formed Eon Productions with fellow producer Albert "Cubby" Broccoli. They tapped a little-known actor named Sean Connery to play the lead part in *Dr. No.*

More than fifty years, twenty-five films, and billions of dollars in revenue later, most people around the world have seen at least one James Bond film. So let's take a quick (and completely unauthorized) look at each in turn.* The following film reviews are out of four stars.

---

* Two key books leaned on for this chapter: *The Incredible World of 007* by Lee Pfeiffer and Phillip Lisa, and *The Complete James Bond Movie Encyclopedia* by Steven Jay Rubin.

### *Dr. No* (1962) ★★★½

**The movie that launched a franchise.** James Bond (Sean Connery, in a star-making performance), initially assigned to investigate the disappearance of a British agent, stumbles upon Dr. No (Joseph Wiseman), a leading member of the terrorist organization SPECTRE, who is out to destroy an American space rocket. Watching this movie now, the most surprising scene occurs when Bond and Honey Rider (Ursula Andress)[*] walk to their dinner engagement with Dr. No: the secret agent admits to being nervous. For all of the later, well-meaning attempts to craft a more "vulnerable" and "sensitive" Bond, this is the secret agent at his most human—and most exposed. Throughout *Dr. No*, he must rely on his wits and ingenuity, rather than silly gadgets or glib retorts, to escape danger.[†] James Bond has never been more real, or accessible.

### *From Russia with Love* (1963) ★★★

**An attempt to quickly capitalize on the success of *Dr. No*.** SPECTRE again makes its presence felt in this complicated Cold War thriller involving Soviet spies and ruthless assassins. The action scenes are effectively executed, if not always original.[‡] *FRWL* is solid entertainment—and Connery is always a pleasure to watch—although the film is not as good as its predecessor.

### *Goldfinger* (1964) ★★★★

**The quintessential James Bond film.** Everything's firing on all cylinders here: Connery is relaxed and yet ruthless as Bond, the main villain has the means and the motive to carry out a massive crime,[§] the sets are spectacular,[*] the gadgets are not only other-

---

[*] Though beautiful, she wasn't allowed to speak for herself—Andress's voice was dubbed. Fans had to wait until *Casino Royale* (1967) to hear her actually speak to James Bond.

[†] One great example: Bond's fighting off of a tarantula in his bed. This scene is still terrifying to watch.

[‡] The helicopter chase is lifted from *North by Northwest*'s crop duster sequence, for instance.

[§] Goldfinger (Gert Fröbe) speaks of his crime as an achievement of the highest order. Coincidently, Fröbe would also play villain Baron Bomburst in *Chitty Chitty Bang Bang* (1968), a film produced by Cubby Broccoli with a script by Roald Dahl (who also wrote the script for *You Only Live Twice*) based off the book written by...Ian Fleming. *Chitty*, his only children's novel, was first

worldly but serve logical plot-driven purposes,[†] the supporting characters are well-developed and memorable,[‡] and the dialogue is highly quotable.[§] *Goldfinger*, a mega-success in its day, is still the most consistently entertaining movie in the series.

### *Thunderball* (1965) ★★★

**A disappointing follow-up to *Goldfinger* is nevertheless a great movie.** The threat is very serious: SPECTRE executes a clever scheme to steal two nuclear warheads, all to extort many millions of dollars from governments around the world. Too many underwater scenes, which drag on for too long, hurt *Thunderball*'s pacing. But Sean Connery is as charming, and deadly, as ever. And Adolfo Celi as Ernst Stavro Blofeld's Number 2 is not only ruthless and sinister but also, unlike Goldfinger, represents a credible physical danger to Bond. *Thunderball* is perhaps the final time Connery treats the role of James Bond with respect.

### *You Only Live Twice* (1967) ★★

**Some iconic moments mask how truly mediocre this film is.** By *YOLT*, Sean Connery had had enough of the role—and it shows.[**] He never seems engaged in the performance. Luckily, there are plenty of one-of-a-kind gadgets (such as Little Nellie,[††] the pint-sided helicopter), exotic locations (such as the islands of Japan), interesting characters (such as Tiger Tanaka), and wild set pieces (such as Blofeld's volcano lair) to distract. Nonetheless, a Bond film rises or falls on the strength of the lead's performance, and *YOLT* is dragged down by Connery's disinterest.

---

published in 1964—the year *Goldfinger* was released. Ken Hughes, who directed *Chitty*, was one of the directors of *Casino Royale*. Everything connects!

[*] The producers weren't allowed access to the Fort Knox gold reserve, although you'd never know it.

[†] Although Bond is initially credulous at the Aston Martin's ejector seat, he makes use of it at an opportune time.

[‡] The most famous of which is of course Shirley Eaton's Jill Masterson, who meets her end painted in gold. Also famous: Oddjob (Harold Sakata), the man with the world's most dangerous hat, and Pussy Galore, because of her name.

[§] "Do you expect me to talk?" "No, Mr. Bond, I expect you to die!"

[**] At a promotional press conference in Japan, he refused to wear a hairpiece.

[††] Cameraman John Jordan lost a limb filming the small aircraft. But he would later shoot the bobsled chase in *OHMSS*.

## *Casino Royale* (1967) ★★½

**Judged as a James Bond movie, it is a creative failure.** To be fair, though, *Casino Royale* has wonderfully entertaining set pieces, a legendary musical score by Burt Bacharach, and a cast for the ages: Peter Sellers, David Niven, Ursula Andress, and Orson Welles,[*] among many others. Sellers is not very good in the role of "James Bond"—the scare quotes are needed since Sellers is not really Bond, just one of many British agents assigned the name James Bond to confuse SMERSH (similar to SPECTRE), a bizarre non-canonical plot device that came about namely because famed producer Charles K. Feldman couldn't manage to snag Sean Connery to reprise the role[†]—mostly because Sellers was chasing after his estranged wife Britt Ekland, a future Bond girl in the silly *The Man with the Golden Gun*. Sellers has a couple funny bits, though, especially opposite Andress. Far more effective is Woody Allen: every one of his scenes is genuinely funny, largely because he rewrote them all himself—though, as he requested, is uncredited as doing so. By the way: without *Casino Royale* and *You Only Live Twice*, there are no *Austin Powers* movies.

## *On Her Majesty's Secret Service* (1969) ★★★★

**This unconventional Bond film is a masterpiece.** Like many great films, this one was critically panned when released and took quite a bit of time to be fully appreciated.[‡] The plot is both realistic and still topical: Bond has to combat the threat of biological warfare. The acting is uniformly high-caliber: Diana Rigg is Bond's best-ever leading lady; Telly Savalas puts a firm stamp on the role of Blofeld; and Australian George Lazenby, a former model, is much better than his critics give him credit for, putting a refreshing and vulnerable spin on the superspy.[§] And composer John Barry

---

[*] Welles and Sellers hated each other so much that they refused to act together on set. Watch the baccarat game closely: clever editing makes it *appear* they are together on the screen, but they are not.

[†] He also couldn't get Eon to produce the picture, leading him to reframe Ian Fleming's first novel as a satire. More than five directors were employed to get the job done.

[‡] Another example of this: *Vertigo* (1958).

[§] A plot idea floated to explain James Bond's new appearance—after all, up to this point, audiences had only known Connery in the role—was plastic surgery (an idea resurrected, sort of, for *Diamonds are Forever*). But plastic sur-

truly outdoes himself. To help celebrate Bond's fiftieth anniversary, the respected *Double-O-Seven Magazine* ranked all the films based on subscriber poll results. *OHMSS* landed in the top spot.

### *Diamonds are Forever* (1971) ★★½

**A return to Sean Connery also brings an unfortunate return to silliness.** Although many set pieces are nice—in particular, the extended Las Vegas chase sequence*—the plot is riddled with holes.† Charles Gray is too tepid and timid as Blofeld,‡ and Jill St. John's Tiffany Case sheds IQ points faster than articles of clothing. But Connery, who, when he agreed to do one more stint as Bond became the then highest paid actor of all time, smoothly and convincingly eases back in to the role—and is always a pleasure to watch.§ He elevates the film, despite the abject stupidity surrounding him.

### *Live and Let Die* (1973) ★★★

**Roger Moore's debut, though dated, is a minor classic.** Moore has the unenviable task of replacing the legend (again), but he mostly succeeds here because he doesn't try to imitate Connery. (For instance, Moore never once orders a "vodka martini, shaken, not stirred.") *Live and Let Die*, with the exception of its amazing McCartney title song, never quite feels cinematic; rather, the movie plays more like an early '70s cop drama and has a very un-James Bond-like score to match (no John Barry for the first time). The absence of Q (Desmond Llewelyn) is a bit inexcusable here; perhaps his absence is due to the filmmakers consciously making every attempt to distance their new Bond from the old one(s). To date,

---

gery wouldn't give audiences enough credit. As Roger Moore has noted, there have been thousands of Tarzans.

* One of the most infamous editing errors of all time: Bond's red Mustang enters a tight alleyway on its right two wheels and exits it on its left two.

† To take just one: Why extort the world for millions of dollars using a space satellite made of diamonds when Blofeld has already smuggled millions of dollars' worth of diamonds needed to construct the satellite to begin with?

‡ Late in the movie, Blofeld informs Bond that "science was never my strong suit." But in *OHMSS*, recall, Blofeld was busy concocting biological-warfare stews. (The actor Charles Gray played another character, Henderson, in *You Only Live Twice*—he unforgivably fumbles Bond's vodka martini drink order—and is stabbed to death right in front of Bond.)

§ He has his best-ever fight sequence in an elevator early in the film.

this is the only Bond film with an African American villain, played by Yaphet Kotto, and he's very effective in the role—as is Jane Seymour, in her star-making turn as Solitaire.

### *The Man with the Golden Gun* (1974) ★½

**What a long, strange trip this is.** For the second movie in a row, James Bond doesn't appear until after the opening credits. (No confidence in your leading man, Cubby and Harry?) Instead, in *Golden Gun*, we see a strange house of horrors: a carnival-type maze of death, created for the pleasure of Scaramanga (Christopher Lee). And although some of the performances are memorable—Lee's and Maud Adams's, in particular—Britt Ekland is terribly unconvincing as Mary Goodnight, who is supposed to be a critical character but is quickly rendered forgettable. Also forgettable: Hervé Villechaize as Oddjob-knockoff Nick Nack. Other than the fantastic twirling car jump,[*] this movie can be best summed up by Bond's reaction to a local wine label: Phu-Yuck.

### *The Spy Who Loved Me* (1977) ★★★½

**This is Moore's finest Bond movie.** After a long hiatus, Cubby Broccoli (sort of) rebooted the franchise with this thriller.[†] Everything from the opening ski jump off the mountain top,[‡] to the submarine Lotus Esprit,[§] to the larger-than-life Jaws (played by Richard Kiel), to the outsized plot (starting a new world, under the sea), to the acting (Roger Moore's found the right tempo for the role) works—and it all works awfully well. Director Lewis Gilbert helms his first Bond movie since *You Only Live Twice* and the design and execution[**] of the picture are nearly flawless.

---

[*] Computers helped to calculate the proper speed and trajectory of the AMC Matador Coupe. Only one take was required, though the stunt is partially ruined by the overlaid whistling sound effect.

[†] Producer Harry Saltzman exited the Bond franchise a year after *The Man with the Golden Gun* was released.

[‡] For which stuntman Rick Sylvester was paid a cool one hundred grand.

[§] Lotus's campaign for getting the car in the movie? The company parked some then-new Esprits at the studio lot. Although beautiful, the cars quickly proved to be unreliable.

[**] Speaking of execution, Roger Moore got seriously injured during a scene in which Curd Jürgens "shoots" him underneath a long dining room table. Ex-

### *Moonraker* (1979) ★½

**The attempt to remake *The Spy Who Loved Me* is anemic.** Lewis Gilbert is back to direct. Jaws is back. A megalomaniac is again bent on the destruction of the world—and the creation of a new one (this time in space instead of under the sea). This is Roger Moore's *Thunderball*: Bigger, but not at all better. *Moonraker* is the apotheosis of creative failure.* Measured in terms of the box office, however, *Moonraker* was a stunning success; amazingly, its world-wide gross total was not exceeded until 1995's *Goldeneye*.

### *For Your Eyes Only* (1981) ★★★

**A solid thriller that ranks among the best Bonds.** Producers thought Moore might not return as Bond, so, in order to establish a link between the "new" Bond and the old ones, *FYEO* begins with Bond visiting his dead bride's grave—the second and last time the Countess would be referred to in Roger Moore's oeuvre. Bond also nicely dispatches of Blofeld, though he is unnamed,† before the opening credits. *FYEO* is mostly serious, somber fare, involving a Cold War revenge plot and multiple double-crosses. Moore is asked to do more than usual here, and he succeeds with aplomb—this is his best performance in the role.

### *Octopussy* (1983) ★★

**A very silly movie that is occasionally entertaining.** It's much more fun than *Moonraker* to watch but nonetheless suffers from many of its same flaws: an uneven tone, a reliance on misplaced humor, and a paint-by-numbers plot. Also, the film's title is something of a cheat since, unfortunately, Octopussy (Maud Adams, in her second Bond movie role) ultimately isn't a critical-to-plot character. Perhaps this movie's biggest claim to fame is its involvement in the so-called "Battle of the Bonds." See the *Never Say Never Again* review below for more information.

---

plosives went off prematurely leaving Moore with "three holes, where most men normally have two," according to the actor.

* To be fair, the first hour or so of the movie works pretty well. Two cases in point: the centrifuge scene and the pheasant hunt. But the script's silliness gets to be so overwhelming that it ultimately suffocates the picture.

† Thanks to a variety of legal machinations over the rights to *Thunderball*, Eon Productions couldn't use the name SPECTRE (SPecial Executive for Counter-intelligence, Terrorism, Revenge and Extortion) again until very recently.

### *Never Say Never Again* (1983) ★★★

**A much better Bond sendoff for Sean Connery than *Diamonds are Forever.*** Not produced by Eon, *NSNA* has its roots in a legal dispute over the rights to *Thunderball.* Connery was convinced to play the secret agent once more,[*] setting up a "Battle of the Bonds"—*Octopussy* and *NSNA* were both supposed to arrive during the summer of 1983, but this film was delayed until that fall. *NSNA* is a more contemporary remake of *Thunderball*, with nuclear warheads again being stolen, and both SPECTRE and Blofeld factor heavily into the plot. Connery, though older (he's about the same age as Moore), is light on his feet and as witty as ever. And Barbara Carrera is especially effective as an over-the-top foil.[†]

### *A View to a Kill* (1985) ★½

**Lots of missed opportunities doom this film.** Roger Moore stars in his seventh, and final, Bond film at the ripe old age of 56. But the problem isn't Moore—it's everything and everyone around him. The plot is a *Goldfinger* rip-off—with microchips being the prize instead of gold—which in and of itself doesn't ruin the film; after all, why not lift from one of the best Bond films? But Christopher Walken is awful, just awful, as Max Zorin, especially in one of his final scenes: he gratuitously guns down scores of his own employees, something that Roger Moore himself very much objected to. Grace Jones is miscast as May Day, and Tanya Roberts's Stacey Sutton is easily Bond's worst-ever leading lady. The special effects are seamless but one of them (the ski chase), like the car jump in *Golden Gun*, suffers from a soundtrack miscue: "California Girls," by the Beach Boys, is inexplicably piped in. *A View to a Kill* is a thoroughly forgettable motion picture.

### *The Living Daylights* (1987) ★★★

**A return to a more serious form.** Initially written to be a bit sillier, most of the script's jokes were excised to permit new James Bond Timothy Dalton to do what he does best: play it straight. And play it straight he does, much to the chagrin of those expect-

---

[*] The film's title comes from a comment Connery made years before in which he declared that he wouldn't ever play the role again.

[†] A character which she more or less reprises several years later on the hit soap *Dallas*.

ing a more fun, lighthearted romp through exotic worldwide locales. But Dalton is outstanding as Bond—likely closer to Ian Fleming's vision of the man than anyone else who ever played the role—and brings a seriousness and gravitas and sense of impending danger to every scene. The plot is complicated, but nowhere near the "incomprehensible" that some critics allege. Another change: Bond is (nearly) monogamous, probably because of the growing awareness of the AIDS epidemic by the end of the 1980s. For comparison, count how many women Bond beds, not even a decade prior, in the lackluster *Moonraker.*

***Licence to Kill* (1989): This film requires two reviews.**

The ★★ review: **Too much of a departure from the classic Bond formula yields too dark a film.** Whereas Moore, with an eye twinkle, a sly smile, or an eyebrow raise, would always signal to the audience that he's in on the joke, Dalton takes the role so seriously that he never once appears to be having fun. In addition, the main villain—Franz Sanchez (Robert Davi)—is simply a two-bit drug smuggler, not a megalomaniac bent on worldwide conquest, and thus doesn't belong as the centerpiece of a James Bond movie. Although the special effects are seamless, at times sequences go on for too long; for example, consider the tanker chase scene: much suspense is milked out of it because of its length. *Licence* (the British spelling of the word is used) was a box-office failure that led to a six-year hiatus between Bond movies.*

The ★★★½ review: **Perhaps the best Bond film since *OHMSS*, Timothy Dalton shines in a role tailor-made for his acting talents.** Although the main villain, Franz Sanchez (played brilliantly by Robert Davi), doesn't have designs on worldwide domination, he represents a lethal threat to Bond. And, this time, Bond actually has a personal motivation for going after him: revenge for the maiming of his friend and fellow spy Felix Leiter (David Hedison, the first actor to reprise the role). The effects are second-to-none, and the plot is always believable. Even Q (Des-

* *Licence to Kill* also suffers from a lackluster score. John Barry was scheduled to compose but fell ill—his throat effectively "exploded" on an airplane flight. Sadly, he would never again compose for a Bond film.

mond Llewelyn) gets in on the act, helping Bond in "the field" (as he called it way back in *Goldfinger*), with his biggest role to date. Although dark, this movie's fresh—we simply haven't seen such realistic brutality in a Bond movie before.*

### *GoldenEye* (1995) ★★★

**Pierce Brosnan's first film is also his best.** Named after Ian Fleming's estate and the first Bond movie in more than six years, *GoldenEye*, though flawed, has a number of great moments, and Brosnan fits very easily into the role—his take on Bond is a sort of "compromise" position between the playfulness of Moore and the sharper-edged Connery, although he is as good as neither. The plot: once a secret agent for MI6, Alec Trevelyan (Sean Bean)† believes that he was betrayed by Bond and seeks revenge. Famke Janssen as the wonderfully named Xenia Onatopp is especially entertaining, and Judi Dench's take on M is highly memorable (she will have a long run, as did Bernard Lee).

### *Tomorrow Never Dies* (1997) ★★

**A very creative story never really takes off.** A media mogul with plans for worldwide domination by starting a war between global powers—this sounds, on paper, like the outlines for a very promising Bond movie. But *Tomorrow Never Dies* repeatedly stalls, despite Jonathan Pryce's excellent hamming-it-up performance as mogul Elliot Carver. Perhaps the problem is Teri Hatcher as Carver's wife: she's completely unconvincing. Or maybe the problem is Michelle Yeoh as Wai Lin: the audience just doesn't buy her derring-do. Or perhaps the problem lies at the feet of Pierce Brosnan: he really phones it in this time, and a convincing James Bond is the one thing a good Bond film can't do without.

---

* One objection, though: at the conclusion of the film, Felix—though he has lost his legs and his wife to Sanchez—is simply *way* too happy when he reports to Bond via telephone that he'll be out of the hospital shortly. Perhaps it's because of all that morphine they gave him.

† Bean was once considered for the role of Bond. He, along with Michael Lonsdale and Jonathan Pryce, enjoys a Bond villains' reunion in the heist film *Ronin* (1998).

### *The World is Not Enough* (1999) ★★

**Several magical moments get buried in a sea of mediocrity.** Let's start with Christmas Jones, played by Denise Richards. Not since Tanya Roberts in *A View to a Kill* have we seen a Bond leading lady so miscast (although Teri Hatcher in *Tomorrow Never Dies* comes close). Next, the plot: *what?* And, finally, Robert Carlyle as main villain Renard is not particularly menacing or interesting. But several things about this film stand out. The main title score, by Garbage, is perhaps the best since *Live and Let Die*'s. Also, the opening pre-title sequence, which runs nearly twenty minutes, is tremendously effective: it almost serves as a stand-alone movie. And, last, the ski scene with Bond and Elektra King (Sophie Marceau) pays homage to a similar scene in *OHMSS*—and, though short, is lovely.

### *Die Another Day* (2002) ★

**Although this movie tries very hard, it's just plain awful.** *Die Another Day* commits a cardinal sin: it doesn't *look* good. The special effects are not convincing. And one gadget in particular, the invisible car,[*] is so stupid that I wouldn't be surprised to learn that masses of people walked out of the theaters at its moment of introduction to Bond by Q (unpardonably played by John Cleese, after Desmond Llewelyn's fatal car accident). The movie starts out strongly, though—Bond is captured and imprisoned in North Korea for a period of years, and MI6 effectively disowns him. The problem is, though, that, save for a few scenes, the psychological effects of Bond's capture and imprisonment are swept under the rug, as if the secret agent's some sort of robot and simply rebooted his personality. Perhaps Brosnan didn't quite have the acting chops necessary to pull off a convincingly tormented James Bond (neither does Halle Berry, who plays secret agent Jinx; unbelievably, the producers, for a short time, were considering filming a spinoff movie centering on Jinx).[†] Not so with Daniel Craig, however, who—after a four-year break—took the helm.

---

[*] I.e., the Aston Martin "Vanish." Not funny.

[†] And to think that Jinx was *this close* to being featured in a spin-off movie boggles the mind.

### *Casino Royale* (2006) ★★★½

**Rebooting was the right decision.** Although Daniel Craig's appointment to the role of James Bond was heavily criticized initially—there were even thousands of fans demanding the unconditional reinstatement of Pierce Brosnan—Craig acquits himself well on-screen and is, without a doubt, better than Brosnan.* This is a new Bond for the new millennium, taking many cues from the gritty, silent, and lethal Jason Borne. But perhaps the most impressive thing about *Casino Royale* is how it takes its time—things never feel rushed, characters are allowed to develop, suspense is permitted to build. Consider, as a good example, the poker game† of which Felix Leiter (Jeffrey Wright, who has played the role in more movies than any other actor) is a part: who figured there could be such breathtaking drama in a single turn of a card?

### *Quantum of Solace* (2008) ★

**The worst James Bond movie of all time.** Intended as a sequel to *Casino Royale*, the shortest Bond film completely falls flat largely because of its editing: chunks of the movie seem to have vanished, leaving confusion (on the part of the audience) in their wake. Daniel Craig does what he can here to salvage *Quantum*, but the damage has been done. Like *Golden Gun*, it was almost a franchise killer.

### *Skyfall* (2012) ★★★

**Another hiatus leads to another successful film.** Four years between movies, and fifty years since *Dr. No*, resulted in this minor classic, which is also the highest grossing Bond film to date. Sam Mendes (*American Beauty*) helms *Skyfall*, bringing a distinctive flair to the proceedings. Javier Bardem is perfect for the role of Silva, the twisted, revenge-seeking psychopath, and Judi Dench does her best work in the series—in fact, with her amount of screen time and the importance of her character to the plot, *Skyfall* might be more aptly described a Bond-M movie rather than just another

---

* In fact, in his book *Bond on Bond: Reflections on 50 years of James Bond Movies*, Roger Moore all but declares that not only is Craig better than Brosnan, Craig's the *best Bond ever*. Although Moore can be charmingly self-deprecating, such a serious statement is clearly not intended that way.

† Of course, James Bond's card game of choice is baccarat, but he can apparently clean up at poker as well.

Bond film. Perhaps *Skyfall* strays a little too far from the tried-and-true Bond formula,* but without innovation the series could not have—and would not have—survived.

(2013)

* Maurice Binder, who designed many of the original title credit sequences, also came up with the famous gun barrel opening. But why is the gun barrel sequence shown during the closing credits for the second consecutive movie?

# PART VI

# RUMINATIONS

# 65.

## Are We in Hell? A Short Treatise on Corporate Life

Some things need to be taken on faith alone. G.K. Chesterton, in his seminal Christian text *Orthodoxy*, said it best: to offer a slovenly defense, with apparent mathematical precision, "proving" the messianic qualities of Jesus,[*] is to wallow in the details.[†]

But proving Jesus is the Messiah is one thing; showing that working in the business world today is akin to hell—or at least a form of purgatory, an endless waiting room with no obvious merit—is another. The believer's fervor and fury may be needed, however, to articulate the truly hellish qualities of the corporate milieu. Like Paul and the early proponents of Christianity, promulgating this gospel of business-as-hell may be enlightening.

So let's pass this cup of knowledge around,[‡] letting the uninitiated partake in bread, wine, and cubicle sacraments aplenty. We've culled four synonyms for the term "hell"—*torture*, *torment*, *anguish*, and *misery*—and we will demonstrate that the distance between these monikers and the corporate environs is more of a gap than a chasm.

*Torture*: For those still not used to the gruesome images of torture that have emerged from Iraq,[§] claiming that staring at a com-

---

[*] Spoiler alert: according to Jewish liturgy, Jesus didn't even come close to fitting the bill.

[†] Of course, proof of any sort is impossible. See: scientific method, falsification. Check out Karl Popper while you're at it.

[‡] Lest the cup runneth over. Sorry, seemed like an appropriate place to drop that cliché in, with all these Biblical allusions everywhere.

[§] Or any other images of torture for that matter. To get a good idea of what traditional forms of torture are like—if you haven't experienced them—you may want to read Christopher Hitchens' article about waterboarding called "Believe Me, It's Torture" in *Vanity Fair*.

puter screen day-in and day-out is analogous to torture may seem a bit misguided. But repetition is a form of torture; like drops falling on one's head without end, or repeated lashings, the mental and the physical are closely intertwined when considering torture; after all, the objective of torture—if it can be called an objective—is to wear down the sufferer's body, mind, and soul, whether it be for questioning or sadistic pleasure. The sufferer is turned from aggressive to passive, from disagreeable to agreeable. In short, in order for a business to work, the minions must be minions—they must not be disagreeable or be capable of begetting chaos within the hierarchical order. Therefore, torture—through the *repetition* of commuting, the repetition of completing cyclical reports—is a must to keep us Epsilons on the straight and narrow track of functionality. A cog in the wheel must stay in the wheel.

*Torment*: If the business of America is business,[*] then the business of business is to torment its underlings into submission. This torment is manifested in many forms, but one of the most devious methods is built into the system[†]—let fellow employees annoy each other to no end; let the mice in the maze block one another's routes to the cheese, so to speak.[‡] The surreptitious planning of cubicle locations and designs facilitates this getting-on-each-other's-nerves organizational structure. For instance, if I am annoyed by my cubicle neighbor's unfortunate habits—such as talking out loud when no one else is there, sighing relentlessly, humming off-key, or unoriginally repeating salutations—there is no recourse for complaint short of alerting other coworkers of the madness over the

---

[*] Calvin Coolidge was prescient. Between afternoon naps, of course.

[†] But to call all of this a "system," or anything a "system," in any and all essays or books on whatever topic is just a convenient shorthand to say: I have no idea why these things are connected, and I don't feel like trying to figure out the causality or the webs of associations and connections, so let me attribute it all to the "system" of this or that and be done with it—because it sounds good and clean and self-explanatory. But isn't the connotation, isn't the meaning, lost when we link and describe every event or mechanism that isn't physical as a "system" or (worse) a "system of systems"? Isn't it all just a little too figurative? Seems like a nested doll of ciphers. But perhaps I'm just too shortsighted and obtuse to understand the latent subtleties of "the system." Oh well.

[‡] Compare this with *Who Moved My Cheese*, that disgusting paean to corporate acquiescence.

wall. But, of course, since everyone's annoyed with at least one other fellow employee, there's a virtual repository of complaints floating around the office. The venom that's spewed by employees about each other hardly falls into the rubric of mere office politics, but rather can be designated taxonomically as a kind of torment. Patience[*] is a skill in short supply, despite the downtime. And the startling abundance of downtime aids minions in spotting and taking note of others' quirks and unusual behaviors. Idle hands are the Devil's workshop,[†] after all.

*Anguish*: Also beyond the pale is that anguish of uncertainty, the tenuousness of our standing. Couldn't hell be constituted as a place one's too afraid to leave because of the consequences, despite it being far from an Endemic realm? The only thing worse than having this job is not having it—what kind of a way to live is that? That's not a pathological modus operandi but, instead, a realistic, sober approach to maintaining some kind of equilibrium in this inescapably awful setting. Satan himself couldn't have designed a better catch-22, and, as we've been arguing, he probably did design it.

*Misery*: All of the aforementioned categories of the hellish nature of work overlap, but misery, in all its forms, is perhaps the central organizing principle of our thesis. Corporate work, *ipso facto*, is misery, is punishment for any and every bad deed we've ever done since birth; it's a sort of karmic retribution, which also is a spot-on characterization of hell.[‡] Dante's *Inferno*? This is worse: imagine never quite knowing when it's going to end, and knowing that, when it does, you'll be too infirm or too feeble to reap the rewards of escape. Eternal damnation it might as well be: without seeing the end, it is for all intents and purposes eternal. Shakespeare wouldn't

---

[*] Patience has been called the art of hoping. Yet there is no hope in this milieu—and thus no patience, either. As Peter Gibbons from the comedy classic *Office Space* declares, "Human beings were not meant to sit in little cubicles staring at computer screens all day, filling out useless forms and listening to eight different bosses drone on about mission statements."

[†] A telling coincidence: most business cubicles are six feet wide, by six feet long, with walls anywhere from four to six feet high. Six-by-six-by-six: a sure sign of the Devil.

[‡] Although, instead of mixing metaphors here, we're sort of mixing religious traditions.

have known whether to categorize this narrative as tragedy or comedy, since it's a bit of both. Hell would be so funny if it wasn't so tragic, so tragic if it wasn't so funny. Misery loves company, and the company is misery—hence we complain. Perhaps we should pray.*

So faith isn't all that's needed to see the gravity of the situation: enumerating the consequences of slaving away in the corporate milieu is satisfactory. It's turned us into fallen angels.†

(2003)

---

* Prayer might not do any good here, though. Recall Ambrose Bierce's definition of prayer in *The Devil's Dictionary*: "To ask that the laws of the universe be annulled on behalf of a single petitioner confessedly unworthy." And, after all, those in the upper echelons of corporate power think us minions terribly unworthy.

† So workers of the world, unite! Just kidding, of course. But, it should be noted, the First World cannot simply expect the Third World to remain the Third World forever: as Thomas L. Friedman has documented in *The World is Flat* and elsewhere, the rising tide of globalization has increased prosperity—and standard-of-living expectations—to countries (teeming with pools of human talent) not heretofore used to the significant advantages of "progress," technological or otherwise: a rising tide lifting all boats. Such countries have had to fast-track the industrial revolution to arrive at a quasi-informational economy, frequently at the expense of the environment. Although luminaries like Al Gore have rightly argued for worldwide pollution restrictions to combat the climate crisis—proffering well-meaning proposals such as the ill-fated Kyoto Protocol—developing nations, on the one hand lacking the beefy infrastructure to have anything but economies of dependence on exporting goods to the First World which these top-tier nations won't subjugate their own workers to make (more accurately, having First World workers make such goods is not cost-effective), while on the other hand suffering through demographic explosions way above population replacement (shades of Thomas Malthus, whose overblown predictions of worldwide catastrophe were based on faulty population data from Benjamin Franklin; lesson here: predictions based on extrapolation are always dangerous), cannot be reasonably expected to worry about the environment when they wish to compete vigorously in a global free-market system. Regardless, the status quo is clearly unsustainable. So, as these developing nations shift to modern economies, who will be left to produce the goods and services that keep the First World afloat?

# 66.

## Culture: The Construction of Americanness

There is a "common" American culture, implicitly shared by most residents of the United States. Essentially, it is: work harder, achieve more, set higher goals, and most importantly, achieve upward social mobility. Most of these American cultural dictates imply a "strive to better one's self"; therefore, many Americans, enumerating the heroes of American culture, would be quick to list sports stars, accomplished presidents (though there aren't many), and successful entrepreneurs.

However, what happens to the American who, wishing to achieve the typical goals of the country's culture, is not physically in the norm, or standard, of the culture itself? Even in today's tremendously accommodating (as compared to the past) American society, there are latent, perhaps unspoken-of, standards that tend to mask accomplishments such an individual has made within the culture. Let me explain what I mean with some examples.

Consider the taxi driver in Ronald Takaki's *A Different Mirror* (1993). While journeying to a conference, a "racial divide" separated the driver and Takaki. The taxi driver noticed Takaki's non-colloquial accent. He asked Takaki the length of time he had resided in the United States. "With a strong southern drawl, he remarked: 'I was wondering because your English is excellent.'" There is irony here: Takaki was headed to a multiculturalism conference.

Takaki was born in America and lived here his entire life. So why does the taxi driver not accept the author as an American, but rather views him as an outsider? The taxi driver's "values are internalized. They provide security and contribute to a sense of personal and social identity... [he] feels threatened when confronted with others who live according to different conceptions...." (from Spradley and McCurdy, "Culture and the Contemporary World"). According to the taxi driver's superficial analysis, Mr. Takaki has "different conceptions" of living—he internally believes that all Americans should conform to a standard of "whiteness"; if that standard is not followed, then, according to the driver, that particular individual is not American, but foreign. However, as Takaki observes, "[O]ne-third of American people do not trace their origins to Europe." The norms of American society are changing; no longer is the European American male exclusively the standard with which to measure an American's background.

The lesson learned from the taxi driver (a man who, on the job, has talked to quite a few people) is more valuable to the author than all of the lectures he attends at the multicultural conference; instead of enumerating the potential problems of integrating cultures in America (at the conference), Takaki receives an opportunity to witness the American attitude firsthand regarding another culture besides white. He is momentarily shocked by the experience of being cast as the Other; nevertheless, Takaki is optimistic that everyone can learn the struggles of various cultures in America by seeing ourselves, as he says, in a "different mirror."

But compared to Takaki, Sucheng Chan, who penned an essay titled "Your Short, Besides!," has a decidedly pessimistic outlook of American culture's ability to change. Chan is an Asian woman with a physical impairment. Although she has many accomplishments, she was persuaded to write about her handicap. Chan describes the history of her health problems and how different societies have reacted to them. "In many East Asian cultures," Chan says, "there is a strong folk belief that a person's physical state in this life is a reflection of how morally or sinfully he or she lived in previous lives." When she grew up in Malaysia, Chan had to "fend off children who ran after [her] calling [her] crippled." The Malaysian society, therefore, contains individuals with very well-defined attitudes about anyone not part of a strictly defined norm.

But when Chan came to America, she noticed a stark difference in people's behavior toward her handicap. Americans were increasingly "protective" of her; they treated her less as a self-sufficient being and more like a helpless child. Why? Because, once again, Americans "feel threatened when confronted with others who live according to different conceptions of what is desirable" (according to Spradley and McCurdy). In addition, Chan writes, "Americans have another way of covering up their uneasiness: they become jovially patronizing. Sometimes when people spot my crutch, they ask if I've had a skiing accident." Such an accident would perhaps be a norm of crutch use; Americans must internalize their social values; and Chan makes Americans uncomfortable because she falls out of the norm of behavior/presentation in American society. She is rightly caught up in a perception of her "low" status: after all, all human interactions, at bottom, are predicated on status, at least according to novelist Tom Wolfe.

However, neither American nor Malaysian culture can accept Chan's impairment; therefore, what makes American culture's treatment of Chan less accepting (or less tolerant) than Malaysian's? Malaysian people, as the author observes, are direct about their gripes, while Americans tend to beat around the bush; they ignore the obvious physical impairment Chan has and, instead, attempt to qualify her in terms of their own accepted norms. This internalizing is wildly inappropriate, because her handicap will never be accepted as part of the norm of American society; instead, since the impairment is interchanged into something definable (and relatable and speak-able) by Americans, the problem is ignored, and her handicap cannot be integrated properly into the norms of the culture—thus not only harming Chan, but others with similar disabilities.

Homosexuality is still perhaps the most difficult norm integration American society has yet to tackle. In the essay "La Guera," the author, Cherrie Moraga, describes her plight dealing with an "abnormal" trait, lesbianism. She was inculcated with American values from an early age and "bleached" of the color that she contained. Of course, prior to discovering (or realizing) her sexual orientation, Moraga's view of homosexuality was more analogous to a typical American's view: that it was inappropriate.

After coming to terms with her own homosexuality, the author examined other common American cultural viewpoints. "How have I internalized my own oppression?" she asks. "How have I oppressed?" She acknowledges the American attitude which forms a tapestry through other discussed individuals' lives: "people feel threatened when confronted with others who live according to different conceptions of what is desirable," according to Spradley and McCurdy.

Moraga does not conform to the internal standards of American culture—and neither do Chan and Takaki. Despite the accomplishments of these three individuals, they are not viewed as American achievers; the overwhelming majority of the country does not label them on their merits, but rather as stereotypes: as a lesbian, a handicapped person, and an Asian. These kinds of judgments are an affront to the meritocracy America aspires to be.

Also, Moraga, Chan, and Takaki all, in their own way, threaten the fabric of acceptable "white" society. Each person brings to light a crack in the dam of ossified intolerant American culture.* And because of their diversity, each of these three exceptional people is arguably more representative of America's norms than the very individuals who attempt to exclude them.

(1998)

* Claiming that those who demand tolerance are oftentimes themselves highly intolerant of others who are intolerant is a silly nonstarter: even if multiculturalism isn't the perfect answer to societal woes, we can all do a lot better to move towards understanding, if not acceptance, of those unlike ourselves.

# 67.

## Dating at the Workplace: A Logic Puzzle

Emily has 8 friends at two different workplaces: MacGuffin, Inc. and DeWitt Co. Her friends' names are Stuart, Bob, Richard, Gavin, Jenna, Zoe, Ashlie, and Carolyn. Emily knows that her 8 friends are dating, she knows that *only* couples who work in the *same* workplace date, and she knows that couples always share a car when coming into and leaving work (there are therefore only four cars between her 8 friends: a VW, a Buick, a Pontiac, and a Chevy), but none of her friends trust Emily enough to tell her exactly who is dating whom. (Emily's a big gossip!)

Instead, her 8 friends each give her one clue. Using these clues, Emily not only was able to figure out who were the couples among her friends, but she was also able to figure out at which company each of her friends worked.

Can you duplicate Emily's feat?

Here are the clues:

- Stuart, who loves *Star Wars*, hates Ashlie because she rejected him years ago when they used to work together.
- Gavin, who is an actuary at DeWitt Co., owns a red VW.
- Stuart and the person who owns the Pontiac work together.
- Jenna was puzzled as to why there were no Buicks or VWs in the parking lot at her historic preservation job.
- Richard and the person who owns the Pontiac do not work together.

- The person who owns the Chevy doesn't work with Ashlie, who is a top-flight bowler.
- Ashlie always avoids Richard whenever they pass each other in the halls at work; they absolutely despise each other. Maybe it's because of Richard's love of Diane Lane films.
- One early morning, Bob and Zoe—who'd rather be homebound, pregnant, and barefoot instead of having to work—were seen driving in together.

(2007)

# 68.

## Sobering Up: A Visit to a Teen Help Center

In the online *Slate Magazine* article "Trick or Treatment: Teen Drug Programs Turn Curious Teens into Crackheads"[*] author Maia Szalavitz documents some of the unintended ill effects of shipping teens off to residential drug treatment facilities. "But what if drug 'treatment' doesn't work for teens? What if, rather than decreasing drug use, teen treatment actually encourages it by labeling experimenting kids as lifelong addicts? What if it creates the worst sorts of peer groups by mixing kids with mild problems with serious drug users who are ready and willing to teach them to be junkies?" If true, this is a classic case of no good deed going unpunished: occasional-user teens in rehabilitation programs, there to wean themselves off their illicit drug use, being exposed to the worst sorts of offenders and modeling their behavior in turn.

At the Rowtown Clinic (a pseudonym) in Pennsylvania, one has to doubt whether the worst sorts of these accusations ring true within their hallowed walls. A massive residential facility, Rowtown Clinic boasts a 55-acre campus with 146 beds, "mature trees, gardens, fountains, and an abundance of greenery," and purports to provide "comprehensive behavioral health services to children, adolescents, adults, and their families."[†] So it's more than just young adults that Rowtown treats—they are one subset of a multipronged setup. But the Clinic claims to provide "individualized treatment" to meet specific needs, despite the breadth of their operations.

Their adolescent program focuses on children thirteen to eighteen years of age. The treatment facility's focus isn't necessarily primarily on issues of drug use; instead, "The goal of this program is

---

[*] Full text, accessed from the Internet May 23, 2008, is available at http://www.slate.com/id/2076329/

[†] All quotes about the Rowtown Clinic come from their promotional materials.

to support young individuals in their struggle with overwhelming emotional problems. Dual diagnosis assessment and education is also provided for individuals with both a primary emotional/behavioral problem and severe chemical dependency issues." Notice the emphasis on *severe*: Rowtown will not necessarily grant residence to the occasional teen drug user, since theirs is a holistic treatment program with addressing teens' core "emotional problems" as the hook, rather than teens' drug use.

The *Slate* article reveals some sobering statistics: "A 1998 study of nearly 150 teenagers treated in dozens of [drug treatment residential] centers across the country found that there was 202 percent more crack abuse following treatment and a 13 percent increase in alcohol abuse. In other words, recent research suggests that parents and schools may be sending binge-drinking/social marijuana smokers off to treatment and getting back crackheads in their stead." It would seem, then, that follow-up programs and treatment in any teen program would be advisable. And Rowtown has just that: "It is extremely important for the adolescent to be followed in aftercare treatment once they have completed the program. The social work staff work collaboratively with families to ensure the aftercare is in place prior to the adolescent's discharge."

Another key criticism that the *Slate* article has of these teen treatment programs is their mishandling of the delicate nature of teens' identities. An eighteen-year-old marijuana smoker and cocaine user named Michael lamented that his $11,000 one-month treatment at the Caron Foundation all hinged on his admitting that he was "powerless" over drugs, even though he didn't believe that. Less than a day after leaving the facility, Michael used again. The article continues:

> Michael's reaction may be the rule for teenagers, not the exception. For an adult who has lost his wife, his job, his health, and his home, admitting to a loss of control might help him recognize that quitting drugs is the only way to solve his problems. But a teenager may not be "in denial" when he says he can control his intake. Most teenagers can. Conversely, forcing a teen to assert that they have no control may do more harm than good, if they have only been experimenting with drugs but are convinced, via treatment, that they are serious addicts.... Since teenage

> identities are fluid anyway, encouraging them to view themselves as powerless addicts may cement an anti-social identity that a teen was just trying on for size.

Although without speaking to a former teen resident I cannot be sure (privacy rules forbid access and dissemination of that type of information), I was impressed with Rowtown Clinic's emphasis on managed care, their assessment process, and their family sessions. Rowtown places a primacy on family involvement, something the *Slate* article notes is important: "Studies show that family therapy and behavioral one-on-one counseling work better for teens than programs modeled on adult addicts." As Rowtown maintains, "Family education and family therapy are essential components of the program and recovery. Prospective clients and their families are informed of the expectations of family participation prior to admission to the program." Rowtown certainly has an effective division-of-labor outfit, split by pre-teens, teens, and adults, and has appropriate family counseling and lavish facilities designed to meet individuals' unique needs.

All of these amenities at Rowtown come at a price, of course. Although specifics are difficult to come by,* if you're a parent of a teen in need of a stay, expect to pay in the thousands of dollars, despite the fact that the average length of a stay is around ten days. Insurance companies won't foot the entire bill, but the Clinic liaisons with most major carriers and managed care organizations.

If one is indeed granted admission for treatment in an "inpatient unit" (in other words, granted a temporary stay at a residence of the Clinic) by the Admissions and Referral Center (the ARC, located in the on-site colonial-style Manor House building), expect only a handful of personal items to be permitted on campus: identification cards, alcohol-free care items such as shampoo and toothpaste, a *list* of all current medications, casual clothing, and comfortable shoes without laces—since laces could be used to harm oneself or others at the facility. Jewelry, food or beverages, cell phones, sharp

---

* In order to get some information on out-of-pocket expenses and general costs, I spoke briefly to a representative of the patients' accounts department at Rowtown. She told me that these costs vary wildly, depending on the length of stay of the patient and the treatment provided. If an adolescent who doesn't have insurance is admitted, the patients' accounts department applies for medical assistance.

or glass objects, money, and televisions, radios, iPods, or electronic games are considered contraband and thus not permitted.

"For kids with minor drugs problems," the Slate article relays, "or for kids who are just being kids, the philosophy must be: First, do no harm." In light of the multiple treatment options, the careful attention to inpatient and outpatient care, the emphasis on family-orientated therapy, and the congenial, helpful attitude of the several staff members that I encountered who work at the facility, it seems that the Rowtown Clinic is well on its way to fulfilling that "do no harm" tenet—and thereby helping children and adults alike.

(2008)

# 69.

## How Do We Improve Schools for Students with Disabilities?

A large, sprawling urban relic, Cerry High School (a pseudonym) just outside of Pittsburgh is anything but friendly to students with disabilities. Although much has been done to improve the situation, it has been done minimally, without passion, only to be in compliance with federal, local, and state regulations. For example, although there are access ramps to assist individuals who require wheelchairs and other mobility-aiding devices, they are there in a perfunctory sense, barely wide enough for a wheelchair. Though bathrooms have been modified to allow easier access for students with disabilities, the extensions seem to have come at the cost of having sanitary facilities—compliance with the law is likely the only driving force behind the restroom assemblage. Much more could be done.

In addition, while inclusion has been effectively pushed and practiced throughout the high school, many regular teachers resist it subterraneously, and a recurring theme emerges: the neglected and isolated student with disabilities trapped in a regular classroom.

"If anything needs fixing, it's the passion of the teachers and the school itself with regard to the kids with disabilities," M. E. Goldberg said. Goldberg, a retired long-time Pittsburgh school administrator, successful high school debate coach, and current Cerry building substitute, said that the problem of passion comes in two forms: the physical considerations, such as improved ramp access and bathrooms, and the cognitive ones, like regular teacher perceptions of students with disabilities. Unsurprisingly, he believes the former is much easier to improve on than the latter.

Goldberg talked with me about a student he observed through the course of a school day this academic year who was confined to a wheelchair. "Mark [his name has been changed], in his algebra class, found it extremely difficult to get involved with the other students in the group activities," he said. "Sure, he could move around well enough, but because of the way the room was made, the desks were hard to shift around. Everyone was simply packed in, and he had to settle for being an observer rather than a participant."

The teacher's measures to counteract Mark's exclusion also discouraged Goldberg. He said that the mathematics teacher displayed little interest in delivering extra help to the student or attempting to involve Mark more in his group's discussion—despite the fact that he was clearly loosing focus in the group assignment. "The teacher just didn't seem to be up to working with Mark when she had twenty-five other kids to deal with," Goldberg explained. "She just can't devote time to one student at the expense of all others."

However, she certainly could have structured the math activities in a way that would have allowed Mark to be more involved to start with. Knowing the classroom arrangement and understanding Mark's special needs should have been a strong consideration. With the ongoing mainstreaming (i.e., inclusion) programs being implemented, so-called regular teachers must not only be experts in the disciplines they teach, but also in the idiosyncrasies of students with disabilities' special needs. This means being acutely aware of the requirements of IEPs (individualized education programs). The problem according to Goldberg is, once again, the lack of passion of the teachers themselves about the details.

"Some of these teachers feel resigned to having students in their classes that they just don't want. It's an unfortunate truth, and the students with disabilities are paying the price," Goldberg claimed. The regular teachers who are uninterested in students with disabilities tend to overtly ignore or isolate them, he said. Treating certain students as vestigial elements in a classroom is certainly inappropriate behavior for any educator and is, in many ways, worse than the lack of an adequate ramp or bathroom stall; the student with disabilities, after a time, begins to submit to the crushing forces of apathy around him—and is left behind.

But what can be done to repair the problems? Goldberg sketched out some general ideas that might be implemented. In terms of the physical facilities, he suggested petitioning the state for additional funding for improvements in access of doors and hallways for people with wheelchairs. An estimate of ten thousand dollars for all improvements was projected. In addition, all of the doors that have round knobs should be replaced with the flat-levered kind. Each knob replacement costs between a hundred- and two-hundred dollars. There are perhaps thirty knobs to change, so the costs for updating the doors would ring in at around three to six thousand dollars.

In terms of the dispositions of the teachers toward students with disabilities, Goldberg's suggestions are more vague. "I'd like to see every teacher appreciate every student's needs, but that isn't going to happen. Maybe a mandatory special education class for all regular teachers would help their perceptions [of the students], I don't know. I still don't think that you can really change a person's mind about something," he said. "We need to put students with disabilities in regular classes with regular teachers who will be passionate about making sure that all of the students are exposed to the same quality learning environment. We need to make absolutely sure that those kids with disabilities are not being put into a class with a teacher who just doesn't care about them." The cost of sending every regular instructor to school to learn about disabilities would be more than the price of fixing the physical facilities, he said. He added that requiring every teacher to enroll in special education classes would not guarantee a change toward students with disabilities.

A solution, then, is to have inclusion in classrooms with regular teachers who are devoted and capable of handling students with disabilities. Yet there is an obvious problem with that notion. "In an ideal inclusion situation," Goldberg said, "the regular teachers that didn't want them [the students with disabilities] wouldn't have them in their classes. But no teacher would admit to not wanting a specific student, I don't think. That would be pretty self-defeating."

Perhaps the only way to at least partially remedy the situation is to check up regularly on the mainstreamed students with disabilities—starting at the beginning of the school year. If they are having difficulties adjusting to the classroom and its environment, they can switch classes, if possible, to better facilitate their learning and inclusion. If that is not an option, then a special education teacher could be assigned to consult with the regular education teacher and discuss concerns. Although the regular education teacher might never fully have that sense of passion about students with disabilities, at least general proper management techniques might be instilled.

"To know how to deal with all of the kids is difficult, maybe impossible," Goldberg said. "Each student is different, whether he or she has disabilities or not, and certainly all teachers need to have some understanding of the students, all of their students, in order to be effective educators.... After all, the teacher isn't the only one in the room."

(2000)

# 70.

## Getting Past the Third Grade

Third grade is awfully challenging. Every day after school, nine-year-old Seth arrives home overloaded with facts. "Mom, there's so much in my head!" he cries. Each night after eating dinner, his mother, Susan, spends several hours helping her child with homework. "The homework shouldn't take anywhere near this long for him to do," she says, "but he has trouble focusing, in part because the Dexatrin has mostly worn off." After the problems in math have been completed, the English homework finished, and the social studies material mastered, Seth relaxes with toy trucks and computer programs creative in nature. Then, he takes a sleeping pill to help him venture into a relaxed, nocturnal state.

Susan, of course, is not the only parent in the country dealing with issues of attention deficit hyperactivity disorder with her child—an estimated three to five percent of all school-age children in the United States have ADHD. Like many children with the disorder, Seth is an extremely intelligent and gifted individual with a severe "stimulation overload" that manifests itself in most school-related activities. However, unlike many with ADHD, Seth was formally diagnosed at a very young age—before his fourth birthday.

"At two years old, when he was in daycare, he tended to be very active and destroy a lot of things," his mother explained. "We knew something was not right, so first we took him to a family doctor, then to a psychologist and psychiatrist. Next, Seth was given medical tests: he had an MRI, an EKG, and an EEG. They were checking him for everything, it seemed.

"The doctors told us to put my son on a Feingold diet to curb his hyperactivity. This was incredibly difficult to do; it was a large strain on the family, and although my mother helped me with it, it just wasn't enough, ultimately," she said. In addition, many other tests were performed on Seth to pinpoint his problems. Within a year, Susan had an explanation for her offspring's instability, and

Seth acquired a formal medical moniker.

"At age three came the 'official' diagnosis: he had ADHD," Susan said. What was once known as "defective moral control" one hundred years ago now affected Susan's son's ability to maintain a normative sense of affective (emotional) and behavioral discipline. By this time, Seth's intellectual capacity was quite advanced. He was able to type out his full name on a personal computer and visually recognize it; discuss, in detail, *Star Trek* and *Star Wars*; and play with a variety of complex software. Of course, the conflicting abilities and disabilities of Susan's child impacted the family greatly. Wildly changing expectations and fluctuating levels of disappointment impacted on daily timetables and engendered states of continual confusion in the family.

Ritalin was prescribed to assist Seth's behavioral control mechanisms, such as his behavioral inhibition and executive functions. "I wasn't happy about him taking the drug, but I suppose I was resigned to it. However, Seth's father was vehemently opposed to it. There was constant turmoil," Susan explained. Of course, to complicate the increasingly difficult issues, Seth was allergic to Ritalin. Dexatrin, a time-release medication, was then suggested. Luckily, the drug has proven relatively effective for Seth.

At close to three years of age, an individualized education program was established for Seth. Once again, the family went through a divisive period, this time about the appropriate placement for Seth based upon his IEP (individualized education program) and other more empirical observations; each member of the household had a notable difference of opinion about which institution should assume responsibility for his education.

However, before Seth began school, patience and energy for taking care of him was running thin. "I had a lot of trouble finding time for him, especially after my mother died, because she had helped a lot," Susan said. "He was like a Tasmanian devil."

Susan was especially concerned about her son's intellectual and social stimulation in an educational setting. Because his IEP stated, quite correctly, that he required more substantive attention from his instructors, Seth's mother worried about the degree of focus teachers would have handling his special needs.

"He has to be kept busy enough so that he doesn't get bored," she explained. "If he gets bored, he'll quickly get into trouble, as we've seen happen many times before with him." Furthermore,

Susan has extremely valid reasons for preventing a sense of boredom in Seth's life. Her sister has two older children who also have ADHD. The severity of "trouble" they found themselves in because of "being bored" was especially high. Susan endeavors constantly to assign her son a variety of interesting activities (once homework has been completed) to assure that he remains on a steady, successful track.

"Another concern I have about the future is that he won't get enough educational assistance from the schools to help with the disorder. There are still some more things I have to find out about how they will deal with him in the upper grades," Susan added.

Perhaps the looming threat of increased homework in those upper grade levels frightens Seth's mother the most. For example, Seth, with Susan's help, currently spends between two and three hours each weekday completing work from school; normally, the assignments should take no longer than a half hour to finish, but his attention span and high level of stimulation deter quick completion. In addition, Susan admits that she herself has some difficulty understanding parts of the work, because school curricula have changed so much since she was in school. Nevertheless, the challenges she faces do not change her overall outlook of Seth's future.

"I just want him to be able to get to his full potential; he has the ability to do anything that he wants and not just waste his life. He is an extremely smart individual," she said.

Because of her firsthand experience with a child with ADHD, Susan believes that many of the stigmatizing labels used to describe children with the disorder need to be reconsidered. Limiting the prevalence of the words "bad" and "evil" to view people with ADHD is a satisfactory first step, she said.

"Also, I want to see more focus from the educational establishment on a different type of learning, a more individualized plan for students with ADHD. We can't treat all these kids like Stepford students in the classrooms," explained Susan. "Although it's hard to do, we need more truly individualized educational programs for these students so they can have the same opportunities as everyone else to succeed in life."

(2000)

# 71.

## Struggling with a Learning Disability

A child's long-term struggle with a learning disability might be equated with a large rock breaking the surface tension of calm waters—the ensuing ripples impact a large area. Extending this analogy, the ripples are large in the classroom, but are even larger and more pervasive in the child's familial network. Special accommodations on both fronts (school and home) must be implemented, necessarily leading to disproportionate magnitudes of time and effort focused on the child with the learning disability. In a classroom, extra resources and specially designed educational techniques equip school faculty, staff, and other representatives with tactics to deal effectively (or at least competently) with the child. But at the home, where a learning disability could be relatively unexplored terrain for a family, the probability of both effectively assisting the child and appropriately altering family structure to handle the lifelong crisis is not particularly high.

Consider the Mendosas (to protect anonymity, all names used in this chapter have been altered) as an example. A mostly "generic" family of the Northeastern U.S., one of their five children has a diagnosed learning disability, and another is classified "at risk" to have an academic learning dysfunction. I talked with nineteen-year-old Lauren Mendosa, the eldest of the four children (she is devoid of learning disabilities, but is partially deaf in one ear). As the sibling of at least one individual with a learning disability, Lauren expressed an amalgam of resignation, resolve, disappointment, and optimism when describing the interactions between family members in her household with the omnipresent hurdle of learning disabilities to continuously traverse.

"Jim [her twelve-year-old sibling with the diagnosed learning disability] gets a lot of help from mom with a lot of things. There's definitely a sense of favoritism there," she said. For instance, Lauren's parents tend to "do anything" (her words) for Jim Mendosa under the veil of accommodation and comfort, even at the expense of other family needs. "They'll say to me, 'Lauren, make dinner for Jim, help him with this, help him with that,' and it can be a burden on me. I love my family, but sometimes I just can't realistically be there for Jim all of the time."

In addition, Lauren's parents frequently have a difficult time accepting the moniker of "learning disability" applied to their child (perhaps because of the seemingly inherent negative connotation of the term), and occasionally engender solutions to Jim's daily dilemmas using denial. Certainly a counterproductive strategy, family tensions centered on the issues of his learning disability are often accelerated and built up rather than alleviated, leading, in some cases, to interpersonal breakdowns in the household.

"My parents are constantly getting distracted with Jim's needs, Jim's comforts, as if he were the only one in the house, and the only one with problems to deal with," she explained. "Sometimes their inability to handle him has really caused problems and really intense arguments, because they just forget about the fact that he has real reasons for these special needs."

Other times, Lauren's parents purposefully use the label of "learning disability" to motivate other family members into accepting inappropriate and often distracting behavior from Jim. For example, Jim tends to be disorganized and rarely cleans his room; although his parents have never condoned such actions from any of their other offspring, Jim is consistently excused because "he has a learning disability." The simultaneous using of the label (in a superficial sense) to explain behavior whilst openly challenging or denying the validity of the term "learning disability" produces a confusing and contradictory situation for all members of the Mendosa household.

Lauren's parents also blame themselves and feel guilty perpetually about his learning disability, "as if it were all their fault," she added. "Some other things he does wrong just get excused for out of their guilt of his situation, I think. That just really annoys me. It just puts added strain on me to be that much better, because they just don't tolerate and excuse me for anything I might do wrong."

A pattern emerges in the Mendosa family: lowered expectations and more lenience for the child with the learning disability, and raised expectations and a lower tolerance for error for the child without the learning dysfunction. Once again, the tensions of the already strained family relationship increase.

"It was always expected that I would excel on my own and not flounder while Jim got extra help, so that put a lot more pressure on me to succeed and prove myself," Lauren said. In a way, though, the added pressure of independence and high achievement ultimately helped to shape Lauren into a very successful student. "Maybe if I had been given all of that attention at a young age [as Jim has been given], I would be utterly dependent and despondent now from it."

Also, Lauren says that her personal struggle with her sibling's disability has affected her deepest convictions about society and people in general. For instance, Lauren wishes to pursue a career in education as a teacher, and because of her daily exposure to an individual who requires assistance to academically function "normally," she feels better prepared to be extra sensitive to children with disabilities in her future career. A small silver lining—but a silver lining nonetheless.

(2000)

# 72.

## A Modest Proposal: The Teacher Exceptionality Information Act[*]

If teachers of any sort are to have the maximum impact on their students' education, both a mastery of subject matter and a mastery of student-teacher relations is necessary. In essence, educators must be as well prepared to handle affective (emotional) student issues as they are to answer in-class queries about their disciplines of expertise. It seems appropriate, then, for instructors to have as much information about their students as possible in order to effectively facilitate the process of classroom information presentation.

Of course, the assumption that knowing (and appreciating) individual student issues as a requirement for an optimal teaching environment is not accepted as valid by all educators; some regard their students' individual needs in the classroom as a concern dramatically subservient to the imparting of knowledge. But this stance is considerably misguided since it ignores fundamental differences in individual learning styles. For a teacher to be required to at least generally learn and understand those differences is of great benefit to all students in the classroom; the efficacy of the educator will increase dramatically.

Since it is not enough to simply promote this humanistic philosophy as a "helpful tool" for the class, legislation must be created to effectively force teachers in all grade levels to at least have a minimum awareness of individual student needs. Especially with the increasing prevalence of inclusionary practices in schools, "awareness laws" should be mandatory. I therefore propose the Teacher Exceptionality Information Act, or TEIA, to help provide teachers with the knowledge they need to form as effective of a learning environment as possible.

TEIA will mandate that all teachers be informed of information

[*] Don't worry—despite its title, this piece is not some sort of Swiftian satire.

pertaining to the exceptionalities for all of their students. A guidance counselor or other school representative would, at the beginning of each school year, present a list of students for each instructor (the list would include only the students in the teacher's current classes; teachers would not have access to the exceptionality histories of students they are not teaching). Enumerated would be the students' past exceptionality history (if they have ever been part of a special education class, if they have ever had documented behavioral problems, if they have ever been enrolled in a gifted class, etc.) in extremely general detail. The teacher would then have the option of learning more about individual exceptionality histories, but only with the approval of the parents or guardians of the students. In addition, in order to avoid any initial dispositions toward or stereotyping of students before the school year begins (due to the exceptionalities), the lists would not be presented to the educators until the end of the second full school week. By that time, instructors will have had ample opportunities to deal with their classes and form their own opinions and expectations about handling the overall classroom dynamics. Learning general information about students' exceptionalities would assist teachers in refining (but not creating) their classroom expectations for the remainder of the school year.

In addition, any students with IEPs from previous school terms would be noted on the list. Without parental consent, teachers of students with IEPs would have the option of viewing the individualized education programs. However, parents would be notified of the IEP contents' inspection, and they would be granted the option of immediately (or at the earliest convenient time for both parties [teacher and parents]) discussing how they feel the short- and long-terms goals of the program are being met for their child; the quality of the accommodations provided so far since the IEP was written; new accommodations that the teacher will implement in dealing with their child's unique concerns; and other issues that may concern them.

The benefits for children with and without exceptionalities are apparent: instead of the generalities of classroom management and material presentation a teacher may implement, a more case-by-case basis for each student's education could be developed within reasonable limits. Obviously, an instructor cannot devote disproportionate amounts of time and energy to certain students' learning at the expense of other students—viewed this way, teaching seems to resemble a zero-sum game. But the teacher can tailor, to a degree, the classroom structure to maximize all students' educational opportunities. How the lists and IEPs determine the classroom instruction are up to the teacher's discretion. Ultimately, and obviously, the individual teacher must decide how best to run his classroom.

Consider the consequences of a teacher not knowing the students: in a text entitled *Teaching Exceptional Children: Cases for Reflection and Analysis for Exceptional Learners*, authors Hallahan and Kauffman discuss a teacher (John McCullum) in the chapter "What You Don't Know Can Hurt You" who did not realize that one of his students had a history of behavioral problems and was enrolled in behavior management classes. Mr. McCullum handled Richard, the student, in inappropriate ways (considering Richard's behavioral problems) and effectively lowered his own confidence in his teaching abilities. The situation might have been avoided with TEIA. Knowing that Richard had behavior issues, John, instead of blaming himself, could have focused his energies on dealing appropriately with Richard. Also note that the entire class suffered as a result of John's mismanagement. TEIA forces teachers to come to terms with the heterogeneity of their classroom environment; everyone, not just individuals with exceptionalities, benefits in the long run* because of an extended awareness of the dynamics of the class. Instead of heuristically diagnosing students' issues, teachers can be formally made aware of the problems and be on their way towards finding solutions.

Implementation of TEIA must emerge solely from a federal level. Creating a generalized list of all school students, and then sorting the list for an educator's classes, does not require funding and is certainly a reasonable requirement under the current provisions of the law (thus it would be a federally unfunded mandate). Although guidance counselors or other school representatives will need time to assemble the lists, the extra work does not seem unreasonable given the value-added benefits to students and teachers. Computer software tailor-made for this process can help. And, if absolutely necessary, outsourcing might be considered, and a mandatory ap-

* Then again, in the long run, we're all dead, as noted caustically by John Maynard Keynes.

propriation of funds from the local government would be the source (not the federal or state government). In this respect, at least, local school decision-making will be maintained (analogous to certain aspects of IDEA). However, the federal government must mandate TEIA for every public school.

In order to ensure compliance, every public school, each school year, must submit a notarized document stating that they have complied with the law and distributed the appropriate lists to every teacher. A failure of any school to comply will result in a ten percent decrease in federal funding for that school over the next two years (starting at the beginning of the following school year, post-violation). If compliance is still not met after that time, stricter penalties will be introduced, including, but not limited to, linear scaled decreases in federal funding and certain school-status privileges temporarily revoked.

Knowledge is certainly power (with all due apologies to Bacon and Foucault)—and TEIA allows teachers some access to information that can dramatically assist their instructional techniques. The more relevant knowledge that teachers have about their students, the better equipped they will be to handle potential volatile and uncomfortable situations in an appropriate manner conducive to maximizing each child's learning.

(2000)

# 73.

## Surrounded by Books and Gossip: An Ethnography

Neolocal residential patterns preclude extended family—beyond the mother and father, i.e., the nuclear family—from providing human association groups; thus, in more "complex" societies like ours, common-interest associations allow an individual to feel a sense of belonging to a group of people.

I work at a public library,[*] and it is an association of common interest. Also, it superficially is a secondary group; we are not necessarily intimate, for example. However, after examining the vocation as a conceptual object, the library appears analogous latently to a primary common-interest group. In order to understand why, descriptions of the library's functions are necessary.

There are twelve staff members, and we refer to each other on a first name basis; surnames are never used. In addition, each employee has at least three years tenure at this particular library; most also have some years of experience at other libraries, so they are familiar with common library procedures.

Each staff member[†] has loosely delineated tasks to engage in. For instance, one employee spends more than a third of her working time typing cards for new books and periodicals; another catalogs adult books; yet another purchases children's reading materials. However, no matter what the specialty, our roles all converge to a common one: handling the desk ("handling the desk" refers to

---

[*] Note that this essay was written right around the time the computer revolution swept though public libraries, so many of the procedures mentioned here have become electronic in nature or have otherwise radically changed (or both). For more information from the front lines of this painful transition, consult Nicholson Baker's library essays in his collection *How the World Works*.

[†] Perhaps the best example of an über-librarian is the fictional Jan O'Deigh from *The Gold Bug Variations*, Richard Powers's sprawling masterpiece of a novel. Alas, I've not yet encountered a librarian who's a polymath like O'Deigh is.

checking out books for patrons). In addition, many of the staff members assume each other's functional roles, at least to a degree. I might catalog adult books, for example. Thus, none of the functional roles are entirely absolute (except for handling the desk).

This cross-changing of roles is latent. When a person is "recruited" onto the library staff (the recruiting process is like that of any other job: a resume is needed, an interview is granted, etc.), he or she (well, mostly she) is given a main functional role and is not expected to assume other roles. But in day-to-day operations, the type and amount of work to be completed determines a staff member's functional roles.

But how is status marked? It would appear that the particular function hired for determines an individual's place in the library hierarchy (the director of the library, for instance, steers the library). However, this is hardly the case; the library "society" is largely egalitarian. Most decisions the director makes have already been influenced by another powerful force: the staff (as a group, not as individuals per se). Being a part of the decision process is not employee-optional but rather something expected; in other words, it is a norm and value of the group.

The group decision-making process is hardly formalized. Instead, it relies on an overlapping complaining/gossiping/morale chain. The complaining portion of the chain is overt; staff members display their dissatisfaction with a potential new policy, for instance, by complaining amongst themselves (the director may or may not be excluded from this process; it depends on the "severity" of the policy being complained about, and from whom the policy originated. The more "severe," the more likely he or she will be involved). The longer something is complained about, the less likely its implementation. This past year, for instance, the director was considering opening the library on Sundays. However, after several "complaining sessions" regarding the new hours (in which the director was involved), the possibility of Sunday work time was nixed. In the complaining/gossiping/morale chain, complaining is often the most effective means to influence decisions.

Gossiping, to be differentiated from complaining, is a much more discreet process among employees. While complaining may have everyone involved, gossiping is much less overt and tends to segment the library staff somewhat. For instance, employees who consistently work on the same night of the week tend to become slightly closer with one another than other staff members. Therefore, the comfort level increases and gossip develops. Gossip usually involves two to three people at once (there are typically three staff members working each night). In addition, to "keep a lid on it," the topics of gossip, while they might be circulated slowly between other close staff members (some people work more than one night a week, so they might be close to two groups of two or of three people; thus, certain gossiping topics might bleed through from the night before, for instance), rarely turn into complaining; instead, gossip impacts staff members' morale.

The most discreet form of decision making is with respect to morale. Morale, as defined in a library context, is the current state of positive job impetus: essentially, Do we want to come in to work each day? Morale is rarely spoken of unless directly asked about, and it involves individuals, not groups of people. The current director of the library can frequently sense when a person's morale is lowered; it might well cause the director to reconsider a decision.

The complaining/gossiping/morale chain has an important function: It allows each person to express her comfort level at the vocation without having to attend formalized meetings or gatherings. Instead, problems are discussed freely during work hours. Free discussion subtly promotes an egalitarian staff: there is no intimidation to speak—or not to speak—at an official staff meeting.

But just as gossip sometimes promotes egalitarianism, it can also sever relationships among individuals. Because gossip frequently divides the staff, serious misunderstandings occasionally occur. Two years ago, a staff member had a minor altercation with a patron; but because of the rampant gossip circles, the situation was blown out of proportion; and, as an eventual result of the gossip, the staff member was terminated (without any explanation).

Thus, in an unfortunate way, gossip is a latent form of social control within the group. Although obviously not all gossip-invoking situations among staff members result in eventual termination from the job, periodic and temporary social ostracizing frequently occurs. For instance, if you are gossiped about, you probably will not be included or even allowed to gossip at all with anyone, even in your own gossip circle (e.g., the other staff members who work with you on the same night). An absence of gossip from an individual, therefore, marks that person as socially ostracized from the staff. Luckily, though, in most cases, gossip is forgotten;

however, the old gossip is replaced by a fresh crop of gossip, and another person may be the target. The cycle continues.

The act of gossiping itself marks membership in the group. It certainly requires several months (at least) to realize exactly how to act properly in a gossip circle. But once "initiated," the individual is marked as a member of the library staff. However, a person is probably not hired because of her gossiping skills; she is selected on the basis of idealized job requirements. More conventional group markers include library jargon use (common to all libraries), casual dress style, and knowledge of book/periodical placement.

Although the library appears to be nearly entirely egalitarian, there are covert statuses that only become apparent after spending enough time in the field. The director does make decisions, so his status as the "top dog" is obvious. However, analogous to a foraging society (the library is to some extent like a foraging society: consider the use of gossip as a means of social control), the director is really no more than a "Big Man" with little power. He can try to convince the staff of a plan's merits, for instance; but if the staff does not approve, the complaining/gossiping/morale chain commences. The key difference between a library director and a Big Man in a foraging society is that the director has the ultimate authority to implement a plan irrespective of staff disapproval (and also the fact that the director doesn't have to hunt for food for the group, of course).

Another covert status marker, and truly the only way to determine who is higher in status at the library, is to have a conversation with the most senior staff member. If she is talking to one employee, she will, without exception, always look that staff member in the eye. However, if she is talking to two staff members, she will, without exception, look exclusively in the eye of the employee with the relatively higher status, even if the employee with the comparatively lower status directly asks her a question (and a staff member with higher status is present; she will look in the eyes of the staff member with the higher status, no matter what the circumstances).

However, what makes this simply no more than her opinion of whose status is higher rather than the reality of the hierarchy of status in the library? Since she has devoted over twenty years to the library, her views are frequently the most respected. In addition, she tends to wield the most gossip-producing "authority," once again largely because of her seniority at the library.

Therefore, we can now describe the latent hierarchy of statuses within the library staff. They have very little in common with a manifest hierarchy except that the top status is given to the director, because he ultimately determines the course of action the group takes. Next in line in the latent hierarchy is the staff as a whole. Its collective use of complaining makes it far more powerful than any one individual. Since the senior staff member denotes the status of individuals in the group with her eye contact, she is next in the hierarchy. And, finally, everyone else is ranked according to seniority. (I have not included the numerous complex gossiping circles in the rankings of this hierarchy—many Venn diagrams would be needed.)

If someone wishes to leave the staff, he or she simply resigns; this is no different than any other conventional U.S. vocation. However, the turnover rate is very low. We now have a logical explanation for the prevalence of gossip: the comfort level between staff members is high because they see each other day after day for years—since staff will rarely leave once they join the library. Because staff members stay in the group for long periods of time, gossip is common.

The library, examined in this latent context of functional roles and relationships between staff members, is much closer to a primary common-interest group than a secondary one. It is rather informal; it has relatively few members (thus, it is a small tight-knit group); there is informal social control in the form of gossip; and because of the cross-changing of roles between staff members (the work load dictates who will do what), the functional roles of the employees are not necessarily always clearly defined. Instead of calling my fellow employees "staff," perhaps I should refer to them as friends, which is what, according to this ethnographic analysis, they really are.

(1998)

# 74.

## Statistics is Stereotyping: A Brief Lament

It is especially ironic that statistics, loosely a branch of mathematics having strong connections to other academic disciplines such as sociology, psychology, and the hard sciences, is on the one hand used to present quantitative evidence of inequities in society but on the other hand practiced in a way that perforce stereotypes groups of people, engages in implicit racism, and grossly oversimplifies human behavior in order to draw inferences from data.

For example, consider the popular statistics textbook *Workshop Statistics: Discovery with Data and the Graphing Calculator*[*] by Rossman et al.: like most statistics books, it stresses analysis of data culled from real-world sources. For instance, one of the Activities (i.e., problem sets) in the text is based on a real study of childhood obesity, another is rooted in information taken from the National Opinion Research Center, and yet another is framed around data culled from *USA Today.* And Activity 6-3, called "Variables of State," is no different. It is based on figures recorded from both the 1990 U.S. Census and the *1996 Statistical Abstract of the United States.* Here, in full, is the Activity description:

> The following boxplots display distributions of variables with states in the U.S. as the cases. Each graph contains four boxplots, corresponding to the state's region of the country. These regions are Midwest, Northeast, South, and West, but they are not necessarily displayed in that order. Your task is to try to identify which region is labeled number 1, which is number 2, and so on. The boxplots are of these variables:

---

[*] The passages that follow refer to the second edition of the book, published in 2002. For more on teaching with this text, see the Appendix.

- The percentage of a state's residents who have a college degree
- The percentage of a state's residents who have never been married
- The percentage of a state's births that are to mothers under age 20
- The percentage of a state's residents who are of Mexican descent

Below the Activity description, there are four comparative box-and-whisker plots, each with a different data display: one for college degrees, one for never-married people, one for young single moms, and one for the percentage of people of Mexican descent.

In order to successfully complete the problem set, though, stereotyping people was required; in fact, stereotyping was entirely germane to the analysis.* The Activity can *only* be solved by thinking in terms of extremes: the Southern/Western border is especially porous, so the Mexicans must be there; the teen girls in the South must be [insert adjective for promiscuousness here], therefore they have the highest rates of pregnancy; et cetera, et cetera.

Consider the article "Unpacking the Invisible Knapsack" (1990) by Peggy McIntosh. She documents her slow but steady realization that she had enjoyed "unearned skin privilege" through her life and was "conditioned into oblivion about its existence," going so far as to describe a "myth of meritocracy" and the protections of whites' privileges that take their form as "silences" and "denials" of that privilege: a sort of unspoken-of conspiracy that has an army of unwitting co-conspirators perpetuating hierarchies of race and class. As Sherlock Holmes famously said, "When you have eliminated all which is impossible, then whatever remains, however improbable, must be the truth." The discovery of the matrix of white privilege around McIntosh seemed at first improbable to her yet slowly revealed itself as the latent truth.

---

* The use of statistics for intentionally nefarious purposes—as opposed to its use here, which is unintentional—has a sordid history. Consider craniometry, a subset of the long-discredited discipline of phrenology, which measured the skulls of humans to classify them; see *The Mismeasure of Man* (1981) by Stephen Jay Gould for pertinent details.

Realizing that stereotyping was the only was to solve this particular *Workshop Statistics* Activity was akin for me to the epiphany Peggy McIntosh has (in part) when she realizes that so-called flesh-colored bandages nicely matched the color of her white skin. Lest you think that this particular Activity is the sole offender in this textbook, let's expand our scope—not only to find several other prime instances of reasoning-by-stereotyping in this book but in another popular statistics textbook as well.

Consider Activity 7-7, "Suitability for Politics," in *Workshop Statistics.* A survey of randomly selected adult Americans are asked their political party, gender, and reaction to the assertion, "Men are better suited to politics than women." The book asks the student to "address the question of whether there is a relationship between political inclination and reaction to the statement or between gender and reaction to the statement. Write a paragraph or two describing your findings." You can imagine students sinking to the basest stereotypes of women in their attempts to explain gender-associated behaviors.

Next, look at Activity 7-11, "Children's Living Arrangements," which asks students to formulate an opinion on whether a "relationship exists between race/Hispanic origin and parental living arrangements." Or Activity 14-12, entitled "Hospital Births," which requires readers to make some racial assumptions about two hospitals—after explaining that about "25% of all babies born in Texas are Hispanic." This Activity, especially, could have made use of some other fabricated or alternative real-life statistic not involving race or ethnicity to illustrate the mathematical ideas.

This call to stereotype is not only endemic in *Workshop Statistics.* Consider another well-known textbook: *Introduction to Statistics and Data Analysis* (2005) by Roxy Peck et al. also has a variety of problems that necessitate negatively stereotyping groups of people in order to analyze data. Here's a sampling: problem 12.25 wonders whether there is a regional difference in the U.S. with respect to people's attitudes toward spanking their children; problem 11.14 asks students whether "girls are less inclined to enroll in science courses than boys"; and problem 9.16 questions whether it would be reasonable to "generalize" the results of a study on Planned Parenthood and parental notification among girls younger than 18. Despite the authors' ostensibly good pedagogic intentions, all of these problems require students to stereotype about race, ethnicity, and gender in order to conduct inferential analyses and generalize conclusions to predict or explain behaviors of populations.

Could statistics be performed without stereotyping? Could the results of surveys and other real-world data sets involving race, ethnicity, gender, class or other groups be utilized and analyzed in ways that avoid this double-bind: namely, that the collection and analysis of data about a race, ethnicity, or gender, so important for the documentation of inequalities and breakdown of the male/white privilege that McIntosh writes about, is *ipso facto* stereotypical? For instance, would a book like *Nickel and Dimed* (2001) by Barbara Ehrenreich be as powerful a read about the struggles of the underemployed in America without the statistics of the underclass presented? And would *Freakonomics* (2005), by Steven Levitt and Stephen Dubner, which relies heavily on statistics to present arguments explaining the most bizarre of phenomena in society—such as the black-white generational patterns of naming children—be anywhere near as powerful, or even exist at all, without the authors' sometimes-blanket statements regarding data analysis which certainly don't sidestep the topics of race and gender? Take a look at this passage from the book, which discusses the issue of "black-sounding" names (from the chapter "A Roshanda by Any Other Name"): "Along those same lines, perhaps a black person with a white name pays an economic penalty in the *black* community.... Maybe DeShawn should just change his name."

How could human behavior be analyzed without drawing stereotypical-type inferences from groups of people? We can't simply *avoid* gathering and aggregating data by these most contentious of groups of association. To argue otherwise is to put forth a full-scale indictment of statistics—and, by extension, sociology and anthropology, which use data to study group dynamics and cultural particularities.

Another problem arises when we cast judgment based on a single standout instance or event, discarding the rest of the data. Think of this as the Jim Marshall effect: Marshall was a National Football League defensive player for two decades, mostly with the Minnesota Vikings. He was a model of consistency and professionalism, getting voted to Pro Bowls, contributing to Vikings' wins in numerous championship games in the 1960s and '70s, and setting a record at the time for most consecutive starts and games played. But for all his success, Marshall is mostly remembered for one mistake he made, considered by many to be the most embarrassing play in professional sports: the "wrong-way run," in which Marshall scooped up a fumble and ran for more than sixty yards to score in the end zone—for the opposing team. Like deeming Jim Marshall's career a failure because of one botched play—one *outlier*—stereotyping an entire population based on a small sample of group members' mistakes is unfair, unjust, misleading, and essentialist. It is proof by example.

A sophisticated and famous critique of essentialism came from the academy in the late 1970s. In his book *Orientalism* (1978), the late Columbia University cultural theorist Edward Said put forth the then-controversial thesis that much of the practice of the Orientalists, those Occident academics that specialized in studying the so-called Orient, was simply justification for the imperialist appetites of their host countries—namely, England, France, and, much later, the United States. These Orientalist scholars defined the "Other" (peoples of the Orient) to their liking, largely in opposition to the culture and mores of the imperialists themselves. The perpetuation of what Antonio Gramsci called "hegemony" over the Orient found its full flourishing not in the battlefields but in the writings and studies of these well-respected Orientalists. Said's text quickly put to bed the entire Orientalist field and spurred the rapid growth of cultural studies in academe.

McIntosh, in her analysis of latent white privilege, confronts power and hegemony in much the same way as Said does in *Orientalism*. But Said extends his ideas further (in part because he develops them at book length) to include how the perpetuation of certain stereotypes and maintenance of specific social hierarchies are promulgated. Here he describes how this perpetuation occurs in contemporary times:

> One aspect of the electronic, postmodern world is that there has been a reinforcement of the stereotypes by which the Orient is viewed. Television, the films, and all the media's resources have forced information into more and more standardized molds. So far as the Orient is concerned, standardization and cultural stereotyping have intensified the hold of the nineteenth-century academic and imaginative demonology of "the mysterious Orient."

So, à la McIntosh and Said, it is extremely important to look carefully at what data is being presented for analysis and of benevolent, non-stereotypical ways of drawing inferences. So, when examining real-world statistics, we must cautiously navigate between the Scylla of avoiding using such data all together and the Charybdis of using the data in a haphazard, irresponsible, and stereotypical manner. Anything less would not only be an affront to meritocracy, but also to common human decency.

(2009)

# 75.

## A Mathematical Approach to Alfred Hitchcock

The systems underlying the films of Alfred Hitchcock are complicated, to say the least. Michel Foucault's *Archaeology of Knowledge*, although he's speaking of the historical process, captures perfectly the incongruity that follows attempts to render such underlying systems transparent. As he writes,

> For many years now historians have preferred to turn their attention to long periods, as if, beneath the shifts and changes of political events, they were trying to reveal the stable, almost indestructible system of checks and balances, the irreversible processes, the constant readjustments, the underlying tendencies that gather force, and are then suddenly reversed after centuries of continuity, the movements of accumulation and slow saturation, the great silent, motionless bases that traditional history has covered with a thick layer of events.

Perhaps mathematics can be used to make the opaque systems of Hitchcock's sui generis world transparent. In its most basic form, mathematics is a tool used to describe a world—whether it is physics, which describes the physical world, or abstract algebra, which describes a "world" that is purely theoretical. By describing and modeling a world with mathematics, we can make deductions and predictions about events or phenomena based on past experiences in that world. Therefore, a "Hitchcockian mathematical system" would describe the Hitchcock "world" with predictive power. What follows is an attempt to construct the framework for such a system.

We will look at the narrative aspect of Hitchcock's films. For instance: Let us assume that in all of his films, there is an "event A" and an "event B" that both could (or could not) occur in the same film. Then there are four "resultant" events:

If both event A and event B occur, then event C is sure to occur.
If event A occurs but event B does not occur, then event D is sure to occur.
If event A does not occur but event B does occur, then event E is sure to occur.
If both event A and event B do not occur, then event F is sure to occur.

So far, we cannot be sure exactly what the specific "events" are assigned to in any of Hitchcock's actual films. If events A, B, C, D, E, and F do in fact exist,* then we probably could not expect to locate them quickly; many events present (and resultant events, if any, from those events) are subconscious decisions on the director's part. The events and resultant events must occur with enough frequency to warrant a "rule" in their favor. In other words, there cannot be 53 exceptions to a rule for each of the 53 films. (It also might be a better idea to think smaller and make these "rules" for only one movie at a time, and not for all films in the aggregate.)

Also, we could expand the rule-making process. Instead of one event dependent on just two events, we might have two events dependent on three events:

If events A, B, and C occur, then events D and E are sure to occur.

This then leads to the notion of having any number of "original" events leading to any number of outcome (resultant) events:

If events A, B, C, D,... occur, then events E, F, G, H,... follow.

Then, we can claim that we can find a discrete number of events in his films (in a specific category, like narrative original events, sound original events, or editing original events, among others), say 100 original events. A 100x100x100x...x100 matrix with rows and col-

---

* Let us assume, for the sake of argument, that event A is the "presence of the male protagonist double" and event B is the "domination of the female protagonist." And let us also say that we have discovered that if events A and B are both true, then event C, "eventual death of the female protagonist," occurs in about 75 percent of Hitchcock's films. These are the types of correlatives to look for in Hitchcock's corpus.

umns having the 100 original events on the axes is a possible way to display the many valid combinations of original events that might occur (which lead to resultant events). For instance, the matrix might have original events A, C, F, and G, but not B, D, E, H, … , that may occur. The cell in the 100x100x100x…x100 matrix that has A, C, F, and G selected as "true original events," or original events that occur, would describe the resultant event. So, to summarize, a matrix could be created to deal with the possible permutations of original events that can occur and describe their respective outcome events.

In addition, resultant events could become original events, thus leading to "chains" of original-resultant-original-resultant events occurring without end to describe continually altering events (events can "double-back" on themselves, so to speak). Perhaps such a mathematical model can be constructed, something more than just linguistically metaphorical, but something that is also by its very composition—as discussed above—incomplete, not closed. Cataloging these events is surely a Byzantine task, since there may be multiple secondary or tertiary systems, and systems may envelop systems ad infinitum as well. Is this cataloging impossible, then? Or is it akin to what Georg Cantor discovered in the late 1800s when playing with infinities: that the rules might be paradoxical and twisted and bent out of shape, but there are indeed still rules? (Cantor literally lost his mind, so this is probably not the best example. Cantor did, though, appreciate the inherent beauty in infinity—he saw that beauty is truth, truth beauty, with apologies to Keats.) Instead of using notions of infinity à la Cantor, let us instead turn to algorithms. Perhaps formalizing these mathematical ideas by introducing algorithms into the mix will make any sort of Hitchcock-system deconstruction more fruitful.

An algorithm is essentially a contained step-by-step finite series of instructions that, when followed exactly, ultimately produces some sort of result, even if that result is simply the following of the instructions to their completion or partial completion, however that is defined.*

* Read through the fantastic *The Advent of the Algorithm* by David Berlinski for a thorough treatment of algorithms and, also, of Gödel's incompleteness theorems. Bertrand Russell's Barber's Paradox best illustrates these theorems for the layperson: consider a small, cordoned off town in which the barber

My applied example of an algorithm here addresses, specifically, the overall concept of the algorithm and the integration of seemingly chance events in a strictly deterministic system:

```
(Line 1) Algorithm: Heads or Tails;
(Line 2) Begin:
(Line 3) Create a numerical variable called "Coin";
(Line 4) The value of Coin equals a Random Number
         (either number 1 or number 2);
(Line 5) If the value of Coin equals 1, Then Display "It is a
         Head.";
(Line 6) If the value of Coin equals 2, Then Display "It is a
         Tail.";
(Line 7) End;
(Line 8) End Algorithm,
```

Although written in what is termed "pseudocode,"* the algorithm above nevertheless manages to combine several facets of a linear finite yet variable system. In terms of the syntax of the pseudocode, the line numbers are present for clarity; the semicolons signal the end of a singly-executable command line; the "Begin:" signals the beginning of the actual "action" of the algorithm; the "End;" declares the end of the "action" of the algorithm; and the "End Algorithm" obviously ends the entire algorithm. The instructions are followed linearly, in numerical order and from left to right on each line. Although most of this declarative abstract grammar appears misplaced it is absolutely necessary if we are to closely follow the more-or-less standard contemporary conventions of algorithmic theory. Although the specific grammatical choices and

---

shaves those people who don't shave themselves. Sounds good—except if we ask, Who shaves the barber? Gödel's Incompleteness Theorem is, in fact, a variant of this paradox, yet it surprisingly applies to all of mathematics, not just to barbers who happen to know their multiplication tables.

* A false code, designed for the express purpose of clarifying the steps of the procedure, rigorously consistent but not syntactically correct for any computer; in other words, there is no way to electronically "run" exactly what is above, but, rather, the lines of pseudocode would have to be initially converted into true computer language code for a machine to understand them. Pseudocode is usually easy to read because it bears at least some resemblance to the English language.

structure of the "Heads or Tails" algorithm was this author's choice, most pseudocodes' syntax follows an analogous pattern.

Of course, we must briefly examine what the "Heads or Tails" program does. (Note that I tend to use the terms "program" and "algorithm" interchangeably, since they have more or less the same meaning in this context.) The first line declares the name of the program, and the second line initiates the algorithm. The third line is vital because it sets up a variable component to the program; although the algorithm is specific in stating that such a variable (called "Coin") must be created at line three, the quantity (numerical) that "Coin" represents is not defined yet. The fourth line takes the "Coin" variable and assigns it to equal either the number one or the number two. Note the latitude of the randomness in this case: although the algorithm gives a dose of "free will" to the variable's value it nonetheless restricts it to a single value: one or two. The integration of a non-heuristic framework of limited chance is apparent.*

However, despite the initial thought that since the "Coin" variable can either equal one or two it automatically subscribes to a binary-like logic, it is in fact lines five and six that demonstrate the inherent binary logic in algorithms. These two lines examine the random value (either the number one or the number two) assigned to "Coin" and determine, based on the value that "Coin" equals, which result of the virtual "coin flip" to display (show on a screen or print out from a printer; it doesn't really matter): heads or tails (one or two). The If/Then commands in lines five and six are the true/false (binary) testers: in each "run" of the algorithm, one of these two lines will always be true, and the other line will subsequently turn out false, because there is no in-between state (the value of "Coin" is always either one or two, nothing else). The reason that line four is not a form of binary logic in the algorithm is because I didn't, when asking for a random number, have to restrict the number to two values. I could have stated that I wanted three values for "Coin"—one, two, and three—and then, in lines five and six said that if "Coin" is equal to the number one or two, then display "It is a head," and if "Coin" is equal to the number three, then display "It is a tail." Thus, the virtual coin I would have creat-

* Although "randomness" is computer science is in actuality pseudorandomness, but that's another story.

ed in the algorithm would not be a "fair" coin, but rather one weighted by a two to one margin in favor of heads; and, the values that "Coin" could have assumed in this algorithm (either one, two, or three) are no longer binary, but trinary. Yet the end result is still either heads or tails—which is binary. Thus, elements of Hitchcock's corpus might lend themselves to reduction and analysis via a complex overlay of such algorithms written in pseudocode.*

Or maybe not. Algorithms are recipes that need to be defined or relayed in advance of a process, but there's so much in Hitchcock that is more organic or at least hard to pin down and systematize in an algorithmic way. Hitchcock is not as—what is the word I am looking for?—*deterministic* as one initially supposes.

So, instead of algorithms, probability theory might be a more appropriate model. Consider *The Black Swan: The Impact of the Highly Improbable* (2007) by Nassim Nicholas Taleb. The book contains many interesting ideas about risk, chance, empiricism, capitalism, the normal distribution (the bell curve), and more, that it might almost be mined forever for fruitful cross-disciplinary ideas. Maybe its ideas could be mapped onto Hitchcock.

Let me briefly summarize a couple of the book's main points (although a cursory summary cannot do the book justice). Taleb's central focus is on how and why we fail at assessing risk and fall short of predicting the "big events," such as 9/11 or the financial collapse of 2008-9. Taleb introduces two types of world models: Mediocristan, a place that's mathematically predictable using the normal distribution, and Extremistan, a place much less predictable. People's heights, among other statistically predictable situations, can be thought of as a data set corresponding to Mediocristan, whereas data points gathered from the stock market can be thought of as corresponding more closely to Extremistan. It is sometimes difficult to tell which world is more appropriate for a given data set or environment you've set out to model. Where these two types of world—the world of Extremistan and of Mediocristan—coincide, at a place called the "Platonic Fold," the eponymous "Black Swans"—those major events of prior unpredictability—pop up. Messy reality clashes with faulty conceptions of it. Fleshing out these notions in a related article he published about foreign affairs,

---

* Read the earlier chapter "Fitting into Kaplan's Suit" for a fleshed-out example; in addition, refer to the Appendix for more on computer programming.

Taleb said, "Although the stated intention of political leaders and economic policymakers is to stabilize the system by inhibiting fluctuations, the result tends to be the opposite. These artificially constrained systems become prone to 'Black Swans'—that is, they become extremely vulnerable to large-scale events that lie far from the statistical norm and were largely unpredictable to a given set of observers."

In his book, Taleb also offers the example of the turkey to describe how most prognosticators were blindsided by the financial crisis: in a related article, he writes, "The life of a turkey is illustrative: the turkey is fed for 1,000 days and every day seems to confirm that the farmer cares for it—until the last day, when confidence is maximal [and the turkey is slaughtered by the farmer]. The 'turkey problem' [i.e., the problem of induction, of predicting the future based on the past] occurs when a naïve analysis of stability is derived from the absence of past variations. Likewise, confidence in stability was maximal at the onset of the financial crisis in 2007."*

Taking a cue from *The Black Swan*, it might be fruitful to read at least some of Hitchcock's films as probabilistic documents, and Taleb's book, amazing though it is, is part of a larger series of texts that analyze real-world events utilizing various aspects of probability theory (such as Bayesian analysis, for instance, named after the Rev. Thomas Bayes, who never published his results). To take just the "turkey problem": one can read *The Wrong Man*'s (1956) Manny (Henry Fonda), a person so committed to routine and order, as having maximal confidence in his agency and control, only to be "slaughtered" by a "farmer": Manny believes he lives in the predictable world of Mediocristan, whereas he actually lives in Extremistan—and his arrest and lockup is the Black Swan of the movie, the Platonic Fold where Mediocristan and Extremistan collide. We see similar types of Black Swans emerge in *Psycho*, *Rear Window*,

---

* David Foster Wallace, in *Everything and More*, presents a similar albeit (probably fabricated) autobiographical example of poultry's ill-fated reliance on induction, this one involving "four chickens in a wire coop off the garage, the brightest of whom was called Mr. Chicken" who ultimately succumbs "when the hired man suddenly reached out and grabbed Mr. Chicken and in one smooth motion wrung his neck and put him in the burlap sack and bore him off to the kitchen."

*The Birds*,[*] and *North by Northwest*, the best James Bond film made while Sean Connery was still driving a milk truck.[†]

Connected to Taleb's systems is chaos theory, which can address semi-rational mathematical problems such as the apparent immeasurable length of the coastline of England or infinitely complex smoke patterns, and is made use of in the physical sciences to model that which eludes systematic description, thus engaging in a kind of poesis.[‡]

Beyond the mathematics, the algorithms, and the probabilities, in order to fully appreciate Hitchcock, perhaps a bit of anthropological ethnography is necessary, too. It is tough to systematize the symbolic realm of Hitchcock ethnographically as participant observers both inside (we live in the same kind of world, emotionally, physically, metaphysically, that the characters in the movies do—since we are human beings) and outside (we are not blatantly actors in a two-dimensional moving fiction, possible objections of Shakespeare notwithstanding) the "culture" in which the films of Hitchcock encapsulate; think of, among many others, Clifford Geertz's essays or Freud's "Totem and Taboo" as paradigmatic attempts to capture ethnographically the manifest and latent systems in a milieu.

Yet whatever rigorous methodology is applied to analysis of the systems in Hitchcock, we are still left with the same old problem noted in anthropology, philosophy, and even mathematics: the perspective one utilizes may be analyzed via a meta-perspective, and that via a meta-meta-perspective and so on, ad infinitum. More of a snafu[§] than a paradox—yet it still makes one wonder if all of these models of systems, mathematics included, are built on quicksand.

(2011)

---

[*] Obviously! It's probably Hitchcock's ultimate Black Swan film.

[†] *North by Northwest* predates any James Bond comic thriller—and manages to supersede them all (with the possible exception of 1969's *On Her Majesty's Secret Service*, George Lazenby's only turn as the secret agent. This is the only Bond movie that successfully transcends most of the silly tropes of the painfully predictable, formulaic series. And John Barry's lush score is so incredible it at times threatens to hijack the whole film). For more, see the chapter "Fifty Years of James Bond Films."

[‡] The author James Gleick elucidates the history and basics of chaos theory effectively in his book *Chaos*.

[§] Look up what this stands for if you don't already know.

# 76.

## THE SUPER BOWL "NUDGE": A DIALOGUE BETWEEN THE STAT G(R)EEKS

*The persons* of the Dialogue:

- EPSILON
- DELTA

*The Scene*: A hotel room in New York City, the morning of Super Bowl XLVIII (Seattle Seahawks versus Denver Broncos).

EPSILON: There was once a Super Bowl Shuffle. Might there also be a Super Bowl "nudge"?

DELTA: What ever do you mean?

EPSILON: Super Bowl games lately have been almost suspiciously close entering the fourth quarter. Where have the blowouts gone?

DELTA: Yes, I have noticed that too. But you would need evidence to demonstrate your assertion.

EPSILON: Very well. Let's examine every Super Bowl from the two leagues' merger onward. Take a look at the following summary statistics. ("Diff.," an abbreviation for differential, is simply the smaller score subtracted from larger score. For the sake of completeness, I have shown the standard deviations of the differentials as well.)

| | Mean of Diff. at Start of 4th | Mean of Diff. at Final | St. Dev. of Diff. at Start of 4th | St. Dev. Of Diff. at Final |
|---|---|---|---|---|
| 1971 to 1979: | 10.8 | 11.2 | 6.3 | 7.1 |
| 1980 to 1989: | 17.7 | 18.6 | 11.9 | 11.2 |
| 1990 to 1999: | 14.7 | 18 | 8.3 | 13.2 |
| 2000 to 2013: | 8.4 | 9.7 | 7.4 | 8.6 |

| | Mean of Diff. at Start of 4th | Mean of Diff at. Final | St. Dev. Of Diff. at Start of 4th | St. Dev. Of Diff. at Final |
|---|---|---|---|---|
| Before 2000: | 14.5 | 16.1 | 9.3 | 11.0 |
| 2000 to 2013: | 8.4 | 9.7 | 7.4 | 8.6 |
| 2004 to 2013: | 5.2 | 6.3 | 4.9 | 4.3 |

DELTA: Ah, that is interesting. Lead me through it.

EPSILON: In Super Bowls of the 1970s, the average score differential entering the fourth quarter was a touchdown and a field goal. By the 1980s, the gap had widened: the average score separating teams entering the fourth quarter was two touchdowns and a field goal. Even in the 1990s, the differential at the start of the fourth quarter was substantial: a bit more than two touchdowns. If not blowouts, many of these games—at least since the 1980s, if not before—could safely be considered decided.

DELTA: I concur. But what has happened thereupon?

EPSILON: Starting in 2000, games entering the fourth quarter were very much undecided: the gap between teams hovered at just a shade above a touchdown. Looking even more recently, since 2004 the Super Bowl has really tightened up—those recent games have been separated by *less than two field goals* when the fourth quarter commenced. Blowouts have become exceedingly rare.

DELTA: There most certainly must be a good explanation for this.

EPSILON: Yes, surely many innocent explanations, besides just mere chance alone, might be proffered. "Parity" is probably the best one. Through revenue sharing, ensuring high draft picks to poor-performing teams, and equitable access to technology for training and in-game analysis, the playing field between professional football teams has been somewhat leveled. To see if parity safely explains the tightening differentials, should we take a look at the games just prior to the big game—i.e., AFC and NFC Championships?

DELTA: Certainly.

EPSILON: Good. For the AFC (the American Football Conference) Championships, summary statistics are as follows.

| | Mean of Diff. at Start of 4th | Mean of Diff. at Final | St. Dev. Of Diff. at Start of 4th | St. Dev. Of Diff. at Final |
|---|---|---|---|---|
| 1971 to 1979: | 11.3 | 13.1 | 7.5 | 8.2 |
| 1980 to 1989: | 10.2 | 12.4 | 6.0 | 5.7 |
| 1990 to 1999: | 10.9 | 14.1 | 10.7 | 13.5 |
| 2000 to 2013: | 7.9 | 11.1 | 5.1 | 5.1 |
| | | | | |
| Before 2000: | 10.8 | 13.2 | 8.1 | 9.4 |
| 2000 to 2013: | 7.9 | 11.1 | 5.1 | 5.1 |
| | | | | |
| 2004 to 2013: | 8.2 | 9.9 | 5.5 | 4.8 |

EPSILON: And here are the data for the NFC (the National Football Conference) Championships:

| | Mean of Diff. at Start of 4th | Mean of Diff. at Final | St. Dev. Of Diff. at Start of 4th | St. Dev. Of Diff. at Final |
|---|---|---|---|---|
| 1971 to 1979: | 9.3 | 16.4 | 9.5 | 9.1 |
| 1980 to 1989: | 11.3 | 13.6 | 6.8 | 8.7 |
| 1990 to 1999: | 11.4 | 14.1 | 7.5 | 9.3 |
| 2000 to 2013: | 9.4 | 12.0 | 10.6 | 11.0 |
| | | | | |
| Before 2000: | 10.7 | 14.7 | 7.7 | 8.8 |
| 2000 to 2013: | 9.4 | 12.0 | 10.6 | 11.0 |
| | | | | |
| 2004 to 2013: | 7.4 | 10.0 | 6.2 | 8.0 |

DELTA: I am puzzled as to why parity doesn't serve us as the best-fit explanation for what we see statistically.

EPSILON: If "parity" really were the explanation, we would expect to see bigger differentials prior to parity's league-wide implementation in the Championship games as well as in the Super Bowl. Championship game differentials entering the fourth quarter would be similarly ballooned in the 1980s and '90s, while the differentials would likewise be substantially smaller in the 2000s and beyond.*

DELTA: But...

EPSILON: ...but that is not what we see in the Championship games—the extremes present in the Super Bowls are tempered quite a bit. The Championship games tend to be closer than the Super Bowls, with more consistent differentials, over the years. Especially with the AFC, the mean differentials are largely unchanged from decade to decade, with a slight contraction from 2000 onward. Admittedly, since 2004 the NFC Championships have contracted noticeably—but even the NFC's highest mean, in the '90s, wasn't that large to begin with: only a differential of slightly more than a touchdown plus a field goal.

DELTA: Ah, but have you tried analyzing the data using more sophisticated methods?

EPSILON: More fancy statistical methods, such as tests of significance and multiple comparison tests, can indeed help us slice and dice the data every which way—but even though our *p*-values from these statistical explorations will be very be low,† innocent explanations for *why* the game has changed are not forthcoming.

DELTA: Am I to assume that you are suggesting a conspiracy?

EPSILON: Well, what about a not-so-innocent explanation for the Super Bowl scoring change? Although conspiracy theories usually fall apart once evidence is carefully and thoughtfully examined, it

* Note that if "rule changes" were the explanation, the Championship games would reflect that, too.

† Using a two-tailed two-sample $t$ test of independent means, comparing Super Bowl differentials since 2004 with those before, we find $p = 0.0095$. Interpreting this $p$-value, we find that if there were indeed *no* difference in scoring between Super Bowls before 2004 and after, the chance of seeing the Super Bowl results we *have* actually seen is less than one percent—meaning that we have very high confidence that the level of scoring in the games is different recently. Note that a small $p$-value—or any $p$-value at all, for that matter—does not give us a reason *why*.

might be worth considering one here: the Super Bowl is (slightly) fixed. Not to the point where the league decides in advance the teams playing on Super Sunday or sets the score before the opening whistle. But perhaps where refs, players, coaches and other officials—the fewer involved, the better, of course—might "nudge" the score closer together as the fourth quarter approaches.*

DELTA: Why risk such a deception?

EPSILON: Why? Consider the price of a Super Bowl commercial: even a thirty-second spot costs millions of dollars. A game that's a blowout—i.e., one safely that's out of reach for the losing team by the beginning of the fourth quarter—might be a Super Bowl that people lose interest in. Televisions being shut well before the close of the game would be devastating to advertising revenue, and thus devastating to the league. The league has every interest to keep their biggest game of the year competitive till the play clock expires, keeping as many people glued to their seats as possible ready to soak up commercialism at its finest. Cue the Sam Spence music.

DELTA: Sam Spence?

EPSILON: He was the NFL Films' composer who set all those slow motion shots of footballs spiraling in the air to music.

DELTA: I see.

EPSILON: Although this Super Bowl "nudge" conspiracy theory might sound initially plausible, it is unlikely to be true, of course. At least, let's hope it's not true!—fixed football would be a tremendous affront to meritocracy. And, in terms of the theory of probability, just because scores are close year after year after year certain-

---

* Anecdotally, for example, recall that Super Bowl XLVII was heading toward blowout territory, with the Ravens up by more than three touchdowns after the half-time show. But then, after a half-hour power failure in the New Orleans Superdome, the 49ers came charging back, closing to within only five points by the time the fourth quarter began. Even Ravens linebacker Ray Lewis later publicly called the blackout a "conspiracy."

ly doesn't preclude the possibility of a non-conspiratorial explanation.*

DELTA: The logistics of executing such a plan—and of keeping it a well-guarded secret—would involve too many people to be feasible.

EPSILON: Sure. Occam's razor rules the day. But conspiracy or no, the question remains: Delta, why has the Super Bowl changed? And where have the blowouts gone?

DELTA: Good queries. But we can continue this dialogue en route. Let us now pack up or we will be late to the game.

EPSILON: Point taken. Be prepared for a close one tonight!

*The Scene*: A hotel room in New York City, the morning after Super Bowl XLVIII.

DELTA: Well?

EPSILON: Never mind.

(2014)

---

* Let's consider streaks. The book *How We Decide*, by Jonah Lehrer, discusses the gambler's fallacy, a common misconception people have when predicting chance events: "The most famous example of such a phenomenon occurred in a Monte Carlo casino in the summer of 1913 when a roulette wheel landed on black twenty-six times in a row. During the run, gamblers bet against black, since they assumed that the randomness of the roulette wheel would somehow 'correct' the imbalance and cause the wheel to land on red. The casino ended up making millions." The notion that such imbalances will "even-out" long-term—as the Monte Carlo gamblers believed—is termed the "law of averages." (Even Edgar Allen Poe subscribed to the law.) Unfortunately, author Jonah Lehrer's career later got derailed for fabricating a single Bob Dylan quote: "I just write them [my songs]. There's no great message. Stop asking me to explain." Certainly nowhere near an affront to journalism as Stephen Glass perpetrated when he concocted whole stories out of whole cloth for *The New Republic*.

# 77.

## So Fake It's Real: Moments of Truth in the WWE

Triple H (Paul Levesque) once said it best: the WWE (World Wrestling Entertainment) is akin to "violent Ice Capes." Professional wrestling, or "sports entertainment" (a moniker the brainchild of the mad-genius promoter Vince McMahon, CEO of the WWE), isn't fake, but merely staged to a degree: sure, matched are "fixed," in the sense that outcomes are predetermined,* but injuries can and certainly do occur.

Author Roland Barthes called it a "spectacle of excess," but there are moments in the spectacle that strain the unfair "It's all fake!" label that professional wrestling has fought for years to shake, largely because the fact that it was staged was a closely guarded secret for such a long time. Let's take a look at three of these moments.

*Moment 1: Owen Hart breaks "Stone Cold" Steve Austin's neck (August 1997)*

At the annual *SummerSlam* pay-per-view, one of the two biggest events the WWE stages every year, wrestler Steve Austin was scheduled for a big "push"—meaning his character was gaining considerable traction with crowds as of late, and, to build on that momentum, management brass were going to place a title on him: the Intercontinental Championship, at the time the second most important title. Austin had worked hard to get to that point, ap-

---

* Knowing that matches' results have been set in advance, but us audience members not knowing the outcomes, should create suspense during the action; but the suspense oftentimes revolves around upper management's prospective decision-making and backstage politics rather than the athletic merits of the in-ring performers—hence the distinction sports *entertainment*, rather than just sports.

pearing in multiple promotions, including the rival WCW (World Championship Wrestling,* now defunct), and adopting dead-end wrestling persona, such as the "Ring Master" gimmick.

Austin's opponent for *SummerSlam* was Owen Hart, son of the legendary wrestler Stu Hart and youngest of the Hart brood—at the time, his older brother Bret Hart was the undisputed top wrestler in the business. Both Owen Hart and Steve Austin were what are termed "technical wrestlers," wrestlers who creatively and athletically bring their matches to life using a mélange of holds and maneuvers rather than adopting a smash-mouth style of brute force, à la Hulk Hogan (Terry Bollea) and other massively bulked-up wrestlers of a previously steroid-suffused generation.†

The *SummerSlam* match between Hart and Austin went smoothly until the finish. After a series of moves and countermoves, Hart picked up Austin, turned him upside down placing Austin's head in between his legs, jumped up, and landed bottom-first on the mat. Done right, this move—called a "piledriver"—has a devastating look to it. Done incorrectly, it can cause serious injury. Many years before, when Hulk Hogan faced the Undertaker (Mark Calaway) at a *Survivor Series* pay-per-view, Hogan received serious injuries that ultimately required back surgery after a slip up during the Undertaker's finishing move, termed the (unsurprisingly) *tombstone* pile driver.

Somehow, Owen Hart botched the move and Steve Austin's neck snapped when it hit the mat. Austin later commented that, for about a minute, he couldn't move any of his limbs—he was convinced the piledriver had permanently paralyzed him. Quickly realizing what had happened, Hart taunted Austin, taunted the crowd, showboated in the ring, and bought time. About two minutes after the piledriver, Austin weakly leaned over and pulled Hart down for the pin, won the title, and had to be helped by WWE staff out of the ring and back into the dressing rooms.

---

* The most famous wrestler to emerge from the ranks of WCW—originally called the National Wrestling Alliance before its purchase by media magnate Ted Turner—is Ric Flair (Richard Fliehr), that stylin', profilin', limousine riding, jet flying, kiss-stealing, wheelin' n' dealin' son of a gun!

† Though those matches between what Bret Hart sardonically termed "dinosaurs" tended to be slower and less graceful than the current-day form, they were still very entertaining.

The two superstars had very career arcs after the match. Austin couldn't wrestle for about a year, but evolved into the biggest face (i.e., "good guy") the company had thus far seen simply by challenging the boss (i.e., Vince McMahon, who by this time had become an evil in-ring character named Mr. McMahon) in an amazing series of promos. But Austin never wrestled in the same lithe, quick way again.

Hart's story is more tragic: within two years of the match he was dead, having fallen a hundred feet into the center of a wrestling ring during a botched aerial entrance at a pay-per-view.*

*Moment 2: Mankind falls off the cell for a second time (June 1998)*

Perhaps the most infamous match in WWE history took place at the *King of the Ring* pay-per-view in June of 1998. Smack dab in the middle of the so-called Attitude Era, the match was lucky to even finish at all.

Mankind (Mick Foley) was one of the WWE's more bizarre creations: a half-masked masochist who unwisely put his body in harm's way, the character reached his apotheosis in the *Hell in the Cell*, an unrelenting chain-link structure surrounding the ring. The Undertaker and Mankind worked a program (a wrestling angle) that culminated in a match within the steel structure.

But instead of the match opening inside the cell, Mankind began by climbing to the top, forcing the Undertaker to pursue. After a scuffle, the Undertaker pushed Mankind off the top of the sixteen-foot cell—and he fell to the announce table below with a sickening crash. Trainers, WWE medical, and Vince McMahon himself quickly congregated around Mankind's prone body. A stretcher was brought out, Mankind placed on it and wheeled down the ramp, the match seemingly meeting a quick, strange end.

That was all planned. But what happened next, according to Mick Foley in his first two sharply observed autobiographical books, was unscripted. Mankind jumps off the stretcher, runs back

---

* Owen's brother Bret also suffered a tragic end to his career. After sustaining multiple concussions upon wrestler Bill Goldberg accidently kicking him square in the face during a match, he was forced to hang up his boots—only to suffer a debilitating stroke several years later when he fell off a bicycle.

to the cell, and climbs it—again. The Undertaker all this time, by the way, hadn't moved from the top of the cell, so he was ready to trade blows again with the masochistic brawler. A quick chokeslam later and the steel structure gave way—dumping Mankind right into the center of the ring.

Mankind was knocked unconscious; WWE medical again converged on his prone body. Like in the Austin-Hart match, there was a lot of stalling for time amid the confusion. The Undertaker jumped down into the ring and began faux threatening trainers and staff, all the while keeping a close eye on his opponent's health: would Mankind be able to continue? Unbelievably, he got up, though very clearly shaken, beaten and bruised—one close-up of Mankind shows a tooth lodged through his bleeding lip—and finished the match, which had "typical" spots of brutality, such as bodies falling on thumbtacks and the like.

Although not by any means pretty, the fifteen-minute match is a testament to how *not fake*, and terribly painful for its performers even in the most controlled circumstances, the WWE can be.

### *Moment 3: CM Punk quits (June 2011)*

In his epic autobiography *Hitman* (2009), Bret Hart listed three qualities necessary for success in sports entertainment: (1) Have a great look, (2) Exhibit in-ring knowhow, and (3) Work well on the mic, meaning, essentially, talk like a wrestler.

Picture the stereotypical wrestler reaming out his opponent on a microphone: there might be lots of shouting and threats and promises to do harm. Not all wrestlers approach the talking (or "promo") part of the job this way, but many do—thus the stereotype.

Very different was CM Punk (Phil Brooks), who broke into the WWE in the mid-2000s. More intellectual and frenetic than most, with move sets that respectfully paid homage to wrestling legends like "Macho Man" Randy Savage, his promos usually cut a fine line between truth and fiction.

But by 2011 CM Punk had had enough of the WWE—and this was not a wrestling angle. Punk felt underappreciated and underutilized, especially by being relegated to the middle of the card of the biggest event of the year: *WrestleMania.*[*] With his contract set to expire in less than a month, Punk was given time at the end of *Monday Night Raw* (amazingly, the longest-running episodic weekly program in the history of television) in late June 2011 to air his grievances—without a script and, for the most part, sans approval from higher-ups (they knew he was going to speak, and for how long, but didn't necessarily know the details word for word).

And air them he did. In a brilliant half-work, half-shoot,[†] six-minute monologue—his so-called pipe-bomb—filled with twists and turns and wrestling references galore, Punk sat cross-legged Indian style at the top of the ramp, microphone in hand, and exposed the dark underbelly of the business—perhaps nothing too shocking for the in-the-know fan, but probably news for the casual fan—and, in the process, elevated himself to the top-tier of the business. No one got hurt, no moves were botched—but pure truth was extemporized to millions, and wrestling was real once again.[‡]

(2013)

---

[*] Punk was slated to work with the third-generation wrestler Randy Orton. But The Miz (Mike Mizanin)—a man of modest talents who parlayed starring in an MTV reality show into a wrestling career—was set to face John Cena, the biggest star in the industry, in the main event of the show. As Punk later explained in the documentary *Best in the World* (2012), management's decision to have Miz headline *WrestleMania* instead of Punk was a slap in the face—and certainly an affront to meritocracy.

[†] In wrestling parlance, a "work" is something that's part of the show (for example: Randy Savage is bitten by Jake Roberts' python in the ring; despite the blood, it was all staged), whereas a "shoot" is an unscripted or unplanned event (for example: Shawn Michaels gets Bret Hart to tap out to the "sharpshooter," Hart's own submission hold, in a *Survivor Series* world title match in Montreal; Vince McMahon ordered the bell rung because he was worried that Hart, who had already resigned, would take the title belt with him to rival wrestling company WCW. The incident has been termed the Montreal Screwjob).

[‡] And, in a case of life imitating art (or the other way around), Punk quit the business, this time for real, only several years later.

# 78.

## Two Unrelated Ideas Perhaps Deserving Your Consideration

***Idea One*:** Promulgation of the term *multisyllabic*, a neologism meaning "a word that, depending on regional pronunciation, has a varying number of syllables."

Examples: *interesting* and *veteran.*

Question: When a word exhibits *multisyllabism*, its pronunciation seems to vary by at most one syllable. Is there a word that varies in pronunciation by *more* than one syllable?

***Idea Two*:** Elimination of daylight saving time in favor of splitting the difference.

Example: Instead of moving the clocks forward an hour for spring, let's move the clocks forward a half-hour—and never change the clocks again.

Question: Why do we still use daylight saving time—is it to conserve energy? I forget.

(2009)

# 79.

# Bullying—

## Five Poems

It's been said that the only difference between poetry and prose is that the poet controls where his lines begin and end whereas the prose writer does not. Award-winning poet Christopher Bursk has a somewhat similar definition of poetry—that it's just text with white space on the left side and white space on the right side of a paper.

Consider the poem "Housecleaning" by Nikki Giovanni—a bitingly short and devastatingly simple description of the author's house cleaning chores, with this kicker at the end: "and unfortunately this habit [i.e., cleaning] has / carried over and i find / that i must remove you / from my life." Or how about Sylvia Plath's gut-wrenching pieces about her family? Or Kathleen Sheeder Bonanno's amazing *Slamming Open the Door*, a book of poetry written in the form of a linear narrative documenting the murder of the author's daughter?*

* This book is so groundbreaking that in 2009 NPR's Terry Gross devoted the entire hour to interviewing Bonanno on *Fresh Air* about it—if you haven't heard the interview, it's worth a listen. *Slamming Open the Door* is the deeply

Poetry may also make manifest the power of the written word to convey the emotion and hurt of being bullied and the tremendous efforts needed to rebuild identity after direct or indirect trauma to the body, psyche, and soul: how bullying has life-long effects; how one can overcome, but not necessarily forget, the painful experiences; how the bully, by her behavior, ultimately pushes others away, isolating herself; how the bully has reasons and justifications for her actions; how one is a disengaged bystander of bullying[*] at one's own peril; and how even the experienced classroom teacher is frequently reduced to *ad hoc* responses when bullying rears its ugly head in a class.

The therapeutic nature of the writing process, it seems to me, cannot be overstated—and not just for the victims of bullying, either. In *True Notebooks* (2003), writer Mark Salzman describes his teaching experiences in Central Juvenile Hall in East Los Angeles. Adjudicated youth, when given proper encouragement and a forum, turn out powerful short stories and poems that at least help them grapple with the tragic twists of fate and wrong turns in their lives. Salzman includes much of their work in his book, and it all makes for an especially eye-opening read.

So *caveat emptor* to those who undervalue the power of the written word. The pen is mightier than the sword, after all.

*The poetry begins on the next page.*

---

moving but never sentimental book that the highly praised prose memoir of loss called *The Year of Magical Thinking* (by Joan Didion) wishes it was.

[*] One can even imagine a new version of pastor Martin Niemöller's poem "First They Came…," with the bully taking on the role of the Nazis (who were the über-bullies)—"First the bully came for the victim, and I did not speak out—because I was not a victim," etc.—and climaxing with the bully coming after "me," the disengaged bystander.

## *This Play's a Wreck*

She came into my class
All rambunctious as usual
Performing and pointing fingers this way and that
Declaring for all: "Mr. Lorenzo, can I have a college rec?"

But K., it's May,
You're a senior,
Aren't we a tad too late?

"No, no, I'm serious."
Laughter from the audience.

And Y. chimes in: "Ha ha, you are out of luck,
You big dumb basketball-playing f—"

Enough!
I don't want to hear another word.

Too late.
Pandora has escaped her box.
A close friend with Y.
J. was visibly upset with the exchange
She resolved to do something about it all.

J. sent me a letter that night
She wrote of how she felt "bullied
In our class"
Which is something I never noticed.

Bullying wasn't in the script!
I just had to read my teacher lines
*(Beat)*
And they had to read their student lines
*(Beat)*
And the play would be over
Applause!
On to next season

A new cast of characters awaits!

A teacher for years
And yet I couldn't read
The bullying part of the script.

J.'s letter to me was a scathing *New Yorker*-like review of
my two-bit off-off-Broadway classroom play
"I hated how you let that happen to Y.
It wasn't fair. Classrooms should be *safe spaces*
And I don't feel safe."

I took J. backstage
Away from the onlookers
And spoke to her in confidence
That next morning.

> I apologize, J.
> I just *have*
> To do better
> Directing my discipline.

Too late. J's father was
A co-head
Of the PTO
And
As such
Had much
Influence.

"Shut down this production!"
He demanded.

A teacher for years
And yet I couldn't read
The bullying part of the script.

Within minutes
My boss would enter the room
To try to catch a glimpse

Of a scene:
Turning a blind eye to the bullies.

> Open your math textbooks to
> *Lines of best fit* in Activity 10-10!
> Let's begin.

All listen.
No one acts up
When the department head is in.

It's too much for K. though
She breaks the fourth wall
And exits stage left, sobbing.
Someone tell me
What do I do now?

A teacher for years
And yet I couldn't read
The bullying part of the script.*

---

* For more detail about the real-life incident that this poem was based on, refer to the chapter "Mediation and Conflict Resolution in High School."

## *Walking Home on a Snowy Afternoon*

How cliché
To claim it feels like yesterday
When I was a boy in seventh grade, hardly built
I trudged home from my bus stop
Up snow-covered hills.

I can still feel the snow
That left my lips burning numb
After Robert and Nick heaved me and my bulky book bag
All to the ground.

I can still hear their cacophonous giggling
Like machine gun rounds
As they, by turns, ran in front of my path
*Ha ha ha ha ha*
Blocking my way inside my house.

I can still smell the oily fluid
In Nick's gray-and-black lighter
Shoved up inside my nostril
Perched to ignite.

I can still feel my body tighten
See my furrowed brow
Reflected in the ice patch I was held upside down over
And then they let go…
Crack! The ice flung away from a center point where my head hit.

I still feel like it was yesterday
I still twitch at the sound of a lighter's flickered start
Or an unsteady step that splits the ice beneath my feet
Or a slowly descending snowflake landing on my lower lip.

I still feel like it was yesterday.

## *A Particular Comfort*

I recently found a particular comfort in
rereading *Dreams from My Father*,
Barack Obama's autobiographical tome,
So beautiful its prose, so lyrical
Its melodies
Singing of a lost world, a far-away
Strange place, an Orient blanketed from
Most of us.

It's on page fifty-nine,
Deeply immersed in the thoughts of a
Ten-year-old boy
Back from an overseas adventure to a
United States that welcomes all;
And it's in Hawaii, no less
That bastion of cultural openness
That Obama is reminded of his Otherness
(with full apologies to Edward W. Said):

> *We sat at a table with four other children, and Miss Hefty, an energetic middle-aged woman with short gray hair, took attendance. When she read my full name, I heard titters break across the room. Frederick leaned over to me.*
>
> *"I thought your name was Barry."*
>
> *"Would you prefer if we called you Barry?" Miss Hefty asked. "Barack is such a beautiful name…." (And the students proceeded to laugh again, louder.)*

Paging Dr. Freud!—
"Barry" should be smoked out by now, right?
Unless I'm missing something,
A cigar isn't just a cigar.
And Freudian couch turn,
Can't help us learn
How even with a childhood hurt,
Young Bullied Barack turned out okay in the end.

An inevitable descent isn't chiseled into stone from birth
And that's why I found rereading *Dreams*
To be of a particular comfort.

## *Eight Ball*

She sets her teacup snugly back into its coaster
Leans forward
And glances down
Puzzled, the tea sloshes back and forth
And as if through a tiny blue window
Revealing an eight ball's insides
A message materializes
On the tea's shimmering surface

"Yes! You were a bully!" the message reads

"Definitely so! You were her judge and jury
You sentenced her
You threw away the key"

I had my reasons
They were all sound
That girl stuck her nose
Way too in my business

How could I have known
Things would turn out this way

A message appears
"Answer not clear. Try again soon"

So many illusions
That she was in the right
But now her best friend
Is gone

Everyone knows

And she's alone

She's all alone

## *On a Shoestring*

There was once a poor man who lived on the street,
and had nothing to do but look at his feet.

"Say, what's wrong bud, why the long face?
Isn't there anything good about this place?"

"My young boy, what little you know,
the key to happiness is money and dough.

"The method and formula to lots of success,
is tons of money in great amounts of excess.

"If I had a ton of dough and a large sum of money,
life would be grand and all my days would be sunny.

"I wouldn't have to sleep under newspaper sheets,
I wouldn't have to constantly gaze at my feet."

"Why not get a job friend, no?
That way you'll make lots and lots of dough."

"Don't you understand, don't you see?
There's nothing left that I could possibly be.

"I once made candles, but set the shop on fire.
Now there's no place that I would be hired.

"I want to be rich like Citizen Kane!
I don't wish to steal food ever again!

"But wait—now I see!
The answer was always right in front of me!

"Instead of looking at my feet,
I'll lie and I'll steal and I'll bribe and I'll cheat!

"I'll make tons of money and lots of dough,
this is the key young boy, if you must you know.

"So let me be blunt:
for all that cash I'll bear the brunt,
of what is sure to be a meritocratic affront."

"But it isn't moral! And it isn't sane!"

"Don't bully me boy—the rich do it again and again!

"Once I make all my money and get in the news,
I can buy what I've always wanted—a nice pair of shoes!"

(2008)

# PART VII

# SHORT STORIES

# 'THE ATWOOD HITCH'

"Let me tell you about my dream last night."

I had met Asa on the first day of college—well, more accurately, the first day of college orientation. We hit it off immediately, becoming fast friends and all the rest. I remember walking with him on the endlessly green campus at Town's College in our first semester, castles on either side of us, him shaking ever-so-slightly—a neurotic rail-thin tall and wobbly presence with a mop of dirty blonde hair—as he took deep puffs of his cigarette alternately talking about the meaning of song lyrics and the meaning of required freshman college courses.

I'll admit it—I was curious. "What was your dream?"

Once second semester hit, we both, by mere coincidence, ended up in the same Acting 101 class with Professor Tina Clowner. Yes, that Tina—the one who referred to Robert De Niro as "Bob" as if she had no better friend in the world. Well, *my friend* Asa and I were given a ready source of material with which to poke fun of Tina Clowner. It was in this class, during this time, that I really learned about Asa. About how he grew up in the area. About how he had once, and only once, smoked pot early in high school—yet still felt aftereffects from it years later (I guess that would explain his neuroses). About how his middle name was Hitch. And about how his last name was Atwood. Which, by mere coincidence, was the last name of my father's boss.

"Well, you were in my dream. I was at the top of a cliff, you were at the bottom, shouting something up to me."

Shit. My friend of two semesters, Asa Hitch Atwood, was my father's boss's son. Great—now things would be different. Now there would be a strained dialogue, a vaguely perceptible link forever-hanging over our interactions. But why clue him in? I would've never figured it out, except my mom asked me during one night how things were going at college and if had I met anyone nice. Well, mom, no girls, but I did meet a guy with whom I became fast friends. Oh, what's his name? Asa. Asa who? Asa Atwood. Shit.

"Okay. So I was moonlighting in your dream. But what was I shouting up to you?"

I didn't see much of a need—now *I* was the one getting neurotic—to mention it to Asa. For, well, years. Yeah—years went by before he figured it out, with a little gentle prodding. But I'm getting ahead of myself.

"You were warning me about Zairah."

The other part of this tale involves a girl (of course). Apparently, although I wasn't a witness to it, Asa and a rich Syrian girl by the name of Zairah met at Asa's sister's wedding, when Christina Atwood decided to shack up with a certain Tom Burton West. Well: at the Christina Atwood and Tom Burton West wedding, a certain Mister Asa Hitch Atwood and a certain Miss Zairah Sami Nafooz hit it off, despite Christina's repeated warnings to both to stay away from each other's ostensibly corruptible presences. And Asa has a way of fixating on things, so it was either good timing or dumb luck that caused him to show up two weeks later at Zairah's doorstep in Santa Monica, California—this Asa Atwood, being of the tiny town of Duryea, Pennsylvania. Three years, a proposal, and an engagement later, and I'm tearing open a wedding invitation.

"Asa, what was I saying about her?"

And what an elaborate invitation! The colors, the design—I suppose it looked chic, but what do I know? "Naseem and Nalida Nafooz and Asa and Amy Atwood [Asa's father was also named Asa] request the honor of your presence at the marriage of their children…at four o'clock in the afternoon / Sand Creek Country Club / Alexandria, Virginia / Reception to follow in Grand Ballroom." I made a hotel reservation and blocked off the day on my calendar.

"You were telling me to break up with her."

Looking back at the wedding now, years on, I think I can see where things went wrong. The morning I left for Alexandria, I had just the right amount of cereal remaining in the box and just the right amount of milk left in the container for a perfectly sized breakfast. I departed at just the right time in the morning, evading all the traffic that is the albatross of the highway traveler, and, despite the lack of a map, ended up at my hotel after a series of random turns somehow turned into the right one. Everything so far went off without a hitch. The mathematical perfection of my day—this day before his big one—was apropos of the groom with the palindromic name of Asa, who was now a struggling math teacher in the interior of Los Angeles.

"Why was I saying that? Why was I telling you to break up with her?"

The wedding rehearsal was in a Greek Orthodox Church right outside of D.C. As a groomsman, I had some responsibilities—like ushering people to the correct side of the aisle. Are you guests of the bride or groom? Oh, the groom? Then take a seat on the right side of the altar.

I also had to walk down the aisle with a bridesmaid. At the rehearsal, the bridesmaids were asked by Leonardo Christopoulos, elder and uncle of Asa, to pair up with the groomsmen. It felt like gym class all over again: waiting to be picked and watching people on either side of me get snatched away until there was no one left so *I'm forced* to pair up with the reluctant party. I'm no looker, but the bridesmaid I got stuck with was—let me be direct—ugly. Regardless, any chance of my connecting with a bridesmaid like my friend Asa did at his sister's wedding was quickly squelched since she barely laid eyes on me.

"Because—you knew."

Here's the thing: I'm not—how shall I put it—particularly sociable. At the rehearsal dinner the night before the Big Day, I was surrounded by about one hundred people—mostly Syrian—at a well-catered, deejayed affair, and only three people took the time to speak with me: Asa, Asa's father (who by now was well aware that my dad was one of his numerous minions) and a nineteen-year-old girl by the name of Delilah. Everyone else, Zairah included, pretty much ignored me. But I do faintly remember Zairah asking me how often I spoke to Asa anymore, considering he now resided in the Great State of California and me more than two thousand miles away. At the end of the evening, all the groomsmen received a "Player's Club: Deluxe Casino Gambling Set," a fitting gift considering what a chance Asa was taking.

A chance made all the more acute because of that dream, which Asa had about two years before the big day. You see, what I knew—the me in his head, the arbiter of reason, the Jiminy Cricket to his neurotic Pinocchio—was that Zairah, who would be too bored with a guy who had a palindromic name like Asa, had eyes for another, a person whom she also met at Christina's wedding. Zairah was, is, an actress. Her tryst with Asa was a mere substitution until a more permanent one could be found.

But at her wedding, in which triplet recessional cello players later doubled (or, I suppose, more accurately, tripled) as belly dancers at the reception in the Great Ballroom, in which bride and groom were lifted on chairs while undulating cheers pierced the air, in which Christina, the maid of honor, barely could get out the words of a clunky speech about the lucky couple without breaking into laughter, in which Zairah's father silenced the crowd with his tales of Asa's frightful asking of permission to marry his daughter, in which I was seated at table 22, in which I witnessed Zairah, the social genius she is, work the room like a modern-day Syrian black-haired, brown-eyed Grace Kelly—the dream found its fully-realized form. The Syrian bride had shown her true colors.

The divorce, which was particularly nasty, occurred only three months after the vows. Asa Hitch Atwood was, for lack of a better description, blindsided and devastated. He was a quivering mass of jelly. We talked many times afterwards, running through the timelines, the mistakes, the routes and alternate routes of our lives, crisscrossing as they had all these years.

And what of his ex-wife? Zairah, that socialite of the crown jewel of the West, California, took well to being the new Mrs. West.

So: if a wedding goes off without a hitch, is that a good thing—or a bad thing?

(2006)

# 'Claudius the Monkey'

Recently, I was so desperate for literary inspiration that I practically smuggled an old-fashioned Underwood No. 5 typewriter in with me when I went to the zoo. Not for me to use, mind you. For the monkeys. No monkeys? Gorillas would do just fine. Luckily I don't have maimouphobia or nikandphobia.*

You see, I had been lead to believe in the "infinite monkey theorem": that a monkey with a typewriter might be able to produce Hamlet. Or maybe something a tenth as good. It didn't matter. Just something.

Let me show you where I got stuck—literarily, of course. Here is my unfinished story, called *The Stoke Song.*

*When it happened, it happened quickly.*

*"I didn't know what hit me," Loraine Tyson, a mother of three, said. "It was at the end of spring. The windows were open. I was getting ready for work*

---

* Though I do have coulrophobia, so you know I'm not clowning around here.

*and the radio was on. It was on in the background, and I wasn't really listening too closely. I reached to open the fridge and my hand just seized up and"—she pauses here—"I don't know, I just passed out. I woke up in the hospital to two doctors pressing my eyelids open, flashing a pin-sized light into my pupils, asking me to look every which way. It hurt to move. I was trapped. I heard the steady beeping of a heart monitor and felt lumps on my chest—there were electrodes running up and down a thin hospital gown I was wearing. Luckily my husband was there, holding my hand. But it was a nightmare."*

*The cause of Mrs. Tyson's nightmare? You probably have already heard: a song by the Carson Brothers entitled...well, I've been told by my editors not to insert the title here (which, again, you probably already know) for fear of lawsuits. Not lawsuits because of intellectual property copyright infringement, mind you; rather, because my editors here at* FORTNIGHT MAGAZINE *are afraid that if you, dear reader, even so much as read the song's title, it might trigger the seizures that thousands of people across the country have suffered from (or, in a few cases, strokes), supposedly due to hearing the three minute, three second pop tune.*

*How strong is the evidence that the Carson Brothers' song has caused this epidemic? According to James Berden, professor of epidemiology at Harvard University, very strong. "Although no experiments have been conducted, and none probably will ever be, statistical patterns of song-play and maladies have been documented," Berden explains. "All signs point to a near-perfect correlation between seconds of the song heard while still conscious and severity of the seizures. In fact, all of the stroke victims reported making it through the entire song before losing balance and, ultimately, consciousness."*

*Berden has a personal stake in this: about two months ago, his seventeen-year-old daughter suffered two successive seizures after hearing the song in a friend's car (her friend wasn't affected). Although the seizures were minor and she's had none since, Professor Berden, along with a colleague at Harvard, Juliet Grobatosky, an assistant professor of neuroscience, has made it his mission to discover why the song adversely affects neural pathways. That search led Berden to a small village in a remote part of the world.*

But: back to the zoo. I found a willing monkey to help me out, help me complete the story. I assumed he was willing because he didn't phone his agent when I presented him with my typewriter. On a wooden stake adjacent to his cage, carved in big, block letters, was (I assume) the monkey's name: Claudius. Sounded Shakespearean enough. Is that irony? I'm not sure. It sounds vaguely ironic, though.*

I think that I needed more than one typewriter, and more than one monkey, but all I had was Claudius. It's probably better if I didn't tell you how I slipped Claudius my Underwood No. 5 typewriter (and the paper) through the steel mesh and how I persuaded him (at least I think I persuaded him) to actually pound the keys and how I ultimately got my typewriter back. I really don't want get into any sort of trouble. (Please don't tell on me.)

I can just imagine it: a knock on my door. Who's there? The police, open up. What did I do? Sir, were you at the zoo yesterday? Um, yes, why? Well, we have a report of a man forcing a monkey to type on an old-fashioned typewriter. That violates Section 3.7c of the No-Typing-Monkeys Code of Pennsylvania. The No-Typing-Monkeys Code? Yes sir. You made that up! No I didn't sir. You have the right to an attorney. Should you not be able to afford one, one will be provided for you…

It certainly would make headlines. Man bites dog story, only with a monkey and a typewriter and some Miranda Rights. Not exactly what I want to be known forever for. My epitaph: Not Quite Shakespeare / He Made Penal History, Nonetheless / Monkeying Around / With Claudius. Now that does sound vaguely ironic.

Do you want to know what Claudius typed? I suppose you do. No need to keep you wondering any longer, so here's all he wrote:

```
GOSFDN XVFREJSF 4R23MFSKVJDS94
FDSJK94NMSF SJHLJKSDVX XV
```

Two hours of waiting, for that.† I'm trying not to let the perfect be the enemy of the good, but what Claudius wrote is certainly not a

* I find irony easy enough to define in theory—meaning the opposite of literal meaning—though tough to spot in practice. In *Brain Droppings*, George Carlin memorably defined irony this way: "If a diabetic, on his way to buy insulin, is killed by a runaway truck, he is the victim of an accident. If the truck was delivering sugar, he is the victim of an oddly poetic coincidence. But if the truck was delivering insulin, ah! Then he is the victim of an irony."

† You'd probably expect, at this point in the story, for me to calculate the probability of those particular letters being typed by Claudius. Think about it this way: if every letter is independent, then even the chances of typing the

cure for what's been ailing me. *The Stroke Song* was supposed to be metaphorical, illustrating how society traps us, cages us all in (or something like that—all fiction has got to have deeper meaning), but Claudius only produced some random drivel as its finish.

I should also probably mention that, after I got home, I had to clean off my Underwood No. 5. It was covered in shit.

That night I had a nightmare. I was at the zoo again, inside Claudius' cage. But Claudius wasn't there. Instead, a crimson half-monkey, half-devil apparition shrieked and danced with a glowing wand, loudly laughing, repeatedly flicking his lizard tongue, taunting me, and I was stuck in the cage. I awoke with a start, shivering.

And I really don't know what I was thinking, but I decided a week later to go back to the zoo. This time I didn't take the chicken salad (okay—I shouldn't have even revealed that because I don't want to get into any trouble,[*] as I said before. But I did bribe Claudius with chicken salad the first time I met him), if only to avoid him shitting all over my Underwood No. 5 typewriter again. (I didn't realize, until I had to, how difficult it is to clean these typewriters, especially between the keys.)

No success, again. I wanted to get the monkey to work like a dog,[†] but I couldn't even get the monkey to type. Not one damn key. What a tragedy.[‡]

Oh well. That's all I got. Another unfinished story, lost in the funhouse of unfinished stories.[§] Guess I'm not so creative after all—so much for that literary inspiration. But when I turned around to leave the zoo, I could swear I heard a monkey laughing.

(2007)

---

word "NO" are 1 in 26x26, or 1 in 676. Coming up with *Hamlet*? Not in the lifetime of the universe.

[*] The great Mr. Barth tells us that "[t]he more closely an author identifies with the narrator, literally or metaphorically, the less advisable it is, as a rule, to use the first-person narrative viewpoint." Indeed: how odd would this narrative be if it were a "confessional" based on a true story? You, dear reader, probably would lose a great deal of respect for me. And, if you didn't, I suppose I'd have to lose respect for you.

[†] Isn't it odd that the expression "to work like a dog" means to work hard? Most dogs I know just lounge around a lot, occasionally begging for food by lifting up a paw or two.

[‡] If I went back to the zoo to try a third time, tragedy would turn into farce.

[§] Sorry, Mr. Barth.

# ‘No Solution’

Mark Jones Lorenzo often reflected on how quickly the years for him had passed but how ever-so-slowly the days of the calendar had turned. Not that he had a problem with slowly passing days: at the cusp of middle age, he looked for ways to stand athwart, hands outstretched, and stop time—but ever the math teacher, he knew that time only grows quicker, as William James noticed, since each coming year is a still-smaller percentage of one’s life already lived.

But Mark supposed that he could at least rekindle old friendships from time to time, hoping that with the rekindling (and the re-rekindling sure to follow after another interminable time of losing touch) a buried vein of recollection would be tapped; routines and images of his past would come rushing into his brain and in their wake youth might be relived, at least for a moment.

It was on just such a vaunted lurch into the past that Mark awoke a hibernating memory—more accurately, a Byzantine web of memories—that were centered not in his head but at the pit of his abdomen, just above his beltline.

"Mark! How've you been?"

"Great, Steve. You?"

"Oh, fine. Wow, amazing seeing you here. I actually heard what happened from Sam at work a while ago. I meant to call you up or at least e-mail you. Sorry," Steve said, as if he were reading from a script.

"That's all right. It happens, y'know? Nothing you can do."

Mark was being dragged into a conversation he didn't want to have. Steve had last worked with him twelve years ago. They were both hired at the school the same summer. Steve was younger, more idealistic than Mark. Mark always held a cynical, pessimistic—he termed it "realistic"—view of things. He had met Steve at a new teacher induction. And they had both met Chloe there.

Steve and Chloe took to each other quickly. Within a month, they were looking for reasons to spend time together. Extracurricular time. Their reasons became less and less about school work and more and more about them—and, despite their natural aversions to workplace dating, they decided to cautiously dip their toes into the romance pool. Steve and Chloe just recently celebrated their eighth wedding anniversary. There's no special significance to an eighth anniversary, short of it occurring at all.

Mark had watched their swing from new teachers to new lovers at the front of life's proverbial theater. He and Steve had, in their first year, plotted strategies to help Steve capture Chloe's interest as more than a friend. Steve, though optimistic, hadn't had the confidence to stick his neck out, lest it get chopped off. But Mark was tailor-made for the role of confidant and backroom organizer. "She came to lunch today and you weren't there, Steve—and the look on her face—oh!—she was clearly upset." Mark had never really been sure about all this—never really been sure that Chloe had the kind of thing for Steve that Steve had for her, although she sure seemed to express it in deed if not in word—but Mark encouraged him to go after her nevertheless. Easy enough, since Mark wasn't the one with skin in the game.

Mark's friendship with Steve cooled after he married Chloe and left for another teaching job. Mark always lamented that, but he had a history of losing touch with people, of letting friendships lapse into silence. So many former friendships-as-artifacts, detritus of a systemic interpersonal failure, markers of regret. As Samuel Johnson once wrote about friendship, "There is no human possession of which the duration is less certain."

Steve motioned for Mark to sit down. Steve sat down beside him.

"I'm just here looking for a book for my son," Steve said. "He has a damn social studies report to write up and I need books on ancient Rome."

"How is Jack?"

"Jack's good, likes second grade a lot. He had some problems with his teacher earlier in the year but it's all resolved now."

"And Chloe? She doing well?"

"Yeah, everything's fine. So how 'bout you, man? Teaching still treating you well?"

Mark didn't want to get into this. He felt his stomach cheerfully tying itself into knots whenever a conversation with anyone got personal. He didn't feel like throwing out even the smallest bit of information that Steve could pick up on and start grilling him about. Keep Pandora safely in her box.

"No problems," Mark said, as a blizzard of nerves set in.

"Good. Glad to hear it. Look, I've gotta go to look for a book but it was good seeing you man. And again, I'm sorry I didn't contact you when..."

"It's fine," Mark interrupted. "Everything's fine. Go get your Rome book. It was good seeing you again," he lied.

Feeling the nerves exit as quickly as they had arrived, Mark felt a slight chill. He turned left at the end of the library's fiction stacks and, with his head down, stepped into the bathroom.

Mark splashed warm water on his face. When he looked up and saw his reflection in the mirror, he was unrecognizable to himself, however momentarily, and that startled him.

He didn't accept what he looked like these days—his rumpled, graying features, his shriveled up yet moist hands, his hunched back, those absurdly massive unmanageable black eyebrows—what he had become; he had had more potential than this. He was waiting for his life to start. How did he land in this waiting room, this purgatory? He was a young man trapped in an old man's body.

Not much use going through the timeline in his mind again, he thought. It'll only serve to justify the past.

To the right of the bathroom's mirror was a large, plate-glass window that revealed a panoramic view of the city. From this angle, cars were hard to make out; buildings shot up like stalagmites, blocking out the slowly setting sun. He heard the soft strings of a train whistle in the distance.

Four or five pigeons were perched on the sill just outside the window. They fumbled around, looking for food, keeping busy, blissfully unaware of being unaware. Mark watched them. And he envied them.

A passive observer. Maybe a voyeur. However Mark labeled himself, he thought, it all probably stemmed back to his upbringing. Oh, what a Freudian approach to the present—blame it all on the past! How convenient. How logical. How defeatist: after all, what can one do about one's past? It is no small claim to make that one's past is chiseled into the hardest of stone.

"Four-fifths of problems we encounter are best solved by ignoring them," his mother used to tell him. It was a breathtakingly, crushingly passive philosophy of life Mark perhaps too broadly applied. Problem, problem, problem, problem, problem. Only address one of them; ignore the rest. They'll go away. And this too shall pass.

But which of these five problems to tackle? Unfortunately, Mark didn't learn that part. His judgment was sorely lacking. He wandered through life like Mr. Magoo, blindly going from point A to point B to point C, blithely unaware of the challenges and opportunities he'd missed. And that was why, he reasoned as his eyes remained transfixed on the busy pigeons outside the windowsill of the public library, he was still alone.

Where did it start, this slowly sloping downwardly depressing ride? When was that one moment of no return, that one moment that Mark wished he could change? These last eleven years were so lonely. Maybe he did have to separate the chaff from the wheat in his mind; he had to stop mentally chasing what Alfred Hitchcock had famously termed the MacGuffin—that plot device that all characters seek but that doesn't matter in the slightest to the story—and begin finding some answers.

Maybe it started the day Rachel and her family moved in two doors down. That was a couple of weeks before second grade started. Mark and his mom and dad crossed two lawns to meet the new neighbors. Rachel asked Mark who his friends were.

"I don't really have any friends," Mark replied.

"I don't understand. No friends?"

"None. Nobody likes me, I guess."

By the sixth grade Rachel, who took the bus home every day with Mark, wasn't, shall we say, simpatico with him. She accused him of a litany of offenses, including (1) still sucking his thumb (not true) and (2) dorkily being able to recite the alphabet faster backwards than forwards (well, true).

Mark hadn't thought of Rachel in years. But Sherry—that's someone who's surely had a profound effect. He had first seen her coming out of Mr. L.'s class in ninth grade. She was a diminutive thing with a shock of blonde hair and gray-blue eyes. She wasn't particularly pretty but had a presence about her that excited him.

He was two grades behind her and, figuring he wasn't ever going to end up in a class with her, discovered that she was a member in good standing of the girls' cross country team—so he deigned to join the boys' team since they traveled with the girls on away meets. On a bus ride home late that season, Sherry spoke to Mark for the first time.

"Want a candy corn?" she asked.

"Uh, no thanks," Mark, slack-jawed, nervously answered.

And that was that. Until Mark, a month later, decided to extend the conversation a bit. He looked her number up in the phone book and, on a particularly cold Wednesday night in April, had a particularly bizarre conversation.

"Hello?"

"Yes?"

"Hi, this is Mark, from the cross country team?" Mark wasn't asking, but his lack of confidence caused the statement to come out as a question.

"Um, okay, hi. What's up?"

"Nothing, I just, uh, wanted to ask about an upcoming meet?"

"You what?"

"I just wanted to ask you about a meet we have coming up? It says here on the schedule that we are going to the George School next Tuesday?"

"Okay?"

"And I wondered how, uh, far away that is 'cause I've never been there before and..."

"It's about forty-five minutes from the school."

"Forty-five minutes, okay, thanks."

"Is that all?"

"Well, um..."

"Yes?"

"I was wondering if..." Mark paused.

"Yes?"

"Never mind. I'm not sure why I called. It was a mistake, maybe?"

"What?"

"Yeah. I guess it was a joke. Okay, bye."

"Uh, okay, bye."

How embarrassing. Mark's sure that the conversation went on a little longer than that—maybe it lasted around seven minutes—but not much was said, and he definitely remembers the end—the "joke" explanation—that was the clownish *deus ex machina* of a rather farcical phone call.

Mark takes a split second to jump three years into the future. It's the first day of sophomore year at college. He finds himself in an English honors class of seven girls, no boys, and—amazingly!—*two* professors who are, of course, female. So much estrogen in the room.

On that first, rather awkward day of class, Mark meets Carrie Donaldson. She has straight dark blonde hair down to her shoulders, the bluest eyes he's ever seen, and wide hips in perfect proportion to her shoulders. And she clearly, undeniably, profoundly dislikes the very sight and being of Mark.

Mark remembers the feeling of bewilderment that comes over him when he first realizes this: Carrie finishes reading a poem she's written and, as an expression of good faith, Mark comments on its effective use of meter.

"Thanks, but no thanks," she snaps. "The meter wasn't good. You're just trying to surreptitiously mock me and I don't appreciate it. Save your comments if they're not serious."

Like a clichéd comedy, where two people who initially virulently dislike each other fall in love by the end of the story, Mark and Carrie take to each other like a clam and a pearl.

They begin what they term an "epic correspondence," via e-mail, handwritten epistle, and phone. They think they are characters smack dab in the middle of a Nicholas Sparks' novel. This is as close as two people could be, they believe.

They are engaged by the time Mark had begun his master's work, after a particularly whirlwind courtship. Mark had learned so much about himself during those years. For instance, he never realized how much he enjoyed...

"Excuse me."

Mark turned around and saw what looked like an apparition.

"Excuse me!"

"Oh, sorry," Mark said.

"Hey, I'm just trying to use the sink here. Could you move please?"

Mark slid out of the way. Apparently the old man, who carried one of the library's newspapers neatly folded underneath his left armpit, couldn't be bothered to use the sink closer to the door. He just had to use the one next to the window.

The sun had disappeared from the horizon. In its place was a pinkish-red shimmering. The pigeons had decamped from the windowsill. And the old man, with a wheeze, shuffled out of the library's bathroom.

Alone in there again, it was back to the past. Mark had many memories of Carrie, some of them good, some of them too painful to recollect. Needless to say, Mark and Carrie terminated their relationship shortly after their engagement. It was a mutual end, or at least that's the reasoning Mark comforted himself with. The central problem was the painful—no, crippling—anxiety Mark began to feel around Carrie as things telescoped from less to more serious.

"Anxiety may be compared with dizziness," Kierkegaard wrote. "He whose eye happens to look down the yawning abyss becomes dizzy." Mark was spinning. He knew he loved her, yes; but at such a young age, he was too uncomfortable with himself to ever be comfortable enough with her. She gave him panic attacks to die for.

Jumping ahead another four years—years marked by sporadic dates with doctors, surgeons, specialists, hospitals, because as time wore on Mark realized he wasn't exactly the healthiest of specimens—Mark landed squarely on the second day of his second year teaching.

It is an in-service day. All the teachers from the entire district are there. A rather plumpish, somber young woman sits down next to him in the school's auditorium. He looks but doesn't recognize her. Not a word is said between them that morning. Not a "hello," not a "this is boring." Not anything. Maybe around eleven o'clock, an attendance sheet is passed to Mark for him to sign. He passes it over to the drab presence next to him. She takes it without comment. Mark sees her sign the sheet out of the corner of his eye. He can't make out her name.

Lunch comes and goes, and Mark returns to the auditorium a bit early. Few teachers are there. He retakes his seat from the morning. A minute later, the young woman retakes her seat next to Mark. Moments pass. Silence. Finally, Mark decides to say something.

"Hi. My name's Mark Lorenzo. How're you?"

She lights up, mumbles something under her breath, and turns to Mark.

"I'm good. This simply could not be more boring!"

"Yes!"

"Are these meetings here always like this?"

"Oh yes. Always!"

"Great. Thirty years of these and I don't know how I'm going to stay awake through this one," she mumbles to no one in particular. "Maybe I'll paint a wall and watch it dry."

Teachers filter back into the room little by little, but by the time the next speaker comes to the stage to discuss some sort of silly new-age method of pedagogy, Mark already knew something was different about this girl. He honestly felt like he had known her for years. What a sharp, dry wit she had! Mark was enticed by her down-to-earth-yet-sarcastic style, her unique way of twisting around words and situations to find the humorous lining beneath. Mark was also struck by how she resembled Tippi Hedren, that two-hit wonder actress from decades ago. Not so much in how she looked—although there was a bit of that, too. It was her intonation, her cadence, her way of carrying herself that gave Mark just the vaguest impression that she belonged in another time.

Mark shot her off an e-mail a couple of days later inviting her to join him and some of the younger teachers at the local bar for a drink. She readily accepted, but complained in her reply how overwhelmed she was, how physically ill she felt from less than a week at this tough new school.

The bar wasn't too far from their school, so they walked there together. Along the way, Mark mentioned to her that he didn't drink.

"That's okay," she said. "My last boyfriend didn't eat meat."

At the bar, she and Mark were exclusive—none of the other teachers even bothered to talk to them. Two weeks passed and this time she invited Mark to go out. And again, they were exclusive in the presence of their fellow teachers. It seemed like she liked Mark. Mark was happy for the first time since Carrie. Things were going well.

He was determined to see this one through, anxiety or not—but first he had to make it a bit more formal, with all the trims and trappings. A true first date would be in order.

A couple of weeks later, after school, paper and pen in hand, he walked down the steps to her room on the first floor to get her number so he could call her up and ask her out on a real date. On the second-to-last step, he slipped and nearly fell. It was an ominous sign. Because when he got to her classroom, this is what happened:

"Can I have your number?" Mark said as he nervously thrust the paper and pen in her hands.

"Yes, here it is," she said as she wrote it, "but in what capacity, because I must tell you—I don't date at the workplace."

"Excuse me?"

"I don't date at the workplace." She handed the pen and paper back to Mark. Her number was written on the paper in large, bold blue lettering.

"But...why not?"

"I had a bad experience at my last job that cost me an opportunity. I'm sorry. It's not you. I just don't date at the workplace."

Mark couldn't believe it. Didn't date at the workplace? What, exactly, were they doing then? Weren't those bar jaunts de facto dates? How could this sudden declaration, this Sherman statement, have not come from her before? You know, before Mark made a complete idiot out of himself?

"We can hang out, Mark. But we can't date. It's not you." She shook her head vigorously and repeated "it's not you" a couple more times for good measure.

Mark paused; he was confused, bewildered; he pursed his lips and was terribly surprised at what came out of his mouth in response.

"Well, I just want to tell you that I really like you. I just wanted you to know that."

She looked at Mark, frozen-faced. Mark half expected her to crumble like a pillar of salt. But she said nothing. Mark, defeated, slumped his shoulders, put his head down, turned around, and walked back up the stairs.

About a year after this relationship failure, Mark was beginning to fancy himself a regular Houdini, a master escape artist when it came to relationships—even when he was trying to get hold of what looked like a no-fail first date, it was never in the cards for him: he had the anti-Midas touch.

Take Sue, for instance. Oh, Sue. Sue of the Internet. Sue of the beautiful posted picture and florid profile. Sue of the intricately woven e-mails. Sue of the emotional, never-ending phone conversations. Sue of the first date at a bookstore—don't bring flowers or any gifts! Sue of the frisk walk out after saying hello to Mark, never to return. Sue for your self-confidence back. (Mark wished he could.)

Mark was sick again, and sick of it—wasn't it Nietzsche who said that "as regards sickness, should we not be almost tempted to ask whether we could in general dispense with it?" A date with an MRI machine that Valentine's Day was too much. It wasn't a cheap date: stretching out inside one of those machines costs around two grand a pop. But, while inside, Mark had time to think. He prayed in that cavernous tomb, as it shrieked and rattled and whistled en route to snapping photos of Mark's head from every angle.

Cupping his hands together, he whispered, "Please, don't let these MRIs show anything special. I don't want to be an MRI model at future doctor-patient fashion shows (or morbidity and mortality conferences). And y'know what? I'm sick of being alone. I'm sick of it. I really want a girl to take to me already, to really like me—for there be to no question of it. It's about time."

Maybe an MRI tube is really a direct conduit to the Almighty, amplifying its occupants' prayers to the heavens above. Or maybe not. Regardless, thank God, the MRI showed nothing pathological. But only because the machine couldn't make out loneliness.

Mark glanced at his wristwatch. It was already one o'clock and he had not yet eaten. He was starving; he had had breakfast much too early this morning. First, though, a quick check of today's news.

As he stepped out of the bathroom at the library, he bumped into Steve again.

"Found your Rome book?"

Steve smiled and said, "Yup—right here. Just checked it out. Jack will definitely be able to use this."

"Great. You probably shouldn't take that book into the bathroom with you, though."

"Oh yeah, right. You leaving now man?"

Mark gathered his thoughts. "No, I think I'm going to go on the computers for a second and see what's going on in the world."

"Well, if I don't see you again, it was good seeing you." Steve thrust his right hand out to shake Mark's. Mark obliged.

"You too," Mark said.

Mark walked to the library's circulation desk and motioned for the attention of the youngest-looking librarian.

She walked up to the front of the circulation desk. Mark was startled at how old she looked up close—she didn't appear to be that old from afar. The hair near her temples was graying. There were lines drooping down from the edges of her mouth. In the movie *Clueless*, one of Mark's favorites, this was termed a "monet"—someone who looks good at a distance but up close falls apart.

"Can I help you sir?"

"Um, yes," Mark said, distracted. Pointing over his shoulder, he said, "May I use one of the computers here?"

"Sure, I just need your library card."

"Have it right here."

"Pick one of the computers to go on to, and, when you're done, come up here to get back your card."

"Thanks."

Mark checked the sports news first. It was right in the thick of basketball season. Teams that appeared to be out of the playoff hunt suddenly were back in it, while other teams that had started the year so strong struggled mightily to remain in contention. Each season played out like an opera, and Mark relished it all.

While reading the sports pages, a headline on the bottom corner of the screen caught his eye:

*Missing your true lost love? Find anyone for free!*
*It's fast, it's easy—just click here!!!*

After the mental sojourn through his past in the library's bathroom, he figured it might be amusing to search for a couple of those long-lost girls he had thought of. He clicked on the advertisement and searched for Rachel and Sherry and Sue. No results found. Then he typed in Carrie's name.

*Carrie Donaldson*
*Female, 40 years old.*
*121 Welt Road, Apartment 2B.*
*Philadelphia, Pennsylvania.*

"Welt Road is only three blocks from here," Mark mumbled to no one in particular. He reached over and grabbed a library bookmark to copy down her information onto. But as quickly as the thought to drop by her apartment flashed into his head, the suffering crush of rationality intruded. He hadn't heard from her, or she from him, in many years (other than one e-mail he excitedly opened, only to quickly realize wasn't from her, but was spam). Mark went home instead.

That night Mark tossed and turned under the covers. The moon was full and bright; its light beamed through his open window projecting a soft glow on the top of his dresser.

Mark got up out of bed and tugged the chain under his nightstand lamp. Now the whole room was lit. He carefully bent down to open his bottom desk drawer. Ruffling through yellowed and dog-eared papers and bills, he found some of Carrie's letters. Sitting on the floor, his back leaning against the desk drawers, he slowly read through each one, taking deep breaths between paragraphs.

He thought again about his prayer in the MRI machine, and recalled one more piece of wisdom his secular mother once imparted in the form of a religious parable: a man prays every night to God to win the lottery. After about a year of this, God is annoyed. With a booming voice, He shouts to the man, "If you want to win the lottery then stop praying to me and just buy a ticket!" God helps those who help themselves.

Mark had clarity: he couldn't keep doing the same thing and expecting different results. Mark still wanted Carrie, all these years later, and he had to help himself. No one else had mattered. How could he have thrown her away? No wonder he was still alone.

As he fumbled to get dressed, Mark thought of Scott Fitzgerald's famous line about there being no second acts in American lives. How wrong he was, Mark thought—living in America is all about reinvention. About being a human cicada and shedding the skin of former lives. About getting those second chances. About stepping into the same river twice, Heraclitus be damned.

So Mark picked up his keys, reached for the library bookmark on his dresser, turned to shut the lights, and tripped a bit as he raced out the door.

(2008)

APPENDIX

# A.

## A (Very) BASIC Introduction to Computer Programming

It is human nature to tackle all sorts of problems using (probably) implicit algorithms. For instance, "How can I go to the bank, make it to the post office, pick up milk at the grocery store, and snag *Electronic Gaming Monthly* before my doctor's appointment?" In order to complete the assignment in the time allotted, the individual must optimize his or her time. However, even if one of the objectives is not met, the overall problem can still be solved, albeit with a decrease in efficiency. Such compromises are also necessary concessions when programming a computer. All of the software ever made involved compromises—the original idea or plan for a computer program usually never makes it to fruition entirely unchanged.

Before examining the programming process, let's discuss a couple of terms. First, a "bug" is an error in a program.[*] There are two types of bugs: (1) *Syntax errors* are created by a misspelling, misuse, or improper location of a keyword in the programming language; and (2) *Logic errors* are caused by the operator,[†] and involve errors only known to him or her. Thus, a computer will run a program with a logic error, but the program might not behave as planned.

Furthermore, there is an important rule of thumb in computer programming: Any program with more than ten lines will have at least one bug in it.

After the reader teaches him- or herself the proper syntax of a computer language and its problem solving techniques, s/he might be properly termed a programmer. But, as a programmer, s/he must realize that no problem can ever be entirely solved in his or

---

[*] This might be apocryphal, but the computer bug supposedly received its name because of a moth, many years ago, causing the malfunction of an entire room-filled computer system by accidently fusing itself between circuit boards.

[†] By operator, I mean user (so why not just say "user," you're thinking...).

her own mind; rather, the problem will be tackled most efficiently by interplay between mind and coding. Sometimes, trial and error is the only method to pursue if a program is riddled with errors of logic—after the program is coded a number of unforeseen errors frequently occur. Therefore, the key to successful programming is gaining experience actually coding, not simply mentally tackling a variety of programming thought experiments.

There is a hierarchy of computer programming languages. At the lowest level is machine language, which allows more or less direct access to a variety of simple commands in the binary form of zeros and ones. It is time consuming and oftentimes wasteful to write a program in machine language, since even the simplest program might contain hundreds to thousands of coded lines.

Assembly language is a bit higher up the hierarchy, and, analogous to machine language, allows a great amount of direct, unmitigated access to a computer's innards. However, it is terribly difficult to learn, master, execute and parse. Thus, it is used mostly today for routines that need great amounts of speed optimization.

Back in 1957, the first so-called high-level programming language was developed: FORTRAN (FORmula TRANslator). A high level language like FORTRAN trades ease-of-use for power. FORTRAN is still used today for some scientific endeavors. Other high level languages include BASIC, Visual Basic, Pascal, COBOL,* ADA, Prolog, LISP, APL,† and PL/1, to name just a few.

C++, which is very popular among programmers today, is neither a strictly high- nor low-level language—the operator is free to decide on a program-by-program basis how to utilize the functionality of C++. The amount of depth permitted is extraordinary, since the programmer is given access to assembly language inputted directly into the coded routines.

The majority of examples following will come from C++ and BASIC (in several forms). However, the languages themselves are

---

* The majority of computer code extant is in COBOL, a very wordy computer language that experienced a popular resurgence in the panic before Y2K: COBOL programmers were in high demand to fix the bugs that could have caused the Big Computer Crash (but didn't).

† Stands for A Programming Language; it is hyper-concise.

not important at this stage—more important are the basic ideas of coding.

Pseudocode is a language-unspecific method of laying out problem-solving code. It is a tool to help the programmer produce structured, readable solutions to programming queries. This "false-code" is an excellent teaching tool as well; therefore, we will begin with a sample problem and solution in pseudocode.

**Problem:** How shall we tie our shoes?

**Solution:**

```
1    Subroutine Tie Shoes
2    Place both hands on
     laces
3    Put one lace over
     top of the other
4    Tie in knot
5    Release laces
6    End Subroutine
```

The code should be at least somewhat self-explanatory; however, if it isn't, here is a line-by-line explanation:

> Line 1: This first line begins a subroutine, or section of a program (i.e., a subprogram); we have given the subroutine a descriptive moniker: `Tie Shoes`
>
> Lines 2, 3, 4 and 5: These are steps in the procedure that describe very specific actions to accomplish the program's objective. Notice how each individual routine is very simple compared with the entire process. (Also notice that `Tie in knot` needs to be unpacked more—this could be a call to a whole other subroutine.)
>
> Line 6. This line ends the subroutine and transfers control back to the main program (in this instance, we do not have a main program).

Also note the line spacing of the code; this is formally called "indenting" and helps the program reader to obtain a clearer picture of the purpose of the algorithm, line by line. Indenting is one key to obtaining readable code; however, if the reader does not feel comfortable using it, then he is free not to. Most computer programming languages syntactically pay no attention to indentations or line spacing.

**Problem**: How should we start our car?

**Solution**:

```
1 Subroutine Start Car
2    Call Enter Car
3    Call Start With Key
4 End Subroutine
5
6 Subroutine Enter Car
7    Walk toward Car
8    Open Car Door
9    Sit Down on Seat
10   Shut Car Door
11 End Subroutine
12
13 Subroutine Start With Key
14   Put Key in hand
15   Put Key into ignition
16   Turn Key
17 End Subroutine
```

The Start Car example illustrates a block approach to programming. The first subroutine, lines 1 through 4, call two other subroutines, in this order: first, `Enter Car` (lines 6 through 11), then `Start With Key` (lines 13 through 17). The program would not be nearly as cleanly structured if it were assembled hodgepodge like this:

```
Subroutine Start Car
   Walk toward Car
   Open Car Door
   Sit Down on Seat
   Shut Car Door
```

```
        Put Key in hand
        Put Key into ignition
        Turn Key
    End Subroutine
```

Note that if `Start Car` were a real computer program, the results would be the identical in both coded permutations. However, as programs become larger and larger, it is good practice to divide similar (and potentially repeated) activities into logical, more self-contained subroutines. But a program can still be a linear, non-stop process if it pleases the operator, as is the second `Start Car` coded example above.

Once again, notice the simple, very specific steps within the subroutines. Even the most complex problems can be broken down into a series of such discrete parts.

We'll now start coding an actual computer program in BASIC (Beginner's All-Purpose Symbolic Instruction Code),[*] using a line-numbered interpreter version (a computer language that requires line number labels for each coded command).

**Problem**: Can we print "Hello" on the screen?
**Solution**: `10 PRINT "HELLO"`

Line 10, the only line of the program so far, prints on-screen the string that is in quotation marks. A string is any series of characters within quotation marks; a calculation is not performed within the string. The output of the program after running it is

```
HELLO
```

However, a question arises. What would be the result if the command line were this?

---

[*] Created by Kemeny and Kurtz at Dartmouth in 1964. Although most versions of the old BASIC language are relatively the same, there are minor syntactical differences between them. GW-BASIC, which these programs were composed and run on, is still robust (though its structure is an affront to modern languages); yet it is still not known for sure what the "GW" stands for.

```
10 PRINT HELLO
```

There are no quotation marks around the string HELLO. Thus, the output is a number:

```
0
```

The 0 indicates that the variable HELLO equals zero, the null value. HELLO is *numeric* data. Numeric data is simply measurement data that can be used for calculation. Observe the following:

```
10 PRINT 2+2
```

The result, not surprisingly, is

```
4
```

However the input

```
10 PRINT "2+2"
```

will produce:

```
2+2
```

Now, the line

```
10 PRINT "2+2=";2+2
```

deals with both types of data: string and numeric. BASIC will first output the value contained in the quotation marks, character by character. Next, BASIC will perform a calculation on the numeric data: 2+2. Notice the semicolon separating the string from the calculation.

The output is

```
2+2=4
```

A variable is like an empty box: the programmer can fill this box with any object, remove that object, and replace it with another one, ad infinitum.

Remember the value of HELLO? The output of the command statement

```
10 PRINT HELLO
```

was 0. The HELLO is initialized to the null value (zero) when it is first appears in the code.

In order to better appreciate the nature of variable declaration and assignment, we will now shift to coding in C++, a compiler. (Line numbers are not required when utilizing C++.) In C++, all variables must be explicitly declared before their use. Therefore, the equivalent statement of 10 PRINT HELLO in C++ is:

```
cout<<hello;
```

The cout is read as "see-out." It sees-out the term after the extraction operator (<<) to the screen. But the statement will cause an error after attempting to compile (getting prepared to execute) the program.

> **Problem**: How do we declare variables in C++?
> **Solution**: `<type> variable;`

The <type> section is allocated for several classes of variables. For the sake of argument, let us assign <type> to int—standing for integer, i.e., the positive and negative whole numbers along with zero. A variable declared as an integer type can range from –32,768 to 32,768 (negative/positive two to the fifteenth power).

```
int hello;
```

In the line above, a new variable called hello has been declared—as an integer-type variable. Therefore, hello mustn't have any decimals, and must stay within the predefined range of integer values. Now, if the two statements

```
int hello;
cout<<hello;
```

are presented to the compiler, the result will be the same as it was in BASIC:

```
0
```

The operator, unsurprisingly, is permitted to assign a non-zero integer to `hello` in the program.

```
int hello;
hello=2;
cout<<hello;
```

Now that `hello` has been designated to equal two before the value is shown on the display, the output will be:

```
2
```

**Problem**: Can two values be assigned to one variable?

**Solution**:

```
int hello;
hello=2;
hello=3;
cout<<hello;
```

What will the output be? Will C++ print `2`, `3`, or both? Remember, after `hello` is declared, it is set to zero. Next, we assigned the variable to the number two, then to three. The output is:

```
3
```

Therefore, a variable "sheds" its previous value into the ether to make space for a new one. After all, the word "variable" means change, and variables are the key to dynamic programs. Also notice a syntactical rule in C++ (which by now should be apparent): every command line must end with a semicolon.

In BASIC, in case the reader is curious, variable declaration is as follows:

```
10 HELLO=2
20 PRINT HELLO
```

And, clearly, the output from this program is

```
2
```

Notice that BASIC does not usually require the operator to concern him- or herself with variable declaration. However, in Visual Basic, a very popular computer language, such declaration is also not necessary but nevertheless important for program readability.

**Problem**: How do we declare variables in Visual Basic?

**Solution**: `hello As Integer`

Visual Basic's environment is very different from other languages, since it allows coding using a variety of GUI (graphical user interface) objects, instead of coding strictly in a central location.

If the reader were the manager/financial advisor of a famous rock band, and decided to take advantage of computer coding (BASIC, for the purposes of argument) to calculate the total amount of money gathered in a single night, how would he or she accomplish this?

**Problem**: If X people attend a concert at $50.00 at ticket, how much money is made?

**Solution**:

```
10 X=100
20 MONEY=X*50
30 PRINT MONEY
```

Several new concepts are introduced above. At line 10, `X` (which, in this instance, is *not* declared as `X As INTEGER`, since the text has returned to line-numbered BASIC, and BASIC does not require variable declaration) is declared to a value of one hundred initially.

In line 20, a new variable is created: `MONEY`. `MONEY` is given a value, but not a single numerical statement like `X` is. In other words, MONEY is not assigned to 66, for instance. Instead, MONEY is assigned to the contents of X (which is 100), multiplied by 50 (the $50.00 price of each ticket mentioned in the problem statement). Therefore, 100 times 50 will be computed and displayed by BASIC as

```
5000
```

If one hundred people attend a concert costing fifty dollars a ticket, five thousand dollars is the total revenue. However, notice the symbol for multiplication, the asterisk (*). It is not the so-called times symbol (i.e., "x"), since the following complication would result:

```
20 Xx50
```

Not only would the line be difficult to read, BASIC would be unable to differentiate the variable X from the multiplication sign x. In most programming languages, with a few notable exceptions, these are the symbols for the key mathematical operations:

| | |
|---|---|
| + | addition |
| - | subtraction |
| * | multiplication |
| / | division |

**Problem**: Create another program, this time containing multiplication and division.

**Solution**:

```
10 X=100
20 Y=10
30 Z=X/Y
40 A=X*Y
50 PRINT Z
60 PRINT A
```

Before attempting a prediction of the output, the reader is advised to pore over each line. Lines 10 and 20 assign two numbers to two variables, X and Y, which do not have to be declared (since the program is in BASIC and not in, say, C++). Line 30 initializes Z, which performs a division calculation between X and Y. In line 40, X is multiplied by Y and assigned to the newly created variable A. The PRINT statements (lines 50 and 60) display the results in successive lines on-screen. The output is

```
10
1000
```

**Problem:** Rewrite the previous BASIC algorithm in C++.

**Solution:**

```
int x, y, z, a;
x=100;
y=10;
z=x/y;
a=x*y;
cout<<z
    <<a;
```

In this C++ program, the output is

```
10 1000
```

First, notice the declaration of the integer values (denoted with `int x, y, z, a;`). After the initialization of the four variables, x and y are given numerical values (100 and 10, respectively). Variables z and a are assigned to computational operations, and then displayed using cout. Now, if every line in C++ ends with a semicolon, then what occurs after the following?

```
cout<<z
    <<a;
```

After the cout<<z, the command line has not ended, since there is no semicolon. The compiler anticipates more instruction related to cout. Therefore, the line

```
cout<<z<<a;
```

is the same command as

```
cout<<z
    <<a;
```

One more thing to notice: there is significant use of indentation. Since both C++ and BASIC ignore any whitespace (spaces) left blank, indenting is recommended for improved readability.

In both mathematics and programming, we must always be cognizant of the order of operations. The order of operations is the sequence in which a mathematical expression is parsed and evaluated. This is the progression:

- First, calculate anything within parentheses (from left to right);
- Then, calculate bases with exponents (from left to right);
- Next, calculate any multiplication and division (from left to right);
- And, finally, calculate any addition and subtraction (from left to right).

For example, the expression 3+4x5 has only one possible result: 23 (doing the multiplication first—5x4 = 20—and then adding the 3). The answer is *not* 35 (3+4 first, then multiplying 7 by 5), because multiplication or division must be carried out before addition or subtraction. However, if we wish for the answer to be 35, a simple fix is possible: since parentheses are evaluated before multiplication or division in the order of operations,

$$(3+4) \times 5 = 35$$

The problem above requires the expression contained within the parentheses (3+4) to be calculated first—and then that result is multiplied by 5.

**Problem:** Create a simple BASIC program illustrating the order of operations.

**Solution:**

```
10 PRINT (2^2+4)+(6*7)*2
20 PRINT 2^2+4+6*7*2
```

What will be the output? (Note that 2^2, or two-caret-two, is two to the second power. Two to the second power is two multiplied by two.)

```
92
92
```

The result is the same; both expressions produce equivalent output because the parentheses are not necessary. In line 10, the first set of parentheses is examined first. Two to the second power (2 times 2) is 4, and 4+4 is 8. Next, the second set of parentheses is evaluated—6x7 is 42. But the 8 result from the first set of parentheses and the 42 result from the second set of parentheses are not added yet; observe the 2 which multiplies the result of the second set of parentheses. That gives us 84. The 84 is then added to 8, and the final answer is 92.

In line 20, the expression of 2^2 is calculated first (which is 4). Then, 6*7 is found to be 42, and the 42 is multiplied by 2. Finally, the 4 (from 2^2), the other 4, and the 84 (from 6*7*2) are added to output a final answer of 92.

In this example program, the results of both calculations turn out to be 92; however, a safe bet is to always use parentheses when unsure of how a mathematical statement will be evaluated.

Without the possibility of entering input during a run, a program becomes no more than a non-interactive slideshow. Permitting user input will be introduced with the following example.

**Problem**: If tax is 7 percent, then what will the tax be on an item costing X dollars?

**Solution**:

```
10 PRINT "What is the cost
     of the item"
20 INPUT X
30 PRINT "Tax is:";X*.07
```

The program allows input of a value, to be assigned to variable X, with the INPUT statement. Line 10 outputs a string to the screen. Line 30 prints two objects: a string and a numerical calculation (which is the tax, calculated by multiplying the inputted cost by 7 percent, or .07). Therefore, the output of the program if a cost of, let's say, 50.00 is entered, is

```
What is the cost of the item
? 50.00
Tax is: 3.5
```

So, here, the tax is $3.50. Note the ?, which is the user input prompt. To make the output cleaner, change line 10 to:

```
10 PRINT "What is the cost
    of the item";
```

Putting a semicolon after the string moves the cursor's position to the end of the string, leading to the following output:

```
What is the cost of the
item? 50.00
Tax is: 3.5
```

Now let's look at a different type of input: strings.

**Problem**: How are strings entered in BASIC?

**Solution**:

```
10 PRINT "What is you name";
20 INPUT X$
30 PRINT "Hello,";X$
```

Notice the dollar sign ($) after the variable X. A dollar sign permits the variable to contain string data. Here are some program runs:

```
What is your name? Madi
Hello, Madi

What is your name? Ali
Hello, Ali

What is your name? Nicole
Hello, Nicole
```

**Problem:** Another string example, please.

**Solution:**

```
10 A$="Hello"
20 B$="Mr. Regan"
30 A=3
40 PRINT A$,B$,A
```

The purpose of the commas in line 40 is to move the output cursor over a <tab> length after successive prints. The output of the program is

```
Hello     Mr. Regan      3
```

Note that A$ and A are two entirely different variables, even though they have identical letter names. One is assigned to string data, the other to strictly numerical data. To illustrate another point, consider the following:

```
10 PRINT "What's your name,
    my pretty";
20 INPUT X
30 PRINT "Howdy,";X
```

The program contains a logic error. Nothing other than numbers can be entered at the prompt, since variable X accepts only numerical data. Look at a possible output:

```
What's your name, my pretty?
Jenna
?Redo from start
?80
Howdy, 80
```

The ?Redo from start error signifies that BASIC will not allow X to be assigned to a string, so it asks for another input. Thus, after 80 is entered, line 30 runs without complication.

Contrariwise, Visual Basic handles inputs differently. Entry can come from a variety of places. Dialog boxes are a common access point, and after the variable has a value (the variable is, in fact, a property, entitled <dialogBox>.Caption) it may be used, either as a string or a number. But other variables might also be declared initially.

**Problem**: How do we declare strings in Visual Basic?
**Solution**: `aString As String`

And C++ has more complex mechanisms to handle string and numerical inputs.

**Problem**: How do we create a number input in C++?
**Solution**:

```
int x;
cout<<"Number?";
cin>>x;
cout<<"Your number is:"
    << x;
```

The output might be:

```
Number?10 Your number is:10
```

C++'s output is spaced closer together than BASIC's. Unlike BASIC's `PRINT` statement, `cout` does not move the cursor to a new line each time it's called—unless a command named `endl` (pronounced "end-ell"), which means "end line," is used.

```
int x
cout<<"Number?";
cin>>x;
cout<<endl
    <<"Your number is:"
    << x;
```

Here's sample output:

```
Number?10
Your number is:10
```

But creating strings in C++ is much too complex for the reader at this stage, since strings rely on "arrays," or collections of variables.

If a program gets too long or too complicated, it is sometimes difficult for the reader to understand the code. Not necessarily the individual line-to-line commands (such as the statement `PRINT "Hello!"`) but the overall gist of the program. Commenting the code will help the reader.

Commenting refers to writing English-based references next to important lines of code, or blocking off parts of a program by marking segments of code with English-style description.

**Problem:** How do we comment code in BASIC?

**Solution:**

```
10 PRINT "Hello"
20 PRINT "What is the tax on
   the item";
30   INPUT T
40  PRINT "What is the cost
    of the item";
50   INPUT C
60 A=T*C
70 B=A+C
80 PRINT "Total cost of item
   is: ";B
```

Note that since the program above is not two or three lines long, time has to be spent examining the purpose of each line. If the code were commented, however, it might be easier to decode.

```
 5 REM TAXING PROGRAM 1
10 PRINT "Hello"
20 PRINT "What is the tax on
   the item";
30   INPUT T   'GET TAX
   INPUT; ASSIGN TO "T"
40  PRINT "What is the cost
    of the item";
50   INPUT C   'GET       COST
     INPUT; ASSIGN TO "C"
```

```
60 A=T*C          'CALCULATE TAX
   ON ITEM
70 B=A+C          'CALCULATE
   TOTAL COST
80 PRINT "Total cost of item
   is: ";B
```

This BASIC program is now easier to understand. Although the comments (the words after the apostrophes and the REM commands) at first glance appear to clutter up the program, they actually bring clarity to each line. If, by chance, other individuals view your program code, comments are necessary for complete comprehension; without them, reading the code becomes like an exercise in untangling hundreds of wires. Even for the programmer himself, comments are indispensible because good chunks of time will probably pass between examining lines of code—some programs take months to complete—and it is much easier to read your own code with comments than without (e.g., you might not remember why you needed a certain command).

**Problem**: How do you comment lines in C++?

**Solution**:

```
cout<<"Hello";          //this
prints "Hello"
cout<<"Hell";           /* this
doesn't */
```

Note that with the first commenting method (shown on the first line, which prints "Hello"), two forward slashes are required to initiate the comment. But the disadvantage of the two-slash procedure is that it can only be used on a single line. Put another way, this is syntactically illegal:

```
cout<<"Hello"<<endl;
//this not only prints
the word "Hello," but it
also ends the line
```

The comment goes beyond the current line to the next line. The C++ compiler would register this as a syntax error, since the compiler would treat the statement `the word "Hello," but` `it also ends the line` as a command line (which, of course, it isn't. The line doesn't even end with a semicolon!).

But the second commenting method in C++ (`cout<<"Hell"; /* this doesn't */`, taken from the example above) does allow you to extend comments for as long as you wish—provided you encapsulate the comment with `/*` and `*/` every time. This particular form of commenting is useful for long-winded descriptions of specific functions of a program. For example:

```
/* the following algorithm will launch
a shuttle to the  moon,  return  it
safely back to earth, eat a candy-bar,
     and  marry another computer */
```

Perhaps the algorithm is a bit unrealistic (!), but (hopefully) the point is well taken.

There are several more basics to learn, however, before coding can be done with any degree of competence.

At this point, we must ditch Visual Basic and C++ as templates for examples—the two languages, especially C++, diverge too greatly from BASIC, which arguably can present foundational concepts the clearest. For example, none of the commands we have learned thus far in C++ can be implemented without a "header file." C++ is paradoxical—on the one hand, it is a very small language, with less than forty fundamental command words. But, on the other hand, there are countless libraries of functions that permit applications of the language to be quite varied—and those function libraries are well beyond our scope here.

Now, with a knowledge of the basics of commenting code, using pseudocode to lay out general algorithms, initiating variables, and applying mathematical operators (+, -, *, /), we can begin learning about loops and `IF/THEN` structures.

Consider `IF/THEN` structures: "IF I get an A on this test, THEN I will pass the class!" or "IF life were something edible, THEN life would be a box of chocolates" or…you get the idea. `IF/THEN` structures are fundamental—most every language has a form of them. They are called conditionals. Put simply, they define branches for a program to follow. Without branches, a program could run in only one direction—straight through each line of code. Let's use pseudocode to learn about the structure of `IF/THEN` commands.

**Problem**: What does an IF/THEN command look like?

**Solution**:

```
1 Create Variable A; Assign
   A to value of 4
2 IF A is equal to 4,
  THEN go to line 5
3 Print "Hello, you no-good
   person!"
4 End the program
5 Print "Hello, nice
  person!"
6 End the program
```

In line 2, the `IF/THEN` command is present—first, though, let us examine the code, line-by-line.

In line 1, a variable is created, named `A`. Then `A` is assigned to the value of 4 (in other words, `A=4`). Line 2 creates an `IF/THEN` condition: if `A` (which was just created in line 1) is equal to the number 4 (which it is; in line 1, `A` was assigned to `4`) then the program is instructed to go to line 5. By going to line 5, any lines between the `IF/THEN` line (line 2) and line 5 are ignored; the code "jumps" past those lines. Therefore, lines 3 and 4 are not run by the BASIC interpreter.

Thus, the words `"Hello, you no-good person!"` are never printed on the screen. Instead, the sentence `"Hello, nice person!"` is displayed. Now, let's rewrite the program, only this time in BASIC code.

**Problem**: How do you write the pseudocode program above in BASIC code?

**Solution**:

```
10 A=4     'assign A to the
   number 4
```

```
20   IF  A=4  THEN  GOTO  50
     'the conditional
      IF/THEN
30 PRINT "Hello, you no-good
    person!"
40 END
50 PRINT "Hello, nice
   person!"
60 END
```

The command END means exactly what it says—it signals the end of the program. Since lines 30 and 40 are skipped over, the words "Hello, you no-good person!" are not printed, and the program is not terminated. But why is the END command needed in line 40? Because without ending the program at line 40, an error arises—a logic error. Let's change the program slightly to examine the problem without an END at line 40:

**Problem**: What would happen without an END?

**Solution**:

```
10 A=4     'assign A to the
   number 4
20   IF A<>4 THEN GOTO 50
30 PRINT "Hello, you no-good
   person!"
50 PRINT "Hello, nice
   person!"
60 END
```

First, we must examine the new aspect of the IF/THEN line (line 20). It means (in yet more spoken English terms): If variable A is *not* equal to 4, then go to line 50. But the variable A *is* equal to 4 (it was assigned to 4 in line 10). Therefore, the IF/THEN structure is not true, because A is equal to 4. Because the program does not go to line 50, it simply continues on to the next line: line 30. Look at the output below.

```
Hello, you no-good person!
Hello, nice person!
```

It is now clear what the END line (previously line 40) did for the structure of the algorithm—it ended the program before line 50 was executed. So, to correct the logic error, do the following:

```
10 A=4    'assign A to the
   number 4
20   IF A<>4 THEN GOTO 50
30 PRINT "Hello, you no-good
    person!"
40 END
50 PRINT "Hello, nice
   person!"
60 END
```

This program will produce the printout of

```
Hello, you no-good person!
```

because the END line is present to terminate the program, avoiding executing the remaining lines.

In order to examine some of the potential of IF/THEN structures in code, consider the following program:

**Problem**: More IF/THENs to work with, please.

**Solution**:

```
10 CLS          'clear the
   screen
20 PRINT "Is your name Bill
    or Jill";
30   INPUT A$  'get input
     from user; assign to A$
35 'the conditional
    structures:
40   IF A$="Bill" THEN PRINT
     "Hiya, Bill!"
50   IF A$="Jill" THEN PRINT
     "Hey, Jill!"
60 END
```

This program is fairly simple; in the first line (line 10) a new command is introduced: `CLS`. `CLS` instructs BASIC to clear the screen, and place the cursor at the top left portion of the display. Line 20 prints a question; line 30 prompts the user for input, and then assigns the inputted text to the string-data variable called `A$`.

Then the conditional structures begin. If the user's response is "Bill," then `Hiya, Bill!` is displayed. If the user's response is `Jill`, then `Hey, Jill!` is displayed on-screen. Notice that an `IF/THEN` structure does not necessarily have to jump to a line; jumping is an option carried out by the `GOTO` statement (which does what it says—it goes to a line).* But, in this program, the `IF/THEN` structures immediately print out a statement; the sentence displayed is dependent entirely upon what the variable `A$` is equal to, which is determined solely by the user's input.

But what if the user's input is neither `Bill` nor `Jill`? Since there is no `IF/THEN` structure to handle any other names besides `Jill` and `Bill`, the two `IF/THEN`s are ignored, and the program simply ends.

Acknowledging that `IF/THEN` structures can get complicated, let's review the basic purpose of the conditional: it calls for the interpreter (BASIC) to make a decision. If a certain condition is true, the `THEN` part of that specific `IF/THEN` line is implemented. If the condition is false, then the `THEN` portion of the command is not executed.

We have already briefly touched on `IF/THEN` syntax. `IF/THEN` allows for several comparisons before deeming a condition true or false. Here is a simple `IF/THEN` statement example:

```
10 IF G=10 THEN PRINT "G equals Ten"
```

---

* The `GOTO` statement is one of the most infamous of all in computer programming because using it without abandon can lead to so-called spaghetti code. The presence of `GOTO` in code is a red flag that the programmer was lazy or inexperienced—any program, even in BASIC, can be written without `GOTO`. (It is not necessary in an `IF/THEN` statement, either.)

The IF/THEN conditional answers a question: Does G equal the number 10? If it does, then G equals Ten is displayed. But if G does not equal 10, then the condition is false; in addition, the entire THEN part of the conditional is ignored because the statement is false. (Of course, since line 10 is not part of a larger program, G is by default equal to the null value—so if this one-line program were run as its own self-contained program, nothing would be printed on the screen.)

**Problem:** What does the AND command do in an IF/THEN conditional?

**Solution:**

```
10 G=10:F=12
20 IF G=10 AND F=12 THEN
   PRINT "Hi"
```

The program above introduces the AND statement. Before we examine AND, however, take a look at the use of the colon (:) in line 10. The colon allows the user to compress what normally would be two or more commands into one line number. Therefore, the colon denotes a "command-stop."

In line 20, two conditions are presented to the interpreter. If and only if* G equals 10 and F equals 12 will Hi be printed on the screen. Examine this program:

```
10 G=10:F=12
20 IF G=10 AND F=0 THEN
   PRINT "Hi"
```

Hi will not be printed because *both* conditions (G=10 and F=0) must be true. But F is not equal to zero; rather, it is equal to 12 (which is assigned to F in line 10).

There is a second conditional operator: OR. OR, if used in the program above, would appear like this:

```
10 G=10:F=12
```

---

* The mathematical abbreviation for "if and only if," which is *iff*, was first used by the mathematician Paul Halmos.

```
20 IF G=10 OR F=0 THEN PRINT
   "Hi"
```

In this case, because of the OR, Hi will be printed on screen. Why? Because either condition (or both) can be true for the IF/THEN statement to register as true. In other words, there are three possibilities for where the statement will be true:

(1) G equal to 10, but F not equal to 0; or
(2) G not equal to 10, but F equal 0; or
(3) G equal to 10, and F equal to 0.

The only possibility for a false register in the IF/THEN statement is G not equal to 10, and F also not equal to 0. In this case, of course, Hi will not be printed.

One conditional operator remains: NOT. NOT was briefly introduced earlier and will now be examined in more detail.

**Problem:** Create a sample program with NOT.
**Solution:**

```
10 H=10
20 IF H<>10 THEN PRINT
   "Yes! Yes! Yes!"
```

Line 10 assigns a variable named H to 10. In line 20, H is given a condition: If (and only if) the variable H is not equal to 10, then print Yes! repeatedly. But, in the program, H is equal to 10—therefore, Yes! will *not* be printed. The back-to-back greater than and less than (<>) symbols denote the "not." What follows is another way to structure the program.

```
10 H=10
20 IF NOT(H)=10 THEN PRINT
   "Yes! Yes! Yes!"
```

In this program, the command NOT surrounds the variable and is the equivalent to <>: the words Yes! Yes! Yes! are not printed, since H is not equal to 10.

Conditional operators can also be combined. This permits multiple routes for the interpreter to decide between.

**Problem:** Create a program with combined conditional operators.

**Solution:**

```
10 T=1:U=2:V=3
20 IF NOT(T)=2 AND U=2 THEN
   PRINT "Ok?"
30 IF T=1 OR NOT(V)=3 THEN
   PRINT "Good?"
40 IF T<>1 AND U<>2 THEN
   PRINT "Nothing?"
50 IF U=3 OR NOT(U)=6 THEN
   PRINT "Hello?"
```

The output of this more complicated program is as follows: Line 20 will print; line 30 will print; line 40 will not print; and line 50 will print.

Certain sections of a program must be repeated. There is no getting around it; repetition is an important task. Imagine, if you will, the statement "Bottles of beer on the wall," repeated 100 times. Here is one approach to the coding:

```
10 PRINT "Bottles of beer on
   the wall"
20 PRINT "Bottles of beer on
   the wall"
30 PRINT "Bottles of beer on
   the wall"
40 PRINT "Bottles of beer on
   the wall"
50 PRINT "Bottles of beer on
   the wall"
60 PRINT "Bottles of beer on
   the wall"
.... etc.
```

Coding the same statement one hundred times is not only an inefficient use of computer memory, but also a monumental waste of time. There is a much easier way to print the same statement on-screen one hundred times.

**Problem:** The easier way, please?

**Solution:**

```
10 CLS
20 FOR A=1 TO 100
30 PRINT "Bottles of beer on
   the wall"
40 NEXT A
```

Let's examine the program in detail. Line 10 clears the screen using the CLS command. Line 20 sets up a FOR/NEXT loop structure (loops were created by Ada Lovelace, daughter of Lord Byron). A new variable is created, named A, which will be used to cycle through the numbers 1 to 100. This is analogous to assigning A to 1, then to 2, then to 3, then to 4, etc., all the way up to 100.

In line 40, the statement reads NEXT A. For every FOR statement, there must be a corresponding NEXT statement, which tells BASIC to quickly go back to the original FOR statement with the variable A (in line 20) and check which number the loop's currently up to. If A has reached 101, then the FOR/NEXT loop terminates.

Now, any lines in between the FOR/NEXT statement are repeated the number of times the FOR/NEXT loop is repeated. In other words, since line 30, which prints Bottles of beer on the wall, is within the FOR/NEXT loop, it is repeated the same number of times that the loop itself is cycled through: one hundred (because of the command FOR A=1 TO 100). Therefore, the program prints out the statement one hundred times on the monitor.

Since the A in the FOR/NEXT loop is really a variable assigned to an increasing number for each pass through the loop (first 1, then 2, then 3, and so on, up to 100), can it be used like any other variable? Yes it can.

**Problem:** Let's refine the program a bit.

**Solution:**

```
10 CLS
20 FOR A=1 TO 100
30 PRINT A;" Bottles of beer
    on the wall"
```

```
40 NEXT A
```

There is a subtle, single change in the program: the addition of A in front of the PRINT statement. A's value will be displayed on the screen, and then Bottles of beer on the wall will be printed next to each value of A. But, since A is increasing, the number on-screen will also increase. Thus, the printout will look like this:

```
1 Bottles of beer on the wall
2 Bottles of beer on the wall
3 Bottles of beer on the wall
4 Bottles of beer on the wall
5 Bottles of beer on the wall
.... etc.
```

But in the "99 Bottles of Beer" song, the numbers start at 99 and descend to 1. Is this descending order programmable with the FOR/NEXT statement? Yes it is—by using the STEP command:

```
10 CLS
20 FOR A=99 TO 1 STEP -1
30 PRINT A;" Bottles of beer
   on the wall"
40 NEXT A
```

Now the numbers descend. Note line 20's modifications; instead of FOR A=1 TO 100, it reads 99 TO 1 to reverse the sequence. In addition, to ensure that the order is reversed properly, the STEP -1 tells BASIC to count down by one number at a time.

**Problem:** What else can STEP do?

**Solution:**

```
10 CLS
20 FOR F=0 TO 60 STEP 10
```

```
30 PRINT F
40 NEXT F
```

The STEP part of the FOR/NEXT line tells the interpreter to count by tens (thus, STEP 10) from 0 to 60. Since line 30 is between the FOR/NEXT commands, the numbers of 0 to 60 increasing by tens are printed on the screen.

FOR/NEXTs are very versatile; they can even be nested within each other.

**Problem:** How can FOR/NEXTs be nested?

**Solution:**

```
10 CLS
20 FOR T=1 TO 10
30    FOR V=1 TO 3
40     PRINT V
50    NEXT V
60 NEXT T
```

Look at the outer loop (with the variable T) first. T is incremented from 1 to 10; anything between the FOR T=1 TO 10 and the NEXT T is carried along for the ride and repeated ten times. Inside, though, is another FOR/NEXT statement; this one repeats itself three times, and prints its value (the variable V) each time. The printout looks like this:

```
1
2
3
1
2
3
.... etc.
```

The one-two-three combination is printed out ten times (as specified by the outer FOR/NEXT loop). Now, for a more confusing variation, consider this:

```
10 CLS
20 FOR T=1 TO 10
```

```
30    FOR V=1 TO 3
40      PRINT T
50    NEXT V
60 NEXT T
```

It is the same program, except for one crucial difference: line 40 tells BASIC to print the variable T (the outer FOR/NEXT loop variable) instead of the V variable (the inner FOR/NEXT loop variable, as specified in the original program). The resulting printout is:

```
1
1
1
2
2
2
3
3
3
....etc.
```

The output begins as one-one-one because the inner loop must repeat itself three times before the outer loop repeats itself once, since the inner loop is contained within the outer loop. For every three increments of the variable V, the variable T increases itself by one unit. Counter mechanisms are sometimes difficult to visualize, so experimentation with FOR/NEXT is recommended.

Now that we have the basics of coding under our belts, let's now analyze, in detail, two BASIC programs written to solve IMP (Interactive Mathematics Program) problems of the week (POWs).*

---

* Though robust, it is still especially challenging to lean on BASIC to code and ultimately solve complicated problems because of how limited and antiquated the language is—perhaps it is like trying to race the 24 Hours of Le Mans with a souped-up Ford Pinto. Also, for a primer on IMP, consult the essay on the Interactive Mathematics Program presented earlier in the book.

## Problem 1—

> *None of the retronymic analog clocks in your house keeps time properly. Every one of the clocks gains or loses a certain number of minutes per hour—but different clocks gain or lose different amounts. At noon today, every clock has the correct time. Will the clocks* ever *be right again?*

What follows is a program that solves the POW.

```
10 KEY OFF: SCREEN 9: CLS: HOUR=12:
   MINUTE=0: CYCLES=0: REALHOUR=12
15 PRINT"IMP POW"
17 PRINT:PRINT"Your clock starts at 12:00.
   We ignore AM/PM.":PRINT
20 PRINT"How many minutes increase per hour
   (input negative number for decrease)";
30 INPUT TIME
35 CYCLES=CYCLES+1
40 HOUR=HOUR+1:MINUTE=MINUTE+TIME
41 REALHOUR=REALHOUR+1
42 IF REALHOUR=13 THEN REALHOUR=1
45 IF HOUR=13 THEN HOUR=1
46 IF MINUTE>59 THEN GOSUB 100
47 IF MINUTE<0 THEN GOSUB 200
50 PRINT "Virtual clock = "; HOUR;
   ":";MINUTE;"and Real Time = ";
   REALHOUR;": 00"
60 GOSUB 300
70 GOTO 35
100 DIFFERENCE=MINUTE-60
110 MINUTE=DIFFERENCE
120 DIFFERENCE=0
125 HOUR=HOUR+1
126 IF HOUR=13 THEN HOUR=1
130 RETURN
200 DIFFERENCE=60+MINUTE
210 MINUTE=DIFFERENCE
220 DIFFERENCE=0
```

```
230 HOUR=HOUR-1
240 IF HOUR=0 THEN HOUR=12
250 RETURN
300 IF MINUTE=0 THEN 310 ELSE RETURN
310 IF HOUR=REALHOUR THEN 320 ELSE RETURN
320 PRINT"Hours to get back to correct time
    is ";CYCLES
330 PRINT:PRINT"Another? (Type Y or N)";
340 INPUT PROMPT$
350 IF PROMPT$="Y" THEN 10 ELSE END
```

Lines 10 through 30 set some variables to initial values (namely, `HOUR`, which is the hour that our virtual clock reads at some moment, and `MINUTE`, which is the minute which our virtual clock reads at some moment; the variable `CYCLES` will track how many iterations the virtual clock has to go through in order to return back to the correct time; and `REALHOUR` will keep track of the "true" time through each iteration of the virtual clock).

Line 35 initiates the `CYCLES` counter, which will track how many times it takes our virtual clock to return to the correct time. And line 40 increases the virtual clock by one hour and however many minutes the program is prompted to increase (or decrease) by per hour.

Line 41 increases the "real" time by one hour. Line 42 makes sure that if we've hit "13 o'clock," the `REALHOUR` counter goes back to 1:00. Line 45 makes sure that if we've hit "13 o'clock," the `HOUR` counter also goes back to 1:00.

Line 46 waits for the `MINUTE` counter to exceed 59; when it does so, the `IF/THEN` statement throws the program to a subroutine (a subprogram) starting at line 100 and ending at the first instance of a `RETURN` command. That subroutine instructs the virtual clock to increase by an hour (accounting for the fact that the clock has now gained at least an hour through our iterations of increase) and corrects the `MINUTE` hand of our virtual clock. For example, if we were increasing the clock by 7 minutes each hour, and the clock went from 1:57 to 2:64, the subroutine would adjust the time to be 3:04, since we've gained more than an hour (and a clock obviously doesn't show 64 minutes).

Line 47 throws the program into the subroutine at line 200 if we had initially prompted the virtual clock to be losing minutes with each hour. Everything that the subroutine starting at line 100 does, the subroutine starting at line 200 does also—except it does it backwards.

Line 50 prints, on the screen, the "current" time on the virtual clock. It also prints the "real" time for comparison.

Line 60 throw the program into a subroutine (starting at line 300) designed to stop the virtual clock if it ever hits the "real" time. It reports, using the value of the variable CYCLES, how many hours it took the virtual clock to match the "real" time. Finally, if the clock has stopped because it hit the "real" time, the user is asked if he or she wishes to run the program again.

The algorithm we've used for this program, although not perfect, could be translated into Visual Basic or C++ relatively easily—the syntax would be different but much else would be the same (counters, loops, and so forth; we'd probably want to construct formal functions instead of using the messy subroutines constructed for the BASIC program here, as well as define the variables, but the program would still have pretty much the same structure).

Running the program, what follows are the results obtained for three examples: if the clock gains 10 minutes per hour, loses 3 minutes per hour, and gains 7 minutes per hour.

- If the clock gains 10 minutes each hour, it takes the virtual clock 72 hours to match the "real" time.*

- If the clock loses 3 minutes each hour, it takes the virtual clock 240 hours to match the "real" time.

- And, if the clock gains 7 minutes each hour, it takes the virtual clock 720 hours to match the "real" time.

This computer program allows us to quickly compile the following set of data for clocks gaining certain numbers of minutes per hour:

* Note that this result assumes, as do all of my results, that the instant an hour of "real" time passes by, the virtual clock increases—or decreases—by the fixed amount of minutes as specified by the operator.

| Gained Minutes | Hours Needed |
|---|---|
| 1 | 720 |
| 2 | 360 |
| 3 | 240 |
| 4 | 180 |
| 5 | 144 |
| 6 | 120 |
| 7 | 720 |
| 8 | 90 |
| 9 | 80 |
| 10 | 72 |
| 11 | 720 |
| 12 | 60 |
| 30 | 24 |
| 35 | 144 |
| 40 | 18 |
| 45 | 16 |
| 60 | 12 |

We can look for patterns in the data. First of all, notice that if we ran the same values for "gained minutes" but instead made them "lost minutes" (the clock would be getting slower, in other words), we would still have identical "hours needed" for each. So, therefore, from this point onward, we shall only consider "gained minutes" for any generalizations.

We can arrive at a formula to calculate when all possible clocks will be correct again, no matter the "gained minutes" values.

Consider the following:

$$\frac{60 \cdot n}{m} \cdot 12 = h \text{, where}$$

- $m$ is "gained minutes" per hour ($m$ is a natural number)
- $n$ is a constant ($n$ is some natural number where $1 \leq n \leq m$ )
- $h$ is the minimum number of hours it takes to match up with the "real" time ($h$ is also some natural number)

We want to minimize $h$ no matter what $m$ is, so we need to minimize $n$. Start with $n = 1$. For any values of $m$ that are factors of 60—such as 2, 3 or 30—$n = 1$ will give us a value of $h$ which is a natural number. Other values of $m$ that are not factors of 60 will sometimes also produce integers for $h$ when multiplied by 12—but not all values of $m$ will do this.

For example, if a clock gains 2 minutes per hour, the number of hours it takes to hit the "real" time again is:

$$\frac{60 \cdot 1}{2} \cdot 12 = 30 \cdot 12 = 360 \text{ hours}$$

But if you encounter a situation where $n = 1$ doesn't work, then you must keep increasing $n$ by 1 until an integer value of the number of hours is obtained. For instance, with "gained minutes" equaling 11, here's what happens, starting with $n = 1$:

$$\frac{60 \cdot 1}{11} \cdot 12 = 65.4545\ldots$$

$$\frac{60 \cdot 2}{11} \cdot 12 = 130.9090\ldots$$
$$\frac{60 \cdot 3}{11} \cdot 12 = 196.3636\ldots$$
$$\frac{60 \cdot 4}{11} \cdot 12 = 261.8181\ldots$$
$$\frac{60 \cdot 5}{11} \cdot 12 = 327.2727\ldots$$
$$\frac{60 \cdot 6}{11} \cdot 12 = 392.7272\ldots$$
$$\frac{60 \cdot 7}{11} \cdot 12 = 458.1818\ldots$$
$$\frac{60 \cdot 8}{11} \cdot 12 = 523.6363\ldots$$
$$\frac{60 \cdot 9}{11} \cdot 12 = 589.0909\ldots$$

$$\frac{60 \cdot 10}{11} \cdot 12 = 654.5454\ldots$$

$$\frac{60 \cdot 11}{11} \cdot 12 = 720$$

Thus, it takes a clock that gains 11 minutes per hour 720 hours to get back to the "real" time.

Notice that when the "gained minutes" equals *n*, the two cancel out, leaving us with an integer number of hours: 720. Since we are looking for a *minimum* number of hours (which has to be an integer) to have the clock return to the "real" time, this implies that 720 is the absolute maximum number of hours a clock could take to return to the "real" time.

**Problem 2—**

> *You are a contestant on a game show. You are asked to choose one of three doors. Behind one of the doors lies the Grand Prize, but behind the other two doors lie booby prizes. The host opens one of the other two doors not chosen by you, revealing a booby prize. You are then asked: "Do you wish to switch doors or stay with the door you originally chose?" Should you switch or stay?*

Not to bury the lede, but this problem has a famous pedigree: it's usually referred to as the Monty Hall problem, after the famous game show. Marilyn vos Savant, who writes the *Ask Marilyn* column every weekend for *Parade Magazine*—and is the person with the highest recorded IQ in the world, according to *Guinness*—in the early 1990s stirred a controversy when she claimed that the correct answer to this problem was to switch doors. Many irate readers, some of them professional mathematicians, wrote to her, disputing her solution. But Marilyn was shown to be correct. What follows is a program to solve the POW.

```
10 KEY OFF:SCREEN 9:CLS:REALDOOR=0:
   PICKDOOR=0:WINSWITCH=0:
   WINSTAY=0:RANDOMIZE TIMER
20 PRINT"IMP POW"
30 PRINT:PRINT"How many trials of switch
```

```
   ing/staying do you wish to conduct";
40 INPUT TRIALS
45 'The first loop code will be for switch
    ing doors every time; the second, for
    staying every time.
49 PRINT"Switching every time...."
50 FOR TIMES=1 TO TRIALS
60 REALDOOR=INT(1+3*RND(1))   'Door the car
   is behind
70 PICKDOOR=INT(1+3*RND(1))   'Initial door
   you decide to pick
80 IF REALDOOR=PICKDOOR THEN 100 'If you
   switch but you were initially correct,
   you lose
85 WINSWITCH=WINSWITCH+1      'If you
   weren't initially right, and a door
   that's wrong was taken away, you win
   when you switch
100 NEXT TIMES
199 PRINT"Staying every time...."
200 FOR TIMES=1 TO TRIALS
210 REALDOOR=INT(1+3*RND(1))
220 PICKDOOR=INT(1+3*RND(1))
230 IF REALDOOR=PICKDOOR THEN
    WINSTAY=WINSTAY+1 'If you never switch,
    you can only win by initially guessing
    the door correctly
240 NEXT TIMES
300 CLS
310 PRINT"Here are your results of ";
    TRIALS;" trials of switching every time
    and staying."
320 PRINT:PRINT"By switching every time,
    you won ";WINSWITCH; "times."
330 PRINT"This is a proportion of ";
    WINSWITCH/TRIALS
340 PRINT:PRINT"By switching every time,
    you won ";WINSTAY; "times."
350 PRINT"This is a proportion of ";
```

```
    WINSTAY/TRIALS
360 PRINT:PRINT"Run another set of trials?
    (Input Y or N)";
370 INPUT PROMPT$
380 IF PROMPT$="Y" THEN 10
390 CLS
400 END
```

Lines 10 through 40 set up the program to perform two versions of the simulation: one in which the player always switches the door, and the other in which the player always sticks with his initial door pick. Specifically, line 10 sets the initial values of the variables `REALDOOR` (used to denote the door that the car truly is behind), `PICKDOOR` (used to indicate the player's initial door selection), `WINSWITCH` (a counter keeping track of how many times the player has won by switching doors), and `WINSTAY` (a counter keeping track of how many times the player has won by staying with the door he initially selected). Line 10 also randomizes the timer, meaning an initial random number seed is generated from the computer's internal clock. Lines 30 and 40 prompt the user to input the number of times the simulation should be run for both the switching and staying scenarios.

Lines 49 to 100 simulate the player switching doors repeatedly. Specifically, line 50 begins the loop—which runs the simulation `TRIALS` number of times. Lines 60 and 70 ask the computer to select one of three doors to put the car behind, and one of three doors for the player to initially pick. If these two values match, then, since the player always switches his door when given the option, he loses on that turn. But in any other circumstance the player wins—since, if his initial guess of a door is wrong, and an incorrect door is revealed, and the player switches to the remaining door, he must be correct. Therefore, line 85 adds one unit to the `WINSWITCH` counter.

Lines 199 to 240 are the analogues to lines 49 to 100—only this time the player always stays put with his initial selection when prompted to switch. In this case, the player can only win if he correctly picks the door the car is behind initially. It makes no difference that an incorrect door is revealed later in the game by the host if the player sticks with his initial selection. Line 230 adds one to the WINSTAY counter only if the player correctly selected the door the car was behind initially.

Lines 300 to 350 display the results of the simulations (in terms of player wins) both in count and proportion form. Lines 360 to 400 ask the user if he wishes to run another set of simulations.

The algorithm we've used for this program, like the previous POW program, although not perfect, could be translated to Visual Basic or C++ relatively easily—the syntax would be different but much else would be the same (counters, loops, and so forth; of course, again, we'd probably want to construct formal functions instead of using the messy subroutines constructed for the BASIC program, but the program would have a similar layout).

Because large numbers of trials can be compiled relatively quickly using the computer program, multiple simulations of ever-increasing sample sizes are shown in the two tables below (one in terms of counts, the other in terms of proportions).

| | Count of Wins | |
|---|---|---|
| **Trials** | **Switching** | **Staying** |
| 10 | 7 | 2 |
| 100 | 63 | 35 |
| 1,000 | 657 | 345 |
| 10,000 | 6,697 | 3,217 |
| 100,000 | 66,685 | 33,652 |
| 1,000,000 | 665,910 | 333,190 |
| 10,000,000 | 6,667,350 | 3,333,303 |

| | Proportion of Wins | |
|---|---|---|
| **Trials** | **Switching** | **Staying** |
| 10 | 0.7 | 0.2 |
| 100 | 0.63 | 0.35 |
| 1,000 | 0.657 | 0.345 |
| 10,000 | 0.67 | 0.322 |
| 100,000 | 0.667 | 0.337 |
| 1,000,000 | 0.666 | 0.333 |
| 10,000,000 | 0.667 | 0.333 |

It is very apparent that as the number of trials increases, the empirical probabilities "settle down" to their true, theoretical probabilities (this is a result in statistics called the law of large numbers)—*assuming* that the algorithmic simulation is an accurate representation of the "Let's Make a Deal" problem.

If the simulation correctly models the situation, then the probability of winning the car by switching your choice is about 2/3, and the probability of winning the car by sticking with your selection (and not switching) is only about 1/3. According to the simulation, you have a much better chance if you switch.

Let's calculate the probability theoretically by considering the possibilities in the "Let's Make a Deal" game; assume for the following discussion that the car is behind door C. First, let's look at what happens if you switch your choice every time:

- If you pick door A initially, then you are incorrect. The host must eliminate door B as a choice (since door C contains the car and the host can't eliminate the grand prize). By switching, you select door C—which is the only door left to select. And you **win**.

- If you pick door B initially, then you are incorrect. The host must eliminate door A as a choice (since door C contains the car and the host can't eliminate the grand prize). By switching, you select door C—which is the only door left to select. And you **win**.

- But if you pick door C initially, then you are correct. Except the host will now eliminate either door A or door B (it doesn't matter which, since there is no prize behind either). When you switch to a door other than C, you **lose**.

Since there are three possibilities listed above, and you win in two out of three of them, the probability of winning the car if your strategy is to always switch doors is indeed 2/3. This result agrees with our computer simulation.

Now, let us calculate the probability of always staying with your initial door pick (the "staying strategy"). What follows are the possibilities:

- If you pick door A initially, then you are incorrect. It makes no difference that the host asks you to switch—you ignore him and stick with your initial pick. Since you didn't select door C, you **lose**.

- If you pick door B initially, then you are incorrect. It makes no difference that the host asks you to switch—you ignore him and stick with your initial pick. Since you didn't select door C, you **lose**.

- If you pick door C initially, then you are correct. It makes no difference that the host asks you to switch—you ignore him and stick with your initial pick. Since you selected door C, you **win**.

Since there are three possibilities listed above, and you win in only one out of three of them, the probability of winning the car if your strategy is to always stick with your initial door pick is 1/3. This result also agrees with our computer simulation.

Therefore, you are more likely to win the car by switching your initial door selection (a 2/3 chance) than by sticking with it (only a 1/3 chance). Note also that not switching your door gives you a 1/3 chance to win and, since there is only one other possibility and all events in a probability experiment must sum to one, switching doors gives you a 1–1/3 = 2/3 chance to win, as expected. All nice to know, should you ever find yourself as a contestant on *Let's Make a Deal.*

(1998)

## *POSTSCRIPT: THE PAPER COMPUTERS*

Back when I was in middle school in the 1980s, I had a mathematics and computer teacher named Mr. Matt. Although an overriding interest in computers wasn't new to me—I had already been programming in BASIC on my own Tandy Color Computer 2,[*] along with avidly reading the monthly *Rainbow Magazine*; computer programming was already the Shangri-La of my (much) younger self—Mr. Matt presented the material in a way that inspired me to extend myself and learn much more.

One day, before the winter break, he showed me the unusual looking Instructo[†]—a computer made of paper and cardboard that he had patented some years before. Although primarily a teaching tool, the Instructo was fully programmable, the way that the electronic TRS-80s in the school's computer lab were. The difference was, however, that Mr. Matt's paper computer relied on human beings rather than electricity as power sources to operate slides, do arithmetic, flip switches, and produce output,[‡] and were thus an affront to Moore's Law and the meritocracy of electronic computing.

The Instructo lit a fire in my imagination, though I didn't really understand much of it at the time. The commands were obscure and low-level, nothing like the high-level BASIC commands I was used to coding. Some years later, after finding out that Mr. Matt was himself inspired by the similar Bell Labs' CARDIAC (a card-

---

[*] A variant of the then-ubiquitous TRS-80s, which were certainly not "Trash-80s," as some critics claimed.

[†] Mr. Matt's manual for the Instructo can be found online (as of February 22, 2014) at an archived version of the *Computer History Museum* website: https://web.archive.org/web/20071011043313/http://www.computermuseumgroningen.nl/mcgrawhill/ipc.html

[‡] Computers, or at least calculating machines, predate society's harnessing of electricity. Besides the abacus, which has been around for thousands of years, the mathematician Blaise Pascal came up with an automatic mechanical calculator around 400 years ago. Most famously, though, Charles Babbage arrived at his Analytical engine in the middle of the nineteenth century. The machine was programmable, using a punched card system similar to that of the Jacquard loom mechanical sewing machine. By the time of the first mainframe computers (like the ENIAC) around World War II, however, vacuum tubes predominated and thus henceforth electricity was needed for computers' operation.

board illustrative aid to computation, probably the first true paper computer),* I would construct an Instructo of my own to experiment with.

I wrote an Instructo program that calculates hailstone numbers, which is shown below.† Comments are designated by the inequality symbols; the `Enter` *N* is not so much a comment as a command to the user prior to the program's execution—a value must be entered by the user into Input A or B (A is used for inputting a single number, while B is used for multiple numbers or letters on a strip of paper; either way, once an Instructo program starts running, there is no way to ask the user for input during the program run itself—rather, prior to the run, all necessary inputs must be completed).

```
00    ENIA, 93    Enter N
01    LDRA, 93
02    DIVA, 10
03    CPRB, 11
04    INDA, 12
05    JBEQ, 15
06    JBGT, 23
07    <Numerical Values>
08    <For arithmetic>
09    3
10    2
11    0
12    1
13    <If value is even>
14    <divide it by 2>
15    STRA, 93
16    PROA, 93
```

---

* The CARDIAC was created by David Hagel Barger and Saul Fingerman; they wrote a very interesting and thorough (but now reads as terribly sexist) manual for the device—it's much more comprehensive and explanatory than Matt's manual for the Instructo—which can be accessed online (as of February 22, 2014) at http://kylem.net/hardware/cardiac/CARDIAC_manual.pdf

† For an explanation of hailstone numbers, please see the earlier chapter "Computers Can't Read."

```
17    LDRA, 93
18    CPRA, 12
19    JAEQ, 31
20    JUMP, 01
21    <if value is odd>
      <multiply by 3>
22    <add 1>
23    LDRA, 93
24    MULA, 09
25    ADDA, 12
26    STRA, 93
27    PROA, 93
28    JUMP, 01
29    <If value = 1>
30    <Hailstone found>
31    PROB, 34
32    PROB, 35
33    STOP, 33
34    SEE INDEX COUNTER
35    FOR HAILSTONE #
```

Program step 00 reads the value the user entered in to Input A, placing it into storage location 93.[*] The value entered must be a positive integer.

Step 01 loads Register A with the value in SS (storage location) 93 which, recall, was what was originally in Input A. Next, step 02 divides the value by 2—and steps 03 to 06 determine, based on the quotient's remainder, if the inputted value is even or odd (also, the Index Counter is incremented by one; this keeps a count of the number of iterations the program needs before terminating).

If the inputted value is even, the program jumps to step 15, where the value is divided by two, printed on the output, and com-

[*] Just like the CARDIAC, the Instructo has one hundred storage locations: 00 to 89 are part of the "Program Storage Unit," while 90 to 99 make up the "Main Storage Unit." Commands, called mnemonic code words, cannot be placed in the Main Storage—it is only for numbers, letters, or combinations thereof.

pared to see if its quotient is equal to one—at which point the program will terminate after running steps 31 to 33. If the value is not equal to one, the program jumps back to step 01 to begin the process anew (see previous paragraph).*

But if the inputted value is odd, the program instead jumps to step 23, where the value is multiplied by three and then incremented by one (notice that storage locations 09 to 12 serve as placeholders for numbers needed for calculations). The result of this calculation is printed on the output, and the program jumps back to step 01 to start again.

If, let's say, `6` is entered in as Input A, the following outputs are produced:

| **Output A** | **Output B** |
|---|---|
| `3` | `SEE INDEX COUNTER` |
| `10` | `FOR HAILSTONE #` |
| `5` | |
| `16` | |
| `8` | |
| `4` | |
| `2` | |
| `1` | |

The Index Counter at the end of the run will show `08`, meaning there was an output of eight numbers till a `1` was reached, including the `1` (as is shown in Output A above).

Like the CARDIAC, Mr. Matt designed the Instructo to be a teaching tool about computers rather than as a pure calculating machine; after all, all the calculating and incrementing and data transfer has to be done by hand (for example, the multiplication and addition in the hailstone program is accomplished off to the side of the paper computer, with paper and pencil—don't use an electronic calculator because it ruins the mood). A local newspaper article re-

* Obviously, the jump mnemonic code is called `JUMP`; the CARDIAC has an analogous command, called the "unconditional transfer," but it's completely numeric: op code 8--, where the "--" refers to the two-digit memory location to unconditionally jump to. Unlike the Instructo, though, the CARDIAC also has a *conditional* transfer: op code 3--, which branches based on sign.

view written shortly after the release of the Instructo was highly critical of the device, calling it "boring," something that confuses the forest for the trees—in terms of forcing the operator to handle too many details, perform too many tasks, largely without supplying the reasoning for them—and it being more appropriate, like the CARDIAC, as an aid to teaching computers rather than as a teacher in and of itself. It just wasn't fun, the technophobic author sadly concluded.

I would add several other criticisms: that, unlike its predecessor, the CARDIAC, which arrived on the scene in the 1960s—well before electronic personal computers—the Instructo was patented and published in the late 1970s, around the time of the Apple II and the Tandy TRS-80. So the Instructo was already an anachronism at its release. Another key problem with the device is its command words (the mnemonic codes). They are excessive, inelegant, and seem less realistically tied to machine-language computing than the codes of the CARDIAC—which are all numerical and are much fewer in number. The Instructo codes are at times reminiscent of a mid-level programming language.

It is also terribly difficult to debug a program on the device. You'd better have thoroughly thought through the logic of an Instructo program before attempting to run it, otherwise you'll have pulled many strips of paper, solved numerous arithmetic problems, and incremented countless counters for nothing.

With that in mind, I thought it might be beneficial to write emulator software for the Instructo. There are at least two emulators of the CARDIAC, one of which was written in Microsoft Excel, so that's what I did—I made an Instructo emulator using Visual Basic macros in Excel. A screenshot of the emulator running the hailstone program (with an input of 6) is shown below.

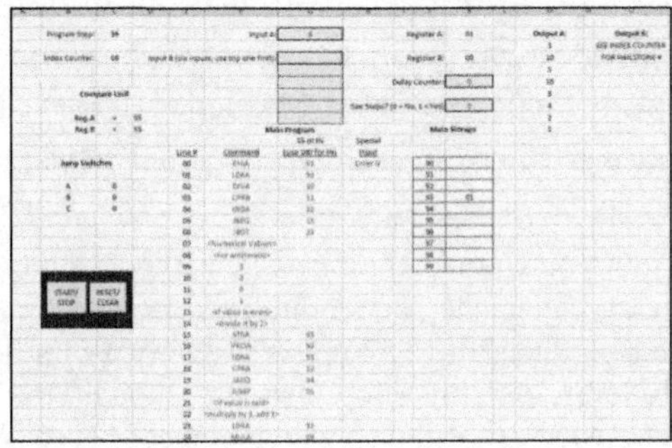

After defining some global variables,[*] a `Do While...Loop` was set to continue until the mnemonic code `STOP` was encountered—which immediately terminates an Instructo program. And every mnemonic code was coded in Visual Basic in a very compartmentalized manner. For example, the mnemonic code `ADDA` adds to the number in Register A the number in storage location SS. The Visual Basic code is

```
If StartCell = "ADDA" Then
    For Delay = 1 To DelayCounter
    Next Delay
     Set TempRegister1 = Range("K2")
     Set TempRegister2 =
               Range("F" & (SS + 13))
     TempRegisterSum =
          TempRegister1 + TempRegister2
     Range("K2").Value = TempRegisterSum
     ProgramStep = ProgramStep + 1
End If
```

Here's another example: the mnemonic code `PABA` prints a mixed fraction on the Output A strip.

```
If StartCell = "PABA" Then
   For Delay = 1 To DelayCounter
   Next Delay
     Set RegisterA = Range("K2")
     Set RegisterB = Range("K4")
     Denom = Range("F" & (SS + 13)).Value
     Range("M" & OutputRowA).Value =
     RegisterA & " and " &   RegisterB &
     "/" & Denom
         OutputRowA=OutputRowA + 1
    ProgramStep=ProgramStep + 1
End If
```

[*] I.e., variables that can be accessed from any subroutine in the program. Numerous counters, locations of input/output tape, and values of Registers are defined globally in the Instructo emulator.

And the mnemonic code REVA reverses the digits of the number in Register A—so, for instance, 123 would be transformed into 321:

```
If StartCell = "REVA" Then
    For Delay = 1 To DelayCounter
    Next Delay
s = Range("K2").Value
Number = Trim(s)
NewNumber = 0
Power = 0
Length = Len(Number)
For i = 1 To Length
    x = Val(Mid(Number, i, 1))
    NewNumber =
          NewNumber + x * (10 ^ Power)
    Power = Power + 1
Next i
Range("K2").Value = NewNumber
ProgramStep = ProgramStep + 1
End If
```

My Instructo emulator can debug programs easily, for two reasons: (1) An option, which can be turned on prior to running an Instructo program, prompts the user before executing each program step, and (2) The tediousness of pushing and pulling paper through cardboard is eliminated in favor of electronics—ironic, since the supposed appeal of the Instructo Paper Computer was to be its independence from electronics. But when used as an emulator, programming on the Instructo, though still cumbersome, is, finally, fun.

(2014)

# B.

## Journal of a New Math Teacher

In 2004, at a crossroads in a still-nascent actuarial career, I made a critical decision—to find a student teaching placement for high school mathematics. The placement was secured quickly enough, and by the end of that fall I met my (future) cooperating teacher, Mr. John M. It struck me how much Mr. M. looked like the comedian Larry David: in his mid-50s with vertex baldness, frizzy white hair, big glasses, a cashmere half-zip sweater—forgive me if I was expecting a nebbish. But looks were deceiving. Mr. M. was an assistant football coach at the high school and nothing if not a very commanding presence around students.

Shortly after New Year's, I tendered my resignation from my desk job for student teaching. I kept a daily account of my classroom struggles and (occasional) victories, which, lightly edited, is presented below.

*January 23*

It is the day before I am scheduled to begin student teaching. I have never taught in a "formal" classroom before (although I have cut my teeth by tutoring a number of students over the years), so, despite logging thousands of hours as a student myself, I have precious little idea of what to expect.

A theory that's recently been percolating in my head: the amount of "energy" in a classroom—the teacher's, plus the students'—is constant, no matter what. Thus, if the teacher comes out of the gate strong, with tons of energy and enthusiasm, the students respond with little energy—and the relationship, the equation, remains in balance. And the converse also applies. I'm not sure how such a theory would or even could be tested.

Starting tomorrow, and through the entire first week, Mr. M. [a math teacher with some 34 years of classroom experience] and I will plan for the second week of my student teaching—and beyond—because the students at the Old School [a pseudonym; Mr. M. and myself, along with about half the faculty of the Old School, moved to the newly opened New School at the start of the second semester] will be consumed with taking finals as they close out their first semester of the school year. But I won't be doing any teaching this first week.

I worked in the actuarial field my entire professional life (since college, for around a half a decade) until this past Friday, when I quit. I voluntarily walked out on a good-paying job* for... well, a

---

* Like teaching, the actuarial profession has many, many hoops to jump through in order to achieve professional stature. An actuary's status is broadly defined by several criteria: actuarial exams passed; years of work experience; and level of business (not necessarily actuarial) knowledge. All three factors are important in the hiring, promotion, and stay of the actuary; however, number of exams passed is perhaps the most important criterion in predicting an actuary's success in any business milieu employing actuaries.

There are two actuarial societies (actually, there are more than two, but the two listed forthwith have the most comprehensive reach), the Society of Actuaries (SOA) and the Casualty Actuarial Society (CAS), both headquartered in the United States. The two societies administer exams. To become a member of the Society of Actuaries, one must pass eight exams and a "professional development" seminar; membership in the Casualty Actuarial Society requires the passing of nine exams. At the time of this writing, the two societies have the first four exams in common, though they are always in flux. Exams for both societies are rooted in mathematics and mathematical notions applied to business. The first four are more purely mathematical in content than the later examinations. The first examination tests students' abilities in the realms of calculus, probability, and risk management theory; the second focuses on finance, theory of interest, and more business applications; and the third and fourth are complementary life insurance-oriented tests. SOA exams at this point diverge from CAS tests to cover financial and life/health insurance theory; in addition, a professional development seminar is required for the full, F.S.A. (Fellow of the Society of Actuaries) designation. (An intermediary moniker, A.S.A. [Associate of the Society of Actuaries], is assigned when the actuarial student has successfully completed the first six exams.) CAS exams five through nine focus on casualty and property insurance concepts, coupled with some detailed accounting and financial theory. Analogous to SOA, CAS has two official distinctions: A.C.A.S. and F.C.A.S. (which stand for Associate of the Casualty Actuarial Society and Fellow of the Casualty Actuarial Society, respectively).

Upon completion of the first four exams, an actuarial student may apply for the M.A.A.A. designation, which stands for Member of the Academy of Actuaries Association. This moniker is only a consequence of passing multiple tests, not something exclusively "earned," as are the other distinctions. All

no-paying internship. Although it's clichéd to say, I definitely feel like tomorrow is the first day of the rest of my life.

*January 24*

On the very first day of student teaching, my school's snow number was called on the radio—the Old School had a two-hour delay.

After I arrived, I observed Mr. M. teach three class blocks in a row [i.e., block scheduling—90 minutes allotted for each class. There are four blocks in an Old School day, and each teacher receives one block off for preparation. Mr. M. taught classes the first three blocks]—all geometry/trigonometry review classes for a final exam coming up this Thursday or Friday morning. It was immediately apparent to me that Mr. M. has an excellent command over the content; that's not surprising, I suppose. What was interesting was how he seemed to have the respect of the entire class—in over two hours of teaching, I only saw him quiet down a single student a single time. He challenged students with more difficult problems,

---

exams (in both societies) are graded on an eleven-point scale (from zero through ten); a grade of zero does not necessarily imply that the student scored incorrectly on every question in the examination, simply that "the paper was very poor." Likewise, a score of ten does not suggest a perfect paper, but merely a "very good paper." Exams in both societies are either administered once every six months (the early examinations) or once every year (the later, more difficult exams). The first four tests are entirely multiple choice (with approximately forty to fifty questions to complete, in a three- to four-hour timeframe); the later examinations, in both societies, are part multiple choice, part free response (and several contain true or false questions).

It must be stressed that scores on an examination on a given date are heavily dependent on the mean score of the actuarial students as a whole; "passing percentages" are determined by cutoffs based on students' performance. Because of the complexity (and, it seems to me, arbitrariness) of selection, the dynamics of the determinations of passing/failing papers will not be detailed here. It suffices to note that at any given sitting, at any given examination, approximately thirty to fifty percent of the students taking the test will obtain a passing score (passing scores are six, seven, eight, nine, and ten; recall that all exams are graded on an eleven-point scale). A higher percentage of students "will be passed" as the exams increase in difficulty; in other words, while only thirty percent of students may pass examination one (or Course One) in May, fifty percent of students may pass SOA examination seven (or Course Seven) that same month.

prefacing them repeatedly with the words "Let's kick it up a notch." Perhaps his students have some built-in expectations I'm not aware of, since I'm catching them at the end of a half a year's worth of instruction.

But how can I achieve that same "control"? Can I ever do it? And what about my expectations? Entering into any American classroom with little expectations of pupils to understand material may turn into a self-fulfilling prophesy: those same students, seeing that you, the teacher, don't expect much from them, might not have the impetus to deliver more than is necessary to satisfy low expectations.

My only criticism of Mr. M. is that he's a bit of a sage-on-the-stage, with his completing-the-sentence style of teaching. Here's what I mean: He threw out many almost-complete sentences to the students, such as "The sum of the vertical angles here is…" and "The sum of the angles of this polygon is…." Perhaps this sort of teaching is more a function of the midterm review itself rather than any intentionality on his part. Time will tell.

*January 25*

Today was again spent reviewing material for the upcoming final exam in Mr. M.'s geometry classes. Essentially, I watched the same sets of problems presented three times in a row—one for each of Mr. M.'s three blocks. What perhaps made these observations unique was Mr. M.'s lack of presentation of any new material. It's all just review, monotonous review, which I'm beginning to suspect not only very necessary, but part and parcel of this job.

I also find that I have to tune out the majority of noises during the day; there is not a quiet moment to be found. Furthermore, I've been incredibly stressed out these past few days. Teaching's clearly a tough job, and the worst of it is that I have yet to actually *teach* even a single minute.

*January 27*

I got to see more of the Old School today, despite the fact that I'm going (along with Mr. M.) to the New School next week.

Mr. M. and I walked around to the three classes that he was giving final exams in (all were proctored by other teachers). I had the yeomen's task of collecting them and calculating final grades.

It was instructive to peek into Mr. M.'s grade book. I noticed that his grades, student by student, had little variation. I suppose that's the criterion for reliability; the final exams were constructed not by Mr. M. but by a committee during inservices.

The remainder of my day was spent at a lunch with several of the teachers, along with a trip to the New School to set up Mr. M.'s classroom—room 230—for next week's school launch. The New School is quite a sprawling campus: a series of large, interconnected brick-and-stucco buildings, surrounded by flat farm land, trees, and homes out in the exurbs, unlike the Old School, which is more of a claustrophobic towering structure set in between a highway and a middle school.

Mr. M. told me not to lose too much sleep over starting with my "own" class, block three, next week. To that end, he mentioned that Ms. Gretchen S., a fellow math teacher also moving from the Old School to the New, still, after nearly a decade of classroom experience, is restless and nervous the night before a semester's first day.

*January 28*

I'm consistently amazed to see how easily and gracefully my presence here has been accepted by both students and especially other teachers. Oddly, the students seem to not really notice me at all; I may be wrong about this—they may be whispering behind my back or talking about me, as in, "Who's that guy in the back of the room watching us?"—but I see no evidence of that.

*Reflections on Teaching: January 30*

Tomorrow I begin teaching. Not all at once—I don't take over Mr. M.'s entire course load—but one of his three classes, precalculus third block, is mine to start fresh. In the first chapter of the *Student Teaching and Field Experiences Handbook (5th Edition)* (2001) by Betty D. Roe and Elinor P. Ross, entitled "Getting Ready," some basic pedagogic methods for neophyte teachers are presented.

The very first page of the chapter has a rather frightening story about a certain Mr. Allen. In the story, Allen, a beginning student teacher, is forced to take the reins when his cooperating teacher, Mr. Wiley, is late (due to unforeseen circumstances) to school one day. Allen tries his best to maintain class order—he's even surprised when he instructs the students to go to their seats and they actually comply—but, ultimately, he doesn't have a good enough handle on appropriate classroom procedures.

As Mr. Allen learns, there's a big difference between just watching and actually being in charge of a classroom. In Allen's defense, he really hadn't been a student teacher long enough to take in all of the details necessary to maintain class functionality, and he shouldn't have been put in a situation where he was the sole adult responsible for the students. Nevertheless, as a teacher, it's vital to be able to adapt to the situation at hand, maintain composure, project authority, and convey leadership. Allen wasn't able to do any of those things effectively.

So the *Student Teaching and Field Experiences Handbook* suggests for student teachers to "[g]et a daily schedule from the cooperating teacher so that you will be aware of the order of classes, times for breaks and special activities, and beginning and dismissal times" (p. 5). What's been especially challenging for me is that the teaching environment I've been in has been in a state of upheaval, due to the transition to the New School (from the Old School). A daily schedule hasn't always been readily available. Also, we will be beginning our math classes tomorrow without textbooks—they weren't delivered yet. I am learning that, as a teacher, planning is only half the battle: responding to the situation at hand, as it develops, is a hallmark of an experienced educator.

*January 31*

Well, I taught for the first time today [third block precalculus]. Mr. M. remarked that I was "very composed," but that I needed to prepare better so I'm not as quick to turn to unknown sources for material.

I agree: I need to know that I'm supposed to do a little bit better *before* I begin to do this without a net. I also need to feel more comfortable with the material that I, surprisingly to me, feel a bit shaky on.

Here's the point: I need to plan better. Period. Although the best laid plans oftentimes go awry, it's better to be over-prepared than under-. Tomorrow I need to make the best of things. It will be at least a little easier, since our textbooks finally arrived.

*February 2*

Mr. M. gave me my first sit-down critique of my teaching. He said that while I am polite and have good time-awareness skills, I need to improve my diagram drawing, and I also need to show more enthusiasm and get more to the point on things. The critique was, of course, totally on-target. I have a lot to improve. The truth is, I keep coming home feeling exhausted, defeated. I'm not getting enough sleep and the hours are already taking their toll on me.

*February 3*

Today was a quiz day, so I only had to prepare about 30 minutes' worth of new material (other than the quiz). What a relief! And yet I'm feeling burned out already, even with only teaching a single class. I don't know when I'll take over Mr. M.'s other two classes; I'm not sure I feel even close to ready for them. A week of teaching and I feel like most of what I thought I'd learned in education classes has completely unraveled. Two weeks ago, I was sitting in the same cubicle I'd practically lived in for nearly five years, and it's beginning to feel like my previous desk-job life was just that—some distant, faraway dream of a memory.

*Reflections on Teaching: February 5*

A week ago I had never taught a single high school class in my life. My teaching experiences were limited to the somewhat sterile and relatively "unrealistic" milieu of the college classroom—I, like the many others who traverse the education route, made many formal graded presentations in graduate and undergraduate classes. But teach a real high school class? I had only read about it, seen movies about it, heard about it—but never experienced it.

The second chapter of the *Handbook*, entitled "Human Relations," presents a multitude of case studies that, purportedly, student teachers like me might be able to relate to. Case Study 2.1 (p.

32) is especially interesting. It is difficult to be spot-on and perfect when you're "on stage" for such long hours, day in and day out. There's an ongoing opportunity for a teacher to accidentally spout an unfortunate remark—like, for instance, a sexist one. But Miss Chambers, in the case study, seems to harbor intentional stereotypes and expresses them in both circular design and practice; consider her planning: "She told the boys to plan and construct a set to look like a festive Mexican home, while the girls located and prepared the foods to be tried." On the one hand, give Miss Chambers points for injecting a bit of cultural diversity into her classroom, and at an appropriate juncture, no less; on the other hand, her execution wasn't particularly praiseworthy: she relied on tired stereotypes, akin to Mickey Rooney's Mr. Yunioshi in the otherwise perfect *Breakfast at Tiffany's* (1961).

Diversity is indeed something teachers need to be aware of—as the book makes plain. But perhaps the author takes things a little too far when he writes, "[C]onsideration of the points of view that groups such as the Tories… had toward the American Revolution may be appropriate in expanding multicultural awareness and understanding" (p. 34). Wait a minute—the Tories?

If I remember correctly, the Tories opposed the American Revolution and even took up arms against rebels fighting the British. There are no Tories left, as far as I can tell; the Tories name is popularly known today in part because Tories are the opposition party to Labor in Great Britain.

Nevertheless, multicultural awareness and understanding is paramount and certainly not something I take lightly.

*February 8*

My class was a bit "unruly" today, and I've been racking my brain all day trying to figure out why. Are my halcyon days over?

Perhaps it's because I began my class by grouping students into pairs and having them write solutions to homework problems on the whiteboard in the front of the classroom; they never quite settled down after that, and they seemed very resistant to the idea of another quiz tomorrow.

*February 9*

I had a chance to observe history teacher Mr. Larry B. in fourth block. The energy Mr. B. injected into his classroom performance was infectious*—but I wondered throughout how he managed to *sustain* his enthusiasm, something that my cooperating teacher has repeatedly mentioned I need to work on.

*Reflections on Teaching: February 9*

"[D]o not lecture straight from your college notes," the *Handbook* instructs. "Remember that your students are not yet ready for material as advanced as the material in your college classes. Use the college notes as background material, and work in information from them only as it is directly applicable and appropriate for your particular students" (p. 133).

That's good advice—especially for me, since this has indeed been one of my biggest temptations: bring in abstractions from those college courses of yesteryear and pound my little greenhorns with the hardest stuff imaginable.

But that hasn't been the best idea, since the more abstract—or, shall we say, less "relevant"—I get, the more they appear to drift away. Some stare through the nearest window, fixated on the deciduous tree limbs swaying ever so gently in the wind. Others find favor in viewing the hard-to-discern images reflecting off their opaque desktops. And a few even find the pockmarked ceiling tiles above them interesting, discovering patterns in sharp relief as fluidly as they might spot a popular cartoon character floating in the sky, made of cumulus clouds, on a bright summer's day.

The authors of the *Handbook* also speak of those two types of assessments, formative and summative, that are the two key pieces of the assessment puzzle. I have, as of now, disseminated and graded two quizzes. Based on summative and formative assessments over the last week or so, the grades on the quiz today didn't show much variation from my preconceived notions ("preconceived" has

* Mr. B. handed me a note halfway through his class which reads as follows: "Basic Level/Almost all are on learning or emotional support/Generally well-behaved/Struggle for good grades/Difficulty focusing, etc."

a bad connotation to it. But I mean it to refer to my prior evaluative processes in this context).

*February 10*

Today was probably my best teaching day thus far. Even Mr. M. told me that I had a good amount of enthusiasm going through the class period. It was simply a review session—I wasn't teaching any new material per se—so maybe the comfort I had with having already taught the content showed.

In any case, tonight is Back to School Night for parents; because of the block scheduling, each New School class lasts only a single semester, so there are two BTSNs per academic year.

*February 11*

Last night at BTSN I insisted on speaking to "my" third block's parents, and Mr. M. acquiesced. I presented course requirements and student expectations using PowerPoint. What was perhaps weird was how *not* weird the whole thing seemed; not to say it was completely natural or anything like that, but it simply didn't feel particularly non-routine to me, despite me not having ever done it.

The material in class is getting more difficult. I have been impressed with two students in third block—C. and K. They are both female, challenging daily the stereotype that only males have a special faculty with mathematics. K. is surely going on to AP Calculus next semester, but we'll see about C., a very introverted tenth grader.

Also, Prof. L., my supervising professor, stopped by for the first time to observe me. "You are clearly making good progress in becoming a professional teacher," she told me. "Your coop., Mr. M. is very impressed with your solid command of the content knowledge. Your self-analysis and feedback from Mr. M. have pinpointed areas needing attention: enthusiasm, energy, student motivation—but you're making progress on these. Keep up the good work and don't be too hard on yourself."

*Reflections on Teaching: February 13*

In the spirit of the *Handbook*, and in the spirit of self-examination, I will now write a vignette of my own to complement the book's many case studies:

### Case Study: A Test Finished By All—But One

Mr. Lorenzo, a student teacher in mathematics, has successfully proctored two in-class quizzes. On his students' third evaluation, a unit test on the first chapter of the textbook, he informs the class that they will have the entire period to complete it. "If you're done early, try to take a look at the next chapter of the book and think a bit about symmetry," he says.

One by one, Mr. Lorenzo's students walk up to the front of the room and hand him test papers; he once again instructs them to take a look at the next unit's material. With thirty minutes left in the class period, all but one student has finished the test. After waiting ten minutes, during which most of the other kids have shifted to working on homework from other classes, Mr. Lorenzo considers asking that last student to finish the test outside the room so that he can begin the next unit's lesson. However, he doesn't want to single that student out in front of his classmates, so he allows the silence in the room to pervade, and only ten minutes' worth of new material ends up being presented before the bell rings.

1. By not removing the slower test taker, did Mr. Lorenzo hurt or help the class as a whole?
2. What could Mr. Lorenzo have done differently that would have not singled out the remaining test taker? Was there anything else that could have been done?
3. Should Mr. Lorenzo have prepared more specific lesson plans for those pupils who finished the test early?

Let me now address my own questions:

1. Mr. Lorenzo did not do anyone in the class any favors by not extricating the student and beginning the new lesson; he lost valuable instructional time. However, as the *Handbook* explains, "Don't be a slave to your schedule" (p. 82).

Student removal would have been a de facto penalty for slower test completion—and, more important, Mr. Lorenzo specifically stated at the beginning of the class period that all students had until the bell rang to finish up the test. Changing rules in mid-stream is more than unfair—it's inconsistent. Inconsistency today hurts credibility tomorrow.

2. I do not believe so—however, this is a question I will ponder in more detail as I develop my pedagogic techniques.
3. Perhaps a worksheet that introduced the new unit by tying it explicitly to the old may have worked. And such a worksheet need not have been a one-off assignment; rather, such an introductory worksheet should have been made and distributed regardless of when everyone in the class finished the aforementioned quiz.

*February 15*

A student from third block, R., who dons fedoras and leather jackets and frequently slumps forward when arguing a point, asked me to sponsor a new extracurricular club—he calls it "Literary Movements & Et Cetera."—and I readily agreed. We stayed after school to draw up a constitution. Here is the preamble:

> *In order to further the advancement of a common interest in the Humanities and, specifically, in the philosophies and with a strong focus in the literary strains of the past and present, and with an especially acute point of convergence on the "et cetera," we hereby establish Literary Movements & Et Cetera.*

I am piqued, though, after Mr. M.'s directive to me to begin teaching first block: a post-precalculus, alternative course to calculus for (mostly) seniors called Advanced Math Concepts, or AMC. I don't feel like I'm ready yet. But he wants me to begin teaching the class this Friday.

*February 16*

Let me just get this off my chest: I hate whiteboards. When I used to study for math exams as an undergraduate in my university's library, I usually slipped into the small study rooms which had small blackboards—and, with chalk in hand, I mapped out the mathematics of problems' solutions. If chalk dust got on my clothes, it could easily be brushed or patted off; my clothes weren't ruined. And I also found it easier to write on the blackboards because of the guiding friction that would take effect when chalk was pressed to board.

In class today, when I wrote a certain problem on the whiteboard, Mr. M. (who was observing) couldn't help himself and broke the proverbial fourth wall to jump in and comment on the problem's presentation in a positive way. That was a small nugget of a victory for me—I feel like I'm slowly pushing the rock uphill.

*February 17*

Today is the last day in which I teach only one class. Tomorrow, bright and early, I begin phase two of my student teaching practicum: taking over AMC, first block. I'll have a class of nearly all seniors with a common affliction: senioritis. And senioritis is always fatal to high school students' academic lives.

*February 18*

Although I was fairly comfortable with the material, my first AMC class did not go especially well. The kids weren't into it at all, and it must've seemed like I wasn't, either, since I just droned on and on and I knew I was doing that!—yet I simply continued. I know I need to improve—and fast—else things aren't going to go smoothly for months to come.

A positive note, however: a student, J., approached me at the end of AMC and told me she appreciated the "time and care" I put into constructing today's lesson and believes things will get easier for me (with respect to teaching AMC). J. participated a number of times during this first class with me—she seemed very eager to call attention to herself,* yet she never said anything to me during the

---

* In some vague way, she reminded me of the Tracy Flick character from the satiric film *Election* (1999). Perhaps seeing her as a movie character wasn't so off the mark: J. would later that year go on to star in her own reality show, produced by America Online, following the lives of several incoming college freshman throughout the country.

weeks I was stuck in the back of the classroom observing Mr. M. deftly teach AMC.

*Reflections on Teaching: February 20*

Am I teaching in an inductive or a deductive way? I think that more than fifty percent of my instruction so far has been deductive: show rules and then apply those rules to problem situations. But I have also made use of some inductive reasoning in the classroom.

For instance, when presenting the transformations and dilations of some parent mathematical functions, I showed my students examples of this or that function and then asked them to generalize from the given data: Do the strictures that seem to be governing the transformations and dilations of these functions hold amongst all parent functions? Are there exceptions to the rules? If so, what are those exceptions and why do they arise?

I enjoy posing these kinds of questions. But as the mathematics gets more difficult, I must accept the fact that there may be times when a correct or complete answer from me to their questions will not be immediately forthcoming.

*February 22*

Today's AMC class went much better. I used PowerPoint to illustrate some complicated ideas, and the class seemed to respond nicely. But, to be completely frank, making PowerPoints takes *forever* and thus I don't know how much longer, realistically, I can continue with them—I'm burned out as it is.

I am surprised, though, at how comfortable I'm starting to feel—five weeks ago I was still plugging away at my former job (in the actuarial field); but things have changed so dramatically since then: my "cubicle" has grown a lot, lot bigger and there are now 30 students bouncing around in it every day.

*February 24*

Things are getting hectic around here. I feel a time crunch taking hold and its grip is tight.

We were let out early today—an early dismissal. I've always wondered, without realizing that I've wondered, what an E.D.

would be like from a teacher's perspective. Now I don't have to wonder anymore. Call this one of my first lessons in being flexible, planning-wise: I lost an entire block. Thus, the test review will have to be tomorrow.

*Reflections on Teaching: February 24*

Am I teaching in a bubble? I told Mr. M. earlier today that, when I was forming my expectations about what student teaching might be like, my worst-case scenarios centered on students throwing chairs and desks at me and the like.*

For my master's degree, I observed classrooms that weren't, shall we say, ideal. In some schools in the inner city, the struggle for classroom control was a battle fought by teachers relentlessly and continuously.† Only twenty to thirty percent of periods in some of

---

* I posed this same question—Am I teaching in a bubble?—to Prof. L. She told me, "Yes, you are working in a 'bubble' of sorts, since the New School has such high-achieving kids—but doing it well. Take on that second block class ASAP."

† One of the math teachers that I observed, in an inner city school's math office, told me to "get out [of teaching] while I could." A little startled at what she said, I asked her why. "Because it's awful. If you were my son, I would never have allowed you to go into teaching! Stay an actuary—don't become a teacher, and definitely don't come here." I was puzzled—her class of tenth graders behaved pretty well. Also, they seemed generally to know the mathematics. Not incredibly well, but competently. However, she seemed continually mad at and visibly frustrated with her students. I couldn't exactly tell why. She told me after the class that in one of her other periods the prior week, a fight broke out in her class and spilled over into the hall, which had never happened to her before. Perhaps I am simply too naïve to fully comprehend her disillusionment, but I certainly hope that I never attain that quality as a teacher.

Not everything about that particular school observation was negative, though. When I arrived at the school in the morning, I had the pleasure of also venturing into the history office. I met three of the school's teachers in there, and they were really, really loud spoken. I next went to the math department office, and found the same characteristic there: everyone spoke really, really loudly, as if people had trouble hearing them. In the first class I observed that particular day, the math teacher spoke really loudly too. When I was in high school, I am not sure I noticed if the teachers did that or not so consistently, so perpetually. But at this school in the inner city, every teacher seemed to speak loudly over an imaginary din.

those schools were spent in a content-related mode; the remaining bulk of the periods were drained by a near-endless discipline effort by the teacher.

I am left wondering: Can a teacher ever regain the respect of the class if it is lost? Can any teacher permit things to go too far and then throttle-back successfully, or is it all too late once those initial mistakes have been made? Classroom discipline is a zero-sum game: either the teacher's holding all the cards, or the students are. There's no halfway.

*Reflections on Teaching: February 28*

"Writing is also a skill that is used in every area of the curriculum," the *Handbook* explains. "In English and language arts classes, students are taught how to write effectively, but in all classes writing provides an effective technique for learning" (p. 150). In my pre-classroom-teaching preparation, I realized early on that interdisciplinary learning is in many ways the most effective kind of learning—it counteracts Nassim Nicholas Taleb's "domain dependence" fallacy. Although the curriculum I am saddled with now is high pressure and covers many topics, I figured it would be nice to inject a little non-mathematical content in there once in a while; having my students compose journals on an occasional basis (which I have been doing) facilitates writing development—perhaps not in terms of writing mechanics or grammar so much as in the systematic construction of clear and concise ideas ("systematic construction" warranted here, since students are forced to put pen to paper about a highly technical topic, mathematics).

Yet another *post hoc* defense of my implementation of the New School's curriculum comes two pages later, when the *Handbook* segues to the notion of enriching lesson plans with literature: "Even in mathematics classes, literature can be useful.... Older students may enjoy and learn from mathematical puzzle books...." (p. 153). And, of course, IMP (the Interactive Mathematics Program)* contains some of the most effective intra- and interdisciplinary ideas of them all—and a host of them involve literature. Reading through Edgar Allen Poe's short story "The Pit and the Pendulum," for in-

---

* See the earlier chapter "A Clash of Complements: Comparing Mathematics Curricula" for more on IMP.

stance, gives students the opportunity to solve an implicit math problem from the story utilizing physics-type modeling.

*March 1*

School was cancelled—snow again. [In my lesson plans for the day, I wrote, "No school—no problem!"]

*March 2*

I was formally assessed by my supervising professor, Prof. L. I never thought that my life-long love of videogames could someday further my career. But it did; here's why: I made a PowerPoint of Super Mario jumping to illustrate parametric equations, and the students seemed to take to it well.* Even Mr. M. told me later that he was so surprised by the lesson that he told a number of teachers about it during his lunch (of which he goes to quite a bit more lately, now that I've taken over two of three of his classes…).

Speaking of lunch—Mr. M. also said that he wants me to go with him to lunch; he doesn't want me to persist in eating alone while planning like a hermit. Usually I'm very reticent socially yet paradoxically I seem to have little trouble speaking in front of people—well, students, that is.

*March 3*

Not a good day. I felt terribly unprepared for first block, though I didn't realize it until the class began: and the unpreparedness was heightened by Mr. M. interjecting during my lesson a mini-lesson of his own. When Mr. M. gets agitated, I noticed, he tends to start a lot of sentences with "Seriously" and "Absolutely," as in "Absolutely, you need to know this," and "Seriously, you've gotta be able

---

* Here's what Prof. L. told me: "You are making excellent progress. You know your material cold. You planned in detail the step-by-step analysis of how to convey even the most difficult concepts to your students. You are developing effective techniques for presentation—and especially for interacting positively and constructively with your students. You have earned student respect and trust. You know all names and call on students even without looking at them. You have developed a very effective way of modeling concept problems on the board and then 'thinking out loud' with students."

to do that." I apparently had a miscommunication with him about what topic was to be covered today, and it was embarrassing. Then again, him taking over instructionally by fiat is certainly well within his rights—it's his classroom, after all.

*Reflections on Teaching: March 5*

There's no question that the hot-topic of diversity is here to stay. This is a serious issue made all the more serious by the inherent, practical difficulties of teaching to a heterogeneous group. Ethnic and multicultural differences are just the tip of the iceberg; special-needs students also fall under the umbrella of this extensive subject.

*March 8*

And it snowed, again. This time with a later start: during second block. By third, students were having a tough time concentrating on the tasks at hand because they were too distracted watching the slowly dancing flakes.

*March 9*

In AMC, we had a full period of assessment. The students didn't do particularly well, so I decided to adjust—well, *curve*—the grades somewhat, letting everyone fall in line with their course averages up to this point. From criterion- to norm-referenced grading in one fell swoop.

Did I neglect to mention just how effective of a teacher Mr. M. is? Even if he is a bit rough around the edges, every class of his I observe reminds me of how far I have yet to go—if I ever make it there at all, that is.

*Reflections on Teaching: March 9*

I would venture to guess that most educators have heard of Howard Gardner. Gardner defines intelligences (originally seven, now eight)—linguistic, logic-mathematical, intrapersonal, musical, spatial, bodily/kinesthetic, and naturalistic—that have seemingly been "influential" in education.

Gardner also seems to be a relativist—not in the sense of Einstein, but in the tradition of the structuralists and postmodernists, like Derrida and Foucault (at least a little bit). Take a look at this sentence, from the textbook *Teaching Mathematics for the 21st Century: Methods and Activities for Grades 6-12* (2000) by Linda Huetinck and Sara N. Munshin: “He [Gardner] finds the logical-mathematical skill to be one way of thinking that is neither superior not inferior to any other in the sets of intelligences” (p. 59). In other words, Gardner—and, by extension, the educators utilizing his intelligences’ schemata—cannot place value judgments on one kind of intelligence over another; they are all equal in significance and importance.

Although it’s above my pay grade to debate the merits of Gardner’s intelligences, I will say that not placing emphasis on any particular intelligence is perhaps an unwise avenue of pedagogical practice *for the mathematics teacher.* As math educators, it is not our duty to find and develop prodigies per se; rather, it is to encourage the logical-mathematical areas of all of our students. For us to treat all types of intelligences, as Gardner has defined them, as equally important in our classrooms renders our vocational purpose moot.

If a school’s *modus operandi* is to educate from the perspective of equity with respect to the Gardner intelligences, perhaps it would be more beneficial to students if special “coaches” were in charge. These coaches wouldn’t be tied to teaching any specific material, but rather would be focused on listening and learning what the pupils might excel at (in terms of one or more of the intelligences) and proceed in some way from there.

Although I am not attempting to sound cynical (although I think it’s coming across that way), my problem with Gardner is that his definitions of intelligence constrict and predestine a student into a role commensurate with his or her kind of Gardner intelligence—or at least this is what I’m reading from his relativistic standpoint regarding the placement of equal value judgments on all intelligences.

Our job as math teachers, it seems, is to highlight, push, cajole, and ultimately help students think about math. But the lessons I’ve gone through about what it is to be a teacher do not, I think, prepare me to encourage anything more than Gardner’s logical-mathematical intelligence.

*March 10*

This morning I taught more than an hour's worth of trigonometry in AMC—because students needed to see a review of that content in order to appreciate the upcoming chapter. I did the review without so much as glancing at my notes, a first for me.

Precalculus time was spent with a quiz on probability.* I will segue tomorrow from a look at their quiz scores to the next unit, statistics, a topic I've had extended exposure to from my actuarial days, something I have already spoken to students about—bringing in as many real-world examples as I can remember that are not proprietary to my former company.

*Reflections on Teaching: March 10*

The technology available at the New School with which to present material is superb; I have been afforded the opportunity to try out many pedagogic techniques—to see what works—in the best possible sandbox.

---

* Probability might benefit by being presented with historical touches. For instance, mathematicians Pierre de Fermat and Blaise Pascal corresponded, hundreds of years ago, on a probability problem called the Problem of Points; their correspondence was the first real attempt at systematizing some notions of probability. In addition, they took luck out of the equation of gambling just a bit by using calculation. The story goes something like this: Fermat and Pascal assumed that they were playing a winner-take-all coin-toss game, but they had to stop in the middle of it for one reason or another. Knowing where they stopped, and who was ahead when they stopped, could a fair distribution of the pot be determined? Realizing the probabilities of the events that could follow—if Fermat and Pascal had completed their gambling game—the pot could be distributed along the lines of the chances each person had of winning.

The fact that gambling has mathematics at its root at all was a paradigm shift. Mark Twain, several centuries ago, wrote a short story (which was based in fact) entitled "Science vs. Luck?" In it, he describes a small town in America that penalized townsfolk caught playing so-called "games of chance." At one of the court hearings for a person accused of playing a game of chance, the defense mounts a case based on the proposition that the game of chance was really a "game of science," rooted in the fundamental, deterministic mathematical operations of probability. The jury rules in favor of the defense and henceforth such games of science are permitted in the town.

The New School has allowed me to experiment with different instructional resources. Calculators—specifically graphing calculators—I used, when I was a student, for a long time as a crutch. Instead of understanding the material as well as I should have before sitting for evaluations, I leaned on the graphing calculators for disproportionate support. There's a fine line to toe between too much and too little technological dependence in math class (and that line is especially tough to find in more advanced courses).

In addition to calculators, I have utilized the computers in the classroom to present material. Perhaps there is some instructional software available for the material I am teaching that would allow me greater flexibility, since I would have pre-packaged resources on tap in addition to those I create ad hoc.

*March 14*

Pi Day. The math-themed "holiday" was spent going over some tough material—very tough. I'm beginning to notice a persistent problem with my teaching: around two or three students dominate class discussion, making it seem like, by some sort of tacit agreement, those silent ones understand what's going on.

Mr. M. spoke to me of "teaching to the middle," and that's precisely what I need to do: teach to the 68 percent of students within one standard deviation of the mean.*

*March 15*

"Think about substituting ASAP," Prof. L. told me when I saw her today, "because that's how you become known!" But, as each day passes, I get more and more nervous about landing a teaching job—anywhere. I'm not really much of a risk-taker, and to leave my job of five years was a huge—no, monumental—leap for me. This is the first year that I truly don't know how I will spend Thanksgiv-

* This percentage refers to the so-called Empirical Rule: that, in any mound-shaped, symmetrical distribution, about 68 percent of the data is one standard deviation from the mean, 95 percent two standard deviations, and 99.7 percent three. Not all data distributions are mound-shaped symmetrical (or normal), although IQ is—though Mr. M. was probably referring to overall ability level rather than just IQ per se.

ing: employed in a school, employed but not in a school, or unemployed. But the days roll onward. Things are getting easier and yet paradoxically harder at the same time.

*Reflections on Teaching: March 15*

"My university supervisor said it's possible to get 20 years of experience in 20 years or to get 1 year of experience 20 times" (*Student Teaching and Field Experiences Handbook* , p. 225). That's a maxim I won't soon forget—and it also makes me wonder: Do my high school math teachers still teach the same way?*

I have a sneaking suspicion that my cooperating teacher never slavishly follows outmoded lesson plans. One of the most salient aspects of Mr. M.'s teaching I've observed is his creation of new lesson plans each and every day; he hasn't recycled old lesson plans. He also—and this is especially noteworthy—solves each and every math problem anew, despite the fact he has (presumably) utilized some of the problem sheets in prior semesters.

*March 17*

I am finding that my students are, in some ways, responding to me better each day; but, in other ways, things are not as efficient as they were even the previous day. The stuff that's better: (1) Rapport, and (2) Pupils' willingness to answer in-class questions. The stuff that's worse: (1) Less respect for me, and (2) Less willingness to take me seriously.

Although I felt like I had a fever by the end of the day, I stayed for the afterschool mathematics faculty meeting—the first department-exclusive meeting I've ever attended. The operative slogan at these rather informal get-togethers—one that was all-but-explicitly stated—was, CYA: Cover Your A—. Quite a philosophy, which has apparently been fruitful for those teachers in attendance.

---

* On BTSN, I ran into my eleventh grade high school mathematics teacher Mr. O., a friend of Mr. M.'s, whose daughter was in "my" homeroom. Too many years must've passed because Mr. O., when saying hello and inquiring how I was doing, somewhat obviously avoided ever addressing me by my first name—which he had clearly forgotten.

*March 18*

Third block finds me funny; the students are loose, maybe too much so. But first block AMC, so early in the morning, is a more quiet and classically "dead" class. Teaching it is sometimes like pulling teeth. One of my students in AMC, B., challenged me today. As a senior, he openly wondered (with Mr. M. safely out of the room, presumably having the first of his four lunch breaks) why he should pay attention to or do anything that I tell him at all, given that the class isn't required for graduation. I countered with a lecture on personal responsibility, my first such non-mathematical deviation from a lesson. And, after grumbling a little, he got to work. "Now you've developed a relationship with students that will make them take what you say seriously," Prof. L. later told me. I'm not so sure; these types of personal responsibility lectures seem to have a short half-life.

*Reflections on Teaching: March 20*

In *Teaching Mathematics for the 21st Century*, four different "learning theories" are presented: behaviorism, social cognitive, information processing, and constructivism. Such theories play fast and loose with reality, deconstructing students and teachers as if they were pieces on a chess board only capable of sets of predetermined, predefined moves and countermoves; even the best of these theories still resort, or at least sound like they do, to such tactics.

Take a look at this sentence, under the heading "Information Processing Theory": "The memory components are: (1) the sensory register, (2) working, or short-term, memory, and (3) long-term memory" (p. 49). Can the lines really be drawn between memory components one, two and three? Or, rather, is memory more along the lines of a spectrum? Although splitting up memory into three parts may indeed be a convenient shorthand for the innards and underpinnings of the brain, the explanation and analysis presented—in this text and others—is not cogent, not convincing, and an affront to students' individuality.

Most important and more to the point, though, conceptualizing memory in this narrow, one-dimensional way constricts your options as a teacher. Following the strictures of information processing theory, for instance, seems misguided and myopic; today, theory "x" is the paradigm, tomorrow, theory "y" is the standard. It is here, at the cutting-edge of pedagogic methodologies, that I do perceive some of those elusive "pendulum shifts" so decried by this text—the pendulum is the paradigm, continually influenced and determined in a kind of dialectical dance between what is perceived to be happening in the classroom and the theories designed to counteract perceived negatives and encourage ever-changing positives.

The perception that roots these theories are frequently vague and ill defined, and the prescriptions for classrooms of efficacy that are supposed to be symptomatic of these theories are also foggy. Consider: "The constructivist approach to teaching requires establishing a community of mathematics learners" (p. 51). After reading this, on the margin next to the sentence, I scribbled a large question mark—this single character of punctuation best expressed my incredulity. A "community of learners" is required? What does that really mean? How can it possibly help me—other than in the most ancillary, auxiliary way—structure my classroom? These theories do not in any significant way assist me in realizing a coherent cosmology of educational practice. Of course, my criticism only extends to personal use; I cannot be certain that these structures have been totally useless to all teachers, and, furthermore, I believe that numbers of education professionals find the theories beneficial in some sense.

*Reflections on Teaching: March 21*

Student learning can be split into two categories: intrinsic and extrinsic.

It is most certainly true that the ideal is intrinsic learning. Intrinsic learning comes from within; extrinsic learning comes from without. *Teaching Mathematics for the 21st Century*, though, treats extrinsic learning as a malevolent force—which seems a bit myopic. Sometimes rewards are required; not everyone is going to love mathematics or any other subject (or anything, for that matter).

"Students are more likely to be intrinsically motivated if they believe they can successfully achieve the assigned task" (p. 60). How shall we get them from non-belief to belief?

Many years ago when I "learned" how to add and multiply negative numbers—and I put the word learned in scare quotes on purpose—I had to accept everything at face value. In other words, my teacher told me that two negatives added together equaled a negative—and I was expected to know that idea come assessment time. He said that two negatives multiplied together made a positive—and that, also, was to be memorized for the test.

Learning negative numbers by memorizing was unfortunate. Come to think of it, I learned much of math that way—by memorization. Treat everything as sacrosanct; ignore rhyme or reason or patterns* and just memorize. What a terrible way to have been exposed to the rudiments of math! Or was it?

Although I had little self-discovery in my math classes, I was exposed to a lot of mile-wide, inch-deep instruction—and memorization did have its benefits for the environment I was stuck in.

Would I have done as well in my secondary-school math classes if I learned with IMP instead of with traditional methods?† Would a

---

* *Teaching Mathematics for the 21st Century* points out that Keith Devlin, a prodigious mathematics author, constructs his math texts on one key notion: that math is all about *patterns*. One of his books has that statement embedded in the title (*Mathematics: The Science of Patterns*); another has it figuring in prominently (*The Language of Mathematics: Making the Invisible Visible*). IMP's first unit is entitled "Patterns." I must consider: were patterns stressed in my high school class? Or was that concept always floating around, without any teacher explicitly pushing it? If memory serves, the concept was never really conceptualized by my instructors—rather unsurprising, since I was exposed to such a "traditional" pedagogy of mathematics presentation.

† However, IMP does not seem to place any more than a modicum of emphasis on the historical roots of mathematics. Math history has much to offer, I believe. Is mathematics discovered (like Columbus discovered the Americas) or invented (like Thomas Edison invented the incandescent light bulb)? The answer is not clear, but a little study—maybe unbeknownst to the student that he or she is even studying it!—could allow a pupil to form an opinion on this still unresolved issue. (In *Teaching Mathematics for the 21st Century*, it is thus bluntly stated: "Mathematics is invented, not discovered…" [p. 177]. To repeat, judging from other mathematical literature I've encountered—such as the text *Journey Through Genius* by William Dunham—the invented-discovered debate is far from settled.)

Should there be any canonical works in high school math? Think of English, for instance: some of the works of Shakespeare are part of the "standard" curriculum, as are Poe's and Dickens' and Dante's. In math, though, rarely are formulas, proofs, or concepts attributed to authors (with one notable exception, the Pythagorean Theorem, which is, somewhat incorrectly, attributed to Pythagoras—an example among many of Stigler's law of eponymy: "No scientific discovery is named after its original discoverer," of which Stigler's law

person like me have excelled commensurately? If, let's suppose, I end up with an "A" average in a traditional class one year, and a "C" average in an IMP classroom the next, am I an exceptional or merely a competent mathematics student? Considering these issues

---

itself is an ironic example). Also, there does not seem to be a body of Great Works required for high school students to study (a Great Work, in my conception, might be an *Elements* or a *Principia Mathematica* or even a *How to Solve It*; surely there are many other such books in a prospective canon). There seems simply to be mathematical concepts that must be touched on in a generic way, such as factoring, proving geometric notions, or graphing equations.

Although I don't think that students should be made to slog through the anachronisms of language and notation present in those older Great Works, perhaps they should be exposed to their contents in a systematic manner. Maybe seeing the derivations and interconnections of the mathematics, as those great scholars from years past realized them, would make math less of a static enterprise.

Let me relay a personal anecdote. It was not until I arrived at college that I knew that math was still being discovered/invented in contemporary times. I don't even recall considering that; I just assumed, I suppose, that all math was just *there*, present in textbooks of more difficulty than I had learned from. But math isn't all just there, and maybe—just maybe—students pondering that idea, of math as a dynamic entity, should be tertiary to *all* lessons.

And, as an extension of that, perhaps more discoverers (or, alternatively, inventors) of math should be credited as new mathematics is learned in the classroom. Science classes frequently reference scientists responsible for discoveries; as mentioned earlier, English, in many ways, structures curricula around the authors of great texts; and history nearly always mentions the actors and effectors of movements and trends. Although I cringe to think of a curriculum of math structured entirely around the "authors" of mathematics since nearly all mathematicians, to use Newton's phase, stood on the shoulders of giants, a little sprinkling now and then of the historical roots of concepts wouldn't hurt, and would better place the subject in the context of history (for instance, imagine a team-taught math-and-history course detailing the Renaissance's impact on the world and the mathematics that helped to pull Western civilization out of the Dark Ages).

Exposing students to some of the history of mathematics has other benefits as well. Many pupils, not really having a perspective on the subject, simply assume that math "is what it is and always has been that way"—that people have always known about parallel lines, how to add two numbers, how to count. It could be of at least some interest for them to hear that, for instance, as recently as one thousand years ago, Arabic numerals were not in use in Europe.

is disconcerting, in a way, since much of my self-concept was the result of traditional classroom feedback!

*March 22*

Another formal observation by Prof. L. Each time she swings by, I get terribly nervous that I'm being watched—despite the fact that I'm being watched by dozens of students (along with Mr. M.) each day. Here's what she said: "Very good use of PowerPoint along with whiteboard demonstrations employing color to note different concepts. Nice touch with the history of the concept being introduced. But are all students *equally* on target? Any need for differentiation?"

*March 28*

Mr. M. handed over his second block precalculus class to me today—but not before telling the students, "You'll like him—he's much nicer than me." Ugh—the kiss of death! I don't want to be known as "nice," I want to be respected. (Wait a minute—are they mutually exclusive?)

The second block lesson today consisted of review, as did the third; but first block, again, is deficient in terms of energy. They are incredibly unmotivated. Sometimes I still miss the solace of my cubicle.

*March 29*

For the final time, Prof. L. stopped by to observe. Although her write-up was generally very encouraging, she offered me a couple pieces of advice. "[You have] exemplary professional attitude and behaviors. The only suggestion is to be more positive and confident in self-evaluation. Negative feelings about self can become all-consuming. Successful job placement will hopefully begin a positive attitude toward self…."

*Reflections on Teaching: March 29*

Is the mathematics classroom an appropriate place for writing? Thinking back to my own not-so-reformed classrooms of math, nothing so bold was ever required of me (perhaps because it would involve a lot more work on the teachers' part, as I've found during student teaching after giving my own student-journal assignments). It's probably important to begin the journal on the first day to establish expectations; and, since the journal will be a big commitment from all of the students, the sooner the better to establish *that* expectation, lest pupils not take it as seriously.

When I was in high school, the subjects were clearly demarcated. In other words, the walls separating different disciplines—like math and English, for instance—were tall and impenetrable. I remember rejoicing on one exceptional day in twelfth grade, when there was a—gasp!—similar discussion in my physics and math classes on graphs of distance against time. The likelihood of such overlaps occurring was so small (even in science and math class) it was as if there was some sort of coordination between departments to ensure it never happened. The *sine qua non* of my high school classes, it seemed, was total independence from all others.

Another especially powerful writing-in-math-class suggestion: give students the opportunity to write their own word problems. Word problems' structure is brought into relief to students by creating the problems themselves. The importance of writing in the math classroom hasn't long been underestimated. Rather, the importance of writing in secondary math has been mostly ignored, to the detriment of our pupils.

*March 30*

C., one of the best students in my third block, told Mr. M. and several other teachers sitting around him that I was "her favorite teacher, ever." I'm flattered—I must be doing something right, though I've discovered it's much easier to figure out why something's not working in the classroom than why something is working.

*Reflections on Teaching: March 30*

The seventh chapter, called "Promoting Communication in the Classroom," from *Teaching Mathematics for the 21st Century*, contains key quotes and theories from two preeminent mathematicians (actually, to be more precise, one was a physicist, but no matter; physics and math are closely related).

"Richard Feynman, a Nobel prize winner and an excellent teacher, said the best teachers are those who can remember what it was like when they did not know the concepts" (p. 261). What an excellent idea! Considering it came from a man who indeed knew most everything in his field—I've heard him called, in more than one place, the second most successful physicist of last century (second to the incomparable Albert Einstein)—it is all the more amazing. Modesty Feynman had in droves; for him to revel in teaching to "the masses" is inspirational, I suppose. I have listened to parts of the audio-only *Feynman Lectures* in physics, and I wish I could have seen him in the flesh. Even listening to the Nobel Laureate was transcendent, his finely-tuned pedagogic practice shining through.

George Polya is the other great mathematician quoted. Segments of his book for the layperson, *How to Solve It*, are sprinkled throughout the chapter. His approach to instructing math classes, at least in the little that I've read of his work, is very Vygotskian. Consider the following: "If the teacher helps too much, nothing is left to the student. The teacher should help, but not too much and not too little, so that the student shall have a *reasonable share of the work*" (p. 269, original italics present). His approach sounds dialectical, and also like the zone of proximal development à la Vygotsky. It certainly doesn't resemble Piaget's stage-driven theories.

Polya also subscribes, somewhat, to what Feynman said. "The teacher should put himself in the student's place, he should see the student's case, he should try to understand what is going on in the student's mind and ask a question or indicate a step that *could have occurred to the student himself*" (p. 269, original italics). I'm not one to disagree with an undisputed master of pedagogy (or, for that matter, mathematics; Polya's extraordinary contributions to mathematics never ceased or slowed throughout his unusually long life).

I do take issue, however, with the assumptions a teacher must amass to "indicate a step that could have occurred to the student himself." Our expectations and perhaps stereotypes, as teachers, will drive this sort of practice; it could lead to pupils detecting negative opinions of their abilities from the instructor, and hence permit self-fulfilling prophesies. I much prefer the catch-all, generalized dictum of Feynman (to repeat, Feynman said for teachers to simply remember what an ignorance of the concepts was like).

*March 31*

I had a game day: all day, math review exercises posing as games. And I'm tired—throughout the day, I didn't realize how much energy I was expending being the "host." I thought it would take *less* energy to do, since so much was prepared ahead of time, but it took so much more. Clearly, I have much to learn.

*Reflections on Teaching: April 2*

"Beginning teachers," *Teaching Mathematics for the 21st Century* explains, "seldom experience difficulties in their classroom due to their knowledge of subject matter; rather, frustrations are most likely to arise from the demands of maintaining a learning environment relatively free from student disruptions" (p. 293). How can I, an inexperienced new teacher, possibly maintain a modicum of control and respect for others in my classroom?

"Maintaining an environment that is advantageous to a community of mathematics learners is your responsibility as a teacher. Thus, encourage students to control their own behavior," according to the text (p. 293). But how? Experienced teachers perhaps have an inner, almost sixth sense of being able to dynamically keep a balance in the classroom between total control and total chaos. It is frustrating that there are no sure-fire methods—no set prescriptions when trouble strikes—in any book. But, as the text concedes, the secondary-school teacher cannot *make* his or her students do anything per se; instead, the instructor can merely motivate and encourage behaviors, reactions, and responses from pupils.

Also, the teacher, eventually, must intervene in some way to address or improve a disadvantaged student's situation—at least within the bounds of the student's classroom stay—lest the environment becomes unbearable. As an instructor, I am not a charity worker, nor am I a counselor. However, I will be confronted with issues requiring attention eventually. Ignoring those problems poses a risk to someone—whether it is to me, to the students in my classroom, or simply to the affected students. The longer problems linger and fester, the more difficult and harder they become to solve.

*April 6*

It's getting tougher for me to get motivated to teach. Yesterday, the district math coordinator dropped by to observe a lesson—but she dropped by first block, and the students were very restless. I think I bombed. Plus, I feel more and more like a lame duck (or perhaps just lame) in the classes; after all, Mr. M. will "assume the office" again very soon when I hand the reins back to the actual, certified teacher in the room. (The stress of not having secured a job, despite putting feelers out, is nagging at me and weighing me down.)

Mr. M. perhaps appreciated me more so than usual today though. He was sick, repeatedly going to the bathroom—but, of course, I was teaching all of his classes, so he had no need to worry. "But John," I asked him, "what if I wasn't here and it was *just* you teaching again? What would you have done today?" Mr. M. paused for a second, and then answered. "Mr. Lorenzo, you've gotta do what you've gotta do." And he left it at that.*

*Reflections on Teaching: April 10*

Is there equity in schools? Can a student get "stuck" in the "low track"? It's an amazing notion: the idea of self-perpetrating loop that students can't escape from easily. From what I know from IMP, this problem is somewhat avoided by a de-emphasis on tracking by ability, with a kind of egalitarian presentation of materials. Then again, I could be mistaken. Is IMP only for the gifted? I'm almost sure this isn't the case, but I do suspect that any IMP materials that teachers cull for their traditional classrooms are almost certainly directed toward higher-ability pupils. Yet it is the lower-level math classrooms that most need exceptional lessons and yet are least likely to receive them.

The unresolved question is of the validity of tracking itself: Should tracking be done at all? Is it really an all-or-nothing proposition? It seems, at least from my still-limited perspective, that it is a bit preposterous to shove all kids of all stripes into a calculus-

* One of his many aphorisms that cut to the heart of the matter. Here's another: "Teaching is more akin to a blue collar job than a white collar job: there's a bell for lunch (there's a bell for everything), no flex time, there are fights to break up, and..." And another: "All of teaching is decisions, all day long."

preparation track in high school. Not because all students wouldn't be able to (eventually) do it, but more so because students develop, mentally, at different rates. Both Piaget and Vygotsky, pedagogy's two big paradigm generators, probably wouldn't have approved of a single classroom for all students, either. A catchall classroom, almost counter-intuitively, is undemocratic.

*April 12*

Running out the clock—that's the operative slogan around here (well, at least in my head). I feel the need to give these last couple of weeks a little extra. But I still have no light at the end of the tunnel—and it is one very long tunnel.

Although the district math coordinator did speak to me during my free fourth block and she praised much of what I did, but not all. An example she wrote to me: "Give specific directions, a specific time limit. It doesn't do any good to talk while they are working. They're not listening—let's get back together so they stop their group work and have them turn around!"*

*Reflections on Teaching: April 14*

## IN DEFENSE OF GIVING TEACHERS ANSWERS TO TEXTBOOK PROBLEMS

Teachers are overworked. Teachers have uncountable responsibilities. Teachers shoulder the burdens of hundreds of students per day. Teachers have to be endlessly creative in the assignments they make, the lessons they teach, the tests they give. Teachers are constantly pitching, trying to sell a product that none of their students wants to buy. In short, teaching is an incredibly difficult, demanding profession. It should not be incumbent upon teachers to also have to answer every one of the math problems they assign.

Although it does place a teacher in a student's position of imbalance—and the teacher, analogous to the perspective of the un-

---

* Although I went on two district interviews in the next two months, I unfortunately didn't make the final cut. Which brings up yet another of Mr. M's aphorisms: "Only those who know those get in"—i.e., it's all about nepotism. Sounds like the hiring process is an affront to, well, meritocracy.

learned pupil, recalls a lack-of-knowing—many rudimentary problems are much too mechanical and time-consuming for the teacher to have to do.

Indeed, there are some problems a teacher should complete on his own. When one does something, one learns it. And, when one learns it, one can teach it. Some non-standard and standard problems the instructor should indeed do; it'll help him think through processes and allow the students flexibility with potential solutions. To wit, many challenging and unconventional and non-routine math queries, despite possibly being time-consuming to solve, are worth the teacher haggling over, if only for his own professional development and mathematical experimentation.

But what of the endlessly mechanical problems—should teachers be forced to do every one of these? Even if they could make the time to solve them, shouldn't their time be spent more wisely—by playing with new and creative teaching methods or making math topics that are normally ancillary relevant to the classroom?

Look, I agree that if a teacher can't do the problems, he should not be teaching. But, although I know of no statistics to irrefutably back this up, there are most certainly teachers in America's classrooms who are not capable of solving some of the problems that they assign their students—and yet they are not resigning their posts en masse. Of course they shouldn't be teaching: it's a tragedy in the making, and our students are unwittingly and unwillingly suffering. Barring a removal of all such teachers, only one option remains: allow them to have the answers to the problems. True, it's like putting a Band-Aid on a bullet wound. Nevertheless, makeshift solutions are sometimes the only solutions.

I'm not demanding that in addition to receiving answers to all mechanical problems teachers be given step-by-step derivations of the answers, but teachers need to have an endpoint, a signpost, so they have a clear idea of the intermediate processes needed to complete solutions. A teacher claiming that he doesn't know the answer or didn't have enough time to complete the homework he assigned (considering how many responsibilities teachers have, this is not necessarily far-fetched)* will be ridiculed relentlessly by his

* Note to new teachers: don't ever complain to your students about how much time you've had to spend grading their papers—they will simply tell you to give them less work, and rightly so.

students, as if a "halo of ignorance" floats above his head—and perhaps he'll never fully gain the class's attention or respect again. And that's a shame, considering how difficult it already is to be a teacher.

*April 15*

A better day today. These days seem to come in cycles—good, bad, bad, good, bad, bad—that seems to be the pattern. I've almost completely forgotten what it was like to work in a cubicle. Is this, the classroom, my destiny? I wouldn't mind.

I also wish I could continue to teach third block—and only third, although second is pretty good too—after my student teaching end date this month. I think I'd do it for free.

*Reflections on Teaching: April 20*

The noted Brazilian educational theorist Paulo Freire, throughout his long life, spoke frequently about the courage and dignity needed to head a classroom: the courage to be who you are, and the dignity that you must show toward others.

Why do I mention this? Because only now, after months of student teaching, do I begin to understand what he was talking about in his countless texts. Freire was a proponent of the individual—and strongly advocated democratic solutions to problems, both from within and without the classroom. The tumultuous milieu he resided for much of his life—a Brazil ravaged by dictators, coups, and human rights abuses—made democracy primacy in his cosmology.

Hegel synthesized the notion of the dialectic; Freire applied it to the classroom. The interplay between theory and practice—between having democracy rule the room and yet still retaining some of that (yes) *autocratic* sensibility needed for teaching—is largely Freire's contribution, though it now seems like common sense or conventional wisdom.

Being up in front of students hanging on my every syllable (okay, that's a terrible exaggeration) forces me to be more conscious of my actions and behaviors than usual. How should I retain democracy while at the same time wielding authority? How shall I have the courage to respect the dignity of the individuals I am teaching?

Where is the line drawn between restraining myself to impose and actually imposing? How much freedom should my students be given?

Freire recognized how difficult pedagogic self-judgment is, and suggested, as many have, teacher observations: let others give you feedback on your practice, even though your practice might be altered by the presence of the watchers (that's a loose analogy to the Heisenberg uncertainty principle,* I suppose, or perhaps to the Hawthorne effect).

*April 29*

My last day. Early in the morning, I ran into L.'s father (L. is, or was, in my third block), who relayed to me that his daughter said I'm a "natural teacher," and that he would send off an e-mail to the principal saying as much.

Walking into first block, I helped J. with a difficult math problem, and then handed out a quiz to my students. At the end of the block, J. handed me a sealed black envelope, which I didn't open till the end of the day.

Second block was uneventful—they had a quiz as well.

But, prior to third block, most of the class came in early to have lunch in the classroom with me. G. ordered pizza for the class. We had a quick review session for their upcoming quiz. C. handed me a set of balloons, one of which read "We'll Miss You!"

In fourth block, I graded the many quizzes. The scores were relatively good—but I was in a generous mood, with partial credit coming in spades.

After filing all the graded quizzes away so Mr. M., who had left school by that point, could find them, I opened J.'s envelope. A red, brown, and white card with her name embossed in cursive lettering on the front opened up to reveal the following:

> *Teaching is like gambling. You're not going to win every time. You won't always reach every student, and sometimes it might seem like all of your efforts aren't enough. But remember the people like me—who care. They care why they are here and they are diligent in what*

* After the 1996 Sokal hoax, it seems suspect to turn physics principles into blanket metaphor.

> *they do. Never turn away someone that needs help, or really wants to learn, find new ways of teaching one idea, no matter how simple it may be, and you will be successful. You will be a teacher, a mentor in which students will say, "I wish I had more teachers like him." Good luck, but I don't think you'll need it.*

I don't know what comes next, but I do know now, without a doubt, that I'm a teacher.

Several months later, after a number of interviews,* I finally landed a job at a nearby public high school—let's call it Madison High. When I was hired there in July of 2005, one of the reasons, as explicitly stated by my new department chair on the good-news phone call, was so that I "could teach probability and statistics to kids."†

After induction late that summer, I went to the high school to pick up my first set of textbooks—but there was no probability book to be found. Instead, I received a package with two instructor's manuals: Precalculus and Algebra 2. Thoughts frantically raced through my mind: Will I have to create the probability course from scratch? Does he (my department head) want me to simply use the probability and statistics chapters from either of these two instructor's manuals? Did they simply forget to give me the book? I went

---

* Teaching interviews are especially difficult for new teachers because an espoused "theory of practice" or "philosophy of teaching" has to match up with answers to situational questions presented on the fly. Going into these interviews, I held fast to five rules: that I must have a willingness to change premade lesson plans, as educational theorist Paulo Freire instructed readers in his *Teachers as Cultural Workers* (1998); allow and encourage so-called grappling, a notion that the authors Sizer and Sizer suggested in *The Students are Watching* (1999); project humility to my students (that's Freire again); always be at my best; and use humor appropriately in the classroom.

† My department chair Mr. B. and I had a number of engaging "theory of practice" conversations that helped to guide my thinking about education, especially in my first two teaching years. Here's something he said to me very early on: "I know you said, although not verbatim, that you left the actuarial field to do something more meaningful. What could be more meaningful than helping young people? What could be more meaningful than empowering people? In my opinion, life doesn't get more meaningful than that."

upstairs to his office and inquired—and his answer caused me great concern.

"Well," he said matter-of-factly, "we haven't received the books from the publisher yet." Oh boy—just what I needed to hear days before my first for-real teaching assignment. To add to my stress, Madison was going through contract negations at the time, and they weren't going well; during induction, no teacher's union faculty showed up to acclimate the incoming freshman class of teachers to the district.

After a bizarre demonstration during the first day of inservice, in which we all lined up next to a flagpole in front of the high school and entered the building single-file, contract negotiations were wrapped up and a strike was averted. But I still didn't get a look at the textbook; it wasn't until the next day, literally hours before I would meet my kids, that I received a copy of *Workshop Statistics: Discovery with Data and the Graphing Calculator, 2nd Edition* (2002), by Allan J. Rossman, Beth L. Chance* and J. Barr von Oehsen. I distinctly remember paging through it for the first time, wondering what in the world the authors were trying to do, wondering what they were trying to get across to students.†

---

* An especially appropriate surname for an author of a book on probability and statistics.

† How come mathematics textbooks, by and large, are so eminently unreadable? How come they're not particularly interesting or engaging, like a good fiction read, for instance? They have lots of symbolic drivel that's not very user friendly.

Consider a novel called *The Gold Bug Variations* (1991), by Richard Powers, a prodigious talent (and a polymath who has publicly decried intellectual specialization). Although fiction, the novel has tons of descriptions of the workings of genetics, since the main characters find themselves so heavily involved in researching and working within the field. The descriptions of the science are unlike anything I have heard and yet they manage to teach. Look at this from the book, nearly culled at random: "Genetic mechanism contains nothing transcendental. Cell growth, organism development conform to the principles of undergrad chemistry. The grammar does not change from generation to generation—only individual sentences do. A simple lookup table, one or more triplets of nucleotides to each amino acid, is universal for all life." Imagine if a math text were written with such fluidity of prose. Pupils would wonder if they weren't in fact in an English class. (The closest Powers ever got to writing something mathematical is his computer science-themed pseudo-autobiography *Galatea 2.2.*)

I was especially puzzled by the "Preliminaries" sections that began each chapter. The questions seemed, to put it mildly, juvenile and silly, hardly befitting what's purported to be—in the introductory pages of the text, at least—a college-level resource for statistics.

And another issue, within minutes of examining *Workshop*, immediately became apparent: where's the probability? With the exception of a small chapter midway through, there just isn't any. That lack surprised me—the course I was teaching was called *Probability* and Statistics, after all. The book just didn't seem like a good fit.*

So, without any real preparation or comfort with the book, and little real teaching experience, I began teaching a brand new Probability and Statistics course at Madison High School. And, putting aside that I am perhaps a bit too hard on myself, I can say without reservation that, at least in the first quarter, it was an unmitigated disaster. By the time I figured out more or less how to teach the course, it was too late: the "honeymoon phase" teachers usually get with their classes was over and I was left to pick up the pieces for the remainder of the year, diminishing returns and all, hoping I could get off to a much better start next school year.

When my department head casually informed me, at the end of my first year, that I was scheduled for an *additional* section of Prob/Stats—increasing the number of sections I teach to three—I felt a sense of panic. I had to rethink and revise the course. I had to be ready.

The following journal entries detail my successes—and my failures—at introducing statistics content to students as a second-year teacher in the fall of 2006. I hope that my teaching practice withstands the tests of both scrutiny and time.

*The Die is Cast*
*Week 1: September 6 to September 8*

It's throwing out as many little details as possible to the kids during this first week that was most important. One of the major prob-

---

* There is only a single chapter of probability in the *Workshop Statistics* textbook—and there's none of the "traditional" probabilistic concepts presented, such as combinatorics.

lems I had last year, my first year, was a lack of focus and a limited understanding of the methodology and approach of the textbook. But now I come into this year's three sections of Probability and Statistics at Madison—the enrollment ballooned—in a much better frame of mind, having a better idea of the structure that the class needs to take almost immediately.

But before describing the implementation of the first week of class, let me note that I spent a lot of time during the summer redesigning the course. Most significantly, I formulated a plan for homework. Of all the problems with my implementation of *Workshop* last year, the biggest problem was far and away the lack of homework—it seems students simply can't take a class seriously if when the class is out of sight it is also out of mind. Although it seems to be patently unfair to grade homework completely for correctness, I believe that I reached a compromise with my "homework formula," which I will quote directly from my Course Expectations sheet:

> Homework will be assigned frequently and will be collected; each individual homework problem, called an "Activity," is worth 5 points (each Activity usually has multiple parts). Therefore, the number of points a single homework assignment is worth can vary from assignment to assignment. Some Activities in a homework assignment will be graded for completion, others for correctness (you will not know which until the graded assignment is handed back to you). You can be sure, however, that if only one Activity is assigned for homework, it will be graded for correctness, but if more than one Activity is assigned, at least one Activity will be graded for completion. Because you are turning in homework to me on a daily basis, I suggest you get a three-ring-spiral binder and stock it with lots of loose-leaf sheets—that way you can easily file graded homework to study. Your homework will constitute 20% of your marking period grade.

With that formulation set, I also had to prepare a better pretextbook introduction to the course. Last school year I fumbled badly on the first day for a variety of reasons, chief among them that instead of devising relevant examples of types of problems and content to be discussed through the rest of the year, I launched into a monologue about casinos, probability, and expected value, something that the book doesn't really spend time on, at least not till much later. Those introductory comments, in addition to being off-topic, were defensive in nature for two reasons: it was my first day of teaching in a new, unfamiliar school of complete strangers, and (unbeknownst to me) I was replacing a hyper-popular teacher who had been removed at the last minute; most of the students in my Probability and Statistics classes had signed up for the class expecting to have him, not me—and their first-day schedules didn't even reflect the teacher change. It was an environment bordering on the hostile toward me.

Not so this year. Although I was still a bit defensive on the first day this year—I'm still not really used to doing this job—things went smoothly and there was a confidence in my tone that comes from knowing the layout of the land, the design of the course.

And yet that was not enough. After a dialogue—well, more of a monologue—about how statistics isn't number crunching, how statistics involves the analysis of genuine data, and how we'll be collecting data from each student, I wanted to *show them*, rather than just keeping telling them, that there are major differences between the math problems of statistics and the math problems of an Algebra 2 or a geometry course. I wrote on the blackboard the equation $x^2 + 5x + 6 = 0$ and informed my students that this is exactly the kind of problem they won't be seeing in this class. Then I handed out a worksheet on statistical thinking, a mélange of simple statistics questions that I instructed them to try and puzzle through as best they could. The worksheet was written in a way similar to the Preliminaries questions that begin each *Workshop Statistics* chapter: they attempt to get the reader thinking about basic notions of statistical theory while also introducing the applications that will be tied to the theory. So my worksheet functioned, I hope, as a sort of "Preliminaries" for the entire course.

Before going over any of the questions on the worksheet, I asked students to give their immediate reactions to the differences between these types of questions and questions that they're used to seeing in a math class. To my amazement, in all three of my sections, students answered in more or less the following way: "There's no math to do." Exactly! On day one, I managed to do exactly what I could only dream about on my first day last year: properly introduce the course.

I thought it especially important, in the next couple of days, to introduce some statistics vocabulary before beginning the first chapter, even though I knew the recitation of vocabulary definitions might induce a sense of fatigue and boredom. And it did, to some degree. But a student named H. commented on how well organized my presentation was, so perhaps things went off better than I give myself credit for.

Not all of my pre-chapter 1 definitions coincided with chapter 1, but most of them did. I thought it important to distinguish between descriptive and inferential statistics, for instance.*

---

* The notion of descriptive statistics, as opposed to inferential statistics, isn't necessarily a theme emphasized by the textbook, but it seems to root each and every chapter: learn how to use tools to display or organize data, then determine what can be gleaned from the data upon inspecting it in this new descriptive context. (Two examples of the contrast, not in the textbook: John Snow's epidemiological dotmap of the 1854 cholera outbreak in London, ultimately pinpointing the Broad Street pump as the source [see Steven Johnson's *The Ghost Map* for the best book-length treatment on the subject]; and Florence Nightingale's creation of the pie graph in order to display Crimean War mortality statistics to Queen Elizabeth, which led to better conditions for soldiers.) This interweaving of descriptive and inferential statistics in the textbook does cause some problems, however. With the textbook's de-emphasis on compartmentalization, it's frequently difficult to differentiate which of the homework assignments is appropriate vis-à-vis the completed classwork Activities. The authors' implicit assumption seems to be that, within a single block of time, all classwork Activities in a chapter must be completed so that any homework Activities in the chapter can be assigned at the instructor's discretion. If only it were that simple: when the very nature of a 45-minute class forces a kind of compartmentalization—today, we'll look at marginal and conditional distributions and tomorrow we'll examine independence and Simpson's paradox—the chunking of material forces a back-and-forth between new skills introduced (the descriptive piece) and associated concepts explored (the inferential piece).

Speaking of Simpson's paradox, last school year I had students complete a Simpson's paradox problem for extra credit. Before assigning it, I had already manipulated the numbers to obtain valid two-way tables (also called contingency tables) using Microsoft Excel. Yet several students were able to do it too, and they did it with just paper, pencil, and calculator during a single class period! Needless to say, I was impressed. Simpson's paradox questions are similar to Sudoku puzzles, in a sense, since in order to create raw totals that conform to the paradox one must consider the consequences of placing certain

By the time Friday, September 8, rolled around, populations versus samples were discussed,* and I assigned each student a number for their Preliminaries' data—they have measured their signature and counted how many states they've visited (these are two of a number of questions the first Preliminaries asks of students).

My first Preliminaries data collection went smoothly—I used an overhead to collect data points, calling out students by number. They copied the class data set, and all three sections already seem to be going exponentially smoother than the smoothest class periods of last year.

*Ungrouping the Course*
*Week 2: September 11 to September 15*

With our Preliminaries data collected, we were ready to begin the first chapter. In addition to all of the work I did on the course during the summer months, I also encountered one of my most (behaviorally) challenging students from last year's Probability and Sta-

---

numbers into the cells of a table. Come to think of it, creating two-way tables that have the property of independence—making sure that the conditional distributions of all of the variables are equal—is also analogous to solving Sudoku.

I'm curious to know if a political candidate could win all of the precincts or districts in the areas he or she was competing and yet, in the aggregate, still have lost the election. The chances, of course, wouldn't be particularly high of such an occurrence, but, at least intuitively, it seems statistically possible. The newspapers and other media outlets, who struggled mightily to explain the nuances of the Electoral College after Al Gore handily beat George W. Bush in the 2000 popular vote, would certainly throw in the towel if forced to clarify a Simpson's paradox defeat of such an unlucky candidate.

Speaking of newspapers, popular author John Allen Paulos, for his part, writes about Simpson's paradox in *A Mathematician Reads the Newspaper* (1995). Unfortunately, his example is rather abstract; he relays a study about two non-existent ethnic groups and the dangers of drawing conclusions about the efficacy of their treatments. But paging through Paulos's book I am reminded of the importance of critical thinking skills when dealing with numbers and analyses based on data. (After all, his most famous text *Innumeracy* is mostly about conveying a sense of number to readers.)

* Though statistician John Tukey advised teachers not to introduce to students the distinction between samples and populations until it was completely necessary, I felt that being able to identify samples and populations in context from the beginning of the course might be helpful.

tistics class at a local mall. After inquiring about his college plans (he graduated in June), I asked him pointedly what went wrong with my implementation of the course last year, and what I could do to improve. He said only two words: "No groups." I can't tell you how much those two words have haunted me as this school year commenced. When I really consider why things went awry last year, why by any measure my instruction last year in Probability and Statistics can be considered nothing short of a failure, the placing of students into groups factors as the cause of the majority of my strife.

What if the in-class *Workshop* Activities (i.e., problem sets in the text) were done a couple of letters at a time,* with everyone working essentially individually, perhaps discussing something with their neighbors here and there? What if there was no formalized group work—and, instead, everyone just loosely worked problems on his or her own? Would that work? So far it has—for the first chapter. All of the in-class Activities were completed by students without the crutch (?) of group work. Last year, I collected group work from in-class and homework Activities that were almost exclusively the province of classwork, but, so far this year, I have collected no in-class Activities—we've just gone over answers to in-class Activities in chunks.

That essentially describes the dynamics of the course so far: a back and forth between students doing work—mostly quietly, mostly by themselves—and a discussion of the answers or ideas that need to be emphasized.

And there have, of course, been supplementary worksheets I've distributed, like **Types of Variables**,† which resembles some of the homework Activities but which I felt was necessary for additional review, and **Counts, Proportions, Percents, and Bar Graphs**, which not only stressed the key notion of the difference between a proportion and a percent but also attempted to function like the chapter in *How to Lie with Statistics* (1954) called "The Gee-Whiz

* By this I mean part (a), then part (b), then (c), and so forth.

† For the sake of clarity, bolded text will be used to denote titles of in-class worksheets or assessments.

Graph" does: demonstrate the deceptiveness of simple visual displays of data.*

On Friday, September 15, students sat for the **Quiz on Chapter 1** (a **Review for Quiz on Chapter 1** was given the previous day). The results were decidedly mixed but nonetheless showed that pupils had a decent grasp on the basic ideas of the course.

Last year I remember hitting a massive wall with instruction in the first and second in-class Activities of chapter 2. Students just weren't ready, plain and simple, for the graphing calculator manipulations called for in the problems, despite the informative screen shots in the textbook. So over the summer I wrote an **Introduction to the Graphing Calculator** packet which, I think, serves as a distilled but thorough tutorial for all of the functions that appear and reappear throughout the text, starting in chapter 2. When used in conjunction with in-class instruction via the calculator projected onto an overhead—and the students' calculators in hand, following along—I hope that chapter 2 will be a natural progression rather than a difficult leap. We'll see—by Friday afternoon, all I had gotten to was setting up the calculator stat editor to show a list. There's so much more to do.

---

* The classic book *How to Lie with Statistics* by Darrell Huff submerges the reader in what I think of as the "culture" of statistics. By culture I mean the vocabulary, critical thinking processes, and everyday real-life examples of statistics. Consider this representative passage from *How to Lie*: "Similarly, the next time you learn from your reading that the average American (you hear a good deal about him these days, most of it faintly improbable) brushes his teeth 1.02 times a day… ask yourself…. How can anyone have found out such a thing?" I'd like the next edition of *Workshop* to perhaps have more of that kind of frame of reference, more of an attempt to show that (if somewhat amorphous, in the way I've defined it) "culture" in action—beyond the true-to-life data sets that form the basis of *Workshop* problems—even if questions need to be explicitly stated and answered by authors Rossman and Chance themselves. This sense of the culture is what I most want my students to take with them years after they have finished my course, rather than correct procedures for entering lists into the calculator or properly calculating *z*-scores. The kind of critical thinking skills that are necessary for success in statistics are certainly, to some extent, required for an educated adult citizenry as well.

*Deliver Us from (Calculator) Evil*
*Week 3: September 18 to September 22*

After the first one and a half days of the week were spent, somewhat boringly, going through the basic statistical functions of the calculator, it was time to transfer the chapter 2 data files (created by the textbook's publisher) to students' graphing calculators. Now, after struggling to figure out how to download not individual lists but groups into my graphing calculator—a situation that was finally remedied by downloading the latest version of the TI-Connect software—a new struggle emerged: getting the data to everyone quickly and efficiently.

Here's what the *plan* was: I give each person in the first row in my classroom (there are desks situated in five equally-sized rows) the files, and they in turn transfer the data sets to the students behind them, and then those students give it to the students behind them, and so forth. But problems quickly emerged.

Why are Texas Instruments' calculators so inconsistent? There are (apparently) subtle differences between their calculators. I'm not speaking of the differences between, let's say, a TI-83 and a TI-84—I know there are differences between those machines. What I'm referring to is the inconsistencies between TI-83s and TI-83-plusses—I'm assuming there are differences in the operating systems. And even between TI-83-plusses and other TI-83-plusses, which cannot be explained away as easily. Sometimes, data groups didn't send, and I've had to send individual lists. Some students didn't even have an "ungroup" option,[*] despite the fact that the groups transferred to their calculators. It seems like data transfers properly only half the time.[†] And all these issues were being thrown at me simultaneously.

---

[*] Since students have an inimitable ability to ruin lists (by forgetting to include a list in a SortA command, for instance), having groups at the ready is a quick and effective fix; in addition, time is saved when transferring lists: why send each item individually when they can all be sent together via a snug data package?

[†] When we assign two events equal probabilities of occurring despite not having supporting evidence, John Maynard Keynes called this the "principle of indifference": "if there is no known reason for predicating of our subject one rather than another of several alternatives, then relatively to such knowledge

Furthermore, this is a high school class, and the level of seriousness about the tasks at hand isn't by default high. So, for instance, person X forgot his calculator, person Y didn't even bother to buy one yet, and person Z has her calculator but the batteries are dead.

Although there is no question that things are proceeding more smoothly and I have a better handle on what needs to be done and the timeline in which to do it than I did last year, my enthusiasm about the appropriateness of the course for high school students at all waned to a distaste for certain aspects of the approach. There's just too much going on at once, trying to get everyone technologically squared away before the lesson or the Activity can actually begin. But, by Wednesday, I did manage to have everyone complete the first calculator problem set, which is the most basic sort of introduction to using the calculator in a statistics situation. And homework due Wednesday allowed students to use the DOTPLOT program (which obviously automatically constructs dotplots on-screen) with a set of genuine classroom data (so the homework students turned in to me had a different answer key for each of my three classes).

On Thursday, I had my students work through as much of the second Activity, on gender splits in medical specialties, as they could. I recall that last year it was this Activity, more than any other one in the textbook, that gave everyone the most trouble. Perhaps it's because the leap that was required from the silliness of doing simple dotplots or bar graphs in chapter 1 to the sorting, viewing and explaining of genuine data in chapter 2 is a bit much. Things went smoother this year; there were fewer problems, probably because of the time I spent going over the basic statistical functions a couple of days before.

Last year, despite the struggles students had with that Activity, I simply pressed forward and assigned more in-class Activities to be turned in. But this year, after students spent Thursday crawling their way through most of it, I took Friday to go through the Activity on the overhead with the entire class, asking people to follow along with me and redo the work. My suspicion is that this reinforcement of the skills called for to complete the Activity will serve my students well as we press on in the textbook. We'll see if my

---

the assertions of each of these alternatives have an equal probability." Just because events subjectively *seem* to be equally likely doesn't mean they are.

suspicions are proved correct—they have a homework assignment to turn in on Monday, and it's a tough one.

*A Sudden Conversion*
*Week 4: September 25 to September 29*

On Wednesday, during a free period, I ran into the district head of math curricula at Madison (whose name escapes me) and Prof. W., who was visiting the high school as part of a Math-Science Partnership grant. After speaking briefly with Prof. W., I turned my attention to talking to the curriculum head; because he was just hired at the end of the previous academic year, he freely admitted to still not being completely familiar with the minutiae of the curricula.

I began talking to him about what I'm teaching, and the discussion (inevitably) turned to the course I'm most focused on this year, Probability and Statistics. I asked him if he had seen the *Workshop* book, and he told me he hadn't. Having a copy on hand, I more than showed him: I tried to convert him to the approach by flipping fervently through it, describing the best Activities, speaking of using genuine data in two ways—through real, published data sets and by obtaining information from students—and was relentless in persuading him of the approach's merits. My defense and—well—preaching of the *Workshop* methodology was reflexive, something I didn't plan in advance, but after it happened I realized that I am, finally, after more than a year, mostly on board with the approach.

My statistics classes this week were riddled with both successes and failures. Recall that I left off last week about half finished with the second chapter.

Last school year, the day before the quiz on the chapter, I distributed (and went over) a review for the quiz problem set that (I believe) gave pupils a fair representation of the content and types of questions present on the upcoming evaluation. This year is no different; after handing out the **Review for Quiz on Chapter 2** worksheet, which I structured similarly to a textbook Activity, it became apparent to me that there was a wider spread of calculator issues than I had suspected: some kids knew exactly what to do, but many others appeared as if they had never turned on a graphing calculator before. This after nearly three days of calculator instruction and a multitude of in-class and homework problems designed to counteract such an eventuality reminded me that there is often a disconnect between what a teacher believes he has taught and what a student has actually learned. This will be my ongoing cross to bear.

The frustration really came to a boil the next day, when the **Quiz on Chapter 2** was disseminated. I've never had to run back and forth as quickly to deal with simultaneous questions and issues in any class period. When five or six hands are up at once, and it seems like there's nothing that can be done to stem the tide, you begin to throw up your own hands and ask: Have I done enough to teach these students about the calculator? Did they really understand anything at all in terms of syntax, or were they just pretending at the time, nodding in waves just to keep the class moving?

But with a new chapter comes a blank slate, and chapter 3 is much less calculator intensive, although we began the next day's period completing the housekeeping issues that'll be done at the beginning of every chapter henceforth: gather Preliminaries data, clear out old lists and groups in the calculator, and transfer the new lists and groups.

After all this was completed, I had enough time only to go through one Activity, which creates a sort of formal checklist for students to analyze the shapes of distributions of data.

*The Daily Grind and Other "Random" Thoughts*
*Week 5: October 3 to October 6*

My three sections are beginning to develop personalities and different dynamics—and I am beginning to become an awfully different teacher in each of those sections, adapting to their struggles and their needs. It's tough to explain why or how this has happened, how I can cover the exact same material hours apart in completely different ways.

First period is relatively dead. For whatever reason, there isn't much interaction in the class. Although the obvious explanation would be that the students are practically still asleep that early in the morning (which happened in my student teaching first block class), this problem (or characteristic) seems to be more deeply rooted than the time of day. Perhaps I am teaching the class differently in first period—my first run-through of the material that day—than in other periods.

Fourth period Probability and Statistics, a class one period before everyone's lunch, is terribly hyperactive and sometimes very silly.* I sometimes feel like Will Ferrell's version of Alex Trebek on *SNL*'s *Celebrity Jeopardy!* It is also more physically demanding for me to get through the content that I found relatively easy to get through in the morning—yet, invariably, it takes less time this period, maybe because I am ever-cognizant of my kids' shorter attention spans so I rush things.

And seventh period is somewhere in between hyper and exhausted. It's usually easy to lecture in this period, yet I have one student in particular who has needs repeated disciplining, unfortunately.

There was so much to cover this week that dealing with these peculiar dynamics was especially challenging. First of all, with the exception of Thursday and Friday, homework was assigned each night. A lot of work for my students, true, but more work for me: I have to grade a portion of each person's homework. Let me detail, day by day, what was accomplished this week (there were only four school days because Madison High was closed on Monday for a holiday).

By the time the bell rings for the start of class, a list of items is displayed on the blackboard: what to do, what we will be doing, any upcoming quizzes or tests, or other special instructions. On Tuesday, this is what was on the board: "Turn in homework into bin; Activity 3-3: Complete/Discuss; Activity 3-18 (not in packet): Complete/Discuss, you'll need group TAM97; Quiz next Tuesday on chapter 3; Homework: Activities 3-9, 3-15." The "Turn homework into bin" refers to a collection bin I have in the front of the room, next to the windowsill. Students have been (dare I say) "trained" to place their homework in there at the beginning of the period.

Here's what was on the board on Wednesday: "Turn in homework into bin; get your homework from yesterday on table; Stemplots intro (worksheet); Activity 3-4; Homework: Activities 3-13, 3-14." The "table" at which students collect the previous day's homework is my desk—I place all graded homework in a pile in

---

* This particular class period would, later in the school year, degrade tremendously; refer to the chapter "Mediation and Conflict Resolution" presented earlier in the book.

alphabetical order by last name, and I write their homework grade on the *back* of the sheets.* Thus, when students go to retrieve their homework and shuffle through the pile, they don't see everyone else's grades. Also, the "Stemplots intro" refers to a worksheet called **Introduction to Stemplots**.

On Thursday, students were instructed to "Turn in your Homework into bin; get your Homework from yesterday on table; Complete Histograms intro." I chose not to use the textbook's introduction to histograms.

Friday was a key day: Against my better judgment, I buckled under self-inflicted pressure and put people into groups of mostly three using playing cards (each student randomly picked a card; all students with aces worked together, all with twos worked together, etc.). Each group submitted one packet of Activities. It was a surprisingly smooth day. I won't, however, be putting students into groups too often for fear that things will devolve like they did last year.

*It's Evaluation Day!*
*Week 6: October 9 to October 13*

This was a most unusual and painful week. Only on Friday did students begin new material; all other days were devoted to reviews and evaluations. The week's structure was an unintended consequence of two factors exclusive to my high school: (1) The slower speed that I'm going at, because of 45-minute class periods, forces me to give more assessments on less material than I otherwise would in a block-scheduled class,† and (2) To prevent students from having too many evaluations on the same day, a "testing schedule" must be adhered to which requires mathematics teachers to give quizzes and tests only on "even days"(essentially, every other day).

So Monday and Wednesday were devoted to review. On Monday, students completed the **Review for Quiz on Chapter 3** worksheet. On Wednesday, pupils worked through the **Review for Test**

---

* A trick I learned years before from Dr. R., a biology professor of mine in college.

† Recall my student teaching assignment at the New School used block scheduling.

**on Unit 1** packet. Giving students the **Quiz on Chapter 3** and the **Statistics Test on Unit 1**[*] were notable for a couple of reasons.

First of all, the quiz took significantly longer for students to complete than the test did—not so much because it was more difficult but because it was certainly a more tedious exercise, involving more descriptive than inferential statistics. For instance, the quiz asked students to construct both histograms and stemplots involving more than twenty numbers each, whereas the test only had a small stemplot. I wrote the test deliberately to focus more on generalities and inference, requiring students to put together some basic statistical concepts.

Second, the test had multiple choice questions that, although relatively simple, allowed students to get a slight taste of the AP exam.[†] Although it's possible (of course) to successfully guess on multiple choice questions, multiple choice requires a different kind of critical thinking—and there's no partial credit.[‡] Plus, since the midterm and final exams in this course are heavily weighted toward multiple choice (for reasons of practicality), it's a good exercise.

Last year my chapter 3 quiz was, to be blunt, a joke. There were five questions, all of which simply asked students to construct possible dotplots given a variety of data collection contexts. By that time last year I still hadn't figured out how to assess students properly—last year's quiz was definitely not valid. (By the time chapter 7 came around in November of last year, however, I had: looking at that quiz now, it seems close to satisfactory.)

By Friday, we were finally ready to begin new material. I had already transferred the chapter 4 data to almost everyone's calculator and had my students complete the Preliminaries questions prior to Friday. But I didn't collect the "Age of Instructor" Preliminaries

---

[*] My first test, distributed on Thursday, October 12, covered what is called "Unit 1" in Madison H.S. parlance—i.e., chapters 1, 2, and 3—but which does not cover the "first unit" (i.e., chapters 1 to 5) that this Appendix details.

[†] I would, starting the following academic year, begin teaching AP Statistics as well.

[‡] I later realized that although multiple choice questions don't lend themselves easily to partial credit with respect to work shown when solving mathematics problems, they do allow for *multiple* choice: students might be permitted to choose two options for answers to each question; if their first choice is correct, they receive full credit, but if instead their second choice is correct, half credit is awarded.

data because Friday was the first Senior Cut Day of the year*—another unfortunate reality of the high school environment—and only a bit more than half of my students were in each of my sections. I will collect this data on Monday.

An Activity which introduces the ideas of mean, median, mode, and sample size was completed and discussed on Friday. I appreciate the use of genuine data in this Activity, although I wish the authors could have picked a better example that had some repetition of observations (all of the Supreme Court justices served a different number of years). I was absolutely startled at how many people didn't know how to calculate a median; these are twelfth graders, after all!

*Statistics Interruptis*
*Week 6: October 16 to October 20 (Excluding October 18 for statewide standardized testing)*

There were two major interruptions this week: on Wednesday there was no class because all underclassmen were taking standardized tests (which I, and most other faculty members, had to proctor), and on Friday a student in the school pulled the fire alarm during one of my Probability and Statistics classes which, unsurprisingly, created a major disruption.

But let me return now to the beginning of the week. Most of my students were back on Monday, after having had the benefit of an impromptu three-day weekend. Those that weren't there asked what they missed. I was conflicted about whether to tell them; after all, in nearly all cases, they decided to cut, so they should be responsible for the material. On the other hand, this is still high school, and teachers aren't quite in the position of a college instructor who can *truly* put the onus on his pupils to keep up.

So I collected the Preliminaries data for chapter 4. It was a bit disturbing for me, however—recall that the only class data collected for chapter 4 is "Instructor's Age." For some reason I expected

---

* It was much earlier this school year than last year; usually, these days take place during the second semester, in which "nothing counts anyway" and seniors, having been infected with senioritis, have better things to do than sit in class. As a reward for those who showed up, I added two points of extra credit to their test scores.

that most people would have undercut my age by years. I got just the opposite, however.* What a bizarre, one-of-a-kind way to determine how (young) people perceive you!

Before assigning the next Activity, in which the relationship between skew and the mean and median is discussed, though, I did sort of spell it all out for my classes. I found last year that a key point—that the mean follows the tail of a data distribution—is just not clear enough.

On Tuesday, I was yet again explicit, this time with the notion of resistant measures, prior to my students beginning the Activity that's supposed to lead them to that idea. Last year, in this chapter, I gave them too much freedom and hardly any direction, letting them realize the main points themselves, and to little avail; by the time the quiz review came around, few knew any of it, and they wondered why I hadn't "taught" this or that. At least I can now say that these ideas were mentioned in class to the class.

Next in the book, the concept of a *weighted average* is implicit but there's no step-by-step method given to calculate it. I think that this is a glaring omission, since most students, when I was introducing it, had blank expressions on their faces. I led them through calculating the weighted average of the following tally chart:

| **Score** | 0 | 1 | 2 | 3 |
|---|---|---|---|---|
| **Tally** | 3 | 7 | 5 | 1 |

In addition, we discussed how to find the median and mode of this tally chart.

By Friday, the day of the fire-alarm pull (or, as the principal awkwardly put it over the loudspeaker after the incident, the "pull-station pull"), I was ready to wrap up the chapter. I handed out **Finding and Interpreting Measures of Center** which has some mean and median "extension" questions.

I'm not sure that I did a better job of teaching measures of center per se, but I am sure that I was much more explicit about the key points of the chapter. Time will tell: next week they'll have their evaluation.

* When I was much younger, I wanted to look older. Now that I'm older, I want to look younger. What I can't figure out is how old I was when I didn't want to look either older or younger.

*Being Observed and Other Problems*
*Week 7: October 23 to October 27*
*(Excluding October 25 for a District Inservice)*

Samuel Johnson once said that when a man knows he is to be hanged in a fortnight, it concentrates his mind wonderfully. Well, I didn't have a fortnight: this was the week I was to be observed—on Friday. But before then, there was a lot to do, and I had to focus. Since the **Quiz on Chapter 4** was scheduled for Tuesday, Monday was spent reviewing measures of central tendency using the **Review for Quiz on Chapter 4** worksheet. In addition, a certain homework Activity,* one of the hardest problem sets in the textbook, was discussed thoroughly because, when grading the Activity the previous day, I was horrified to find a specific set of recurring mistakes on people's papers.

By Tuesday, I felt that students had been given thorough going-over of the material and were ready for the assessment. About half of the quiz was multiple choice—the review the previous day had sample multiple choice questions, so the format did not come out of left field for them—and the remaining parts were fill-in and free-response questions. Which stands in stark contrast to the chapter 4 quiz I gave last year: it was *entirely* multiple choice. Not a particularly appropriate way to test students on the material, considering that all the Activities required calculations.

After the unproductive fare of an inservice, students returned Thursday to start chapter 5—and to work through, as a class, an **Introduction to Measures of Spread and the Boxplot** worksheet. I was reminded, on that day, of the power of lecture to deliver content quickly and efficiently; by the next day, students were adept at (at the very least) constructing boxplots and obtaining the five-number summary and IQR (i.e., the interquartile range, the middle fifty percent any data set).

So by Friday, when an administrator visited my first period class for a formal observation, pupils were more than ready to work through the chapter's first Activity.† Although my first period class worked fast enough to begin the second Activity in the textbook—

* This interesting problem set centers on finding weighted averages between two classes of different sizes.

† On finding measures of spread and constructing skeletal boxplots.

on calculating standard deviation—my other two sections did not; I managed to get them through only the first problem set in their respective periods, perhaps because it was a Friday and they were burned out, or perhaps because I didn't manage the clock as well, given the numerous disruptions that occur my fourth and seventh period classes (*especially* in my seventh period class).

It's that heterogeneous mix of students,* a quality that this class but no others in the Madison mathematics department truly have, that perhaps is surfacing yet again as a major source of the problems in the later-in-the-day Probability and Statistics classes. After all, in my seventh period class alone, there are students who barely managed to pass Algebra 2-T (the most basic track of Algebra 2) sitting next to kids who did well in the Algebra 2-E (enriched, a higher-level approach) courses sitting next to kids who already had or are taking precalculus concurrently with this course sitting next to a kid whose background involved a two-year stint in the Madison alternative school.† It's been a tough challenge, and it's not likely to get any easier this year. I hope to be more buttoned-down next year.

*Wrap Up*
*Week 8: October 30 to November 3*

This week wrapped up chapter 5, the last chapter in the marking period. Let me reflect on the events of the week.

On Monday, I conducted a visual-mathematical demonstration of what standard deviation is—well, sort of. Two dotplots were on

---

* But a larger question still remains: Is *Workshop* the right approach to teaching statistics to all high school students with a good algebra background? I appreciate the prodigious research that went into the book; the data sets are at times enlightening and at other times truly spectacular—better examples could not be unearthed. Nevertheless, I have been continually haunted by the words at the beginning of the text: "Providing a one-semester introduction to fundamental ideas of statistics for college and advanced high school students…." My population of statistics students is a heterogeneous mix of those who signed up for a fourth year of math—some have had, some take it concurrently, and some will never see precalculus. This mélange of pupils requires, more than most classes, differentiated instruction.

† A teacher, who is currently at the high school, had this particular student in his class in the alternative school several years ago. His comment when I told him that I now have him in my class? "Sorry."

the board when students walked in; one of the dotplots had five numbers spread out equally, the other one also had five numbers—but three of them were clumped in the middle and the other two were spread equally apart from the median. The range of both dotplots was the same, but the standard deviation of each was, of course, different.

I instructed students to find the mean and range of both dotplots. Then students were told to calculate the distance of each of the observations from the mean of the dotplots. Finally, students were asked to find the mean of these distances. Thus they calculated mean absolute deviation (MAD) and not standard deviation—which I specifically pointed out—but I believe that it gave them a sense of the importance of coming up with a single number to describe the way the observations are spread out, just like the mean and the median are single numbers used to describe the center of a distribution.

And it was then that I assigned the chapter's second Activity, which also leads pupils through calculating MAD and then standard deviation. A 35-year veteran teacher at Madison, who retired last year, once told me that in his Algebra 2 classes he required students to obtain standard deviation by hand. But the process of cranking out the standard deviation of a data set is so incredibly tedious that I made a conscious decision, last year, to never (in this particular course, at least) require students to do it by hand—it seems to me to be a major distraction and timewaster, especially since (a) the calculator, which everyone has access to, can find it quickly, (b) exposure to the process of obtaining MAD is sufficient to get a quick and dirty sense of the notion of a measure of deviation from the mean, and (c) the textbook really doesn't require students to calculate standard deviation by hand.

Tuesday was Halloween and I figured I was in for a rough day—it's tough to concentrate on statistics when you're dressed as Miss America (not me—some of the students). But my kids were surprisingly mellow throughout the day,* and we covered a lot. One Activity in particular is especially good since it's so analytical. The only problem is its formatting: like last year, when asked to match boxplots to corresponding five-number summaries, students didn't

* Well, except for in seventh period, when A., a female student, arrived late to class dressed up as a pimp.

know where to look for the boxplots (they're printed on the next page). I hope that this formatting error will be corrected in the next edition.

Last year I had found the Empirical Rule to be one of the most difficult concepts for the kids to assimilate. Working through an Activity didn't give them a good foundation with which to solve other Empirical Rule problems, so all three of my sections on Wednesday were exclusively devoted to lecture. In introducing the rule, I used the well-worn example of IQ: mean 100, standard deviation 15, and mound-shaped. And, surprise!—students were able to solve the problems on the **Interpreting Standard Deviation** worksheet that I distributed to them at the end of the period.

Thursday was spent on the *z*-score questions, and on Friday we went over the **Review for Test on Unit 2** packet. Class by class, I believe that I've made things very predictable for my students: gather Preliminaries data and get the calculator files, work through in-class Activities and perhaps a worksheet or two, have a quiz or test review, then take the quiz or test. In fact, the fifth chapter was the most unpredictable of the lot since there was no end-of-chapter quiz—I had to jump right to the test because the marking period's coming to a close next week. The **Statistics Test on Unit 2** will be given this Monday. And then we'll collect the next set of classroom data and the predicable routines of my classroom will continue to structure the days and weeks and months—and years—ahead.

*The Seventh-Period Stretch: A Lamentation on Class Control*

The realities of high school, and the day-to-day implementation of curriculum, don't exactly go according to plan—even from period to period. Although I have, by any measure, vastly improved my execution of the course this year as compared to last, I was reminded of the gaps in my newfound teaching abilities by a parent.

Ruth (a pseudonym) is a student in my seventh period Probability and Statistics class; I also had her last year in my Algebra 2 class. In an October e-mail from Ruth's father, he expressed concerns to me on multiple fronts.

> I am Ruth's father. She is in your afternoon class and I was speaking with her a few days ago and she happened to

> mention that [there are behavior problems]—by at least a few students.
>
> Ruth does not know that I am emailing you… but I was concerned to hear about the problems. Is the behavior situation negatively impacting on your ability to teach the subject and to keep the seniors interested (including Ruth)?

Needless to say, the e-mail caused quite a bit of consternation on my part. Were things out of control? Was I not doing my job? Was I not planning enough, or not being interesting enough?* I felt it prudent to respond the day he wrote. Because my e-mail encapsu-

---

* I remember asking a colleague of mine this past winter why he spent such an exorbitant amount of time lesson planning (he was, like me, a first year teacher, but in the business department). Why not just lean more heavily on the textbook(s) you have, instead of burning yourself out? Why not just copy the supplemental worksheets and be done with it? Why care about bringing in outside examples, videos, materials, and the like? Be prepared, or even over-prepared, but why give up your limited time at home in favor of kids who probably wouldn't know the difference anyway?

He said that although it's true that he could do a more than competent job by just using the standard curricular materials, he was concerned that the students wouldn't find it all *interesting enough.* Believing that learning is best facilitated by raising students' interest levels, he spent (from what he's relayed to me) his days and nights and weekends preparing for his daily show.

And yet, while I admire his devotion, it all seems a bit too much. Although I was certainly more prepared for this school year than I was for the last one, permitting me more time this year to fill in gaps and pull in some outside resources, perhaps I can best raise the interest level by simply being more passionate and overtly committed to the ideas, examples, and learning styles propagated by the textbook (whatever it may be)—in essence becoming a preacher for the pedagogic style, allowing nary a word of dissent—rather than attempting to pull in too much extracurricular content which could be a distraction and which may not be all that interesting to begin with. Because, with an instructor who's committed to the ideas and ideals of the *Workshop* approach (for instance), the Activities, *ipso facto,* come to life—it's certainly better than a teacher passively assigning Activity after Activity without even a modicum of interactivity or discussion. This notion of synthesizing interest by showing passion—not, dare I say, putting on a dog-and-pony show every day attempting to disguise the underlying "blasé" nature of the content, but instead presenting with an instructional delivery that displays not only a command of the content but a love of it—can perhaps both garner interest as well as sow the seeds of intrinsic learning. After all, isn't this, as educators, what we're all supposed to be trying to do?

lates many of my feelings and repeated frustrations with this course, I include it in full below.

> The class that Ruth had me in last year was an exclusively Enriched class—and, to be perfectly honest, the quality of the students were uniformly very high. The reality of the Prob/Stats class is that it is a heterogeneously mixed group; the academic backgrounds of the students in the same classroom are very, very different (and not just in mathematics). For instance, in Ruth's class alone, various students came from: (a) Algebra 2-T, (b) grade-level Algebra 2, (c) Algebra 2-E, (d) Precalculus, (e) Precalculus-E, (f) Algebra 2-Honors, and even (g) Alternative School. In another period of this class, I have a student who took AP Calculus last year sitting next to students who struggled to make it through Algebra 2-T. It's a unique situation; the Prob/Stats course is the only such "untracked" math class in the high school, and I am thus far the only person to have ever taught it here.
>
> The behavior challenges come from three fronts for me: (1) Students who perhaps are somewhat apathetic to the idea of a fourth year of math because of their prior struggles with it, (2) Students who are finishing in-class assignments too quickly because they are extremely capable in mathematics, and (3) Nearly all students are seniors who have, to varying degrees, already checked out—not just of math class but of school (I can't tell you how bad the attendance is in my senior-only classes, let alone the frequent cutting that occurs).
>
> I started off much, much stronger this year than last year in my Prob/Stats classes, trying to figure out how to best mitigate the many issues and challenges I encountered last year. But I haven't eliminated the problems; I haven't gotten my Prob/Stats to (yet) be as smooth as my Algebra 2 or my precalc class was (or is). But things have improved considerably over last year's Prob/Stats course, in terms of behavior, curriculum, instruction, and assessment.
>
> Therefore, I would strongly disagree with Ruth's assessment that things are "pretty much out of control." It is true that there are two or three students in the class that

present me with many behavioral challenges and have indeed been disruptive from time to time. I have taken various actions to deal with this, and sometimes my actions have had the desired outcome, and sometimes not. But I have dramatically improved in dealing with these sorts of situations from last year to this year, and I will continue to improve. The content is being covered, on schedule, and completely on pace with my other two sections of the course. The learning environment is not. (And, unfortunately with the timeline, the most difficult material comes at a time when my seniors' bags are packed and they've already checked out, in some cases literally.)

Prob/Stats is a different kind of class than Algebra 2 was for her with me last year—in that class, I lectured most of the period and there wasn't much student interaction. The textbook was of a "traditional" style. I had very little group work or other such activities. But the Prob/Stats class cannot be run as pure lecture—the textbook simply doesn't lend itself to it, and by its very nature a heterogeneous grouping of students requires individualized, differentiated instruction that a pure lecture format can't allow. When a teacher, any teacher, disavows the use of lecture, the class dynamic changes from one of sitting upright, listening to the teacher at the board, to interacting with peers. And that's both good and bad for a teacher: good because as a teacher you want to see kids talking about the material, but also bad because you've opened up Pandora's Box in the sense that students won't *just* be talking about the material with each other no matter how much you press them to stay on task.

And that's more or less what Ruth's seventh period class is like: a class of almost all seniors, some completely checked out, others extremely mathematically capable but not particularly interested in the subject, and still others who are working really hard and struggling to stay afloat in the class. The class is completely on schedule (I am ahead of where I was last year)—we just hit page 93 in the book today, and we've done problems on every single page. But, let me answer your question directly: Is the behavior situation negatively impacting on my ability to teach the subject and to keep the seniors interested (including Ruth)? The

> answer is certainly no because, put into the context I stated above, there really isn't a "behavior situation." Those who want to learn and want to work hard will do so and will receive encouragement and support from me; those who don't will be prodded by me to do work during class and if necessary receive disciplinary action (which I have meted out this year, in her class).
>
> One more thing: If Ruth is not as engaged in my math class this year as she was last year (which is possible but I'm not sure yet), then it might be more a function of her simply being too bright and mathematically inclined (and therefore a bit bored) rather than any classroom dynamic that's causing an adverse effect. An AP Statistics course, which would have used the same text[*] but focused in on much more complex ideas much more quickly, would've been more appropriate for Ruth. The catchall course of Prob/Stats isn't necessarily the best-fit for all of the students who are in it—but it's the only game in town right now.[†]

Ruth's father responded that night, thanking me for my quick response and also writing that he wondered why I didn't just kick out the disruptive kids—permanently. A seemingly good idea but, alas, not exactly an option in a public, comprehensive high school.

Since the e-mail exchange, I have addressed and cajoled the class, and those individuals in question, about their behavior and their actions. Things have improved.

*The End*
*November 2006*

As I write these words over the Thanksgiving break, nearly a month has passed since chapter 5 was completed, and there's a lot to be thankful for. I'm now deep into chapter 7 with my classes,

---

[*] Although I would go on to teach AP Statistics with *Workshop Statistics*, heavy supplementation by me would be required because the textbook isn't considered an AP-ready textbook.

[†] The appeal of Probability and Statistics as a catchall course diminished somewhat with the arrival of an AP Statistics class at Madison High, since de facto tracking—now for statistics too—went into effect.

with a quiz scheduled for next week on the idiosyncrasies of two-way tables. And, with this past month to reflect on my progress, I have been struck again by how substandard my Probability and Statistics classes were last year. The ship was righted this year; the classes are now perhaps, on a good day, better than average—but their mere averageness throws my first-year teaching into sharp relief.

I have become a better teacher, and that's not a subjective statement. Things in the Probability and Statistics classes are relatively smooth—I can actually *speak and teach* in front of these classes, day after day!—and I am truly grateful that, for whatever the reasons, if a mastery of the teaching of this course has not yet been achieved, then I am certainly on the road toward it.

Yesterday everyone in the Madison H.S. mathematics department received an e-mail from the math department chair. "I will be recommending, at the next principal's cabinet meeting, an AP Stat course since a lot of parents have requested it." He spoke to me privately about it, telling me that he expects me to teach it. Next year should be interesting: statistics and more statistics! If I'm not careful I'll start being typecast.

But I will almost certainly also have to share at least one section of the Probability and Statistics course with another math teacher. I have cornered the statistics market for too long; with enrollment in this course due to balloon yet again, I won't be able to hold on to all of the sections.

The one-man show will end, and I'm not sure how I feel about that: being, by default, the high school's resident expert on the content and the course, will I have to teach a neophyte teacher the pitfalls and the perils of this material and this textbook?* I suppose I

---

* Flying solo, having no one to truly explore the logistics and dynamics of this approach with, is of course antithetical to the collaborative nature of the course and has been to my students' detriment. I can only professionally reflect to a limited degree in a monologue. On the other hand, there is something to be said for being the sole "owner" and instructional deliverer of the material: I have complete control and am not answering to another instructor's timeline. For instance, if teacher X concurrently taught statistics, then, in a sense, I would be (or would have been) beholden to another's timeline and progress. In a sense I was lucky not to have that pressure and be allowed a breadth of flexibility in my first teaching year.

will. The next person who teaches this will have an advantage I never had: namely, me.*

Perhaps I'm being overly dramatic about this, and a little selfish to boot. After all, I was completely petrified this past summer, worrying that three classes per day this year, my Prob/Stats classes, would be complete washes with no learning. But fortunes changed quickly; I truly have a handle on the course now. There's been no sophomore jinx (yet).† It's that sense of confidence, more than anything else, that's been a boon to my implementation and instruction. It's a confidence instilled not only by hours of planning and preparation,‡ but also of feeling a comfort level with the material, the text, and the teaching as never before. And that, more than anything else, is something I have to be thankful for this Thanksgiving.

(2006)

---

* That proved to be true years later, when enrollments skyrocketed again and course sections needed to be spun off.

† Unfortunately, I spoke too soon here—see the chapter "Mediation and Conflict Resolution in High School" for the details.

‡ Redoing the Activities during the summer break also reminded me that expressing mathematical ideas in sentence format is required in every chapter. Since this is likely the first time students have to do this in any extended, protracted way—the cursory emphasis on open-ended problems for standardized-test preparation not withstanding—perhaps an introductory chapter should be devoted to proper writing skills. Sure, students may pick it up as they go along, but I found (possibly due to my inexperience at teaching the content and at teaching in general) that, last school year, the length of the responses to the open-ended Activities' questions were positively correlated with the students' mathematical background knowledge and motivation. Let's face it—it's a tough course for any student. A real technical competence (if not mastery) has to be achieved in order to properly deal with the calculator; a strong grasp on statistical ideas and concepts must be attained in order to solve problems; a degree of literacy must be met in order to read and understand the questions; a high degree of writing ability must be realized; and an understanding of psychology and at least a cursory awareness of ethics is necessary for the sampling and experimental design chapters—and all this in only the first half of the book! And the instructor has the hardest job of all: in addition to being fluent in all those areas, he has to also be a coach to students, manage the groups (keeping them on task), determine what should be lectured about (sometimes on an ad hoc basis) and what should be left to student self-discovery, write assessments that are both valid and reliable, and grade accordingly. It's a tremendous challenge that I'm only beginning to appreciate despite my prior experience with the course—one that demands a high level of commitment, devotion, and hard work.

# A Note on the Author

**MARK JONES LORENZO** is a teacher.
He lives in Pennsylvania with his dogs.
This is his first book.

Printed in Great Britain
by Amazon

36458605R00374